D0848278

Flying
MacArthur
to Victory

TEXAS A&M UNIVERSITY
MILITARY HISTORY SERIES
1

Flying
MacArthur
to Victory

By Weldon E. (Dusty) Rhoades

Texas A&M University Press
College Station

Library of Congress Cataloging-in-Publication Data

Rhoades, Weldon E., 1906–
    Flying MacArthur to victory.

    Includes index.
    1. Rhoades, Weldon E., 1906–   –Diaries.
2. World War, 1939–1945–Personal narratives, American.
3. Air pilots, Military–United States–Biography.
4. United States. Army Air Forces–Biography.
5. MacArthur, Douglas, 1880–1964.   6. Generals–United
States–Biography.   I. Title.
D811.R478A3   1987   940.54'4973'0924 [B]   86-26105
ISBN 0-89096-266-9

This book
is dedicated to Zelma Kibler and Donald Reardon.
Without their encouragement, constant prodding, and selfless work,
this material never would have reached publication.

Contents

Illustrations

Maps

Preface

I started this diary when I first became an active participant in World War II. One purpose was to assign myself a task that would impose strict personal discipline—a duty that I would have to perform each and every day. Another purpose was to preserve a record of sorts for my children, who were too young to know the meaning of war.

Much of the material is entirely personal. To the random reader that material may therefore be of little interest, except perhaps in one unique way. Written history is replete with overviews and results, but almost nowhere to be found is a personal account, religiously maintained over a period of time, by an individual who records much of what he saw, felt, and reacted to during a "convulsion" of civilization. What did the Revolutionary War soldier do and think about during his long days of enforced idleness or during his brief periods of intense activity? What did the California gold rush forty-niner really do, think, and feel over a prolonged period? What motivated the ordinary little guy day after day to produce on some unpredictable occasion a sometimes spectacular, almost superhuman performance when required? Did these individuals too suffer enormous and almost unbearable fatigue after tremendous expenditures of effort? Did they too experience an indescribable ecstasy from their minor successes? Did they too suffer grinding boredom when idleness was forced upon them?

The first half of the diary covers a period of time when I was actually (unwittingly) training myself for greater responsibilities. In those days airport and navigation facilities were primitive compared with those of today, and skill in long overwater operations (which were a rarity then) and self-confidence in the arts of navigating and flying into strange places and unfamiliar weather patterns were acquired only through long experience.

The second half of this diary treats the period from my initial meeting with Gen. Douglas MacArthur and assignment to his personal staff to the date of my separation from active duty early in 1946. This latter portion describes my personal relations with and observations of General MacArthur and his chief of staff, Lt. Gen. Richard K. Sutherland. My role in their historic accomplishments was insignificant.

My observations of and communications with Generals MacArthur and Sutherland were privileged and could not ethically be disclosed at that time. For this reason, any of the things I heard them discuss and the words they used are necessarily reconstructed from memory because I, like most people, do not possess the "total recall" capability that would be required to make verbatim quotations.

My written records, which serve as the sole source of many of the events related here, are in themselves complete except in two respects. First, I could not record any classified material in my diary and notes. Second, on many very long, exhausting, and dramatic days, my physical and mental fatigue acted to limit the quantity and details of events I recorded; on dull and featureless days, of which there were also many, and when I had an excess of spare time, there was little of interest to relate.

Another annoying limitation was that army regulations forbade the maintenance of a diary because of the possibility of enemy interception. I interpreted this liberally to mean that the diary should not be kept in the theater of operations. My continuing contact with my many United Air Lines pilot friends, who were flying to our area almost daily, presented me with a solution. Whenever I accumulated a few pages of handwritten material, I sent them to my wife in Atherton, California, by one of my friends. When I did not have an opportunity to write everything I wanted to on an eventful day, I made a short memorandum to myself, and at first I usually found time later to include these notes in the body of the diary.

As the war became more exciting and eventful, however, I found myself unable to incorporate all these memoranda into the diary. Consequently, I shipped some of these notes home with pages of the diary. As the war progressed, more of these notes had to be sent home before integrating them. After the war, I incorporated the remainder of them into the main diary before it was typed, keeping the verb tenses uniform throughout. The material contained in these original notes, whether written in the war zone or written after the war, is enclosed in brackets.

Since this diary was not written for publication, I have edited the entries to improve the occasional awkward phrase or unclear passage. In addition, some unimportant material that is likely to be of little interest to the reader has been deleted to reduce the whole to a manageable size. Spelling and terminology have been made consistent with standard English usage and editorial style.

One unabridged handwritten copy of the original diary (without notes) is located in the Hoover Library at Stanford University and another is in the Bureau of Archives of the MacArthur Memorial in Norfolk.

Millions of words are spoken for each word recorded. Millions of acts are performed for each deed that receives recognition. Thus, history is deprived of much of the human interest and supporting background that precedes or triggers the major events of which it does take notice. It is my hope that what is written here will be useful in clarifying the character and relationships of these two diverse personalities (MacArthur and Sutherland) and that it will add some to the understanding of the administrative methods used by them as principal directors of the World War II military campaigns throughout the vast western Pacific area. One man had his eyes upon history. The other was a man of the present with more personal and pragmatic objectives and was more subject to human foibles. Both men were controversial in an entirely different way. A great deal that has been said and written about them has been grossly distorted.

Frequently I have been asked how I happened to be chosen as General MacArthur's personal pilot. My actual selection for the position was pure happenstance, as will be related later in this document.

Abbreviations

AACS	Army Aviation Communication Service
AST	Australian Standard Time
ATC	Air Transport Command
AWT	Alaska War Time
	Algerian War Time
	Atlantic War Time
	Australian War Time
BWT	Bering War Time
	Brazilian War Time
CINCPAC	Commander in Chief, Pacific Area Command
CWT	Canton War Time
	Central War Time
EWT	Eastern War Time
	Egyptian War Time
FWT	Fiji War Time
GHQ	General Headquarters
HWT	Hawaiian War Time
IWT	India War Time
MWT	Morocco War Time
	Mountain War Time
NCWT	New Caledonia War Time
NZWT	New Zealand War Time
OPA	Office of Price Administration
PCA	Pennsylvania Central Airlines
PDG	Plaine des Gaiacs
PWT	Pacific War Time
	Palestine War Time
RAAF	Royal Australian Air Force
RAF	Royal Air Force
RCAF	Royal Canadian Air Force

SWPA   Southwest Pacific Area
SWT   Samoa War Time
            Senegal War Time
USAFFE   United States Army Forces in the Far East
USAFPAC   United States Army Forces, Pacific Area Command
(AFPAC)
WAC   Women's Army Corps
YWT   Yukon War Time

Flying
MacArthur
to Victory

1

Starting Out

New York, N.Y., June 1, 1942   1345 EWT

Nine years ago today I began my career on the airline. Today a new phase begins. Today the poisonous blood of war has worked its way at last into the very sinews of our economic existence. Today I start to work indirectly for Uncle Sam in the direct furtherance of the transportation phase of total war.

It is a rainy, gray day at La Guardia Field today. One hundred seventy of us, all airline personnel from various companies, are now en route in fourteen army cargo airplanes to Presque Isle, Maine, where we are to be separated into three groups, to be stationed at Presque Isle, Maine, Goose Bay, Labrador, and Bluie West 1, Greenland, from which bases we shall transport important cargo and personnel to Iceland and perhaps England. The United pilots are Bob Ashley, Johnny Roberts, Jimmie Allen, Tex Irvine, George Tremble, J. O. Stewart, and myself. We should arrive about 5:00 P.M. at Presque Isle, at which point further instructions will be issued.

Presque Isle, Maine, June 1, 1942   2100 EWT

All arrived at Presque Isle to find everything in a state of confusion. Huge barrack buildings completely devoid of furniture, and not a single bunk or blanket available. Everyone milling around, praying for a place to sit down. No instructions—everything completely unplanned. We have a meeting scheduled for 8:30 in the morning, at which time we hope to learn to which point we are supposed to fly.

[At this time it might be well to recount some of the past events which led to this activity.

In the early morning hours of December 7, 1941, I flew a United Air Lines trip in a reliable DC-3 from Chicago to Denver on my routine scheduled assignment, arriving at my home in Denver a little past 10:00 in the morning. I was tired after being up all night on the seven-hour flight and looked forward to a rest in the afternoon. But my plans were upset by a sudden flurry of news on the radio, which was beginning to bring in fragments of information describing the Japanese attacks on Pearl Harbor.

Together with the rest of the nation, my family and I desperately awaited developments as the country shook off its lethargy and commenced to adjust to a state of war.

Confusion was rampant. The news media either did not know or were incapable of providing the vital information needed by many people to rearrange their lives and objectives. I had been trained as a pilot by the United States Army Air Corps and had served three years as a cadet and as a second lieutenant. Now, as an active reserve captain and pilot in the Air Corps, I knew I would be involved in some capacity in the war effort. I increased my activity in the reserve unit at Lowry Field near Denver and continued to fly my assigned schedules for United Air Lines between Denver and Chicago.

The holiday season that year was a sad one. Some of our friends began receiving orders to active duty with the army or navy. Many were given only a couple of days' notice before having to report. The Air Corps, at that time organizationally an integral part of the army (it did not become an independent entity as the United States Air Force until well after the termination of World War II), had been caught in the emergency with only a minuscule fleet of obsolescent transport aircraft. It therefore instituted a program to requisition a large portion of the airlines' airplanes. For the most part these were Douglas DC-3s.

Hourly I expected to receive my active duty orders. But none came.

After having taken a large percentage of pilots and airplanes from the airlines, the War Department announced in the spring of 1942 that it would no longer continue to requisition men and equipment from this source. In addition it ordered that those aircraft and aircrews retained by the air carriers be frozen in that capacity in order to ensure the continuity of domestic air transportation, which was belatedly recognized as being so essential to the war effort.

I felt uneasy in my safe role as a civilian reserve officer during a total war situation. However, it was not long before things began to change. The army soon learned that it did not have enough pilots skilled in weather and instrument flying to operate all of the aircraft it had requisitioned from the airlines. Realizing it could not meet its own requirements for air transportation, the army therefore decided to enter into contracts with the various airlines to provide the necessary airlift. In May of 1942 I was asked by United Air Lines if I would volunteer to fly for the army, using the airline or army airplanes under the direction of the army but remaining an employee of United Air Lines. This I readily agreed to do since it helped appease my conscience and I felt I would be contributing more directly to the war effort. Additionally, I could satisfy a lifelong ambition to see as much of this earth as possible.]

Northern Maine is beautiful beyond description. Limitless rolling hills thickly covered with scrub forest and generously sprinkled with irregular, transparent lakes—and on many of these lakes the unusual appearance of the huge, mushroomlike forms of floating pulpwood logs.

Walked two miles into town tonight. Once a quiet, quaint village, it is now ridiculously gay with soldier-brought prosperity.

New York, N.Y., June 2, 1942   2300 EWT

Today was without doubt the most confused and confusing day of my life. It is not fair to the army to state that the day's happenings were typical of the army method of operating, but it was quite discouraging to those of us who were incidental to the essential operations of the day.

Last night we finally retired with the feeling that the morrow would find us actually engaged in some useful work for Uncle Sam. However, upon our reporting to the officers' mess today for breakfast, it was obvious that changes were afoot. And what changes!

Last night, we thought that several hundred airplanes and our allotment of 300,000 pounds of emergency cargo were to move eastward to England via Labrador, Greenland, and Iceland. But this morning the airplanes were to move to the west coast of North America. Such a reversal could not be made without confusion, of course. And the combat outfits were naturally the first to be considered.

After the first surprise had subsided, rumors grew to astounding proportions. The Japs had bombed California; the Japs had taken Dutch Harbor; the army had suddenly grown jealous of the task the airline pilots were about to do and had ordered them off the job. At any rate, we finally received verbal orders to take off with our transport airplanes and proceed with certain personnel to Bangor, Maine, and Manchester, New Hampshire. We arrived at Bangor after a fine trip over this indescribably beautiful northern Maine country.

At Bangor the confusion was even greater. More rumors. The airline pilots were to take the cargo airplanes with loads to California; the army was angry with airline pilots and was ordering them out of the territory. All of these rumors eventually were proved to be incorrect. After some delay I received orders to proceed to Manchester, New Hampshire, with the group of navigators I was carrying. This I proceeded to do, enjoying a perfect trip over this colorful country.

At Manchester I reported personally to General Hunter, a dashing but severe gentleman with an enormous mustache which easily out-Stalined Stalin. He ordered me to return to Bangor immediately to carry twenty additional navigators to Westover, Massachusetts. En route to my airplane I was suddenly advised by a Colonel Gerhardt that my orders had been remanded and that I was to stand by for further orders from General Hunter. Further orders from the general failed to arrive. I finally proceeded back to New York in company with Captain Russel, aboard an army cargo airplane. Captain Russel was aide to General Hunter, and he assured me that even the general did not know what had happened to cause the Army General Staff to reverse its plans of movement.

[We were not told at the time, but later, of course, it was revealed that the Japs had attacked Dutch Harbor on Unalaska Island in the Aleutians. Until overall strategy could be reassessed, our efforts might have to be redirected to the west rather than toward Europe.]

En route New York–Chicago, June 3, 1942   1400 EWT

Now en route home, tired and disappointed. But there are compensations. The country I visited was new and thrilling, and although no constructive work was accomplished by the trip, still all personal reward does not derive from a feeling of work well done.

En route Chicago–Cheyenne, June 3, 1942   2300 CWT

Am now en route home, ferrying an airplane to Cheyenne for overhaul. A tired man.

Denver, Colo., June 4, 1942   2200 MWT

A day of rest and relaxation. Nothing useful accomplished, but now I am rested and ready for what ever else may come along. The verification of the Japanese attack on Dutch Harbor completely substantiated the reasons advanced for the cancellation of our recent mission to Greenland.

En route Denver–Chicago, June 5, 1942   2300 CWT

Now en route to Chicago on my regular trip. Cleared up odds and ends of business at Denver. An uneventful trip tonight. Perhaps something interesting will develop tomorrow.

Denver, Colo., June 6, 1942   2300 MWT

Returned on my regular trip from Chicago this evening. Trip routine except for a few thunderstorms and a new copilot on his very first trip. Exciting news today, and once more I try to further the war effort. Tuesday I leave for Alaska, with the hopes of going all the way to Dutch Harbor. I will go as observer, as this is my qualifying trip. It will be much fun, but there will be considerable work involved in trying to get the general idea of the terrain and other facts useful to flying over the landscape.

Denver, Colo., June 7, 1942   1600 MWT

Little activity today. Have spent most of the day clearing up odd jobs necessary before departing for a stay of a week or more.

It's a gloomy day, with much rain. We had intended going for a drive, perhaps one of our last in view of the freeze on the purchase of tires, but the day's weather has been entirely inappropriate for any kind of an outing.

2

North by Northeast . . . by Northwest

JUNE–AUGUST, 1942

Presque Isle, Maine, June 8, 1942   1900 EWT

My, how times do change! When I closed this epistle last evening I was certain, or relatively so, that I was going to Chicago and Alaska. About 6:00 P.M. the field called to advise me that I was to ride from Denver to New York last night in order to depart from New York at noon today for Presque Isle, Maine, to complete the mission we set out to do a week ago. After a nice airplane ride of seventeen hours, we arrived in Presque Isle at 5:30 P.M. today, completing another journey over this incomparably beautiful Maine country.

Things were considerably better organized here than they were on the previous trip. Dinner was ready, rooms were assigned, and now we are prepared for a fine night of sleep.

We go to an operations meeting at 8:00 P.M. to learn what we are to do tomorrow.

2300 EWT

Just returned from the operations meeting. We are to fly from Presque Isle to Goose Bay, Labrador, to Bluie West 1, Greenland, to Reykjavik, Iceland, and perhaps to Scotland. We had a brief outline of facilities, which are few, and a short description of probable operating conditions. It will be very much of an individual affair, with little help to be expected in case of trouble. The chances are that the airline pilots will fly for the most part between Presque Isle, Maine, and Greenland, and that army crews will be used in combat zones from Greenland to Scotland.

The same United Air Lines personnel who came here originally are again here on this mission. There was no indication of how long the assignment may last, but it seems that it will be more than a week. The first mission for each crew will be only as far as Goose Bay, Labrador, about

600 miles and return. The affair starts at 1:30 tonight, but that means little, since from Goose Bay northward it is quite light throughout the night. As yet we do not know when we will be scheduled out. We'll learn about the schedule tomorrow.

Well, I suppose it's what we asked for. Wonder how the family is tonight? Wish I could communicate with them, but have so little definite information to tell them.

Presque Isle, Maine, June 9, 1942   2200 EWT

More delays, more discouragement. It seems that an army colonel has been placed in charge of our mission here, and he has had no experience in transportation. From the general trend of pep talk by the colonel, it does not appear that any mission under him can be done very efficiently.

At any rate, when volunteers were called for to fly the various legs of the route, United pilots all volunteered to fly the overwater section, while TWA and PCA crews refused to fly over water. We will leave at 6:00 A.M. tomorrow for Goose Bay, Labrador, to be based there and fly eastward. The land-loving crews will fly from Presque Isle to Goose Bay.

I spent all morning working on maps and courses, checking my octant and navigational supplies, etc. Then I sent a telegram in code to my family to inform them of our next immediate plans.

[Some time earlier I had a premonition that I might be assigned to fly almost anywhere in the world. I decided to teach myself to navigate by the use of celestial bodies, an art that had long intrigued me, and I purchased an octant (a sextant that had its own built-in artificial horizon in the form of a small air bubble floating in fluid) together with the pertinent textbooks on the subject. Celestial navigation was at that time the only direct, self-contained means of determining one's position over water or large expanses of the then unsurveyed or unmapped landmasses. I spent weeks in intense study at home and subsequently several more weeks sharpening my skills by practicing during various flights. From that point on I never undertook a long trip without access to an octant and an air almanac if radio aids were not available. As a result, I was never thereafter disoriented for long.]

Presque Isle, Maine, June 10, 1942   2300 EWT

Well, we are still in Presque Isle tonight! We were to be ferried to Goose Bay by army crews, but it seems that the weather was a bit bad, so we are still holding for an indefinite departure. It has been a most monotonous day. Largely it has been a problem of killing time.

Perhaps we depart at 6:00 A.M. tomorrow, but no one seems to know.

Greenland Sea

GREENLAND

Baffin Bay

Reykjavik **ICELAND**

•Blue West 1
Tunugdliarjik Fjord **Cape Farewell**

SCOTLAND

Prestwick (Glasgow)•

LABRADOR

Goose Bay•

NORTH

ATLANTIC OCEAN

•Presque Isle
MAINE
•Bangor

Much confusion and boredom, especially for a group of normally active men.

Things are not all bad. Have met many old army acquaintances from early cadet training days; much flying talk, etc. The food is poor because it is too substantial and all starch. They feed us as though they expect us to row the cargo to Europe!

We sincerely hope tomorrow will bring a bit more action.

Presque Isle, Maine, June 11, 1942   2300 EWT

Another day has passed and we are still in Presque Isle. More of the same army inefficiency and red tape. The weather at Goose Bay was overcast, so we waited until it *improved* from a 6,000-foot ceiling down to 800 feet and then, of course, the army couldn't fly there. (Two airline crews went into Goose Bay without incident, however.) We listened to another two-hour harangue by our most intelligent colonel and in two hours learned exactly nothing. Now we are again scheduled to depart at 7:40 A.M. tomorrow but we have practically given up hope of ever going beyond this place. If the American army is fighting the war as inefficiently as is the colonel of the Sixtieth Transport Group, then the Axis should win easily by autumn. The mechanics and radio operators are about to rebel and go home. They came to me in a group tonight for advice and assurance, and I'm sorry I could not paint a very cheerful picture for them. However, to avoid a total collapse of our efforts here, I tried to persuade them to stay long enough to make one trip, which they finally agreed to do. It is my honest belief that if we can ever get over to Goose Bay and start operating in spite of army opposition, we will soon learn for ourselves that most of the tales of dangers to be encountered, etc., will prove to be based on some facts and much imagination.

Perhaps tomorrow is the day we leave Presque Isle. Who knows?

Goose Bay, Labrador, June 12, 1942   1000 LWT

At last we are in Goose Bay, Labrador, after a fine trip. This morning there was the usual delay because the weather at Goose Bay was 2,500 feet and unlimited visibility. Apparently they are waiting for a clear day before we can go there. However, the squadron commander finally agreed to let his squadron take off. I went as Lieutenant Nigro's copilot, and found him to be a thoroughly accomplished pilot in every respect and a fine gentleman. We were somewhat delayed at takeoff due to the fact that "my name's Malone—*Colonel* Malone" issued orders that no airplane could take off until General Spaatz had departed for England.

Although a part of the trip to Goose Bay was through very hard rain, the remainder was beautiful. Labrador is the most grimly beautiful land I have seen. The same uncounted lakes, but this time thickly spread through a country whose trees are less numerous and are stunted because of their precarious purchase along valleys between massive knobs of worn granite. Not a sign of human habitation for 250 miles, not a single house nor road nor visible trail in this strange wilderness. Utter loneliness for anyone who might venture here, but to venture into this wilderness by any means would be a most difficult task.

Accommodations here at Goose Bay are anything but adequate. About fifty of us are quartered in a newly constructed garage, without even a place to wash our hands. The food, however, is much better than that at Presque Isle.

Now to bed, for we may leave for Greenland tomorrow.

Goose Bay, Labrador, June 13, 1942   2200 LWT

Raining this morning and, although the weather on Greenland is excellent, the army refuses to clear anyone. However, it begins to appear that the airline pilots may be able to take things into their own hands a bit more than we have been permitted to do up until our arrival here. At least we are farther removed from so many army inefficiency experts.

Since no flying was to be permitted today I took a walk through these queer Labrador woods to an Eskimo village and to an Indian village about four miles up the bay. The Eskimo village was undoubtedly the filthiest human habitation I have ever seen. In the marshy, moss-covered forest, where with each step I sank into the muck almost to my knees, the Eskimos had built a half-dozen houses of logs and had sunk the houses into the ground to a depth of three feet. The walls protruded above the ground to a height of about four feet. Mud was eight inches deep inside and outside, throughout the village. The stench was almost unbearable. Gnawed bones and skins were as numerous in the mud inside the houses as outside. Human excrement was no farther than two feet outside the door, which was the only opening into each hut. Enormous laziness could be the only excuse for such a miserable existence, since they possessed ample tools with which to fashion from wood most of the essentials and conveniences for an adequate existence. One mother, a half-breed with blue eyes, was shaving a half-rotted sealskin from which to make some of their crude boots. A baby, no more than two months old, was, from all outward appearances, no worse off for its surroundings. I suppose only the hardiest can survive childhood. Some of them spoke passable English. One boy, not larger than a normal two-year-old child, told me he was eight years of age.

Huge white husky dogs ran everywhere. All of the puppies had thongs tied around their mouths. One old Eskimo indicated, in very broken English, that this was done to break them of their universal habit of howling, as this howling attracted the huge Labrador wolves from the woods to the vicinity of the villages. Apparently they greatly fear these wolves.

Farther down the bay was a Siwash Indian village. Here conditions were much better. They lived in tents, and in each tent was a very adequate stove. The floors of the tents were covered with freshly cut spruce boughs. Industry was evident among the women. Freshly killed deer were hanging in the camp. For some undetermined reason, they had recently stripped the bark from the lower trunk of most trees of the village.

After a long walk back to the army post, I was quite tired. Then I learned that I must attend another meeting at 8:00 P.M. This was about the tenth meeting in half as many days, and it dragged on for hours without accomplishing much.

[Incidentally, it was on this operation that I first experienced an operating obstacle that was to be a chronic source of irritation to the airline pilots who flew under contract for the army. In the airline business, schedule reliability was one of the most important objectives. It was axiomatic and always uppermost in my mind that one could not complete a trip unless one started it. Inclement weather was usually only a nuisance to be overcome. Of course, adequate measures to protect the safety of the trip had to be taken in the form of available alternate airports, adequate fuel reserves, etc. But in the Air Corps before the war any inclement weather often was an excuse *not* to fly. (This may have been a carryover from the disastrous experience of 1934, when the Air Corps was ordered to carry the U.S. mail.) As a result, I found many army air bases staffed with junior operations officers who had been conditioned not to clear flights into any type of weather other than that of unlimited ceiling and visibility. It was vexing to have at least half of my early assigned trips delayed or canceled for this reason alone.]

Weather permitting, I am to leave for Greenland at 5:30 A.M. tomorrow. So now to bed.

Goose Bay, Labrador, June 14, 1942   2400 LWT

Today was the day. Arose at 6:30 and was off to cross the longest jump of the Atlantic at 9:05. Incidentally, the army now has us operating on Greenwich Meridian Time, so the official time is rather early in the day in reference to local time.

The trip was quite monotonous except for the thrill of the idea. We were on instruments throughout until within fifty miles of the Greenland coast. Here we made landfall and headed for a fjord midway between Cape Farewell and Cape Desolation. I flew the trip at 9,500 feet and made good speed, considering the decreased power setting I chose. The greatest hazards were mechanical, poor navigation, or insufficient weather data. At any rate, I arrived off Julianehaab just four hours out of Labrador, then proceeded for fifty miles up Tunugdliarjik Fjord in a semiexploratory trip, and culminated a successful flight in a nice landing on a metallic landing mat at Bluie West 1. We found the accommodations to be excellent in view of the circumstances.

My writing ability is not adequate to attempt a general description of Greenland. It is both forbidding and inviting. There is no part of it that is not rugged, and everywhere its granite cliffs rise vertically from the blue, blue water. Innumerable icebergs are floating in all of the available water, and the blue color of these icebergs in this water defies comparison or description. The trip up Tunugdliarjik Fjord, which ended all too soon, surpasses any similar trip I have ever taken. This fjord is where Leif Ericsson's father made his first base in North America. The very ancient ruins are still visible.

We had only a glimpse of the ice cap, which covers all of Greenland except for a narrow border near the sea. The glaciers, which are direct streams of ice from this ice cap, spill into the fjords. In fact, one of them sends its icebergs into the fjord at one edge of the landing field. On the next trip I plan to fly across the edge of this cap on the return portion, when the airplane is comparatively light.

After an excellent lunch in the visiting officers' club, we departed for Labrador and arrived at 10:00 P.M. after a long but uneventful trip. After a hasty dinner I wrote a letter home and fell into bed to make this entry before sleep could overtake me.

Goose Bay, Labrador, June 15, 1942   1500 LWT

No flying for me today, as some ignition trouble which I had noticed and reported on my airplane on the return flight over the Atlantic yesterday proved to be quite serious, and today my airplane is out of service for a double magneto change on one engine and a single magneto change on the other. I hope the trouble will be completely corrected as I am scheduled to fly to Greenland at 10:00 A.M. tomorrow. Engine trouble in the middle of the Atlantic would be uncomfortable, to say the least.

There are no facilities for personal cleanliness. I have not washed or shaved for four days. A latrine was hastily constructed yesterday for sanitary reasons. It is a four-holer on the "chick sales" model, but the designer, an English carpenter, evidently believes that all American males are of tremendous stature. I almost need a ladder to climb up on the bench, and the smallest of the four holes is at least eighteen inches in diameter. Some of the remarks made about this are classic but unrepeatable.

Now to bed to get some much-needed rest for a long trip tomorrow.

Goose Bay, Labrador, June 16, 1942   1600 LWT

Yesterday the army boys had a hard time trying to get into Greenland, and almost lost a half of the airplanes which went over. The army authorities suspect that favorable weather reports were broadcast by enemy stations in our secret codes, which led us to believe the weather in Greenland was good, when actually it was quite bad. Our radio communications with Greenland are very unsatisfactory, and it would be quite within the range of possibility for the enemy to substitute false information. At any rate, we were quite fortunate that the army boys finally landed there without mishap.

Today we had only occasional weather reports, and they were all bad. So all flying to Greenland was canceled, and now I am scheduled out again at 10:00 A.M. tomorrow. We operate by using airline crews one day and army crews the next.

Just heard that I can leave tonight at midnight for Greenland instead of tomorrow. So now I'll go over to check the weather.

Reykjavik, Iceland, June 17, 1942   1000 IWT

Made a landing at Reykjavik, Iceland, not more than fifteen minutes ago and in broad daylight! A surprise trip indeed. Didn't get away at midnight last night, but rather departed from Goose Bay, Labrador, at 8:00 A.M. Proceeded to Bluie West 1, Greenland, without incident, but upon arrival learned that some particular freight must be expedited to Iceland. Roberts and I agreed to take it over. We gathered what information was available concerning the aircraft challenging system, friendly answering codes, dangerous areas, etc., and we finally departed from Bluie West 1 at 6:40 P.M. The trip was rather long due to unfavorable winds, and although we landed just before midnight, nevertheless the sun was still shining almost directly from the north. We had been alarmed considerably by reports that we would be fired upon by pursuit airplanes and antiaircraft if we did not answer all challenges immediately. We were not once challenged on our approach, but, of course, all defending units had been advised of our impending arrival. The flight to Iceland was purely a matter of dead-reckoning and celestial navigation, as all radio aids are inoperative.

We are now in bed in an iron-covered igloo, tired but happy. Tomorrow we are scheduled to return to Labrador at 11:00 A.M.

En route Bluie West 1–Goose Bay, June 18, 1942   1400 LWT

Now en route from Bluie West 1, Greenland, to Goose Bay, Labrador. This morning I arose at 8:00, had breakfast in an igloo with a major general, hurried down to have a quick look at Reykjavik, a quaint little city of 38,000, and was on my way back to North America.

Reykjavik was something of a disappointment. Perhaps it was the attitude of the people, perhaps it was the usual feeling of disappointment after a romantic place in one's mind is finally actually seen. The people were very grim. Not a smile on any face and a very definite anti-American feeling everywhere. The poor people apparently do not yet realize how much better it is to be left alone by the Americans than it is to be overrun and exploited by the ruthless Germans. The town had an aspect of determined respectability so often seen in poor, but proud, communities. I could not help but notice that all of the women had pinched, set facial characteristics. All of the natives had ruddy cheeks, but very fair complexions.

For the most part, the houses were constructed of corrugated sheet metal or concrete. The streets and buildings were almost ruthlessly clean, in spite of prevailing strong winds and much lava dust, which was continuously being blown about. If the Danish people were responsible, it seems that they made a great mistake in not calling Iceland Greenland, and Greenland Iceland.

We finally departed at 11:30 A.M. after having been considerably delayed by the stuffy English, who insist on having eveything done exactly in their own stilted, unimaginative fashion, regardless of the ideas of others. The return trip was beautiful, with excellent weather and another crossing of the incomparable Greenland ice cap. This is without doubt the most desolate spot on the face of the globe, with its plateau averaging about 8,000 feet high and stretching for hundreds of miles—level, glaring ice. Near the sea the ice literally flows down the gorges between the jagged mountains and continuously breaks off into the sea. We had a quick trip to Bluie West 1, arriving at 4:00 P.M. After a rugged lunch and refueling, we took off at 6:00 for Goose Bay.

To me it is almost inconceivable that I, who am ultraconservative by nature, should be up here flying the North Atlantic in airplanes without sufficient fuel to go to any other place than the point of intended landing. And a stranger thing is that I asked for it and I like it. Perhaps men like to live just a little bit dangerously rather than in a world where most things are considerably ordered or controlled.

Goose Bay, Labrador, June 18, 1942　2300 LWT

Arrived here in Goose Bay at 11:00 P.M. after a round trip to Iceland in thirty-six hours, twenty-two of which were spent in the air. So I shall not delay long in going to bed. A tired but happy man, cheered by the satisfaction of a hard job well done.

Goose Bay, Labrador, June 19, 1942　1400 LWT

Arose this morning at 8:00 A.M. after a short but refreshing sleep. No one else was awake, so I had breakfast and walked down to the Indian village alone to try to buy some trinket to take home. The Indians were very shy, and none of them spoke any English. After an hour and a half, and with the aid of seven bars of candy and two dollars and much patience, I finally obtained a pair of deerskin moccasins. By sign language and by drawing pictures on birch bark, I finally got the idea over to one of the squaws that I wanted a small pair of moccasins suitable for my "squaw." They are crude, but very characteristic of the people who make them. She indicated by signs that they would be ready for me tomorrow. Hope I shall be here so that I can obtain them. Rumor has it that I will finish my task here by tomorrow.

2000 LWT

No more startling developments today. I have one more trip to take to Greenland, and then we hope this task will be finished. However, there is a persistent rumor that there are 130 more men waiting at Presque Isle, Maine, to be flown with full equipment to Greenland. This would mean about twenty additional trips for us.

Goose Bay, Labrador, June 20, 1942　1400 LWT

A very fine letter from home has made the world a much finer place. Although it is raining and gloomy here, I feel much cheered to know that all is well at home.

Am still due out for Greenland, pending the arrival of an airplane in which to go. Our equipment has been in use almost continuously without adequate servicing facilities, and as a result many minor troubles are developing.

This morning I arose early and walked again to the Indian village. The old squaw had made the moccasins as per instructions. It was a beautiful walk through this tundra wilderness in a softly falling mist. I saw several of the common birds of the States, but all were very shy.

2400 LWT

No further developments except that an airplane for me to make my last trip to Greenland is expected sometime early tomorrow. Am now going to retire. Wrote a letter home but hope I'll be there before it is.

Bluie West 1, Greenland, June 21, 1942   2330 LWT

This morning I departed from Labrador and arrived here at 2:00 P.M. after a long trip on instruments. The weather back at Goose Bay is such that they will not clear us back there, so we are remaining here overnight, expecting to clear sometime tomorrow. Our task here will be over as soon as we return to Presque Isle, and I am looking forward to seeing my family again in a few days.

There is an overgrown black gnat here which is probably the most persistent fly of its kind in the world. It does not bite, but merely flies into one's eyes and nose and ears and will not be brushed away. The one nice thing about it is that it will not bother one inside the house but rather seeks only the daylight at the windows.

Tomorrow perhaps we will get away and our task here will have been completed.

Presque Isle, Maine, June 22, 1942   2200 EWT

Back in the U.S.A. at last! This morning we were up bright and early in Greenland and departed in the face of nasty weather for Goose Bay. Somehow we managed to get into that place and then took off for Presque Isle, arriving here at 5:30 P.M.

Most noteworthy of events was that the Coast Guard sank a submarine which they caught off Tunugdliarjik Fjord.

Upon arriving here I wired my wife Grace that I would be returning to Denver immediately, and then proceeded to have my first shower bath in two weeks. Now the bed is calling. We are proceeding to New York at 10:00 A.M. tomorrow, thence to Denver and home.

Chicago, Ill., June 23, 1942   2200 CWT

This morning at 11:00 A.M. we departed from Presque Isle in an army formation of forty-four planes and went to New York via Burlington, Vermont, and Albany, New York, account bad weather down the coast. The trip was beautiful but long. Upon arrival in New York I caught a United plane for Chicago at 5:30 P.M., but was unable to get through to Denver so remained here in Chicago. Am anxious to get back to my family now.

It would appear that I will get little rest this month as most of the airline men have flown about their maximum allowable hours for the month.

En route Chicago–Denver, June 24, 1942   1430 CWT

At last I am on the final leg of my homeward trip, on a priority ticket, so I am certain to arrive there about 8:00 P.M. It's going to be great to see my family again.

One item I just learned. The morning I left Reykjavik and skirted the convoy off the harbor, one of our navy PBY patrols inadvertently broke out of the clouds over the convoy and, upon failing to answer the challenge immediately, was promptly shot down by antiaircraft. All men were saved but three were injured.

Denver, Colo., June 25, 1942   1300 MWT

A pleasant day with the family. Tonight I fly a regular airline trip to Chicago. Rather tame, but relaxing. All's well in life today.

Chicago, Ill., June 26, 1942   1200 CWT

Leaving this afternoon for Denver on my regular airline trip. Routine except for a little en route weather. Learned this morning that I go to Alaska now for a permanent assignment—that is, as permanent as any assignment can be these days. I will have until July 2 to rest up and enjoy my family. Grace and I plan on a fishing trip for a couple of these days.

Denver, Colo., June 27, 1942   1800 MWT

A pleasant day, spent in shopping for life in Alaska and for our fishing expedition, proposed for Monday. Ran across this clipping in *Time*, June 29, 1942:

Aviation

Magic Carpet

Privately owned U.S. airlines are doing their biggest and most sensational job ever. Some of the details leaked out of Washington last week. When an army post in fog-wrapped Alaska screamed for huge 10,000-gal. gas tanks and 4-ton gas trucks to go with them, the airlines sliced up the tanks and trucks with acetylene torches, stuffed the pieces into airplane bellies, flew them right to the post. Mechanics in Alaska welded them back together.

One day this month over 30 heavily laden planes rumbled off rough, badly lighted fields in Labrador, winged across 800 miles of stormy water to secret airfields in Greenland. All records later topped when 60 round trips were made in three days.

Denver, Colo., June 28, 1942   2200 MWT

A quiet Sunday at home today. Much fun with the family and some preparations for the fishing trip tomorrow.

Black's Ranch, Parshall, Colo., June 29, 1942   2000 MWT

A wonderful outing, but poor fishing. Grace and I went over Loveland Pass to Dillon and then up the Blue River, where we tried fishing with no success. Then we went on to Kremmling and to Sheep Creek, but no luck.

Denver, Colo., June 30, 1942   2100 MWT

Home from a nice trip.

The airport advises that my first trip to Alaska has been indefinitely postponed due to lack of equipment. The army took all airplanes assigned to Alaska and sent them to some secret destination. Now I am to stand by for further advice as to when I shall go to Alaska.

Denver, Colo., July 1, 1942   2100 MWT

Spent today preparing Grace and our son Jim for their trip to visit the family farm in Missouri. They depart tomorrow for a two- or three-week stay. It will be Jim's first experience with chickens and pigs and all those wild animals, as well as with trains.

Denver, Colo., July 2, 1942   2100 MWT

Put my family on the train this afternoon, bound for the farm.

No further information about my schedule to Alaska. Am still wasting time when I could do something for the war effort. Organization is a queer thing. You can't get much accomplished without it, and yet its ponderous movements often are the best indications of its inefficiency.

Denver, Colo., July 3, 1942   2100 MWT

Tomorrow I leave for Chicago and Alaska. Am due out of Chicago the night of July 5, but I'm going back a day early to do what I can toward studying the route, etc. Am looking forward to this trip and hope I shall not be disappointed.

It's been a lonesome day without the family. Took a long walk tonight.

Denver, Colo., July 4, 1942   1100 MWT

A beautiful day here. Have been packing for my trip and am now ready.

Edmonton, Alberta, July 5, 1942   2330 MWT

Arrived here at 10:30 P.M. after a long, long flight from Chicago. Departed from Chicago at noon, and the weather was excellent, but the winds were quite strong. It is 1,500 miles and I made one stop for fuel at Fargo. Much too tired to say a lot tonight. The first noticeable thing about Canada is the mosquitoes.

Edmonton, Alberta, July 6, 1942   2300 MWT

Spent the entire day working on maps and gathering data for the trip north from here. It's an enormous country up here—almost too large for comprehension. Flying here is going to be a feat of ingenuity and endurance.

Have excellent living accommodations in the MacDonald Hotel, one of the Canadian National chain. A number of old acquaintances from the West Coast are here. They are stationed here on a temporary basis, to continue for one month, and are all flying north from here.

Edmonton is a bit of a disappointment. It's quite spread out, and a typical country small city. The Hudson's Bay Company, a romantic name since my childhood, has nothing more than a typical Sears, Roebuck store in the States, whereas I fully expected to see a trappers' outfitting store.

Chicago, Ill., July 7, 1942   2000 CWT

Arrived here at 2:00 P.M. after the 1,500-mile flight back from Edmonton. I was scheduled out to Fairbanks this morning when quite suddenly a trip came into Edmonton with seventeen soldiers who were war casualties and who were being rushed to the States for hospitalization and treatment which could not be given in Alaska. There was no other pilot available to bring them to Chicago, so it necessarily fell to my duty.

The trip down was fast, but when I arrived I found I had to take a physical examination for license renewal. Now I am going to go to Des Moines by air tonight and then ride the bus to Missouri to visit the farm.

Harris, Mo., July 8, 1942   2100 CWT

Arrived in Princeton on the bus at noon. We went directly to the farm where I was born and reared and to a huge farm dinner, and then my brother Wayne and I cut oats with the binder and tractor until 8:00 P.M. Tonight I'm so tired I can hardly stay awake.

Harris, Mo., July 9, 1942   2100 CWT

It rained last night and we were unable to finish cutting oats this morning. However, we did finish this afternoon, and I shocked oats until 8:00 P.M. Am unaccustomed to such labor so I am tired.

Harris, Mo., July 10, 1942   2200 CWT

A lazy day today, doing as little as possible. I milked a cow for the first time in several years. Farm life wouldn't be so bad if it became necessary again.

Harris, Mo., July 11, 1942   2200 CWT

I chopped thistles all afternoon while Wayne cut hay for stacking on Monday. My hands are a mass of blisters. Perhaps I'm getting soft.

A telegram came with advice to the effect that I can expect to be due out of Chicago for Alaska on Monday night. I now plan to board a United plane at Des Moines tomorrow night.

Des Moines, Iowa, July 12, 1942   2400 CWT

Wayne, Grace, and Jim took me to Princeton, where I boarded the bus for Des Moines. I leave here at 2:30 A.M. on the plane for Chicago.

Chicago, Ill., July 13, 1942   2200 CWT

Arrived here at 4:00 A.M., and today I have accomplished many odd tasks necessary for my next trip to Alaska. Among them were such things as the purchase of a mosquito hat to guard against those enormous Alaskan mosquitoes.

I had three inoculations—typhoid, tetanus, and smallpox—and tonight I am suffering from multiple reactions. It now appears that I will not be scheduled for Alaska for two or three days yet.

Chicago, Ill., July 14, 1942   1800 CWT

Have spent the day working on maps and other material applicable to the Alaska run. The reactions from the inoculations have now run their courses and I now feel quite well again. My schedule to Alaska is still indefinite.

Chicago, Ill., July 15, 1942   2300 CWT

No further news on my schedule. No planes are returning from Alaska, so there is nothing for me to fly.

When I arrived back at my hotel after dinner I found Sid Nelson staying in my room. He is departing for Alaska in the morning, so that makes me due out next. We are having much conversation about flying to Alaska.

Chicago, Ill., July 16, 1942   2000 CWT

Another useless day. Went to the airport and had lunch with Ray Gohr and Tom Plunkett, but there was no further information regarding when I may depart for Alaska. It was very warm here today. Read a mystery novel.

Chicago, Ill., July 17, 1942   2200 CWT

Nothing worthwhile accomplished today. Still no planes are arriving from Alaska, and this waiting is growing most tiresome. That is especially true in view of the heat wave we are experiencing. It was the hottest July 17 on record today — 100 degrees — and very humid. There is little one can do to escape the heat in Chicago.

Although I am not a particularly ambitious individual, a few experiences such as this one are enough to show one the folly of seeking a life of ease. By no stretch of the imagination can it be construed to be fun to sit here in complete idleness, with absolutely nothing which has to be done. How much more fun it would have been to have remained on the farm, where I could have worked in the fields and known the grateful feeling of physical tiredness!

Chicago, Ill., July 18, 1942   2200 CWT

Still no action! However, a plane is en route to Chicago from Alaska and is due in about midnight tonight. It will be mine to take back, when and if it goes back. The dispatch office says it will leave about 6:00 A.M. tomorrow, but I doubt this.

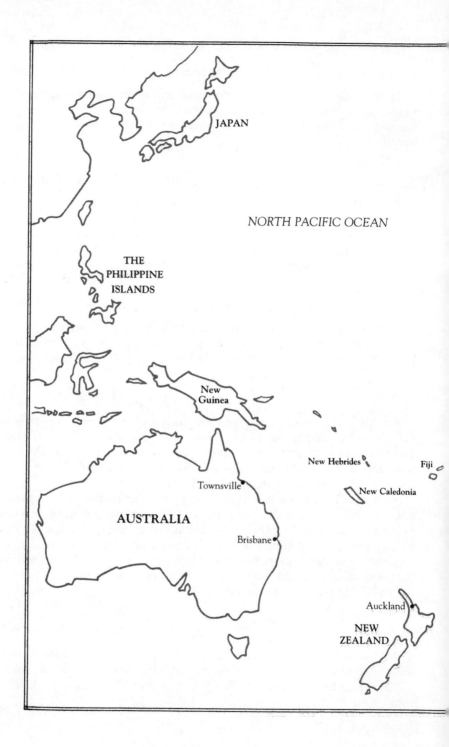

JAPAN

NORTH PACIFIC OCEAN

THE
PHILIPPINE
ISLANDS

New
Guinea

New Hebrides

Fiji

New Caledonia

Townsville

AUSTRALIA

Brisbane

Auckland

NEW
ZEALAND

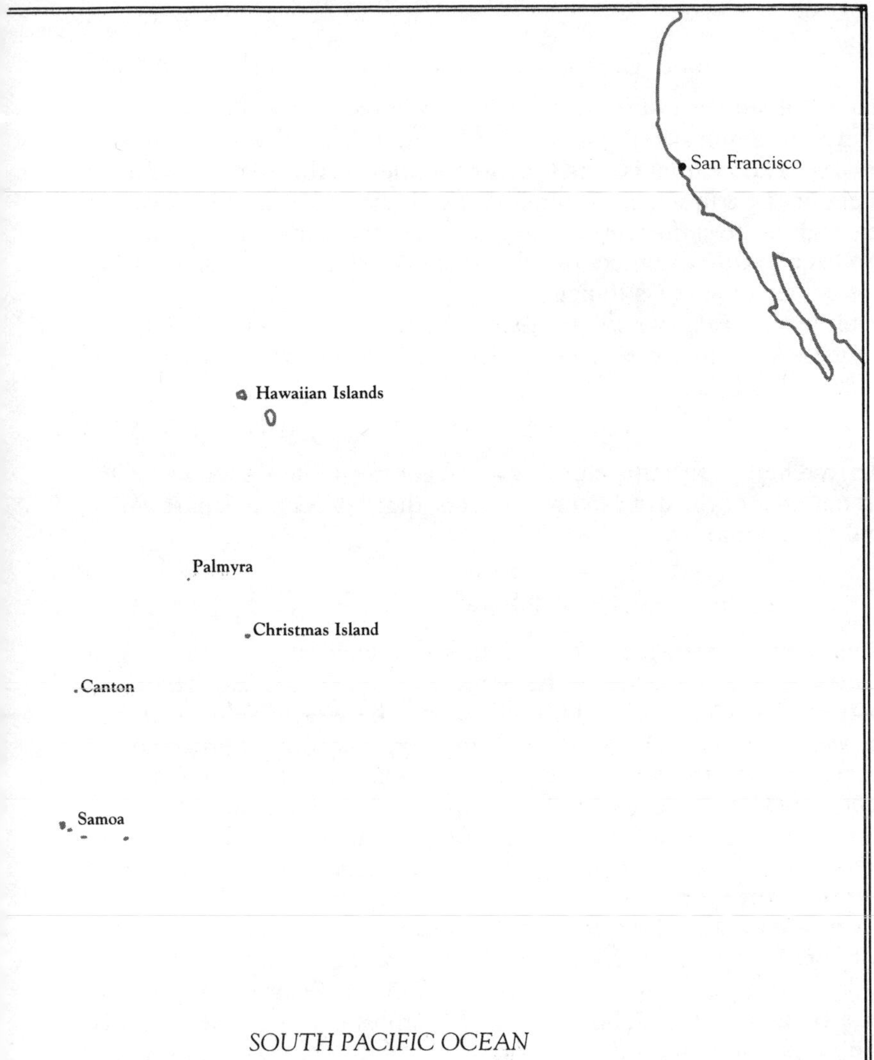

San Francisco

Hawaiian Islands

Palmyra

Christmas Island

Canton

Samoa

SOUTH PACIFIC OCEAN

En route Chicago–Edmonton, July 19, 1942   2300 CWT

We are about thirty minutes out of Fargo now on the way north. It's a relief to be going at last, and more relief to be away from the Chicago heat wave. The weather is good tonight and there is that certain exhilaration about the trip which so often comes from flying in good weather when engines are performing perfectly through the star-studded night sky. I have been taking a number of celestial navigation fixes with a considerable degree of success tonight.

After leaving Fargo we will have about six hours of traveling to Edmonton, where we will arrive after daylight.

Edmonton, Alberta, July 20, 1942   2300 MWT

Arrived here at five this morning and slept until noon, then rested for the remainder of the day. No news, except that I expect to depart northbound early tomorrow.

En route Whitehorse–Edmonton, July 21, 1942   2300 MWT

This morning we departed at 10:30 with a load of eighteen enlisted men for Whitehorse, Yukon, with instructions to return to Edmonton immediately. The distance is 1,000 miles, and the weather, although not good, was not too bad. We worked a simulated instrument procedure at each of the stations as we went northward, with the exception of Fort Nelson, where a very extensive forest fire was in progress and the country, for a distance of 200 miles, was completely enveloped in a dense, white smoke blanket. The trip up required six and one half hours and was both beautiful and instructive.

I had never realized the immensity of the northwestern part of this continent. This journey of 1,000 miles, seen as a line on the map, is almost lost in the broad spaces of northern Canada. To sit in the airplane for five or six hours, grinding away at 175 miles per hour over country which is monotonously alike but invariably beautiful, and then to accomplish only a "couple inches" on the map seems almost preposterous; but nevertheless it is true. Unlike so many other parts of the continent, everything is green. Forest and brush cover almost every inch of the land, and broad rivers and lakes of all sizes are to be found almost everywhere. The country from Fort Nelson northward is quite rough, with mountains occasionally rising to 8,000 feet.

We arrived over Whitehorse at 11,000 feet in a heavy snowstorm, and with the army radio there is no reception in precipitation. After a few anxious moments we found an area where the precipitation was light and we were able to spiral down to contact.

Whitehorse is an interesting town, but with very little activity. Its interest is largely in its history as it is now only a shell of its former self, and ruins from its former prime are everywhere in evidence.

After about two hours in Whitehorse, we departed for Edmonton. However, as it was time for dinner when we approached Watson Lake, we landed and had an excellent meal. The field is located on the shore of a beautiful lake, and the men stationed there reported the fishing to be excellent.

After dinner we departed for Edmonton, and we will now arrive there in a short time.

En route Edmonton–Fairbanks, July 22, 1942   2300 MWT

Slept late today, then gathered with Dutch Schram, Johnny Johnson, Eddie Eshelman, Art Derby, and Leo Allen to drink a few beers. We went out to dinner early, and the field called to say that Schram and I would depart for Fairbanks about 10:00 P.M. This we did and are now nearing Grande Prairie. There is considerable weather involved, so I have enough to keep me awake. The 1,500 miles to Fairbanks is too far to go without refueling, so I plan to stop at Whitehorse if the present doubtful weather permits.

The Whitehorse Inn, Whitehorse, Yukon, July 23, 1942   2300 YWT

A hectic day! We arrived at Fairbanks about 5:00 A.M., and decided to have breakfast and return as far as Watson Lake. We made short stops at Big Delta and Northway, Alaska, and then proceeded on to Whitehorse. Fatigue overtook us on this leg: we had been up over twenty-four hours and had flown over thirteen hours.

Finally, we arrived at Whitehorse to find that all our plans, which we had flown so long to carry out, could not be fulfilled. We would not be able to go on to Watson Lake after all. Dutch Schram had had engine trouble here at Whitehorse last night, and although his airplane was flyable, he did not believe its condition made it desirable to proceed to Fairbanks with a large load. Consequently, I agreed to take his airplane back to Edmonton and let him have mine with which to proceed, with his cargo, to Fairbanks. My copilot Cole and I were too tired to go on without rest, so Cahill and Quinby, our mechanics here, allowed us to use their beds to get some rest. Vacant rooms are simply not available in Whitehorse. We have had a good sleep now, and are going to proceed to Edmonton in an hour. Moreover, the boys are off work now and want to occupy their beds for the short rest they will get.

This is a very famous (or infamous) hotel, built during the gold rush to Alaska. It is interesting to have stayed here, but I have seen better hotels.

Salt Lake City, Utah, July 24, 1942   2300 MWT

What a day this has been! We brought the disabled airplane down from Whitehorse and arrived in Edmonton about 8:30 A.M. After breakfast and bath we were in bed about 10:30, throughly fatigued. At 11:30, soon after we had fallen asleep, the field called to say they were unable to effect the necessary repairs on the airplane and asked if we could possibly ferry it to Salt Lake City for the necessary work.

This we did, arriving in Salt Lake at 7:30 P.M. after a flight of 2,000 miles from Whitehorse since 2:00 A.M.! We came down via Calgary, Lethbridge, Great Falls (where we landed for the Customs), Helena, Idaho Falls, Pocatello, and Ogden. Now, after an excellent dinner and rest, I'm going to bed for ten long hours (I hope).

Tried to telephone the family in Denver but there was no answer. Guess they have not returned from the farm or Chicago.

Denver, Colo., July 25, 1942   2200 MWT

Much disappointment tonight. Arrived home from Salt Lake City for a day, while an engine was being changed in my airplane, and found that my family had not returned from their visit to Chicago. So what was to be a pleasant evening at home has turned into a lonesome one. Have spent the evening in bringing my correspondence up to date, etc.

Salt Lake City, Utah, July 26, 1942   2200 MWT

Came back here by air from Denver this afternoon in preparation for the return to Edmonton tomorrow morning. Spent a lazy day at home alone, then a quick trip here. To bed early tonight.

Edmonton, Alberta, July 27, 1942   2200 MWT

Had to test-fly my airplane after the engine change, and then there were many typical red tape delays at Salt Lake and Ogden before we were finally properly loaded at Ogden and en route to Edmonton. The trip back via Pocatello, Helena, Great Falls, and Calgary was pleasant and short. After a fine dinner, am now going to retire in anticipation of a trip northward to Alaska tomorrow.

Edmonton, Alberta, July 28, 1942   2100 MWT

No trip for me today. It seems that the work to be done here is gradually decreasing. Two airplanes went south to the States, and I'm the fourth man due out northward. Cole and I took a long hike this afternoon, and it was pleasant except for mosquitoes, which breed most prolifically and grow to immense proportions.

Big news today: Chicago telephoned to ask how Hudson, Brown, Fay, and I would react toward flying to Australia. It seems that United has signed a contract with the army to fly DC-4s and B-24s from San Francisco to Australia, and they expect to start operation in about a month. I would go to school in San Francisco for about a month to brush up on navigation and check off on those types of airplane. I replied that I would definitely go providing the operation was at all logical. In other words — if I were to be based in San Francisco rather than on some South Pacific island, etc. It will be great fun if it materializes. Don't know how they arrived at the particular four of us. I certainly do not rate it purely on a seniority basis.

To bed now, as I might be called for a trip early tomorrow.

Edmonton, Alberta, July 29, 1942   2100 MWT

No trip out for me today as there were no planes out from the north. A quiet day. To bed early tonight, as I expect to be called sometime during the night to go north.

Anchorage, Alaska, July 30, 1942   1600 AWT

As we more or less expected, we departed from Edmonton at 2:30 A.M. and arrived here after a trip which was beautiful all of the way. I had not been beyond Fairbanks before, and the trip from Fairbanks to Anchorage was inspiring. Came alongside Mount McKinley en route and saw moose along the Susitna. We were delayed two hours in Fairbanks because we had a load of enlisted men and no one knew where they were going. They had not been told, and no one could be found in Fairbanks who possessed the information. At length it was decided we should proceed to Anchorage with them.

Upon arriving here, Cole and I purchased some old ivory, had a good dinner, and now plan to retire at once. Tomorrow we proceed to Nome with another group of soldiers, weather permitting.

Nome, Alaska, July 31, 1942   1200 BWT

In Nome at last! And what a place! The Eskimos and bad weather really are kings here.

We finally departed from Anchorage at 8:30 this morning after nearly three hours of army red tape delay, and we had a beautiful trip for most of the way over. The weather was fine on the eastern portion of the route, and Mount McKinley and its lesser satellites protruding through a lower overcast formed an impressive spectacle indeed. The terrain for a considerable distance west of Anchorage is as rugged as any I've ever seen. From McGrath westward, however, it is of low altitude and relatively smooth. We crossed the Kuskokwim, upon the lower reaches of which four acquaintances a few years ago struck a platinum deposit which netted them some four million dollars.

Over Norton Sound we fervently hoped that we might spot a group of whales, but we were not so fortunate. Near Nome the weather became very bad and we were rather fortunate to have just sufficient ceiling and visibility to land there.

Cole and I went into town here to inspect the place. It is certainly not much of a town. The houses are all small and very weatherbeaten. The entire place gives one a sense of impermanence — as if each and every one of the inhabitants were merely biding his time, awaiting a chance to move to some more hospitable place. The place has a gray, dismal appearance, and the wind blows in from the ocean in a constant effort to steal the warmth from one's clothing. Eskimos form a large part of the population, and each house presents its long rows of salmon drying on stakes and poles out of the reach of the huskies.

We had a poor but expensive lunch of reindeer steak and are departing for Fairbanks in a few minutes.

En route Whitehorse–Edmonton, July 31, 1942   2400 AWT

We landed at Fairbanks, Tanacross, Northway, Whitehorse, and Watson Lake and are now on our last leg to Edmonton. It was interesting country from Nome to Fairbanks. The terrain is almost treeless, but covered with brush and moss and quite green. As in most of the rest of Alaska, there are innumerable lakes. The Yukon is very wide and muddy and very similar in appearance to the Missouri or Mississippi rivers.

We discovered a black bear up on top of a ridge, where he was probably feasting on berries. We circled him quite closely at a low altitude and since he had no cover in which to hide he became infuriated. He stood upright and made futile efforts to strike out at us as we went around him. We also sighted a large herd of caribou and numerous moose. Wildfowl abound on every lake.

In a few hours now we shall be back in Edmonton, where we can get some rest. We will have flown about sixteen hours and have been on our way continuously for over twenty-four hours by the time we arrive in Edmonton.

Above: A military C-47 transport airplane. Courtesy McDonnell Douglas Co.
Below: A military C-87 transport airplane, a cargo version of the B-24 bomber.
Courtesy U.S. Army Air Force.

Edmonton, Alberta, Aug. 1, 1942   2200 MWT

A day of rest today, but I also received notice that I am definitely going on the Australian run and that I will have to report to school in San Francisco not later than August 6. I am to fly a trip down from here to Chicago tomorrow morning, and then to proceed to Denver for a couple of days at home.

En route Chicago–Denver, Aug. 2, 1942   2200 CWT

An uneventful trip from Edmonton to Chicago today and soon I shall be in Denver and home! Learned some of the details of the Australia run. Will fly C-87s, flying all the way through with rest stop at Honolulu each direction. Will be based in San Francisco, and will move my family there. The run starts September 1 but, since I am the most junior man on the run, I will probably not leave on my first trip until much later than that. In the meantime, I will be going to school and moving my family.

Denver, Colo., Aug. 3, 1942   2000 MWT

This was a fine day, spent largely in becoming acquainted with my family once more. In a way it is nice to be away so much because homecoming is so pleasant.

There were many business matters to attend to, and now to bed for a fine sleep in my own home.

Denver, Colo., Aug. 4, 1942   2400 MWT

Another quiet day at home and then a little farewell celebration with a dinner at the Buckhorn and a movie. Now for a couple hours of sleep before I board the airplane at 3:00 A.M. for San Francisco and a new task.

3

Hot and Cold

San Francisco, Calif., Aug. 5, 1942   2100 PWT

Arrived here this morning after a nice flight from Denver and found details of our school quite disorganized. Reported in and then went to the hotel for some sleep. However, Sid Nelson, with whom I am rooming, wanted to go to Palo Alto to inquire about houses for rent, so we boarded a train, met a realtor in Palo Alto, and discussed our problems.

San Mateo, Calif., Aug. 6, 1942   2330 PWT

I inherited quite a task today. I am now the instructor in celestial navigation for the entire group here, which consists of seventy-eight captains, first officers, and navigators. I see where I am going to be a busy man during the next few weeks. There was no organization when I came, and I spent most of the day in dividing and organizing the group so that the number of students in any one group would not be too large to handle. I'm afraid my lecturing technique can stand a bit of improving. I ran the first groups through the preliminaries today and then held a stargazing performance on the roof of the hotel here tonight. All of this left very little time for anything else.

San Mateo, Calif., Aug. 7, 1942   2330 PWT

Another day spent in playing schoolteacher! It's very difficult for me to maintain an even disposition after answering the same questions for the hundredth time each hour.

After a long and tiresome day in the classrooms, we had an early dinner and then held classes on the roof of the hotel until 11:00 tonight, identifying stars, etc.

San Mateo, Calif., Aug. 8, 1942   2300 PWT

Classes lasted only until noon today, then Sid Nelson, John Roberts, L. H. Smith, and I went to Palo Alto on a house-hunting expedition.

San Mateo, Calif., Aug. 9, 1942   2200 PWT

Today Sid Nelson, Smitty, and I went bus riding through Redwood City, Atherton, and Palo Alto, visiting real estate agents and looking for houses. Tonight we were back at the hotel in time for another session of star-gazing and measuring star altitudes from the hotel roof. I'm retiring early to allow the boys to play with the stars without interference from me.
A fine letter from Grace makes the world a finer place.

San Mateo, Calif., Aug. 10, 1942   1800 PWT

A tiring day today. Hours of classroom work and hundreds of questions to answer over and over until my head fairly rings with "right ascension," "declination," "meridian altitude," etc. There will be no stargazing tonight, thank God, because the sky is completely overcast.

San Mateo, Calif., Aug. 11, 1942   1800 PWT

Another day of schoolteaching, but at last most members of the class are beginning to get the idea, and my task becomes progressively easier. Jack O'Brien, our chief pilot, has asked me to grade the class and pick out the ones that should be eliminated, but I have refused, on the premise that I do not wish to have any part in the administration since I too am merely a member of the class and, as such, should properly have no jurisdiction or responsibility in such matters.

Tomorrow I am going to take a group down to Los Angeles in a DC-3 for a dual purpose. Each embryo navigator will take sun sights on the way down and star sights on the way back, and while we are in Los Angeles we will visit the planetarium, where the machinery will be at our disposal so that we may view the celestial sphere, which will concern us on flights to Australia at various seasons of the year.

Los Angeles, Calif., Aug. 12, 1942   1800 PWT

A long but interesting day today. I departed from San Francisco with twenty-five student navigators in a DC-3 and en route to Los Angeles they each had ample opportunity to take altitude observations of the sun and plot position lines. Upon arrival here we proceeded to the Griffith Observatory, where Dr. Cleminshaw gave us a most interesting lecture and quite vividly illustrated, by use of the planetarium, many of the features of celestial navigation which were vague or indefinite in the minds of the students. This lecture lasted about two and a half hours and included sights of the celestial sphere at all latitudes, particularly those of Australia.

I'm now back here at the Burbank airport waiting to depart for San Francisco after dark, in order that the students may have an opportunity to take some star altitude measurements from the airplane en route back to San Francisco.

San Mateo, Calif., Aug. 13, 1942   2200 PWT

I arrived back at the San Francisco airport at 1:00 this morning after hours of delay at Burbank due to army regulations.

Today in class we had a review of dead-reckoning navigation, and for once I had the opportunity of doing a bit of studying for my own account. There were a number of things which I wished to review, and I also practiced taking some radio Morse code, a feat which I had not even attempted in over twelve years. It was surprising, however, how rapidly one could regain some skill in an almost-forgotten accomplishment.

Too little sleep last night will force me to an early retirement tonight, but only after I have written the family at least a note.

San Mateo, Calif., Aug. 14, 1942   2200 PWT

Another dull day of schoolteaching today, but now, fortunately, all of the students have progressed to a point where I have very little instructing to do. Brought up a few vague points about celestial today, and even had time to do a little studying for myself.

San Mateo, Calif., Aug. 15, 1942   2400 PWT

Today there were no classes, so Sid Nelson and I spent the morning doing such tasks as opening a bank account, etc. Sid, Smitty, and I returned to San Mateo early and then went to the movie to see *Mrs. Miniver*, which proved to be an excellent show but not at all similar to the book, which was also good.

San Mateo, Calif., Aug. 16, 1942   2100 PWT

After a late breakfast, Sid, Smitty, and I went to Palo Alto to try to locate houses to rent, when and if the company tells us it can approve our moves. Smitty located an ideal house and rented it for occupancy after September 10. Sid and I found two houses in which we were interested but did not make any definite commitment on either of them.

The three of us are going to the roof of the hotel to make some practice observations of the moon, which is visible now for the first time since we started the navigation school.

San Mateo, Calif., Aug. 17, 1942   2000 PWT

A routine day in the classroom today until about midafternoon, when Jack O'Brien came to ask if I would like to go to Honolulu tonight. Of course the answer was in the affirmative. It seems that a routine trip was scheduled to go and I could go as observer to collect as much information as possible concerning the methods of operation, navigation, etc.

I rushed to the hotel to obtain sufficient personal effects to use for a few days and then returned to the airport at all possible speed. I was to be flown to Hamilton Field, from which point the trip would depart for Hawaii. About this time the dispatch officer at Hamilton called to advise that the trip would be held until tomorrow morning to permit certain important personnel to arrive from the East in time to connect with it. Now I am at the hotel, where I can have a fine sleep and be much more rested for the trip tomorrow. Seeing Honolulu again will recall a lot of almost-forgotten memories.

San Mateo, Calif., Aug. 18, 1942   1800 PWT

Am leaving for Honolulu tonight about ten o'clock. An airplane will take me over to Hamilton Field, where I will depart, as observer, on a trip in a C-87 with a crew from Consolidated Aircraft Corporation. Today has been routine here, with the usual classwork and the answering of many questions, when my mind has really been centered on the impending trip.

En route San Francisco–Honolulu, Aug. 18, 1942   2330 PWT

Here we are, over the ocean about 300 miles out from San Francisco, and all is going well. The crew is very congenial and consists of Captain Jackson, Copilot Jamieson, Navigator Lyon, Engineer Stanley, and Radio Operator Olson. Preparation and execution of the flight have been extremely interesting to me as this is my first experience at such operations. The airplane, the same general type which we shall use, was interesting and appeared enormous. We expect to arrive in Honolulu about 10:00 A.M. PWT, which is 7:30 A.M. HWT.

Honolulu, T.H., Aug. 19, 1942 1700 HWT

Arrived here at 7:30 A.M. and went to bed immediately to get some much-needed sleep. Honolulu appears the same as when I last saw it just ten years ago. The barbed wire along Waikiki is of course incongruous with my memories of the place. There is still considerable evidence remaining of the bombing raid of December 7. The hangars at Hickam Field and the upturned hulks of warships in Pearl Harbor are mute evidence. The quarrelsome myna birds are still chattering away, oblivious to the meaning of war, but the perpetual whining of airplanes overhead reminds one of the constant threat by further invasion by hostile forces to the peace of this beautiful island. We depart tonight at 7:30 for the good old U.S.A.

San Mateo, Calif., Aug. 20, 1942 2100 PWT

Arrived at Hamilton Field at 10:00 A.M. today after a fine trip of eleven hours and fifty-five minutes from Honolulu. The weather was excellent and I learned much about the method of operation over the Pacific. Upon arriving at Hamilton Field, I called United at San Francisco to try to get an airplane to come for me, but, although they were willing, the army would not approve any such flight through a restricted zone. I proceeded by bus and train to San Mateo, and this required four and a half hours. I was so tired and sleepy that it was almost impossible for me to stay awake on the way down. I went to bed upon arriving at the hotel and slept for a few hours. After all, a round-trip from San Francisco to Honolulu to San Francisco in twenty-four hours is rather rapid traveling for 1942. Perhaps my children will regard it as horse-and-buggy speed by 1962.

San Mateo, Calif., Aug. 21, 1942 2200 PWT

Today I gave all of the information I had collected to the entire class. The members were very much interested in all details of the trip, from the navigating problems to the operation of the airplane.

The world is a fine place tonight. After a fine dinner I'm now ready for a good sleep, secure in the knowledge that my family thinks I'm fine and that life is very good to me.

San Mateo, Calif., Aug. 22, 1942 1800 PWT

No school today except for those who needed to practice radio code. Perhaps I should have practiced, but I was too lazy. Did some of the personal odd business tasks this morning, and this afternoon I had a fine game of tennis.

San Mateo, Calif., Aug. 23, 1942   2200 PWT

A day of ease today. This morning Sid, Smitty, and I played tennis, then we had a session of study in the afternoon, and tonight some more practice with the stars. The first day of complete relaxation since we have been here.

San Mateo, Calif., Aug. 24, 1942   2200 PWT

Today I inherited a new task. The United States Marine Corps sent twelve young pilots to our newly founded navigation school to have us check them out in celestial navigation. I inherited the job, so I spent the day with them, trying to determine just how advanced they were. I had them work a number of problems, and this afternoon we took a trip in a C-47 to Redding, Reno, and return in order to give each of them an opportunity to take celestial observations and plot sun lines of position from the airplane.

San Mateo, Calif., Aug. 25, 1942   2200 PWT

More hours of classroom instruction for the marine pilots today. Two of them returned to Camp Kearney in their airplane to obtain material which they had failed to bring, and the balance of us had a "cram session."

Had my first meeting with the FBI today. I was approached by one of our guards and informed that an FBI special investigator wished to talk with me. After a short period of apprehension on my part, he disclosed the fact that he was seeking information concerning an acquaintance of mine, a former pilot with United Air Lines. The person in question is suspected of being a Nazi sympathizer, and I believe I was able to give the investigator certain information which may be of considerable value to him. If the suspect is really guilty, then I will do everything in my power to see that he is apprehended. Even though I once considered him to be my friend, if he is now engaged in activities contrary to the best interests of this country, then there is no one who would be more desirous of seeing him properly punished.

Tried all day to obtain permission to take the marine pilots in their own airplane out to sea to do some celestial practice tonight. This permission was not forthcoming from the Army Interceptor Command so the proposed flight had to be postponed.

San Mateo, Calif., Aug. 26, 1942   2300 PWT

More flying with the marines today for the purpose of practice in taking and plotting sun lines. At noon the company announced that all of us here in the school would go on leave for two weeks, pending the signing of United's contract with the army for the trans-Pacific operation. The contract is being delayed due to arguments about pilots' pay, etc., and it's a possibility that it may not be signed.

Salt Lake City, Utah, Aug. 27, 1942   2300 MWT

This morning Sid and I went to Palo Alto for the purpose of house hunting. I signed a lease for a lovely house in Atherton.

Upon returning to the hotel we found a message from the airport to the effect that a ferry trip was departing for Salt Lake City at 1:45 P.M. and that we could ride it if we could be at the airport by that time. This allowed us only fifteen minutes, but we packed and made it by virtue of the fact that they held the trip a few minutes for us. Now here in Salt Lake City it appears almost certain that we will be able to get space on the trips eastbound about midnight.

Denver, Colo., Aug. 28, 1942 through Sept. 6, 1942

I spent this period at home in Denver awaiting developments. Although I made an entry into my handwritten diary each day, there were no events of significant interest to anyone but my family, which consisted of Grace, Jimmy (now two years old), and a fourth family addition, due to be born in early December.

On September 6 I received a telegram from United Air Lines saying I would be assigned to the Alaskan route again while awaiting the signing of a contract with the army for operation to Australia.

En route Denver–Chicago, Sept. 7, 1942   2300 CWT

On our way to Alaska for an assignment which no one particularly relishes. Other, more interesting things are in the wind, and since we have already seen so much of Alaska, I feel as though I am only marking time here. Flying will be considerably more hazardous in view of the fact that winter has started in Alaska, and the transition from summer to winter presents more hazards to flying.

It was difficult to part with the family this afternoon. They are so uncertain of the future, as to where they will live, etc.

En route Chicago–Edmonton, Sept. 8, 1942   2330 MWT

We are on our way tonight, fourteen of us including three flight crews and mechanics. Others will follow tomorrow as soon as airplanes become available.

I was unable to find anyone in the company in Chicago who was willing to commit himself as to whether or not I should move my family to San Francisco.

Edmonton, Alberta, Sept. 9, 1942   2300 MWT

Back here again for some more of the old grind. Looks as if we will do a lot of sitting around on this expedition as there are too many pilots for the number of airplanes we have.

A very unexciting day today. Not much to do but await the arrival of another airplane. It appears that we may get away for Alaska sometime tomorrow.

Fairbanks, Alaska, Sept. 10, 1942   2300 AWT

Had a long flight up from Edmonton, and now I must await an army loading crew to load my airplane. It will be four hours and is typical of army efficiency.

The weather was not good today, and at this time of year darkness comes early. At Whitehorse there is as much lack of daylight as there once was lack of darkness. It is truly a black hole to try to get into under bad weather conditions at night. The navy lost a DC-3 there a few nights ago with fourteen passengers aboard. The wreckage has not been located as yet.

Yesterday I saw one of the many hypocrisies of our civilization in Edmonton. There was a great parade, for which the entire town turned out. The occasion was the return of five RCAF pilots, who had, less than forty-eight hours previously, bombed Saarbrücken, Germany. The local populace was quite vociferous in its welcome to these boys who had so recently hurled death down upon other supposedly civilized people. Without going into the justification therefor, it makes thinking people wonder when they see peace-loving people fired to the point of bloodlust. Our civilization is a fine influence, but one which can so easily be cast aside when its existence is threatened. Putting the cloak back on will probably be far more difficult.

We plan to proceed to Anchorage tonight, get some rest there, and then return to Edmonton tomorrow. That is, of course, providing the army has no other plans for us.

En route Tanacross–Whitehorse, Sept. 11, 1942   2000 AWT

We slept in NCO barracks at Anchorage until 9:00 this morning and then proceeded to the operations office, expecting to go to Yakutat. However, they had loaded our airplane with cargo destined for Galena, which is out toward Nome. We had a beautiful trip out there, passing alongside Mount McKinley, which for the first time I had seen it had no clouds about its summit.

The scenery here is magnificent. The valleys are a blaze of color, since the frost has turned the leaves of the aspen and other deciduous trees. Fresh snow covers all of the mountains down to a low level, but the lakes and streams are as yet unfrozen. There is a fascination about the country that is not quite describable. To those fortunate people who are attuned to the land, it must afford an unending thrill.

Galena is expecting 500 airplanes through on the way to Russia in the next three weeks. We went to Fairbanks from Galena, and there we encountered many Russians, who are here to ferry the lend-lease airplanes through Siberia to the fighting fronts in Russia. On studying some of their maps, it would appear that they will have a rough journey through Siberia.

[In talking with an interpreter for these pilots it was interesting to learn that these airplanes (mostly P-39s) are quite successful when used against German tanks and truck convoys. The P-39s have not been very successful when we have used them against enemy fighter airplanes, since they cannot outrun, outmaneuver, or outdive the enemies' counterparts.

Doubtless the Russians will lose many of the airplanes on the long ferry trip, but it is hoped that those that do arrive on the eastern front will be effective.]

We were considerably delayed awaiting loading at Fairbanks, but finally departed for Edmonton, with stops at Tanacross, Whitehorse, and Watson Lake. We may, or may not, get into Whitehorse, as the weather is doubtful, and no reports have been received for the last few hours. With luck we should arrive in Edmonton about 6:00 in the morning.

Saw two moose and a black bear this afternoon.

Edmonton, Alberta, Sept. 12, 1942   2100 MWT

Slept a few hours after arriving here at 0530, and am still somewhat dazed after the long trip. Nothing a good night's sleep will not correct, however. Other crews are arriving, so it will be some time before I go back to Alaska.

Edmonton, Alberta, Sept. 13, 1942   2200 MWT

This has been a dull Sunday. Edmonton has blue laws; there are no Sunday newspapers, no movies, nothing. Have been reading most of the day and am now retiring with the expectation of going to Fairbanks tomorrow.

Fairbanks, Alaska, Sept. 14, 1942   2300 AWT

Attended an operations meeting at Edmonton at noon today and then departed on my trip at 1530. The trip up was uneventful except for some snow, ice, and static from Whitehorse to Fairbanks.

I am staying at the Nordale Hotel, but I have seen better. The toilet is some distance away. Food is very high—a bowl of soup, forty cents; a hamburger sandwich, forty cents. The town appears to be much less prosperous than Anchorage, but, of course, the army is much less active here.

Tonight I wonder just what the family has done about moving. Perhaps they are out on the street, but there's so little I can do about it from here.

Fairbanks, Alaska, Sept. 15, 1942   2100 AWT

None of our airplanes came in from the south today due to bad weather around Whitehorse, so we are stranded. There is little enough indication of when we shall get away from here. I have covered the town completely now, street by street, and although nature is at its most beautiful point, nevertheless I would like to get away so that I could be doing something useful.

Fairbanks, Alaska, Sept. 16, 1942   1600 AWT

Still no airplanes have arrived from Edmonton. We have hopes for tonight, but nothing definite.

Today Dawson, Stropes, Dixon, and I took a long walk out into the country to view the muskeg, etc. It was a beautiful trip, as the aspen leaves are at the height of their color. Mount McKinley and Mount Hayes were visible far to the south.

This afternoon we rented an automobile and drove about twelve miles out to Esther, where American Smelting operates a huge placer mine. We spent some time in observing the dredging operations, where they are taking out about half a million dollars in gold weekly. About one hundred feet of topsoil and muskeg must be washed away with huge streams of water, and the gravel must be thawed before the gravel bearing the gold is ready for the dredges. It is a tremendous operation, but it is profitable. At the present rate of operation there remain about twenty years of dredging. It's a far cry from the methods employed by the old prospectors, but far less romantic.

We inspected Alaska University, which normally has about two hundred students but which now has only a fraction of that enrollment due to the war. The museum was very interesting.

Edmonton, Alberta, Sept. 17, 1942   2000 MWT

We departed from Fairbanks at midnight last night and arrived here at 1000 this morning after making short stops at Northway, Whitehorse, and Watson Lake. Winter is rapidly moving southward, as there was considerable snow even on the plateau south of Fort Nelson. Temperatures at flying levels were below zero. The weather was generally the best I have ever encountered on this route.

No letter from the family.

Edmonton, Alberta, Sept. 18, 1942   2200 MWT

Two letters from home today advising me that the family has stored the furniture and is moving into an auto camp to await word concerning moving to California. It's a most unsatisfactory solution, but I know at least that they are all right.

Today Vaughan, Peternell, and I went hunting for ducks. It was a beautiful day, really too good for duck hunting, but we hired an automobile and drove about twenty-five miles into the country northwest of Edmonton. Ducks were very plentiful, but they were flying high, and the marsh at which we hunted afforded no cover.

Edmonton, Alberta, Sept. 19, 1942   2300 MWT

Frank Wittenberg, Jack Sorenson (a native Swede), and I went duck shooting today at Egg Lake, about thirty miles from Edmonton. I killed seven and should have had more, but my marksmanship was not too good. We have just returned to the hotel, tired but happy, and were it not for my concern over my family, life would be fine.

There is no further word concerning the Australian contract with the army.

En route Watson Lake–Edmonton, Sept. 20, 1942   2330 MWT

A surprise trip for me today. The field called this morning to advise that I would have a trip to take to Whitehorse and return. We departed at 1300, had a slow but beautiful trip up, and are now on our return trip after having stopped for an excellent dinner at Watson Lake. We are now settled comfortably for the four-hour flight from Watson Lake to Edmonton. The weather is excellent, the engines are singing a merry tune, and all is well.

We followed the new Alaska Highway from Whitehorse to Watson Lake, and I've never had a more beautiful journey. In spite of many heavy frosts, the aspen still hold their bright red and yellow leaves, and the pine trees furnish a solid background. As we were going down Teslin Lake at sunset, the coloring could not have been more brilliant. A rising three-quarters moon cast its silvery path into the lake from the southeast, and a brilliant red sun provided a dazzling reflection from the southwest and painted the lower cloud surfaces a delicate pink. The lake was completely bound by dense growths of yellowed aspen, and from the surface of the lake literally hundreds of wildfowl struggled into the air to flee the monstrous, noisy airplane. I shall never forget the beauty of that sight. There is something about this country that gets into one's blood, and it has certainly left an indelible impression upon me.

The new highway has progressed almost phenomenally. If the army fails to accomplish a lot of its objectives in this war, the highway at least will be a tribute to engineering ingenuity and hard work.

Edmonton, Alberta, Sept. 21, 1942   2200 MWT

This is a beautiful Indian summer day here, and as I have nothing better to do, I have been spending it in a lazy, languorous fashion. No further news about when we will be finished here and can proceed on the Australia run.

Edmonton, Alberta, Sept. 22, 1942   1530 MWT

At last good news has arrived! We are to withdraw from Alaska now and proceed to San Francisco immediately. Some of us expect to get away from here tonight, and the remainder tomorrow. The world is already a finer place. Perhaps I'll be with the family again by tomorrow.

Denver, Colo., Sept. 23, 1942   2200 MWT

Flew to Chicago from Edmonton and then rode to Denver by air. Found the family fine but crowded in their tourist cottage.

Denver, Colo., Sept. 24, 1942   2100 MWT

Spent today doing the many last-minute jobs incidental to moving. We plan to drive through to San Francisco starting early tomorrow.

Salt Lake City, Utah, Sept. 25, 1942   2200 MWT

Drove fifteen hours today at a conservative forty miles per hour to conserve rubber. The countryside through the mountains was beautiful in its early-autumn blaze of color. Fatigue is rapidly overtaking me.

Fernley, Nev., Sept. 26, 1942   2300 PWT

Another fifteen hours of driving today and then much trouble locating a place to sleep. The only consolation is that tomorrow we will have a much shorter distance to go to our destination.

San Mateo, Calif., Sept. 27, 1942   2200 PWT

Arrived here at 1630 after an easy trip down from Fernley. There was no mechanical trouble with the automobile throughout the entire trip. There seems to be little activity on the Pacific setup, but tomorrow I'll go to the airport to learn what I can.

San Mateo, Calif., Sept. 28, 1942   2000 PWT

Went to the field today and learned that it would probably be some time before I would be making a trip or even be making familiarization flights in the airplane. As soon as the army delivers an airplane it expects a trip to be flown with it immediately. This, of course, is almost impossible in view of the fact that none of us has ever had an opportunity even to fly the C-87 type of airplane.

San Mateo and Atherton, Calif., Sept. 29, 1942 through Oct. 16, 1942

During this time my family and I settled into our new home in Atherton. Although I made an entry each day into my handwritten diary, there were no significant events to report, and the daily entries have been deleted in the interest of brevity. I checked out as pilot on the C-87 aircraft.

Atherton, Calif., Oct. 17, 1942   2300 PWT

Grace and I spent the day in San Francisco shopping for our new house. Lots of fun along with it, however, and we ended up with a Chinese dinner. Just as we arrived home, the airport telephoned to advise that I might be called out about three o'clock in the morning to test-fly a C-87 which is scheduled out to Australia tomorrow. Naturally I hope I will not be called, as a shopping trip in San Francisco is a tiring thing for anyone.

Atherton, Calif., Oct. 18, 1942   2300 PWT

Sure enough the airport called me out for the test hop this morning after I had been asleep only thirty minutes. I did not arrive back home until 6:30 A.M. and Jim kept me from sleeping most of the morning.

Atherton, Calif., Oct. 19, 1942   1800 PWT

This morning the pilots had a long meeting with Walt Addems, the United system chief pilot, to try to learn something concerning our contract. There was little news forthcoming, and some of the pilots are becoming so dissatisfied with the lack of information and action that they are seriously considering leaving United to go with other companies. We were almost certainly promised some kind of news before the end of the week.

More ground school this afternoon, and then I was advised that I would be leaving as observer on a trip to Australia tomorrow afternoon. Now I have to get my personal effects ready for the trip.

Atherton, Calif., Oct. 20, 1942   2300 PWT

Our trip did not leave today as the airplane could not be made ready in time. I had a written exam on the airplane.

Hamilton Field, Calif., Oct. 21, 1942   2100 PWT

At last we are on our way! We arrived here about 6:00 P.M. from San Francisco, and are now making last-minute preparations for our journey. I am observer on the trip and the crew is Clarence Hudson and Virgil Vaughan. We are looking forward to a good, but exciting, trip.

4

First Steps in the Pacific

OCTOBER, 1942–JANUARY, 1943

Honolulu, T.H., Oct. 22, 1942   1200 HWT

We arrived here at about 8:00 A.M. after a trip of thirteen and a half hours. The trip was long but uneventful, and Hawaii presented its beautiful landscape to our tired eyes. There is much more activity here than there was two months ago when I visited this place so briefly. I'm staying at the fine old Moana Hotel, where I had so many pleasant times when I was a bachelor second lieutenant pilot here in the army from 1930 to 1932. The breakers from Waikiki come up under my window to spend their final effort on the sands of the beautiful beach. Very shortly they will lull me to sleep after my thirty hours of wakefulness.

Tomorrow morning we depart at 7:30 for Canton Island.

Canton Island, Oct. 23, 1942   1900 CWT

Ten and a half hours of flying brought us to this pinpoint in the Pacific. The trip down was beautiful. The blue, blue ocean had hardly a ripple on its vast surface, and equally blue sky was generously sprinkled with small white cumulus clouds. We were all less tired after a refreshing rest at Honolulu, and much better able to enjoy the trip.

We arrived here about 4:30 P.M. local time, and I spent an hour on the beach watching the strange hermit crabs, which varied in size from that of a pinhead to the size of one's fist. They are so jealous of the shells they have appropriated for their own use. The island itself is a beautiful spot—merely a circular island about eight miles in diameter, with a lagoon in its center which leaves a rim of coral formation about a mile wide around its perimeter. The contrasting coloring between the lagoon, the coral, and the ocean forms a most beautiful picture. The island is infested with rats—a field variety which is not particularly obnoxious, but they managed to search our luggage rather thoroughly each time we placed it within their reach. There are crickets and flies on the island, but no mosquitoes. A form of low shrub and a type of bunch grass grow sparsely.

Tonight we visited the officers' club for a few minutes. It's a far cry from the clubs I have known.

Nandi, Fiji Islands, Oct. 25, 1942   1800 FWT

We lost our day as usual when we crossed the date line.

Today has been a most interesting day, partly because of the misfortunes of others. Yesterday an army B-17 carrying Eddie Rickenbacker left Honolulu about the time we did, but he failed to reach Canton Island. When last heard from he was believed to be in the vicinity of Palmyra, but there was a possibility that he might have made a crash landing on one of the uninhabited islands. Consequently, we conducted a search of three of these islands by detouring from the direct route between Canton and the Fiji Islands.

First we visited Enderbury Island, which lies southeast of Canton. It is a rectangular coral island about two miles long and one mile wide, and, although it is now uninhabited, it has the remaining buildings of a small settlement. It is the nesting place of many frigate birds and other seagoing birds, and is visited occasionally by commercial collectors of guano. There is some small vegetation and the usual lagoon in the center.

Next we visited Phoenix Island, which is also uninhabited. It is triangular in shape, with a perimeter of only three miles. It is a nesting place of birds and is also visited by guano collectors.

Then we proceeded to Sydney Island, which is not often heard of but which appeared to be the typical romantic South Sea island. It is triangular, about twelve miles in perimeter, and is inhabited by a considerable number of Polynesians. Vegetation grows luxuriously, and there is the usual central lagoon. The natives live in thatched-roof buildings, and have converted most of the island into coconut groves. They came out onto the beaches in great numbers to watch us go thundering overhead as we made our search. The grass skirts of the women were plainly discernible from our low altitude. This is the island to which I think I shall retire when I grow tired of it all.

Needless to say, we saw no trace of the lost airplane, so we proceeded on to the Fiji Islands and arrived here in midafternoon.

These are beautiful islands, rugged and with much and varied foliage. After a thorough personal cleanup campaign in the officers' quarters, we went about four miles into the native village. The natives here are typical of the many pictures we have so often seen of them. Most of the buildings in the village as well as those on the army post are of thatch construction, and afford no protection from the swarms of mosquitoes. The natives are rather solemn, at least around Americans, and seem to take great delight when we return their most dignified military salutes.

Brisbane, Australia, Oct. 26, 1942   1700 AWT

Arrived at Amberley Field, Ipswich, about twenty miles out of Brisbane, at 3:15 this afternoon, after a trip of nine and a half hours from Fiji. Although we passed directly over New Caledonia, we did not see it because of clouds and rain there.

Australia was a welcome sight, and many unusual things were immediately noticeable. Two RAAF Spitfires challenged us as we approached Brisbane, and upon proper recognition they escorted us to Amberley Field.

The first things which caught my eye in the landscape were the brilliant blue jacaranda trees and the scarlet poinciana trees. I have never seen anything to compare with them in color, and I consider it strange that I have never even heard of them.

We were driven in an army car over the long, winding road into sprawling Brisbane. One's first impression is that Australia is about twenty years behind the United States in general physical progress. The highways are poor, the automobiles are largely antiquated American models, the railroads are obsolete by our standards, and the central portions of the cities are constructed on the horizontal plan rather than the vertical. Soldiers are everywhere, both Australian and American. The sanitary conditions which prevail are certainly not up to our standards, but I suppose that depends largely on what one is accustomed to.

Brisbane, Australia, Oct. 27, 1942   1700 AWT

Today we spent in seeing the town of Brisbane. For hours we walked through various parts of the city, buying trinkets, observing customs, and talking to the people. By our standards it's a queer place, although it has a certain charm.

We wished to buy some shorts for flying, and other minor articles of clothing. In order to do so we first had to go to visit an Australian captain in charge of military rationing for this area, and obtain a ration book from him. This book, and good American money, enabled us to buy what we needed.

The city is not unlike any Midwest American city, except that poor transportation and congestion make it a much more confusing place. Most stores are small and there is a complete lack of large department stores such as we know. There are no buildings more than five stories high, and air raid shelters are located strategically over all of the city. Traffic congestion is aggravated considerably by the fact that in the downtown area many bomb shelters are built above ground in rows down the center of the streets. Brisbane has not had an air raid as yet, although there have been several alerts.

It rained most of the day, and this detracted somewhat from the pleasure of our sightseeing.

Citizens here are limited to two gallons of "petrol" per month, and, as a result, many automobiles have been converted to charcoal-burners. The apparatus weighs about three hundred pounds and is usually mounted on the rear of the car, where, due to unbalanced weight, it causes very rapid wear of the rear tires.

Brisbane, Australia, Oct. 28, 1942   1600 AWT

No airplane arrived for us to fly in to San Francisco, so we spent another day in acquainting ourselves with Brisbane. We visited the botanical gardens and the zoo. A sight of the flora and fauna of Australia almost makes one believe he is in a new world. In many cases we in America have no counterparts for the various animals and plants found here.

The residential areas of town are entirely different from ours. There is apparently little effort at zoning between business areas and residential districts. Almost all houses are built on stilts at considerable height off the ground, and nearly all have tin roofs. Another strange custom is that houses along a street are not numbered, but rather are named, and addresses consist of house name, street name, section, and city, so that a postman must have a really good memory. A typical address would be Hull House, Anne Street, Bulimba, Brisbane. It appears to be a usable system, however.

Tomorrow we hope to get away.

Brisbane, Australia, Oct. 29, 1942   1600 AWT

No airplane arrived today, so we took a trip on a boat about fifteen miles up the Brisbane River, where a zoo is located at Lone Pine. Here among other things they had a number of koala bears, which are about the most intriguing little animals I have ever seen. They are typical teddy bears and they take delight in hanging about one's neck. They eat only the leaves of eucalyptus trees.

There were also emus and a cassowary bird, neither of which I had seen before. I also learned to distinguish between kangaroos, wallaroos, and wallabies.

Upon returning tonight we learned that an airplane had arrived, and we are to start our return trip at 2:00 A.M. tomorrow.

Nandi, Fiji Islands, Oct. 30, 1942   1730 FWT

We departed from Amberley Field, Ipswich, Australia, at 2:30 this morning and, after an uneventful trip, stopped at Plaine des Gaiacs, New Caledonia. Among our passengers were Col. Jim Davies and Colonel Rodieck. Jim Davies and I were on army duty together in Hawaii, and he has been in the entire Southwest Pacific campaign to date and has been awarded many honors for his excellent work in Java and the Philippines. Rodieck was formerly my squadron commander and is now on the General Staff in Washington, but is now here on some type of inspection.

New Caledonia is the most primitive place we have yet visited. It is almost entirely undeveloped. The men are extremely dark and have unusually muscular physiques. There are about six native men for each woman, and each wife lives peacefully with a number of husbands.

We departed from New Caledonia after trying to eat an inedible breakfast. Bill Eddy of Consolidated Aircraft had some bad luck while we were there. We had brought a spare nose wheel tire to him to replace one that had punctured. After effecting the replacement, he started to taxi out to resume his trip and the nose wheel strut collapsed, causing serious damage to the airplane.

We arrived in midafternoon at Nandi, where we are spending the night.

Canton Island, Oct. 31, 1942   1800 CWT

Arrived here late this afternoon after an uneventful trip from Viti Levu (Fiji). We detoured slightly en route to go by Tana Island, where there is an active volcano—600 feet above sea level.

I spent some time on the beach here observing the very interesting hermit crabs, and collecting seashells. We plan to leave here in about an hour and go on through to Honolulu tonight, arriving there early tomorrow.

Today is my birthday, as well as that of my son. By local time tomorrow will also be my birthday, since we crossed the date line today.

Honolulu, T.H., Oct. 31, 1942   2100 HWT

Sure enough I had a birthday which lasted two days. It would have been so much more pleasant if I had been able to spend it with my family.

We arrived here about 8:00 this morning after a long, all-night trip from Canton Island. I slept for three hours and then spent the remainder of the day on Waikiki Beach. It was most relaxing, and I shall do more of it tomorrow.

Our present plans are to depart from here for California at about 6:00 P.M. tomorrow.

Honolulu, T.H., Nov. 1, 1942   1600 HWT

Today is a leisurely, restful day. I'm staying at the Moana Hotel, where I had a fine breakfast this morning, including fresh, *ripe* Hawaiian pineapple such as I haven't tasted since I was in the army here years ago.

I spent all morning on Waikiki Beach, where I collected about all of the sunburn I could stand. I swam out about a half mile through the breakers and returned, so that now I'm pleasantly tired and will probably have difficulty in remaining awake on the trip tonight.

We are leaving the hotel at 4:30 this afternoon, with a proposed departure time of 6:00 P.M. for San Francisco. So I'll be seeing the family again tomorrow.

Atherton, Calif., Nov. 2, 1942   2000 PWT

Home at last! Arrived here about 1:30 this afternoon after an all-night trip of thirteen hours from Honolulu and much delay at Hamilton Field. I found the family all well and happy, and now I'm going to bed for some well-earned sleep.

Atherton, Calif., Nov. 3, 1942   2030 PWT

A fine night of rest made the world a better place. Today I was lazy, secure in the belief that I would have nothing to do but rest for a few days. However, I was rudely shaken from that belief today when the field called to advise that I would have to attend school for five days at the Oakland airport, starting tomorrow at 8:00 A.M.

Jim and I had great day today, becoming reacquainted and enjoying life in general. I find that he has developed a fear of Snoopy, the little black cocker spaniel we got for him. Snoopy is a bit large, and inclined to be too playful to please Jim. Perhaps when Jim grows in proportion to the size of the dog he will be better able to hold his own.

Atherton, Calif., Nov. 4, 1942   2030 PWT

A long trip over to Oakland to school today. I learned nothing. It was a review of navigation systems, all of which I have used in actual practice. We made an arrangement whereby I could conduct the school at the San Francisco airport, thereby eliminating the necessity of going all the way over to Oakland each day.

No further news of the contract.

Atherton, Calif., Nov. 5, 1942   2030 PWT

Another day of school, but we managed to cover all of the required subjects so that now our school is finished, at least for the present. I have to stand by to test an airplane about midnight tonight, providing the mechanical work on it is completed in time. Perhaps now I can have a few days off. I am scheduled to make a talk before the navigation class at Oakland Monday morning, and beyond that it would appear that my life will be my own for the next few days.

Atherton, Calif., Nov. 6, 1942   2330 PWT

Today I worked in the yard, caught up with other odd jobs, and then Sid Nelson and I played tennis. Tonight we celebrated by having my long-overdue birthday dinner with all of the trimmings, and it was really quite a feast. The Nelsons and the Smiths were here for dinner.

During the course of the dinner Jack O'Brien called up with bad news. Sunday I am to leave to ride to Australia again in order to have a relief crew there, so that airplanes will not have to remain idle there but rather that they can return immediately with the relief crew aboard, while the inbound crew gets its much-needed rest and returns on the following trip. I am the most junior man in the schedule, so the job of riding to Australia falls to my lot.

Atherton, Calif., Nov. 7, 1942   1700 PWT

Today I have been busy preparing for my long, long trip. I now know so much more what I need to take in the form of supplies, etc. It's quite a task to pack as lightly as possible, and yet take everything needed.

I'm still standing by to test the airplane and to check out my copilot so that he will at least be familiar with the cockpit before we have to take off from Australia in the dark and with an overload.

Atherton, Calif., Nov. 8, 1942   2330 PWT

Today I went to the airport early in order to check out my copilot, Stropes. The weather was quite bad and we were able to make only one takeoff and landing. We then went by automobile to Hamilton Field in order to board the airplane there for Australia. However, the pilot, George Douglas, did not like the prevailing weather en route to Honolulu so the trip was held for departure tomorrow night. We drove back to the San Francisco airport, and I finally arrived home a few minutes ago.

En route Hamilton Field–Honolulu, Nov. 9, 1942   2300 PWT

Another early trip to the airport today to try to get my copilot checked out ended in failure. The airplane I was to use developed brake trouble and was out of service.

We flew to Hamilton Field at 3:00 P.M. today, departed there at 9:20 tonight, and are now on our way. It will be a long ride so I'm taking it as easy as possible. I'll bring this same airplane back as far as Honolulu and have my rest there. We are very crowded in the airplane, having only half enough seats. Probably will not get much sleep.

It's a beautiful night—clear overhead with a stratus overcast below. We have a trip forecast of thirteen and a half hours, so that we should arrive in Honolulu about 8:30 A.M. local time.

Honolulu, T.H., Nov. 10, 1942   1900 HWT

Arrived here at 8:30 A.M. and after much delay at the field we finally got to bed at the Moana Hotel at 1:00 P.M. Up at 6:00 P.M. without enough sleep, and now we are going to the airport at Hickam at 8:30 in order to depart at 10:00 P.M. Frank Wittenberg is the captain from Honolulu to Australia.

It was a beautiful day in Honolulu, but I was too tired to enjoy much of it. On the return trip perhaps I'll have time to spend on the beach.

Canton Island, Nov. 11, 1942   0700 CWT

Landed here after a nice nine-hour flight from Honolulu. The weather was fine, the stars bright, and the navigation excellent. We had breakfast here, watched the hermit crabs for a time, collected coral, and are now ready for departure to Nandi, Fiji, where we will spend the night.

Nandi, Fiji Islands, Nov. 12, 1942   2200 FWT

It was a fine trip down from Canton today, and we are in this beautiful spot for the night.

In the morning we leave early for Plaine des Gaiacs, New Caledonia, and then Brisbane.

Amberley Field, Australia, Nov. 13, 1942   2000 AWT

Another nice ride into Australia, broken only by a short stop at New Caledonia. I was so tired upon arrival that I was most unhappy to learn that there were no rooms available in Brisbane and that we must stay on the post in tents. I tried to get permission to leave tonight and go back to Fiji, where we could at least have a bed in which to sleep. However, the army had other ideas, and we are staying here, departing tomorrow night for home.

En route Australia–Fiji, Nov. 14, 1942   0200 FWT

Here we are in the middle of the night on our way back to the good old U.S.A. This of course is the first trip I have actually flown as pilot on this route, so at last I feel as though I am accomplishing something. My crew is performing well enough considering their experience, and all is well.

The takeoff at Amberley tonight was not too comfortable, in view of the fact that I had never before handled a fully loaded airplane and only my flight engineer had flown in one before.

We are passing over New Caledonia and expect to arrive in Fiji well after sunrise. It's quite a thrill to be all on your own in this huge airplane out here, where the entire responsibility rests with you and the only possible help lies in your own resourcefulness. I can readily see how those who are not certain of their own ability to navigate must be quite apprehensive on these trips.

Nandi, Fiji Islands, Nov. 15, 1942   1600 FWT

Arrived here this morning after an entirely uneventful trip from Australia. We plan to rest here overnight and to go directly on to Honolulu with only a fuel stop at Canton en route.

Canton Island, Nov. 16, 1942   1600 CWT

Practiced navigation on the way here today to see if I could find the island without the use of radio. The plan worked out very well, so I am more reassured than ever.

We are stopping here for only a few hours, long enough for dinner and a short rest, and then we are proceeding to Honolulu tonight.

I'm getting quite a thrill out of this first trip in which I am in full command.

Honolulu, T.H., Nov. 16, 1942   1200 HWT

This leg of the trip was not so uneventful. All went well until we were about 400 miles south of Honolulu, when we came upon an enormous thunderstorm. Not being certain of how much rough air this airplane can stand, I did not wish to enter headlong into the storm. I tried to climb above the storm, but at 13,000 feet was still unable to see the top of it. I then elected to go to the left around it, and I had to proceed more than a hundred miles westward before I could successfully skirt it. Radio was useless due to static, so we had to find Honolulu from an unknown position by dead reckoning. This we did, but were delayed about an hour and a half by the unusually long detour.

Upon arrival at Hickam Field we found that there was an alert due to the fact that some Japanese naval units had been spotted within 400 miles of Oahu. The army wanted us to leave immediately so that in case of an attack our ship would not run the risk of being damaged. However, having flown nineteen hours out of the past twenty-four, I did not consider it safe to proceed. Consequently, we are laying over here until tomorrow night before proceeding to San Francisco.

It is certainly fine to get back to our type of civilization, where baths and good food are possible.

Honolulu, T.H., Nov. 17, 1942   1800 HWT

We were scheduled to depart at 5:30 this afternoon, so we went to Hickam Field and learned that the army through Major Stevenson desired that we not leave on schedule due to some bad weather approaching the West Coast. Although the weather appeared flyable to me, I did not insist, but rather agreed to depart at 2:30 tomorrow morning providing the weather was to the major's liking.

Had a nice day here today. Arose late and had a leisurely breakfast with a double order of fresh pineapple.

Now that we are holding for an early morning departure, we are remaining here on the post at Hickam Field, where we can obtain more rest than would be possible if we returned to the Moana Hotel in Honolulu.

Atherton, Calif., Nov. 18, 1942   2200 PWT

Home again! After the age of thirty-five that's about the most wonderful thing that can happen to a man.

We departed from Honolulu at about 3:30 this morning and had a fine daylight trip over after a short mechanical delay at Hickam, caused by a defective throttle lock. We made fair time across, but were plenty tired upon arrival. There was the usual confusion and delay at Hamilton Field, especially in view of the fact that we arrived there after dark.

I'm going to bed now for a long, long sleep, Jimmy and God permitting.

Atherton, Calif., Nov. 19, 1942   2000 PWT

Did manage to sleep a bit late this morning, then up to complete some of the long-delayed small business matters. There are always so many details to attend when one has been away so long.

I found the family all well and happy.

I went to the airport today to check in and turn in my report of the trip, get the latest mail, etc.

Atherton, Calif., Nov. 20, 1942   2230 PWT

More business details today and then a pilots' meeting in San Mateo to determine whether or not the pilots will continue to fly to Australia after each pilot who is assigned to the operation has made one trip. It was agreed that rather than stop this essential operation, we will continue to fly but only on a trip-to-trip basis, and if the contract isn't signed soon, we can cease operations any time we deem it advisable.

Went to the airport after the meeting, and then tonight we went to the local movie. One of these nights before too long we will be arising at some unconventional hour and journeying to the hospital to add another member to our family.

Atherton, Calif., Nov. 21, 1942   1900 PWT

A rather lazy day today. Some business in Palo Alto this morning, and then I made some progress on the winter garden this afternoon while the rest of the family had their naps.

Everything is under control now, but I'm still not entirely rested from my trip. It appears that I will not be due out again for some time, so I'll have plenty of time for rest.

Atherton, Calif., Nov. 22, 1942   2050 PWT

Another lazy day—Sunday—with nothing pressing to be done. Have begun to get a bit restless now, however, and want something to do.

Atherton, Calif., Nov. 23, 1942   2100 PWT

Today I went into San Francisco to the State Department to get a passport. It seems that the British and Australians aren't satisfied to have us help them win the war, but now they are more concerned to be sure that we do it legally. Consequently, we who go into English-controlled territory such as Fiji or Australia must have passports as well as visas from the British consulate, so I spent all day in San Francisco, where I had to provide six photographs, one birth certificate, my army officer's commission, a letter from the company to the effect that I have business in Australia, and $13. Friday I can return and pick up my passport, then I must go to the British consulate, pay them an additional $5, and get the proper visa. I would say that the British are in this war with, among other purposes, that of not losing money.

Did some minor shopping, stopped at the airport for the mail, and returned to my very fine family.

Atherton, Calif., Nov. 24, 1942   2200 PWT

Worked in the yard and garden for most of today. I am preparing a much larger winter garden, in view of the fact that the government announced today that there would be no more fresh vegetables on the market after the present crop was harvested, due to lack of transportation.

I was tired tonight, and had retired early to read. I had been in bed only a few minutes when Cherri Smith telephoned to tell me that her husband, Smitty, had cracked up today in New Caledonia. She wished me to do what I could to learn whether or not the report she had was complete. The report said that there were some slight injuries to the crew, but nothing serious. There is nothing I can do tonight. This is the first accident in our new operations, but I have much confidence in Smitty's ability, and it was, no doubt, due to some mechanical failure of the airplane.

Atherton, Calif., Nov. 25, 1942   1900 PWT

This morning I telephoned the airport to learn what I could of Smitty's mishap. What I learned was essentially the same as what had been told Cherri Smith. Thereafter, we called on Cherri to comfort her but found her in a very fine mental state.

Atherton, Calif., Nov. 26, 1942   2200 PWT

Today was Thanksgiving Day. Even among our small troubles we have so very much to be thankful for, and we are so much better off than most of the people in this troubled old world.

Conditions were not so bad but that we could still have our turkey dinner, and that's something that most of the people in starving Europe could not do. Mrs. Smith had dinner with us, and others, including Mrs. Sawyer, the Broerens, and the Hal Taylors, had cocktails with us prior to the dinner. There was no further news of Smitty or his accident, and naturally Mrs. Smith was not in too good spirits.

A long walk with the family, and now to bed early.

Atherton, Calif., Nov. 27, 1942   2030 PWT

Most of today I spent in going into San Francisco to pick up my passport (#51556) and to get a visa from the British consul. After all of this red tape, I can now enter the Fiji Islands, New Zealand, or Australia with the complete legal sanction of the British government. That's quite nice of the British, I think, to make certain that we are legal while we help win the war.

Atherton, Calif., Nov. 28, 1942   2000 PWT

After a lazy morning, Grace, Jimmy, and I went this afternoon to a plant nursery and obtained various plants for the vegetable and flower gardens. I worked until dark tonight getting all of the plants set out, as the weather indicated rain in the offing and I wished to have the plants in the ground before the rain started.

Still no word from Smitty up until this evening. Nelson arrived yesterday and we expected he would possibly bring news, but he did not do so. Now we must wait until Dick Crane returns, perhaps tomorrow.

Atherton, Calif., Nov. 29, 1942   2030 PWT

Dick Crane arrived today with the first authentic news regarding Smitty's mishap. He had brought all of the crew back with him with the exception of Smitty, and he reported that no one of our men was injured. It seems that the runway was muddy, and that, upon applying brakes, the airplane skidded into some posts. I did not learn how badly the airplane was damaged.

Today was a quiet day. We took two long walks, and I worked in the garden for a couple of hours. Tonight I am catching up with accumulated correspondence.

Atherton, Calif., Nov. 30, 1942   2000 PWT

Went to Palo Alto today to do the miscellaneous errands necessary before gas rationing goes into effect tomorrow. There will be few trips in the automobile from now on, and we will resort to a lot of walking henceforth.

Am engrossed in reading two good books now, *The Golden Bough* and *Look to the Mountain*, one classical and the other popular and modern.

Smitty will arrive tomorrow.

Atherton, Calif., Dec. 1, 1942   2100 PWT

Six months ago today I started writing this little letter. At times I've been on the verge of giving it up, and probably I should. However, when I read back over it, it recalls a great many incidents which I have already forgotten. So now I suppose I shall continue it for a while longer at least.

Atherton, Calif., Dec. 2, 1942 through Dec. 8, 1942

I remained in Atherton during this period. I made an entry into my handwritten diary each day, but nothing of importance occurred. We were impatiently awaiting the arrival of the fourth member of our family.

Atherton, Calif., Dec. 9, 1942   2100 PWT

Well, today was the day. We got to bed rather late last night and this morning at 0515 things began to happen. We went to the hospital at 0645 and then, after much pacing of the corridors for me, little John Emmerson arrived on this earthly scene at 1545 today. He is a fine little fellow of six pounds, twelve ounces in mass and nineteen inches in length. He is very red and has much long, dark hair. Grace is groggy but well.

Being a father is an awesome thing. The responsibilities are frightening when one ponders them too long. It's a thrill I wouldn't miss for the world, though, and when these boys reach maturity I only trust we will have reared them in such a manner that we can be proud of them.

Atherton, Calif., Dec. 10, 1942 through Dec. 20, 1942

Troubles started on December 10. Jimmy came down with chicken pox and, of course, Grace and newborn Johnny had to remain in the hospital in order not to be exposed. For these ten days I cared for the sick child and ran the household as best I could. Fortunately, I did not have to go on a trip during this period.

Daily diary entries have been eliminated in the interest of brevity.

Atherton, Calif., Dec. 21, 1942   2100 PWT

Today the family came home from the hospital. Now there are four of us, and only such a short time ago there was only myself. It is difficult to imagine myself the father of two boys. I'll wager, however, that the realities of the situation will not allow me to forget it for long from now on.

Tonight home is a fine place. There is a cheerful fire in the fireplace, and we are, for the minute, so snug and secure in our fine home. Wonder how long it will last.

Atherton, Calif., Dec. 22, 1942   1800 PWT

The family was all happily settled at home again this morning, so I went to the airport to clean up a lot of details and business with the company. Things were quiet there, due to bad weather. It now seems that the army wishes to have us resume operations to Alaska early this spring—this time operating out of Seattle with C-46-type airplanes. It will be an interesting variety to the Pacific operation.

I am now the twelfth man due out, so it will probably be at least three weeks before I depart on my next trip. I'm anxious to get started again.

Atherton, Calif., Dec. 23, 1942   2000 PWT

It rained all day today, so that I spent most of the day indoors. Jim and I went to Palo Alto today to get haircuts and to do some shopping. Johnny is doing very nicely.

The field called this afternoon to advise that I would have an airplane to test at 0900 tomorrow. It will be fun, but I hope the weather will have improved somewhat before that time.

Atherton, Calif., Dec. 24, 1942   2000 PWT

Spent two and a half hours this morning testing a C-87 prior to its outbound trip. It was fine to fly an airplane again after such a long rest.

This afternoon there were the usual preparations for Christmas Eve. Our Christmas this year is to be a very quiet one, in view of our new baby and in view of the war. I have to go to the airport early in the morning to test another airplane.

Atherton, Calif., Dec. 25, 1942 through Jan. 14, 1943

I was most fortunate to be able to spend the holidays with my growing family. I made regular entries into the handwritten diary but there were no important events transpiring as far as my participation in the war effort was concerned. This material has been removed in the interest of brevity. My only duties were several airplane test flights, a couple of physical exams, and some inoculations.

Our festivities were quite low key, and we had many callers—not only to see the new baby but also to help us celebrate.

Atherton, Calif., Jan. 15, 1943   1800 PWT

After weeks of inactivity, today at last ushered in a new era of excitement. This morning I was feeling much improved from my bout with a cold, so was up and around when the field called to request my presence at a special meeting there at 1:00. At the meeting a special mission was vaguely outlined to us.

[Four of us pilots and our crews were asked to take two C-87s from San Francisco to Western Australia on a very secret mission. We were not told the reason for the trip at the time.]

There are so many things to do in preparation, that I'm going to be a busy man. The four of us spent all afternoon in San Francisco outfitting ourselves with special equipment, etc.

Atherton, Calif., Jan. 16, 1943   1900 PWT

I still have my packing to do, and it will be more difficult than ever to say good-bye to my family this time. The trip will be more hazardous than former ones, and now my family is larger than it has ever been before. It seems that the more responsibilities one has, the more one hates to go away and leave them—this in spite of the fact that we all probably have times when we feel that we would like to leave everything behind and get away from it all.

Tonight we are having a quiet evening at home. Tomorrow night we expect to have guests, so this is our last real evening together for a long, long time.

Atherton, Calif., Jan. 17, 1943   1800 PWT

Today has been a beautiful day, and I've had little I've had to do except to finish my packing. The whole family took a long walk this morning.

We have a roaring fire going in the fireplace now, and we are awaiting the arrival of the Torrisons from San Francisco. I want to get a good night's sleep tonight as tomorrow will be an almost endless day.

5

Down Under

En route San Francisco–Honolulu, Jan. 18, 1943   2330 PWT

Well, we are on our way on what may prove to be the finest adventure of my career. We departed from Hamilton Field tonight in an airplane equipped with everything but the proverbial kitchen sink. Even we do not know exactly where we are going or what we are to do, but it promises to be fun.

There are two airplanes, with four of us captains aboard in order that we can push right on through without stopping for rest. We alternate with our flying and our resting. Aboard our airplane, a C-87, are Johnny Johnson and myself as captains; Emory Wishon, navigator; Hank Strzelecki, flight engineer; Tom Minor and Ray Wolf, radio operators; and Roy Miles as steward. The captains aboard the other airplane are Rube Wagner and Johnny Roberts. We will arrive in Honolulu after daybreak tomorrow and then will depart directly for Canton, where we will have to stop for refueling.

The army dispatchers tried to discourage us from leaving Hamilton tonight due to supposedly bad weather. However, to date it had been a beautiful night and the weather has been perfect.

It was most difficult to part with the family today. Jimmy and his mother drove me to the airport and I hated to say good-bye. It will be a long time before I see them again, and of course there's always the possibility that I might not come home from one of these trips.

En route Honolulu–Canton, Jan. 19, 1943   1130 CWT

We had a splendid trip over to Honolulu, albeit a bit long. Landed at Hickam at 9:00 this morning, had much delay getting briefed, and at last are on our way to Canton. We should arrive at Canton about dark, and the army powers that be, who are controlling our movements on this trip, have decided that we should remain overnight at Canton rather than push on through to Brisbane. To go on through without stopping would mean an afternoon arrival in Australia, and the colonel who is directing our mission, Col. Milton Arnold, of the Air Transport Command, would be unable to transact the necessary business before the following morning anyway. So we will rest and arrive in Brisbane in the morning. Which suits me.

This is a beautiful day and a fine trip today. The weather is perfect. There are only a few puffy white clouds below us, lazily dragging their reluctant shadows across the calm blue ocean. This is an enormous world when one finds himself out here in the center of the Central Pacific.

En route Canton–Fiji, Jan. 20, 1943   0830 CWT

We landed at Canton last night after a very fine trip from Honolulu. We had a good sleep of seven hours and are now on our way again. We plan to arrive in Nandi, Fiji, in the early afternoon and remain there until near midnight and then depart at such time as to arrive in Australia early in the morning. It is interesting to observe that from San Francisco to Canton, approximately 4,300 statute miles, we averaged 155 miles per hour elapsed time, even including our four-hour stop at Honolulu.

Everything is going nicely, our equipment is all performing perfectly, and conditions could not be better. We are about to start through the ever-present tropical front now, so I had better go back to work. Sometimes it gets a bit rough.

En route Fiji–Brisbane, Jan. 21, 1943   0430 AWT

We are about one and a half hours out of Brisbane now and proceeding nicely according to schedule. We expect to proceed to Townsville on the northeast coast of Australia after a four- or five-hour stop in Brisbane.

There is considerable military activity at Nandi now. Three battleships and an aircraft carrier are there, among other units, and a large air force is there also. Looks as though some activity is going to develop soon, and we may be in on some of it on this mission before we are through.

Hope to get a few hours of sleep in Australia today, as I've had entirely too little of it since leaving San Francisco. To be in Australia just two and a half days out of San Francisco naturally requires a sacrifice of several things, not the least of which is sleep.

En route Brisbane–Townsville, Jan. 22, 1943   0530 AWT

Many delays and changes of plans developed yesterday, so that we did not get away from Brisbane as soon as we had expected. Upon arrival it was decided that we would go directly to Port Hedland on the west coast of Australia by a route directly over central Australia, but that we would stop overnight at Charlieville, about 450 miles west of Brisbane, and make the long flight during daylight today. However, it developed that we would have to go to Darwin on our way, so then we decided to leave at 4:00 local time this morning. When we started to plan our trip at the airport this morning, we found that we would not be permitted to enter the war zone directly, but that it would be necessary for us to go to Townsville after all in order to pick up necessary identification codes, procedures, etc., for entering the war zone. We are on our way at last and are now about two hours out, proceeding up the northeast coast of Australia.

The trip is a beautiful one. The land is green with luxuriant vegetation, and the ocean is of the deepest blue. Almost the entire coastline is bordered by a beautiful strip of rose-tinted coral sand, with the perpetual surf rolling in over it up to the reddish earth of the rocky soil. The mainland is quite rough and broken, but few of the hills exceed 2,000 feet in height. We have just reached the southern tip of the Great Barrier Reef, and it is an impressive sight indeed. I can understand why it is often called the eighth wonder of the world.

Our two passengers, who are directing this mission, are Colonel Arnold and Captain Elkins. They are splendid, likable men, and they are quite as vexed as we are at the difficulty we are having with the army authorities in obtaining proper information and permits for our trip.

If all goes well, we may be able to get through Townsville without much delay, and then proceed on to Darwin before dark. More often than not, however, delays are much more extensive than one anticipates.

En route Townsville–Darwin, Jan. 23, 1943 0700 AWT

Well, Townsville was interesting for a lot of reasons. We arrived there in time for lunch and then went back to the operations office to collect what information we could regarding airports and facilities along the west coast of Australia. We expect to be there about a week or ten days, and we learned many things concerning conditions we can expect to find there.

In the first place, we will probably have to sleep out in the open as there are few places where the RAAF can provide us with quarters. There is considerable malaria and dengue fever there, so we had to completely equip ourselves to guard against mosquitoes while living in the open, and starting today, we are on a diet of quinine. Fresh water is very scarce, and all military personnel are limited to two gallons per day for all purposes. Guess we will need a bath by the time we return.

Today we are flying directly across the northern part of Australia. The landscape is quite varied. For about a hundred miles out of Townsville

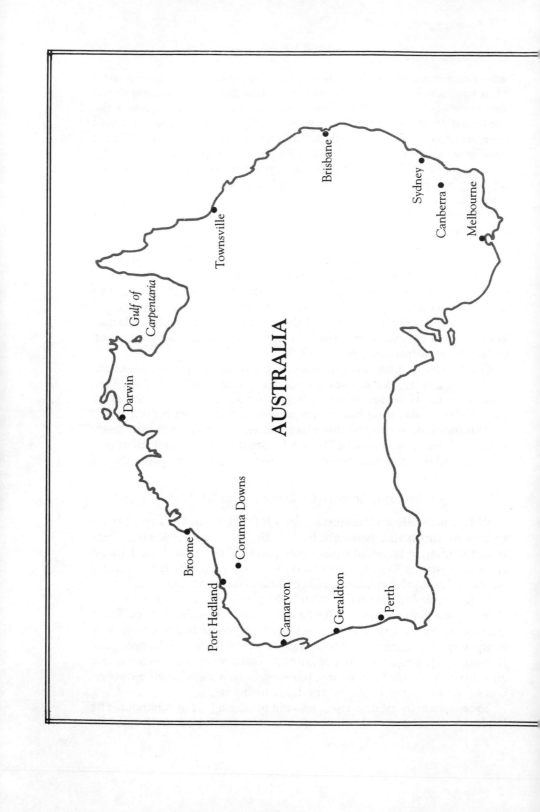

AUSTRALIA

Gulf of Carpentaria

Darwin
Broome
Port Hedland
Corunna Downs
Carnarvon
Geraldton
Perth
Townsville
Brisbane
Sydney
Canberra
Melbourne

the ground is very rough and is covered with dense jungle growth. The rainfall here is heavy. Farther westward there lies a drier, timbered plateau, still rather rough. There are practically no roads, but occasionally trails appear to arise out of nowhere, to lead to native villages. The great Gulf of Carpentaria is much like our own Gulf of Mexico. It is shallow and muddy near the shoreline, and the land bordering is tide flat or marshy. Numerous short, wide rivers empty into the gulf. There are occasional water buffalo to be seen wallowing in the mud flats.

We will arrive in Darwin in the early afternoon, and expect to remain there overnight. There are still some articles of equipment we must obtain, and Colonel Arnold has certain contacts to make.

En route Darwin–Corunna Downs, Jan. 24, 1943   0600 WAWT

Darwin is no more. Before the Japanese attack it was a famous little town of about 3,000 people, but now it has no civilian population. There is not a single building standing in the city or at the airport. In the first attack the enemy came over with 120 bombers and worked at their leisure, unopposed by so much as a single antiaircraft gun. Only one Australian airplane got off the ground, and it was immediately shot down. It is estimated that at the end of the first week of bombing 3,000 people, civilian, military, and sailors, had been killed. Now, of course, the place is amply fortified, but there's nothing there to protect. It is a scene of utter desolation. These things we do not hear of in the States.

We were taken care of by the RAAF in Darwin and had a pleasant stay except for a bit of apprehension concerning the safety of our airplanes. The Japs had raided the harbor the two preceding nights, but they did not come over last night. Our two large airplanes would have been a choice target for them.

Today we are headed for Corunna Downs, where we hope to find a suitable airport. With characteristic British inefficiency, no one seems to know much about anything except his own area and job. Corunna Downs has become famous for one thing—that of having set a worldwide temperature record. It has had 160 consecutive days and nights during which the temperature has not fallen below 100 degrees. And this is now the summer season. In fact yesterday in Darwin was one of the most uncomfortably warm days I have ever experienced. We have to keep our shirts buttoned at the neck and our sleeves down to guard against mosquitoes. We are now on a ration of ten grains of quinine daily, and it has some adverse reactions. We also are now adding three drops of iodine to each canteen of water we drink. That doesn't improve its taste, especially when we drink so much of it.

We crossed over the Timor Sea this morning, and it was unusually calm.

Soon we will be over the Indian Ocean. The land we are crossing over now is beautiful from the air, but indescribably desolate. There has been no sign of human habitation since we departed from Darwin. The land is extremely rocky, with almost no soil. Gum trees grow sparsely—enough to make a pleasing contrast with red rocks. Anthills pockmark the ground every few rods, and some of them are built up to an unbelievable height, appearing from the air to be thrown up to at least fifteen feet. They seem to be capable of withstanding severe rain without washing away, and they look very much like miniature castles. Incidentally, we have had a severe thunderstorm each night since we have been in Australia.

Our present plans are to land at Corunna Downs to learn the condition of the field at Port Hedland. If the field there is suitable we will go on to it and set up our base of operations. It appears that we will operate out of Port Hedland for about a week.

En route Carnarvon–Port Hedland, Jan. 25, 1943   0630 WAWT

Yesterday we arrived over Port Hedland in the early afternoon, carefully inspected the field from the air, and then proceeded to Corunna Downs, where we landed. This is really a hot spot and the place is literally alive with a small type of fly which insists on landing on any exposed flesh it can find, regardless of opposition. It does not bite, but rather seeks to gorge itself on one's plentiful perspiration. We found the place interesting but primitive. It is at the center of a rich gold-mining area, but there are actually very few people here. It is estimated that there are 60,000 kangaroos on the military reservation.

After checking on the condition of the airport at Port Hedland, we proceeded on to it and found living facilities much better than we had expected. We are stopping in a small, dirty hotel, but at least we have beds to sleep in. Sand flies (similar to what we call no-see-ums) are everywhere, and they bite continually. They go through any kind of mosquito net, and I already have welts all over me from their bites. Last year Port Hedland had twenty-three inches of rain in twenty-four hours.

This morning we were up at 4:45 and off to the airport to unload our cargo and to take off for Carnarvon to inspect the airport. Our trip down was very interesting. This is the center of the sheep country, but still it is practically uninhabited. The sheep stations (ranches) run up to as large as a million acres and have as many as 80,000 sheep each. They are attended by only three or four men, and shearing is done by traveling crews with the necessary machinery. The sheep get their water from wells equipped with windmills. When roundup time comes, all windmills are turned off except a few in the vicinity of the shearing pens. Thirst finally drives the sheep to these wells and they are penned up and sheared.

There is little market for the meat, so most sheep die a natural death.

We saw perhaps 3,000 kangaroos on this short trip down, and we also saw about a hundred emus. We flew for miles at not more than fifty feet off the ground, and the kangaroos were terrified at our roaring airplane. The huge anthills were still prevalent through all this country. I learned that they are built by white ants, which live largely on cellulose, and that many of the hills are deserted. The ants move on or die out when their food supply is depleted by drought or other causes.

Carnarvon has several banana plantations, a new venture for this part of the country.

Port Hedland, Australia, Jan. 26, 1943   1400 WAWT

We found Carnarvon to be by far the best small town in Western Australia. The town is clean and has a nice airport and port. It is the first clean place we have found, although cockroaches are still abundant. We had lunch at the hotel, walked around the town, ate our first ice cream in Western Australia, and then proceeded homeward. We found many kangaroos on this trip back. We inspected the airport at Onslow on the way and found it to be not too good.

En route Port Hedland–Broome, Jan. 27, 1943   0700 WAWT

Last night we did not depart from the airport for our hotel until 8:30 due to poor servicing facilities. We shared a poor dinner of tough mutton with several dozen cockroaches, and fell into bed exhausted after a very long day. Sand flies fed on my blood all night, but I was hardly aware of it until this morning. We were up at 6:00 this morning and are now on our way to Broome to inspect the airport there.

The temperature has been very high and it is impossible to maintain a decent appearance under the circumstances. Today promises to be the hottest day yet.

Last night the aircraft tender *Heron* arrived in Port Hedland with supplies for us, and is to remain there and help us in any way possible until we have finished our mission.

Carnarvon, Australia, Jan. 27, 1943   2030 WAWT

Today turned out to be a very hectic day after all. We proceeded to Broome without incident and accomplished our work there. That was the place where the Japs caught the refugees from Java. Several hundred women and children were killed there, including all of those aboard two air transports which were shot down in the harbor immediately after takeoff from the field. We saw the wrecks of the planes still lying partly submerged in the harbor.

We returned to Port Hedland shortly thereafter, and it was not long until our other airplane, which had taken Colonel Arnold to Perth, returned also. We set up a guard and went into town for the night. Soon after we had settled down in town, we received word that we might expect a Japanese attack at any time to try to destroy our airplanes. Thereupon we made hurried preparations and departed for Carnarvon, 440 miles farther down the coast, arriving here at dark. Our immediate plans now are obscure, but we know that we are out of the striking range of Japanese aircraft for the time being.

En route Carnarvon–Port Hedland, Jan. 28, 1943 0800 WAWT

Yesterday we had a lazy day of it, with nothing to do but to clean up our airplanes, relocate cargo, and take life easy. I explored the town a bit and walked out along the ocean to see my first mangrove swamps at close range.

This morning we were up early and took off at 7:00 for Port Hedland. We are having an excellent trip except for some tropical rain showers.

En route Port Hedland–Carnarvon, Jan. 29, 1943 0900 WAWT

We arrived over Port Hedland a short time ago, and as we approached, the aircraft tender, *Heron*, began signaling us with her light. We didn't have a radio operator aboard, so I had a bit of difficulty in taking down code and flying the airplane at the same time. They signaled us that there had been almost a cloudburst last night and that the runways were very soft and unsafe for landing. That was self-evident, as the whole countryside was under water. I advised them by code that we would return to Carnarvon. Tonight I am officer of the day so will be up all night.

En route Carnarvon–Port Hedland, Jan. 30, 1943 1600 WAWT

Last night I stood watch as officer of the day from 8:00 P.M. until 1:30 A.M. It was a beautiful night, and I had my first good opportunity to study the stars of the Southern Hemisphere. After my tour of duty was over I slept in my airplane until 8:00 A.M. today and then departed for Port Hedland. We arrived there in due time, accomplished our mission, and took off for Carnarvon. Upon arriving over Carnarvon we found that a willy-willy was in progress, and that the wind was blowing about fifty miles per hour and the dust was so thick that the visibility was zero. We circled the place where we believed the airport to be but were unable to find it. So there was nothing to do but to return to Port Hedland and spend the night, regardless of the Japs.

We will have to endure the filth and the cockroaches in the hotel at Port Hedland tonight in spite of anything we can do.

En route Port Hedland–Carnarvon, Jan. 31, 1943   1000 WAWT

Last night we went into the hotel at Port Hedland to find that the entire town had closed up to go to the local movie, which was showing *Alexander's Ragtime Band*. After much arguing, we finally got the hotel cook to feed us some cold mutton and bread, but I managed to get only about half of my serving, as the cockroaches took the rest away from me. We had a good sleep, arose late this morning, and tried to eat breakfast, without much success. Finally we went over to the aircraft tender *Heron*, and had some coffee with Commander Mundorff and Lieutenant Burgess. It was the first coffee we'd had since Honolulu.

The dust storm at Carnarvon yesterday put all radio communication there out, so we were unable to get any report on the weather or the field condition. Therefore, we are now proceeding there, hoping we will be able to land. There is some indication that the climax of our expedition may come tomorrow, and then we will probably start a fast trip back to San Francisco.

En route Carnarvon–Perth, Jan. 31, 1943   1430 WAWT

When we arrived in Carnarvon today Colonel Arnold advised us he would like to have us proceed on to Perth immediately to take a couple of sailors to the hospital. They had been injured during the storm at sea yesterday. Now we are on our way and are remaining overnight. Perth has the reputation of being one of the finest cities in Australia. We expect to arrive there before dark and to return tomorrow morning.

The climate at Perth is supposed to be similar to that of San Francisco. I hope so in order that I can escape this infernal heat in which we have sweltered since leaving Honolulu. Perhaps also we can get some fresh fruit and vegetables to eat.

En route Perth–Carnarvon, Feb. 1, 1943   0800 WAWT

Perth was something of a disappointment. Perhaps our hopes had been built too high. At any rate we arrived there in the late afternoon and found that they had a nice airport, but that its approaches were quite bad. Upon landing we encountered the usual Australian inefficiency, and it required an hour and a half even to obtain a fuel truck: it was teatime and nothing could disturb that old custom. After we obtained the truck, it broke down twice while delivering only 500 gallons of fuel. Trying to hurry an Australian is as futile as trying to drain the Indian Ocean. We finally got into town to find everything closed, but after much walking we managed to find some eggs and toast to eat.

Perth resembles Brisbane very much. It is low and sprawling, with winding, unplanned streets, and is not too clean. The countryside is quite fertile, and vineyards, orchards, and sheep are in abundance. The country between Carnarvon and Perth is all flat, sandy desert except for a small area around Geraldton which is farmed. The Indian Ocean is beautiful here and is bordered by miles of sandy beach.

En route Carnarvon–Perth, Feb. 2, 1943   0830 WAWT

We arrived in Carnarvon yesterday without incident, and for lack of something better to do we played poker.

Colonel Arnold had gone up to Port Hedland in the other airplane, and he remained there aboard the *Heron*. Incidentally, I forgot to mention the other day that the *Heron* has quite a record. It is an 1,100-ton ship which came over to Asia from the United States in 1922 and has not returned since. It has served all through the present war, slowly retreating from China to Manila to Java to Australia. At one time it was under attack from Jap aircraft for seven hours, and the bomb marks are still visible over all parts of the ship.

Colonel Arnold sent word back for both airplanes and all personnel to proceed to Perth, where facilities are available to do some much-needed work on the airplanes. We have to stand by for immediate moving orders, which he will send to us by radio. We expect to start the important part of our mission at any time now, and our airplanes must be in good condition, because it is probable that we will fly almost continuously for several days once we leave the west coast of Australia. Another advantage in being in Perth is that we will be free from possible Japanese attacks.

Perth, Australia, Feb. 3, 1943   1100 WAWT

Today we have relaxed here in Perth, while the much-needed work is being done on our airplanes. We have no idea how long our stay will be, but it probably will not be too long.

I have been walking around the town, which I find not very impressive. It certainly isn't much of a city, but to the Australians it is important in that it is the only town of more than a few hundred population in an area as large as the entire United States west of the Mississippi River. I still haven't seen a screen on a door or window, although flies and mos-

quitoes are plentiful. We are staying at the Esplanade, the best hotel in
Perth, and we still have to provide our own mosquito nets in order to get
any sleep. Tap water is not for drinking, and pasteurized milk is unheard
of, but beer flows from almost every tap at the slightest excuse.

The accent of the people here is pronounced, in fact almost not understandable for an American. This difficulty is aggravated by the use of many
idioms with which we are not familiar. As an example, I did not know
whether to be insulted or not the other day when a squadron leader approached me and said he would "like to yarn with me a bit when I had
time."

Tomorrow I am officer of the day and will spend twenty-four hours
at Pierce Field, where our airplanes are stored. It is twenty-eight miles
out of Perth.

Pierce Field, Australia, Feb. 4, 1943   1100 WAWT

I am on duty now here at the airport but there is very little to do. This
morning I waited two hours for a driver who was supposed to pick me
up at the hotel at 7:30. They are very cooperative, but a time schedule
means very little to them. I just had lunch at the officers' club, and it
was very nice if you liked mutton.

The other airplane took off a short time ago for Port Hedland to get
Colonel Arnold. His radiogram was sent last night but did not arrive
here until 10:00 this morning. It would seem that we must be remaining here for some time longer in view of the fact that the colonel is coming here. Our airplane is not in flying condition at present due to some
troubles found during recent inspections. It does not appear that it will
be flyable even tomorrow.

I expect the other airplane to arrive with Colonel Arnold at about 9:00
tonight.

[After the Aussies had set out the flares it was obvious that these did
not offer very good guidance to Rube Wagner for a safe landing on a blacked-
out runway at night. I got the Aussies to gather all of the old scrap lumber they could find and pile it at each end of the runway. Just before we
thought the airplane was due to arrive we set the lumber ablaze, creating
two flaming targets for Rube to align with for landing. The airplane landed
without any difficulty, Rube being the splendid pilot that he is.]

Perth, Australia, Feb. 5, 1943   1900 WAWT

This morning I went off duty at 8:00, came into town, and have done
very little all day. Went to the navy commissary at Fremantle to get some
shirts and razor blades. Was driven there by a girl who is now employed

by the navy as a driver. She is South African Dutch, and although she is only twenty years old, she has been through nearly all of the war. She was visiting in Holland when the invasion occurred, escaped to London, went to Java, and was evacuated from there when Java fell. She is a very intelligent girl and tells some gruesome stories of her experiences with the Japs.

At the airport I learned an unusual thing. All of the Australian pilots appeared to be at least as old as I was, but theirs was nevertheless a combat unit. Upon inquiring, I found that none of them was over twenty-six years of age, and that the average age was twenty-two. They appeared to be almost middle-aged, but this was due to the fact that most of them were bald and had few remaining natural teeth. This condition I imagine is due to their poor diets, as milk and green vegetables are almost never served, even here where they are plentiful. I notice that even when the menu offers both beef and mutton they almost invariably eat mutton, with lots of potatoes.

Perth, Australia, Feb. 6, 1943   1300 WAWT

Today there has been little to do. We have played some poker and have walked about town a bit. There is absolutely nothing to be bought that is worth taking home. Tonight we are going to take our little Dutch girl-friend to dinner and to a movie. Her name is Mary Hartman and we have adopted her as a sort of mascot. She expects to come to the United States when the war is over.

I have learned a great many things concerning the aborigines through talking to several Australians who have spent years among them. Whether or not all of the stories are true, I have no way to ascertain. They are among the most primitive of peoples, and they have developed some unusual customs, the strangest of which deal with sex. They practice sterilization of unfit individuals and engage in strongly sadistic rites in determining the fitness of the adolescent youths to become adult members of the tribes. Girls are sexually initiated at a very young age by the oldest men of the tribe before they are turned over to their husbands.

It now appears that we will leave here about February 12, and will proceed directly overland to some point on the east coast of Australia. Tomorrow I am going up to Port Hedland to pick up certain of our supplies, which we left there on our way down here.

En route Port Hedland–Perth, Feb. 7, 1943   1300 WAWT

We did a bit of experimenting on our trip up to Hedland this morning. We climbed directly to 25,000 feet out of Perth in order to try out our equipment, etc. The airplane and its accessories performed very well indeed, and a few interesting things occurred. We obtained a 235-MPH airspeed with normal cruising power, and the airplane responded well. Matches would not strike at all, and a fly we had in the cockpit could still manage to fly, but only in short jumps of about an inch each. It was surprising that it could develop any aerodynamic performance at all, considering the rarefied atmosphere. The temperature was minus fifteen degrees Centigrade, and when we descended into Port Hedland, where the ground temperature was well over one hundred degrees Fahrenheit, it was rather hard to adjust.

We are almost back to Perth now, and will have made a 1,600-mile trip in less than eight hours. I am relieved that I have gone in and out of Port Hedland for the last time. The airport is much too small for safe continued operation of these airplanes, and I've almost been expecting a nasty accident in that godforsaken place. Our airport here at Perth is very good indeed in comparison.

Perth, Australia, Feb. 8, 1943   1000 WAWT

I had a talk with Colonel Arnold this morning concerning orders to active duty for myself in the army. He promised to try to find a suitable place for me when he returned to Washington; if he is able to do so, he can have me ordered to duty in such a manner that I can be granted a leave of absence from the airline. I told him I would like a flying job, but he explained that that would be impossible in view of my rank and experience. So if I go to duty, it will be in an administrative capacity of some kind and will probably be in Pacific Operations. My conscience would be a bit easier if I could do so.

Perth, Australia, Feb. 9, 1943   1530 WAWT

Today we took a bus to Scarboro Beach, where we had a fine swim and much sunburn. It is one of the finest beaches I've ever seen, although the swimming is not too good, due to heavy swells and considerable undertow. The sand is clean and white and stretches for miles. It's fun to have been swimming in the Indian Ocean.

No further news about the probable time of our departure, but we expect to go on the alert at most any time now. It will be a long, hard grind when we start.

Perth, Australia, Feb. 10, 1943   1300 WAWT

Today has been a lazy one. We had some supplies to pick up this morning and then a late lunch. I'm standing by here at the hotel in case some important news comes. Colonel Arnold and I are going to play tennis this afternoon.

Perth, Australia, Feb. 11, 1943   2000 WAWT

Today has been an interesting day. First we received news that we might be leaving here soon, but, as it later developed, all plans were postponed due to deteriorating weather conditions. Then, tonight, Mary Hartman, the little Dutch girl from Java, invited me out to her home to meet some officers of the Dutch navy who are now working out of here. Among them was Captain de Meester, who played an important part in the evacuation of Java and in the Battle of Makassar Strait. It was very interesting to me to hear all of the tales of conditions there, both before and after the coming of the Japs. The story came out that Miss Hartman and her mother and sister were on a boat ready to be evacuated about ten days prior to the arrival of the Japs in Soerabaja. Mary wanted to stay to do what work she could among the much-bombed natives. Her mother wouldn't tolerate this, of course, so just as the boat sailed Mary returned ashore. She continued to work there in the face of constant Jap attacks until the Japanese entered the city, and at the last minute she was evacuated on a naval vessel. She was awarded a medal of honor for her work there. Her mother did not have any idea what had become of her until they were reunited in Perth some weeks later. Her father remained behind to help destroy oil wells, etc., and has not been heard from since. These people really understand how terrible war can be, and their hatred of the Japs is so great that they can't even talk about them. The Hartmans were once wealthy people. Now they are dependent entirely upon the meager income of the two girls, who are working here for the American and the Dutch navies.

Perth, Australia, Feb. 12, 1943   2030 WAWT

Have not been feeling good today. Do not know what the trouble is, and I have broken out with some bad cold sores.

Tonight Colonel Arnold approached me with a rather startling proposition. I had been talking to him at various times about going on active duty, and he had agreed that upon his return to Washington he would see if he could have me ordered to duty in some manner so that I would not have to resign from United. Colonel Arnold is assistant chief of the Air Transport Command, and as such has considerable power in Washington. Yesterday he received a radio from the chief of staff instructing him to obtain all information possible concerning facilities available for our type of operation at Geraldton and the Cocos Islands. This leads him to believe that there must be definite plans afoot to close the gap in our

Above: I (*far left*) and fellow United Air Lines captains Johnny Roberts, Rube Wagner, and Johnny Johnson inspect a chart showing the route to Western Australia. *Below:* Members of our two crews pass the time in Perth. I am hatless in the right foreground.

around-the-world operation now existing from Eastern Australia to India. Last night he asked me if I'd be interested in coming to Perth or Gerald-ton to become control officer for the army to supervise the operation be-tween Ceylon and Brisbane. This, of course, providing the plan of the General Staff is to extend the operation over this section. I naturally told him I would be very pleased with such an assignment, and he said he believed he could get my promotion to major at once. I don't care much for Western Australia, but I would get some very valuable operations ex-perience on an around-the-world operation. I hate to leave my family be-hind, but after all this is a war, and I've felt since it began that my place is really in the army. It will be interesting to see what develops.

Bad weather in the Indian Ocean is still holding up our expedition here. Perhaps by Monday we can start moving.

Sent a cablegram to the family today.

Perth, Australia, Feb. 13, 1943   2030 WAWT

Today we had lunch with the Dutch officers aboard the Dutch light cruiser *Tromp*. It is based in the harbor at Fremantle and works out of there. The visit was very interesting, and we found the Dutchmen to be very much like Americans. They had all learned to speak excellent En-glish during the past year. We had the usual ceremonial drink of Bols be-fore dinner.

We played poker again this evening, and I won eighty dollars.

Perth, Australia, Feb. 14, 1943   1730 WAWT

This morning Colonel Arnold and I played Ralph Johnson and Emory Wishon a handicap match of tennis, and we finally won after much fun. This afternoon we played poker again for lack of anything else to do. I won sixty-five dollars. This is Sunday and everything is closed up tightly —no movies, no beer, nothing. I'm going to bed early to try to sleep in this smothering heat.

Perth, Australia, Feb. 15, 1943   2100 WAWT

Today we again expected that our mission here would start, but noth-ing developed. Colonel Arnold wanted us to stand by, however, so we could not get far away from our hotel. I played four sets of tennis in the blister-ing sun, winning two and losing two. This evening the gang of us took Mary Hartman to a movie.

I suppose it is safe enough now to outline the purpose of our trip here. When President Roosevelt and his staff decided upon the now historic conference at Casablanca, it was determined that upon its termination certain members of his staff would continue on around the world, holding a series of military conferences at various of the worldwide headquarters. There is at this time no existing air transportation link between India and eastern Australia. The services of a Pan American Clipper have been enlisted to carry these members of the staff from India to Western Australia, and we are to pick them up here and take them back to the United States, stopping at certain points where they expect to visit en route. Ours is the most difficult assignment in the entire plan, due to an almost complete lack of communication and other facilities in this part of the world, and due to the great length of our operation from here to San Francisco. We have been set up here for about ten days, ready to receive the Clipper from India, but a tropical hurricane which developed in the Indian Ocean off the coast of northwest Australia has until now made it impossible to clear the Clipper safely to Australia. Now the storm has dissipated, and we can expect to be under way at almost any time. We are anxious to get started, but our responsibilities from this point on will be tremendous. To lose this cargo would be a great blow to the war effort of the Allies.

Perth, Australia, Feb. 16, 1943   2100 WAWT

Well, the Clipper is on its way from India to Australia, and is now about halfway across. We do not know, of course, just how or where the passengers will desire to go when they arrive, so we have to be prepared for any development. At least we are starting home tonight, and that's something. We have no idea whether we will be three days or three weeks on the way, but at last I'm starting back to see my wife and my two boys. We are not at all sure of the route we will take back from Australia.

Tonight we had a short poker game, and my luck held. I won thirty dollars, so I'm now very much ahead of the game.

Perth, Australia, Feb. 17, 1943   2230 WAWT

One airplane — Rube Wagner and his crew — got away homeward bound tonight. It looked as though we could start too, but it was decided at the last minute to hold us here until the Clipper got away to be certain it ran into no difficulty. Our important cargo turned out to be General Wedemeyer and his two aides. Others who were supposed to be aboard changed their plans and returned to Washington the other direction.

We left the hotel today at 2:00 P.M. and did not go back tonight as we are unable to get rooms in Perth without much trouble. Tomorrow will be a long day to spend here at the field.

En route Perth–Brisbane, Feb. 18, 1943   1930 WAWT

Incidentally we are making history in that this is the first airplane which has ever flown nonstop from Perth to Brisbane. Our route is 2,000 nautical miles, directly across the center of Australia, and the trip is most interesting. We have been out about four hours now, and expect to make the trip in about twelve hours. We passed over Kalgoorlie, the famous mining center, two hours ago. Central Australia is without doubt the greatest expanse of total desert I have ever seen. Much of the ground is completely bare, and where vegetation exists it is composed of sparse scrub. There are vast expanses of alkali flats where I don't believe there are even rabbits. We crossed the trans-Australian rabbit fence just west of Kalgoorlie.

We expect to arrive after daylight in Brisbane, where we will get further orders from Colonel Arnold.

Ipswich, Australia, Feb. 19, 1943   1400 AWT

When we arrived this morning we were greeted with some sad news. One of our trips crashed into the ocean off Canton Island a few nights ago, killing Captain Pickup, navigator Judd, mechanic Adams, and my regularly assigned radio operator, Paul Carlson. The copilot, Moninger, swam about two miles to shore. Fourteen passengers were killed and two passengers escaped. The cause of the accident is unknown, but the airplane was in its final approach for a landing.

When we landed, Colonel Arnold, in Rube's airplane, had not yet arrived from Sydney, so we were unable to learn just what we were supposed to do. The colonel is now here and is at General MacArthur's headquarters trying to determine our next move.

2100 AWT

Colonel Arnold has just returned from headquarters and still has little definite information other than that we will probably go up into the war zone of New Guinea, Guadalcanal, and Noumea and spend ten or twelve days there. We think it is a waste of personnel and equipment to keep both airplanes here, but that's the way General MacArthur wants it done. Plans change without notice, however, and I'll wager that by tomorrow some change will have occurred.

Amberley Field, Australia, Feb. 20, 1943   1400 AWT

This morning we came out to the airport after an unpleasant night at the Palais Royal in Ipswich, and sure enough there were new plans in the air. Now it would seem that the general's party will go to New Guinea in an armed B-17, and Rube Wagner will wait with his airplane either here or at Noumea and take the party on to San Francisco. Ralph Johnson and I will take our airplane to Honolulu tonight with a load of cargo, and for the purpose of having some much-needed work on the airplane. Then we will return here not later than February 28 to pick up General Mac-Arthur's staff and take them to Washington for a conference there.

Colonel Arnold has gone down to General MacArthur's headquarters now to confirm this arrangement, and if it is satisfactory we will probably leave for Honolulu tonight sometime after 9:00 P.M. That will be much better from our viewpoint than sitting here at Brisbane with nothing to do.

Sydney, Australia, Feb. 21, 1943   1600 AWT

Plans really do change in a hurry. MacArthur wouldn't approve of our trip to Honolulu, so on short notice we came down here to Sydney to try to obtain some cylinders which we need for our engines. This is Sunday and everything is closed, so tomorrow I expect to start trying to get the much-needed parts for our airplane.

My first impression of Sydney is a good one. It appears to be a cosmopolitan city, and much like San Francisco. It is beautifully located on a large harbor, and there is much timber in the area. House roofs are largely of red tile, and the contrast between them and the water and the trees and white beaches is almost startling in its effect.

Sydney, Australia, Feb. 22, 1943   1300 AWT

Today I was able to locate the cylinders we needed for our airplane engines. Now we can put our airplane into good shape for the long trip back to Washington.

I spent the balance of the day seeing the city of Sydney, buying additional uniforms, and trying to find a suitable present for Grace. I tried every store in the city, and could find nothing suitable for a present. There's nothing here which is not inferior in quality to similar products in the States. All interesting things had long since been purchased by American soldiers who had their headquarters in Sydney so long. This is a splendid city—the only good one in Australia. It has a definite American air. Above all it is clean, a fact unique among Australian cities. Streets are all crooked, in the manner of Boston—doubtless a carryover from the early necessity of conforming to the outline of an irregular and rocky harbor. The Sydney Harbor Bridge, a byword for magnificence in all Australia, would be dwarfed by even the ancient Brooklyn Bridge. There are few large stores, but rather an endless expanse of small shops throughout the city. Trinkets à la Woolworth are the largest obvious stock in trade. They have a peculiar custom in Australia of building arcades stretching from street to street through the centers of most business blocks. These arcades are lined with a succession of very small shops, a great many of which are now out of business due to wartime curtailments.

Tonight we plan on going out to another of the night spots for one last good dinner in Sydney. Tomorrow we return to Brisbane.

Ipswich, Australia, Feb. 23, 1943   1830 AWT

Rube Wagner lost an engine yesterday over the ocean while returning from Noumea, and his airplane is now out of service due to an engine change. We are now the number-one airplane, and must stand by for any immediate orders from General MacArthur.

I'm tired tonight and plan on going to bed immediately. I'm getting homesick now and want to return to my family. That will be some time yet, however, as we probably will not depart from here before March 1. The five days between now and March 1 are going to seem endless. It will probably be at least ten days after we depart for Washington before we finally arrive at home. "I hate war—."

Brisbane, Australia, Feb. 24, 1943 through March 3, 1943

We and our airplane were detained in Brisbane by General Kenney, chief of the Fifth Air Force, and by General Sutherland, MacArthur's chief of staff, until they were ready to depart for Washington, D.C., on March 4, 1943. There was little for us to do except to kill time and wait, and this period was from our viewpoint completely unproductive.

General Kenney made a formal request that we remain with him in the States and fly him back to Australia when he was ready to return.

Although I made daily entries in my handwritten diary, they have been consolidated into these paragraphs in the interest of brevity.

Tontouta, New Caledonia, March 4, 1943   1700 NCWT

We departed from Amberley at 7:00 A.M. and arrived here at 12:30 today. We have more army rank on our airplane than I've ever seen in one place before. We have Lieutenant General Kenney, Major General Sutherland, Brigadier General Chamberlin, and four of lesser rank, including Captain Chase, who is General Kenney's aide.

Tontouta is about the most unpleasant place I have ever visited. It has rained steadily for nine days and is still pouring rain. The temperature is about 110 degrees, and you can't distinguish your own perspiration from the rain. Mosquitoes are more plentiful than I have ever seen anywhere except in Alaska. Mud is at least a foot deep everywhere, and it is impossible for us to present a perfect appearance such as a general's pilot should do.

The harbor here at Noumea is literally packed with naval vessels— seventy of them—and all of the aircraft from the carriers are parked at the airport. This adds greatly to the confusion, and decent quarters are simply not available.

Nandi, Fiji Islands, March 5, 1943   1800 FWT

Arrived here this afternoon after an easy trip from Tontouta. Everywhere we go it rains, and it has been generally pouring rain since we landed.

It seems that General Kenney is in no great hurry, so that we are going to travel only by day where possible. Our three generals are splendid men, and I'm proud that our military efforts are being directed by such capable men. General Kenney has just received word that his airmen have sunk the last of the twenty-two Japanese ships in the convoy which was headed for Lae, and he is so pleased that each time I talk with him he goes over and over the strategy involved in the weeks of planning for such an operation. General Sutherland likes to fly the airplane, and spends most of his time on the flight deck. I have had some interesting talks with him, and he has practically asked me to become his and General MacArthur's pilot. That might not be a bad idea.

Canton Island, March 6, 1943   2100 CWT

We had a nice flight into Canton, arriving at early afternoon. We are jinxed by the rain, as it has followed us here, the first rain I've ever seen at Canton.

We are departing for Honolulu at 6:00 tomorrow morning. It's good to get back toward home, with hopes of seeing the family again. General Sutherland informed me today that I have to take them not only to Washington, but also back to Australia. So unless they permit me to return to San Francisco during their business stay in Washington, it may be some time before I can more than speak to my family.

Incidentally, General Twining is accompanying us in a B-24. Nate is one of the finest men I have ever met and used to be my squadron commander when I was in the army. Now that he is a major general, he has not changed in the least. He even wanted to get into our poker game, but could hardly do so under the circumstances.

Honolulu, T.H., March 7, 1943   2400 HWT

We arrived here this afternoon after a fast trip from Canton.

Rube and his crew are here, and we plan to depart for San Francisco tomorrow afternoon unless our generals change their minds. It now appears that we will spend a few hours in San Francisco—long enough to say hello to our families— and then will depart for Dayton and Washington that same evening. All of the rank in the army and navy is converging on Washington. General Kenney now says he is going to keep us in Washington during his stay there, and that he may wish to make quite an extensive tour of the United States before he goes back to Australia.

Atherton, Calif., March 8, 1943   1900 PWT

Home at last! Life's really worthwhile after all when a man can come home to a beautiful wife and two handsome boys. I found them quite well, and they had been so throughout my absence. Jimmy is so much better behaved than he was when I departed, and Johnny has changed so much now that I wouldn't have recognized him.

We had a nice trip over from Honolulu, but upon arrival were unable to land at Hamilton Field due to weather. This suited us perfectly as I was able to land at San Francisco, then home to see my family. Previously I had expected to see only Grace at Hamilton Field.

I'm leaving at 6:00 in the morning for Dayton, Ohio, and then Washington. My available time with my family is so short that I will not waste more of it writing.

Dayton, Ohio, March 9, 1943   2300 CWT

We departed from San Francisco at 7:30 this morning and came here by way of Bakersfield, Daggett, Albuquerque, Amarillo, Oklahoma City, and St. Louis. There was some bad weather on the direct route to Dayton. So we detoured to the south. We made 240 miles an hour on the way over.

We are leaving here at a reasonable hour tomorrow for the easy hop into Washington.

Washington, D.C., March 10, 1943   1500 EWT

Well, we delivered our generals safely this afternoon after the very long trip from Brisbane. It is a relief. There's one disappointing note now, however. We will not be able to go back to San Francisco to spend any time with our families. General Kenney now wants us to go no farther away than Chicago, and he wishes to have us back here available for use by the morning of March 16. We plan to go on to New York this afternoon to spend the night, and then proceed on to Chicago tomorrow to have some maintenance work done on our airplane.

It will be fine to have a good night of rest for a change.

New York, N.Y., March 11, 1943   2330 EWT

Did not go to Chicago today, as the weather was so bad that not even the airlines were flying. Our airplane is not equipped to carry much ice either.

Chicago, Ill., March 12, 1943   2100 CWT

Arrived here about 4:30 this afternoon after a nice flight from New York. It was a typical hazy, chilly early spring day in the East.

There was little to be done at the airport when we arrived, as most of the people I wished to see had gone home from work.

Chicago is miserable and cold, with dirty, sooty snow everywhere. I had almost forgotten how uninviting Chicago can really be. I think I'd almost prefer Australia.

Chicago, Ill., March 13, 1943   2300 CWT

Today I went to the airport early to do certain business matters which have been neglected almost too long. I saw Walt Addems and he organized a luncheon party at the Barn, where Ralph Johnson and I had a most pleasant time talking about our trip to Walt, Jack Herlihy, Bill Williams, and Bert Lott, all of United Air Lines. We then went home with Bill Williams to spend the night, but we called on the Addems family en route. We have had a most pleasant evening here discussing various things with Bill and Walt, and now I'm pleasantly tired and ready for a night of sleep.

New York, N.Y., March 14, 1943   2000 EWT

After a leisurely departure from Chicago today we had a fast trip over here to New York. The weather was fine and there was little to do on the way. We obtained excellent accommodations here at the St. Moritz. I feel at last as though I'm about to become rested from the long trip we have spent so much time completing.

Tomorrow we will have to go to Washington unless we get some definite word to the contrary. I am not looking forward to this with much pleasure, as we probably will be there for some time and decent living facilities will be hard to obtain.

I hope General Kenney soon will be ready to return to Australia, but I rather doubt this, as the morning papers carried an item to the effect that he is to confer with President Roosevelt in the next two or three days.

Washington, D.C., March 15, 1943   2300 EWT

Today we were advised by General Kenney's aide that we should return to Washington at once in order to be ready to go as soon as the general might desire to go. As a result we arrived here from New York about 5:00 P.M. and are now comfortably quartered on Bolling Field awaiting developments. It does not appear that we will depart tomorrow, but there's always that possibility.

There's a chance that we might return to Australia via the eastern route, so we have begun to assemble data with that in view. It would be most interesting, and if the general even hints of it we want to be ready to give him all available information. It would be a trip of about 16,000 nautical miles as compared with 9,500 back the way we came.

Washington, D.C., March 16, 1943 through March 28, 1943

For twelve days we sat idly by in Washington. On several occasions we thought we were about to depart, but our departure always was postponed. I explored much of the city on foot and several nights played poker. I found a couple of young disbelievers who thought their poker game was better than it was. I ended up about eight hundred dollars ahead.

Our highlight was that I could telephone Grace frequently to learn of family activities and health.

Although I made an entry each day into my handwritten diary, these have been consolidated here in the interest of brevity.

Bolling Field, D.C., March 29, 1943   2300 EWT

Today was a great disappointment. We got ready to go at the set time, and General Kenney and his wife came out to go. But Generals Sutherland and Chamberlin were not there. Then they disclosed to us that we were to go only to Dayton and return to Washington to pick up the balance of the party tomorrow and take them to Dayton. This we did, making a fast round trip to Dayton, and now we are back in Washington. Tomorrow we go to Dayton to remain overnight, and then Wednesday we are to proceed on to San Francisco. General Kenney has announced that I have to remain with the ship all of the way back to Australia, but I'm going to try to talk him out of it if I can. I've been away so long there are a lot of personal things I must do at home, and also the company needs me very badly at San Francisco.

Dayton, Ohio, March 30, 1943   1800 CWT

Left Washington this afternoon at 1:00 as planned and had a slow trip here. At last it appears that we are on our way. We are to leave at 6:30 tomorrow morning and should arrive in San Francisco about 5:30 in the afternoon, local time. That will be a happy day in my life.

Am staying at the Biltmore Hotel, and accommodations are much better than before, as General Kenney arranged for them this time.

I am going to telephone Grace tonight to tell her of our plans. It will be good to hear her voice again.

Atherton, Calif., March 31, 1943   2200 PWT

Arrived here late this afternoon after a twelve-and-a-half-hour nonstop trip from Dayton. Came almost the direct route, which took me over my farm at Harris, Missouri. Couldn't see anyone, due to one small cloud directly over the place.

It's so fine to be home again! Grace is beautiful and fine, and the boys have grown beyond belief. Life is worthwhile after all.

I couldn't get out of going on back to Australia on this trip, as General Kenney insisted on keeping me on. So now we plan to depart at 5:00 tomorrow afternoon for Hamilton and Honolulu.

6

Island Hopping

APRIL–JULY, 1943

Hamilton Field, Calif., April 1, 1943   1900 PWT

Well, we are on our way again after a too short stay at home. We are having a little mechanical delay here but will soon be off for Honolulu. It was hard to leave the family today after such a short visit. But I'm sure they will be even more attractive upon my return.

Honolulu, T.H., April 2, 1943   1200 HWT

It was a long trip over, fifteen and a half hours in spite of a forecast of thirteen and a half hours which they gave us at Hamilton. I'm so tired I can hardly remain awake, so I plan on going to bed now to sleep through until tomorrow morning. Our schedule is to depart at 8:30 A.M. for Christmas Island.

En route Honolulu–Palmyra, April 3, 1943   1200 PaWT

This morning after we had our engines started, General Kenney suddenly decided to go to Palmyra instead of Christmas, as the navy supposedly had good facilities and comfortable accommodations there. We are about an hour out now and it appears that the weather will not be too good around Palmyra. Our trip down has been fast.

Palmyra Island, April 4, 1943   1900 PaWT

Arrived here in time to have a fine swim before dinner. We find that Palmyra is not too comfortable after all. It has rained almost continuously since an hour after our arrival, and it shows no signs of quitting.

Palmyra is a beautiful island, of coral and only a few feet above water, but covered with vegetation, including many groves of palm trees. I climbed one of the trees and gathered twelve coconuts, but someone ran off with them while I was having dinner. The island is a nesting place of black-and-white terns, and there are literally clouds of them, all very tame. The island has 230 inches of rainfall a year, and I can easily believe it after seeing the sample we are now getting.

Played poker a while tonight and won thirty-five dollars. Could have won more if I hadn't lost my temper to a drunk who came into the game.

We plan to depart at 7:30 tomorrow morning for Nandi, Fiji, where we will spend the night.

Nandi, Fiji Islands, April 5, 1943   1800 FWT

Our trip here was uneventful today except for some rather critical engine trouble on takeoff at Palmyra. One propeller governor failed to operate, and we were too heavily loaded to attempt to land again. After about thirty minutes we succeeded in overcoming the difficulty sufficiently to proceed, but we had a few anxious moments.

This is our last stop before Brisbane and I, for one, will be glad when we deliver our precious passengers safely to their destination. It has been a bit of a mental strain, even though we haven't exactly realized it.

Saw Sid Nelson and his crew here tonight. They are northbound and were on Canton Island when it was bombed. Sid tells comical stories of the event.

Am very tired tonight, so am going to bed very early.

Brisbane, Australia, April 6, 1943   1700 AWT

At last our mission is safely over! Arrived here after a fast trip from Fiji, and delivered our passengers in good shape. Now we are remaining until day after tomorrow in order to rest up and to enjoy a small party tomorrow night on the invitation of our generals. We should have some good fun and much poker playing.

We were really met in style at the airport, and I never saw so much brass in all my life. We were brought into town with a flourish in General Kenney's three-star limousine—probably the only one I'll ever ride in. Now we are comfortably established for a good night of rest. Our airplane is being held on General Kenney's order for our return trip.

Brisbane, Australia, April 7, 1943   1500 AWT

A lazy day today, with nothing to do but rest. I was up early and out to buy the beautiful agate jewel case I had wanted to get for Grace. However, I found that it had been sold and that no more would be available until after the war. Disappointing. This evening we are to go to the Lennon's Hotel to a party in our honor, to be given by General Kenney. Expect to have much fun.

Brisbane, Australia, April 8, 1943   1600 AWT

The party last night was fun, but they gave us too many drinks and everyone got quite sleepy.

Nandi, Fiji Islands, April 9, 1943   1800 FWT

Arrived here after a slow trip from Amberley, including the usual unpleasant stop at Plaine des Gaiacs.

Saw Col. Andy Anderson, who is now operations officer here at Nandi. He was on duty with me in the army at Honolulu from 1930 to 1932.

Here is a clipping from the Brisbane paper concerning the arrival of our distinguished party in Australia:

U.S. MILITARY MISSION BACK

Lieut. General George C. Kenney (Chief of the Allied Air Forces in the Southwest Pacific) and Major General R. K. Sutherland (Chief of Staff), who headed General MacArthur's mission to Washington, have returned to Australia.

This was officially announced at Allied Headquarters yesterday.

Members of the mission were entirely reticent about the conference in Washington. It was stated that they had fully presented the military situation in the Southwest Pacific area and General MacArthur's comments and recommendations thereon.

Members of the mission, which also included Brigadier General S. J. Chamberlin, one of General MacArthur's Assistant Chiefs-of-Staff, left Australia on March 4 but it was not until March 16 that their arrival in America was released.

Commentators immediately suggested that they were in Washington to seek reinforcement of Allied air strength in the Southwest Pacific area, and to give last minute information on the military situation to President Roosevelt and other Allied war leaders.

Since then both the U.S. War Department and service chiefs in Australia have preserved silence about the results of the mission.

Played poker for a few minutes tonight, but did not feel lucky, so quit even. Tomorrow we are going through to Honolulu with only a fuel stop at Canton, as the Japs have been bombing Canton again and we do not want to run the risk of losing our airplane. It will be a long and hard trip.

Honolulu, T.H., April 10, 1943   1500 HWT

Arrived here early this morning after a long trip of eighteen and a half hours through from Fiji with only a refueling stop at Canton. At Canton we heard that the Japs were carrying out a heavy raid on Funafuti in the Ellice Islands. We passed within about 250 miles of it while the raid was in progress.

I slept only about four hours and am now up again to prepare to go on to San Francisco tonight. I'll be plenty tired when I finally get home tomorrow. This will be the fastest trip I've made.

Atherton, Calif., April 11, 1943   2000 PWT

Home at last! Arrived here about noon today after a nice trip from Honolulu. Found the family well and happy, and now I'm going to bed for a nice long sleep.

Atherton, Calif., April 12, 1943   2200 PWT

Today I got reacquainted with the family, went to Palo Alto on business matters, and then spent the remainder of the day at the field, checking in and bringing myself up to date on company affairs. Tonight I have worked on my income tax report until I can't think straight. It is quite involved this year.

Atherton, Calif., April 13, 1943   2000 PWT

More business matters in Palo Alto today, and then much more work on income tax returns. I've completed the latter now, and we will go into San Francisco tomorrow to pay the taxes. They are enormous this year, but necessary if we are to win the war and are to have any of our economic institutions remaining after the war.

Atherton, Calif., April 14, 1943   2400 PWT

A nice day today. Grace and I went into town, paid our income taxes, and then celebrated. We had lunch, shopped a while, and then visited the cocktail bars, including the Top of the Mark. Properly happy, we then had a Mexican dinner and went to see Gilbert and Sullivan's *Pinafore*. After the opera, we had a long and sleepy drive home to our very nice family.

Atherton, Calif., April 15, 1943 through May 1, 1943

During the above period I spent all of my time at home, becoming re-acquainted with my family, paying income taxes, planting Liberty gardens, etc. In view of my long absence, United Air Lines did not schedule me out again until May 2. Although I made daily entries into the handwritten diary, I have consolidated them here to save space.

Atherton, Calif., May 2, 1943   2030 PWT

About the time I was ready to depart for the airport this morning, I was advised by telephone that my airplane could not be made ready for departure tonight and that I would not leave until tomorrow. A bit of a letdown after I was all ready to go.

Hamilton Field, Calif., May 3, 1943   1800 PWT

On our way now, for what should prove to be a good trip. We departed from San Francisco at 2:00 P.M. and have now completed our final preparations here for our takeoff at 1900.

Had a nice chat with Major Elkins and Colonel Barrie here. They want me to do what I can tonight toward searching for a B-24 which went down in the ocean about midway between Hamilton and Honolulu. There will probably be little I can do at night, but I'm taking extra fuel in case there is anything I can do. There were fifteen men aboard, and searchers believe they have heard radio SOS calls from them.

Honolulu, T.H., May 4, 1943   1230 HWT

The trip over was fine and fast, and we arrived almost an hour ahead of our estimate, so that we had to make a partial instrument approach and a night landing. Was very tired, so went to the Moana Hotel immediately and to bed without bothering about breakfast. Had a three-hour nap and then got up for lunch. Now I'm going for a swim and a sleep on Waikiki Beach. It's a beautiful, lazy day here. It now appears that I will be here until the day after tomorrow.

Honolulu, T.H., May 5, 1943   1230 HWT

This has been a lazy day. Went to bed last night at sundown, so arose this morning at 6:30, had a leisurely breakfast, and then stayed on the beach until noon. I'm completely rested now, and anxious to be on my way, before I suffer from too much sunburn here on the beautiful beach.

Should know definitely tonight whether or not I'll be leaving in the morning.

Honolulu, T.H., May 6, 1943   1245 HWT

Only one airplane came through from the States last night, so I didn't get away this morning. However, another one is on the way over today, so that I may get away tonight. In fact, the field has just called to advise that they have set up my departure for 10:30 P.M.

En route Canton–Fiji, May 7, 1943   1000 CWT

This has been a long grind, and I'll be most happy to reach Nandi so that I can go to bed. Left Honolulu at 10:30 last night, reached Canton after daylight, and remained only two hours before taking off for Fiji. Departed from Honolulu along with seven B-24s, one of which got lost in the vicinity of Canton. We have just heard by radio that he was finally brought into Canton a short time ago with less than thirty minutes' fuel remaining.

The flight today has not been very pleasant as it has been raining all of the way. Have had to depend on radio for navigation, as we have been on instruments most of the time.

En route Fiji–New Caledonia, May 8, 1943   0900 FWT

Had a fine, much-needed rest in Nandi last night, although it rained all night and the rain soaked my bed without even making me aware of it. The weather is better today, and we are on our way in to Australia, but we have to stop at Plaine des Gaiacs, New Caledonia, on the way. Just passed over Tana Island, where the active volcano is smoking away.

Brisbane, Australia, May 9, 1943   0800 AWT

Arrived here in good order yesterday afternoon and had a fine sleep last night. This morning I have been doing a lot of minor errands, such as delivering messages and packages, including one for General Sutherland.

Will be leaving tonight at 1:00 A.M., which means a departure from the hotel at 10:30 P.M.

En route New Caledonia–New Hebrides, May 10, 1943   0930 NCWT

Last night I had dinner with Hank Godman, the current GHQ pilot, and then we departed at 10:45 for Amberley Field. We took off from Amberley at 1:00 A.M. and arrived at daybreak at Plaine des Gaiacs, where a surprise awaited us. The airplane southbound from Espíritu Santo failed to meet us, and we learned that he had wrecked a wing tip at Espíritu. So we went down to Tontouta, obtained the required wing tip for the airplane, and are now on our way up with it.

Espíritu Santo is the nearest advance base to Guadalcanal and is in the New Hebrides Islands. It will be interesting to see.

Tontouta, New Caledonia, May 11, 1943 1830 NCWT

I now have a load of twenty combat pilots going to Auckland, New Zealand, for a well-earned rest. Would have taken them on down tonight except for the fact that the airport at Auckland is unlighted, and I could not land after dark.

Espíritu Santo was interesting and different. It is really a jungle island, with vegetation so dense that it would be impossible for a man to make his way through it. Sunlight never reaches the ground through the thick vegetation, and huge vines literally cover the tops of the trees. Looking down upon it from an airplane, one sees it in much the same way that a fly must see the top of a bed of ivy. Rainfall is heavy, and an oppressive steam rises from the ground all of the time. Mosquitoes more than abound—they swarm.

The military establishments occupy large coconut plantations, where British soap manufacturers once produced copra for their factories. These plantations serve admirably for their present purpose, affording a certain amount of camouflage as well as brush-free ground for quarters and equipment. It isn't at all the type of setting one would expect to fight a war in.

Must get some sleep now, as I've already been up thirty-six hours and must be up early again in the morning for a 7:00 departure for New Zealand.

Auckland, New Zealand, May 12, 1943 1930 NZWT

An interesting trip today. Came over Norfolk Island, which is almost halfway between New Caledonia and New Zealand. It is a beautiful spot, only four miles in diameter and about 400 miles from the nearest other land. It is well farmed, and once was a prison island of the British Empire. It also figures in a sequel to the mutiny on the *Bounty*, as some of the mutineers later made their way from Pitcairn Island to Norfolk Island.

Arrived here in Auckland in midafternoon and learned that I will be here for at least a day, as there is another crew here.

My first impression of New Zealand is a good one. The countryside is green and well tended, and the city is clean if not too prosperous. Auckland reminds me somewhat of Reykjavik. People are very friendly. Tom Torrison and I walked about the city for a while and then had an excellent dinner. Tomorrow I expect to cover a large part of the town on foot as this might be my only chance to see much of the place. It is about the same distance south of the equator that San Francisco is north, and it appears to have a similar climate. It is now autumn here and the air is quite crisp.

Auckland, New Zealand, May 13, 1943   1900 NZWT

Today has been a most interesting day. I walked for hours about the city, and gained a fair impression of the people and their country. These are more nearly like the United States than any others I have seen, excepting Canada, of course. The people are as violently anti-British as the Australians are pro-British, and they look to the United States for their future security and development.

The best part of the day I spent in the War Memorial Museum. It is the most complete collection of its type I have seen anywhere. The exhibits pertain to the Maori peoples of the Southwest Pacific, the development of New Zealand, and the plants, animals, and minerals of the country. Among items of historical interest was the original iron anchor of the mutiny ship, *Bounty.*

The climate here is not too good. The sun rarely shines and the average temperature is about sixty degrees winter and summer. There is no heat in any of the buildings, and, as a result, the only way I can keep warm is to walk or to stay in the shower bath. Baths are forbidden after tomorrow, however, as there is now a severe water shortage. The New Zealanders are rather rugged people.

Auckland, New Zealand, May 14, 1943   1430 NZWT

Spent more time today walking about the city, trying to find something suitable to buy to take home. There's nothing to be had worth taking home. The entire marine force which was used to capture Guadalcanal has been brought here to rest and recuperate, and members of this force have bought all of such desirable things as were available.

The airplane which I will take out of here in the morning is being brought in this afternoon by Jack O'Brien. Have to get up at 4:30 A.M. to get away at daylight.

Espíritu Santo, New Hebrides, May 15, 1943   1800 NZWT

The trip up from Auckland today was uneventful except for a few minor troubles. The departure from Auckland was accompanied by various minor army-caused delays. Then, upon reaching Tontouta and attempting to get away with as little delay as possible, there was no gas truck available, causing a delay of an hour. Finally we reached Espíritu before dark but failed to establish radio contact with the control tower, due entirely to army stupidity.

Tonight before dinner we had a walk down to the waterfront to see the spot where the *President Coolidge* sank 300 feet from shore when it hit a mine which the navy forgot to tell the captain about.

Mosquitoes are very bad here, and dengue and malaria fevers are quite prevalent. I've had several bites, but I hope the mosquitoes were not infected.

Food here is about the best I've seen in the Pacific. That's fortunate as it's about the only pleasure the men here can indulge themselves with.

Nandi, Fiji Islands, May 16, 1943   1600 FWT

Today has been a comedy of errors. The flight from Espíritu must depart before dawn in order that it can change crews at Plaine des Gaiacs, then land at Tontouta, and still arrive at Auckland before dark, as there are no field lighting facilities there. We were up and ready to take off at the prescribed time, but the control tower operator wouldn't bother to wake up and give us radio direction or even turn on the field lights for us. Since delaying the trip long enough to awaken the men to provide radio and lighting facilities would have meant that the trip couldn't make Auckland before dark, I decided to take off in absolute darkness and without radio. The field is situated in a dense jungle, and that was probably as hazardous a takeoff as I'd ever made. It was further complicated by some cows wandering across the runway in the dark. Any mechanical difficulty after we left the ground would have been tragic as we could never have located the field again, and we had no radio contact with anyone. Fortunately everything went well, but this is really a haywire operation.

Upon reaching Plaine des Gaiacs, where Sullivan and his crew relieved us on the shuttle, there were further army delays. Finally we got away, arrived here in midafternoon, and will be able to get a night of rest.

Canton Island, May 17, 1943   2000 CWT

More troubles today. Had set up our departure for 8:30 this morning, but at the prescribed time no transportation was available and no lunches had been prepared for ourselves or passengers. When we finally overcame these difficulties and arrived at the airplane, we found a leaking brake expander tube, which necessitated removing a wheel.

At last we got away from Nandi at 11:00 A.M. and arrived here after dark. I had planned my operation to go on to Honolulu tonight, but upon arriving here was advised that I would not be cleared until I had had eight hours of rest. So here we stay for a morning departure.

Honolulu, T.H., May 18, 1943   2130 HWT

Had a nice day on the beach today and collected much sunburn. Then I went to Hickam Field for the purpose of registering some gripes with the army. There I was met by Seeley Hall, vice-president UAL, who wanted to know what I wanted to tell the army authorities. After I told him, he requested that I refrain from saying anything at present, as he was having some rather delicate talks with the army powers that be and my gripes might queer his efforts. I agreed to do this, pending the outcome of his conferences.

Honolulu, T.H., May 19, 1943   1400 HWT

We are leaving this afternoon at 6:00 for San Francisco. Have been on the beach most of the day, and now we are going out to Hickam Field early in order to do some shopping at the post exchange. It will be a long trip, but that's quite all right, for I'm going home to see my fine family.

Atherton, Calif., May 20, 1943   2100 PWT

The trip over required fourteen and a half hours, and I arrived in SF at noon to be met by my lovely Gracie. Now the world is a good place once more, in spite of the army. My boys were both well and happy, so there's little more that I can ask, other than for a few days of rest. I flew 108 hours in sixteen and a half days, so now can use a few days in which to recuperate.

Atherton, Calif., May 21, 1943 through May 30, 1943

I spent this period at home in Atherton, resting, enjoying my family, and accomplishing a few business chores. Although I made daily entries in this diary, they are of little general interest. I have eliminated them in order to save the reader boredom.

Atherton, Calif., May 31, 1943   2000 PWT

Today is an anniversary for this diary and for myself.

This entry completes one year of scribbling, each and every day, into this book. Entries have often been made under most trying conditions—

and in all kinds of surroundings. The bleakness of Iceland and Greenland and Labrador contrasts so strikingly with the desert of Western Australia and with the teeming fecundity of tropical Espíritu. From Perth to Reykjavik, from Auckland to Nome, this diary has been my constant companion. As a literary effort, it is futile. As a stimulant to fading memories, it is a help. The trying and unfortunate part is that on the days when interesting things do happen, physical fatigue and inhospitable surroundings combine to defeat my desire to set down my mental impressions. On days when there is no fatigue and when my immediate surroundings are pleasant and conducive to writing, then nothing of interest occurs. But I'm learning that that is the way of most things in life.

This is also a personal anniversary of mine with United Air Lines. Today I have completed ten years with the company. I sometimes try to analyze my feelings toward United. Shortly after I came to work here, I felt as if I were working *with* the company — as if the company were partly mine. Now I feel quite definitely that I am working *for* the company. When things go better for a while, and I do not happen to be confronted with some stupid policy, I grow quite content, and even a little proud of the company. I suppose I'm even a bit more loyal than the average employee with ten years of continuous service behind him. At any rate, I think I shall stay here a while longer unless the company feels otherwise, but I'd much rather feel toward the company the way I felt when I was a new employee.

Atherton, Calif., June 1, 1943   2100 PWT

Went to the airport today on miscellaneous errands and then stopped for short social calls on the Stropeses and the Odells. The airport is the usual confused place, and I spent over an hour trying to exchange an unserviceable suitcase for one which I can use on my next trip. It now appears that I will depart on Saturday.

Atherton, Calif., June 2, 1943 · 2300 PWT

Today has been a queer one. We suddenly decided to can some cherries, and, due to lack of foresight and experience, we spent most of the day and evening at the task. However, we ended up with twenty-two quarts of nice fruit, which will be very welcome in view of probable increased rationing.

Atherton, Calif., June 3, 1943   1830 PWT

This has been a routine day, but not so tonight. We are going into San Francisco with the Odells, the Craines, and the Stropeses to a dinner and dance as a celebration before going out on another trip. It promises to be fun.

Atherton, Calif., June 4, 1943 2200 PWT

We had a fine time in San Francisco last night. We went to the St. Francis, and the place was literally jammed. As an indication of wartime prices, our bill for eight drinks and sixteen turkey sandwiches was $30.50. We didn't have either napkins or water, but we did have much fun.

The Stropeses came down today and we played a lot of tennis. He is my copilot and this next trip will be his last one, as he is being transferred east for upgrading.

Atherton, Calif., June 5, 1943 2000 PWT

The airport advised this morning that I will not be due out until Monday now, as mechanical difficulties are delaying the operations somewhat.

Have spent a lazy day, with only some halfhearted work in the garden. Have collected the things necessary for my trip but as yet have not packed anything. I hope this trip is a bit more pleasant than the last one.

Atherton, Calif., June 6, 1943 2000 PWT

A lazy Sunday today, with some visiting with the neighbors and the necessary last-minute preparations for my trip. It's a beautiful day here, and such a pleasant time in which to do nothing.

I have my home here in very good condition so that I can leave it without too many things going wrong in the yard and garden. Should be leaving tomorrow night unless there is some further unexpected delay.

Atherton, Calif., June 7, 1943 2300 PWT

This morning I went to the airport to test an airplane which was due out this afternoon. This required an hour and a half, and included a trip to Hamilton Field. There have been some schedule delays, and I'm not due out now until day after tomorrow.

Would like to be away on my trip now, as it's always a bit of a letdown to get all ready to go and then be so long delayed.

Atherton, Calif., June 8, 1943 2000 PWT

Another day of useless waiting. However, I was advised this afternoon that I would be leaving definitely tomorrow.

It was a fine day here, so I was lazy all day.

Hamilton Field, Calif., June 9, 1943   1900 PWT

On our way at last. Came over here at 4:00 this afternoon and am now all ready for takeoff. Probably will depart about 2000 PWT. This will be my 13th crossing to Honolulu and my 11th crossing of the Pacific.

Hated to say good-bye to my family today. I miss them so much, but I suppose all good things must end. The boys change so much during my absence that I feel as though I lose out on some part of the fun of having them. This promises to be a short trip, however.

Honolulu, T.H., June 10, 1943   1700 HWT

The trip over last night was the best I've ever had. The weather was favorable and the winds good, and but for the fact that they would not permit us to land here until after daylight, the trip would have been under twelve hours.

Slept until noon and then spent a couple of hours on the beach. It now appears that we will leave here tomorrow morning.

This island is more beautiful than ever now that summer has come and its emerald hills are in full foliage. It's difficult to believe that now we are at war and this island is our enemy's most coveted objective.

Honolulu, T.H., June 11, 1943   1800 HWT

No airplane came out of San Francisco last night, so we did not get away this morning. It's now probable that we will leave tomorrow morning.

Spent three hours on the beach this morning and acquired about as much burn as I could comfortably stand. This afternoon has been a lazy one, with some rummy playing to pass away the time.

En route Honolulu–Canton, June 12, 1943   1230 HWT

We took off from Honolulu this morning for what promises to be a nice trip to Canton. Our only difficulty is that our airplane is so poorly loaded that we are unable to obtain a reasonable speed from it. We have the cabin half full of cargo, and then twenty passengers draped around the cargo. In order that they may have someplace to be comfortable, they have to go back into the tail of the airplane, and this shifts the center of gravity far to the rear.

En route Canton–Fiji, June 13, 1943   1130 CWT

Our overnight stop at Canton was not too pleasant. Yesterday we had Spam sandwiches to eat. Last night at Canton we had absolutely nothing to eat except Spam and cheese and sour pickles. Today we again have Spam sandwiches. After the war the makers of Spam had better go out of business, because there will be about twelve million men who will never eat it again.

Our trip today is fine and without incident. Some of our cargo came off at Canton, so our passengers are a bit more comfortable, and the airplane flies more nearly normally. Have one New Zealand general aboard.

En route Fiji–New Caledonia, June 14, 1943   0800 NCWT

Had a little delay getting out of Nandi this morning because our New Zealand general overslept. However, we are now almost into Plaine des Gaiacs, New Caledonia, and as soon as they are able to service the airplane, we will depart for Australia. The trip today has been excellent in every way, and we have again passed over Tana Island, where the active volcano is smoking and smoldering away. Should arrive in Australia about midafternoon.

Brisbane, Australia, June 15, 1943   2200 AWT

Disposed of most of our passengers and cargo at New Caledonia and had only a short delay for that station. Came on to Australia and landed here about 3:00 P.M.

There were no rooms to be had until 10:00 P.M., so we went to see a very poor show in order to pass the time until we could go to bed.

En route New Caledonia–Fiji, June 16, 1943   1000 FWT

Had our golf game today, and, surprisingly enough, I shot 101.

We departed from Amberley Field for Plaine des Gaiacs at 1:30 A.M. local time, in a brilliant moonlit night. Had a fine trip over except for rather bad weather conditions along New Caledonia. We are now on our way to the Fijis and will arrive there about midafternoon.

En route Samoa–Christmas, June 17, 1943   1100 SWT

Departed from Nandi at 3:30 this morning and came by way of the Samoan Islands. We landed at Pago Pago (pronounced Pango Pango) on Tutuila, American Samoa, and were most pleasantly surprised by the appearance of these beautiful islands. They surpass anything I have seen yet in beauty and romantic appeal. Then the fact that Tutuila is under navy control lends to its attractiveness, as the navy always appears to make its bases far more livable than does the army. Anyway, Samoa appears to be the ideal South Sea island paradise. Its striking green foliage on the rough mountains, the islands set in a turquoise sea and bordered with palm-fringed white coral sands, form a picture which I shall not soon forget.

After an hour and a half in Samoa we took off for Christmas Island, where we will spend the night. I have not been on Christmas before, and will have to make a night landing there. I don't particularly care to do this on my first time in the airport, but there will be a full moon tonight, which will help.

En route Christmas–Honolulu, June 18, 1943   1000 HWT

We found Christmas Island to be another beautiful spot. It is about thirty miles long, but quite low and flat. It has many large coconut plantations, and we saw many large crabs of the variety which lives on coconut meat. We spent some time in husking coconuts to obtain the milk. It is such a chore without proper tools that it is hard to imagine the crabs doing it with only their claws.

There was some excitement on the island this morning. Two members of a ferry crew of a B-25 had gone fishing in an outrigger canoe. They had failed to return last night and were presumed to be lost. However, an aerial search, started at dawn today, located them on the beach of a nearby small island. They will be rescued this morning.

One of our passengers is Sgt. Grady Gaston. He is a big, overgrown farmer boy who has had one of the most astounding experiences of this war. He was lost for 141 days on the bleak, barren salt flats of the southern shore of the Gulf of Carpentaria in northern Australia. He was a member of a crew of a B-24. They became hopelessly lost in a storm and ran out of fuel, so they parachuted from their plane at night. Sergeant Gaston and three officer members of the crew got together and tried to hike out of the marshes. They had no idea where they were, and, unfortunately, started out in the wrong direction. They parachuted on the night of December 1, and he was found on April 21. The last of the three officers died on February 24. When found Sergeant Gaston weighed only 100 pounds but now he weighs about 185 pounds. They saved their last match for a fire on Christmas Day. They had no tools other than their bare hands, as their pistols rusted so much from saltwater that they were useless after the first few days. Mosquitoes, flies, hunger, and lack of the will to live caused the deaths of the three officers. Sergeant Gaston lived on dead fish and snakes and bugs, which the officers could not tolerate. He also ate snails and newly hatched young birds which he found in nests. He believed that his farm training gave him a certain "know-how" which the officers lacked. During the last few days before a native bushman found him, he was barely able to drag himself along. A full military funeral had already been given him, both at his station and at his home. He is now on his way home. A remarkable coincidence is that I flew directly over the spot where he and the last surviving officer were camping on January 24. I was on my way from Townsville to Darwin.

I tried to talk Sergeant Gaston into the idea of collaborating with some good author to produce a book about his experiences. It would make better reading than any *Robinson Crusoe.*

We will arrive in Honolulu in midafternoon today. Hope we are able to remain there for a couple of days.

Honolulu, T.H., June 19, 1943   1800 HWT

Went shopping today and then spent several hours on the beach. We are leaving for San Francisco at 11:30 tonight. Would prefer to remain here another day to rest up a bit, but our airplane is on its way here now.

Atherton, Calif., June 20, 1943   1800 PWT

Home again! So tired I'm going to fall in bed immediately. Haven't closed my eyes for thirty-eight hours.

Atherton, Calif., June 21, 1943 through July 18, 1943

I spent this long period at home, and during this time I accomplished a number of things. There were two physical exams to take, I attended ground school for the new airplane we were to use—the C-54, and I checked out on the airplane and then instructed other pilots in order that they could be qualified to fly it. I was asked by United if I would go to Seattle to fly for sixty days out to the Aleutian Islands chain to Attu, which our armed forces had recaptured from the Japs. I agreed to accept this assignment providing I could return to the Australian operation as soon as the Aleutian emergency airlift was completed.

This period at home was a most enjoyable one which allowed me once again to be with my beautiful family.

The daily entries in the diary have been eliminated here in the interest of brevity.

Atherton, Calif., July 19, 1943   2030 PWT

A quiet day until midafternoon, when the field called to advise that they now want me to go to Alaska as soon as possible. That of course means that I will not go on my Pacific trip, but, instead, will go to Seattle sometime this week. There will be a great many things to do to prepare for the trip, inasmuch as it will be an entirely different type of flying. Will be using DC-3s, which I haven't flown for about a year, and the weather out on the Aleutians will be usually bad. It should be an interesting diversion from the monotony of Pacific flying, however. I'm to be on the assignment for sixty days and should get to Attu sometime during that period. Grace now plans to come up to Seattle during my tour in Alaska, and to have her first vacation in a year and a half. It will be nice to go back to visit the city in which we had our second home, after being married.

Atherton, Calif., July 20, 1943   2100 PWT

Went to the airport today to make final arrangements about going to Alaska. Also got a bicycle for Grace. I had bought it in Australia some time ago, but was unable to bring it back on my last trip. One of the other pilots brought it through on his trip yesterday.

Will be leaving for Seattle via airline on the morning of July 23, and will be flying out of Seattle for Anchorage on the twenty-sixth. Will have plenty of chores to do between now and the time of my departure.

Atherton, Calif., July 21, 1943   1530 PWT

Have spent the entire day today in getting my piloting information in order, packing an emergency kit in case of a forced landing in the Aleutians, and assembling the proper clothing for flying and living in the northland. No doubt I'll forget some of the most essential items.

Tonight Grace and I are going out to do a bit of celebrating. Will not see my family again for quite some time.

Atherton, Calif., July 22, 1943   1630 PWT

Grace and I had dinner at the Fox Shoppe and then went to a movie last night, so that we were late getting to bed.

Today I've been very busy doing last-minute things before going away. Chores have included going into town to buy some more army uniforms suitable for cold-weather use.

The airport just called to advise that it would not be necessary for me to go to Seattle in the morning on a regular airline trip. An airplane will be ferried to Seattle, leaving about noon tomorrow, so I can ride on it. This will be more satisfactory and less crowded than the regular airline trip.

Hate to part with my family this time. I expect Grace to be able to visit me in Seattle.

Atherton, Calif., July 23, 1943   2000 PWT

Spent nearly all day at the airport waiting for someone to make up his mind as to when he was going to fly the ferry to Seattle. Finally, at 5:00 P.M. I became so thoroughly disgusted at not being able to get any definite information that I got a reservation on the regular airline trip for tomorrow morning, and returned home. This will give me one more night with my family. The way this operation is starting out, it appears that things may not run so smoothly.

7

Anchorage to Adak

JULY–OCTOBER, 1943

Seattle, Wash., July 24, 1943   2100 PWT

Had a fine ride up to this place today, without a cloud in the sky. Upon arrival I learned that I had to have some kind of a special pass required to go into Alaska, and I had only one and a half hours in which to go into town, have pictures taken, and get the pass. I am to depart for Anchorage, Alaska, at 0700 tomorrow, so I rushed around and finally obtained the necessary pass.

Anchorage, Alaska, July 25, 1943   1800 AWT

This has been a long day, but a very fine one. Was up at 4:15 this morning in Seattle to be ready for takeoff at 7:00 A.M. at Boeing Field. We got away on time, and the weather was perfect, so that I had the incomparable pleasure of watching the beautiful northwestern scenery roll by below as we inched our way along over the interminable expanse of lakes and sounds and straits and capes and islands of the tree-shrouded coastline. At length we reached Ketchikan, where we landed on Annette Island for fuel. This is the island on which the famous wealthy Indian settlement is located at Metlakatla. The trip to Ketchikan took us across the heart of beautiful Vancouver Island, where some of the finest timber, fishing, and scenery in the world are to be found.

Out of Annette we passed outside of Juneau, but went over Sitka with its many strange Russian names which recall the days of rich sea-otter hunting and strong living. Baranov chose a beautiful spot for his settlement, but he did not allow for the relentless ferocity of the Indians whose lands and waters he had appropriated.

We landed at Yakutat, where the army has built one of the finest airports in one of the finest locations I have ever seen. Here we refueled and departed for Anchorage. The weather was not too good, so I didn't

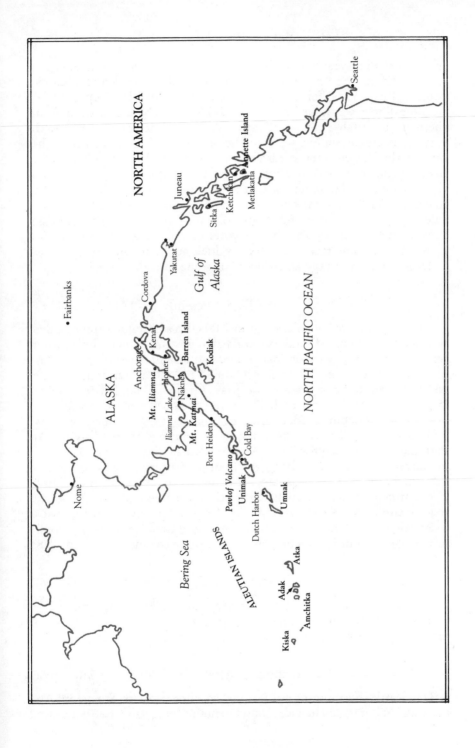

NORTH AMERICA

Seattle

Juneau

Yakutat

Sitka

Ketchikan

Metlakatla

Annette Island

Gulf of
Alaska

Cordova

Fairbanks

Anchorage

Kenai

Homer

Barren Island

Mt. Iliamna

Iliamna Lake

Naknek

Kodiak

ALASKA

Mt. Katmai

Port Heiden

NORTH PACIFIC OCEAN

Cold Bay

Pavlof Volcano

Unimak

Umnak

Dutch Harbor

Nome

Bering Sea

ALEUTIAN ISLANDS

Adak

Atka

Kiska

Amchitka

see Cordova or Portage Pass. In fact, I had to make an instrument approach into Anchorage. At Anchorage, accommodations were adequate but expensive. I paid $2.50 for a steak, potatoes, and bread for dinner.

After dinner we walked down to a small river about 200 yards from the hotel to watch a couple of men fish for salmon. They fished with very crude tackle—only a weighted hook tied to a line. They threw the hook to the far side of the stream and pulled it back hand over hand. The hook caught in the side or back of a salmon as it swam upstream, and the fish was pulled to shore. Most of the fish were worthless humpbacked males, weighing about three pounds, but occasionally they caught a silverside or dog salmon weighing about ten pounds. About every third cast netted a fish. Next trip I'll have a layover of a day in Anchorage, so I'm going to take some tackle and try my luck at the fishing.

I'll be called at 5:00 A.M. so now I'm going to bed.

Portland, Ore., July 26, 1943   2245 PWT

This morning we left Anchorage at 7:00 with a hospital airplane filled with sick and wounded soldiers attended by an army nurse. The weather was not good, so we were on instruments almost all of the way from Anchorage to Ketchikan. We were scheduled to land at Yakutat, but the weather there was not good, so we passed it up and landed at Annette Island near Ketchikan for fuel. Then we continued directly on to Portland without stopping at Seattle, as our wounded were destined for a hospital at Portland. The trip down required about ten hours of flying. At Portland we met with bad luck. An army truck which was parked near our airplane to receive the baggage of our passengers pulled out and ran into the left wing of our airplane. It damaged the wing tip and aileron of the airplane to such an extent that they must be replaced. This will require two or three days, so now I'm deadheading on the airline back to Seattle at about midnight tonight. Am very tired and must get some rest, as I'm due out for Anchorage again early in the morning of July 28.

Seattle, Wash., July 27, 1943   1500 PWT

Didn't get to bed until 2:00 A.M. so slept until 10:00 this morning. Now I'll have a full day, writing Grace, preparing my maps, and making other preparations for going to Anchorage again tomorrow morning.

Anchorage, Alaska, July 28, 1943   2100 AWT

Left Seattle this morning at 7:00 and had a fine trip here. Stopped at Annette and Yakutat, and had less than ten hours' flying time to Anchorage.

When we arrived it was raining, but I went fishing anyway. My luck was not too good, but I caught about eight fish from three to six pounds each and got thoroughly soaked.

The survey flight returned from the Aleutians this afternoon and had some interesting stories to tell. It would appear that the flying out there will be plenty rough.

I had a very small steak and a bottle of beer for dinner tonight and the price was $3.20. The proprietor admitted he was out to make the greatest possible profit while the getting was good.

En route Yakutat–Ketchikan, July 29, 1943   2200 AWT

Unfortunately for us, four trips arrived in Anchorage late this afternoon, and the army wished to turn one of them around. So I had to depart this evening and am making an all-night trip back to Seattle.

The weather is not too good tonight, and it does not appear that we will get into Ketchikan. I plan on stopping at Vancouver, British Columbia, anyway to discharge Maj. Dan McDonald, a former UAL employee who is now with the army and based in Edmonton. We should finally get to Seattle about 4:30 A.M. if all goes well. I don't like these all-night trips, because of the extreme fatigue from which I suffer.

Mercer Island, Wash., July 30, 1943   2300 PWT

Arrived in Seattle at 0500 this morning and got to bed an hour later. The telephone started ringing at 0800, and after many calls I finally gave up trying to sleep and got up at 1000.

I had to go out to the airport because one of the passengers I had brought in was a civilian and the immigration authorities had failed to meet the airplane to check him in. We had landed in Canada on the way down, so he was technically entering the U.S.A. from a foreign country. I had to go out to identify him as the same man I had brought in. Much red tape, especially since this individual was a government employee.

Seattle, Wash., July 31, 1943   2030 PWT

I stayed all night at the Parkers' (friends from my year of work in a logging camp) and came home to the hotel about noon today. I'm soon going to try to get a small apartment, as there is so much noise and confusion here, with crews coming and going and the telephone ringing quite frequently. If I can find an apartment, that will solve Grace's housing problem when she arrives.

I'm now scheduled out for Anchorage again tomorrow morning. Don't know whether or not my trip will go on out on the Aleutians, but hope it will.

The weather here has been cloudy and cool, and not at all the same as I remembered it being in Washington when I was flying out of here with United in 1937. Perhaps this is only temporary, and it will improve. Seattle is crowded and spoiled as a city and not much fun at all. Prices are almost unbelievably high.

Anchorage, Alaska, Aug. 1, 1943   2230 AWT

The trip north today was fast and uneventful. We got a late start but landed only at Annette and Yakutat, so arrived here in good time. The Alaskan scenery is becoming more beautiful with the definite approach of a change of seasons.

Anchorage, Alaska, Aug. 2, 1943   2000 AWT

Today has been quite rainy here in Anchorage, and that has spoiled what might have been a good day of fishing. I did go, however, and, among the numerous humpies, did manage to catch one good dog salmon of about ten pounds, which I am taking back to Seattle.

En route Portland–Seattle, Aug. 3, 1943   2345 PWT

This has been a long and hard day. Departed from Anchorage early this morning with a hospital airplane bound for Barnes Hospital in Portland. We landed only at Annette Island on the way and are now ferrying our empty airplane back to Seattle. Will be glad when this trip is over. Will probably be moving to an apartment tomorrow.

Seattle, Wash., Aug. 4, 1943   2100 PWT

We had to sleep in a sample room at the hotel last night, so today I moved into a small apartment in the President Apartment Hotel. It will be adequate for a place for Grace to stay when she arrives.

Seattle, Wash., Aug. 5, 1943   2200 PWT

Ray Wolff and I took about a ten-mile walk out through the University of Washington and return today. Did little else, but the exercise was good for me.

Seattle, Wash., Aug. 6, 1943   2230 PWT

Another rainy, gloomy day here. Am about to change my opinion about Seattle summer weather.

Have spent a lazy day. Took a walk this morning, bought a history of Baranov called *Lord of Alaska,* and have been fascinated by it. This evening I took an airplane down to McCord Field at Tacoma to have an IFF secret radio installed in it and arrived home only a little while ago.

No further definite information about our Pacific accident at New Zealand, but there is a rumor that the pilot was Laughlin. It seems that the airplane caught fire on takeoff, and crashed when they tried to get back into the airport with it. It will probably be some time before we hear the true story through all of the army censorship.

Seattle, Wash., Aug. 7, 1943   2100 PWT

Still another rainy day. Haven't been very active today. Went to the airport for a briefing on the Aleutians, and now my schedule has changed again. I'm now starting on a trip to Alaska tomorrow. Probably will not get away from here very early and will go only as far as Anchorage tomorrow night.

Have been deeply engrossed in the book about Baranov. When we think we have troubles, it's enlightening to read a story of someone who really did encounter difficulties.

I had a nice letter from home today, which allayed my worries as to the welfare of my family.

The Parkers wanted me to go over to Mercer Island tonight, but I declined.

Seattle, Wash., Aug. 8, 1943   2000 PWT

Didn't get away today as planned, due to mechanical difficulties with the airplane. We are now scheduled to depart at 0700 tomorrow, which means a 0430 call.

Took a long walk out to Volunteer Park and visited the museum there. Have done little else except read. One reaches an anticlimax when he is fully prepared for a thing to happen and then is delayed.

This trip and then one more, and after that, Grace arrives!

Anchorage, Alaska, Aug. 9, 1943   2200 AWT

The trip up was most unpleasant, with instrument weather most of the way. And upon our arrival, we had bad news. The army wants all airplanes back in Seattle as soon as possible to bring certain emergency cargo to Anchorage. It may be that I'll have to return to Seattle without making a trip to the Aleutians this time. However, my present orders are to hold here in Anchorage. Perhaps an airplane will come in tomorrow and I can take it to the Aleutians the following day.

Anchorage is gloomy and rainy tonight with a feeling of autumn in the air. We had considerable snow at 9,000 feet on the trip today. Summer is definitely on the decline here and daylight is growing noticeably shorter each trip I make.

Anchorage, Alaska, Aug. 10, 1943   2100 AWT

Have done very little today. It has been a nice day but I slept until late and then went out to the army field to get more information on the Aleutians. While I was at the field, Ralph Johnson came in from Amchitka, tired but pleasant as usual.

Late this afternoon I went fishing but without success. The river was high and swift, and I didn't catch even one humpback. Had a fine hike through the woods, however, and enjoyed the outing thoroughly. In the morning I am leaving for Adak Island, weather permitting.

Adak Island, Aleutians, Aug. 11, 1943   1930 BWT

The trip down was one of the most interesting ones I've had. Departed from Anchorage at 0700 this morning and flew at low altitude and contact by way of Kenai and Homer to inspect the landing strips there, then crossed Cook Inlet to Lake Iliamna, past Iliamna Volcano, and on to Naknek. Had to do an instrument procedure into Naknek, where the weather is almost invariably bad. Went along to the west of Katmai Volcano.

Out of Naknek we flew contact under low clouds at 200 to 500 feet to Cold Bay, inspecting the airport at Port Heiden on the way. This was the most interesting part of the trip. The northern part of the peninsula along here is quite flat, and about half of the surface consists of small lakes. There are no trees of any type west of Naknek, but the tundra is quite green with grass and moss. In this area alone I saw at least 150 pairs of huge trumpeter swans, nesting egariously along the lakes, and most of them had three or four half-grown goslings. So perhaps these magnificent birds will not become extinct after all.

[At Cold Bay I had an annoying experience which finally turns out to be almost comical when looking back upon it.

I had to work an instrument procedure down to about 100 feet in order to land. I refueled and signed my takeoff clearance to proceed onward. A young second lieutenant was operations officer (a nonpilot officer). He refused to sign my takeoff clearance because the weather ceiling was reported to be 100 feet, when his procedures manual said that the ceiling must be 300 feet or better before a clearance could be authorized. I argued with him in vain because he was adamant in his position. Even though I had been able to land under the restricted ceiling and visibility conditions, he would not change his position.

Cold Bay is a very isolated and lonely place. I told him that since it was so difficult to clear out of the place, I would have to recommend to my fellow pilots that they avoid landing at Cold Bay unless it was because of an extreme emergency. I told him that of course the people there then would get no mail and no fresh food, which we normally brought in by air.

Not surprisingly he caught on very quickly and immediately signed my clearance.

I will report this incident back to my chief pilot to see if we cannot correct the practice. We airline pilots have been given explicit approval to authorize our own clearances.]

Surprised one huge Alaskan brown bear that appeared to be as large as a horse. He was infuriated as we dived to within a few feet of him. I saw perhaps two hundred caribou, those awkward creatures with such huge antlers. They looked like cows with rocking chairs on their heads, as they fled from the approach of our airplane. They have peculiar gaits when they run, no doubt caused by the effort necessary to hold their antlers aloft.

We cut across Bristol Bay and saw a school of porpoise and several huge blackfish.

The Pavlof Volcano was in the overcast and we were unable to see it spouting its smoke into the air, as it does every six minutes.

The weather at Dutch Harbor was zero-zero so we were unable to get a look at the place. We landed at Umnak for fuel. The closer we came to Kiska the more activity we saw, although flying conditions are far from ideal anywhere west of Anchorage. Out of Umnak we flew across the Bering Sea directly to Adak. The weather was not too good, but we arrived at Adak without incident.

Here at Adak there is no question but that we have a war to win. The harbor is full of ships, and there is activity everywhere. An airport has been carved out of this rugged island, and now it is the main base used against the Japs. It's a relief at last to see some of our army and navy really at work winning the war.

One incident today brought the war a bit closer to me and gave me a queer feeling. Soon after we landed, one of the officers said that twenty-four bombers were due in from a raid on Kiska. In a few minutes the bomber formations appeared, but one airplane was missing from each squadron. Wonder where those poor boys are tonight—

The Aleutians impress me in an unusual way. They are cold and aloof and mysterious—their green and brown crags hide behind perpetual curtains of fog, to appear only occasionally in the clear, like memories that you can't quite grasp and pull back to consciousness. I believe their cloak of mystery will never be quite removed. After the war they will probably return to their realm—half real, half mythical.

When we landed, the army asked us to take our cargo on to Amchitka, but it seems that some limitation in our contract makes it impossible for us to do so.

Here I sit in an army-type igloo with an oil stove and in comparative comfort. Such a short time ago I was sweltering in the jungles of the South Pacific. Tonight I will sleep in an eiderdown sleeping bag. This island of Adak is almost as far west as the Fiji Islands and as far south as the northern tip of Vancouver Island, yet there is snow on the mountains above our igloo.

Will depart early in the morning for Anchorage.

Anchorage, Alaska, Aug. 12, 1943   2100 AWT

Today's trip back was quite as fine as the one yesterday, but a bit different. I had a hospital ship filled with wounded soldiers and consequently was unable to fly low over the terrain. We were on instruments along the Aleutian chain until well along on the Alaska Peninsula. From about Mount Pavlof to Anchorage we were out in the clear, and the weather was perfect. We went alongside the Katmai Volcano and watched it pour its smoke into the sky to color the air for a hundred miles to leeward.

We turned over to Kodiak Island and flew across it, in hopes that we would see some of the famous Kodiak bears, but we were flying too high to be able to spot them. Flying across Afognak Island, the Barren Islands, and the tip of the Kenai Peninsula, we descended into Anchorage in late afternoon after an eight-hour nonstop trip.

Seattle, Wash., Aug. 13, 1943   2200 PWT

Arrived here at 1945 after a long, long trip, but one flown in very fine weather. I'm quite tired. Have flown for forty hours in four days, and that's enough.

No news from the family, but I suppose Grace is busy with the two boys and with making preparations for her vacation.

According to the present schedule, I'm due out on August 18 again, which will be about right. I'm to go out to the Aleutians on that trip, so should be back here not later than August 25. Grace plans to arrive on August 27, and I'll have flown almost one hundred hours, so can't be scheduled out again before August 31. I'm looking forward to her visit as I'm getting just a bit homesick.

Seattle, Wash., Aug. 14, 1943   2000 PWT

Slept late today, and have done very little else except to take a long walk. Had a fine letter from home with pictures of the two boys, but that served only to make me more homesick. I will not be very long until Grace will be here, and then we can have fun.

Seattle, Wash., Aug. 15, 1943   2100 PWT

Another entirely useless day. Have not felt at all good the past three days.

It has been a fine day here today, warm and cloudless. Didn't quite feel up to taking my usual walk, or it would have been interesting. Perhaps tomorrow I'll be ready to go again.

Seattle, Wash., Aug. 16, 1943   2300 PWT

Spent most of the afternoon in the library, browsing for various bits of information I'd been wanting to look up. Then tonight I took the Johnsons and Claire Wittenberg out to dinner to a place where we had a fine seafood dinner. Tomorrow I'm going to play squash with Ralph Johnson at the Athletic Club, and then he wants to organize a poker game for the afternoon.

It still appears that I will be due out on August 18 on my next trip to Adak.

Seattle, Wash., Aug. 17, 1943   2100 PWT

Played squash with Ralph Johnson at the Washington Athletic Club today, and later this afternoon Ralph, Frank Morton, Ed Hoy, and I played poker. I lost at squash but won at poker.

It has been a fine day here, with much sunshine and warm. It is more nearly like the Seattle I remember.

Had hoped for a letter from home but none came. I get so I depend so much on letters. Would like to see my family tonight—

Anchorage, Alaska, Aug. 18, 1943   2300 PWT

Although we were at the airport ready to depart from Seattle at 0900 this morning, our airplane was not finally ready until 1400 hours. Consequently, we have had a very long day of it.

The trip up was fine, with weather much better than forecast. We landed only at Annette Island and arrived here just at dark. We are leaving early tomorrow for Adak.

Atka Island, Aleutians, Aug. 19, 1943   2200 BWT

The trip today was quite long, due to strong headwinds the entire distance. The weather at Adak was zero-zero, so we stopped and are holding here at Atka for the night, and expect to go on to Adak tomorrow morning.

We flew from Anchorage to Naknek contact and did some sightseeing. We found three large moose on the peninsula near Kenai, then we went across to fly over the smoking Augustine Island volcano. From here we went through Bruin Bay Pass to Lake Iliamna, and thence to Naknek. We flew low over the charred remains of the army transport airplane that crashed on a mountainside a few days ago, killing the passengers, including Miss Gardner, the army nurse.

From Naknek to Cold Bay the weather was quite bad and we were unable to do much game hunting. We landed at Cold Bay, and after leaving there we hedgehopped on out to the tip of the Alaska Peninsula and on across most of Unimak Island. Here we saw many caribou, including three different herds of at least a thousand animals in each. We came upon a beautiful red fox in the center of an open field, and we had much fun with him before he finally reached the shelter of his den. We also came upon a small tidewater island which was literally crowded with fur seals.

We were unable to get into the regular airport on Umnak Island, due to weather, so we landed at Reindeer Pass on the north side of the island. Just offshore near Reindeer Pass we came upon a tremendous flock of dark brown seabirds which I believe were shearwaters. I would estimate that there were at least 100,000 birds in the flock, as they extended along the surface of the water for several miles in a flight at least 200 yards wide.

We cleared from Reindeer Pass to Atka, hoping that the weather at Adak would improve sufficiently to permit us to continue on, but such was not to be the case. So here we are, spending the night in comparative comfort in our eiderdown sleeping bags in a cozy Quonset hut. We will be up early in the morning for a try at Adak and then a return trip to Anchorage.

Anchorage, Alaska, Aug. 20, 1943   2230 AWT

This day has been long and difficult. We were up early in a pouring rain at Atka and departed for Adak, where we landed with no weather margin to spare.

At Adak we finally got the true story about Kiska. Our troops made well-planned landings on Kiska some days ago but were unopposed. As of yesterday, reconaissance parties had covered all parts of the island except the active volcano and had found no enemy forces. In fact, the Japs had removed all of their installations, including their huts, and had completely evacuated the island. The navy was just preparing to fly over the island, advising the Japs (who were not there) to surrender, as they had no chance of escape. For days the navy had been pouring high-explosive shells into the abandoned island and talking about what a tough fortress it was going to be. Someone high in authority is going to have the difficult task of explaining why so many millions of dollars have been spent in taking an abandoned, undefended rock, and of explaining how the 7,000 Japs escaped through the navy's "ring of steel." Aside from the accompanying embarrassment, however, the pleasant fact remains that we are now in possession of the island, which might otherwise have cost a huge sacrifice in American lives had we been forced to neutralize it before occupying it.

We departed from Adak in heavy rain with our airplane loaded with hospital patients. We were on instruments until over Dutch Harbor, but from there to Anchorage the weather was good.

Mount Pavlof was in the clear and spouting its smoke with characteristic regularity. We circled its cone and watched the unusual spectacle of smoke and rocks belching forth to soil the perpetual snow which covers the steep slopes of the mountain. It is indeed an impressive sight and one which very few people are ever privileged to witness.

We proceeded on along the southern coast of the Alaska Peninsula. When we were about abreast of Naknek, that station called to beg us to stop to pick up an emergency hospital patient. This required about 150 miles of extra flying, but we did it and worked an instrument procedure into Naknek. We remained there only long enough to load the patient, then came on into Anchorage, arriving here just at dusk.

Anchorage, Alaska, Aug. 21, 1943   2000 AWT

This has been a day of fine weather. Got up late and then this afternoon we went for a walk along the river. Tried trout fishing for a few minutes, but without success. Tonight we have played rummy to pass away some more time. We are expecting to depart for Seattle tomorrow morning.

Anchorage, Alaska, Aug. 22, 1943   2100 AWT

It has rained almost continuously today, so we have been unable to get outside. The airplane that we were supposed to take to Seattle today developed engine trouble at Juneau on its northbound trip, so we will not get away until tomorrow.

I know of no place more uninteresting on Sunday than Anchorage, unless it is Brisbane. Had long discussions about religion with my crew members, Wally Gehlaar and Ray Wolff, both of whom are Catholic.

Seattle, Wash., Aug. 23, 1943   2200 PWT

Had an interesting trip down today. Got out of Anchorage early and landed at Yakutat to discharge a passenger. When we arrived at Annette Island the reported weather was 100 feet and three-quarters of a mile visibility, but I decided to make an attempt at landing there in view of the fact that I had six passengers for the place. It was an interesting approach, and we did get in there all right.

We had as passengers Major General Pearts and his staff. He is in the Royal Canadian Air Force and is in command of the defense of western Canada. He led the Canadian units that landed on Kiska, and he related many interesting tales concerning the operation. Contrary to the first reports we had, the Japs abandoned almost all of the equipment they had on Kiska. They destroyed their installations and evacuated only their men. They probably did this by using destroyers as troop carriers, and then under cover of darkness and fog. He said their attempts to establish a base there were almost pitiful. They had practically no power equipment and were in the process of building a landing strip by using only handcarts and shovels. Bombings and marine shellings had made their installations almost untenable, in view of the inclement weather.

We landed at Vancouver to discharge the general and his party and then arrived in Seattle about 1930 this evening.

I have my flying time in for the month and will not be dispatched again before September 1. A letter from Grace tonight assures me she will be here on August 27 as planned. That will be good—

Seattle, Wash., Aug. 24, 1943   2100 PWT

Slept until late today, then went to the airport to type some letters.

It has been a beautiful day here, warm and with much sunshine. Hope this lasts until Grace arrives.

Seattle, Wash., Aug. 25, 1943   2200 PWT

Today I did various small errands, including making reservations on the boat for Grace and me to go to Victoria on Sunday, August 29. It should be a nice outing.

Day after tomorrow Grace arrives. How nice it will be to see her again!

Seattle, Wash., Aug. 26, 1943   2200 PWT

A lazy day with some walking and little else. Located a used movie camera which I'll go to see tomorrow and probably buy. I don't want to allow the boys to grow to be men without something of a record of their process of growing up.

Less than twenty-four hours now until Grace arrives. Don't know when I've been more anxious to see her. She is already on the train and on her way here.

Seattle, Wash., Aug. 27, 1943   2300 PWT

It was a long day today, waiting until Grace arrived. Her train was only a little late, and since her arrival we have had so many things to talk over. It's good to see her again and get all of the news concerning the two boys. They are well and growing, except that Johnny has had some more bee stings.

Seattle, Wash., Aug. 28, 1943   2345 PWT

We slept until late today and then went to the railroad station to recover Grace's baggage. This afternoon we went over to the Parkers' on Mercer Island and later went to a picnic at the Moss home there. Had a generally fine evening. Grace was not feeling well.

En route Seattle–Victoria, Aug. 29, 1943   2300 PWT

Grace and I are now on our way over to Victoria, British Columbia, where we will spend tomorrow and return to Seattle tomorrow night. Although the boat is crowded, we have a nice stateroom and will have a comfortable night.

We did very little in Seattle this lazy Sunday before departing on this good ship *Iroquois*.

Victoria, British Columbia, Aug. 30, 1943   1600 PWT

The weather has been bad today with much drizzling and cold. We arrived late and then took a tally-ho ride behind horses to see the high spots of town. It was quite interesting. Grace was not patient enough to wait until tea was served in the lobby of the Empress Hotel, so we never did learn just how it is done.

Now we are about to start a long struggle with immigration authorities over the process of getting back into the United States. This wartime travel simply isn't worth the effort necessary to accomplish it.

Seattle, Wash., Aug. 31, 1943   2100 PWT

We finally arrived back in Seattle last night after much delay caused by customs and immigration inspections. I suppose all of this is necessary, but is appears to be carried to almost absurd lengths, especially between friendly countries such as ours and Canada.

The company called this morning to advise that they want me to go to Edmonton, Alberta, tomorrow to make several trips between Edmonton and Fairbanks, Alaska. This will seem almost like homecoming again. As now planned, I'll leave here tomorrow morning and will be away about a week. Am sorry I'll be away so long, in view of the fact that Grace will be here alone on her vacation.

We telephoned Atherton again tonight to make certain the boys were both well.

Edmonton, Alberta, Sept. 1, 1943   2100 MWT

Came here from Seattle today and am now waiting to take a trip north to Fairbanks at midnight tonight. It's going to be a long trip and a long time without sleep. I sometimes wonder why I continue to do this difficult, dangerous, and exhausting type of work when I could go back on the domestic line and live sensibly again. Perhaps it's because I still have a streak of adventure left in me, or perhaps it's because I still want to be doing something for the war effort in a more direct manner than holding down my regular peacetime job.

We are based at the MacDonald Hotel again, and the town of Edmonton doesn't seem to have changed much in the year since I was last here.

Fairbanks, Alaska, Sept. 2, 1943   2000 AWT

We were tired men when we arrived here about 1000 hours today. Had been out of bed thirty hours and in the air fifteen hours. The trip to Fairbanks was not pleasant, as we had considerable weather to combat almost all of the way. We landed at Watson Lake and Tanacross. Whenever we were able to see it, the Alaska Highway was a pleasant sight. The improvements in the airway and highway facilities here in the past year have been remarkable. From Tanacross to Fairbanks the weather was good and the landscape beautiful. Alaska is at its best just now. Frost has colored all of the deciduous growth until the lower slopes and valleys are a blaze of color. Fresh-fallen powder snow covers the hills above this color line, and the resulting contrast is a masterpiece of beauty indeed.

We are poorly billeted here in a large, cold barracks where there is much noise and confusion and little opportunity for rest. Soviet pilots are here in great numbers, so living facilities are scarce.

We expect and hope to get away tomorrow morning. Now for some sleep—I hope.

Edmonton, Alberta, Sept. 3, 1943   2200 MWT

We had a long and tiring, but very interesting trip down today. We departed from Fairbanks at sunrise this morning and followed the Alaska Highway all the way down. I took some colored movie pictures, which I hope catch most of the exquisite coloring that is now so profusely splashed around the countryside.

We landed at Whitehorse for fuel and passengers, then continued on to Fort Nelson. The highway route between these two centers is quite tortuous, so built to avoid the muskeg country along the more direct air route. The resulting trip was consequently much longer than normal. After a short stop at Fort Nelson, we continued on to Edmonton, with favorable winds and weather, by way of Saint John and Grande Prairie.

I'll probably make one more trip northbound before continuing back to Seattle. Hope to do this soon in order to see Grace again before she departs from Seattle on September 10.

Edmonton, Alberta, Sept. 4, 1943   2000 MWT

Today has been a cold and rainy day with little to do for diversion. Too nasty to get outdoors, so I've spent the day reading and playing rummy. Sent a telegram to Grace but still was unable to tell her when I would be going back to Seattle. No further news about when I take another trip northward.

Edmonton, Alberta, Sept. 5, 1943   1700 MWT

Nothing exciting today. Sunday in Alberta is comparable to a Sunday in Australia. It's a beautiful autumn day, and I did manage to take a short walk. I am now due out tonight sometime after 1900 hours. Our airplane is here now, but it requires some mechanical work before it will be ready to go. It will be another all-night trip. They are so fatiguing after being up all day. Hope we get a break on the weather so that the trip will not be too disagreeable.

Fairbanks, Alaska, Sept. 6, 1943   1700 AWT

The trip up last night was really a nightmare. We didn't get away from Edmonton until 2100 hours, and it took us thirteen hours to make the trip. I get so tired on that kind of trip that I almost give up, because it means at least thirty-six hours without sleep. The weather was excellent in spite of the strong winds, and we were treated to an almost continuous display of aurora borealis. We stopped at Fort Nelson and Whitehorse, and arrived in Fairbanks well after daylight. We will depart about nightfall and have another all-night trip southbound tonight. Only had four hours of sleep today in dirty beds in the louse-infested Nordale Hotel.

Edmonton, Alberta, Sept. 7, 1943   1900 MWT

Another all-night trip last night has left me nearly exhausted today. Slept about five hours after arrival and am now ready to go back to bed again.

Tomorrow we are leaving for Seattle, as our task here has been completed. It will be good to see Grace again. I'm afraid her vacation hasn't been too pleasant, as she has been alone there most of the time. Had a welcome telegram from her when I arrived here this morning. Two or three more trips from Seattle to Anchorage and then I can go back to California and see my boys again!

Seattle, Wash., Sept. 8, 1943   2200 PWT

We had a late start from Edmonton this morning and then had to go by way of Great Falls, Montana, on the way to Seattle. As a result, I didn't arrive here until after 2000 hours.

Gracie was waiting patiently for me when I arrived, and it was good to see her again. Tomorrow she is going to try to get her train reservation changed to a later date so she can remain here a few more days.

Seattle, Wash., Sept. 9, 1943   2345 PWT

Today Grace and I took in the downtown section of Seattle, bought some presents for our boys, bought some new phonograph records, etc., and generally splurged. She managed to get her train reservation changed to Sunday so that she will now have two extra days to spend here.

Tomorrow I must go to the airport to do a lot of chores there.

Seattle, Wash., Sept. 10, 1943   2200 PWT

Was up early and went to the airport to complete my business. Then Grace and I went to a movie and then enjoyed a Chinese dinner. To bed early tonight to make up for lost sleep last night.

Seattle, Wash., Sept. 11, 1943   2200 PWT

Today we took a ride to Bremerton and return on the ferryboat. Tonight we had intended going out to dinner and dance with the Parkers, but they were unable to go at the last minute because Betty had contracted a cold. We are home early tonight with nothing to do.

We talked to Jimmy over the telephone last night and found both him and Johnny to be well. I'm anxious to go home and see the boys. This is the longest period I've been away from them continuously. Grace leaves at noon tomorrow for Palo Alto.

Seattle, Wash., Sept. 12, 1943   1500 PWT

Grace got away on time at 1230 today, so I'm all alone again, just putting in time until I can return home and see my family once more. I am due out for Anchorage at 0900 tomorrow, and I have three more trips to make before I can leave. If airplanes are available, I should be able to complete these trips in about ten or twelve days.

Anchorage, Alaska, Sept. 13, 1943   2230 AWT

We were delayed in departing from Seattle today, but finally got away and had a splendid trip up here. Weather was unusually good so that we were flying contact most of the time. Stopped at Annette for fuel and then went up the inside route via Juneau to Yakutat. The scenery along south of Juneau is certainly beautiful. The rich blue waters of all of the innumerable channels and straits are broken only by the sheer, tree-covered islands and peninsulas which rise so precipitously from the ocean floor. Among the green fir trees are just enough of the deciduous varieties, now brilliantly colored by frost, to create a blaze of color. It's an unforgettable sight.

Along the beach south of Yakutat we came upon about twenty black bears, out feeding on salmon in the late evening light. It was too dark for pictures, but I did take some movie shots of Malaspina Glacier and of Mount Saint Elias and Mount Logan in late afternoon sunlight. I hope that they will prove to be good. Arrived here well after dark, and the days here are noticeably shorter than they were two weeks ago.

Anchorage, Alaska, Sept. 14, 1943   1500 AWT

No airplane in which to return to Seattle today, so I'm staying over until tomorrow. Dick Crane is also stranded here.

Slept late this morning and have done little since rising. It's a cloudy, gloomy day, and not one conducive to getting outside. Perhaps a card game will relieve the monotony later. Then there's the possibility that Dick Crane and I may take one of the airplanes that arrive this afternoon and go out to make some terrain altitude surveys for the Civil Aeronautics Authority.

Seattle, Wash., Sept. 15, 1943   2330 PWT

The trip down from Anchorage today was the most unpleasant I've had so far. Collected heavy ice over Portage Pass and couldn't maintain altitude to safely clear the Chugach Mountains, so had to go out to sea to descend to allow the ice to melt. Then strong headwinds made the trip unduly long. Landed at Yakutat, Juneau, and Annette and was twelve and a half hours in the air to Seattle. South of Yakutat the weather was good and I took many color movie scenes, which I hope are as colorful as the brilliant landscape. Saw many more black bears, but the lighting was not favorable for pictures.

Am thoroughly tired now, and will be in bed in a few minutes. Am now due out on the first trip day after tomorrow.

Seattle, Wash., Sept. 16, 1943   1600 PWT

Slept late this morning and then have been busy doing all of the necessary chores. Had a nice letter from Grace with many enclosures of other letters from the folks in Missouri. Wayne reports the quail hunting will be good on the farm this winter, and I should like to be able to get back there for a day or two. Grace found our two boys in good condition after her absence and reports that Jimmy is growing by leaps and bounds, literally and figuratively.

Anchorage, Alaska, Sept. 17, 1943   2200 AWT

The trip up today was fine but rather long. Good weather enabled me to take several movie shots, at least some of which should be good. Got several shots of black bears on the delta near Yakutat. Took these with a telephoto lens and I hope they turn out all right. We stopped only at Annette and Yakutat.

Will not be returning tomorrow, as ours was the only trip northbound today. There will be no airplane available for us. Can look forward to another dull day in Anchorage.

Anchorage, Alaska, Sept. 18, 1943   2000 AWT

Today it has rained continuously here, and I haven't been outside the hotel. No place can be so dull on such a day. Even the conversation around the hotel lobby is dull and unenthusiastic.

An airplane arrived tonight and we will be taking it south to Seattle in the morning. One more trip and then I can return home and see my family!

Seattle, Wash., Sept. 19, 1943   2200 PWT

The trip down today was quite the most unpleasant one I've had. On the ground it was raining all the way from Anchorage to Seattle, and at flying levels we had ice and snow and rain throughout the entire 1,500 miles, with no radio reception much of the time. The transition from summer to winter is abrupt and severe in this country and presents its problems in flying. Hope my next and last trip will be more pleasant so that I can be more kindly disposed toward Alaska when I leave it.

Am now due out again the day after tomorrow. Plan to go back to San Francisco on September 24.

Seattle, Wash., Sept. 20, 1943   1700 PWT

Have been trying to recover from the effects of my trip, but still feel quite tired and lazy. Am just marking time now until I can depart for home. Have done all the necessary chores today in preparation for my trip northbound in the morning. Have made reservations on the noon trip to San Francisco September 24.

Anchorage, Alaska, Sept. 21, 1943   2000 AWT

Had a fair trip up today with weather about average. Had some movie camera shots of some bears near Yakutat.

All I can think of now is getting home to see my family. It seems that the time simply will not go by fast enough so that I can get back to see Grace and the boys. Just three more days—

Anchorage, Alaska, Sept. 22, 1943   1900 AWT

Today has been another typical rainy Anchorage day, with no opportunity to even get outside. Have played some rummy and done some reading. There's nothing else to be done.

Am departing tomorrow morning at 0600 hours and should be in Seattle by nightfall.

Ralph Johnson and Frank Wittenberg just arrived in town on their last trips northward. Soon the operation will be over as far as we are concerned.

Seattle, Wash., Sept. 23, 1943   2300 PWT

Arrived back here late tonight after a long instrument flight down from Anchorage. The weather was bad throughout, but at last we arrived after landing only at Annette en route, and now I am through with the operation here.

Tomorrow I go back to Palo Alto and my family!

Atherton, Calif., Sept. 24, 1943   2200 PWT

Although the trip down from Seattle today was pleasant and fast, it seemed as though we would never reach San Francisco. When we did arrive, Grace and Jimmy were at the airport to meet me and Johnny was here at home, laughing and happy. It's almost enough compensation for being away from home, to be able to have the pleasure of returning, especially when a fine family awaits your arrival.

Atherton, Calif., Sept. 25, 1943   2200 PWT

This has been a day of relaxation and play. Have spent the hours in becoming reacquainted with my boys, in doing a bit of paperwork, and in being generally lazy. Hope to be able to spend several more days in just this same manner.

Atherton, Calif., Sept. 26, 1943   2300 PWT

Today I worked on my income tax report, worked in the yard, and played with the boys. Tonight Grace and I went to Dinah's Shack for dinner, and there we fell in with the Ted Boerslers and another couple, and we had a splendid evening together. Tomorrow I am going to report in to the airport to get the latest news on Pacific Operations.

Atherton, Calif., Sept. 27, 1943   2345 PWT

My trip to the airport today was not too productive. Learned that I will be due out to Australia about a week from today and that I will have to fly both a C-87 and a C-54 and check out my copilot sometime during this week. There are quite a few changes in operational procedures on Pacific Operations.

Atherton, Calif., Sept. 28, 1943   2030 PWT

Have been at home all day today, working in the yard, trimming trees, etc. I went on a strict diet on September 12 in order to lose some excess weight. The diet is a success in that I've lost thirteen pounds in sixteen days, but I find that I am unable to do much heavy work on account of weakness and easy fatigue. A few more days and I'll be down to my desired weight.

The company called to advise that I'll have shakedown flights in a C-87 and a C-54 tomorrow, so that I'll be gone most of the day. Grace and I had planned on going in to San Francisco to file our income tax returns, but this will now have to be postponed. Tonight Grace is at school— learning Spanish.

Atherton, Calif., Sept. 29, 1943   2100 PWT

Went to the airport today and made a shakedown flight of a new C-54. Took it to McClelland Field at Sacramento, where I found the weather to be plenty warm. It seemed quite strange to be in a large airplane again. There was no C-87 available for flight today. It still appears that I will depart for Australia on Monday, October 4. I accomplished very little of the necessary work around the house today.

Atherton, Calif., Sept. 30, 1943   2030 PWT

Today Grace and I did many odd chores around Palo Alto, including trying to find any type of usable washing machine, and then we went into San Francisco on the bus to file our overdue income tax returns. This required most of the day.

Tonight we are saddened by the departure of Elva, our good and faithful servant, who has completed her year's contract with us and is now going to work in a shipyard here for a month before leaving for her home in Denver. We will all certainly miss her, including Jimmy and Johnny.

Grace is at Spanish class again tonight, so I'm keeping the boys.

Atherton, Calif., Oct. 1, 1943   2100 PWT

Have spent the day preparing for my trip to Australia. There is so much paperwork to do as well as clothing to pack, etc. It still appears that I'll be going Monday evening, October 4. Could have used a few more days at home in order to get the yard and garden in shape. The rainy season probably will have started by the time I return from this trip. It seems that one can never quite catch up.

Atherton, Calif., Oct. 2, 1943   2230 PWT

This morning I rode Grace's bicycle into town on an errand. That was really an experience for me, but I'm gradually becoming master of the contraption.

This afternoon I went to the airport to get some instrument practice in the C-54 with Jimmy Johnson. After we completed that, I stayed to give my copilot, Wally Gehlaar, some landing practice, both day and night. I guess I almost ended my career sometime during the flight. When we quit for the night, we found that at some time during the flight a large section of the lower side of the left wing had failed. The skin surface for a length of twelve feet and about eighteen inches wide was carried away, and a large structural member was loosely hanging from the hole. Had this member been carried away by a little more flying, it would probably have taken a part of the tail section with it, or at least a part of the landing flap or aileron. We would have crashed into the bottom of San Francisco Bay and it would have been another case of "pilot error."

Atherton, Calif., Oct. 3, 1943   2000 PWT

This has been a lazy Sunday, but we have had plenty to keep us busy in caring for the two boys. Just keeping them fed leaves little time for anything else. Among other things Jim and I took a long trike-bike ride.

There has been no change in schedule so far. I'm still due out tomorrow night in a C-87. Had hoped I would get a C-54, but then I'll probably pick up one somewhere en route.

Atherton, Calif., Oct. 4, 1943   1300 PWT

Have been busy this morning getting my packing done for the trip, etc. Must be at the airport at 1600 hours, and I'll depart from there for Hamilton, where I'll remain overnight, and take off for Honolulu at daybreak tomorrow morning.

8

Back to the South Seas

OCTOBER–NOVEMBER, 1943

Honolulu, T.H., Oct. 5, 1943   2100 HWT

Well, we had the best trip today that I've yet had. Flew a C-87, but a good one, and we found that the navigational facilities had been greatly augmented and improved since our last trip. The weather was perfect and it was daylight throughout, so we couldn't have asked for anything better. Made it in 13:11, which was good time for a C-87.

The islands are as beautiful as ever, but quite warm. Quite a contrast with Alaska and the Aleutians, which I so recently left.

Honolulu, T.H., Oct. 6, 1943   1500 HWT

Today I was up early and went to town to try to find a Chinese table the Odells wanted. Having no success, I returned to the hotel and spent two hours on the beach. Can't stand too much sun now, as I lost all of the fine tan I had acquired before going to Alaska.

The airport called to advise that we will be departing this evening at 2110 for Canton Island in a C-54. It should be a good trip, and I'll be able to see how a C-54 performs with a load and on a long flight.

Canton Island, Oct. 7, 1943   0900 CWT

We were delayed in departing from Honolulu last night because the army had chosen that night to do some antiaircraft firing and had failed to notify us until we reached the airport. However, we did finally get away and had a fine night trip, arriving here after sunrise. The performance of the C-54 fully met all expectations, although we were so loaded that the airplane was not well balanced.

[I am carrying a pouch of secret documents "For MacArthur's Eyes Only."]

The temperature is higher here than I have before seen it. There is no breeze, and sleeping in the daylight is impossible.

The army has improved living conditions here immeasurably since I was last here. We even have individual huts to sleep in now.

En route Fiji–New Caledonia, Oct. 8, 1943   1000 FWT

We departed from Canton at a little past midnight and reached Nandi about sunrise. The weather there was very low—300 feet and half a mile visibility—but we managed to get in, which is not an easy task in a large airplane such as the C-54. We breakfasted there, then took off for New Caledonia, where we will probably be relieved by another crew, and will have to spend the night or at least wait until another airplane comes along. The trip today has been excellent, with perfect weather west of Nandi.

Ipswich, Australia, Oct. 9, 1943   1700 AWT

When we landed at New Caledonia, our relief crew there had gone to a native festival of some kind, as they had not expected us to arrive due to the bad weather around Nandi. We were faced with the decision of whether or not to break the army's flight time limitation and continue on to Brisbane, or to allow the airplane and its passengers to be delayed at Plaine des Gaiacs for an indefinite time until the relief crew returned. We decided to continue on to Brisbane, hoping the army would not be too tough on us for flying sixteen hours without rest.

[At Brisbane I decided to rid myself of the courier package I was carrying to MacArthur before I started my rest. I shaved, bathed, changed uniform, and ordered up an army staff car to go into the city to deliver the packet of documents. I had been given many and sometimes menacing admonitions on how to protect the documents, how never to let them out of my possession and to deliver them only to General MacArthur in person. I wanted to be free of the responsibility as soon as possible.

Obviously I knew who General MacArthur was but knew very little about him. I had only moderate expectations of finding him in his office. Little then did I know about his work habits! Arriving at his headquarters, the AMP building in Brisbane, I stated my mission and was quickly ushered upstairs to his office. He was pacing the floor and looked at me curiously when I introduced myself and gave him the packet. As I turned to leave the room he asked me to sit down for a moment. He opened the packet, briefly inspected the contents, then turned his attention to me.

My dress was a standard army officer's uniform, but the insignia thereon was a special one worn by civilian flight crews operating Air Corps transport airplanes for the Air Transport Command. General MacArthur took instant notice of this insignia, which apparently he had not seen before. He inquired about it and asked a number of questions about the type of work I performed.

I explained to him that although I was a civilian, I wore the army uniform and insignia so that if perchance I were brought down in enemy territory I would be treated as a prisoner of war and not be subjected to the more drastic treatment applied to enemy spies. He asked about my personal status, about my technical background, and about my activities both before and after the U.S. entry into the war.

I told him I was a captain in the Air Corps Reserve but that I had been frozen in my status as an airline pilot. The company for which I worked, United Air Lines, was operating military aircraft under contract in furtherance of the military effort. I tried to be brief and accurate but he continued to question me, always extracting more information. I felt somewhat embarrassed at monopolizing so much of his time. He kept me there for an hour, sometimes talking about the New Guinea campaign and dwelling on the lack of men, equipment, and transport he needed to properly wage the war. He frequently emphasized it would be a long and taxing campaign unless he were allocated the necessary facilities to be able to go on the offensive.

Needless to say, I was astounded. Here I was, a perfect stranger, being made a one-man audience to a monologue on a subject about which I had very little detailed knowledge. Later I was to learn that this was not an unusual characteristic of the general's.

After a while, he stopped pacing the floor, faced me, and quite abruptly asked if I would like to join him and become his personal pilot. He said he currently had a very good pilot, Lt. Col. Henry Godman, but that Godman had not had much experience in instrument and long-range flying. Moreover, being a career military officer, he should, to further his career, get more experience with a combat unit. The general said that although he personally did not fly very often, members of his staff needed to move about the theater constantly. He indicated I would be expected to assemble a stable of different types of airplanes and flight crews for different purposes and that I would be able to requisition my aircraft from the Fifth Air Force as required.

Obviously I was startled. My somewhat confused reply was to the effect I would be flattered and delighted to become his pilot. I said that I had a very patriotic feeling about my country after having been trained by the army and, in a sense, I was uncomfortable at not having been called to duty when war was declared. But for the training the Army Air Corps had given me I would not have been able to enter into and to advance in the splendid profession I was in as an airline pilot. I told him I had worked hard as an officer in the Air Corps Reserve and had attained the grade of captain.

I also told the general that since I was frozen in my civilian job, some action on his part would be required to obtain a release from my assignment to United Air Lines. He asked what action he should take, and I suggested that perhaps a simultaneous cablegram to both the War Department and the president of United Air Lines might accomplish the objective. He said I should proceed back to San Francisco and await developments.

After I left MacArthur's office, and in fact all the way back to San Francisco, I puzzled over what had occurred. Why had he suddenly chosen me for a job most pilots would have been most eager to have? Certainly not because I had any special technical or personal advantage over the dozens of other available military or airline pilots. I never learned the basis of his selection. I could only conjecture that he intuitively felt that our temperaments might mesh and that our mutual objectives in the war effort would coincide. Whatever the reason, his request converted me from an indifferent admirer of his to a most loyal disciple.

I flew back to San Francisco and with mixed feelings discussed with my wife the meeting with General MacArthur. If I were called back to active duty, a momentous change would come over our lives. We agreed that since there were several contingencies which had to be explored before I could accept the proffered assignment, we would not discuss it with anyone else. After all, General MacArthur might forget all about our conversation.]

We are now staying at the dirty old Palais Royal Hotel in Ipswich for lack of any better accommodations.

This is early springtime here, and the countryside is beautiful.

Ipswich, Australia, Oct. 10, 1943   1800 AWT

Another Sunday in Ipswich leaves little to describe. If possible, the place is a bit dirtier and more run-down than before. As usual, there is absolutely nothing to do for recreation or amusement, so we have played a little poker. It has been almost impossible to find food to eat, as all but one of the restaurants are closed.

Jim Belding, whom we passed up at New Caledonia, wishes to return in his normal place in schedule, so that we will not be going out tonight. It now appears that we will leave early Tuesday.

Ipswich, Australia, Oct. 11, 1943   1400 AWT

Today has been dull. It has been sprinkling rain, and there is little to do. I was up at 0700 hours but could get no breakfast until 0900. The Australians are certainly a queer lot, and the unsanitary conditions in which they live impress me more than ever this time.

Will be departing from Amberley Field at 0430 tomorrow morning, which means arising at 0230. Will have a C-54 as far as Nandi at least.

Nandi, Fiji Islands, Oct. 12, 1943 1700 FWT

Had a fine trip from Amberley with a stop at Plaine des Gaiacs. The C-54 performed perfectly and I had a good load of passengers. Nandi is very hot, with lots of mosquitoes. It appears that we will be here until tomorrow afternoon, when we will depart for Canton.

Canton Island, Oct. 13, 1943 0900 CWT

Our trip here was at night, and we made a night landing very early this morning. Our weather en route was supposed to be very bad, but it did not materialize, and I've never had a better trip. The moon was full and beautiful, and it was almost as light as day for our landing here on this white coral island.

Got very little sleep, as the heat was stifling by sunrise, and then the army chose this day to paint the hut in which we are living.

The army expects a raid by the Japs here tonight, as the moon is full and they usually come over at this time. The reception committee is prepared for them.

We expect to depart from here shortly after midnight for Honolulu.

Honolulu, T.H., Oct. 14, 1943 2300 HWT

When our C-54 arrived in Canton last night, it had a broken exhaust stack on one engine. Since there was no spare, this had to be welded. This required about three hours, but when we ran the engines prior to take-off, we found that No. 4 engine had a number of bad spark plugs. Changing these required an additional four hours, so we did not depart until after sunrise. We arrived off Honolulu after dark to encounter antiaircraft firing and were delayed some time because of it. We finally did get in, only to learn that we are due out at 0950 tomorrow morning. This means arising at 0600 without sufficient sleep, and then a long trip to the States.

En route Honolulu–San Francisco, Oct. 15, 1943 1700 PWT

After arising early and rushing to the airport for an early morning departure, we did not depart until well after noon. Our airplane was late in arriving, and then it required considerable work before redispatching. Now we are well on our way on the last leg of our trip and should be at home at least by sunrise.

It will be so good to get home. This has been a fast trip as we will have been en route only eleven days. Much of our flying has been at night, so that we haven't had much rest. It now appears that fog may prevent us from landing at Hamilton or San Francisco upon our arrival, and this may force us to go on to Sacramento or elsewhere.

Only a few more hours now until I'll see my family again.

Atherton, Calif., Oct. 16, 1943   2000 PWT

Arrived home at daybreak this morning to find the family well and thriving, although Grace seems a bit tired, what with caring for the two boys and holding down the house all by herself.

I slept all day and still feel plenty tired. Didn't even awaken in time to go to the airport to have my physical examination.

Atherton, Calif., Oct. 17, 1943   2000 PWT

Today has been a lazy day, spent largely in playing with the boys and generally doing nothing. It's so fine to be home again that I'm simply letting the pleasant feeling soak in for a day or two before I start to work on the necessary chores.

Tomorrow I have to go to the airport to check in and make the usual routine reports. Also take a physical exam.

Atherton, Calif., Oct. 18, 1943 through Nov. 5, 1943

I spent this period at home, enjoying the family life, taking physical exams, doing regular business chores, and doing all the other tasks that get neglected when one is away for an extended period. During this time, General MacArthur and General Sutherland sent word by Lieutenant Colonel Godman that they still wanted me to come to Australia as their personal pilot. I cautiously questioned the local United Air Lines personnel about the possibility of a military leave, but they were noncommittal.

We took Johnny into Palo Alto one day on a routine shopping trip while Jimmy was in school. We usually did not take the children into public places too often because polio was rather prevalent.

The diary entries for this period have been condensed for brevity.

Atherton, Calif., Nov. 6, 1943   1945 PWT

This morning I went to the airport for my physical exam, and then I had some information to get from Ralph Johnson. The trip required most of the day.

Tonight Grace made arrangements for someone to come in to keep the boys, and then we could find no movie or play which we particularly wanted to see.

The airport just called to advise that I'll now be due out tomorrow instead of Monday.

Atherton, Calif., Nov. 7, 1943   1430 PWT

This morning I have finished the last-minute tasks before leaving. I'll go to Hamilton Field at 1830 this evening and then depart from there tomorrow morning at 0740 for Honolulu. Have just been advised that I'll have a C-87 for the long hop instead of a C-54.

Honolulu, T.H., Nov. 8, 1943   2130 HWT

We had a very fine trip over from San Francisco today. We spent the night at Hamilton Field last night, and then were up early this morning for a takeoff at sunrise. There was some weather en route, and we could not be too certain of our navigation, but, as it happened, we were never far off our course. The trip required 14:15, which was rather long, and it was well after dark when we landed at Hickam Field. These daylight trips are so much more pleasant than those at night, and I always feel much better physically at the completion of one of them.

There is one crew here ahead of us southbound, so it appears that we will depart from here on Wednesday morning, perhaps on the trip which goes by way of Christmas Island, Samoa, and the Fijis. One advantage in going down this route is that the crew keeps the same airplane throughout, and misses the New Zealand shuttle, which is now flown out of New Caledonia.

Honolulu, T.H., Nov. 9, 1943   1800 HWT

Was up rather early this morning and then spent about three hours on the beach. The weather is perfect, but somewhat cooler than it was on the last trip.

No further report as to when we will depart southward, but we still expect to go tomorrow morning.

Wonder how Grace is getting along with all of her work and caring for the two boys. I know she has plenty to do.

Honolulu, T.H., Nov. 10, 1943   1400 HWT

This morning I was up early and on the beach to collect some more tan, when the airport called to advise of a great change in plans for me. The War Department has issued orders for myself and crew to be in Washington, D.C., by Saturday, November 13! This is perhaps in connection with the request of General MacArthur and General Sutherland, but I did not expect anything to develop from it in such a short time.

At any rate we are returning on a trip tonight and will be in San Francisco tomorrow morning. I have no idea of the details—whether we will fly an airplane back to Washington, whether we will go on the airline, or what—but whatever we do, it will be a change from the regular routine.

[Although I do not know it, this order from the War Department probably is a direct result of my conversation with General MacArthur in his office a month previously.]

I suppose I'll be inducted into the army on Saturday or a short time thereafter. Never a dull moment—

Must prepare now for a pickup to go to the airport.

Atherton, Calif., Nov. 11, 1943   1600 PWT

The trip from Honolulu to San Francisco was routine, but not the news upon my arrival. At Hamilton Field I was taken up to headquarters to meet General Ryan and others, and they explained as much of the proposed mission on which I am going as they were able to do. After that, I called Colonel Barrie in Washington, D.C., and he explained still more details.

It seems that an important party of general officers is going on an extended trip, and they have requested specifically that I fly them. I am to take a C-54 to Washington tomorrow night and be there Saturday morning. The mission will go eastward out of Washington, and I have been instructed to bring all the information which I have collected concerning Western Australia. Of course that means that we will go on around the world by way of India, and make the long hop from India to Australia. The mission is expected to require 240 hours of flying, which means that there will be many side trips in addition to the straight-through route. I am to have all of the help in flying that I may require, and I am to get this by means of borrowing TWA crews anywhere en route. I am speculating that we will call on each of the Allied command headquarters around the world. I hope this includes Moscow and Chungking. I imagine that General Sutherland is going, and I feel that he must be the one who insisted on having me fly them.

I certainly feel flattered to have been chosen from among all the airline and army crews to head this mission. And they went to great trouble and expense to jerk me out of the middle of the Pacific Ocean to go on it. To my knowledge, no other crew has ever gone around the world over this route, as the long hop from India to Australia is too difficult and uncertain. Here's hoping I get a good break with equipment, etc.

Am to depart from here at 1700 hours tomorrow, and I have a hundred things to do in preparation. And I am so very, very tired tonight after my long trip!

Atherton, Calif., Nov. 12, 1943   1700 PWT

This has been a hectic day. I don't know just where I am going or how long I will be away, so I've had to prepare for almost any eventuality. Getting enough clothing together, both heavy and light weight, settling the household for an indefinite period, etc., have kept me plenty busy.

Now all is in readiness, and we are about ready to depart for Washington.

9

"See the Pyramids along the Nile..."

NOVEMBER, 1943–JANUARY, 1944

Washington, D.C., Nov. 13, 1943   2015 EWT

We had a fast trip across the States last night, arriving here from San Francisco after a flight of ten hours and forty-five minutes. Upon arrival I went to my quarters and slept for two hours and then reported in to headquarters at Gravelly Point. Here I found everything in its usual state of utter confusion, and I spent the entire day, up until 1800 hours, trying to get a few bits of information which should have been available in an hour. Finally I got my orders and found what I am supposed to do. We take off at 1000 hours Monday for a crossing of the South Atlantic, and will go by easy stages, stopping at Miami, Puerto Rico, Belem, Natal, Dakar, and Marrakech. At Marrakech we will meet General Sutherland on November 19 and will travel at his command to the Cairo Conference, then through the Middle East and the Far East, and then will eventually go from India to Australia, leaving General Sutherland in Brisbane. After that I suppose we will go into regular Air Transport Command schedule at Brisbane and return on a regular trip to San Francisco. At any rate, the next thirty days promise to be interesting ones.

I'm so tired I can hardly stay awake now. Got a letter off to Grace tonight, and now I'm going to bed. Tomorrow I will be busy the entire day, being briefed on the route and test-flying my airplane to be sure that it is ready to go.

Washington, D.C., Nov. 14, 1943   1345 EWT

Was up bright and early this morning to get at all of the million and one things I have to do to be fully prepared for the mission. Am unable to get a complete briefing here, but rather will get it by steps as we go along. Met Captain Hanson and Captains McGlone and John Rodgerson of Pan American, and they were most helpful about various things. We are planning now on departing at 0800 tomorrow morning for Puerto Rico with a stop at Miami. About 1600 hours today I am going to test-fly my airplane to make certain that everything is in readiness.

2000 EWT

Our airplane is still being fitted out, so we have called off our test flight and will make the test en route tomorrow. Hope all new equipment works all right, as it will be difficult to obtain good maintenance from this point on.

It is interesting to note that I am starting on this trip, which should be the best of my career to date, on the exact fourteenth aniversary of the date I made my first solo flight as a cadet at March Field, California.

Borinquen, Puerto Rico, Nov. 15, 1943   2300 EWT

Today has been a difficult, yet interesting, day. We were up at 0500 in Washington and made an 0800 departure for Miami. We went via Richmond, Raleigh, Savannah, Jacksonville, and West Palm Beach, and arrived in Miami about 1300 hours. Here we met with much confusion and resistance from the army. We had to go through a minute briefing and then an involved clearance through customs, and, as a result, we finally got away from Miami about 1700 hours instead of 1500 as we had planned.

We flew a direct course to Puerto Rico, passing north of Cuba and then skirting historic Haiti. Weather was not too good, and I was too tired to enjoy the trip to the fullest. It was well after dark when we arrived here, and now I'll get three hours of sleep only as we are planning to depart at 0400 hours in order to reach Belem before dark.

Although I'm so tired I can hardly stand up, I'm having the time of my life. I wonder how Grace and the boys are getting along.

Belem, Brazil, Nov. 16, 1943   2000 BWT

This morning we were out of Borinquen after some delay at 0500 hours. We proceeded southeastward through the Lesser Antilles, past Trinidad and Venezuela, to the coastline of South America at British Guiana. We passed Georgetown and then continued along the coastline rather than take the more direct inland route over the steaming jungles of the Guianas. An airplane forced down in these jungles would be hopelessly lost, even if its occupants survived the crash.

We continued by Zandery, Surinam (Dutch Guiana), where the huge bauxite mines are busily feeding their rich aluminum deposits into the war effort. Then we proceeded over famous (or infamous) Devil's Island off French Guiana, thence to the northern coast of Brazil. Along the entire northeastern coastline of South America, the ocean is very shallow and muddy from the numerous sluggish rivers that empty their loads of silt into it.

Strangely enough, the most impenetrable jungle is in the Guianas. When one reaches Brazil, the country changes. It is still quite low and flat, but vegetation is comparatively sparse, with large areas of bare ground. The ocean, however, is still shallow and muddy.

We reached the northwest bank of the Amazon River an hour out of Belem and it took us an hour to cross the river. It is 200 miles across at this point, but is somewhat of a disappointment. It is shallow and sluggish and muddy, and is choked with mud flats and islands.

We arrived at Belem about 1730 hours. It is located on the east bank of the Pará River and is the third largest city in Brazil, having a population of about 300,000. I did not go into the city, as passes to leave the field were very difficult to obtain and I was also quite tired. It is regrettable that I missed it.

Natal, Brazil, Nov. 17, 1943   2000 BWT

This morning we were up at 0600 and departed for Natal at 0800 hours. It was an easy, interesting five-hour trip. From Belem to São Luís there is considerable jungle country, and then the landscape changes abruptly. The country from São Luís to Natal is quite dry and rough, with only scattered vegetation. There are low mountains through the area, and one could very easily mistake it for west Texas. The vegetation resembles mesquite and sagebrush, and the soil is very sandy. The ocean along here is still shallow and muddy.

We arrived at Natal about 1300 hours to find an excellent airport and good accommodations. Briefing, mechanical work on our airplane, etc., required several hours, and then we got passes to go into town. Passes were difficult to obtain because the army did not want its men to come in contact with the natives, many of whom were infected with various contagious diseases.

The trip into town was interesting, but almost repulsive. It's impossible for us to imagine the absolute poverty, filth, and laziness of these people. The people are short and slight of stature, rarely exceeding five feet in height, and are of all shades of brown. They dress with complete simplicity, the men wearing only a pair of cotton trousers and the women only a straight cotton dress. Practically no one wears shoes. The only means of transport is on foot or on burro-back. There are dozens of burros everywhere, and one often sees heavily laden trains consisting of twelve to twenty of them.

The housing is of the crudest type imaginable. Houses are built by

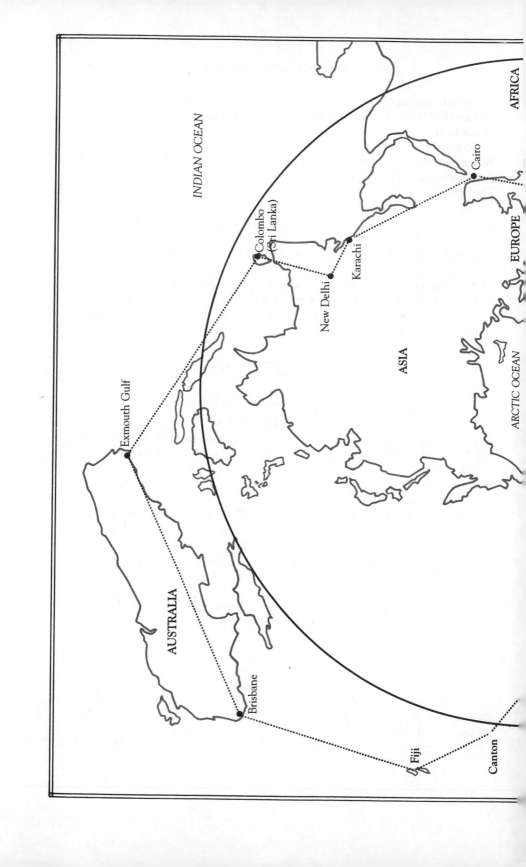

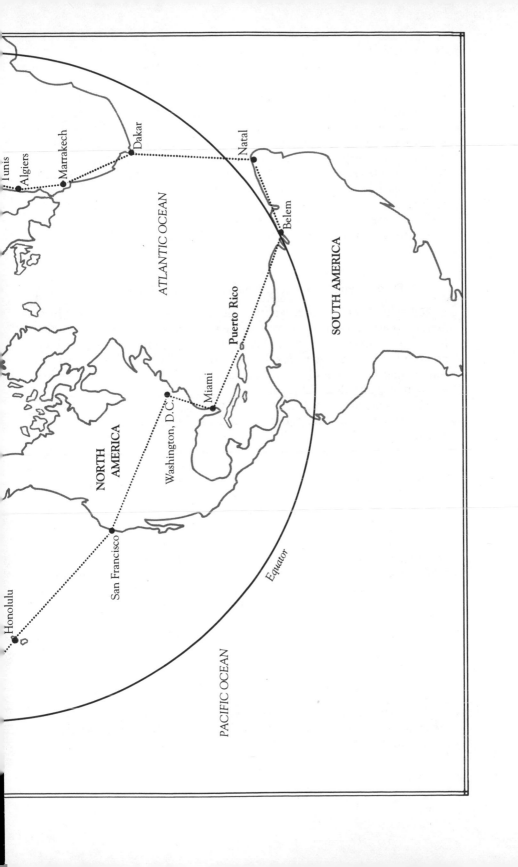

making a strong framework of brush, and then plastering over this with adobe mud. I peered into the interior of some of these houses and found them to contain only the rudiments of furniture, sparsely distributed on the dirt floor of the one room of each house. The room is usually occupied by the family as well as the family burro and chickens.

The people are cheerful and happy and dirty and, apparently, continually hungry for food and sexual appeasement. They appear to lack any ambition, because their living conditions could be improved greatly by the mere application of some physical work.

We are arising at 0200 in the morning in order to take off for Dakar at 0400.

Dakar, Senegal, French West Africa, Nov. 18, 1943   2000 SWT

Today has been a long and partly monotonous day. We departed from Natal at 0400, groggy and only half awake, and then flew for ten and a half hours across the water to Dakar. We landed here at Rufisque about an hour before dark and were taken in hand by Pan American. Their station manager, Mr. Manning, certainly did everything in his power to make our stay comfortable and pleasant.

This is an interesting place but we were unable to get into Dakar itself. The French here are not too friendly, and the natives are very black and very surly. The country is largely low desert, quite rough and rocky. The army does not use this place extensively, except for ferrying combat airplanes.

Mosquitoes are bad, and the army has a greater percentage of malaria here than at any other place where the Air Transport Command operates. We have started our daily dose of Atabrine, and I hope I have not gotten any mosquito bites while here.

In Natal the ATC pulled a fast one on me and removed three of my passengers in order to make space for General Bartron and two colonels. I did not know this had happened until we were well under way, and it was in direct contradiction to my army orders. Two of my original passengers arrived here tonight, so I will recover them, but the third is still in Natal.

We are taking off at 0700 hours tomorrow for Marrakech, at which point our real mission is to start.

Marrakech, French Morocco, Nov. 19, 1943   2100 MWT

Today has been a most interesting day. We departed from Dakar at daybreak and flew six hours across the Sahara Desert and then another hour across the peculiar Atlas Mountains into Marrakech. I had wanted to follow the coastline up, but the army would not permit this, as we would have been off Río de Oro most of the way, and that is Spanish territory. Had we been forced to land anywhere along there, we would have been interned for the duration of the war. As it was, I'm glad we came across the desert. It was an inspiring spectacle.

There is absolutely no vegetation, and the sand dunes are constantly drifting. There was a solid blanket of blowing sand extending to about 8,000 feet and often there was not even vertical visibility from our flight altitude of 9,000 feet. At the earth's surface the blowing sand must have been almost unendurable. And yet, in spite of this condition, which appeared to exist much of the time, native huts and camel trails were occasionally visible. These must be hardy people indeed who can exist under these conditions. We flew over places with such intersting-sounding names as Méderdra, Iryn, Idjibitan, Bel Azziam, and Oum Anman, only to find that they contained perhaps a half dozen mud huts and were located in the middle of the desert, where no visible means of water or food supply existed.

At length we came to the Atlas Mountains, and they were queer indeed. They are composed largely of sandstone and are sharply eroded into precipitous gullies and almost vertical cliffs. These mountains extend upward to 14,000 feet and are absolutely barren. The surprising thing is that every few miles there are small villages containing a few mud or stone houses, and all with high surrounding walls of stone or adobe. They are situated in the most unlikely places — often on the top of vertical cliffs with only one narrow means of entrance. One can only guess as to how these people obtain food and water, and they apparently make war among themselves continually, if they put so much effort into walling their villages in the manner that they do.

We finally reached Marrakech in the middle of the afternoon, to find the weather overcast, so that we had to work an instrument procedure down from the high altitude we had been flying in order to clear the mountains. From the air, Marrakech is a beautiful town. It is located in a fertile valley among rich green olive groves and is built entirely of brown adobe. The old city in the heart of the present city is entirely walled with a rock and adobe wall about twenty feet high and six feet thick. Many other sections of the modern city are also walled.

We landed and learned that General Sutherland had arrived earlier in the day and had gone on to Algiers, leaving instructions for us to follow him there immediately. However, the airport at Algiers is unlighted, and we had some mechanical repairs to make on our airplane, so we are staying here overnight. Briefing, etc., kept us at the airport until 1800 hours. Here I found Major Chatfield, whom I took to Iceland last year on one of my first flights for the Air Transport Command.

We were billeted in the Hôtel de La Mamounia, the best that Marra-kech affords, and our trip into town was an experience indeed. I wish that I could record all of my impressions, but that would require much longer than time permits.

The native Arabs are tall and dark and bewhiskered, and speak a type of poor French. They invariably wear ankle-length, heavy woolen parkas with attached hoods, and they are all filthy. Some of the women are veiled and some are not. They travel about on burros or camels and often block the streets with their herds of sheep, which they seem to be always driv-ing through town. They are inveterate beggars, and many have trinkets for sale, for which they ask exorbitant prices but which they will sell for one-third of their asking price. I was able to practice my almost-forgotten French while trying to buy some souvenirs.

After walking about town for an hour, we went back to the hotel for dinner. The hotel would be considered very ordinary by our standards, but to the local French it is the ultimate in luxury. There was running water, but no baths, and the rooms were bare, poorly lighted, and dismal. There was no heat of any kind. Strange as it may sound, the temperature fell to a point below freezing as soon as the sun went down, and we are quite miserable in our tropical dress.

We had dinner at the hotel, and it was about as elaborate as any dinner I have had recently. The dining room was large and formal, with spotless linens and faultless service. We had good wine with the dinner, and the food was excellent. It was all entirely out of keeping with everything else in the city. Many French officers and their *dames* had dinner there.

We are departing at 0700 hours tomorrow for Algiers, and I hope that we will be able to make contact there with General Sutherland.

Algiers, Algeria, Nov. 20, 1943   2100 AWT

This morning we took off just at sunrise. Below us, after we had gotten into the air, was a high-walled enclosure in which several hundred Arabs were kneeling facing the east. It was interesting indeed to see them in their long gray parkas with their pointed hoods all indicating the direc-tion of Mecca, and was quite a contrast to our modern transport plane and all of the Western civilization that it represented.

Our trip to Algiers required about four hours over interesting, rough country dotted with the ever-present walled houses and villages. The low hills were all snow covered, which I had not expected. We went out over the Mediterranean Sea for the novelty of doing so.

When we arrived at Algiers, we were told that General Sutherland was not in town and had left no instructions. After an hour of inquiry I found that he was here awaiting our arrival, but for the moment was having lunch with General Giraud. He called about 1500 hours and said he would like to leave at 0830 hours tomorrow morning.

We went into town about dark to try to find rooms. It was all my meager French could do to get us around, but after much walking we finally located our hotel, if you could call it such. My room was eighty-seven steps up and contained only a double iron bed with two army blankets on it.

After checking in at the hotel, we set out to find some food. We walked about two miles before we finally located a dirty restaurant which would feed us. This town is quite the most congested place I have ever seen. In addition to many soldiers and sailors of all Allied nations who are based here, the city is crowded with European refugees and refugees from bombed-out Tunisia. Food is scarce and poverty rampant. Queues of people stand for hours awaiting buses or streetcars. The city itself appears to be substantially built, and in peacetime is probably a thriving place. They say it is as typically French as any city in France proper.

I forgot to mention that at the airport mess the cooks and dishwashers are all Italian prisoners. It was also strange to see German Air Force pilot prisoners walking around the airport, with practically no restrictions, in full uniform and chatting with RAF pilots. Only a few weeks before, they were trying hard to shoot each other down.

It is miserably cold here tonight—well below freezing, in fact. There is no heat in any building in Algiers, and I'm so cold and tired that I can hardly write. I must be up at 0600 hours tomorrow to get to the airport and be certain to have everything prepared for a departure at 0830 hours.

Tunis, Tunisia, Nov. 21, 1943   1630 AWT

We were up in the cold hours before dawn this morning, and were practically frozen stiff before we arrived at the airport and had breakfast. The Italian prisoners did well by us, though, and fed us cold powdered eggs and cold mush, but much hot coffee. I slept not at all last night, what with the cold and with worrying about being awakened on time. I got practically no cooperation from an uninterested, half-awake army, so as a result General Sutherland arrived about five minutes before we were entirely ready with the airplane. However, he is a considerate gentleman and was not at all perturbed. We had an interesting two-hour flight to Tunis, landing at El Ouina before 1100 hours. We saw many marks left by the bitter battles which occurred in these hills near Tunis and Bizerte. The harbor is completely bombed out, and bomb craters mark all parts of the airport and town. From the air, many demolished airplanes and tanks can be seen scattered around the countryside, left to corrode at whatever point they ended their bitter, martial careers. I suppose all of the men who went to their deaths with the machines have been removed.

We were better received here, of course, because the general was along. He has bidden us good-bye for a couple of days while he takes a side trip up to the battlefront in Italy. We are now about 250 miles from the main battle line to the north of us. We will now have time to do some work on our airplane and to get some much-needed rest. I have flown 17,000 miles with only one twenty-four-hour period out of the air in the past thirteen days. That day off was the hectic one spent in Washington.

We came into town after lunch and are quartered at the Hôtel Transatlantique. Accommodations are not as bad as those at Algiers, but the city itself is worse. The filthy and crowded condition is aggravated here by the debris left from the bombing and shelling of the city. War is not a pretty thing. We walked about the city this afternoon. The place is in no way pleasant, with the conglomerate population so dirty and undignified, and with their universal begging tendencies. Incidentally, there are many Turks living here.

1930 AWT

A big change of plans has occurred. The operations officer just telephoned to inform me that we will be taking off at 0630 hours in the morning for Cairo! And I'm so much in need of rest, but now I'll be up most of the night. We have a magneto off of our airplane and the whole departure will have to be reorganized. Not a dull moment—

Cairo, Egypt, Nov. 22, 1943   1900 EWT

This morning was a nightmare. We were up at 0400 hours, expecting everything to have been organized as we had planned last night. However, this was not true. Our transportation did not arrive, and when we did arrive at the airport, I had to awaken everyone concerned, including weatherman, briefing officer, operations officer, etc. No mess attendants were there so we had no breakfast. The general arrived promptly at 0630, but they did not even have the airplane loaded. We finally got away at 0700 hours, and the general took it in good spirits.

The number-one man of this mission stayed here yesterday, but he departed for Cairo last night—Franklin D. Roosevelt.

Today we had one of the most interesting flights thus far. Off of Tunis, we flew across the Mediterranean to Tripoli and then again across to Benghazi. From here we followed the historic battle route across to Tobruk, Mersa Matruh, and on to the El Alamein Line, extending from the impassable Quattara Depression to Mediterranean, where Rommel was finally stopped only a few miles from Alexandria. Remaining marks of these extensive drives are to be seen everywhere. Abandoned tanks and trucks line the roadsides and shell and bomb craters mark the sands of the desert everywhere. Crashed airplanes can be seen littering the sands. I saw probably five hundred of them, left to corrode where they were shot down. The barricades at El Alamein are still standing, and there isn't an area of one hundred square feet anywhere that is not marked by a shell crater from the terrific artillery barrage the English laid down when they finally broke through the German defenses. Benghazi and Tobruk are mere shells of cities.

The sands of the Sahara make a beautiful contrast along this area with the very blue waters of the Mediterranean. The desert here is all the same and contains no signs of vegetation or life of any kind. You can imagine our surprise when, as we approached Cairo, we could see in the distance a sharp, dark line on the desert. This was the green vegetation of the Nile valley. There is no gradual change from the desert to fertility, but rather a very sharp line separating the inhospitable from the hospitable.

As we came in over the valley, it was as green as anything I have ever seen. The native Egyptian villages are generally of uniform size, about half a mile in diameter, and surprisingly numerous, averaging only about two miles apart. They are walled and built entirely of grayish brown mud. The roofs are all of straw and mud. Storks are to be seen everywhere on the rooftops. They say that these villages are unbelievably filthy and that practically all the natives born, live, and die in this filth and never leave their native village. Every square foot of this land is intensely cultivated. Each village contains one white-domed church.

We landed at new Payne Field here and found ourselves to be the last of the sixteen C-54s in this mission.

Cairo, Egypt, Nov. 23, 1943   1830 EWT

Today I did something I had never (before this trip) expected to do during my lifetime. I went out and visited the Sphinx and the Pyramids.

I was up at seven after a most refreshing night of sleep and had a fine breakfast. Then we had our briefing for our trip east to Karachi, so that we would be fully prepared whenever it came time to go. Then I checked on the work being done on the airplane, and was free for the day.

I took a bus which went directly through the heart of Cairo, across the historic Nile, on through Giza and Memphis to the Pyramids. The city was very interesting and much larger than any we have seen so far. It is quite unkempt according to our standards, but the buildings are larger and better maintained. Both men and women wear only long flowing robes that greatly resemble our old-fashioned nightgowns. About half the women have their faces veiled. About half the men wear the identical red fez with a black tassel, a symbol of their Mohammedan faith. Personal cleanliness appears to be unimportant to them. Most of them understand English well, and speak it brokenly. There are many religious edifices, and most of the architecture has a distinct Turkish motif. Many natives travel about the streets in oxen-drawn or burro-drawn carts, or perched far back on the rumps of tiny burros or seated uncertainly and bouncingly on the rocking humps of plodding camels. A few splendid horses are in evidence.

The Nile River and its myriad canals were something of a disappointment, but I suppose I expected too much. It was colorful, especially with its many small sailboats, all equipped with the queer triangular lateen sails which are used extensively in no other place in the world except the Nile valley.

Just before reaching Memphis we had to detour down through one of the queer, dirty native villages, because "Franklin and Winnie" were housed at one of the villas in Memphis. MPs were stationed everywhere. The native village was one of those strange ones built of mud, and I have never encountered a stronger stench or more putrefaction. Burros, camels, water buffalo, storks, and people all live together in the dirt, and all appear to be half starved. Brazil was bad, but I believe this is worse, because added to it all is the overpowering stench of the irrigated swamplands of the Nile valley.

The Pyramids stand on a limestone cliff about one hundred feet above the Nile valley. The Sphinx lies between the first two of the three large pyramids, and all face the Nile and the rising sun. About ten miles to the southeast can be seen the nearest group of smaller pyramids.

I went through the Temple of the Sphinx, which is built of huge slabs of pink granite. The Sphinx itself is somewhat smaller than I expected and is rather much in ruins, what with its missing nose which Napoleon shot off while using the statue for artillery practice. I hired a native guide who spoke fair English, and walked on up to the largest of the Pyramids, Cheops's. I walked around it, and it is a massive structure indeed. It is on a square base, 754 feet on a side, covers thirteen acres, and was originally 480 feet high. I went into its dark and odorous interior and climbed up a steep ramp to the exact center of the structure to the king's mausoleum. It is a cubicle about 40 feet on a side, and in its exact center is the king's sarcophagus. The room is built of huge slabs of black granite, and has two ventilating shafts to the outside. On the way down I went into the queen's chamber, which was about half as large and not nearly so elaborate. It is located at exactly one-quarter the distance to the top.

As I was coming down from the pyramid, Winnie (Winston Churchill) and his staff were on their way up. He was chewing his ever-present cigar.

I came back here to the airport on the bus, again via the heart of Cairo.

I went to operations immediately, as I had to report in every four hours, and I had been away somewhat longer than that. There were no instructions, however, so I had a splendid, large dinner after my pyramid climbing, and now I'm ready for another night of rest. Tomorrow I may go into Cairo and inspect it more closely.

Cairo, Egypt, Nov. 24, 1943   1900 EWT

The general telephoned to tell us that he would not need us today, so we were all up early for a trip into town. Ray Wolff and I took an early bus into Cairo to see the city and do some shopping. We started at the world's famous Shepheard's Hotel, which is Cairo's best but which is rather dark and dismal and dirty. We were accosted by so many Egyptian boys and men asking to be our guide that we decided it would save much time and nervous wear and tear to hire a guide. We got a good one at the hotel, and at least he kept the other boys away from us. Their continuous shouting becomes almost unbearable after a while, and they continually grab your arms or clothing as you walk along in order to have you pay some attention to them. They are inveterate beggars.

We went down to the native bazaar and it was entirely different from anything I have ever seen. The funny, dirty, winding alleys with open shops selling just about everything imaginable are unique indeed. The noise of chattering, shouting, etc., is deafening. The merchants never expect to get more than a fraction of the asking price on their merchandise. After a couple of hours of walking and looking, I finally bought two ounces of fine perfume for Grace, and a very nice carved sterling silver jewel case. I tried to find a good star sapphire, but that proved to be impossible.

At length Ray and I went back to the Shepheard's Hotel and had lunch. It was elaborately served in the best French manner, but the food was very mediocre.

After lunch we went on a special bus to see the mosques. First we visited the Mosque of Hasan, built about 1300 as a place of worship and as a tomb for Sultan Hasan. When Napoleon captured Egypt, he looted it and then fired cannonballs into the minaret in order to try to raze it. However, the structure was too sturdy, and the cannonballs still can be seen lodged in the limesone walls. Next we visited the Citadel, built in 1166 as a fort to protect the city. Most of the structure is still intact. From there we went to the Mosque of Mohammed Ali, which is still used as a place of worship. It was finished in 1840, and contains the most beautiful dome I have ever seen. The dome is lighted in daylight by the most exquisite of stained-glass windows, and enormous glass chandeliers provide the illumination at night. It is a magnificent building, according to any standards. Our guide told us much about the religion and customs of the people.

From the hotel we took the bus to the airport and I am now tired and ready to retire.

Cairo, Egypt, Nov. 25, 1943   2000 EWT

Today is Thanksgiving Day, but it has not meant much to me. I was up for an early breakfast, and then we flew our airplane on a test flight to make certain that there was no further maintenance work to be done.

This afternoon I sent a radiogram to Grace. At least she will have some idea where I now am. It would do me a lot of good if I could see her and the boys. As long as I am busy, I don't miss my family so much, but when I have a day to myself I begin to get homesick for them.

Tonight we had our army Thanksgiving dinner. It was excellent, turkey and all of the traditional trimmings, but the environment was not right. It would have been so much better to have had hamburger at home with my family.

No further word as to the time of our departure. Hope it is soon so I can be home by Christmas.

Cairo, Egypt, Nov. 26, 1943   2000 EWT

Today I've done little besides wait for something. Have stayed at the airport all day on the alert but have not been called upon to fly.

Am quite rested up now and anxious for something to develop. Maybe we will be moving again tomorrow.

Cairo, Egypt, Nov. 27, 1943   1900 EWT

Today has been a lazy day, spent here at the airport standing on the alert for any developments. This afternoon General Sutherland called to advise that he desires to go to Jerusalem at 0800 hours tomorrow. It will be fitting to spend the Sunday in the Holy Land.

To bed now, as I am arising at 0530 hours tomorrow.

Jerusalem, Palestine, Nov. 28, 1943   1500 PWT

This morning we were up at 0530 to allow plenty of time to be ready for the general's arrival at 0830. Sure enough he arrived exactly on the minute and we took off for Lydda, Palestine. We came across the historic and well-defended Suez Canal, where we had to fire the colors of the hour to identify ourselves so that we would not be fired upon. We came on past historic Jaffa, which figured so prominently in the great Crusades during the early centuries of our era. Then we passed Gaza, where General Allenby campaigned so vigorously during the First World War, and where Lawrence of Arabia occasionally came in from the desert to confer with the general. Upon landing at Lydda, which is an RAF base, we were met, as prearranged, by staff cars, and we drove about thirty miles through colorful but poverty-stricken countryside. We were met by Father Pascal, a Franciscan friar, who guided us through Jerusalem and Bethlehem and proved to be the most informative and efficient guide I have ever seen.

First, we went into the old walled city, up Mount Zion, and into the church of the Holy Sepulchre. Here we saw Mount Calvary and the rent in the live rock where the cross was planted. Then we came to the final resting place of the body of Christ. All of these spots are now converted into places of worship, and there are some of the most decorative and magnificent altars in the world. No expense was spared; all of the various sects of Christianity vied with each other to see which one could obtain possession of the most hallowed spots, and build thereon the most magnificent place of worship. This is particularly true of the various branches of the Catholic church. Many of the altars are beyond description, consisting of exquisite mosaics of gold and precious stones. There has always been much strife in Jerusalem over these venerated spots.

The Jews and the Moslems own and control the country and its politics. Neither group believes in Christ. The Christians, on the other hand, have nothing to say about the country, its politics, or its laws, but are vitally interested in the various spots which have historic and religious significance. The Jews and Mohammedans previously recognized this fact and bartered various spots of land for fabulous sums to the fanatical Christians. Other spots, such as that of the Last Supper, are still in possession of rich Mohammedan families and cannot be bought for any price. Their possessions represent almost infinite wealth and do not fluctuate in value as does money or gold, because the Catholic church will always pay any price to possess them.

The English govern Palestine as a protectorate. In the 1920s the New Zion movement started to bring the Jews back to Palestine, and in twenty years they increased from 100,000 to 450,000; the exodus of Jews to this, their native land, was hastened by Hitler's policy in Europe. At the end of the last war the English were friendly with the Arabs, and there was little trouble then with the greatly outnumbered Jews. Then pressure was brought to bear upon England, and she soon found it expedient to shift her sympathies to the Jews. Eventually, open warfare broke out between the two peoples, but now England has swung back to the side of the Arabs because they represent the greatest power in the Middle East. This vacillating policy breeds trouble, and after this present war ends the matter will probably have to be forcibly settled.

We drove on down to Bethlehem and went down into the rocks to the stone manger where Christ was born. This, of course, is one of the really holy spots, and is surrounded by altars which could not be richer or more beautiful.

We then came back to Jerusalem to visit the Garden of Gethsemane, where now stand the most elegant church and altar of all. They were donated by the Catholic churches of America, and the decorative mosaic work is unsurpassed anywhere in the world. Here we saw the stone where Christ sweat blood on the evening before his crucifixion.

After seeing all of these things, my impressions are somewhat mixed. I have always believed in the reality of Christ, and certainly no man in history has made such a mark upon the Western world. However, the efforts of the various churches to venerate the places where he lived and taught, and the spending of untold wealth to create *the* showplace of the world, when this wealth could better be used more directly to benefit mankind—all of this seems just a little outside the teachings of Christ himself. Another thing strikes me as being most incongruous: Christ was a great teacher of cleanliness, yet here stand these wonderful edifices and altars commemorating his teachings, surrounded by human filth and poverty which are a shame to mankind.

I might mention that this whole country is about as infertile and inhospitable as it could possibly be. There is practically no soil, and the countryside is composed of precipitous hills and valleys of outcropping limestone, to which cling precariously the gnarled and ancient olive trees. Incidentally, when land is sold, the ownership of the olive trees thereon does not go with it. This leads to great complications. Herds of poor sheep and camels graze over the barren hills, and occasionally a fruit tree is terraced into a hillside.

The people are a very poor lot. They are lazy, dirty, and indifferent, and there is much blindness. Many of them have diseased eyes—probably a result of uncleanliness. There are alms seekers at every turn of the narrow, winding streets. Most of them live from the spending of the rich Catholic church.

After we had completed our tour, Father Pascal took us to the American School, which he heads, and refreshed us with some excellent wine and peculiar hard cakes. We are now about to depart for Cairo.

Cairo, Egypt, Nov. 28, 1943   1900 EWT

We departed from Lydda at 1600 hours and swung down over the Dead Sea en route to Cairo. It is the lowest spot on the earth's surface—1,350 feet below sea level. We were supposed to cross the Suez Canal before 1700 hours, as its corridor is closed to air traffic after that. We made it at 1701, fired our colors of the hour, and passed on unmolested. We landed here at Cairo after dark. Tomorrow we will be idle, but Tuesday we expect to go to Luxor.

The general was certainly most considerate in giving us this specially conducted tour, which we could not have arranged for ourselves for any price.

Cairo, Egypt, Nov. 29, 1943   1930 EWT

Am having my troubles today. A mixture control lever on the airplane broke, and it took Strzelecki and Carroll about fifteen hours of work to repair it. Then I discovered that Walker, our navigator, had never been inoculated against yellow fever. India will not allow anyone into the country unless he has been inoculated at least fourteen days prior to the date of entry. I had him inoculated today at a cost of $2.50 to the government, and I'll have to take a chance that the Indian authorities will not notice the date. If they do, I may have to leave him in quarantine at Karachi, and pick up an army navigator.

Then, on top of these troubles, Gehlaar, Walker, and Strzelecki are developing dysentery. Gehlaar is in bad shape. I have borrowed a Pan American copilot for the trip to Luxor tomorrow morning. We are departing at 0745 hours and will visit the famous Valley of the Kings of the ancient Egyptians.

Cairo, Egypt, Nov. 30, 1943   2015 EWT

Today has been one of the highlights of my life to date, and one which I shall never forget. However, it started out very badly.

I was up at 0530 hours to be certain that everything would be set to take the general to Luxor, departing at 0745 hours. When I awakened, both of my arms were so sore that I could hardly move them. I had had inoculations yesterday for typhus and cholera, which the doctor advised prior to my entering India, even though I had had them once before.

When I finally got moving, I was suddenly advised that the Pan American copilot I had arranged to borrow to replace Gehlaar for the trip would be unable to go since that crew had been ordered out on another flight. I appealed to the army to provide me with an army copilot, and they agreed. Thirty minutes before departure time he had not appeared, so I went to his quarters, to find him still in bed. I got him to the airplane in time, and while I was waiting for General Sutherland, General Eisenhower and his party drove up, thinking I was their pilot. General Eisenhower introduced himself and started to climb aboard my airplane. I'm not in the habit of stopping full generals, but I had to explain to him that this was General Sutherland's airplane. It so happened that Eisenhower's Pan American crew didn't have their airplane started up yet, so I thought for a minute that General Eisenhower was going to requisition me and my airplane and leave General Sutherland without transportation. Although General Eisenhower was a bit perturbed, he accepted the situation much more gracefully than did his aide. He was delayed about thirty minutes by the Pan American crew. Then General Sutherland arrived and chided General Eisenhower a bit about not selecting a good crew.

We finally departed a few minutes late, and flew about 350 miles up the historic Nile valley to the present city of Luxor. Visible all down the valley were the various processes of human existence, which have changed little throughout the era of recorded history. All along on the river itself were hundreds of small boats and rafts with their queer, tattered triangular lateen sails, plying their slow and weary way in local commerce. Along the banks of the river were bucket brigades of men and women, lifting the life-giving waters of the Nile in their strange animal-skin buckets and passing these buckets back along the human conveyor belt to the thirsty silt of the fertile fields. At many places, camels hitched to strange large waterwheels plodded their slow and weary way in endless circles, lifting earthen jars of water from the river or from the wells, to pour it into pitiful wandering canals, which in turn spread the water over the fields.

We landed at the excellent airport maintained by the RAF at Luxor and were met by a well-educated Egyptian guide who had been in the employ of Thomas Cook and Sons for twenty-five years.

The present city of Luxor is located on the ancient site of the city of Thebes, so famous in early Egyptian history. The Egyptians and their Roman conquerors have left their permanent marks here. The ruins here represent life after the development of the mature and complex religion of ancient Egypt, and date back to 500 B.C. (The pyramids, of course, date back to about 2600 B.C. and represent an age which had simpler concepts and a less sophisticated religion.) The ancient city of Thebes was divided into two parts: the city of the living on the east bank of the Nile, and the city of the dead on the west bank.

We rode in ancient Ford cars from the airport to the Nile River. Here we boarded one of the strange riverboats along the same route the ancient kings took on their final earthly journey to their magnificent tombs. Here we again took to Fords, and the general and I were driven in style in our car by the number-one boy, an ancient, wrinkled black man whose driving was inspired, but unorthodox. We traveled up the tortuous Valley of the Kings to the site of the tombs.

On this spot, fifty-two tombs of the pharaohs have been discovered to date. Most of them were robbed and vandalized by thieves hundreds or even thousands of years ago, but a few have been discovered intact, just as they were when sealed, some 3,300 years ago. We went down into the tombs of three of the kings: Tutankhamen of the Eighteenth Dynasty, Ramses VI of the Twentieth Dynasty, and Seti I of the Nineteenth Dynasty. Of these, only the tomb of Tutankhamen was discovered intact, but that of Ramses VI was by far the most complete.

The typical tomb has a shaft, cut down into the living rock at about a thirty-degree incline, starting near the top of the mountain. The shaft is about 12 feet wide and 15 feet high, and extends down for a distance of 375 feet. At the base of the shaft is a large room, in which are located the sarcophagus and the accompanying food and drink for the soul whenever it chooses to return. The walls and ceilings of the shafts and tombs are covered with hieroglyphics chiseled into the stone and highly colored. These depict the life of the king and list all of his possessions, and they are very beautifully done. We saw the mummy of Tutankhamen, resting just as it was found.

From the Valley of the Kings, we went to the Temple of Deir el Medineh, where the bodies were mummified and lay for forty days before burial. It is a tremendous heap of gigantic stones, all carved and built into an almost unbelievable temple of worship. Many of the brilliant colors of the figures remain as bright as on the day they were stained.

Next we went to the Colossi of Memnon, two gigantic, monolithic figures about fifty feet high and thirty feet across, sitting all alone on the plain of the valley and marking the entrance to the city of Thebes.

Then we recrossed the Nile and made a quick walk through the Temple of Luxor and the great temple complex of Karnak. This area covers about 1,000 acres and contains hundreds of tremendous pillars and statues as well as the famous Avenue of Sphinxes. Here also are located most of the obelisks remaining in Egypt.

I walked into a typical native mud house here, in order to get an idea of the manner in which they live. The walls and roof were of mud, and the floor was of dust at least six inches deep. The complete furnishings consisted of one pot-bellied mud stove and two earthen jars. There was no larder or food of any kind in sight. The children wore little or no clothing and were filthy and covered with sores. There were flies by the hundreds, both inside and outside the house.

We returned to the airport after being treated to a show by a snake charmer and his cobras — for a fee — and took off for Cairo just before sunset. Our trip here was quick and fine, but when we landed there was no sign of Gehlaar. I imagine he is in the hospital at Camp Hukstep, but will have to wait until morning to verify this.

Cairo, Egypt, Dec. 1, 1943   2000 EWT

By telephone this morning I located Gehlaar in the hospital at Huk-step, so this afternoon I went over to visit him. He has recovered from the worst phase of his dysentery, but is still rather weak. The doctor says that unless complications develop, he will be well enough to travel with us, but will be unable to do any work for a while. General Sutherland can act as copilot, and we will not have to leave Gehlaar here to dead-head home, as it first appeared that we might. However, Strzelecki and Walker are showing more symptoms of the dreaded disease, and all I can do is to keep my fingers crossed.

The general has indicated that we probably will not depart from here eastbound before December 4 or 5, so we have ample time to have every-thing in readiness. Our airplane is in good condition now.

I've begun to get a little homesick. For a time I had hopes of being able to spend Christmas with my family, but now it appears unlikely that I can do so. When I am idle I keep wondering if the boys are all right and whether or not Grace is working too hard trying to keep them under con-trol. It's very hard on her because she has no way of getting away from them when I am not at home.

Cairo, Egypt, Dec. 2, 1943   1930 EWT

Today has been a day of little activity. I have had nothing to do except to rest and to read. Gehlaar is much better but will remain in the hospi-tal until we are ready to depart.

The big conference, which we were instrumental in transporting to this place, was announced to the world today. Also the No. 1 party re-turned here from Teheran today, and reported that they had had an ex-cellent meeting with "Uncle Joe" (Stalin).

Cairo, Egypt, Dec. 3, 1943   1930 EWT

Today has been a long day of waiting. There is no news as to our de-parture, but the No. 1 party went down to Luxor this afternoon sightsee-ing, and I imagine they will be there tomorrow. Perhaps tomorrow we will know something about our schedule.

I know I'm definitely homesick now. Every few minutes I find myself thinking of Grace and the boys, and I almost feel sorry for myself because I can't see them, even for a few minutes.

Cairo, Egypt, Dec. 4, 1943   2000 EWT

Today has been another one of waiting. No developments—no news. I cannot help but feel that things are about over here, however. President

Inonu of Turkey arrived this afternoon, and he is about the last possible one who could come to the conference.

Gehlaar returned from the hospital today, and Walker and Strzelecki are much improved.

I can't seem to throw off this affliction of homesickness I'm having. My thoughts continually turn to Grace and the boys, and I find myself checking on the local time at San Francisco and wondering what they are doing at each particular moment.

Cairo, Egypt, Dec. 5, 1943   1000 EWT

News at last! General Sutherland just telephoned to advise that he desires a tentative departure of midnight tonight, but that he will call me back at noon today to give me definite confirmation. So I guess we will be on our way at last. He desires to arrive in Karachi tomorrow afternoon and then go on over to Delhi Tuesday. Now I have to set the wheels in motion to ensure that all will be in readiness.

1630 EWT

Bad news again! The general telephoned to advise that he cannot get away tonight but expects to be able to depart tomorrow night. He will telephone definite confirmation of this tomorrow morning. It seems that the conference is about to break up at last, and we all will depart about the same time. There are sixteen four-engine planes here on this mission, and we have all been idle since November 22. It's a tremendous waste of equipment and manpower.

Cairo, Egypt, Dec. 6, 1943   1930 EWT

This morning General Sutherland called to advise that he was still unable to give me definite information as to our departure, but that he would telephone me again at noon. At noon he called, but said that Churchill had invited him to luncheon tomorrow, and that it was one of those things which couldn't be refused. He will have to stay for that, and then he will want to go to Delhi, India, as rapidly as possible. He arranged to telephone me again tonight. Tonight he said definitely that he wanted to go tomorrow night, so we have tentatively set up a departure for 1830 hours tomorrow, flying nonstop to Karachi, India, and then on to Delhi, arriving at about 1630 hours local time.

My homesickness got the better of me today, and I sent another cablegram to Grace. Wonder what she is doing now. She is fortunate in one way—at least she can see and talk to our two fine boys.

Over Baghdad, Iraq, Dec. 7, 1943   2100 EWT

We departed from Cairo for good tonight, and now are well on our way to India. We crossed the Suez with the usual secret identification procedure and then headed out over Jerusalem, on across the Dead Sea and Transjordan, and into Iraq. We are now over this famous old city of Baghdad, and I wish I could stop and see it. If all goes well, we will reach Karachi, India, well after sunrise tomorrow.

I have aboard more brass than I've ever hauled on one trip before. I have nine general officers, including General Wedemeyer, who was involved in our other special mission to Western Australia last winter.

We were not permitted to lay our course directly across Saudi Arabia because in the past natives had inflicted some weird and terrible tortures on our pilots who were forced down there. I carry a special letter written in Arabic, instructing the natives to treat us well and advising them that they will be generously rewarded for returning us safely to any Caucasian station.

New Delhi, India, Dec. 8, 1943   2000 IWT

The flying last night was not quite as pleasant as I had hoped. When we were well out over the Persian Gulf we ran into a severe storm, and it lasted until we were over the Arabian Sea. We were on instruments about three hours and had considerable ice. We were tossed about for some time, and finally cleared the storm just at daybreak as we skirted the west coast of India.

I had a sobering experience this night which I am a bit reluctant to describe because it reflects upon the thoroughness of my flight planning. I had been unable to obtain any aerial maps of the route between Baghdad and Karachi. However, in Cairo I did obtain some surface maps, prepared by the French but printed in English. I plotted my desired flight track on them. We started out over the Persian Gulf south of Abadan, then headed inland on a direct line to Karachi. These maps indicated that the highest terrain over which we would fly on one portion of the flight would not exceed 5,000 in altitude, so I felt comfortable with a 10,000 cruising altitude. Wally Gehlaar, the copilot, was still weak and ill with dysentery, so I sent him to the cabin, where he could be comfortable, and General Sutherland was in the copilot's seat. It had been a very long day— all of us had been awake for at least twenty hours—so I told all of the flight deck crew to relax and sleep while I struggled with the task of maneuvering to dodge the thunderstorms, which were violent but scattered.

While we were on and off instruments, with our altitude varying between 8,000 feet and 10,000 feet, there was a vivid flash of lightning. Directly ahead of us about a mile distant there appeared in a break in the clouds an enormous mountain mass towering far above us. In another dozen seconds we literally would have plowed directly into it in the dark. I did an abrupt climbing 180-degree turn with that large airplane, headed back along our previous track, and gave myself time to figure out the puzzle. What I was seeing simply could not be true! I again looked at the map, and sure enough it indicated that the terrain altitude was 3,000 to 5,000. Almost in desperation I turned the map over and there, printed in French in very small type, was a notation that all terrain altitudes were shown in *meters*. If we had hit the mountain it would have gone into the records as another of those unexplained accidents. I can only thank that timely lightning flash that I am here writing about this incident. It was perhaps the nearest I have ever come to killing myself in an airplane.

I haven't told the rest of the crew of this event yet. I shall do so later. Of course, it was my fault for taking too much for granted. I must concede that some power, which was more aware than I, compensated for my carelessness by providing that most fortunate and timely bolt of lightning.

We arrived at Karachi and were well received. We had a good breakfast, were passed through a very strict quarantine which is guarding specially against yellow fever, obtained our briefing as far as New Delhi, and took off for this place. We are now comfortably settled here in the Marina Hotel in the new part of the city. I expect to remain here tomorrow and see something of the life of India.

I have never been so surprised with any place as I have with India. I had expected to see much jungle and thick vegetation everywhere. Instead of that, almost all the country in western and northern India, over and along which I have flown about six hours now, has been rough, barren, and treeless, without many signs of human habitation. Of course, in the wide valley of the Indus River there is much fertility, and many native villages, but aside from that there is nothing but bleak desert in this section. I was beginning to wonder where all of India's teeming millions lived until I reached Delhi. Now I know at least a part of the answer. The climate here is quite cool at this time of year, which fact also surprises me. In fact, the temperature falls to near freezing at night.

I am quite weary now, having flown 3,200 miles without rest in the past twenty-four hours. Tomorrow should be an interesting day.

New Delhi, India, Dec. 9, 1943   2000 IWT

Today is Johnny's birthday, and I am almost exactly on the other side of the world from him. Wonder how the little rascal is. Expect he is giving his mother a bad time.

I am billeted with Captain Cox of the Coast Artillery here, and he is one of the friendliest men I have met. This morning he took me in his jeep and we covered this city, including Old Delhi. It would be useless indeed for me to attempt to describe the filth and poverty and hopelessness of the people here. Truly I had a glimpse of India's teeming millions. The streets are narrow and crowded and lined with human and animal excrement. They are so crowded with sacred cows and human beings that there is hardly space in which to drive a jeep. Their religion forbids the people to kill these strange humped cows, and there is one cow for each three of India's people, even though the people are starving to death. Thousands of the people have no homes, and simply sleep wherever they happen to be. One can see them even eating grass. The dung of the cows is used to plaster walls, to burn as fuel, etc. Many of the people chew betel nut, and they seem to take delight in spitting it on the walls of what few nice buildings the English have built. The situation appears hopeless, and I don't see what can ever be done about it. The people don't appear to want to have their conditions improved, so it would seem that the white race should withdraw and leave them to their own devices. Following is a direct quote from the morning paper here, which portrays actual conditions better than I could ever describe them. This concerns only one of India's large cities:

Hunger Victims
The following is a summary of the official statistics concerning starvation cases in Calcutta and suburbs for December 7 issued on Wednesday:—

Died in Hospitals	29
Admitted to Hospitals	50
Discharged	36
Bodies disposed of by Relief Organizations	41
Total admissions of starving persons in hospitals between August 16 and December 6	15,948
Total deaths among such admissions	5,928
Bodies ascertained as disposed of by the Police Corpse Disposal Squad and the two non-official Relief Organizations from Aug. 1 to December 4	8,929
Total deaths among 'paupers' recorded by the City Corporation Health Officer between Aug. 1 and December 4	15,743

After we had covered a part of the city, I had to go to the airport to see that all was in readiness for our departure tomorrow morning. Captain Cox drove me to the airport, and when I arrived there was a note for me to call General Sutherland at Lord Mountbatten's residency. When I did this they sent a car around for me, and I was rushed up to Lord

Mountbatten's office. Although I did not meet him personally, I worked for a time in the room with him; he looks very much like King George.

I was provided with everything I could possibly need for the trip on to Australia, and then I was sent back to my hotel in an official car. Wing Commander Wilson was my guide around the regency.

Back at my hotel, my bearer, or personal servant, drew my bath, laid out my clothes, and generally took care of me. The fee for a bearer is thirty cents per day for an American, and half that for an Englishman.

Colombo, Ceylon, Dec. 10, 1943   2100 IWT

We were up long before daylight this morning and were almost frozen in the early morning cold. We arrived at the airport and had a cold breakfast in the mess there, and then were ready to take off when the general arrived. General Wedemeyer was out to see us off.

We flew low down over Agra to have a look at the Taj Mahal, and then on down through central India, past Hyderabad, and on out over the Bay of Bengal to steaming Ceylon. Central and southern India is rough but fertile, and appears to produce all types of grains and livestock. There is no jungle in this section either, but we found plenty of it when we reached Ceylon.

The climate here on this large island is incredibly warm and humid, even though this is their cool season. The island has a large clump of mountains in its center, but the perimeter is flat, marshy ground for a distance of about twenty-five miles from the coastline on all sides. Almost every available foot of the flat country is planted in coconuts, rice, or rubber, and tea plantations extend up the sides of the mountains to about the 5,000-foot level.

We landed in midafternoon, and after carefully inspecting the airport I decided that it would be satisfactory for our heavily laden airplane. I spent all afternoon making all of the many last-minute preparations so necessary for the safety of a flight such as the long one we shall undertake tomorrow.

I obtained a car and driver and went into Colombo to see the city. It is much better than the cities of India, and the natives seem infinitely more prosperous. All of the plantations provide food for export, and this produces wealth with which to improve their standard of living.

This is a crown colony and is politically not a part of India. The people are small and wiry and of all shades of color. The women dress in brightly colored long skirts, which are made by wrapping several yards of gauze round and round their hips. The influence of the white race has been considerable here. The city itself is not much to brag about, however, and the heat is almost unendurable.

It is pouring rain here now, as the monsoon has not quite ended for this season. It will rain all night, stopping only at daybreak.

The RAF officers here at the club have a pet mongoose — the first I have seen. It is a playful and affectionate little animal.

We are taking off at 1230 hours tomorrow for the long hop, so I'm going to assure myself of some rest tonight by the use of Seconal.

Over the Indian Ocean, Dec. 11, 1943   2300 IWT

Well, we are almost two-thirds of the way across now, and if the engines keep running, the trip will be routine from here on in. This hop is 3,200 miles long, and I've taken infinite pains to ensure its maximum safety. We have no radio contact with the rest of the world because of the proximity of Jap bases. The takeoff at Colombo was uncomfortable and with no margin of safety. I had 68,500 pounds gross weight. The temperature was very hot, so that we had a density altitude of 1,500 feet. There was a direct, strong crosswind. I used almost the last foot of the runway and then had to make a sharp climbing turn immediately in order to clear some trees. But we made it, thanks to the performance of these fine engines, which I overboosted by two inches of manifold pressure.

I planned my departure from Ceylon so that I would make landfall on Western Australia just at daybreak. This will give me the stars for navigation right up to our arrival time, and we will thus be able to arrive more nearly at the desired point. There is no radio in Western Australia on which we can base our navigation close in. The only disadvantage was that we had to parallel Jap-held Sumatra and Java for six hours during daylight, and there was the possibility that they might intercept us. I set up a watch by my passengers in the cabin, but no one spotted any aircraft. We are running without lights now, and there is no possibility of interference from this point on.

We passed the Cocos Islands a while back, and are now going down the home stretch.

Over central Australia, Dec. 12, 1943   2300 AWT

My plans and navigation worked out perfectly. I took every second celestial fix myself and had the navigator cross-check my calculations. We made landfall exactly at dawn and arrived within one mile of the intended airport at Exmouth Gulf. I'm really proud and General Sutherland was amazed. We landed just before sunrise.

There are practically no amenities for living at Exmouth Gulf, but the U.S. Navy detachment stationed here did their best for us. It isn't every day that I sleep in the same room with Gen. George C. Marshall and have lunch and dinner with him, along with six other general officers. General Marshall was in good spirits and was on his way to confer with General MacArthur.

I said "sleep," but that was hardly the word for it. The temperature started rising with the sun, and continued rising until it reached 117 degrees. Along with the heat were numerous flies, and two hours of sleep was all I could manage in spite of my fatigue and grogginess.

In disgust, we held a conference to determine whether or not we should wait until nightfall to take off for Brisbane or whether we should go on at once. The generals agreed that if I was not too tired to proceed, we should go on without rest. I agreed because it was much more comfortable aloft than in this almost intolerable place. So we departed this evening for Brisbane, rather than wait until morning as we had originally planned. Now we are almost halfway across the great desert of central Australia, and will arrive in Brisbane about 0900 hours tomorrow. This 2,600-mile hop across here seems almost trivial now, but I am very tired.

Brisbane, Australia, Dec. 13, 1943   1900 AWT

We landed here at Amberley Field after an eleven-hour trip across Australia. I had some arrangements to make at the airport, then we came into Brisbane. I drank two glasses of beer, ate lunch, and collapsed. I have completed my mission successfully! I slept all afternoon, got up for dinner, and now I'm going back to bed. Don't believe I'll ever feel completely rested again.

Brisbane, Australia, Dec. 14, 1943   2000 AWT

I slept as late as I could this morning and then put on my best clean clothes and went to General MacArthur's office. There I had a long discussion with General Sutherland relative to being called back to army duty. General MacArthur is sending a radiogram to Mr. Patterson, president of United Air Lines, asking him to release me on a leave of absence. If the plans materialize, I'll bring my next regular trip to Brisbane and be called to duty in Australia. I will be made a lieutenant colonel if regulations permit. If not, I will be inducted as a major and will be promoted to lieutenant colonel at the end of six months. General MacArthur will radio me when he receives word from Mr. Patterson and has all other details arranged. At last it appears that I will be able to get into the army. My job will be interesting and will probably include some more trips from Australia to India. I will be on the general staff under MacArthur.

Have spent a lazy day resting up for the trip back to San Francisco. I am departing at 0400 hours tomorrow.

Nandi, Fiji Islands, Dec. 15, 1943   1900 FWT

We departed from Brisbane as planned this morning and had an easy trip into Fiji, with no weather involved. We are resting here and will depart early in the morning for Canton. Three more days and I'll be home with my family! That seems to be the only thing I live for now.

Canton Island, Dec. 15, 1943   1800 CWT

Arrived here without incident after a fine short trip. Will depart for Honolulu at 0300 tomorrow.

I've now gained a day in my life. Having gone around the world from west to east, I'm living through two December 15s and am only being charged with one of them on the calendar. Perhaps I'll pay for it in my old age, however.

Honolulu, T.H., Dec. 16, 1943   1900 HWT

Had a nice trip up from Canton, but I'm tired now and I can hardly hold my eyes open. Almost home! Two more landings and I'll have flown the same airplane around the world! Good old 276 has been a faithful airplane. I'll have some very interesting statistics to record here when we finally complete the trip.

Now I'm going to bed—even without dinner because I'm too tired to bother.

Honolulu, T.H., Dec. 17, 1943   1400 HWT

Was up early this morning after a refreshing night of sleep. Had breakfast to the tune of the lapping surf here at the Moana Hotel, and then shopped for another nice present for Grace. We are departing at 1800 today for San Francisco and home! Once more I'll be with my fine family.

Atherton, Calif., Dec. 18, 1943   2000 PWT

Home at last! Around the world successfuly, and now I can relax. It was quite a relief when the wheels touched the ground at San Francisco.

The company has received the wire from General MacArthur relative to my active duty, so it appears to be all set. I will be granted a leave of absence for the duration.

A few statistics concerning the flight around the world: I flew 31,200 miles in making the circuit, and landed only twenty times. The flying period covered nineteen days, or parts thereof, and required 157 hours and 15 minutes in the air. About 32,000 gallons of fuel was used. Allowing for takeoff and taxi times on the ground, the overall speed was more than 200 miles per hour average for the entire trip.

I found the family here not too well, with influenza having invaded their sanctuary. However, it does not appear to be a very virulent type, so perhaps it will run its course soon and we can have a happy family holiday.

Atherton, Calif., Dec. 19, 1943   2300 PWT

Slept quite late this morning and then was as lazy as possible all the remainder of the day.

Tonight Grace and I slipped away to Dinah's Shack for a small fling together at our favorite eating place. It was a delightful evening, and would have been perfect except for our worry over Johnny. There was nothing we could do to help him by remaining home the two hours, however.

Atherton, Calif., Dec. 20, 1943   2300 PWT

I spent most of the day in Palo Alto today, catching up on my business affairs and doing much shopping.

Tonight Grace and I went to the Stanford University Chapel to a beautiful concert by Yehudi Menuhin. Some of it was a bit over my head, but he is certainly a wonderful artist.

Atherton, Calif., Dec. 21, 1943   2200 PWT

This morning I caught an early bus to the airport to start in on the many things necessary in preparation for leaving my job here for the duration of the war. It will require several days to sever my connections here, but I accomplished much today. Then I went on in to San Francisco to order a new army uniform and to do other necessary shopping there.

Arrived home late, tired but happy. This is my first full evening at home, and the children are feeling much better, although Grace is about to come down with the influenza now. It's really good to be home!

Atherton, Calif., Dec. 22, 1943   1700 PWT

Today has been a dark and gloomy day, but I have been indoors all day working at my desk. Many business matters to try to straighten out on a long-term basis.

The boys are much better today—almost normal in fact. In a few more days I hope to have all of my work done so that I can relax for a few days and do nothing but enjoy my family.

I depart for Army duty.

Atherton, Calif., Dec. 23, 1943 through Jan. 4, 1944

I spent this period at home. I received official orders to return to Australia and to be called to duty there.

We had a quiet family Christmas at home, then Grace and I went to Carmel-by-the-Sea for a few days to ourselves.

There were many business chores to be done, and I purchased a new uniform.

Although I made daily entries in my diary, I have condensed these here in the interest of brevity.

Atherton, Calif., Jan. 5, 1944   2200 PWT

This morning I went in to Palo Alto and had my picture taken for the family—full uniform and all. Then this afternoon I completed the last of my business affairs, packed my belongings, and am now ready to go. Tonight we sat until late hours before the fireplace, playing our beautiful musical recordings and consuming our last bottle of champagne. These are the things I'm going to miss while I am away.

Atherton, Calif., Jan. 6, 1944   1330 PWT

This is the final day. I am to be at the airport at 1530 hours to depart for Australia. Will go to Hamilton Field tonight and depart from there for Honolulu at dawn tomorrow morning. I'm physically ready to leave, but emotionally I'll never be quite ready. Wonder how long it will be before I'll see my dear family next. I have a feeling it will not be as long as my mind tells me it will be. In the meantime I'll have no distractions and should be able to apply myself to whatever task lies ahead of me. It's nice to know that the boys will be in the finest care possible.

10

To War—For Good

Honolulu, T.H., Jan. 7, 1944   2000 HWT

Went to the airport as planned yesterday and was interviewed by the company publicity man about my recent trip around the world.

We stayed at Hamilton Field last night, and I called Grace by telephone to tell her one more good-bye. We were both rather low, as at last we were beginning to realize just what this separation is going to mean to us. No longer can we depend on each other for advice and comfort in our little troubles, and then I'll miss those two sweet boys so very much. They will almost be young men when I see them again. I'll have all the more incentive to do my utmost to help get this war over as soon as possible.

We departed from Hamilton Field at dawn and landed here at sundown, and had a perfect trip over. I am observer on Jimmy Johnson's trip. I plan to remain here tomorrow, departing tomorrow night for Canton Island.

Honolulu, T.H., Jan. 8, 1944   1800 HWT

Had a lazy day here today. Spent a little time on the beach, played some poker, and am now preparing to depart this evening for Canton.

I can't seem to throw off this blue feeling about breaking away from my family. If anything happens to them during my absence, I'll never forgive myself, as I could have gotten out of this army duty if I had really wanted to. However, I would have felt very cowardly about not having done my duty toward my country if I had tried to avoid the army duty. So all I can do now is to work hard and pray that all goes well at home. If I had a less capable wife than Grace, then I probably could be justified in worrying.

Canton Island, Jan. 9, 1944   1900 CWT

The trip down was uneventful last night, and we arrived shortly after sunrise.

The day has been quite warm, and sleeping is almost impossible. I took a sunbath and then had a long walk along the lagoon.

There is a hurricane in the vicinity of the Fiji Islands, and the weather and winds are adverse there. The trip is holding here until 0100 hours and may not depart then if the weather does not improve considerably.

En route Canton–New Caledonia, Jan. 10, 1944   0500 CWT

This is the day I lose until I cross back over the date line again eastbound, so I will not say much more about it at this time. Hope to be in Australia tonight if all goes well.

Ipswich, Australia, Jan. 11, 1944   2000 AWT

This has been a very long and monotonous day. We departed from Canton at 0345 hours this morning, passed up Fiji account local weather. Then we stopped at New Caledonia. We were there a couple of hours, and then came on into Amberley Field here, where we landed about 1830 hours. I was observer on a crowded airplane, and the trip was not pleasant. Now, however, I am here by the time I had told General Sutherland that I would be, and I'm mentally and physically ready for induction into the army. Tomorrow I will report in to GHQ.

Ipswich, Australia, Jan. 12, 1944   2100 AWT

This morning I was up early and went to Amberley Field to get transportation to go into Brisbane. Reported in to General Sutherland and General MacArthur at 1030 hours and started through the mill to go on active duty. This is somewhat complicated, as it turns out. I could be inducted immediately on a 63-type examination, but then if I failed to pass any part of the 64-type exam for flight duty, I would find myself in the army and not on flight status, so that I would have to have a desk job only. Therefore, I have insisted that I not be inducted until the results from the 64 exam can be obtained. This requires about three days due to development of X rays, Kahn blood test, etc. I completed the examinations today but will probably not be sworn in until Saturday.

Still being a civilian somewhat complicates matters, as I am unable to obtain billeting in Brisbane, so must stay here at Ipswich. I believe it is a wise move, however.

Two trips are coming up soon: one to Sydney on January 15, for which I probably will not be ready, and another to Honolulu on January 22, which I hope to be able to make.

Ipswich, Australia, Jan. 13, 1944   2100 AWT

Today I decided to stay here at Ipswich and await developments. There is nothing I can do in Brisbane, and it's quite comfortable here. Have spent a lazy day with Sid Nelson, discussing various and sundry things and drinking some good Australian beer. Tomorrow I think I shall force the issue a bit and move into Brisbane.

Brisbane, Australia, Jan. 14, 1944   2300 AWT

This morning I was up early, and I obtained a staff car and took my belongings into Brisbane. Upon checking in at GHQ I found that I was to be billeted at the Lennon's Hotel, so I moved in there in a hurry before someone changed his mind. This hotel is air-conditioned and by far the best one in Brisbane. This is where General MacArthur lives with his family. I have a small room, but one with private bath, and I am physically far more comfortable than I had any hope of being.

Although my physical needs are well provided for, that is not quite true of my mental needs. I could find no books, magazines, or other suitable reading material in town, so I've already been most miserable for lack of it. There is simply no material available of the type to which I've always been accustomed, and I'm going to miss books greatly. Sid Nelson has promised to bring some good books, but that will be at least a month hence.

Brisbane, Australia, Jan. 15, 1944   1900 AWT

Another day of disappointment. I made the rounds this morning to see if the results of my physical exam had come through channels as yet, but no such luck. General Sutherland sent a tracer on it, so I expect results by tomorrow. Headquarters works seven days a week, so Sunday will be no obstacle.

Perhaps I'm just a bit homesick, but I've had to get out the pictures of Grace and the boys and study them a couple of times today. They constitute a mighty fine family and are really something to go to war over.

It's very hot here now, and this air-conditioned room is something to be appreciated. I have to use a fresh uniform every day, and laundry service requires ten days, so I have to buy a large supply of them.

A study in strategic distances.

Brisbane, Australia, Jan. 16, 1944   2000 AWT

No developments today, and I have accomplished very little. Was up early and over to the adjutant general's office to see if they were yet ready to induct me into the army, but my physical exam still was not back. They finally admitted that they had misplaced my blood sample and that that was the cause of the delay.

Brisbane, Australia, Jan. 17, 1944   2130 AWT

This morning I was up at 0600 to accompany General Sutherland to Archer Field, where we spent an hour flying famous old *CXE*, his private C-47. He does an excellent job flying in it, and I acted as his copilot.

[I was surprised to find that Sutherland was a skilled pilot. He said he had been graduated from the flying school operated by the Philippine Army. However, he was not a rated pilot in the U.S. Army and therefore could not officially fly our aircraft.]

After the general had finished his flying, I remained at the field, learned my way about the place, and met many of the officers there. This afternoon Henry Godman and I flew the B-17, General MacArthur's airplane, *Bataan*, for a while, and I made a couple of landings in it. I like it very much, but of course am not too familiar with it as yet.

Upon returning to GHQ General Sutherland advised me that I would be going to Melbourne on Wednesday in *CXE*. I'm still not in the army, but he guarantees me that I will be, and when he says that, it is pretty certain to happen. It will have to occur tomorrow if I am to fly the trip to Melbourne.

Brisbane, Australia, Jan. 18, 1944   1900 AWT

Tonight I am a major in Uncle Sam's army. When things started to happen, they really happened fast, and I was called to duty as a captain and promoted to a major in the same order, which was predated effective January 12. Guess the general was a bit peeved at the delay, so he cut through the red tape.

[There are many things I do not know about the modern army, how it functions and how GHQ accomplishes its mission. I am also at a loss as to how to learn about it. My immediate boss is General MacArthur, but obviously I cannot be running in to him all the time asking my simple questions. I keep a very low profile and try not to display my lack of sophistication. Colonels Francis (Woody) Wilson and Herb Wheeler on General Sutherland's staff realize my predicament, have taken me under their expert "wings," and will attempt to educate me in matters of protocol, "pecking order," etc. To them I owe a great deal. As soon as possible I start learning about airfields and facilities in eastern Australia by taking flights over the area.]

As soon as the paperwork was finished, I went to Archer Field and flew *CXE* for an hour to see if I could still fly a C-47.

Melbourne, Australia, Jan. 19, 1944   2200 AWT

This morning we departed from Archer Field at 0730 hours for a direct flight to Melbourne. The weather was excellent, and we had a fine five-hour flight to this fine city. Among others, I brought Gen. Richard Marshall and General Alexander.

I like Melbourne better than any of the other Australia cities, excepting Perth. The city is much more like an American city than Brisbane, and is quite clean for a change. Although the place is somewhat crowded now, it lacks the confusion of the other places.

I am staying at the Menzies Hotel, which is Melbourne's best and is very, very British. The service and customs here at the hotel are all done in the best British manner, and hardly a breath of the war finds its way into the peace and tradition of the hotel.

Melbourne, Australia, Jan. 20, 1944   2100 AWT

Today I saw what I could of this fine city. I took several long walks, including visits to the library and museum, and then I got a staff car to drive about the residential part of the city. The weather appears to resemble that of San Francisco. It is certainly one of the more choice parts of Australia.

It seems that we will be departing tomorrow for Brisbane, but General Marshall has as yet not given me definite instructions. I'm getting quite a kick out of my own reactions to all of the consideration and deference I get, simply because now I am *Major* Rhoades. I'm not accustomed to it, and I'm afraid I'm not always quite as dignified as I am supposed to be.

Brisbane, Australia, Jan. 21, 1944   2200 AWT

We departed from Melbourne at 1330 hours and had a fine, fast trip back here to Brisbane. The weather was good, and we delivered our party in good shape.

Tonight I have written a long letter home and caught up with some odd work here in my room. I'll have to admit that I'm just a little bit homesick. It would be worth a lot to me to be able to see Grace and those boys.

Tomorrow morning I have to see about the trip to Honolulu. Will not have very long to prepare for it, if we leave Sunday morning as planned.

Brisbane, Australia, Jan. 22, 1944   1900 AWT

Today I did many chores around town—things which had to be done relative to pay, quarters, etc., while living here in town.

Everything is ready for our departure for Honolulu tomorrow morning. We are taking off at 0700 hours, and I am going as Godman's copilot. It should be a nice trip and I'll see several of the United crews. When I reach Honolulu I'm going to have a funny feeling, being so near my family and then not being able to see them.

Tontouta, New Caledonia, Jan. 23, 1944   2000 AWT

We departed from Brisbane as planned this morning and had a fine four-and-a-half-hour trip to this place. Tontouta is the same dirty, inexcusable hole that it was a year ago, and apparently no effort has been made to improve it.

En route New Caledonia–Canton, Jan. 24, 1944   2200 CWT

Departed from Tontouta at 1830 hours today and was plenty glad to escape from the hole. We are now well on our way to Canton, where we should arrive about daybreak. We plan to refuel there and to continue on, without rest, to Honolulu. Our passengers include General Sutherland and General Chamberlin, both very fine gentlemen, and both most considerate of us.

Honolulu, T.H., Jan. 24, 1944   2230 HWT

Although this is a different day, we crossed the date line and it's still January 24.

We were in Canton about one and a half hours and then came on here, landing at Hickam just after dark. It was a fine trip, but rather slow. The old B-17 functioned perfectly, and I'm growing fond of the airplane. Its official name is *Bataan*, and I shall refer to it hereafter by that name.

We obtained rooms at the Moana Hotel and will be comfortably situated during our stay. We have flown 3,400 nautical miles in the past twenty-two hours, so I'm very tired. Now for bed and some sleep, my first in forty hours.

Honolulu, T.H., Jan. 25, 1944   2330 HWT

Arose late this morning and then went into town to do some shopping for certain supplies which are unobtainable in Australia. Also sent a small gift home to Grace by air mail. This afternoon I went swimming.

Wrote a letter to Grace and certainly wish I had one from her to read. It's a shame I can't get into *Bataan* and cruise over to San Francisco to pay a visit to her and the boys. Wonder what they are doing tonight. It would be a lot of fun to look in upon them.

Honolulu, T.H., Jan. 26, 1944   2030 HWT

Went to the airport this morning, extended my shopping, and had lunch there with Charlie Wrightson, the United station manager here. Came back to the hotel, played poker, and generally managed to be lazy.

No news about when we may expect to depart, but it will probably be on Friday or Saturday.

Honolulu, T.H., Jan. 27, 1944   2030 HWT

Have done very little today except to take life easy. Went downtown this morning and then went swimming this afternoon. Visited with several more of the United crews who were going through. Tomorrow will probably brings news concerning our proposed departure time.

Honolulu, T.H., Jan. 28, 1944   2100 HWT

Today I spent most of the day at Hickam Field, trying to obtain some good information on the performance of the Wright engines used in our *Bataan*. It is surprising how little is known about this engine. Or perhaps much is known but is simply not on file in places accessible to me.

Returned to the hotel and had a swim late this afternoon. Tonight we were informed that we would be departing for Australia at 0700 hours tomorrow morning. There were the usual arrangements to be made concerning the departure, and now I'm ready for my sleep.

Canton Island, Jan. 29, 1944   2000 CWT

Had some delay in leaving Hickam field this morning, due to failure of our ground transportation, but at length we got away. We had a nice trip down here, but it was rather long. We are remaining overnight, and then going straight through to Brisbane with only a refueling stop at Plaine des Gaiacs.

International Date Line, Jan. 30, 1944   0900 CWT

This is the day we lose by crossing the date line.

Brisbane, Australia, Jan. 31, 1944   2200 AWT

We departed from Canton at 0400 hours today and landed at Plaine des Gaiacs just eleven hours later. Had considerable rain en route. We were there only long enough to refuel our *Bataan* and ourselves, and then we came on to Brisbane in four more hours. Archer Field was closed because of mud, and we landed at Eagle Farm Airdrome.

I'm thoroughly tired and ready for bed after fifteen hours in the air today.

Brisbane, Australia, Feb. 1, 1944   2030 AWT

Was up at 0700 hours this morning to a leisurely breakfast, but when I reported to GHQ, there was excitement. An immediate trip for me back to Washington was in the offing, and there was much planning going on. I went to Archer Field and to Amberley Field on some necessary errands, and when I returned to my office at GHQ this afternoon, it seemed that the proposed trip to the States had fallen through. Naturally I was disappointed, as I would have had an opportunity to see my family for a few hours on the stopover on the West Coast. Now I suppose there will not be much for me to do for a few days.

Brisbane, Australia, Feb. 2, 1944   2230 AWT

Not much activity today. Worked out a schedule for General Sutherland and then checked with the field to see if an airplane was available to fly, but no use.

Still no letter from home. I'm really getting worried now, as I know that they have all been ill, and it's not like Grace to allow such a long interval to pass without writing to me. The other officers here are regularly receiving letters from home by air mail in six days, but none arrive for me.

Brisbane, Australia, Feb. 3, 1944   2130 AWT

This morning Hank Godman and I went to Eagle Farm and moved our airplane back to good old muddy Archer Field. No other airplane was available to fly, so I came back to the office and did some paperwork for the remainder of the day. General Marshall has informed me that he wants an airplane to go to Sydney and Melbourne in the next day or two, but I doubt if I'll go. Either Henry or I will have to stand by to fly *Bataan* if needed, and I'll probably stay.

Still no letter from home.

Brisbane, Australia, Feb. 4, 1944   2145 AWT

Today I flew *Bataan* for one and a half hours, including a trip out to inspect the fields at Johndaryan and Cecil Plains. I like the airplane better all the time. Intended to fly the C-47 this afternoon, but it was not in service.

Sent another letter to Grace today, but still received none. Now I'm really worried about what has happened to her and the boys.

Brisbane, Australia, Feb. 5, 1944   2100 AWT

Went to Archer Field early today and flew *CXE*, our C-47, for two and a half hours. Practiced under the hood for an hour and then went down to Evans Head to look at the airport there. It will afford a very good alternate when weather is bad around Brisbane. It's fun to fly the old C-47 once more.

Tonight I went to Colonel Lehrbas's room for a drink, and he gave me a bottle of Scotch whiskey. That's really something here, as it's almost impossible to get now.

I wrote a letter to Jimmy tonight. My, how I wish I could see the little rascal and his mother and Johnny! For some reason, I feel particularly lonesome tonight, and if I could only see my wonderful family all would be well.

Brisbane, Australia, Feb. 6, 1944   2115 AWT

This has been a very quiet day. The airplanes are out of commission, and since there's nothing to fly, I have spent most of the day in the office. I don't have any definite duties here as yet, so it's largely a matter of killing time. I took two long walks, as that is about the only kind of exercise I can get here. With so much time on my hands, it would be easy to get soft and out of condition, as many of the officers here have done. I'm determined that I am going to come out of this war as good a man, physically and morally, as I went into it. That certainly is not going to be true of the majority of the people I've seen here.

It is quite warm here, with considerable rain and high humidity. The countryside is at its best, with its solid background of green, highly colored with a profusion of flowers. It's an easy life these Australians have.

Still no letter from home.

Brisbane, Australia, Feb. 7, 1944   2350 AWT

The airplanes were still not in flying condition today, so I was unable to do any practice work. I'm afraid the maintenance isn't all it should be at Archer Field. In the past seven days, *Bataan* has been flyable only one day. This is really ridiculous as measured by the standards to which I am accustomed.

Still no letter from home. I've been away just one month today. I'm afraid my letters have been misplaced somehow and will probably all be sent back to Washington now, to determine where I am to be located.

Brisbane, Australia, Feb. 8, 1944   2000 AWT

This morning I was up early and to the office, hopeful of some mail, but no such luck. Then I went to Archer Field and took an instrument check ride in a C-47 to get a regular army instrument authorization card, so that I can be cleared in instrument weather. The check pilot was not very experienced, and he hardly realized what was going on until it was all over. It was good practice, and I enjoyed it. *Bataan* is still not flyable.

Wrote a letter home, and have enjoyed a quiet evening in my room. Still no letter from Grace.

Brisbane, Australia, Feb. 9, 1944   1625 AWT

Today I went to Eagle Farm and flew a 22-B, a small Dutch pursuit airplane. It's quite a machine, and much fun.

Sid Nelson is arriving today, and I hope he will have some news for me about Grace.

I'm leaving for New Guinea early tomorrow morning and expect to be there about two weeks. Will land at most of our airfields there and will no doubt see Maury Wiley. It should be an interesting trip.

Just returned from Ipswich, where I saw Sid Nelson. He assured me that my family was now all right, that none of them was still in the hospital, etc. So I feel much better about the situation. Sid also brought me a bunch of books, most of which I am taking up to New Guinea tomorrow to distribute to the men there. I now plan to take off from Archer Field at 0700 hours tomorrow for Townsville and then Milne Bay, New Guinea.

11

Into the Jungle

Milne Bay, New Guinea, Feb. 10, 1944

At last I'm in this amazing island of New Guinea! We departed from Brisbane at 0700 hours this morning and had a nice trip over the monotonous land of Australia to Townsville. It was raining there, but we landed and refueled, took on two finance officers and half a million dollars in cash, and departed shortly after midday for Milne Bay. We had excellent weather and sighted the shoreline of New Guinea about three hours out of Townsville. An hour later we landed at this much-bombed, much-fought-over bay, and it is indeed a beautiful spot.

Along most parts of the coast, the green-carpeted, almost-sheer mountains rise abruptly out of the reef-fringed blue ocean, and their height is almost incredible. Every little cove has its settlement of the strange, friendly "Fuzzy-Wuzzies," who live almost entirely on and by virtue of the coconut. They waved cheerfully at us as we flew over.

Our installations for warfare are tremendous, and it gives one a thrill to see the actual jumping-off place of an army. The activity here is almost unbelievable. The bay offers an excellent harbor, and it is being fully utilized.

After landing, I had a minor mishap with my airplane. In taxiing into a revetment as security against a Jap bombing raid, one of the control elevators struck an oil drum and was slightly damaged. Not much effort will be required to repair it, however.

We had an interesting drive into base section headquarters, about twenty miles from the airstrip. Along the way we saw the famous Turnbull Field airstrip, where the Jap forces were finally pinned down in their invasion of this bay. Although the jungle has reclaimed most of the scene of the conflict, still there are many signs of the battle. Many of the coconut palms are without tops, and they stand as mute reminders of the bitter struggle that went on in the steaming jungle beneath them.

We are very comfortably housed in a screened hut, which is characteristically enough constructed of the fronds of the coconut trees and is located on the very shores of the bay, so that the surf almost laps at the base of the stilts upon which it is built. There are some mosquitoes, but not as many as I had expected. There is considerable malaria, however, and I'm certainly not forgetting to take my daily pill of Atabrine.

Milne Bay, New Guinea, Feb. 11, 1944 2000 AWT

Was up early this morning after a refreshing night, and took my mechanics back to the airstrip to get our airplane in readiness for operation tomorrow. On the way, Sergeant Cicerello, my radio operator, showed us various foxholes and places from which he had helped to fight the Japs when they attempted to take Milne Bay a year ago. He showed us the pit in which they had buried all of the Jap dead when the battle for Turnbull airstrip was finally over. We found the damage to the airplane's elevator to be even less than we had expected.

I took a jeep and went on an exploring expedition by myself. I drove about forty miles along roads and trails, and got well up onto the mountainside on one trail. From my vantage point I had a wonderful view of the beautiful bay and harbor with all of their war-stimulated activity.

I got a Fuzzy-Wuzzy to climb a coconut tree and pick a half dozen fine nuts for me. It's unbelievable how they can scale the bare, perpendicular tree trunks. We could talk quite well to each other in Pidgin English.

It rained most of the afternoon, and although we obtained a jeep to drive about in, it was not too pleasant and we soon called it off.

This is an amazing land. The dense, almost-impenetrable jungle covers everything with its crawling vines. Parrots and kookaburras scream and laugh incessantly from their jungle refuge, but one can rarely spot them for all of their noise. The jungle vines and trees even cover the almost-vertical slopes of the precipitous mountains.

To fight a war in this country is indeed a gigantic undertaking. It's very heartening to see the tremendous effort that is being expended here at Milne Bay. Of course there is terrific waste of material and manpower, but it probably is impossible to eliminate it in an undertaking of this scope.

The Fuzzy-Wuzzies are queer little people. They have these enormous mops of fuzzy hair, of which they are very proud. They constantly rub lime juice into their hair in order to bleach it, as they seem to like light-colored hair. In fact, they almost worship some of our soldiers here who have blonde hair. They chew betel nut and their lips are crimson red. They are very friendly and helpful. The women are all kept back in the villages in the hills and are not permitted to come about our camps. A wise plan.

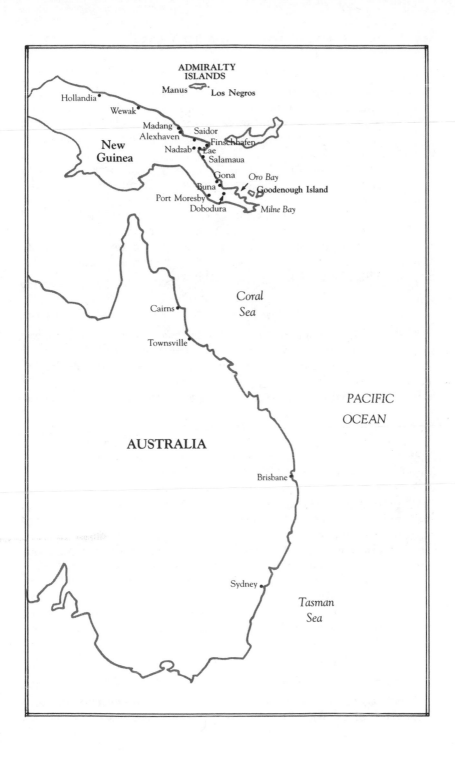

ADMIRALTY
ISLANDS
Manus   Los Negros

Hollandia

Wewak

Madang   Saidor
Alexhaven   Finschhafen
New   Nadzab Lae
Guinea   Salamaua

Gona   Oro Bay
Buna   Goodenough Island
Port Moresby
Dobodura   Milne Bay

Coral
Sea

Cairns

Townsville

PACIFIC
OCEAN

AUSTRALIA

Brisbane

Sydney   Tasman
Sea

Goodenough Island, Feb. 12, 1944   1500 AWT

Here I sit in a comfortable screened thatched hut on the banks of a roaring mountain stream, in a perfect tropical setting. The only catch is that it rains perpetually, and malaria and scrub typhus are rampant. This is a beautiful island when the clouds and rain permit one to see it, and it isn't too warm.

We departed from Milne Bay at 1100 hours, and were only thirty minutes en route here. We spotted a smoke bomb on the water on the way over. It was of the type used by aircraft in distress, but we were unable to locate any lifeboat or other indications that an airplane had landed on the water in the vicinity. We spent some time in searching.

Everywhere we go we are cared for in the best manner, and it has its advantages, but also its disadvantages. I don't have much of an opportunity of seeing the unpleasant side of the war.

Oro Bay, New Guinea, Feb. 13, 1944   2200 AWT

This morning we departed from Goodenough Island early while the weather was still clear, and circled the beautiful island before we set out on our way to Dobodura. En route we passed Cape Nelson. We landed on one of the excellent airstrips at Dobodura, and then were taken by jeep to Oro Bay, which was so hotly contested during the Buna campaign. We are living on the beach in most comfortable style. This afternoon I sunbathed for two hours.

Among others of our party is Colonel Baedcke, who led the American troops in the historic march across the Owen Stanley Mountains and defeated the Japs at Buna and Gona. He is a remarkable man, has really suffered in this war, and is one of its outstanding heroes. He is now in GHQ in Brisbane, only because of extremely poor health. He is riddled with malaria and is one of the few men who has had scrub typhus and has recovered from it. He is not very talkative, but occasionally I can draw him out a bit concerning his experiences. He is almost fanatical about getting back in the field with his regiment, which is now at Finschhafen, but of course GHQ will not permit it, because he would probably soon die of malaria if exposed to it again.

Don't know what the plans are for tomorrow. I think our party is going on to Finschhafen, but we are not permitted to take our unarmed airplane there.

Oro Bay, New Guinea, Feb. 14, 1944   2100 AWT

Today was one of the most instructive days I have ever spent. Early in the day Colonel Baedcke asked me if I would like to accompany him on a trip to the battlefield of the old Soputa Track near Sanananda Point. It was here that he engaged the Japs after his historic march over the Owen Stanley Range.

We drove about thirty miles in a jeep after I had outfitted myself with proper clothing and a gun. (Two Jap stragglers gave themselves up only last week, although this battle was fought fifteen months ago.) On our way we visited the American cemetery, which is located in a beautiful valley and is well kept, but which has all too many graves marked unknown. And in it lie only about 60 percent of our dead because the others could never be found in the dense jungle. We also visited the nearby Jap cemetery, which represents only a token effort on the part of the Australians to abide by international covenants. All of its dead are marked unknown, and what few grave markers have not been stolen by souvenir hunters have been drilled with many bullet holes by our own troops.

We came, finally, to the battlefield, and we set out through the dense jungle on foot. All of my ideas of warfare were upset immediately. This battlefield has never been cleaned up and still remains much as it did when the battle ended. The opposing front lines averaged only about fifty to one hundred feet apart, and the jungle growth was so thick that rifles were almost useless. All of the fighting, except for sniping from the trees, was done by mortar fire and hand grenades. The Jap pillboxes and our own foxholes are still there, although the jungle is rapidly obliterating the scars. The bones and skulls and equipment of the Jap dead lie about in great quantities, and even these last traces will not survive much longer. It gave me a strange feeling to probe among and walk over these bones of what had once been fanatical Jap soldiers, bent on the destruction of our boys for some strange reason which they probably never understood. Before the battle, if they had suspected that they would come to such a ignominious and unknown end here in this lonesome, stinking jungle, I wonder if they would have been quite so eager to die. I'll have to admit that I had no great compunction in walking over skulls. They seemed little different from animal remains. Our boys were in this battlefield for twenty-eight days, and the superior number of Japs was finally defeated, more by the will of our men to win than by any other factor.

I don't believe I've ever been quite so hot in my life as I was in hiking through this jungle. We finally got back to our jeep and returned to Oro Bay for a welcome shower and a change of clothing.

Oro Bay, New Guinea, Feb. 15, 1944   2000 AWT

Today has been a very lazy day. Our party went on up to Finschhafen and we will pick them up again here about Sunday. In the meantime, I plan to go over to Port Moresby for a couple of days.

Port Moresby, New Guinea, Feb. 16, 1944   2300 AWT

This morning we were up at a reasonable hour and departed from Dobodura for Moresby. We had a nice trip across the "hump," and the weather was good. We came here over Kokoda Pass, where our troops crossed the ridge at 7,000 feet on a crude foot trail to engage and defeat the Japs at Buna and Gona. That was a feat which will long be remembered. Our ground forces were equipped and supplied entirely by parachute packs dropped by our troop carrier airplanes.

At Moresby, I checked in at GHQ and then proceeded to look up Maurice Wiley. I soon found him at Wards Field. He is a lieutenant colonel and is group operations officer for his troop carrier group. He is well provided for and is living in a comfortable house atop a steep hill. Maury and I went into GHQ for dinner, and then I came back here to stay all night with him.

Port Moresby, New Guinea, Feb. 17, 1944   1730 AWT

Maury and I were up at daylight and cooked our own breakfast here at his place. We had oranges, basted fresh eggs, toast, and coffee. I then took my airplane and went down to Hood Point, about sixty miles southeast of here, and landed in a small grass field there. A native Fuzzy-Wuzzy village is located about three miles from the field, and we walked into it through the sweltering heat. We spent about four hours in the village, talking to the natives and observing the manner in which they live.

Their thatched huts are built on stilts out in the bay, where a breeze blows and keeps most of the mosquitoes away. The people are friendly, simple, and crude. Their main staple is the coconut, although they do cultivate taro and yams. They do some fishing in the bay. The men wear only a scanty loincloth and the women wear a grass skirt and nothing more. All of the children up to the age of twelve wear no clothing at all. The little babies are about the cutest I have ever seen. Many of the people have running tropical sores on their legs and bodies, but in this vicinity they are not afflicted to the extent that many of them are in other localities; bathing in saltwater is said to decrease the size and number of these peculiar sores. Most of the adults chew betel nut. Their mouths and teeth are brightly stained. They had nothing worth trading for so I got no souvenirs from them.

A violent rain shower caught us just before we took off, but we got away all right. I flew on northwest of Port Moresby to inspect the landing strip at Thirty-Mile. It affords an excellent alternate field for Moresby. We landed at Wards Field in a rain and saw the crack-up of a B-25 which apparently overshot the field. I returned to GHQ, where I took a bath and changed clothes after our long and sultry hike. Otherwise, I had a very lazy afternoon.

Oro Bay, New Guinea, Feb. 18, 1944   2000 AWT

This morning we were up early at Port Moresby and went out to the airport to take off for Dobodura. However, no airplanes were flying, due to so-called bad weather. We finally convinced the operations officer that we should take off and have a look at the weather at any rate, and we could always return if we found it to be too bad for safe flying. We took off at 0930 hours and landed at Dobodura an hour later, and were not in so much as a single cloud all the way over. I've begun to wonder about this "bad" New Guinea weather.

Oro Bay, New Guinea, Feb. 19, 1944   2000 AWT

It was rainy and cloudy all day today, so that I was unable to lie on the beach as I had hoped. Consequently, I was very inactive, and spent most of the day reading a murder mystery. Wrote a letter home and then tonight we started a poker game, but it lasted only a few minutes as one of our players was called away on business.

Port Moresby, New Guinea, Feb. 20, 1944   2130 AWT

This morning I had information that my passengers wanted to depart from Oro Bay for Port Moresby at 0900 hours. We were up early, but did not finally take off until 1330 hours.

The trip across the hump was uneventful, and we arrived here in time for a good Sunday dinner of fried chicken. The army eats better here in New Guinea than in any place I've seen.

Went to a movie tonight and wrote a letter to Grace. Tomorrow night I'll be in Brisbane, and I hope I'll have some mail from her at last.

Brisbane, Australia, Feb. 21, 1944   2030 AWT

Departed from Port Moresby at 0900 hours this morning. Had an un-eventful four-hour trip to Townsville across the Great Barrier Reef. There was some weather involved. We stopped there only long enough for re-fueling, and then came on to Brisbane, arriving here at 1830 hours. I rushed into town to try to get to the office before it closed. Sure enough, there were four letters from Gracie, and now the world is a much finer place.

I guess it's difficult for the folks back home to realize how much their letters mean to us here. I'll spend much of the night reading and reread-ing these letters. It's so fine to know that the family is well and thriving.

Brisbane, Australia, Feb. 22, 1944   2300 AWT

Slept rather late this morning and then went to Archer Field to fly *Bataan* for an hour and a half. Have now just finished writing a long let-ter to Grace. Must get to bed to be ready for a navigation flight in *Bataan* tomorrow.

Brisbane, Australia, Feb. 23, 1944   2330 AWT

Today was a long but interesting day. I was up early and took off in *Bataan* for a practice navigation flight to Lord Howe Island, about 400 miles off the coast from Brisbane. It's a beautiful island, probably 3,000 acres in extent, some of it level and the other part mountainous, rising to 2,500 feet. The climate is ideal, and it would be the perfect place to settle down to forget the rest of the world. From the air it would appear that about one hundred people live there. The cliffs offer haven for many birds.

Returned to Archer Field about 1500 hours, had an early dinner, and then played bridge until 2300 hours.

Had a nice long letter from Grace but it was old. It was written on January 31.

Brisbane, Australia, Feb. 24, 1944   2100 AWT

Didn't do much today. Gave Captain Oviatt a lesson in celestial naviga-tion. Day after tomorrow, United Air Lines starts operating into Townsville instead of here, and I will not see much of my former United associates.

Had a nice V-mail letter from Grace today, written on February 14. The family is all well again and Jimmy is in school once more. That's a relief.

Brisbane, Australia, Feb. 25, 1944   2300 AWT

Spent the day in town doing little of importance. Went to the dentist this morning and had a tooth filled, and found that I had almost procras-tinated too long, as the cavity was nearly too large for filling.

This afternoon I checked in with General Willoughby concerning a ground job I'm supposed to have. He doesn't seem very anxious to have me work in G-2.

Brisbane, Australia, Feb. 26, 1944   1800 AWT

This morning I went to Archer Field and flew the B-25 for over an hour. It is a fine airplane, but with a high wing loading.

Tomorrow morning I am going to take General MacArthur north to the battle area in *Bataan*. It will be an interesting trip for me. I do not expect to be away more than four or five days. Hoped I'd get another letter from Grace before leaving, but no luck.

Port Moresby, New Guinea, Feb. 27, 1944   2200 AWT

We departed from Archer Field early this morning, and proceeded to New Guinea with a stop at Townsville. We had General MacArthur and Admiral Kinkaid aboard. We narrowly averted a crack-up at Townsville when we landed on a short runway and the brakes failed to hold. We departed from Townsville and went to Milne Bay, New Guinea, where we left all of our party; then we proceeded on to Port Moresby to spend a couple of days waiting. We had good weather throughout our trip, which was fortunate. Tuesday afternoon we will go to Finschhafen, where we will pick up General MacArthur and take him back to Brisbane.

Tonight I played some rummy and now I'm a bit tired.

Port Moresby, New Guinea, Feb. 28, 1944   2100 AWT

Was up at a reasonable hour this morning and went to the airport to see Maury Wiley. Unfortunately, he had just departed for Darwin. I was caught in a terrifc rain which lasted about two hours and almost washed my jeep out from under me. Took a tour to Jackson Airport, but there wasn't much activity there in the rain.

Was lazy this afternoon, reading and writing a letter home. Tomorrow we will be leaving for Finschhafen, to pick up the general on the following morning.

Finschhafen, New Guinea, Feb. 29, 1944   1800 AWT

Had a most interesting trip today. We departed from Port Moresby at 0900 hours and took a leisurely tour to Finschhafen by way of Wau, the Markham River valley, Nadzab, and Lae. All of these points were most bitterly contested only a couple of months ago, but now the Japs are really on the run. I saw the enormously rich goldfield at Wau, and I saw enough mahogany timber to furnish almost every house in the United States. Someday, I imagine, someone will exploit some of this unbelievably productive country. Certainly the Germans will never again be permitted to come into this land.

We landed at the single strip here at Finschhafen, and the activity here is almost unbelievable. In a few short weeks the Seabees and the army engineers have transformed this jungle into a bristling army and navy base. It is only ninety miles from the front lines at Saidor and is the jumping-off point for our present offensives. The Sixth Army HQ is here.

We got an army jeep and drove all over the place. I got some pieces of teakwood from the timber here, and I'm going to try to fashion some candlesticks of them. Accommodations here are very rugged, but one cannot expect much in a zone as far forward as this. We expect to depart tomorrow for Port Moresby.

Port Moresby, New Guinea, March 1, 1944   1900 AWT

We met General MacArthur and Admiral Kinkaid at Finschhafen this morning and brought them down here to Moresby. The weather was not good, but not sufficiently bad to prevent us from getting in here.

General MacArthur was in rare good humor this morning. He had accompanied troops in their landing on Manus Island yesterday, actually having gone ashore with them. The landing had been a complete success, and our troops had captured the airstrip with the loss of fewer than ten soldiers. There is considerable cleaning up still to be done on the island, but it appears that the Jap resistance there has been broken completely. This leaves Rabaul and Kavieng practically at our mercy. Not a single Jap airplane opposed the landing.

Tomorrow we will take General MacArthur back to Brisbane.

Brisbane, Australia, March 2, 1944   2200 AWT

We departed from Port Moresby early this morning with General MacArthur and Admiral Kinkaid aboard. The general was most pleased over the success of the landings in the Admiralty Islands. He personally had gone ashore and walked the full length of the airstrip less than two hours after the first troops had reached the beach. I hate to see him take these chances, but he wants to do it and it instills respect in his troops, I guess.

The trip down was without incident, as the weather was quite good. We landed at Townsville for lunch, and then arrived at Archer Field at 1630 hours. I stopped at GHQ on the way in to get my mail, and sure enough there were five letters. I've already read them over two or three times, and I feel much better. We have delivered the general back safely, and the letters tell me that all is well at home, so what more could one ask? Well, I could ask to see Grace and the boys.

Above: General MacArthur used *Bataan*, a B-17 bomber, for his own transportation in the Pacific theater. Courtesy U.S. Army Air Force. *Below:* General MacArthur with troops on Los Negros Island. Courtesy U.S. Army.

Brisbane, Australia, March 3, 1944   2230 AWT

Today has been rather aimless. I've learned something about my ground job in G-2. It is most interesting, and I certainly get all of the latest information on the Japs. There is a trip to Sydney and Melbourne tomorrow in the B-25, and I could take it, but I have a dental appointment which I do not want to miss. So Colonel Godman will go on the trip.

Seeley Hall, vice-president of United Air Lines, was in town, so I drove out to Amberley and visited with him for an hour. He assured me that everything on the airline was going well, and that there would be plenty of work for me to come back to when the war was over.

Brisbane, Australia, March 4, 1944   1900 AWT

Spent two hours at my job in G-2 this morning and then attended the daily operations and intelligence meeting on the war situation. This is always an interesting meeting. The latest developments with ground, naval, and air forces are outlined and discussed. Of course it is all very secret information.

Admiral (Bull) Halsey came to call on General MacArthur today, and he is one tough-looking character. I guess his disposition matches his character. I'd like to be listening to him and General MacArthur in their discussions.

My boss is due for congratulations. The following clipping appeared in today's paper:

Promotion for MacArthur's Chief of Staff
WASHINGTON, March 3 (AAP): President Roosevelt has nominated for promotion to the rank of lieutenant-general Major-General Richard K. Sutherland (Chief of Staff to General MacArthur) and Major-General Holland Smith (Marine Corps) who led the Tarawa and Kwajalein invasions.

No letters today. Guess I'll go to bed early, nurse my aching jaw, and feel sorry for myself.

Brisbane, Australia, March 5, 1944   2045 AWT

This morning I was up rather late and went directly to the office. Had some interesting work to do there relative to the Jap air force, attended the regular situations conference, and then went to Gregory Terrace for lunch. My tooth extraction was not bothering me today.

This afternoon I went to Archer Field and flew *Bataan* for a couple of hours just to practice and keep my technical skill at an acceptable

Gen. Richard K. Sutherland with his third star.

level. I'm a firm believer in the adage that practice makes perfect, and I can't afford to be much less than perfect.

No letters today. That always makes me a little sad, but when they do arrive there will be more of them.

Brisbane, Australia, March 6, 1944   2300 AWT

I worked in the office until noon today and then went to Archer Field and flew the B-25 until about 1630 hours, having much fun with it. To-night Colonel Baedcke and Captain Oviatt came by and had dinner with me. We had a very pleasant evening of conversation.

No letter for me today.

Brisbane, Australia, March 7, 1944   2045 AWT

Just two months today since I departed from San Francisco and all that is dear to me. Still no letters for me today. I've had only nine letters in two months, and I've really begun to feel sorry for myself. Everyone else gets letters every day, and I go weeks without any. Wonder if my family has forgotten me. Of course I know that is not true, but I do get very lonesome.

I remained in the office all day today, not feeling too ambitious. This afternoon I saw the first official, but secret, showing of the moving picture taken of the Arawe and Cape Gloucester landings. It was a very interesting picture, and most instructive concerning the way in which an amphibious landing is planned and executed.

Tomorrow I will probably depart for Finschhafen and the New Guinea battlefront again. A trip is going and I'm not just certain whether Hank Godman will take it or whether I will. I've been unable to locate Hank today.

[I have begun to notice a subtle but distinct change in my personal status around GHQ. Up until now, when not occupied with flying duties, I have been a bit of a lost soul. I spend considerable time talking with General Sutherland, both on his frequent early-morning recreational flights with me and in his office. Only occasionally do I talk with General MacArthur, and then usually about airplane matters. I have complained mildly to General Sutherland that when not busy with aircraft affairs I am bored with inactivity while on my assignment in G-2. I do not think General Willoughby appreciates my presence in G-2, due to my direct access to Generals MacArthur and Sutherland. General Sutherland has gone on a quick trip to Washington; he said he would make some other arrangements for me when he returned.

The reason for his trip is that his mother has died unexpectedly. Also, our successful conquest of Cape Gloucester and the Admiralty Islands has given General MacArthur the assurance he needs to bypass Hansa Bay and Wewak on the north coast of New Guinea. But this will expose our right flank to any long drive directly to Hollandia, since the Japanese conceivably could come out of the islands to the north with heavy naval forces and attack our huge convoy. We will need protection by our own heavy naval vessels located in the Central Pacific. That will require approval by the Joint Chiefs of Staff. General Sutherland has taken elements of the plan to Washington since he will be there anyway. He told me also that he had developed an elevated blood pressure and wanted to see if doctors at Walter Reed Hospital in Washington had any better medication that might help.]

Brisbane, Australia, March 8, 1944   2300 AWT

Today I got the trip all arranged to depart at 1500 hours, and even went to the airport, and then Colonel Godman announced that he would be taking the trip. That's a good example of the way the army does things, however. Rank accounts for everything. Of course I have to take it in good form, because I also get certain privileges by virtue of my rank, and a good soldier has to take orders as well as give them. I will certainly be pleased when General Sutherland returns.

No letters today. I'm a forgotten man.

Tonight I played bridge with Colonel Wilson and Colonel Thomas.

Brisbane, Australia, March 9, 1944   2030 AWT

Today has been a dull day. Worked in the office most of the day as it was rainy. Received a package from Grace and it contained a bottle of rum, my hunting knife, my notebook, a can of popcorn, and 120 of my favorite razor blades. Then late this afternoon I got two V-mail letters from Grace. There was not a word concerning the two boys, but she apparently has her hands full as Elva has arrived there but is very ill.

Brisbane, Australia, March 10, 1944   2100 AWT

Spent this day in the office, not having the inclination to fly. Have felt pretty low the last few days, with no flying to do and everything more or less against me. Perhaps it's my imagination, but I think there is more and more resentment against me here. I suppose that is only natural. With General Sutherland away, more and more people find reasons to put me in my place.

Brisbane, Australia, March 11, 1944   2300 AWT

This morning I spent in the office and accomplished little. This afternoon I went to Archer Field and flew the B-25 for a couple of hours. Can't seem to shake off this feeling of depression. If only I had more work to do I could be much happier. Tonight I had dinner with Colonel Wilson and Colonel Thomas. Wrote another letter to Grace but received none. Now to bed—lonely and blue and restless.

Brisbane, Australia, March 12, 1944   1915 AWT

Today I had very little to do. I took a long walk this morning, and then at the office there was very little to be done. I wrote four letters to people in the States. When the chief of staff finally returns, if he ever does, perhaps things will start happening. I still have hopes that he will obtain a C-54 for us while he is in Washington.

Brisbane, Australia, March 13, 1944   2015 AWT

This morning was rather dull, with only a few communiqués to read to pass the time. At noon I received a letter from Wayne and Marge, giving me all of the news from Missouri.

The afternoon was equally dull, and I was in my room at 1800 hours when Colonel Lehrbas called to tell me that General MacArthur wished to see me. I reported to the general's office immediately, and he advised me of a proposed trip a few days hence. I shall not give details here for security reasons. He made me commit myself that *Bataan* would be ready for service, even though I was aware that two engines were being changed in it. I called the field to have them get the night crews busy, because if the airplane is not ready, it will certainly be my neck.

I set up a trip for myself to Townsville and return tomorrow in the B-25. I want to see how the airplane performs on a trip, and I also want to look over some of the airports on the way up.

No letter from Grace today.

Brisbane, Australia, March 14, 1944   2200 AWT

Was up rather early this morning and took off from Archer Field at 0900 hours for Townsville. Had a most pleasant trip up along the coastline and looked over the airports at Rockhampton, Mackay, and Bowen on the way. Returned this afternoon, having made the round trip of 1,400 miles in six hours and twenty minutes. Not bad. Karl Oviatt went with me. The B-25 behaved very well and I like the airplane more each time I fly it. The chief criticism is the extreme noise level present while flying.

Above: A B-25 light bomber used extensively in New Guinea. *Below:* The B-24 bomber. Photographs courtesy North American Aviation (Rockwell International).

Brisbane, Australia, March 15, 1944   2330 AWT

Today was quiet until about 1600 hours. At that time General Marshall came into my office and told me to plan on taking Colonel Sverdrup to Momote airstrip on Los Negros Island in the Admiralties in the B-25 on Friday. This was a surprise, as our ground forces are still fighting the Japs over this airfield. The trip will be quite an experience for me, and I'm most pleased to get the assignment. My only regret is that I shall miss taking General MacArthur to Canberra on Friday.

There are many details for this trip which will have to be carefully worked out. We will have to go armed, as we can expect Jap interception around the Admiralties, and I'll want some good gunners with me. I'll also want to be fully equipped for jungle or water survival in case we should be shot down. I'll be busy tomorrow, testing the airplane, the guns, etc. It will be fun.

Still no more letters from Grace.

Brisbane, Australia, March 16, 1944   2000 AWT

Spent the morning making all of the small preliminary preparations relative to my trip tomorrow. I'm quite thrilled about it because it will be the first time I'll actually be in an area where active fighting is occurring. The airstrip where I am planning to land is still in range of gunfire from the Jap forces and is still being attacked by their air force. Test-flew the airplane and fired all of the guns out at sea this afternoon, and now all is ready for our departure at 0700 hours tomorrow morning.

Had two V-mail letters from Grace today so now I'm much happier. For the first time she has told me something about the boys and their development.

Finschhafen, New Guinea, March 17, 1944   2000 AWT

We took off from Archer Field in the B-25 this morning and proceeded to Townsville, where we landed only long enough to refuel. Then we departed for Finschhafen. We flew the 1,600 miles between Brisbane and Finschhafen in just seven hours. It was a fine trip in every way, and we had three fine passengers aboard: General Hutchings, Colonel Sverdrup, and war correspondent Earnie King.

Here at Finch I got all of the information relative to approaching and landing at Momote Airstrip in the Admiralties. Fighting is still going on at the strip, and even our own antiaircraft gunners have quick trigger fingers. We are departing tomorrow morning at 0800 hours and are now faced with an unpleasant stay here at Finschhafen. Living facilities here are unimproved since our last visit.

Port Moresby, New Guinea, March 18, 1944   2230 AWT

Today has been one of the most exciting days I've ever spent. We departed from Finschhafen as planned and had an uneventful trip of one and a half hours to the Admiralties. We saw no Jap airplanes and had fair cloud cover most of the way. We very nearly had a minor crack-up in landing on the Momote strip, however. The strip is quite short for use by a B-25 type of airplane, as it lands rather "hot" when loaded. I landed as short as was possible, but when I applied brakes to stop the landing roll, the left brake failed to function. This threw the airplane violently to the right, and I almost ran into a mound of coral before I could regain control. Fortunately the emergency air brake worked and I escaped what could have been a nasty spill.

Fighting is still active here around the strip. The airplane which landed directly ahead of me circled a bit too widely around the field and received eight bullet holes in his wing. If I was fired upon by the Japs from the ground, at least they were unable to hit me.

After landing, we went down to the command post, where my party conferred with General Krueger and General Swift. Then I was free until 1400 hours to look over the battlefield from as close as I desired to get to it. Sporadic shooting was continuing all the time. I looked over three Jap Zeros which had been captured and then went down to where some land action had occurred. To date our forces have buried about 1,500 Jap dead here in the vicinity of the airstrip, but dozens of them remain unburied. The stench of the rotting human flesh is almost unbelievable. The putrefaction and the flies working together here in this hot sun remove the flesh from the Jap skeletons in two days, but the stench remains. The reason why the bodies have not been buried is that they are located in areas where land mines are planted, and we haven't been able as yet to spare enough men from the fighting to sweep the area.

In many cases our Seabees covered over many of the Japs still alive in their foxholes, using bulldozers to overrun them. Our boys aren't showing the enemy any mercy. I talked to several of the soldiers who are doing the fighting, and they are plenty tough men. One can have all of the Jap souvenirs he wants by merely picking them off the rotting dead Jap soldiers, but I can't work up much enthusiasm for that sort of thing.

General Hutchings was ready to depart at about 1400 hours for Milne Bay, and we had a nice trip down, making it in three hours. The weather at Milne was not too good, but we got in all right. After refueling we came on here to Port Moresby.

Port Moresby, New Guinea, March 19, 1944   1900 AWT

We are remaining here today to get some work done on our B-25, as it needs a new set of brakes and a new generator. We will go back to Momote early tomorrow morning to pick up our party and take them to Saidor and Nadzab. I went to the airport this morning to get the work under way on the airplane. Went back to the airport again this afternoon to pick up some fresh newspapers from the States. Also took a sunbath and wrote a letter to Grace.

Nadzab, New Guinea, March 20, 1944   2015 AWT

This has been a long and tiring day. Was up at 0500 hours this morning at Port Moresby and took off for Momote. Arrived there at midmorning without encountering any Jap air interception.

Since Colonel Sverdrup was not ready to depart, I took the opportunity to spend a couple of hours on the battlefield. A ground battle is something about which I know very little, but in a short time I saw enough to realize that war is not a pretty thing. Rather heavy firing was continuing in the jungle, and our artillery located alongside the airstrip was firing support over our heads. This sort of thing has a weird fascination which I suppose finds its roots in the ever-present thrill of danger. The dead and rotting Japs were fascinating because of their grotesque, mutilated forms and their almost-fleshless grinning skulls. The soldiers who were fighting in this sector were Arizona Indians, and they are certainly living up to their reputation in this type of warfare. I brought up about two dozen copies of late magazines from the States, and distributed them to the men on the battlefield. Some of the soldiers almost cried upon receiving this one small, impersonal contact with home.

We departed in late morning for Saidor, which is only a few miles from the Jap airstrips at Madang and Alexhaven. Although we were thoroughly prepared for it, we again got no Jap interception. We remained at Saidor about two hours and then went to Finschhafen, where we stayed for an hour. In late afternoon we took off for Nadzab, which is the main base of the Fifth Air Force. I met General Wurtsmith again, and he told me that if I ever got tired of flying for GHQ, then he would always have a job for me. He is a nice guy. He put me up in the general officers' quarters for tonight, and I am indeed well provided for.

Port Moresby, New Guinea, March 21, 1944 2130 AWT

After a fine breakfast this morning we took off for Lae. We were there only a few minutes and then went to Milne Bay. This took us well out of the war zone. I had thus made at least one landing at every forward airdrome and did not see a Jap airplane except for a few on the ground. A pleasant disappointment.

We remained at Milne Bay about four hours, and the heat was almost stifling. From Milne Bay we came here to Port Moresby, where we are spending the night in comparative luxury. Tomorrow we will return to Brisbane.

12

Planning the Next Move

MARCH–MAY, 1944

Brisbane, Australia, March 22, 1944   2230 AWT

Up at 0500 hours again this morning and then an easy six-hour trip to Brisbane with a short stop at Townsville for fuel.

It's interesting to note that on this trip I flew 7,200 miles in thirty-three flying hours, and I've become quite fond of the sturdy B-25, even with all of its tricks.

I'm a tired and relaxed man now and am enjoying a fine bottle of beer.

Brisbane, Australia, March 23, 1944   2030 AWT

Early this morning I had an hour's visit with General Sutherland. He was in good humor, and he kept generals and admirals waiting outside his door while we talked flying. He told me all about his trip to the States and his many experiences there.

[I told him that my work in G-2 was most unsatisfactory from my standpoint and that I was wasting some mental assets that should be usable somewhere. Shortly after that he arranged for me to have a desk in the anteroom near his and General MacArthur's offices. He explained to me he had wanted to make me his aide and thought he could do so when he received his third star. However, his analysis of the army's table of organization at that time was that it did not permit any chief of staff to have an aide. He said he would arrange with the clerical staff to see that most of the interesting incoming radiograms and other documents would be routed over my desk insofar as was practicable; if I were out of the office on flight duties, or other activities, the material would merely bypass my desk. I would also be given the responsibility of preparing certain outgoing documents for transmission.

This arrangement is entirely satisfactory to me and provides me with a vantage point enjoyed by few others in the command. Additionally, it affords me an opportunity to observe much of the day-to-day interaction between the commander and his chief of staff. This is an intriguing situation, involving two men who complement each other, who need each other, who are intimate acquaintances rather than intimate friends, and who have great respect for each other.

Much to my amazement I am accepted immediately as an audience of one even when the most involved strategic concepts are being debated by the two of them. When I am in General MacArthur's or General Sutherland's office and the other enters to continue some aspect of a long-standing discussion, they talk freely in my presence and do not suggest that I leave. To me it is a fascinating experience. I am rapidly gaining an insight into how these two men work together. Rarely do their discussions involve any subject not related directly to the military effort or to the top-echelon commanders who are executing it. Neither of the men engages in small talk in my presence, and I doubt if they do so at other times. I have come to realize that, after the morning dispatches have been digested each day, both men have many hours of boredom, during which they often like to have someone to talk with or to act as a sounding board.

Perhaps General Sutherland is the only individual in the theater who can and does stoutly voice disagreement directly to General MacArthur when he feels the commander in chief is wrong. I believe such opinions often are appreciated.

In the army hierarchy the commander in chief always has the ultimate responsibility and authority for all policy decisions. If he does not like the way his chief of staff is performing, he can remove him at will. The chief of staff directs the operations, and all headquarters personnel, except for the personal staff of the commander in chief, come directly under his command. Obviously the two must act as a team if the various missions are to be accomplished efficiently. In our theater there certainly is no individual other than General Sutherland who has the knowledge, experience, and perspective to advise General MacArthur.]

I was disappointed when General Sutherland told me that we're not getting a C-54 for the present. However, it appears that he is going to keep me busy enough with the equipment we now have, and in the office. I'm to take him north next week to the battle area to confer with the generals in the field. His three stars look good on him and he certainly deserves the promotion.

Brisbane, Australia, March 24, 1944   2330 AWT

Made many preparations for the trip north with General Sutherland next week. These included drawing new charts and preparing them, and going to Archer Field to check on the status of the airplane. Things really get done, and I'm feeling much better about my job now that General Sutherland has returned from Washington. His presence seems to electrify everything here around GHQ. He certainly is one of the finest and most capable men I have ever had the pleasure of knowing.

[In addition to General Sutherland, the five officers on the staff whom General MacArthur relies on for prosecuting the war carry the bulk of the unheralded effort.

Maj. Gen. Stephen J. Chamberlin (G-3) is a most dedicated and experienced soldier who does a plodding but superb job in planning the details of the operations. He is a native of Kansas, was a graduate of West Point in 1912, and served in the Philippines in 1915. During World War I he was in charge of moving one and a half million troops to Europe from New Jersey. Shortly after World War II started he went to Australia to spearhead the running of the Japanese blockade of the Philippines and succeeded in delivering some supplies to the besieged MacArthur in Manila.

Lt. Gen. George C. Kenney is the aggressive commander of the Fifth Air Force. Although he was born in Nova Scotia in 1889, his parents were American. He was graduated from MIT, worked as an engineer in Quebec, and completed flight training with the Signal Corps in 1917. He was a fighter pilot in France in World War I. He remained with the Air Corps and in July, 1942, joined MacArthur in Australia, where he activated the Fifth Air Force. (In June, 1944, he was given command of the Far East Air Forces, to which he added the Thirteenth Air Force.) By accomplishments and insight he helped to convince MacArthur that command of the air was an absolute essential for successful sustained ground and seaborne offensives.

Vice Adm. Thomas C. Kinkaid of New Hampshire was born into the navy tradition, since his father before him had been an admiral. He was a graduate of the Naval Academy in 1908. He had participated in several engagements in the Pacific before joining MacArthur in November, 1943, for the battle of New Britain. (From that time on, through the Philippine campaign, he remained with the general as commander of the Seventh Fleet.) He is an astute expert on naval strategy but occasionally appears to be indecisive. At times I believe General MacArthur becomes impatient with him, and I know General Sutherland does. Fortunately he has an aggressive assistant in Rear Adm. Daniel E. Barbey, who commands the amphibious forces on most landings.

Lt. Gen. Walter Krueger is the patient and cautious commander of the Sixth Army. He was born in Prussia in 1881 and brought at an early age to the United States, where he attended schools in the Midwest. He enlisted in the army for the Spanish American War in 1898. He advanced through the ranks, served in the Philippine insurrection in 1901, and was promoted to second lieutenant. He attended many military training schools. He was made a brigadier general in 1936 and advanced rapidly to Major General, then to Lieutenant General in 1941. In February, 1943, General MacArthur requested his assignment, and he was sent to activate the Sixth Army. He carries the major responsibility for ground and amphibious action throughout New Guinea. By nature his actions are deliberate and methodical, and at times MacArthur expresses some impatience with these traits.

Maj. Gen. Charles A. Willoughby, chief of intelligence (G-2), was born in Germany in 1892 and became a naturalized citizen of the United States in 1910. He retains the appearance and bearing of a Hollywood version of a Prussian officer, even including a distinct German accent. He was schooled in various army training colleges and was on Corregidor when the Japanese attack came. He presides over his organization in a pompous and ironhanded manner and at times is inclined to be abrasive.

Thus the six men upon whom General MacArthur depends to plan and execute the war are a heterogeneous combination. Two are graduates of the national military academies (Chamberlin and Kinkaid). Two are foreign born (Krueger and Willoughby). Two were selected by MacArthur to accompany him when he departed from Corregidor for Australia (Sutherland and Willoughby). Although all are career military officers, each individual except Sutherland had been so preoccupied with his own military specialty that none had acquired the broad outlook and vision necessary to toss around the various aspects of the total war effort with the commander in chief. Also, I do not believe any of them have the temerity to argue with General MacArthur even if they think the general is wrong. Some might express mild doubts, but I believe that would be the extent of their protests.

Krueger, Kenney, and Kinkaid are referred to around the shop as MacArthur's KKK. Of course, no one uses that nomenclature in MacArthur's presence because the implication might be misunderstood.]

Brisbane, Australia, March 25, 1944   2000 AWT

Had two talks with General Sutherland today, and each time I seem to come away inspired. I guess such reactions in his subordinates are the secret of his extraordinary leadership.

General Sutherland took me into General MacArthur's office with him to discuss a possible trip.

[The commander in chief began by saying that the subject under discussion was not to be mentioned outside that room under any conditions, that my personal safety as well as the lives of many others might depend on complete secrecy.

Many groups of guerrillas had been carrying on as best they could in the Philippines, and our only very limited communication with some of them was by means of submarines and occasionally radio. Most of the freedom fighters were unaware of this very secret operation, as it was quite difficult for these groups to communicate with each other. One group on Mindanao had relayed out the information that they believed they could properly accommodate an airplane if it could be flown into and out of their area. General MacArthur asked me to explore the possibility of such an undertaking, using what meager information was available, and report back to him my opinion on its feasibility.

There were several people in headquarters each of whom had bits of information about the area involved. No detailed mapping had ever been done of most of Mindanao. General MacArthur told me as much as he knew. The facts generally were as follows. The Filipinos, mostly Moros in this area I believe, had laboriously cleared a dirt landing area in a jungle well to the northwest of the coastal village of Cotabato in western Mindanao, north of Illana Bay near Sugar Loaf Mountain. As they had prepared the ground, they had built on it a native village, consisting of a number of small lightweight thatched huts. These had been constructed so that they could be picked up and carried off the airstrip by many groups of men. The huts afforded splendid camouflage not only for their work but for the end product of their efforts—the landing area. The idea was that the Filipinos would carry the huts off the cleared area the night the landing was to be made and replace them in their original positions immediately after the landing. The airplane would be concealed throughout the following day by covering it with palm fronds and other vegetable matter, which they would cut and hold in readiness. The return trip takeoff would be made after dark the next night.

The general said such an operation, if successful, would be electrifying for many of the natives, who by this time must have been wondering if they were not engaged in a completely hopeless struggle. Word of a successful flight would spread rapidly, at least through Mindanao. He asked me carefully to calculate the amount of cargo I could take aboard the aircraft. It would consist almost entirely of sulfa drugs and counterfeit Japanese-printed Philippine peso notes of small denomination. We had obtained specimens of this paper money, and millions of pesos' worth of the notes had been printed for such use as we could make of them.

The general explained the drugs would be most helpful to the natives for treating some of the wounded and for certain illnesses. The paper peso notes would enable the guerrillas to purchase what items they could from the occupational army and might be useful in bribing some individuals in the enemy forces. He told me the guerrillas had been able to steal a number of drums of gasoline, which he hoped would be suitable to use on my return trip.

The general then handed me a note on which was handwritten, without any title, the following:

8° 09'N, 123° 20'E—30 Km from Silos in Silos Valley, just north of Sugar Loaf Mountains. Runway bears 10. Cultivated around field. Line of hills to north but east of approach from N. runway 7000' × 200'. River at each end.

He cautioned me not to rely too much on the exact location of the area, since all the maps were unreliable. He asked me to plan very carefully and report back to him by April 20.

I left his office with my mind reeling, trying to grasp the many avenues that had to be explored. There were such items as fuel consumption, fuel replenishment possibilities, navigation problems; spare parts for the aircraft to be carried; point of departure (would Hollandia or Biak Island possibly be available in a few weeks, or would I have to plan for a longer flight starting from Darwin, Australia?). Where did the Japanese have radar installations? Could I possibly install airborne radar in my plane, primitive as it was at the time, to avoid colliding with rocks and islands en route during very-low-altitude flying over the ocean? What skills would I need among crew members?

General MacArthur had not said specifically that I was to operate the flight personally, but I felt that that was what he intended. On the way out of the office I asked General Sutherland if he thought I was to be the pilot. His reply was very flattering. He said it was just possible that General MacArthur thought I had become too valuable around GHQ to risk on the trip and might want me to select another pilot for the mission.

At any rate, I did not have the opportunity to plunge into these planning problems immediately, as General Sutherland said he wanted me to take him to New Guinea early the following morning.]

I spent most of the day working on a new set of charts for the trip north. I'm taking an Air Force colonel as my copilot, and I think he is somewhat burned up. The general wants it that way, however, so that's the way it will be. Colonel Godman took the B-25 north yesterday and is now down with engine trouble at Port Moresby. Perhaps I shall be able to recover my map case from him as we go through on our trip north next Monday.

Had two letters from Grace today and they were such fine letters. All about herself and the boys and so full of news and human interest.

Brisbane, Australia, March 26, 1944   2000 AWT

Will not get away on my trip tomorrow as expected, because Admiral Nimitz is in town and he and General MacArthur are having long conferences. It now appears that it will be at least Tuesday, and perhaps Wednesday, before we can depart.

I have been rather busy today. Have talked to General Sutherland twice and have also test-flown the C-47. It may be just as well that we are not going tomorrow, as there is a deep tropical disturbance over the Coral Sea off Moresby.

Brisbane, Australia, March 27, 1944   1930 AWT

Spent all day at Archer Field getting a new-type radio compass installed in the C-47. General Sutherland had asked Colonel Godman to do it two months ago, and when he found that it had not been done, he requested me to do it. Just about completed the installation today, and tomorrow I'll be able to check it in the air. Our trip north has now been postponed until Wednesday because the weather is quite bad north of here. It has been cold and rainy here all day, reminiscent of San Francisco weather.

The big conferences here have ended, and now I guess we are to start to work carrying out the plans. The next two or three months are going to be most interesting. Big things are about due to happen.

Grace has been writing very faithfully here of late. I have just finished a long letter to her—no news to tell, but just a lot of visiting.

Brisbane, Australia, March 28, 1944   1945 AWT

I spent the entire day at Archer Field getting some last-minute work done on the airplane and making certain that everything was in readiness for our departure tomorrow morning at 0600 hours. I have learned by hard experience that the best way to be certain is to be present on the job myself. I talked to General Sutherland a few minutes ago and he is going to telephone me this evening as to the exact hour of our departure. He is a busy man and cannot always do as he would like.

Shucks! Just had a call from the general and he will be unable to leave now until Thursday morning. I have all of the food ready, etc. Oh well, that's what I'm paid for. The weather is still quite bad up the coast.

No letters today, but then I expect the bad weather has had something to do with that.

Brisbane, Australia, March 29, 1944   1830 AWT

This has been a long and discouraging day in many ways. I'm merely waiting for the general to catch up with his work so that he can get away on the trip north. I had a long talk with him again today, and he told me many secret and exciting things, but they are so secret that I shall write nothing about them in this diary. I asked him for permission to do one of the pending trips as I think I am the most capable man in the theater for this sort of thing.

We are definitely leaving at 0530 hours tomorrow morning. I hope the food hasn't all spoiled. I made another trip to Archer Field this afternoon to check and see if all was in readiness. Also checked the weather, and it appears that we should have a good trip.

Port Moresby, New Guinea, March 30, 1944 2000 AWT

We departed from Brisbane at 0645 hours this morning and came here, with a stop at Cairns, Queensland, for fuel. The weather was generally good except in the area around Cairns. General Sutherland and WAC captain Bessemer-Clark were our only important passengers. Tonight Maury Wiley and Major Tillman came over from their base to have dinner with me.

Must be up very early again tomorrow.

Nadzab, New Guinea, March 31, 1944 2030 AWT

This has been an interesting day. We came out of Moresby early this morning and inspected the old battlegrounds of Salamaua and Lae. Then, immediately after landing here at Nadzab, we went directly to the advance headquarters of the Fifth Air Force. The big aerial strike against the Japanese at Hollandia was in progress, and we spent several hours listening to the returns while Generals Whitehead and Wurtsmith put on their usual energetic interpretation. This was most interesting to me, as was the process of preparing orders for missions to be carried out the following day. Although all this was excitement enough, more was to follow. At noontime a fire started in the kunai grass in the valley below. A strong breeze carried it along rapidly, and by 3:00 P.M. the fire had reached a huge ammunition dump. Fortunately the dump contained only incendiary bombs, pyrotechnics, and light ammunition, but no large demolition bombs. With considerable apprehension we watched the approach and inevitable culmination of the spectacle from a vantage point in headquarters about 500 feet above and half a mile away from the dump. As the fire gained headway in the storage area, there were great flames and numerous explosions of small bombs. Then without warning there occurred a single terrific blast, which literally knocked us off our feet and displaced the side of the building from the veranda of which we were watching. Several tons of photoflash bombs had exploded simultaneously. It could only be described as a horribly beautiful and "awe-ful" spectacle. Brilliant white magnesium flares and smoke shot hundreds of feet into the air. The resulting concussion wave damaged many remote buildings. The dump burned for many hours, with large parachute flares continually being thrown into the air in all directions. In time the fire progressed sufficiently to engulf a machine gun ammunition storage. These shells began exploding, casting their beautiful red tracers indiscriminately in every direction. The fireworks continued into the night until finally all was quiet.

Tomorrow we leave early for Finschhafen and points north.

Finschhafen, New Guinea, April 1, 1944   2200 AWT

I had an early breakfast with the Fifth Air Force communications officer to learn what I could about the effectiveness of airborne radar. I was attempting to determine if it would, in its primitive state, be useful on my pending secret trip into the Philippines. He suggested I contact the navy since they had done much investigation of radar for use in aircraft for detecting surface obstacles and ships on overwater flights.

Had a nice trip from Nadzab to Finschhafen this morning, and General Sutherland conferred for some time with General Krueger of the Sixth Army. Following this we flew up the coast to Saidor to meet General Gill. General Sutherland invited me to sit in on these conferences. We remained at that congested and dusty place for three hours, and then returned to Finschhafen. We are remaining overnight at GHQ, Sixth Army.

Tonight I saw the movie version of *The Song of Bernadette*, having previously read the book. Very good.

Port Moresby, New Guinea, April 2, 1944   1900 AWT

Arose leisurely this morning and had a beautiful trip over the Owen Stanley Mountains to Moresby. New Guinea is truly a ruggedly beautiful country when seen from the cool, comfortable vantage point of an airplane at 10,000 feet. It is not nearly so inviting, however, from any point on the ground.

It's always nice to get back to the comforts of a comparatively civilized place and to be able to wash away the dirt and grime of the forward battle areas. I'm so much more fortunate than the boys who have to live up there for months on end.

2200 AWT

The general has just informed me that we will not be going back to Brisbane until Wednesday. We will remain here tomorrow, go to Goodenough Island Tuesday, and return home Wednesday.

Port Moresby, New Guinea, April 3, 1944   1800 AWT

This has been a most unpleasant day for me. I've been vomiting and chilling alternately most of the day, and am feeling most wretched. I'm thankful that this was a day of inactivity, as I would not have been able to do much flying. I'm a little afraid I have a touch of malaria or dysentery, and I'm trying my best to hang on until I get back to Brisbane, as

I would hate to get stuck in the hospital here. Maybe I'll be all right to-morrow. Did manage to get a short letter off to Grace today.

Aboard U.S.S. *Blue Ridge,* April 4, 1944—2100 AWT

Today has been most interesting. We were up early for a 0630 takeoff for Goodenough Island. After a nice trip over, we were met by Generals Eichelberger, Irving, Hardy, and Byers. General Sutherland held a conference with them relative to the present task force, and I was invited to sit in on it. I had lunch with the generals, which is rather unusual for a mere major, and then we departed for Dobodura. There we were met by Admiral Barbey's aide, and brought on a launch out here to the flagship.

As we started to board the *Blue Ridge* from the launch an amusing but embarrassing event, for me, occurred. At the foot of the accommodation ladder leading up to the deck of the ship, I stood aside in the launch to allow General Sutherland to precede me, thinking at that time that senior officers always went first. However, the general kept pushing me and said I should go ahead of him up the ladder. I did so, but when I reached the deck I was not aware that I should first salute the flag, then salute the officer of the deck and request permission to come aboard. I did neither. Later he took me aside and briefed me on various aspects of military etiquette. He said that the reason for the junior officer's going up the ladder first was lost in antiquity. Perhaps at some time long ago some high-ranking officer had been dumped unceremoniously into the water when a ladder had collapsed. Now, to ensure that this did not happen again, the junior officer was symbolically sacrificed for the potential dunking.

Already General MacArthur had instructed me about entering an automobile with a senior officer. The first time I rode from the office to our hotel with him the vehicle was parked in such a manner that we both had to enter the rear seat from the right side. I thought it was proper for me to wait for him to enter first, but he pushed me in ahead of him, then entered. He explained that senior officers sat in the right rear seat, and if the junior officer could not enter from the left side of the auto, it was he who had to do the undignified scramble across the hump in the floor to the opposite side.

There are aspects to my job other than flying airplanes.

I again had dinner with the generals and admirals in the admiral's cabin and then sat through one of the most interesting discussions I have ever been permitted to hear. A variety of subjects were covered, including the naval operation in conjunction with this present task force. Then the discussion turned to the war in Europe and the present implications of world politics. General Sutherland told us a lot about what happened on the inside at the Cairo and Teheran conferences, and a lot more about what is happening and what is to happen in Europe before July. He certainly has his finger on the sources of information in world affairs.

Tonight I'm retiring in style in a stateroom on the top deck of the flagship. The navy goes in for a life of comfort while at sea, but then of course I'm enjoying (temporarily) the facilities provided only for the grade of admiral.

Port Moresby, New Guinea, April 5, 1944   1800 AWT

Had a leisurely breakfast aboard the *Blue Ridge* this morning in typical navy style and then "launched" to the airport. We had a nice trip across the Owen Stanleys to Moresby, and will remain here today and then return to Brisbane tomorrow.

Took a run up into the hills this afternoon for the exercise.

Brisbane, Australia, April 6, 1944   2100 AWT

We departed from Port Moresby early this morning and had a nice trip down. We stopped at Cairns only long enough to refuel, and we arrived here about 1700 hours.

There were six letters awaiting me and I've had a fine evening "living" with my family through the letters. It's so nice to hear all about them. I'm quite tired now, and relaxed after a successful trip.

Brisbane, Australia, April 7, 1944   2300 AWT

Today is Good Friday and the city of Brisbane is closed for a three-day holiday. One would hardly know there was a war on. I had a lot of personal chores to do, but was unable to do any of them.

Spent most of the day in the office, and tonight I went out to Colonel Wilson's to play bridge. I think some big news is going to break for me tomorrow.

Brisbane, Australia, April 8, 1944   2130 AWT

Went to Archer Field this morning and flew *Bataan* for one and a half hours, and then when that ended I went up in a C-47 for two hours of instrument practice.

The trip to New Guinea had cost me several days that I had expected to spend planning the mission to the Philippines, but I had done considerable thinking about it. Since I was committed to give General MacArthur an answer concerning its feasibility by April 20, I went to talk to him immediately to learn if he had any additional information. He did, and said that due to weather conditions and Japanese activities in the area completion of the airstrip had been delayed. I suggested that I go into Mindanao and make a parachute drop of the important cargo. He promptly discarded the idea, saying much of the value of the trip would result from the guerrillas' having participated in a plot to foil the enemy and have an American airplane and crew in their midst. He said I should continue to plan the flight and have all the elements ready when the airstrip was complete. The plan as developed was rather simple. I would use a C-54. On the trip to the Philippines I would fly just above the water under cover of darkness to avoid visual or radar searches. Moreover, if I could fly within approximately 100 feet of the water in the "ground effect" I could obtain considerably better fuel consumption. We would carry a kit of spare parts, consisting of magnetos, spark plugs, a mounted wheel and tire, a wheel jack, tools, hydraulic fluid, engine oil, etc.

I would take a copilot and three mechanics, one of whom would be a radio operator, and I would do my own navigating. The plan was to depart Darwin, Australia, on the night of a full moon, or the night after, in order to have a setting moon to provide some light in crossing the jungle of Mindanao and for landing. The landing would be made a few minutes before sunrise. The guerrillas were to be instructed to build one bonfire on the upwind end of the airstrip and two bonfires on the downwind end. I would land over the two fires and toward the single one. En route I would manage the fuel burnout so as to have at least one tank of pure aviation gasoline remaining for takeoff and climb-out from the airstrip. On the ground during the day we would refuel the other tanks aboard the plane with the automobile gasoline that had been stolen from the Japanese. This presumably had an octane rating well below that normally used by aircraft engines. However, it could be used satisfactorily at reduced cruise power operation, and even if it resulted in damage to one or more engines on the return trip, that would be the least of my worries. If the mission were delayed until after the capture of Hollandia or particularly Biak, the length of the trip would be considerably less.

Brisbane, Australia, April 9, 1944   2100 AWT

Had another letter from Grace today, which was a help. Spent a good part of the day organizing the mission and instructing my crew. There's so much to do.

Brisbane, Australia, April 10, 1944   2200 AWT

Today has been another busy day, with much planning, etc. Now it's a matter of continued planning and preparation until word is received that everything is prepared there to receive us.

Among other things, I flew the C-54 for an hour today. It had been four months since I had flown one, but I managed to handle it satisfactorily. Had a nice letter from Wayne and Marge. Wish I had time to answer it.

Brisbane, Australia, April 11, 1944   2130 AWT

Spent the entire day doing more planning and gathering information. I am trying to spot all Jap troop and airplane dispositions and to memorize them in order that I may avoid them insofar as is possible.

Tonight, after a hard day, I was invited out to Colonel Wilson's house for a surprise birthday party for him. I stayed only a few minutes as most of the guests were generals and I was the only major present. I didn't want to cramp the style in which they were letting their hair down.

Brisbane, Australia, April 12, 1944   2115 AWT

Another morning of checking and rechecking plans, navigation data, and emergency equipment. Then this afternoon I flew the C-54 for a couple of hours. Saw General Sutherland late this afternoon and he wants me to fly with him at 0700 hours tomorrow. That means a 0530 call. Tonight I took a long walk to break in a pair of heavy GI shoes which I will wear on the trip. Then I spent some time studying the stars to make certain that I knew their locations in the heavens, etc.

Brisbane, Australia, April 13, 1944   2210 AWT

This has been a day of checking and rechecking every conceivable item which has to do with the security of my trip. Nothing exciting—just a lot of routine.

Had three letters from Grace today and they were so nice. I can't describe my feelings when I get all the intimate news of my dear family.

Brisbane, Australia, April 14, 1944   2030 AWT

Another day of waiting and endless checking. I am awaiting only a go-ahead signal from the other end now. I am getting splendid cooperation from everyone here.

Had a long talk with General Sutherland tonight at his apartment concerning the details of the trip.

Have been taking two hours of strenuous exercise each night for the past week to put myself in condition for jungle survival if that becomes necessary. I hope it will not.

Had another nice letter from Wayne and Marge.

Brisbane, Australia, April 15, 1944   2030 AWT

Pappy Gunn and I spent hours today planning and rechecking the trip. We went to Amberley Field to inspect the airplane and to test the new fuel system. Then tonight General Sutherland called me in to tell me that the entire Jap First Fleet was moving into the very area where we planned to land. To go ahead with our trip would be almost certain suicide now, so we must postpone it until some future date when the Jap fleet may vacate the area. I'm discouraged in a way, but on the other hand it's a relief to get out from under the great tension which has necessarily accompanied my preparations during the past week. After all, I am not anxious to become a Jap prisoner of war, and I don't particularly desire to have my widow and orphans collect a handful of medals.

[I first became privileged to hear Generals MacArthur and Sutherland engage in their discussions regarding our theater problems and strategies about the first part of April. The first subject concerned the problem of two theaters of operations, the South Pacific and the Southwest Pacific commands. The immediate objective of both commands was completion of the recapture of the Solomon Islands and the conquest of New Guinea. Although there still remained many cleanup operations ahead, in the New Guinea area particularly, there certainly was no continued need for two separate commands. Would they both be consolidated? Would a drastic change be made to have ultimately a single command for the entire Pacific? Would the main thrust be to recapture the Philippines? Or would it be to bypass the Philippines and head for Formosa and the Ryukyu Islands, from which to assault Japan proper, a course apparently favored by the navy?

General MacArthur was adamant in his position that we could not afford to bypass the Philippines. Not only would we be deserting our one and only good friend in the western Pacific, but if the Japanese were left in undisturbed occupation of the Philippines, and we cut off their supply lines to Japan, the Filipinos would suffer even greater deprivation as their bare necessities for existence diminished and were further requisitioned by their captors. He expressed his absolute conviction that if we failed to aid our friends at the earliest possible time, then in future years — long after this war had ended — we would find ourselves completely friendless and unsupported along the vast expanse of the east coast of Asia.

Regarding one of the other alternatives, if we directed our next offensive toward Formosa and the Ryukyus without first invading the Philippines, we would be committed to a lengthy campaign with very long and vulnerable supply lines, exposed on both flanks without benefit of protective land-based air cover. Moreover, our left flank in particular would be unprotected against formidable and nearly self-sufficient, experienced Japanese forces with sanctuaries in the Philippines, China, Indochina, and Indonesia. After the war we would have to withdraw at least from

Formosa, thus leaving us with no suitable military representation off the Asian mainland.

Often General Sutherland would play the devil's advocate, pointing out that our real mission was the capitulation of Japan; that probably the most expeditious way to accomplish this objective would be to strike at the heart of the Japanese homeland, take our losses, and end the conflict as soon as possible. But nothing could deter General MacArthur from his single-purpose reasoning that we had to go by way of the Philippines.

These discussions occurred over a period of several weeks. Many times flight duties interrupted my exposure to the dialogues. On my early-morning recreational flights with General Sutherland, he usually brought me up to date with the latest considerations. If he forgot to brief me, I would ask him, having finally developed the courage to do so, and he did not seem to mind my questions.

There was much discussion between the two men concerning the political implications of the growing effort in the United States to nominate General MacArthur to run against Roosevelt for president. They speculated at length on how this might be prejudicing the decisions which soon had to be made regarding the next objective in the war and who might be the ultimate military commander.

By the end of April General MacArthur obviously had come to a decision that his contribution to the military effort was more important to him personally than belatedly trying to enter the political arena at the top by campaigning for the presidency. He composed a message and sent it on, I believe, April 30, 1944, to the chairman of the Republican National Committee. It definitely and unambiguously stated he would not accept a presidential nomination even if it were tendered him.

In the week following the general's announcement denying his possible candidacy we began receiving newspapers and magazines from the States which contained many editorials relating to his decision. It was interesting to read the variety of reactions. We who had been near him had suspected what his decision would be, but of course did not have the temerity to express an opinion on the subject. It is no small honor to be considered seriously for the world's number-one position. Any normally ambitious man likely would savor the compliment as long as possible.

Some political leaders earlier had made needling statements which had cast aspersions on the general's abilities as a professional soldier. As he stated to General Sutherland, this, and his resentment that the administration held a trump card which it played none too subtly, determined the timing of his rejection announcement. His resentment was that his military status for the remainder of the war might be at stake because of political circumstances.

For the assault on Hollandia, we had assembled an amphibious force far larger than any previously used in the Pacific area. It was considered advisable to establish a temporary advance headquarters echelon at Port Moresby in order to shorten communication lines. Finschhafen was anything but hospitable for this type of establishment, due to weather conditions and lack of continuously accessible port and aircraft facilities, and for the accommodation of large-scale aircraft operations.

During the days prior to the operation all of my flight crews and airplanes were busy flying men and equipment between Brisbane and Port Moresby.]

Tuesday I am to take General MacArthur and his party to New Guinea. So I'll have to make careful plans and do a bit of practicing at flying *Bataan*. I expect to remain in the north for two or three weeks this trip. Then when I return I'll probably resume my plans to go to the Philippines.

Brisbane, Australia, April 16, 1944   1730 AWT

Have spent today in preparing for the trip north with General MacArthur. Went to Archer Field and flew *Bataan* for an hour. I went to Amberley Field to set up the C-54 for a cargo load to Port Moresby for General Sutherland. With GHQ moving temporarily to Port Moresby, much equipment must necessarily go.

Tomorrow I'll fly *Bataan* again for a final check as to its condition. No mail for a couple of days now.

Brisbane, Australia, April 17, 1944   2100 AWT

Many troubles today. Flew *Bataan* again to make certain that it was ready for General MacArthur tomorrow. After I landed it was found that the oil consumption was high on No. 3 engine, but I pronounced it safe to fly, since our stops would be frequent. However, at 1800 hours tonight the engineering officer called to advise that he was grounding the airplane for an engine change. This really put me on the spot, because I had just informed General MacArthur that the airplane was ready to go. We finally arranged to have General MacArthur go in General Kenney's airplane, and tonight we are changing the engine in *Bataan*. On Thursday I will take General Kenney north and then return with General MacArthur when his mission is complete. Worries, worries.

No mail today, but I've been too busy to miss it.

Brisbane, Australia, April 18, 1944   2215 AWT

Had a long chat with General Sutherland this morning, during which I offered my apologies for having let General MacArthur down in not being able to have his airplane ready. He was not much perturbed about it, however.

It's been a hectic day. Among other things, I had to arrange to have the C-54 make two trips to Moresby and two trips to Darwin during my absence. Many details. And I can't get much help from Colonel Godman.

Townsville, Australia, April 19, 1944   2200 AWT

Last night General Sutherland called up to see if I could fly with him this morning at 0700 hours. Of course the answer had to be yes, even though I had already arranged to test *Bataan*. I was unable to contact God-man as he was "sick" but not to be found in his usual hangouts. Finally I arranged to have Seidel test *Bataan* while I flew with the general. After all arrangements had been completed at a late hour, Godman finally called me to tell me he would not approve of Seidel's flying *Bataan*. Anyway, this morning I tested *Bataan* and he flew with the general. I'm certainly having to labor under difficulties and many reversals of statements from Godman. Hope my patience endures.

This afternoon I took off with General Kenney for Townsville and had a nice trip up except for mechanical troubles. About thirty minutes before arrival, the entire electric and hydraulic systems both failed on *Bataan*, and I had to continue on in under real difficulties. I could not lower the landing gear except by hand and had no landing flaps. I had no instruments or radio and no landing lights. The landing was after dark and hazardous, but successful. General Kenney was burned up as our troubles were directly attributable to poor maintenance, all of which comes under his direct control. Perhaps we will get better maintenance control now than we have had in the past.

My airplane is in the repair depot tonight, undergoing a thorough inspection. If the necessary work is completed, we will depart early tomorrow for Nadzab.

Nadzab, New Guinea, April 20, 1944   2015 AST

After a delayed departure this morning, we had a most pleasant trip. Arrived here at 1230 hours and had intended to go back to Port Moresby immediately, but General Kenney asked me to wait until 1500 hours and take General Chamberlin back with me. I waited until 1730 hours and then finally called the general to advise him that we should depart very soon, or the weather and darkness at Moresby would conspire to prevent a safe landing there. Whereupon he decided to remain here overnight and depart at 0600 hours tomorrow. We are very poorly billeted, what with the place so crowded due to the start of the big strike tomorrow.

Port Moresby, New Guinea, April 21, 1944   2015 AST

The trip over the Owen Stanley Mountains this morning was excellent. I really believe General Chamberlin is beginning to like to fly with me. When I took him back to Washington over a year ago, he was very ill at ease in an airplane, but now I think he actually enjoys flying.

I expect to remain here for a few days and then go up to Finschhafen to get General MacArthur.

Port Moresby, New Guinea, April 22, 1944   1830 AST

Had a talk with General Sutherland this morning about some personnel changes among the enlisted men of our airplane crews. Then he told me about the progress of our landing offensives, which began this morning up the coast of New Guinea as far as Hollandia. The operation seems to be progressing much better than the general had even dared to hope.

This afternoon I gave Captain Oviatt, my copilot, some practice landing in *Bataan*. Conditions were a bit against him, so he will need more practice before I can safely check him out.

Had my usual two-mile run and hill-climbing exercise this morning. I'm getting back into fair physical condition again.

Port Moresby, New Guinea, April 23, 1944   2000 AST

A fine, lazy Sunday today. Had intended to fly, but *Bataan* was being worked on. Had my exercise and then remained around my quarters, reading and writing letters.

Tonight General Sutherland telephoned to advise that General MacArthur will arrive by cruiser at Finschhafen early tomorrow morning. I am to be at Finschhafen with *Bataan* not later than 0700 hours, which will mean that I'll have to take off at 0530. Hope I can give the general a nice trip across the hump, as he will be quite tired already. He went ashore with the troops at three places during the landings on the north coast of New Guinea. He is getting rather old for all of that activity.

Port Moresby, New Guinea, April 24, 1944   1930 AST

Was up at 0400 hours this morning and arrived at Finschhafen at 0700 hours. The *Nashville*, with General MacArthur aboard, was just casting anchor as we landed and we made perfect contact. The general was in rare good humor due to the success of our landings. He even got familiar with me and now calls me "Dusty." Quite a tribute, coming from him.

Everything clicked on the trip down. I was fortunate enough to make a perfect takeoff and landing, and there was not a ripple in the air en route.

I'm almost proud of myself, as one of my tasks here is to build up his confidence in me so that he will lose the aversion he now has toward flying.

[On the way to Port Moresby the general stood in a cramped position in the cockpit and wanted me to point out the battlefields of Lae, Morobe, and Buna and then the summit of the Owen Stanley mountain range.]

At my quarters, I found nine nice letters awaiting me, including four from Grace. It would be almost unbearable here if I were not able to visit with her constantly through the delayed medium of our letters.

It was raining today, so I passed up my usual run for exercise.

Grace sent a fine package to me. It contained many items which I need very badly and which I am unable to buy here.

Port Moresby, New Guinea, April 25, 1944   2030 AST

Had two talks with General Sutherland today, one about the progress of the war and the other about obtaining some radar equipment. I'm going to take a B-25 over to Nadzab tomorrow morning to get some of the apparatus. Have been studying something about radar this afternoon. I am going to go to school for a couple of days when I reach Brisbane.

I took my usual run this morning and tonight went to a movie.

Port Moresby, New Guinea, April 26, 1944   2330 AST

The B-25 was not flyable today so I took *Bataan* to Nadzab and obtained the radar equipment I wanted. Had a beautiful trip over and back and took a load of the GHQ officers along to see the country. Most of them had never been north of Port Moresby.

Port Moresby, New Guinea, April 27, 1944   2300 AST

Took General MacArthur to Milne Bay this morning, and the weather was not good. Managed to get in all right, but it poured rain nearly the whole time we were there. We returned in the afternoon, and had much better weather. The general was in good humor and I'm definitely "Dusty" to him now.

Had two fine letters from Grace today.

Port Moresby, New Guinea, April 28, 1944   2030 AST

Had an inactive day today. Went to the airport for a while, then had my daily run.

I almost blew my top tonight. General MacArthur wanted to go to Dobodura early tomorrow morning, so I made all arrangements for early calls for myself and crew, transportation, etc. Then a few minutes ago Colonel Godman telephoned to tell me that he was going to take the trip. Some more of the "war of nerves" between the two of us, and I almost lost my temper, which would have been bad. The least he could have done was to advise me earlier, but he is famous for not being able to make up his mind. He is acting very much like a spoiled child, but there is little I can do about it except to await the inevitable showdown between us.

Port Moresby, New Guinea, April 29, 1944   2330 AST

Did little of a practical nature today. Godman took the trip to Dobo-dura and I flew locally with General Sutherland. Had a nice flight. Tonight I played poker and won about fifty-five dollars.

Port Moresby, New Guinea, April 30, 1944   2030 AST

Took General Sutherland to Nadzab and Finschhafen this morning. Had fine weather and we were back here for lunch. This afternoon I set up a trip to take General MacArthur back to Brisbane tomorrow with a stop at Townsville. The advance echelon of GHQ is moving back to Brisbane, since the Hollandia operation has been virtually completed.

Brisbane, Australia, May 1, 1944   2100 AST

This has been a fine day. This morning I was up early to make certain that all was in readiness for General MacArthur's departure. He arrived at the airport on schedule and said something very complimentary to me. Upon entering the airplane, he said, "You know, Dusty, I never worry about the weather or the airplane when you are flying me." We had an excellent trip down, with a stop at Townsville for lunch.

[The general was fascinated with the aerial view of the Great Barrier Reef, and he remained in the cockpit as we detoured away from the coast-line to inspect it from a low altitude.]

Had some mail, and now, after a fine dinner, I am relaxing among the accepted comforts of civilization once more.

Brisbane, Australia, May 2, 1944   2115 AST

Have had a busy day. Have again started to work on the trip into the Philippines, and am now installing certain radar equipment in the airplane. There are so many details to be planned and executed. I am trying to get everything set for a departure on Saturday night.

Brisbane, Australia, May 3, 1944   2015 AST

Had a long conference with General Sutherland this morning and then spent most of the day at Amberley Field supervising the installation of the radar equipment, etc. Am now going to try to depart on the special mission on Saturday night.

Tomorrow I am taking the *Bataan* to Townsville to place it in the air depot for a general overhaul. I will return tomorrow night, by which time I hope that the C-54 work will be almost completed.

Brisbane, Australia, May 4, 1944   2100 AST

This morning I was up early and took *Bataan* to Townsville for a complete overhaul. Had a rather slow trip up, delivered the airplane to the depot, and then rode back here to Brisbane in a B-25, which came to Townsville to get me.

When I arrived here tonight there were two letters from Grace. My, how I love that woman!

Brisbane, Australia, May 5, 1944   2015 AST

Went to Amberley today to check on the radar installation in the airplane. Then I returned to the hotel and refigured all of the navigation, power curve, and fuel consumption data for the trip for the nth time. By tomorrow night I'll be entirely ready to go, although I have definitely postponed the departure until Sunday night.

Two more nice letters from Grace.

Brisbane, Australia, May 6, 1944   1700 AST

When I talked with General Sutherland this morning he told me that he had just about made up his mind to call off the entire Philippine project. I was surprised by this announcement, since I had labored so long and so hard over the mission, and felt almost certain that I could get by with it. However, he is so much more able than I am to get a good perspective of the undertaking that he no doubt knows best. Moreover, I flatter myself enough to think that he has grown fond of me now and hesitates to have me undertake a mission on which perhaps I could be lost. At any rate he will give me a final and definite answer tomorrow morning.

Brisbane, Australia, May 7, 1944   1730 AST

Disappointment was definitely awaiting me this morning! General Sutherland finally told me he thought General MacArthur was going to cancel my trip to the Philippines. Apparently the Japs had received word of our coming, and yesterday they knocked out most of our communications there by bombing.

[For some reason this information precipitated a sudden reaction of frustration and anger on my part. I had spent an inordinate amount of time and effort in planning the trip. I guess I exploded my feelings to General Sutherland. He said General MacArthur wanted to see me, but, observing my anger, suggested I take fifteen minutes to "cool down" before going in to see the commander in chief. I took his advice. When I finally went in to see the general, he also must have detected my unhappiness. Without saying a word he approached me, placed both hands on my shoulders, gazed steadily into my eyes, and said, "Do you know why I canceled your trip? I know that if anyone could have completed the mission successfully, you could have done it. But I guess I was afraid you might not come back and I would lose you."
He then seated me and spent thirty minutes explaining developments which made completion of the flight impractical if not impossible.]

Went to Amberley Field this afternoon and flew the C-54 for two hours, testing the newly installed radar equipment. It's working fine, but now I haven't much need for it. It's fun to fly the big airplane again anyway.
Early tomorrow—0230 hours—I'm taking off for Darwin in the C-54 to relieve my own tensions and to do a dry run for a part of my canceled mission. If I'm not too tired, I plan to come directly back tomorrow night.

Darwin, Australia, May 8, 1944   1300 AST

Departed from Brisbane at 0240 hours this morning and had a delightful eight-and-a-half-hour trip, with perfect weather. I had almost forgotten about the thousands of miles of absolute wasteland in the interior of Australia, and this trip gave me a better opportunity for observing it than any former trip had afforded me. There are stretches of five hundred miles where there are no signs of life of any type, and from the air there are not even the slightest indications that man has ever set foot there. The vastness of the desolation is almost beyond comprehension.
Here at Darwin I was well attended by the navy. Conditions are a lot different than they were eighteen months ago when I was last here. Much reconstruction of a military nature has occurred, and order now prevails where chaos once held sway.

Brisbane, Australia, May 8, 1944   2330 AST

Had a fine, fast trip back, under perfect flying conditions. I made the round trip of 3,600 miles in seventeen hours, so I'm somewhat weary now. Had I been headed toward San Francisco, I would now be halfway home. Guess it does no harm to dream about seeing my family—

Brisbane, Australia, May 9, 1944   2345 AST

Eight o'clock found me still in bed this morning—the first time since I'd gone back in the army. I was really tired, and haven't quite succeeded in throwing off my lethargy all day.

General Sutherland has gone north to Hollandia, so I have nothing to do. There are no airplanes here, and I am temporarily up to date on all of my chores. It appears that I will now have a couple of days of idleness.

A fine letter from Grace today. Jimmy is "Heil Hitler"ing all over the place now, to her embarrassment. Imagine that, and he is only three and one half years of age. It's hard for me to realize how rapidly he is developing.

I sent a small package and a cablegram home today.

Tonight I played poker for about three hours. Didn't have any great luck, but managed to win twenty-five dollars.

Brisbane, Australia, May 10, 1944   2030 AST

An idle day today, with no excitement and nothing much to do. I got up to date with many of my personal chores and then did little else. Tonight I played poker again. I thought I was getting into an ordinary and reasonable game. I agreed to bank the game, and much to my surprise the players bought over $1,000 worth of chips to start with. I decided to risk $75 and then to quit, but at the end of one and a half hours I was winner by $145. Thereupon I promptly quit. I don't care to gamble for such high stakes, as the consequences can be serious.

Had two fine letters from Grace today. I envy her all the fun she is having with Jimmy and Johnny.

Brisbane, Australia, May 11, 1944   2000 AST

Another day with little accomplished. General Sutherland is still in New Guinea, and when he is not at his desk there is a distinct decrease in activity around GHQ.

Brisbane, Australia, May 12, 1944   2315 AST

General Sutherland returned from New Guinea today, so now perhaps I'll have something to do soon. For me this was another day of comparative idleness. Read some communiqués, wrote some letters, and that's about all.

13

Stuck in the South Pacific

MAY–JULY, 1944

Brisbane, Australia, May 13, 1944   2330 AST

A quiet day at HQ today. I had a talk with General Sutherland today, and made a proposition to him which he accepted. I haven't enough to do to keep me busy a large part of the time, so I suggested that I occasionally fly C-54 trips out of here to New Guinea. He agreed, so I will go out on my first trip at 0200 hours on Monday. I would have gone out early tomorrow morning, but some work is needed on the airplane and the Australian maintenance crew took the afternoon off to go to the races, thus effectively tying up a $750,000 airplane for twenty-four hours.

Hereafter I shall occasionally record certain facts and theories concerning the political and strategic aspects of this war. They should provide interesting comparisons with events as they actually do occur during the subsequent prosecution of the war and the peace to follow.

The war of nerves brought on by the imminent opening of a second front in Europe is rapidly approaching a climax. Churchill's almost intolerable petulance increases daily, and with good reason. At Teheran, so I am told, Roosevelt and Stalin agreed upon the time and place of the development of the military undertaking, even though Roosevelt knew that our casualties would be extremely high. Churchill, however, remembered too well his political and military degradation resulting from the disastrous operations at Gallipoli in World War I. No amount of persuasion could convince him that the second front should be undertaken, so he was finally and decisively overruled by Roosevelt and Stalin. Churchill knows that British losses will be great, and he believes that his constituency will overthrow his government in a reaction embittered by these losses. Regardless of his stand, plans are proceeding toward D day, which is to come on one of the last days in this month of May or in early June. To place the maximum of emphasis on his final arguments, Churchill has informed Roosevelt and Stalin that he will resign from his position as prime minister to His Majesty's government. Such a move would certainly not displease Stalin, although Roosevelt no doubt is not cheered by the prospect. As the fateful day relentlessly approaches, the tired old man at No. 10 Downing Street grows more truculent. In a few days we will know whether this truly great man will make good his childish threat, or whether he will "see it through."

Brisbane, Australia, May 14, 1944   1930 AST

Another lazy Sunday. I've had no duties today, and even tried to sleep for an hour this afternoon in preparation for my trip tonight. I'll have to get up at midnight for a 0200 departure.

Wrote a long letter to Grace today and then took a walk. It's raining this evening; however, it is the first rain we have had for a very long time.

Tomorrow I hope to see some of the UAL crews in Port Moresby. I'll be there only about two hours before returning to Brisbane.

Brisbane, Australia, May 15, 1944   2130 AST

It has been a long and tiring day. I went to Amberley Field at midnight last night and took off in rain and fog for Port Moresby at 0230 hours this morning. The trip up was slow, with considerable headwind. I spent about two hours in Moresby, and obtained some late newspapers and magazines.

My trip back from Moresby was made under considerable nervous strain. The hydraulic system in my C-54 failed on takeoff, and I did not know whether I would be able to lower the landing gear upon arrival. I decided to continue on here to Amberley Field, where, in case of an accident, maintenance facilities are available. I managed to get the wheels down and locked all right, but had no wing flaps or brakes. I made a nice landing without mishap and got the airplane stopped well within the limits of the airport. From there I had to be humiliatingly towed to the hangar as I did not wish to jeopardize the airplane by trying to taxi it without brakes.

Having been awake for forty-two hours continuously now, I'm ready for bed.

Brisbane, Australia, May 16, 1944   2030 AST

I have been somewhat groggy and sleepy today, so haven't done much. I tried to remain in my room for a while, but the telephone kept up a constant clamor, what with Colonel Whitney, Colonel Unger, etc., calling about this and that. I finally gave up and returned to the office. Had a letter from Grace, wrote one to her, and quit for the day.

Things are looking up a bit in Italy and Germany these days. It will be such a relief to us here when things are finished in Europe. Stalin made the definite commitment to Roosevelt at Teheran that if we stuck it out in Europe and opened the second front on schedule, he would, upon cessation of hostilities there, declare war upon Japan and give us his full support in neutralizing Japan. Of course we have probably given him adequate excuse to repudiate his promise, what with all of our delays in starting the second front. I am of the opinion, however, that he will live up to his commitments, as he seems to have a better record on that score than do most statesmen. If Russia does enter the war against Japan soon, our task here will be infinitely easier and the war will be over before too long.

Brisbane, Australia, May 17, 1944   2300 AST

This afternoon I flew *Bataan* for a couple of hours and gave Captain Oviatt some practice in it. Late this afternoon, when I returned to the office, Colonel Godman was waiting for me, and he started bawling me out about my attitude, etc., and informed me that hereafter I was to take orders from him. I informed him that that was not my idea of my working arrangement here, and that we had better both go to see General Sutherland and get our status straightened out. This we did, and General Sutherland informed us that hereafter Colonel Godman would run the schedule but that he would have no other control over me. This is quite satisfactory with me, and I hope that it operates to our mutual advantage.

Brisbane, Australia, May 18, 1944   2300 AST

This has been a quiet day with little excitement. I've had nothing to do, and no airplanes are in flying condition. We are all awaiting news of the Wakde landing and the Soerabaja strike, although no great difficulties are anticipated.

Brisbane, Australia, May 19, 1944   1830 AST

Another quiet day, although I've been busy. I've been preparing a set of maps for General Sutherland for his use in flying. I'm spending considerable time on them in order to accomplish a fine product. He will appreciate the effort, I'm sure.

Two fine letters from Grace today.

I am to fly with General Sutherland at 0700 hours tomorrow. So I plan to spend a quiet evening, although I was invited to a poker game tonight.

Brisbane, Australia, May 20, 1944   2330 AST

I worked all morning on a set of flight maps for General Sutherland. This afternoon I played tennis for the first time since I came to Australia. I played with Colonel Melnick; Colonel Wang, of the Chinese Army and a graduate of West Point; and Mr. Chen, a prominent local Chinese.

I did not fly with General Sutherland this morning. While I was preparing to go to Archer Field at 0545 hours, he telephoned to advise that he was in bed with a cold and could not come.

Brisbane, Australia, May 21, 1944   2230 AST

Spent this morning working on maps, but this afternoon I felt as though I was getting a cold, so I've remained in my room most of the time since then. I have a few aches and sore muscles from my tennis games of yesterday too.

Tonight I attended a buffet dinner at Colonel Wilson's home. A number of army dignitaries were there, including Lieutenant General Harmon, who once was (as a major) my commanding officer when I was a flying cadet at March Field, California, in 1929.

Admiral Halsey and his staff are in town, and there has been much activity in General MacArthur's office today.

Brisbane, Australia, May 22, 1944   2230 AST

I finished the maps for General Sutherland, and when I presented them to him he seemed to be quite pleased. I did an excellent job on them.

Today has been foggy and rainy, and as there was an inspection at Archer Field, there was no flying.

Brisbane, Australia, May 23, 1944   1900 AST

Another rainy day with little activity. Had intended doing much flying locally, but the weather was not too suitable, and I spent the day in the office.

Tomorrow morning I plan to go to New Guinea in the B-25 and will be there for several days. Will go to Finschhafen tomorrow and then on to Hollandia the following day. We have had possession of Hollandia for only three weeks now, so conditions there will be rather grim.

Finschhafen, New Guinea, May 24, 1944   2230 AST

The trip up was without incident and the weather was good. We stopped at Townsville for refueling and arrived here before 1500 hours. There was much confusion here as usual, as this is one of the most disorganized places I have seen in this theater. After two hours at the airstrip, we finally got transportation to Base Section Headquarters, but it required over an hour to negotiate the twelve miles of road. The engineers have failed to do their usual good job here, and recent frequent rains have rendered the roads impassable to all except the most rugged four-wheel-driven trucks.

A few minutes ago, Colonel Unger, who is one of my passengers, asked me to report to him. When I did so, he advised me that we would be unable to land the B-25 at Hollandia tomorrow due to restrictions imposed there by the Fifth Air Force. That unit is moving into Hollandia en masse now, and there is so little dispersal space available for aircraft that they refuse to allow any itinerant airplane to land there.

Finschhafen, New Guinea, May 25, 1944   1900 AST

I've had a completely quiet day today. There has been absolutely nothing to do, and I have been reasonably comfortable in a thatched hut located on the site of the old Dutch village of Finschhafen. The sky has been overcast, so that I haven't been able to take a sunbath.

Finschhafen, New Guinea, May 26, 1944   1700 AST

This morning I took a long walk up to a native village in the hills back of the harbor here. When I got there, I was not able to enter the village due to army restrictions. At any rate, I got some valuable exercise.

It has been raining again today so I have been lazy. Have been watching some interesting natural processes here in my thatched hut. Although the hut has been erected only a few days, the termites are well on their way toward its destruction.

Then there are dozens of lizards scurrying here and there and everywhere in search of insects to satisfy their ravenous appetites. There would be plenty of insects for them if their tastes were not too delicate, but they pass up most of them in search of special ones which are apparently more delectable. They are colorful and fascinating little creatures.

Finschhafen, New Guinea, May 27, 1944   2000 AST

This morning after breakfast General Baker came over to inform me that he had just had a message from Hollandia, Dutch New Guinea. It

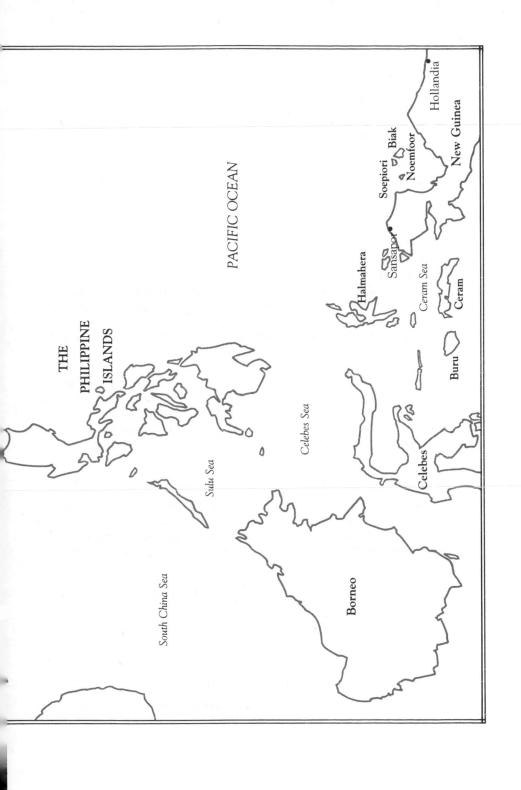

was to the effect that the Hollandia airstrip was now open to transient aircraft and that we were to proceed there immediately to get our party of officers and return here tonight. We lost little time in getting away and had a fine trip. We went along the coast past Madang and Alexhaven, which were taken from the Japs only three weeks ago, and then on past Wewak, where our forces have about 40,000 Japs cut off completely and are now in the process of starving them out. We negotiated the distance to Hollandia (600 miles) in two and a half hours.

Hollandia proved to be a beautiful spot, but not too suitable for a large base from which we could carry out big-scale operations. Practically all of the terrain is either precipitous or marshy, and harbor facilities are limited. The airstrips are merely good at best, and flight approaches are quite poor. Lake Sentani, behind the harbor, affords the setting for many quaint native villages.

I have never witnessed so much aerial destruction as we found at Hollandia. Our Fifth Air Force had attacked the place prior to our occupation, and had destroyed about 250 Jap planes on the ground in addition to many ground installations. Wreckage lay everywhere, and disabled Jap aircraft literally covered the ground. I don't think the Japs ever realized what hit them.

We departed from Hollandia in early afternoon and had a fast trip back. En route we spotted an active volcano on an island about forty miles offshore, so we went out to look it over. We also flew in close to Wewak, but failed to draw any Jap antiaircraft fire. This afternoon the enemy carried out an air raid at Hollandia. Glad we got away ahead of it.

Finschhafen, New Guinea, May 28, 1944   1930 AST

Early this morning we departed for Manus Island. It is one of the finest bases we have in SWPA, and although the weather was quite warm, I enjoyed our six-hour stay there. Among other things, I contracted a beautiful sunburn. Before nightfall we were back here in our comfortable quarters.

It does not appear that we can possibly complete our mission and return to Brisbane before June 1. What was supposed to be a four-day trip will not be terminated under eight days. These delays always find me without sufficient clean clothing. I'm impatient to return and read my nice letters from Grace.

Finschhafen, New Guinea, May 29, 1944   1900 AST

Today has been a day of rest. Colonel Unger is working here, and there is little for me to do except to wait. I took a cruise for a couple of hours

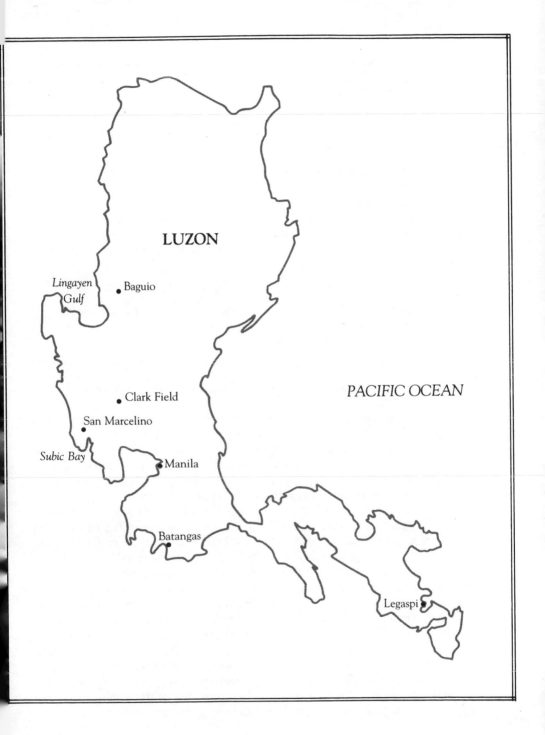

LUZON

Lingayen
Gulf

• Baguio

• Clark Field

San Marcelino
•

Subic Bay

Manila

Batangas

PACIFIC OCEAN

Legaspi •

in General Baker's private launch. Visited Sixth Army Headquarters and the airstrip. This afternoon I wrote letters and read stories. Tomorrow we go to Lae and Oro Bay.

Oro Bay, New Guinea, May 30, 1944   1915 AST

The trip to Lae was made under quite difficult flying conditions, as was the flight on here to Oro Bay. The tropical rain came down in a solid sheet the whole way, and the ceiling was never more than 300 feet. All radio was inoperative.

We are comfortably quartered here on the beach. Tomorrow we go to Milne Bay. I'm growing impatient, waiting to go to Brisbane to get my letters from Gracie. Will probably arrive there the day after tomorrow.

Milne Bay, New Guinea, May 31, 1944   1900 AST

Arrived here at noon in rather bad weather, and it has rained hard all day. Have been unable even to take a walk.

Brisbane, Australia, June 1, 1944   2000 AST

It was two years ago today that I started keeping this diary. What momentous changes have occurred during those two years! The revolution has affected not only the world but also the most minute details of our private and personal affairs. Life can never again even resemble that which we knew and liked so well in prewar days. Whether the changes will be for better or for worse remains for history to decide. Personally, I cannot become appalled at the prospects of these changes. Whatever new forms of economy or society or government we may substitute for the old order, I feel that most of us, as individuals, will find a level therein which will be comparable to that to which our abilities have enabled us to climb within our present scheme of things. I feel that a return to the simpler, more fundamental things of life would not be undesirable.

The intrinsic value of this diary is nil. I have persisted with it for a number of quite selfish reasons. During the past two years few people have enjoyed a more varied or interesting life. I have been able to see and to do things which only the extremes of good fortune could have made possible. Whether I record my experiences and impressions in an interesting manner is somewhat beside the point. I have recorded herein most of the salient events, which should provide guideposts for certain delightful memories. These otherwise would inevitably grow dim with the passage of time. My children may be interested in my adventures. I can turn back and see what occurred on any particular day.

Many nights, when the time comes for me to make my daily entry herein, I am so utterly weary that I have no desire to attempt even to be interesting. But the mere fact that I have to do it, and that I *do* do it, gives a decided boost to my pride in myself. So I think I shall continue with it, even though I may never be able to take all of this scribbling out of Australia with me. The censors may object.

We departed from Milne Bay early this morning in most unfavorable weather. However, conditions improved near Townsville, where we stopped for lunch. The trip to Brisbane was fine, and we arrived here without incident at 1530 hours. I stopped at the office only long enough to get the seven letters from Grace, which had arrived during my absence. Now I'm reading and rereading these and generally relaxing. It's good to have a wife who loves you.

Brisbane, Australia, June 2, 1944   2300 AST

There hasn't been much for me to do today as all of our airplanes are undergoing maintenance. I talked to General Sutherland for a half hour, wrote letters, and got up to date with my personal living chores.

Brisbane, Australia, June 3, 1944   2345 AST

Another dull day. No airplanes to fly so I was in town all day. I called on various officers I have to deal with and generally got in their way. I wrote some letters and then quit. After all, it was Saturday afternoon and I felt somewhat justified. No one is too busy these days, as we are now passing through one of those inevitable lulls which intervene between operational thrusts in the combat area.

[These are days of consolidation in New Guinea, and we are battling to take Biak Island. We need bases closer to Borneo so that we can more effectively bomb the Japanese oil production facilities from that area.]

Monday I expect to go to Sydney to take Mr. Atherton, head of the American Legion.

Brisbane, Australia, June 4, 1944   2000 AST

I was up early this morning in spite of my late retirement last night. I went to Archer Field and flew the C-47 for one and a half hours. I actually do very little handling of flight controls in this airplane since I'm usually with General Sutherland in it and he wants to do all of the flying. So I needed a bit of practice on my own.

Much excitement in General MacArthur's office today. The Jap First Fleet is moving down on our forces at Biak in great strength, with one or more battleships and troop carriers. After all the talk our navy has done about wanting the Japs to come out and fight, they now find themselves unable to get our heavy units here in time to intercept. So once more we will have to rely upon our air force to destroy the Japs while the navy will be safely back east. The impending battle can be a major test of our air force.

[Biak Island would be a far superior air base and was shortly to be highly developed for that purpose, but the conquest of Biak had so far been a bitter one; although we had believed there were only about 2,500 Japanese troops on the island, we had found there were several times that number. It now looked as though reinforcements were arriving: we learned that the Japanese task force consisted of one battleship, two heavy cruisers, and a number of light cruisers and destroyers, escorting cargo ships and troop transports toward Biak. Their combat ships could easily have overcome our maximum strength of four light cruisers and several destroyers that remained after the heavier units had been withdrawn to the mid-Pacific following our successful Hollandia operation. There were many tense hours until suddenly, for reasons unknown to us, the Japanese naval force changed course and headed for the Vogelkop Peninsula on the western tip of New Guinea. This was only one of several occasions on which the Japanese, without apparent reason, suddenly changed their objective and failed to take the opportunity to inflict severe damage upon us.]

Sydney, Australia, June 5, 1944   2100 AST

I talked to General Sutherland for a time this morning.

[When I had not been away on trips I had noticed General MacArthur was spending much more of his time at his desk writing and studying than was his normal habit. He usually paced the floor much of the time when he was in his office, presumably to get exercise. Later, when I asked General Sutherland what was concerning the commander in chief, he said the general was distilling his thoughts of his ideas on the future course of the war. One of his previous concerns had been removed with the decision to merge the South Pacific Area into the Southwest Pacific Area. But he wanted to be fully prepared to express effectively his arguments in favor of a Philippine campaign if he had the opportunity.]

This afternoon I took off from Brisbane for Sydney, and had a nice trip down, arriving here just at dusk. Among other high-ranking passengers were Mr. Atherton of the American Legion and General MacNider. The military reception we received at the airport here was presented with more fanfare than any I have ever witnessed with any of my passengers, even including General MacArthur. There was a band, an inspection of troops, etc., all amidst the constant twinkling of photographers' flashbulbs. Politics is quite a thing.

Tonight I'm billeted in the swank Australia Hotel, which is really the sin center of this wide-open city. There are continuous parties in almost every room, but I'll be able to sleep in my luxurious bed in spite of the noise.

Sydney, Australia, June 6, 1944   2000 AST

I spent some time walking about the city this morning. This afternoon I went to a movie and saw *The Human Comedy*. It was quite as refreshing as the book.

Late this afternoon we received the first news of the Allied invasion of France. Of course I'm living with one ear glued to the radio in order not to miss any of the news, and will probably get little sleep tonight. It is unlikely that we will receive much real news of the progress of the operation for some days yet. I'm also wondering how we are making out with the Jap fleet northwest of Guinea. When I am away from General MacArthur's office, I get none of the inside news.

Sydney, Australia, June 7, 1944   2000 AST

Have spent another day in delicious idleness. Did some walking and window shopping but could find nothing to buy. The weather is brisk and fine.

This afternoon I went down to the dock, intending to take a ride with Mr. Atherton and his party. However, there was so much fanfare that I slipped quietly away and returned to the hotel. I don't care to be associated with so much foolish display at a serious time such as this.

As the schedule now stands, we will depart tomorrow at 1100 hours for Brisbane.

Sydney, Australia, June 8, 1944   2100 AST

[Before I departed from Brisbane with Mr. Atherton, General MacArthur had requested that I remain in Sydney with Mr. Atherton and bring him back to Brisbane on June 7.]

My annoyance was great this morning when Mr. Atherton advised me that he would not return to Brisbane until tomorrow. I've lost most of my respect for the American Legion and all of it for Mr. Atherton. He is here on an extended party at army expense, and from all I can tell he is just a fat playboy, out for a good time. He seems unable even to carry on an intelligent conversation. As far as aiding the war effort by partying here in Sydney, that is impossible.

General MacNider and Colonel Hipps got fed up with the detail and departed for Brisbane by courier airplane this morning.

[I informed General Sutherland of my predicament. He said General MacArthur did not want to irritate Mr. Atherton as he might return to the States and report unfavorably on the conditions and leadership that their sons had to endure while serving in the South Pacific. General Mac-Arthur relayed word to me to hunt up Mr. Atherton and advise him that the only time the general's schedule would allow him to grant Mr. Atherton an audience was at 11:00 A.M. the following morning.]

It has been cold and miserable here today. I've spent a useless day.

It's disappointing how little real news is coming to us concerning the European invasion. I have a feeling that it isn't going too well.

Brisbane, Australia, June 9, 1944   2100 AST

We had a nice trip to Brisbane and I reported immediately to General Sutherland. Among other things he informed me that he wanted to fly early tomorrow morning in a C-45. I hadn't flown one before, so I spent an hour at Archer Field this afternoon checking out in one. It's a nice little airplane, much smaller and more responsive than anything I've flown recently.

Brisbane, Australia, June 10, 1944   2145 AST

Was up at 0530 hours this morning and flew two hours with General Sutherland. We had a lot of fun in the C-45. Immediately afterwards I flew *Bataan* for an hour and a half, and the contrast between the two airplanes is most pronounced. I stopped at Amberley Field to get a package which Grace had sent over to me by one of the pilots on the trans-Pacific run.

Brisbane, Australia, June 11, 1944   2015 AST

Had a long talk with General Sutherland this morning. Then I set up two trips to go out tomorrow—one to Hollandia and one to Melbourne. The general will not allow me to go on either of them, as he wants me to take him to Bougainville on Wednesday in a C-54.

This afternoon I went to Archer to send a package to Melbourne for Captain Bessemer-Clark. It has rained this afternoon and evening, so I've done little else.

Brisbane, Australia, June 12, 1944   2100 AST

Went to Amberley Field this afternoon to test the C-54. Had a nice ride and that was about all. The airplane is in good condition and should be ready for the Bougainville trip Wednesday.

Brisbane, Australia, June 13, 1944   2045 AST

This has been a busy day, what with hunting airplane supplies, preparing for the trip, etc. I went to Amberley Field this morning to try to determine the reasons why the ATC has been unable to show a better performance with the C-54s. So I got myself involved in a jurisdictional dispute between the ATC and General Sutherland. He is under the impression that they should operate the airplanes as he sees fit, and they contend that Washington has told them to do nothing about operating them. I'll have to get General Sutherland's viewpoint during the trip tomorrow.

Had a nice letter from Grace and one from Wayne today. Didn't get away from the office until 1930 hours tonight. I have to get up at 0400 hours tomorrow, so must go to bed.

Bougainville, Northern Solomon Islands, June 14, 1944   1930 AST

It was with great difficulty that I rolled out of bed at 0400 hours this morning. However, I reached Amberley Field on schedule after a thrilling ride through thick ground fog behind a driver who was not too familiar with the tortuous highway. Was off the ground at daybreak in a C-54 and landed only a few minutes later at Eagle Farm. Here, as he always does, General Sutherland arrived on schedule, and we took off for Bougainville. We had some difficulties with the functioning of a propeller governor shortly after takeoff. Possibly we should have returned but I made the decision to continue, with the well-considered reasoning that the trouble could be repaired with little difficulty if its source lay where it appeared to be.

We had an excellent trip throughout, and landed here at 1420 hours. We found that our mechanical troubles were easily repairable. We are now billeted with the pilots of the Twenty-fourth Marine Air Group and are quite comfortably situated. In many respects, Bougainville is one of the best bases in the Pacific area. The soil consists of volcanic ash and gravel, and although there are frequent torrential rains, there is never much mud.

The jungle has been well cleared from our base here, although it is practically impenetrable only a few yards from the airstrip.

Bougainville, Northern Solomon Islands, June 15, 1944   2030 AST

Today I had few duties, so that time permitted me to walk about the country here and gain a firsthand knowledge of it. The rank tropical vegetation and the many forms of bird life were most interesting to me.

About 15,000 Japs surround the perimeter of our beachhead here, but they are gradually becoming impotent insofar as any sustained military effort is concerned. Starvation and jungle conditions are slowly decimating their numbers and their effectiveness. Only yesterday they dropped thirty-six mortar shells on the airstrip, but only six of those detonated. The remainder had defective fuses, etc. Their food has become a problem to them, so they have cleared certain areas and have planted war gardens therein. Now one of the daily missions of the marine pilots stationed here is to spray these gardens with creosote and oil from devices which they have rigged onto their aircraft. It is only a question of time until few Japs will be left alive here.

[I sat in on some of the conferences General Sutherland is having here regarding consolidation of some of the elements of South Pacific command with that of Southwest Pacific.]

Went to a movie tonight, but it was most uncomfortable. A tropical downpour was presented free along with the movie. Incidentally, the movie theater is in the open air at the edge of the jungle, and at various times Jap soldiers have been caught sneaking into the area to watch the movie in the dark alongside our own troops.

We depart at 2200 hours tonight for Brisbane. Hope the C-54 functions all right.

Brisbane, Australia, June 16, 1944   2230 AST

This has been a tough day on me. As planned, we departed from Bougainville last night at 2200 hours. The airplane functioned perfectly on takeoff, but we had been out about ten minutes when the oil quantity gauge on No. 2 engine began to indicate a rapid loss of oil. There was no indication of oil leakage on the surface of the airplane, so I thought the apparent trouble might lie in a defective gauge. However, a few moments later the oil pressure on that engine dropped suddenly, and I feathered the propeller, immediately, as only about ten seconds of rotation without oil will do irreparable damage to the bearings. Then the problem was to decide upon a course of action which would afford maximum safety for the flight. To return to Bougainville would allow the quickest termination of the flight, but would present the problem of a hazardous landing on the ill-lighted field, which was located adjacent to very rough terrain. To continue to Port Moresby required about three and a half hours of operation through rain on three engines, which was safe enough, providing the other engine on the same side of the airplane did not also fail. I decided upon the latter course of action, partly because the hazards were no greater and because repairs could probably be effected with less delay.

We arrived at Port Moresby at 0200 hours this morning. It was soon discovered that the oil loss was due to a missing oil plug in the scavenger pump. A similar plug on No. 3 engine was also loose. I strongly suspect that this is a case of sabotage, as it is extremely unlikely that two plugs would become loose on the same airplane at the same time. However, to prove such a contention would be impossible. These plugs are supposed to be "safety-wired" in place.

We repaired our troubles in about thirty minutes, and General Sutherland remained with us, as we expected to depart for Brisbane in short order. But we were not to have such good fortune. We started the engines —that is, all except No. 2, and it refused to start regardless of our efforts. It had been dragged through the rain too long in an inoperative condition. After an hour of fruitless effort, we admitted defeat, and sent General Sutherland off to bed. We labored over the engine all night and at last got it to run. Then I lay down and had an hour of sleep between 0600 and 0700 hours, and was up again to make certain that all was in readiness. General Sutherland did not appear until 1200.

Our trip from Port Moresby to Brisbane was without incident, and we delivered the general at Eagle Farm shortly after nightfall. I then took the airplane on over to Amberley Field, but had to wait an hour for my car. Consequently, I arrived at the hotel at 2100 hours and am now so thoroughly tired that I want to sleep for hours.

[As a result of this incident I have initiated a guard system over all headquarters airplanes when they are away from home station. Our aircraft maintenance is uniformly excellent, considering the conditions under which the mechanics have to work.]

Brisbane, Australia, June 17, 1944   2230 AST

I have been most lazy today. I was up at a late hour and went to the office for my mail, then I came back to the hotel, wrote letters, and generally did nothing.

Brisbane, Australia, June 18, 1944   2245 AST

This morning I caught up with my duties at the office, and then this afternoon I flew *Bataan* for a couple of hours. Tonight, while I was out for my before-dinner walk, I came upon Hunt Bassett, a colonel in the Air Force and a classmate of mine at the flying school. He is currently located in Washington as chief of Army Air Force Meteorology, and is on an inspection trip to this theater. We had a fine visit for a couple of hours.

Brisbane, Australia, June 19, 1944   1900 AST

Spent the entire day at Archer Field. This morning I completed Karl Oviatt's checkout in the B-17, and then this afternoon I practiced instrument flying under a hood in a C-47. I try to get at least an hour under the hood each month to be certain that my instrument flying technique does not deteriorate. Tonight I plan a quiet night of letter writing and reading.

Only two letters from Grace in seven days. Jimmy has been sick again, however, so no doubt she has been quite busy. Jimmy undergoes a tonsillectomy on June 26, and we hope that it will result in an improvement in his general health.

Brisbane, Australia, June 20, 1944   2315 AST

My day today was not very exciting. I accomplished nothing of importance, and received no letter from Grace. Late this afternoon I had a long talk with General Sutherland about certain impending problems. Hereafter I am going to test-fly each airplane for a few minutes immediately prior to a flight on which General Sutherland or General MacArthur is a passenger. Guards are now provided for the aircraft according to a routine procedure at each station, but I feel that it is increasingly necessary to provide a guard to guard the guard, since the regular guard often is unhappy in his job and thus often has an inherent dislike for all "brass hats," whom he instinctively blames for his hard lot of being assigned to New Guinea.

Brisbane, Australia, June 21, 1944   1020 AST

This morning I ran some errands for General Sutherland.

No letter from Grace today. I'm beginning to become a bit worried now.

I'm flying with General Sutherland at 0700 hours tomorrow, which means a call at 0530 hours for me.

Brisbane, Australia, June 22, 1944   1930 AST

Was in the air two hours this morning with General Sutherland. After that I accomplished only a few minor chores. This afternoon I took a long walk in this fine, crisp winter air to get more exercise.

Once more I am becoming worried because of lack of mail from Grace. It is unlike her not to write, but of course there is always the possibility that an airplane was lost en route here with all of its cargo of mail. Perhaps tomorrow will bring relief in the form of some letters.

Brisbane, Australia, June 23, 1944   2030 AST

I went to Archer Field this morning to fly the C-47 for the purpose of calibrating a new positive radar altimeter which we have installed in it. This proved to be an interesting task, although I may have further work to do on it before the calibration is perfected.

This afternoon General Sutherland asked me to fly with him early tomorrow, and he also asked me to take a C-54 on a nonstop trip to Hollandia Sunday night. This trip is for the purpose of transporting eighteen staff officers of the new Eighth Army, which is being organized there. I set up the trip, and then tonight he telephoned to advise that he could not let me go and that one of the regular C-54 pilots would have to take it. Prime Minister Curtin is arriving back in Australia, and General MacArthur will offer him the use of *Bataan* to return to Canberra. So I will have to stand by to fly the prime minister in case he accepts General MacArthur's offer.

After the general's flight tomorrow morning, I plan to fly *Bataan* for a couple of hours to calibrate its radar altimeter. Then Major Beezley, who is General Kenney's pilot, wants me to give him an hour of instrument instruction; so I'll have a full day of flying.

Two nice letters from Grace today broke the long silence.

Brisbane, Australia, June 24, 1944   1945 AST

This has been a busy day, yet a fine one because I like to be busy. Was up early and flew almost two hours with General Sutherland, and then I took *Bataan* up for a test flight for over an hour. When I landed I had a note that General Sutherland wanted me to call him. This I did, and he asked me to arrange to get thirty-six staff officers to Hollandia instead of the eighteen he mentioned yesterday. I'm doing this by sending twenty-eight of them to Hollandia in the C-54 and taking the other eight to Port Moresby myself in a C-47 early tomorrow. I'll return Monday and be ready for Prime Minister Curtin, who is now supposed to arrive on Tuesday.

Had a two-hour flight with Major Beezley this afternoon, during which I showed him some of the shortcuts and tricks in instrument flying. He is very appreciative of my help.

Tonight I had another talk with General Sutherland, and now I've just finished packing. Another 0500 call.

Port Moresby, New Guinea, June 25, 1944   2100 AST

The trip up was very fine, with good weather and good winds. We stopped at Townsville for refueling and for lunch and arrived here in mid-afternoon. Among my passengers was Gen. Bob Shoe.

Another 0500 call for tomorrow. I'm getting tired of such frequent early rising.

Brisbane, Australia, June 26, 1944   2130 AST

Only 7:45 elapsed flying time with a stop at Townsville, so I arrived here quite early. Two nice letters awaited me, so I'm quite happy. The trip down was entirely routine.

I didn't report in to General Sutherland tonight as I was dirty and tired and he had a full list of appointments. Will see him tomorrow morning. I don't know whether Prime Minister Curtin will be flying back to Canberra or not, but at any rate he is remaining in Brisbane for another day or two. Colonel Lehrbas told me he doubted that the prime minister would fly down as he disliked flying and had had too much of it on his trip to London and return.

Brisbane, Australia, June 27, 1944   1930 AST

Went to see General Sutherland the first thing this morning and he had good news for me. I am to take him to Honolulu this week, departing about Friday or Saturday. He is undecided as to whether he will take *Bataan* or a C-54. If it is the C-54 we will make only one stop, at Tarawa. If it is the B-17 we will make two stops, probably at Guadalcanal and Baker Island. We will be in Honolulu only two or three days and then will return. Too bad we can't go on to San Francisco to see the family. I hope we use the C-54. At any rate, I spent the afternoon at Amberley and Archer fields, making early preparations to have the airplanes both ready, pending his decision on which plane to use. We should have a fine trip. It will be fun to see some American-type civilization again and to eat good American food once more.

Today Jimmy is to have his tonsils removed. It hurts me to think of the poor little man's having to be hurt, but of course he will suffer much less in the long run for having had the operation. I shall be uneasy until I hear how he stood the ordeal.

Brisbane, Australia, June 28, 1944   2000 AST

General Sutherland advised me this morning that he will take *Bataan* to Honolulu, departing Friday noon. We will stop at Plaine des Gaiacs and at Canton Island only for fuel and will continue directly on. This will require about twenty-five and a half hours of flying time. I'll take two radio operators and two engineers, but will have to relieve the navigator myself. I do hope we have no mechanical or weather troubles, as I want very much to give the general a good trip. The date of my promised promotion is drawing near.

This afternoon I was busy at such details as arranging for food, checking on the airplane, etc. The general instructed me to take another navigator instead of Markovich, so I'm taking Lieutenant Ansbaugh, from one of the C-54 crews. He appears to be capable.

General Sutherland wants to fly at 0700 hours tomorrow, so this means a call at 0500 hours for me. I'm keeping plenty busy these days, but that's the way I like it. I feel much more as though I'm doing my bit toward the war effort.

Brisbane, Australia, June 29, 1944   2100 AST

It's been a long and tiresome day. I was up at 0500 hours and flew with General Sutherland for an hour and a half, and then I flew *Bataan* for an hour and a half to make certain that it will be in perfect condition for the start of the trip tomorrow. Also had to get my radioman briefed on the proper use of the trans-Pacific radio circuit. As of tonight, all is in readiness. We depart from Archer Field tomorrow at 0900 hours.

Had another nice letter from Grace today. Jimmy's operation has been postponed definitely until July 5 now as the doctor couldn't make the schedule of June 26. It's going to be very disappointing to get to Honolulu and not to be able to go on over to San Francisco to see the family. It will help just to be that near to them, however. One of these days perhaps we will be taking a trip which will not terminate at Honolulu.

En route New Caledonia–Canton, June 30, 1944   2200 AST

We got away this morning as planned and had a fine trip to New Caledonia. We remained there only long enough to refuel and took off again for Canton. We are now in a storm area, and the tropical rain is pouring down. It is going to be a long trip before we reach Honolulu. All is going well and we've been singularly free of mechanical troubles with *Bataan* so far. We will land at Canton Island for fuel shortly before daybreak.

Honolulu, T.H., June 30, 1944   2330 HWT

We crossed the date line last night so it's June 30 again today.

I think a law should be passed prohibiting the writing of entries into diaries at nighttime. All entries should be made before breakfast because so often after an active or interesting day one is much too tired to do justice to the events of the day. We arrived here at 1900 hours after a flight of twenty-six and a half hours which we made in the elapsed time of twenty-nine hours. For forty hours I haven't closed my eyes, having traveled 4,800 miles, and now I'm much too tired to write, let alone to try to be interesting.

Our entire trip was uneventful, and now I'm in a comfortable room here at the Moana Hotel, ready for ten hours of sound sleep.

Honolulu, T.H., July 1, 1944   2130 HWT

Was up at 0800 hours this morning, as I belatedly realized that this was Saturday and that all shopping would have to be completed before 1200 hours. I had many small items to purchase for various friends in Australia, as well as a present for Grace. So I rushed about madly all morning.

This afternoon I telephoned General Sutherland and he advised that he wanted to take a sightseeing flight over to the island of Hawaii tomorrow. I now have the trip set up for a departure at 1400 hours. Then on the following morning we will depart for Australia at 0800 hours, going by way of Canton, Guadalcanal, Hollandia, and Brisbane. That will be another long, straight-through trip, started even before my present fatigue has worn off completely. Perhaps I'm not as young as I once was, but I don't seem to recover too quickly from these long trips now.

Honolulu, T.H., July 2, 1944   2000 HWT

Our sightseeing trip was very fine. We departed from Hickam Field as planned and made a leisurely flight to the island of Hawaii by way of Molokai and Maui.

This is indeed beautiful scenery. In fact I think it is more nearly perfect than any other part of the Pacific. Molokai with its windward shoreline dropping precipitously into the sea and decorated with its myriad sheer waterfalls is a sight not soon forgotten. Then the vast, dead crater of Haleakala on Maui brings one back in a startling manner to the realization of the immensity of nature and her works in comparison with the puny scars which man, with prodigious effort, finally manages to scratch out on certain places of the earth.

We went on to Hawaii, and by climbing rapidly we gained sufficient altitude to circle Mauna Kea, to see its dazzling patches of snow clinging so incongruously to the very summit of this tropical land. Thence we flew across to Mauna Loa, the world's largest single mountain mass. This really brought back memories to me as we circled the smoking crater of Halemaumau. Just about twelve years ago, Capt. Fish Salmon and I climbed to the summit of this 13,700-foot mountain in an eventful three-day hike. Five of us started the trip, but only two of us completed it. As I looked down upon the tortuous trail over the lava where Fish and I plodded upwards, retching from our exertions and freezing at night, an entire lifetime flashed through my mind.

After Mauna Loa, we circled the crater at Kilauea, turned back past Hilo, and then returned to Oahu along the north coast of Hawaii and its endless miles of sugar plantations. We flew over Lanai, the pineapple center of the world, and thence across the leper colony on Molokai to Hickam Field.

General Sutherland thoroughly enjoyed his trip, even though I made a terrible landing at Hickam. He informed me that he would be unable to complete his conferences here in time to depart tomorrow morning, and that we would very likely leave on Tuesday morning. This pleases not only me but also my crew, as we will all be more completely rested in another day. He invited me to sit in on the meetings he was attending, but I declined as I was still weary.

Honolulu, T.H., July 3, 1944   1900 HWT

This morning I went for a swim at Waikiki, and this afternoon I shopped for a present for Grace. I'm sending it to her by Smitty, who departs for San Francisco tonight. Have been resting most of the day as I have to arise rather early tomorrow. We depart then for Brisbane direct, with stops only at Canton and PDG. Must write to Grace now and then get to bed. I only wish I could be traveling east instead of west tomorrow.

En route Canton–Fiji, July 4, 1944   2200 FWT

What a long day! We were off at Honolulu at 0900 hours this morning and had an uneventful trip to Canton. At Canton we found the main runway closed for repairs and had to land on the auxiliary strip directly crosswind and during a rain squall. The B-17 handles notoriously poorly in a crosswind, and it took all of my skill and a good left brake to avoid serious consequences. Upon landing, we were informed that the field at Plaine des Gaiacs had been abandoned and that we would have to change our plans. After consulting with General Sutherland we decided to proceed on without delay, landing at Nandi for fuel. We are well on our way now and will reach Fiji after midnight.

I am now relieving the navigator, who is having a bit of sleep. Making a flight as long as this places considerable strain upon me, as I try to relieve each other man on the crew at regular intervals. Yet there is no one to take over so that I can get some rest.

It's a beautiful night, with a full moon and fine weather. It's fun to do celestial navigation on a night such as this.

En route Canton–Fiji, July 5, 1944   0000 FWT

This is the day which doesn't exist as we have crossed the international date line. I make this entry only to keep the record straight.

Brisbane, Australia, July 6, 1944   2000 AST

Home at last, a tired and pleased man. We arrived at Archer at 0930 hours this morning, and encountered a bit of local weather. However, we landed safely and terminated our grueling trip. Another twenty-six and a half hours in the air out of twenty-nine. I went to the office only long enough to get my mail and then I went to bed for four hours. I got up for dinner and a drink, and now I'm going back to bed again. After forty hours without sleep, I need a lot of it. The important thing is that the trip was entirely successful.

Brisbane, Australia, July 7, 1944   1930 AST

Today I've spent in doing many personal chores. Haven't accomplished much and I'm still somewhat groggy.

Had two more fine letters from Gracie. The world is almost a fine place once more.

I've spent a large part of the day delivering various things I bought for people while in Honolulu. It's fun to do things for people who are appreciative.

Brisbane, Australia, July 8, 1944   2115 AST

It was raining all day so that I couldn't do anything out of doors. I went to Archer Field to check up on *Bataan* and got thoroughly soaked. Back at the office there was nothing to be done, so I wrote three letters. It's another of those periods of waiting. I have an idea that something is in the air which may affect me. I can't tell just what it is, but some important trip is involved. Whether I will go on it or whether someone else will be the pilot, I don't know as yet. I have an idea it may be another world conference, and if so, and if I go on it, I'll probably go in the capacity of command pilot rather than as the one in actual control of the airplane. All of this is conjecture of course.

Brisbane, Australia, July 9, 1944   1900 AST

This day started out with rain and fog, but the weather improved by noon. The airplanes were out of commission and Archer Field was too muddy to fly out of, so I remained in town all day. Having little else to do, I walked for two and a half hours steadily this afternoon, covering at least twelve miles. I should sleep soundly tonight.

Had three letters from Grace and one From Wayne and Marge. That is really all right.

Brisbane, Australia, July 10, 1944   1930 AST

As the result of retiring early last night, I was awake and up early this morning. Our rain had ended at last, so I had my usual morning walk before breakfast.

I had a long discussion with General Sutherland this morning, and he informed me in great secrecy that I am to go with General MacArthur to a world-important conference a long way from here before the end of this month. Recently the newspapers have been carrying speculative discussions about President Roosevelt's probable attendance of a conference in England soon. It would appear that all of that is merely a blind to obscure the facts in the case. At any rate, I'm to be in on it in a rather strange capacity. It will be fun, but much work and worry for me.

Went to Archer Field this morning and flew with Major Beezley for an hour. I showed him a few things I'd learned about a B-17 since I'd been here. Then I took Captain Skov up in a C-47 to see if he would be a suitable pilot for our new organization. I walked home from Archer—nine miles in exactly two hours, so I've had my exercise.

No mail today. I'm anxious to have the first report on Jimmy's operation, but it will be a few days yet before a letter can reach me.

Brisbane, Australia, July 11, 1944   2315 AST

It has rained steadily all day today so there has been little I can do. It's quite a task for me to kill time when I can't have something constructive to do.

Brisbane, Australia, July 12, 1944   2000 AST

At last the rain has stopped. I went to Archer Field, hopeful of being able to fly some airplane this morning, but I found the field closed because of mud. I walked back to the office from Archer, again making the nine miles in two hours.

Had quite a talk with General Sutherland about various things. Today completes my six months here, and according to my agreement with the general I was supposed to be promoted at the end of six months. Apparently he has forgotten the date, and I suppose I'll eventually have to remind him. However, I'll wait a few days before I do so.

[Charles Lindbergh suddenly appeared at GHQ in Brisbane. I do not believe either General MacArthur or General Sutherland expected him when he arrived with General Kenney. He had been flying with some of the fighter squadrons out of western New Guinea and Biak Island. He had been sent to the area by General Motors, the manufacturer of the Allison engines used in P-38 fighter aircraft, to demonstrate to the pilots of these planes how they could significantly increase their range by proper altitude selection and by refined methods of engine fuel adjustment. The added range was badly needed so that they could provide fighter escort for the bombers and attack airplanes over their targets farther into the island chains leading to Borneo and toward the Philippines.

It was not exactly according to protocol to have Lindbergh, a civilian, flying fighter aircraft in combat, but certainly no one at this stage was about to challenge his authority to do so. General Sutherland asked me to talk to Lindbergh while he was awaiting his appointment with General MacArthur. He was his usual quiet, charming self but appeared to have aged considerably since I had first met him, some years previously.

MacArthur talked with him for half an hour. Although I am not certain of this, some things Lindbergh said when he came out of the meeting led me to believe that the general, while greatly appreciating what he had been doing to help our fighter pilots, nevertheless told him he should not be risking his life flying illegal missions.]

Early tomorrow I fly with General Sutherland. This means a call at 0500 hours.

Brisbane, Australia, July 13, 1944   2300 AST

I spent a couple of hours this morning flying with the general and then came back to the office. It rained again this afternoon. I started to fly *Bataan* but upon checking the airplane before takeoff I found the No. 2 engine had a defective magneto, so I never got off the ground with it.

This afternoon I had a letter from Grace, which she wrote immedi-

Above: General Sutherland and I in the cockpit of a C-47. *Below:* P-38s as flown in New Guinea by Charles Lindbergh.

ately after Jimmy was operated on on July 5. He had not yet recovered consciousness after the operation, but everything had gone off OK.

Brisbane, Australia, July 14, 1944   2200 AST

Went to Archer Field this morning but found the airport too muddy for any except necessary flying. I walked the nine miles into town again, wore two blisters on my right foot, and had a fine shower bath. Upon reporting to the office I found very little to do.

Two more letters from Grace today assured me that Jimmy was convalescing well from his operation, although his condition had not been good prior to that time. The letters were written July 6.

Brisbane, Australia, July 15, 1944   1930 AST

I went to Archer Field this morning and flew the B-17 off of the muddy place. Then after lunch I flew the B-25 for an hour and a half. I hear a rumor that we are going to move our airplanes from Archer to Eagle Farm, which, if true, will be a decided change for the better. Eagle Farm is a modern airport in every way, and we will be free from the mud and the dust at Archer. The men are not in favor of the move, as living accommodations are not as good.

I walked back from Archer again and my blisters are bothering me. Will probably have to give up these walks for a few days until my feet are well again.

No letters from home.

[General MacArthur called me into his office today and said he wanted me to fly him to Honolulu on July 26. He questioned me at some length about the trip—how long it would take, how many stops we would make, etc.

We did not have a suitable aircraft for General MacArthur to make the long twenty-six-hour flight from Brisbane to Honolulu for the conference with the president. Our beloved B-17, *Bataan I,* although ideal for operation in New Guinea, had a crowded passenger compartment and insufficient headroom to permit the general to do his methodical pacing. The two C-54s available to us were cargo-type planes without insulation and soundproofing, hence cold and very noisy. They were equipped only with foldable metal benches for seats.

I had been given authority to requisition almost any airplane in the theater if I had a compelling need for it. Pan American Airways was operating some passenger-equipped military C-54 airplanes into Brisbane under military contract. I exercised my authority and arranged for one of these desired aircraft to arrive in Brisbane on July 20. We would replace three rows of seats with a comfortable innerspring cot for the general's use, since the twenty-six-hour elapsed time trip through three time zones would be very tiring even for a younger man. We also would install a radio that could receive standard broadcast frequencies in case the general wanted to hear news reports.]

This impending trip is causing some speculation around General MacArthur's office. It could mean a shake-up in the commands in the Pacific area, but I'm inclined to believe it is largely politics. A few pictures of the president conferring in the Pacific with General MacArthur certainly wouldn't lose the president any votes in the coming election. On the other hand, to remove General MacArthur or to decrease the size of his command could have grave political repercussions at the polls in November. We shall soon know.

Brisbane, Australia, July 16, 1944   1900 AST

Had a long, informal conversation with General Sutherland this morning. We discussed details of the impending long and important trip. Then I asked him pointedly what had happened to my expected promotion to Lieutenant Colonel. He said that, since the time of his promise, a new army regulation had been enacted which prohibited promotions under the grade of major with less than six months in grade, and from major to lieutenant colonel with less than nine months in grade. He said that he had not forgotten his promise and that he would promote me at the earliest possible moment. This assures me that we are not at variance in our respective understandings of our agreement about my case. Consequently, I feel better about the whole thing, even though I am naturally disappointed at having to wait longer than I had expected.

Brisbane, Australia, July 17, 1944   2215 AST

Was up at 0500 hours and flew with General Sutherland until 0845. After I let him out at Eagle Farm, I flew over to Amberley Field on business concerning the C-54s. My blisters still were bad enough to prevent me from walking into town again from Archer.

Tonight I took Chief Warrant Officer Paul Rogers, from our office, and his new bride to dinner with me. He is a very capable boy, and a fellow alumnus of mine from William Jewell College. He came out of the Philippines with General MacArthur and General Sutherland and has been a right-hand man to them since that time. Then a master sergeant, he was the only enlisted man to come out in the general's party.

Another letter from Grace assures me of Jimmy's further improvement. Children always have such an astounding recuperative power, but from all reports his tonsils were very bad.

Brisbane, Australia, July 18, 1944   2300 AST

Remained in the office this morning and then early this afternoon I flew *Bataan* for a couple of hours. Went out to work the instrument approach procedure for Jondaryan and also one at Eagle Farm. We will soon be moved to Eagle Farm and will thus escape from the mud and dust at Archer. After landing, I walked the nine miles into town in 1:56, the best speed I've made thus far.

Brisbane, Australia, July 19, 1944   2345 AST

This morning I drove out to Amberley Field on business in connection with the forthcoming important trip. It was a beautiful drive through this fine crisp winter weather. I returned to Brisbane for lunch and then went to Eagle Farm on a private errand for General Sutherland.

Tonight I played poker at Gregory Terrace and won eighty dollars. It was a good, congenial crowd and I enjoyed the game very much.

No mail today.

Brisbane, Australia, July 20, 1944   2330 AST

Went to Archer Field this morning to fly *Bataan* over to Eagle Farm. We will hereafter be based at the latter field, as we have moved all of our facilities out of muddy, dusty Archer.

The C-54 which we are to use on our forthcoming trip arrived at Amberley today. Tomorrow I'll be occupied with arranging details of its equipment, etc.

Two fine letters from Grace today.

Brisbane, Australia, July 21, 1944   1915 AST

This has been a long and busy day for me. Was up at 0530 hours to go to Eagle Farm to fly with General Sutherland. Afterwards I returned to the office to find the Pan Am crew of the C-54 awaiting instructions concerning the pending trip. I then went to Amberley Field to inspect the airplane. I returned to have another discussion with General Sutherland.

Brisbane, Australia, July 22, 1944   2115 AST

This day I spent attending to many of the necessary details in preparation for our trip. I went to Eagle Farm and then to Amberley Field in connection with getting the airplane ready, and then I spent most of the afternoon bothering with details of food, service en route, etc. If all of the people do all of the things I've asked them to do during the following two days, everything will be in readiness.

The morning newspapers carried the report that President Roosevelt had arrived at a navy base on the west coast of the United States.

No more letters from home today.

Brisbane, Australia, July 23, 1944   2345 AST

Still more planning and checking of preparations. This afternoon I walked out to Eagle Farm and back, a distance of eleven miles, and I got a fine lot of exercise. I always feel so pleasantly tired afterwards. I walked the eleven miles in exactly two and a half hours, which isn't bad for a thirty-seven-year-old man. If I had proper shoes so that blisters would not bother me, I could do better.

Had a long discussion with General Sutherland, and he scheduled a local flight for early tomorrow morning and later canceled it.

Tonight I played poker again for a few hours and won thirty-three dollars. Still no mail today—

Brisbane, Australia, July 24, 1944   1915 AST

Another hectic day, spent largely in checking up on airplanes, food, etc. This afternoon I flew *Bataan* down to Amberley Field and back to Eagle Farm, for official business as well as for keeping the airplane in good flying order as a standby in case trouble develops with the C-54.

Had another conference with General Sutherland and now I believe everything is set for the big trip.

Still no mail from Grace today.

Brisbane, Australia, July 25, 1944   2000 AST

Another day of dashing about and checking on details. Had to get a new rug to cover a part of the floor of the airplane. We brought the airplane over to Eagle Farm late today, and now all is in readiness for our departure at 0800 hours tomorrow.

The war news is looking much better, so perhaps this conflict will end somewhat earlier than the private guess I had made of July, 1946. It will be such fun to get back to civilian life once more.

14

View from the Top

En route New Caledonia–Canton, July 26, 1944   2300 AST

General MacArthur was fifteen minutes late in arriving at the airport this morning, but we took off at 0815 hours for Tontouta, New Caledonia. Aboard the airplane as passengers were General MacArthur, General Felers, Colonel Lehrbas, Colonel Chambers (doctor), and the Pan American flight crew.

[As General MacArthur had not previously been aboard a C-54, I made him familiar with its interior arrangement. Although he appeared quite pleased with it, he seemed somewhat preoccupied, which was not his usual public manner.

We had planned the flight with refueling stops at Tontouta, a naval base at the southern tip of New Caledonia, and at Canton Island. We could have made the trip with only one stop, at Tarawa, but, knowing the general's habit of walking almost constantly while in his office, it seemed preferable to stop at least twice to allow him to stretch his legs.

The flight to Tontouta required about four and a half hours, and the weather was excellent. Since it was daylight, General MacArthur did not use the cot at all but paced back and forth in the aisle. When we parked for refueling I preceded the general down the stairway to see that all was clear for him. As he stepped to the ground, he paused for a moment, and said: "Dusty, I just realized that this is the first occasion since the war started that I am setting foot on soil over which I am not the commander in chief."

In other words it was the first time he had been away from his own command.

The general walked about the ramp until we were ready to resume the flight. When he boarded I invited him into the cockpit to watch the takeoff, but he refused. I suggested he lie down and rest, as we had about a ten-hour flight to Canton Island and would arrive there before daylight. But he appeared tense and irritable, and for the first time was somewhat abrupt with me. He paced back and forth in the aisle for the entire trip, only occasionally resting for a short time in a seat.

About halfway to Canton Island I went back to offer the passengers some food and coffee. The general ate sparingly, but it was apparent that he wanted to talk. He said if I was not needed in the cockpit I should sit beside him and relax while I had some coffee. He then started one of his characteristic monologues, to which I was not expected to reply.

Obviously I cannot quote verbatim what General MacArthur said, but the crux of his dissertation was that he was trying to prepare himself mentally for any development that might result from his meeting with Mr. Roosevelt. He could not fully comprehend why the president would pull him away from his command at this time, when the Japanese were definitely on the defensive in New Guinea and it was imperative to keep every possible pressure on them. He said the possible results of the pending conference could run the gamut, all the way from his being removed from his command, to his command's being reduced in order to provide a holding action in New Guinea, to his being given the green light, together with men and equipment, to mount an assault on the Philippines. MacArthur said he had been preparing for weeks to make the strongest possible case for the latter course of action. He believed that, it being an election year, with the president reputedly in poor health and facing some general opposition on principle, as a candidate running for unprecedented fourth term, perhaps Roosevelt had summoned him for the simple purpose of providing publicity pictures for the president, showing him conferring with his top Pacific area commanders (i.e., the general and Admiral Nimitz). He said he hoped that since he had been ordered to make this long trip and suffer some indignities thereon, the purpose would be more useful than that.]

Honolulu, T.H., July 26, 1944   1800 HWT

This is still Wednesday because we crossed the date line last night.

[When we landed at Canton, the general's mood already was one of guarded resentment and obvious apprehension. An incident soon to happen at Canton Island did nothing to improve his equanimity. We landed there before dawn on July 26 and were met by a courier carrying a radiogram from Admiral Nimitz. The message requested that General MacArthur delay his scheduled 2:30 P.M. arrival in Honolulu until 5:00 in order that Admiral Nimitz could meet him. No other reason was given. The general, now having been awake for some twenty hours and experiencing many other mental uncertainties, blew his top. To have a commander whom he considered junior to himself even to try to tell him *how* to make a trip was a bit too much.

His first reaction was to order me to send a radiogram back to Nimitz saying that if the admiral could spare even an ensign to meet him and show him to his quarters, that would be sufficient, but that we would arrive at our planned time. The radiogram we actually sent was not quite that abrupt. We did arrive almost on our estimated time at 2:45 P.M. and Admiral Nimitz was there to meet us. The admiral had thought he had a problem in that President Roosevelt, aboard the cruiser *Baltimore,* was due to arrive at the same time we were. Obviously Nimitz, as the host officer, had to meet the president. The *Baltimore,* however, arrived late, so the problem disappeared.

As we approached Honolulu we could see the sky literally filled with aircraft that had just become airborne and were maneuvering and assembling to fly a review for the president, approaching in the cruiser off Diamond Head.

Admiral Nimitz greeted the general warmly and the two departed together. MacArthur had not slept for some twenty-eight hours and his uniform was rumpled and in disarray, but he was alert and walked briskly to the automobile.

As a side comment, I could not fail to be amused by some newsmen and reputable authors who reported in great detail how General MacArthur arrived in Honolulu in *Bataan,* his famous B-17. Except for the fact that they each have four engines, there is not much resemblance between a C-54 and a B-17. One wonders how many other "facts" were as carelessly witnessed or reported.]

With considerable difficulty I got a room at the Moana Hotel, and I'm going to bed now to sleep at least twelve hours if I can. We made our landing here this afternoon just twenty-five hours and ten minutes after departing from Brisbane.

Honolulu, T.H., July 27, 1944   2230 HWT

I got thirteen hours of sleep last night but I still felt a bit dazed this morning. However, I was up at a reasonable hour and off to a busy day of shopping; I had a list of about fifty items to purchase for friends in Australia. These chores required all of the morning, and then this afternoon I got a car and went to Hickam Field to initiate plans for the return trip to Australia. I don't know just when we will depart, but I had to make arrangements for food, make certain the airplane was being properly prepared, etc.

This evening I met a number of my friends from United Air Lines.

I wonder how General MacArthur and President Roosevelt are getting along. I hope for the best, but I fear the worst. The man who refused to help the general with so much as the use of a single destroyer at Bataan now uses him to make political hay.

Above: President Roosevelt, General MacArthur, and Admiral Nimitz meet in Hawaii. Courtesy Associated Press. *Below:* General MacArthur, President Roosevelt, Admiral Nimitz, and Admiral Leahy confer in Hawaii. Courtesy U.S. Navy.

Over the Pacific, July 28, 1944

This is the day which doesn't exist because we have crossed back over the international date line.

Tarawa, Gilbert Islands, July 29, 1944   2330 HWT

Early this morning General MacArthur sent word to me that he wanted to depart for Brisbane after his lunch with the president. When he arrived at the airplane at 2:30 P.M. I could tell he was in rare good humor. I fell in step with him and had the temerity to ask if he had obtained what he wanted. He looked around to see if anyone could overhear him.

He said, "Yes, everything. We are going on."

I asked, "To the Philippines?"

He answered, "Yes. It will not be announced for a few days yet, but we are on our way."

We finally got away at 1440 hours and had a fine trip here to Tarawa in the Gilbert Islands. This is the bloody island where almost 1,000 of our marines died so heroically.

[The general is in a rare good mood, like a child with new toys. This is in stark contrast to the depressed mood he had been unable to conceal on our way to Honolulu a few days ago. He was eager to talk, and after we were well under way he discussed at length with me the manner in which he had presented his arguments to the president. He felt that in Washington the president was not receiving a balanced viewpoint concerning the situation in the Pacific, and that the president, being a navy man himself, perhaps was too much inclined to listen sympathetically to the high-ranking naval officers advising him.

He said the president had committed to him many things that would ensure the success of an operation to recapture the Philippines. One of these was that the recently activated Eighth Army would be brought up to strength as soon as possible. Another was that the Fifth Air Force would be provided with more and later-model airplanes. He said his greatest concern about a direct assault on the Philippines would be a lack of ground-based air cover for the necessary amphibious landings during their critical phases of vulnerability. He said the president had assured him he would have the full support of the naval carrier-based aircraft until such time as land bases could be prepared to provide his own ground-based air coverage.

The general said he was shocked at the president's physical appearance and marveled at the spiritual strength Roosevelt obviously possessed in order to retain his mental acumen and his wit in the face of evident physical deterioration.

During the flight from Tarawa to Brisbane I went to the cabin to have a sandwich. I sat by the general, who was still in a talkative mood. He spoke of many things, but one item stands out in my memory. He said, "You know, Dusty, if you reach for the stars you may never quite grasp them, but you'll never come up with a handful of mud." I do not know whether this observation was original with him, but I have heard it or read it several times since. Up until this occasion his discussions in my presence had generally been about factual matters, rather than in a philosophical vein.

We landed in Brisbane at 9:45 A.M., just twenty-three and a half hours after departing Honolulu, establishing what I believe is a record. Several generals of his staff met him at the airport, and as he deplaned he cautioned me to say nothing about our discussions.]

Brisbane, Australia, July 30, 1944   1945 AST

Three letters from Grace were awaiting me at the office. All is well at home. Needless to say, I'm very tired. I slept four hours this afternoon and will retire again now for another ten hours of rest.

Brisbane, Australia, July 31, 1944   2330 AST

Reported in to General Sutherland this morning and told him all about the trip. This afternoon I spent in doing my personal chores and in delivering purchases I had made in Honolulu for friends here.

Had two fine letters from Grace today and all is well at home.

Brisbane, Australia, Aug. 1, 1944   2030 AST

I went to Amberley Field this morning and then spent most of the day there trying to determine just how we could convert one of our new C-54Bs into a suitable personal airplane for General MacArthur. He was so pleased with the performance on our trip to Honolulu that he will never again be satisfied to fly in *Bataan*. The reconversion of our present cargo-type airplane to one suitable for his use would be an enormous undertaking, and this afternoon I recommended to General Sutherland that we not try it, but rather that we get the Douglas aircraft factory to make the integral changes at the time they build a new airplane. This he will try to have done.

Had a fine letter from Gracie and one from Wayne today.

[Now, almost immediately after General MacArthur's return, the tempo around GHQ has begun to increase. Although no announcement has yet been made that our next objective will be the Philippines, all of the personnel seem to sense it. Generals MacArthur and Sutherland have many long discussions on how best to plan the assault on the objective. General Chamberlin is also involved in many of these discussions, and occasionally I am privileged to listen in.

One possibility they have pursued is to land on and take a defendable base on the island of Mindanao, which is known not to be heavily defended; establish naval, air force, and supply bases; then work northward, much as New Guinea has been neutralized. Another is to go directly to Luzon, the main island that is strongly defended but that affords much better roads and other communication facilities. The third is to bypass lightly held Mindanao, attack and secure an island in the middle chain, then invade Luzon, which, of course, is the ultimate objective. General Chamberlin's G-3 is immersed in coming up with answers to many, many questions that his superiors keep throwing at him.

A subtle change is developing in the relationship between MacArthur and Sutherland which I cannot help but recognize. It has come slowly, and perhaps most of GHQ is unaware of it. I am affected directly because I report to both of them, depending upon their individual needs for my services. If MacArthur wants something from me, he discusses it with me and gives me orders directly. At all other times I receive my orders from Sutherland. My position in a very short time has developed into the most interesting one in the theater. I often can hear the discussions during which a pending campaign is conceived. I can watch the detailed planning for it and later, on some occasions, go with one of them to the scene of action to watch the execution of the operation. Thus it is of personal concern to me that these two men continue in this splendid relationship. Otherwise I will be torn by my loyalties to each of them. But a coolness between them slowly and surely is intruding. They have started treating each other with more formality and their discussions occur less frequently.

The commander in chief is the visionary, the architect, the historian, the idealist, the global philosopher, albeit the "softie" in many personal contacts. The chief of staff is the exact reciprocal: the administrator, the driver, the precise and coldly calculating brain who can and does get things done, even ruthlessly if necessary. As a team they complement each other. General MacArthur's life has been examined microscopically by many biographers, but perhaps no one has completely isolated all of the ingredients that make him tick. General Sutherland, on the other hand, is a complete enigma and still remains one to many people. But to a great extent, not realized by most, he is the real executor of the war. Doubtless it was inevitable as the war drama unfolded that MacArthur's popularity and recognition would increase with each successful campaign while Sutherland, saddled with many necessary but often unpopular decisions dealing with personnel and their activities, would slowly decline in stature and popularity. It is unfortunate that Sutherland does not receive a greater share of the credit.

General Sutherland is temperamentally a unique person. When it comes to discussing himself, he is without question the most taciturn individual I have ever known. He talks to me about any and all other subjects. I estimate that I spent upwards of one thousand hours with him or in his presence during the war years. He *never* volunteers any information about his past. When the occasion presents itself, I ask a few questions, but all I learn is that in 1944 Sutherland is fifty-one years old and that he was graduated from Yale. His father was a U.S. senator from West Virginia. He is married and his wife is acquainted with Mrs. MacArthur. He has at least one child, a daughter. He served as a private in the National Guard on duty on the Mexican border. He then was commissioned in the National Guard and as an infantry captain served for a time in France in World War I. He was on duty in China in 1938 when he was transferred to Manila, where he joined General MacArthur in an attempt to build up the Philippine Army. The General brought Sutherland out of Corregidor with him, along with a small cadre of others, to Australia before the fall of the Philippines.

His physical health appears average except for high blood pressure, a problem that at times appears to obsess him. His concern for this causes him to mention it to me frequently. Although he always appears calm and unruffled, I have learned that in highly stressful situations he often is seething within. He can make an involved decision or mercilessly rebuke a subordinate for unacceptable performance without batting an eye, but he has a habit of grinding his teeth after a stressful incident. This may or may not have contributed to the very poor condition of his teeth. I believe I am his only friend and confidant in GHQ, but in reality I certainly do not know the man on an intimate basis.

(I have my opinion about the inception and development of the schism between MacArthur and Sutherland. It is based on my close observation of the two men over a period of many months and on things that General Sutherland told me in various conversations.

I do not believe anyone would categorize our progress in the war in the Southwest Pacific prior to the time I arrived in the theater as a spectacular success. There were many reasons for this; it is doubtful whether any other leadership, given the same resources, could have done as well. Jungle warfare was a strange adventure in a new type of combat for the novice troops, who in order to survive had to learn their fighting techniques for the first time by participating in actual combat. Also, the Air Corps originally had lacked continuity of capable guidance as well as sufficient and suitable aircraft. General MacArthur was reported to be unconvinced of its usefulness.

The general had suffered defeat in the Philippines, and stopping the Japanese at Buna and Gona in New Guinea had been bloody and costly. By this time he may have had some carefully concealed self-doubts, and thus he needed all the moral and decision-making support he could get. Sutherland filled this support requirement perfectly. He was calm, perceptive, analytical, and forceful. He was not intimidated by MacArthur.

He could stand up to the commander in chief in effectively presenting his ideas. The two men made a great team. They could and did rely upon each other.

Then the tide slowly began to turn. Cape Gloucester, the Admiralties, Hollandia, and stubborn Biak were unarguable successes. MacArthur's confidence was being restored. It was upset again temporarily when he went through the worrisome waiting period preceding his critical meeting with President Roosevelt. He could even imagine himself being relieved of his command. But the meeting with the president reinforced his ego, setting him back on top of the world. By the time an advance GHQ was being planned for Hollandia, MacArthur was definitely back in the saddle and was now dominating Sutherland. The two did not talk as often as before. MacArthur was privately becoming critical of his chief of staff, although he continued to let him run the operation because no one else could do it as well. He no longer thought he needed so much support from General Sutherland. On one or two occasions I heard him mildly rebuke Sutherland for some relatively minor decisions the chief of staff had made, which were of the same type he had routinely made in the past. MacArthur did not want to be bothered by too much detail, but Sutherland began to be somewhat confused about what he himself could and could not do. I sometimes thought that Sutherland even "baited" MacArthur merely to determine just how far his own sphere of freedom extended.

There was another factor entering the picture. It is occasionally labeled "stars in the eyes." When it became apparent that there would be a tremendous increase in the size of the command in preparation for the Philippine campaign (i.e., the addition of the Eighth Army), all personnel realized there would be many promotions to staff the enhanced military units. A few of the general officers who disliked having to report through Sutherland used various methods to bypass him and go directly to General MacArthur with their problems. I suppose they hoped to impress the top man with their personalities. Some used the age-old pretext that Sutherland had not exercised field leadership under battle conditions and therefore could not properly understand their problems as MacArthur could. Strangely enough, MacArthur tolerated these minor breaches of discipline. Perhaps such action on the part of MacArthur was intentional, for the purpose of indicating to his chief of staff just who the boss was.

Whether precipitated by a single cause or rather, as I choose to believe, a multiplicity of causes and perceptions, the close, interdependent relationship between the two men that had existed during the Australian sojourn of GHQ deteriorated slowly but perceptibly.)]

Brisbane, Australia, Aug. 2, 1944   2100 AST

It has been a long day for me. I was up at 0500 hours and out to fly with General Sutherland for two hours. Then I took *Bataan* up for nearly three hours and made a flight south along the east coast of Australia almost to Sydney. It was a wild, windy day, and I saw many thrillingly beautiful spots where the wind-harried waves were pounding upon the incomparable beaches and upon the worn cliffs along the shoreline.

I returned to the office about 1500 hours, then did some paperwork there until dark. Had an early dinner and have spent the evening writing three letters. I received two nice letters today.

Had considered playing poker tonight, but later decided against it. My luck has been too good lately. I'm getting impatient for another trip to the north, but few people seem to want to travel. Someone else takes what few trips there are. I sometimes suspect that General Sutherland keeps me here purposely so that I'll always be available to him.

Brisbane, Australia, Aug. 3, 1944   1900 AST

Upon reporting to the office this morning I found little to do there, so I decided to walk to Eagle Farm and fly our new C-47. This proved to be such fun that I spent much of the day there, and then walked back to town late this afternoon. This eleven-mile walk is about the proper amount to assure me of a sound sleep. Will have to arise at 0500 hours again tomorrow, as General Sutherland wishes to fly before going to the office.

No letters today, and nothing else of interest occurred.

Brisbane, Australia, Aug. 4, 1944   2200 AST

It was a beautiful dawn this morning. Again I can vouch for that fact because I was up early to fly with General Sutherland for an hour before he had to go to the office. Afterwards I came back into town and did a few chores around headquarters.

[General Sutherland called me into his office to meet Maj. Jesus A. Villamor, who was, I believe, the only successful Filipino combat pilot. He had been assigned to headquarters after having attended various army schools in the United States. We went into General MacArthur's office for a short introduction, and the general requested that I check him out in one of our C-47s. This was not an easy task. The major, having flown very little during the previous three years, had only limited total flight experience, and that was all on small training or fighter aircraft. (As it eventually turned out, I was never able to bring him up to a proficiency level where he could be used as pilot in command, but he was useful to us on some trips as a copilot. I am sure that Major Villamor greatly resented the fact that I would not permit him to fly as pilot in command. A few months later he was transferred to other duties. After the war I believe he became head of the civil aviation authority of the Philippine government.)]

Brisbane, Australia, Aug. 5, 1944   2300 AST

At Eagle Farm this morning I flew both *Bataan* and *CXE* to calibrate the new radio altimeters which we have installed in them. This task required all morning. This afternoon I relaxed in the office and accomplished little. I did finally manage to get Captain Oviatt his well-deserved promotion to major, and also got Technical Sergeant Burden promoted to master sergeant. Perhaps this is some little accomplishment, as no one else would intercede in their behalf.

No mail today.

Tonight I played poker at Gregory Terrace for three hours. My luck was fair and I won twenty dollars. Except for the fact that I can usually win, I don't particularly like to play with this crowd. The officers are a rather rough lot and don't quite meet my standards of congeniality.

Brisbane, Australia, Aug. 6, 1944   1900 AST

It was a beautiful morning when I arose. Everything pointed to a splendid day. However, when mail call came, there were still no letters for me. The day was ruined. If the people at home could only realize how very much their letters mean to us, they would make every effort to write with regularity.

I did very little useful work today. Remained at the office all morning and then took a nine-mile walk this afternoon. Now I'm physically tired, but mentally restless. This morning I had a talk with General Sutherland. It now appears that I'll be going to New Guinea about August 11 for a few days. In the meantime I have to start Major Villamor in his flight training.

Brisbane, Australia, Aug. 7, 1944   1915 AST

It's seven months tonight since I told my family good-bye. Wonder how long it will be before I see them again. On the martial side, things have begun to look much better recently. I do not believe the Germans can stand up to our massive blows much longer, and certainly nothing is going to stop the wonderful fighting machine of the Russians. When Japan is left to stand alone against all of the world, I cannot believe she will long continue her suicidal efforts.

Today I had one letter, the first in many days, but it has given me new heart. The sky is a bit brighter, although it is raining.

I spent the morning in the office, and this afternoon I flew for two and a half hours with Major Villamor.

Tonight General Sutherland told me I am to take a load of cargo in a C-54 to Hollandia tomorrow night. That will be fun, as I'll go straight through nonstop in my favorite airplane. I am to fly with the general tomorrow morning at 0700 hours, so tomorrow will be a long day for me.

Brisbane, Australia, Aug. 8, 1944   1845 AST

Watching the sunrise is quite a regular thing with me now. We flew early this morning, and then I spent considerable time at Eagle Farm obtaining certain radio equipment for General Sutherland's airplane.

This afternoon I slept a couple of hours in anticipation of my trip tonight. Plan to depart from Amberley Field at 2300 hours and arrive at Hollandia about 0830 tomorrow morning. I'll probably return the same day.

No letters today.

Hollandia, Dutch New Guinea, Aug. 9, 1944   2100 AST

Late last night General Sutherland telephoned me to tell me that there would be a slight change in my schedule. Instead of going nonstop to Hollandia, I would have to stop at Merauke to pick up General Casey and General Sverdrup, who had been forced down there with engine trouble. We took off from Amberley Field at 2330 last night and had a fine trip through some inclement weather. We reached Merauke shortly after daylight.

[This is a famous, unkempt little village located on the edge of the vast crocodile-, mosquito-, and snake-infested swamps and savannahs of southwestern New Guinea. Before the war it had gained a notoriously infamous name and was the principal port of call for many tramp steamers passing through the Timor and Arafura seas. Upon my landing, the two stranded generals were only too glad to climb aboard the big C-54 and leave the swamp to the crocodiles and mosquitoes. Having plenty of fuel aboard, I asked them if they would like to do a little exploring en route to Hollandia. They eagerly agreed as long as we did not go too far west into the Vogelkop area, where the Japanese still might be operating a few fighter aircraft.

We took off on what was to be one of the most spectacular and incredible flights I had ever flown. Although flying has always afforded me a feeling of the ultimate superiority of man over his environment, certain flights stand out in my memory, with vivid perceptions of a higher dimension than that of an earthbound biped who is forever aspiring, but never quite attaining, the supreme goal of freedom. This was one such trip.

As we climbed out of Merauke, the swamps gave way to higher ground to the north and west. Here the jungles appeared to be impenetrable and almost like a bright green carpet on which the undulating treetops and vines climbed desperately over each other in search of sunlight. The mahogany and teak trees were distinguishable by their characteristic shades of green. There were numerous muddy creeks and rivers winding toward the sea. The entire panorama was frighteningly hostile, yet intriguing. What a horrible place to have to make a forced landing!

This was unmapped country. As we proceeded, we expected to encounter the usual foothills rising to the Oranje mountain range, but this proved not to be the case. There were small low-level cumulus clouds that prevented us from seeing the mountains as we approached them. But, suddenly, there they were, those spectacularly awesome and towering jungle-encrusted peaks! We had to circle to gain altitude, and when we climbed above the cloud layer, the vista was even more inspiring. Stretching away to the northwest was the rocky spine of New Guinea, second largest island in the world. Here, almost on the equator, the higher peaks were snow covered. Most of the slopes appeared far too steep for climbing but nevertheless were heavily jungle covered up to about 12,000 feet. Above that altitude the peaks were starkly barren, near-vertical upthrusts of rock. There were numerous knife-edged ridges leading to the bare upper peaks, and in some areas there were narrow fertile valleys between the ridges.

Judging from evidence visible from the air the native population was considerable, and it is probable that at that time most of them had never seen a white man. Probably the natives were perpetually at war with each other. Most of the villages were located astride crests of the knife-edged ridges, with the only possible approach to them being along a narrow path leading up the spines of the ridges from the valleys below. The narrow valleys had many cleared areas an acre or two in extent that appeared to be walled by barricades of large logs, as though used for farming and defensive stockades. Some of the villages were located above 11,000 feet, not far below the altitude limit for vegetation. We proceeded northwest along the crest of the range to the highest peak at about 17,000, which at that time I believe was called Mount Wilhelmina, before turning toward our destination of Hollandia. To the north of the range the terrain fell away more slowly than on the south but was inconceivably rough and completely shrouded by steaming jungle. Even the broad, swift rivers that tumbled down from the higher mountains were nearly hidden by the jungle's canopy of vines.

Thus ended an inspiring, instructive trip, a bit out of routine, and it cemented a bond of friendship that had developed over the months between General Sverdrup and myself.

A word about this remarkable, gregarious man. Jack Sverdrup was born in Norway, the son of an illustrious family of educators and businessmen. He came to the United States at the age of sixteen and attended various engineering schools, including the universities of Minnesota and

Missouri. He founded the firm of Sverdrup and Parcel in St. Louis. After the war he was instrumental in designing and/or constructing and consulting on such notable projects as the Lake Washington floating bridge in Seattle, oil pipelines in the Middle East, the huge supersonic wind tunnel at the Arnold Engineering Test Center at Tullahoma, Tennessee, the Chesapeake Bay Bridge-Tunnel complex, and the investigation of the failure of the Tacoma Narrows Bridge. His principal duty during the war was to locate, design, and build military airfields for use by the Air Force as we advanced through New Guinea and the Philippines. I flew him on many occasions in New Guinea on these survey trips to scout out possible locations for such installations. These flights, made at treetop level, were often wild and interesting and always challenging. Later he would go in, on foot if necessary, to the more promising locations and determine whether such sites were feasible from the standpoint of soil conditions, drainage, availability of building materials, and other factors to be considered in the construction of the airstrips.

After an inspection of progress on the new construction at the GHQ site at Hollandia that was to be our new home in a few weeks, I prepared to return to Brisbane early the next morning.]

This afternoon I tried to regain some of the sleep I lost last night, but there is as yet entirely too much construction work in progress here at the base. In order for Morpheus to win in a bout with a bulldozer, fatigue must indeed be great.

Brisbane, Australia, Aug. 10, 1944   2000 AST

We were up before dawn to prepare for an early takeoff from Hollandia. As there were no hitchhiking generals to be picked up en route, we were able to make the trip nonstop to Brisbane with forty passengers aboard. The highlight of the trip was, of course, the crossing of the Oranje Mountains. We landed at Amberley Field with a record to our credit: the 2,000-mile trip required only eight hours and fifty minutes! Thirty-nine passengers were happy, and one Colonel Bird was quite disgruntled because I would not permit him to smoke en route.

Brisbane, Australia, Aug. 11, 1944   2310 AST

I've been pleasingly lazy today, having done only the essential chores of existence. General Sutherland is away and there is nothing for me to do, so that I tell myself I am justified in procrastinating a bit.

Had three letters from Grace today. My disposition is improving as a result.

Jack Benny and his troupe came by the office to call on General Mac-

Arthur this afternoon. They have had a rugged tour of New Guinea and are returning there for further soldier-entertainment.

Tonight I played poker and had only moderate luck. Won twelve dollars.

Brisbane, Australia, Aug. 12, 1944   2100 AST

This morning General Akin requested me to take him to Melbourne tomorrow. I went to the airport to fly *Bataan* and *CXE* and to set the trip up for a 0800 departure tomorrow.

Melbourne, Australia, Aug. 13, 1944   2000 AST

We departed from Brisbane at 0800 hours this morning and had a fine five-hour trip to this city in *CXE*, Weather was excellent all the way. We will remain here tomorrow and then go to Sydney on Tuesday afternoon.

It is very cold and gloomy here, the temperature being only forty degrees, and there is no heat in the hotel. Since it is Sunday, the place is very dead—no movies, no people on the street, no shops of any type open for business. The war is over, as far as this city is concerned. I'm approaching the point where civilians and their unconscious attitude toward the war thoroughly disgust me. I know I should be more tolerant, but I can't help my feelings in the matter. It's much as though the people not in the military services, having gotten us all overseas, have settled back into their own smug ways and now say, "Now that you're over there, you'll have to go ahead and finish the war before you can come back anyway, so why should I worry about it?"

Melbourne, Australia, Aug. 14, 1944   2115 AST

I slept as late as possible this morning, because the bed was the only place one could be thoroughly warm in this wintry place. Then I was up and after breakfast took a long exploring trip around Melbourne on foot. Tonight I had several beers and much conversation with Dr. Klopsteg of Northwestern University, who is now research director of the National Research Institute. He is a most interesting person, albeit professorial. I will have further discussions with him at breakfast tomorrow. I'm anxious to return to Brisbane, as I understand that Washington has approved a C-54 for General MacArthur as a private airplane. There is always the possibility that I might get to go to the States to fly it over.

Sydney, Australia, Aug. 15, 1944   2100 AST

This morning I did more hiking about Melbourne, and then at 1500 hours we departed for Sydney. The weather was particularly good, for which I was thankful because I had not before seen this section of Australia. The snow-covered mountains were an unusual sight, to say the least.

We passed over Canberra and inspected it carefully from the air. It is interesting in that it is an unusual experiment in government. When the Commonwealth was formed, the various states could not agree as to the location of the federal government. Finally a compromise was decided upon. A separate plot of ground was set aside as belonging to no state, and then the supposedly model capital city was founded thereon. It is a small city, and communications with the remainder of Australia are quite inadequate. Australians generally are not too proud of the results, and the word Canberra is often heard used with particular vehemence.

We landed here at Sydney at nightfall, and there was a tie-up in our transportation. At last we got into town from the airport, and I'm billeted at the Australia Hotel. General Akin always seems to have transportation difficulties, and it's amusing, as he is signal officer and his department handles all requests, etc.

Had a fine, leisurely dinner, wrote another note to Grace, and now I'm ready to retire to read my newspaper. Bob Hope arrived in town at the same time we did, and he created quite a commotion.

Brisbane, Australia, Aug. 16, 1944   2200 AST

It was a long, dull day at Sydney, waiting for General Akin to complete his conferences so that we could depart for Brisbane. Finally we got away at 1600 hours, after I had taken several short walks about town. Our trip to Brisbane was short and perfect, and we landed at Eagle Farm soon after dark. At the office I found I had considerable mail, including two fine letters from Grace.

General Sutherland arrived here from Hollandia tonight also, and I'll have much to discuss with him tomorrow.

Brisbane, Australia, Aug. 17, 1944   2130 AST

Have been very busy since early this morning, when I talked with General Sutherland and he told me to take direct charge of the operation of the C-54s and to move them to Eagle Farm as soon as I could make the necessary arrangements for personnel, etc. I spent most of the day at Eagle Farm investigating various possibilities, etc. Now tomorrow I have to go to Amberley Field to look at the problems from the other angle. It's most interesting to me, as I'll actually be operating quite an airline of my own, with all its attendant personnel problems and operating difficulties. I couldn't ask for finer experience, but I suppose it will bring its troubles.

Brisbane, Australia, Aug. 18, 1944   2315 AST

This morning I went to Amberley Field to work out the details of a seven-day mission for one of the C-54s in New Guinea. Then when I arrived back in the office there was a mix-up about the handling of a group of generals who wanted to go to Hollandia. This required much diplomacy, etc., but was finally settled to the satisfaction of all concerned.

I'm not to move the C-54s to Eagle Farm now because I'm going to Hollandia on September 1 to be based there. There would be too many attendant problems, with no one to solve them while I am away.

I'm to take another trip to Melbourne and Sydney in the next few days. Apparently about the same sort of trip as the last one.

Brisbane, Australia, Aug. 19, 1944   2000 AST

I flew *Bataan* for an hour this morning. I was originally scheduled to go to Melbourne on Monday morning, but after a close study of the weather map I recommended to General Sutherland that I go tomorrow instead. Of course the change in plan caused some confusion, but I believe I was justified in making the change in view of possible inconveniences otherwise.

Last night General Sutherland called me to state that GHQ will be departing permanently from Brisbane by September 1 and we will be located at Hollandia. He said I should start preparing to conduct the air operation involved.

Melbourne, Australia, Aug. 20, 1944   2300 AST

This morning we took off from Brisbane for Melbourne and had a fine trip down. Major Latoszewski came as copilot, and we are enjoying each other considerably. Among other passengers, we brought four-year-old Anthony Bessemer-Clark, who is the grandson of Sir Norman Brooke and Lady Brooke. He is a fine youngster and reminded me somewhat of Jimmy. Lady Brooke met us at the airplane, and she insisted that I have dinner with her tomorrow night. I accepted largely because it will be the first chance I've ever had to observe British nobility in their home atmosphere. Lady Brooke appears to be a most likable person.

Melbourne, Australia, Aug. 21, 1944   2315 AST

This morning Lato and I were up reasonably early to catch a tram into the city in order to do some shopping. We had a fine lunch at the Menzies Hotel, went to a show, and then rode the tram back to St. Kilda Beach, where we are staying. A car called for me, and I arrived at the Brooke estate at 1845 hours. Sir Norman Brooke, Lady Brooke, Lady Cynthia Smith, and I were all there were except for a few butlers, nursemaids, etc. They have moved out of their "big house" in order that it can be used as a hospital, and are now living in the "small house," which, to my impractical eye, appeared to be large enough.

We had some delightful drinks before the fireplace in the elegantly furnished drawing room, and then we drove in to the Menzies Hotel for a very fine dinner. Lady Brooke and I got along very well together. She is coming to Brisbane for a few days next week, and she invited me to her home there. After dinner we went to Victoria University to see some movies of various war operations. Lady Brooke is commandant of the Women's Air Training Corps of Australia and as such wears the uniform of a colonel. We returned to Lady Smith's home and had late tea, and then I came back to my cold, humble hotel room at St. Kilda Beach.

It was a most interesting evening for me. I felt very much at ease and thoroughly enjoyed myself. These people are not so very different from upper-class Americans. They place much more emphasis on family and heritage and much less on material wealth. They are enormously rich, yet they always play down that theme. Most of their efforts are expended on charities and hospital work. I had the impression that they could and would stoop to any task which might be necessary in the national interest if it were only for a limited time. However, I believe they would soon break if confronted with meniality or loss of wealth and power over any protracted period of time. I shall look forward to seeing Lady Brooke if I'm in Brisbane next week.

Sydney, Australia, Aug. 22, 1944   2200 AST

When we arrived at the airport to take off from Melbourne this morning, we found that someone had broken the lock from the door of our airplane in an effort to get into it. We had difficulty in opening the door, and we also discovered a bad leak in one of the fuel tanks. As a result, we were delayed a few minutes. We arrived here in Sydney before 1300 hours, however. After a late lunch, I did little this afternoon except to write some letters. Tonight we had an invitation out to an English lady's home, but I declined because I wanted to write a letter to Grace. Lato accepted the invitation and has not yet returned.

Brisbane, Australia, Aug. 23, 1944   2245 AST

We had a leisurely morning in Sydney and then departed at 1430 hours for Brisbane. The weather en route was very bad, and to complicate matters I lost all gyro instruments and one radio set in the airplane. When we arrived over Brisbane the weather was 300 feet and half a mile. I had considerable difficulty—and fun—in trying to land on the unlighted field in the dark and in pouring rain. The airport authorities refused to turn on the runway lights. After about five futile attempts I finally managed it, much to the relief of my passengers. A few minutes ago General Sutherland telephoned to ask if I had arrived safely. He knew I had departed from Sydney and was anxious to know whether I had been able to land in the prevailing bad weather.

Had three nice letters from Grace and all is well at home. Now to bed.

Brisbane, Australia, Aug. 24, 1944   2100 AST

At the office this morning I learned several surprising and pleasant things. All of GHQ is moving to Hollandia, the move to be consummated not later than September 15 instead of September 1. I will be going up on September 1. The Americans are going to leave Australia entirely and forever, insofar as it is possible to do so. Also, Colonel Godman is being transferred to Biak Island, and I will be in full charge of the GHQ aviation section.

It now seems this latter move was inevitable, though it is also somewhat regrettable. Colonel Godman was not reasonable or logical in some of his dealings with and attitudes toward me. Since I couldn't deal with him in an open and straightforward manner, I chose not to have an open break with him, since he held a higher rank in the army. Instead, I decided to combat his offensive and obstinate attitude with a policy of pleasant and deferential service. It would appear that I have won out in the contest of personalities.

Brisbane, Australia, Aug. 25, 1944   2330 AST

Remained in the office most of the day. Had two nice letters from Grace and one from Wayne and Marge. My childhood sweetheart, Mary Susan Clark, has remarried since the death of her husband.

Tonight I played poker at Gregory Terrace and won thirty-four dollars.

Brisbane, Australia, Aug. 26, 1944   1900 AST

Spent considerable time at Eagle Farm today, making certain that the airplanes were ready for our big move to Hollandia about September 1. Came back into town this afternoon and had a talk with General Sutherland relative to the many details of the move. Tonight I'm packing my personal belongings in preparation for my departure about August 31. To-morrow morning I'm to fly with General Sutherland at 0700 hours.

Brisbane has been a comfortable place for me to live from a physical standpoint, but mentally I have often been ill at ease here. I feel that now that we are departing from Australia we will be able to get on with the war in a more satisfactory manner. I'm really looking forward to the next few months.

Had a nice talk with Col. Phil LaFollette, three-term governor of Wisconsin, this morning. He will telephone Grace when he arrives in San Francisco in a few days on leave.

Brisbane, Australia, Aug. 27, 1944   2000 AST

Was up at 0500 hours this morning to go flying with General Sutherland. It was a perfect day, and we had much fun. The balance of the morning I wasted at the office.

I expect to leave for Hollandia with the general about August 31. After that I will possibly have only infrequent short trips back to Australia. Which will please me greatly.

Now I'm pleasantly tired after my long day and some excercise. So to bed.

Brisbane, Australia, Aug. 28, 1944   2315 AST

Was up early and to the office, where General Sutherland outlined the plans for the move to Hollandia. After much telephoning and running about, I have most of the details worked out. The first of the airplanes will leave tonight and then the other will follow along in order. I'll be flying General Sutherland up on August 31.

I gave *Bataan* a test flight this afternoon. Tonight I played poker at Gregory Terrace and won five dollars. It was a most unpleasant game, as we had a drunk sitting in.

Brisbane, Australia, Aug. 29, 1944   2030 AST

This has been a terrible day. Great waves of depression have swept over me in unending succession. I don't feel well physically. Everyone who speaks to me makes me angry. It's a beautiful day, yet nothing is right. I have had a fine letter from Grace; still I wonder why she doesn't write more often. Weathermen might claim there's a low-pressure area moving in. I think it's just one of those days—

The gem cutter who promised to have two sapphires for me today went back on his word. He doesn't have them and apparently doesn't plan to get them, so I guess poor Gracie doesn't get a Christmas present from me.

Brisbane, Australia, Aug. 30, 1944   2015 AST

Tonight is my last night in Brisbane. Yet I'm not at all depressed at the prospect of leaving the place. I've been comfortable enough here, but I and many others could have been doing much more for the war effort.

I was up at 0530 hours this morning and flew with General Sutherland. Spent the remainder of the day in preparing for our departure tomorrow. I'm taking General Sutherland to Hollandia via Port Moresby. I have a feeling now that I may be back with my family within a year.

Port Moresby, New Guinea, Aug. 31, 1944   2200 AST

We departed from Brisbane on time this morning and landed at Cairns, Queensland, five hours later. We were there only sufficiently long to refuel, and then we took off for Port Moresby. Upon arriving here, we encountered quite reduced visibility, peculiar to this area. There is a volcano some miles to the east of here which infrequently erupts, but when it does, it throws out enormous quantities of fine volcanic dust, which very rapidly spreads through the atmosphere for miles to a depth of many thousands of feet. It's an interesting natural phenomenon, and I've looked a number of times for the particular crater from which the dust emerges. To date I've been unable to locate it among the maze of jungle-covered mountain ridges.

Tonight I had dinner with General Sutherland and Colonel Bartella. After dinner we had a private showing of a movie, which was not sensational. Tomorrow we fly on to Hollandia.

15

Back to the Philippines

Hollandia, Dutch New Guinea, Sept. 1, 1944 2000 AST

En route across New Guinea we flew over Mount Hagen, which is a very advanced native area deep in the center of this fabulous island. It is a broad valley whose elevation is about 6,000 feet. The valley is intensely cultivated, and the general intelligence and accomplishment are apparently far ahead of those of the remainder of the native portion of the island. The farms are laid out symmetrically, and often in such order as to create unusual geometric patterns as seen from the air.

From Mount Hagen we went down the Sepik River and out to sea along Wewak and the starving Japanese Eighteenth Army.

We arrived here at noon and had some confusion concerning transportation. I'm now located in my new home and am quite comfortable. It's only a temporary arrangement, and I'll probably be moved a time or two before I settle down permanently. I expect to be much busier here so will not miss the lack of many conveniences.

Hollandia, Dutch New Guinea, Sept. 2, 1944 2230 AST

Was up at 0500 hours again this morning, and off to Los Negros Island with General MacNider. The weather was not good, and when we arrived at our destination there was really a tropical downpour in progress. We got in all right, had lunch at the Thirteenth Air Force officers' club, and then returned to Hollandia. We arrived back here at 1600 hours.

Things are more confused here than ever. More and more officers and men are arriving every day, and there is insufficient space available for quarters and messing. This confusion probably will continue for some weeks until the poor harassed, overworked engineers can construct more buildings.

Have to be up at 0500 hours again tomorrow for another trip.

Hollandia, Dutch New Guinea, Sept. 3, 1944   2000 AST

Had some bad luck and some good luck today. I was to depart for No-emfoor Island with General MacNider and General Sutherland aboard at 0700 hours. When we started to taxi out for takeoff, a tire blew. It was fortunate to have it happen at that time, as such a mishap could have serious consequences should it occur upon a landing. We changed the tire and were off an hour later. Had a fine trip along the endless, jungle-choked swamps of northwest New Guinea, past famous Wakde Island, Owi Island, and Biak Island, and on to Noemfoor Island. This island is circular, entirely of coral formation. It is covered with jungle foliage, but is quite flat. There are two excellent coral airstrips on the northern side of the island.

I had lunch with General Sutherland, General Patrick, and General MacNider, and was most interested in hearing their discussion of both past and pending operations. The Japs on Noemfoor have been reduced from 3,000 men to an estimated 20 men, now led by a fabulous lieuten-ant colonel who still has with him his two elaborate swords. Every Amer-ican on the island is trying to kill this man in order to recover the swords.

We departed for Hollandia soon after lunch. The return trip was un-eventful, and my only disappointment was that there was no letter from Grace. I haven't been turning in a very good performance in letter writ-ing myself.

Tomorrow I have no flying scheduled. I'll be able to spend the day in accomplishing some long-neglected personal chores.

Hollandia, Dutch New Guinea, Sept. 4, 1944   2130 AST

Didn't do much of interest today. Went to the airstrip to check on the airplanes and to try to find some additional crew members for our grow-ing GHQ air force. Much of my time was taken up by the red tape neces-sary to get Sergeant Cicerello returned stateside due to the serious ill-ness of his father.

I passed up a good movie tonight because I felt that I needed my sleep more.

Hollandia, Dutch New Guinea, Sept. 5, 1944   2215 AST

This morning I flew CXE over the whole area of Humboldt Bay and the surrounding terrain to measure various elevations and to try to work out a good location for a radio range. It is a difficult task to work out an acceptable instrument letdown procedure because the terrain is rough and the adjacent mountains very near and precipitous.

Last night we had a torrential tropical downpour. My shelter was inadequate and it rained on me most of the night. As a consequence I was not too full of ambition today.

Hollandia, Dutch New Guinea, Sept. 6, 1944   2030 AST

This has been a fine and busy day. Two brand new second lieutenants, complete with shoulder-holstered pistols, reported in to me, fresh from the States. They are Second Lieutenants Normile and Shoemaker. Put one of them on a C-54 and sent him to Brisbane within an hour of the time he reported in. He is to serve as copilot with Oviatt on a return trip in a C-47. The other one I took with me first on a local flight in a B-25 and then on a local flight in a C-47. He was quite amazed, especially with the B-25, since the largest aircraft he had flown in previously was a Cessna.

Had two fine letters from Grace today. Everything seems to be well at home.

I walked the five miles from the airstrip to GHQ this afternoon. It's a climb of 1,000 feet and is splendid exercise except for the dust which is raised by the almost-constant stream of truck and jeep traffic. I'm pleasantly tired now and shall retire early.

Hollandia, Dutch New Guinea, Sept. 7, 1944   2045 AST

We had another torrential rain this morning. Little activity was possible during the storm.

This afternoon I went to the airstrip on business, and on the way back I stopped in at the 820th Air Evacuation Unit to say hello to 2nd Lt. Jean MacQueen, who is a former stewardess with UAL. She is very busy here, serving as nurse on planes which carry the wounded back from forward areas.

Hollandia, Dutch New Guinea, Sept. 8, 1944   2100 AST

General Sutherland was supposed to fly locally at 0900 hours this morning, but General Eichelberger came to call on him, and meanwhile I waited unknowingly at the airplane down on the strip. Finally he did fly at 1400 hours.

Hollandia, Dutch New Guinea, Sept. 9, 1944   2200 AST

Was up early this morning and took Sergeant Cicerello to Nadzab in a B-25 to catch the trans-Pacific airplane back to the States.

Tonight I had to attend a conference with General Akin and Colonel

Nichols relative to radio aids to flying in this theater. General Suther-land just telephoned to tell me he wanted me to take General Sverdrup on a tour of all bases to the west of here. I'll be arising early again to-morrow.

Had a nice letter from Grace today.

Noemfoor Island, Sept. 10, 1944   2130

A long and busy day today. We left Hollandia this morning and made the 600-mile trip to Middleburg Island and Sansapor. These are our most advanced points in the war at present and are still being attacked con-stantly by the Japs with what little strength they can muster. And that amount is pitifully inadequate to be more than a nuisance. There is great activity here, as the bases are being rushed to completion. I saw no Japa-nese aircraft in the air.

We landed at both Middleburg and Sansapor, and then late this after-noon we departed for Noemfoor Island, where we are spending the night. Food is almost uneatable at these places, but I shouldn't complain, be-cause the poor soldiers here have to eat it all of the time.

This island is a beautiful coral island, but it's very near the equator and very hot. I don't expect to get much rest tonight on my bare blanket. I don't mind these hardships because I have to tolerate them only very occasionally, while the soldiers based here have no comforts to look for-ward to for months to come. I think none of us has any grounds for com-plaint unless he is in combat and has to accept the very real risk of being maimed or killed.

There is much malaria and typhus. Hope I am not unfortunate enough to catch the latter. It is not often fatal, but almost always leaves the vic-tim with an impaired heart, due to the fact that the 106-degree fever usu-ally lasts for five or six days.

We leave here tomorrow for Biak Island, where we will spend the night. A good movie tonight, but I'm much too tired to sit through it.

Noemfoor Island, Sept. 11, 1944   1930

Instead of getting away as planned, we had a lot of excitement sub-stituted for our projected trip. I spent a lazy morning waiting for General Sverdrup to complete his business here and then I went to the airstrip to prepare for our takeoff at 1600 hours. I took a short sunbath.

[I was awaiting the arrival of General Sverdrup. He and General Mac-Nider drove up under the right wing of the B-25. As Sverdrup started to climb aboard through the belly hatch of the B-25 I noticed an Australian P-40 landing on the runway. The fighter airplane started to swerve directly toward us, and when a collision appeared inevitable I yelled for all to run. Sverdrup and I got about fifty feet away before the collision occurred, but MacNider froze in his jeep's driver's seat. The propeller of the P-40 cut through a fuel tank of my B-25 containing about 1,000 gallons of gasoline, which spurted over the P-40's hot engine and over MacNider. Miraculously no fire developed. But both of the aircraft and MacNider's jeep were damaged beyond repair, what with the very limited maintenance facilities available in this part of the world. The Australian pilot had been strafing Japanese installations on the Vogelkop Peninsula with his P-40 and had taken some machine gun fire in return. This gunfire had ruptured the airplane's hydraulic system, so that the pilot had no brakes. I sent a radiogram to General Sutherland informing him of our plight.]

Tonight I am billeted in General MacNider's house and am much more comfortable on a hospital bed he provided than I was last night. It's a great life, and not entirely devoid of excitement. At least no one was killed, and that is the important thing. More airplanes can always be built.

Noemfoor Island, Sept. 12, 1944   1000

Here I sit with rain pouring outside my tent, waiting for someone to arrive to fly me back to Hollandia. I feel the way an unhorsed horseman must feel. There's nothing I can do except to wait until transportation arrives to carry my crew and me back. We are going to feel keenly the loss of our B-25 as it was our best aircraft for making quick trips around the theater.

2130

I'm afraid General Sutherland has let me down. He didn't answer my radiogram today. Nor did he send an airplane to return us to Hollandia. Perhaps he believes that the accident yesterday was somehow my fault and he is punishing me for it. I know I am entirely too sensitive about it, but when I suspect someone doesn't approve of me even though I'm expending my best efforts, I have a tendency to become quite depressed. Sort of a feeling that perhaps I'm inadequate to meet the requirements of the job.

Have written two letters to Grace today, as my thoughts always seem to turn to her when the going gets tough.

I've made arrangements to return to Hollandia by air freight tomorrow morning. It will be a bit unusual for me to be riding in a cargo airplane.

2330

Played poker for a while this evening and lost heavily. I guess this is simply not a lucky period for me.

Will be glad to get away because I hate to infringe on General Mac-Nider's hospitality any longer than is necessary. Perhaps tomorrow I can get away.

Hollandia, Dutch New Guinea, Sept. 13, 1944   2100

Early this morning I had a radiogram from General Sutherland to the effect that he was sending a C-47 down to get us. Major Oviatt arrived at 0830 hours, and by 1145 hours we were back here in Hollandia.

Had a letter from Grace and one from Wayne. My desk was piled with papers, so I'll be busy for a couple of days, bringing things up to date.

I reported to General Sutherland concerning the loss of our airplane, but he already had the complete story from General Sverdrup. He was not nearly as unhappy about our loss of the aircraft as I was.

[When I returned to the office in Hollandia there was a new element of excitement in the air. Until that time G-3 (operations) had been planning, as the next moves, the capture of Mindanao, then Leyte, and finally Luzon, in that order. I asked General Sutherland what was causing the furor. He said General MacArthur had received a message from the Joint Chiefs of Staff in Washington asking whether or not the next advance could be made directly to Leyte, thus bypassing Mindanao, and if so what timetable could be met. Sutherland said he was on the spot, since this was the type of decision MacArthur reserved for himself alone and he could not get MacArthur's approval because the general was aboard the *Nashville* engaged in the Morotai landing. The cruiser was maintaining radio silence. Sutherland made the decision in the affirmative and advised MacArthur that he had done so (the *Nashville* could receive messages but was not sending any)].

Hollandia, Dutch New Guinea, Sept. 14, 1944   2200

I spent the early morning at my desk, and then went to the airstrip to fly *Bataan*, which I hadn't been in for some weeks. After lunch I flew with General Sutherland for an hour and a half. He promised me I could get another B-25 in a few days.

It appears now that I'll be going to Brisbane and Canberra in about a week. I may remain there for about two weeks. As yet, I do not know.

Tonight General Sutherland instructed me to take a trip to Nadzab and return in a C-47.

Hollandia, Dutch New Guinea, Sept. 15, 1944   2100

The trip to Nadzab and return was uneventful. I was disappointed to find that the latest package Grace had dispatched to me had not yet arrived at Nadzab, but when I got here last night I found that some kind soul had already brought it to me.

Also had a fine letter from Grace. I feel like I'm having a ten-minute furlough from all my troubles when I get a letter from her.

Hollandia, Dutch New Guinea, Sept. 16, 1944   2230

[General MacArthur had arrived back from the landing on Morotai and was in very good spirits.]

Attended a conference this morning and then drew up plans for a building for a lounge room for my men at the airstrip. They have little enough of the comforts and they at least deserve some shelter from the rain and dust. Late this afternoon General Sutherland decided to fly for an hour, and we had quite a visit while aloft. He told me of various changes in war plans, which were most thrilling but very secret. I asked him if I could go in on one of the landings, and he said he would see if he could arrange it on the *big* one. It would be the culmination of thrills for me if I could go, as the day that General MacArthur sets foot on the soil of the Philippines again will be a day that will be remembered in history.

Hollandia, Dutch New Guinea, Sept. 17, 1944   2000

Went to the airstrip this morning to fly *Bataan* for an hour. When I returned to the office I had considerable mail, which is always pleasing.

This afternoon I had to work with the engineers on the proposed site and arrangement of our building at the airport.

Tonight General MacArthur informed me that he might wish to depart for Brisbane early tomorrow. I had my crew on the alert, but at 1900 hours he said that he would not leave until Tuesday morning. It will be a welcome relief from the heat and the jungle here.

[Yesterday or today the first open break occurred in the relationship between MacArthur and Sutherland. I did not witness it, but I certainly felt the repercussions. Sutherland had ordered his Australian WAC friend to Hollandia, and she was performing some hostess-type duties at the various activities in GHQ. This was contrary to MacArthur's sense of propriety, and Sutherland knew it. There are many female military per-

General MacArthur confers with Admiral Barbey during the Morotai operation. Courtesy U.S. Navy.

sonnel, including hospital nurses, evacuation nurses, and others, in Hollandia, and I suppose Sutherland reasoned that if it was proper for them to be there it was proper for his friend also. To me she did not seem to be particularly out of place here. When MacArthur learned of her presence, however, he reportedly was furious.

Additionally, although General Sutherland had made the correct decision, to bypass Mindanao, and had advised the Joint Chiefs of Staff, it is my opinion that General MacArthur somehow resented his having done so. It is possible that MacArthur might have accepted the fact that Sutherland had made the strategic decision on his own but for the fact that all high-level commanders, including those in the navy, knew that Sutherland and not MacArthur was the source of the decision. This made it appear that Sutherland was usurping some of the commander in chief's authority.

At any rate, General Sutherland related to me some of the facts concerning the very heated argument he had had with General MacArthur. He said it had been such a disagreeable event that he doubted a complete rapprochement between the two was possible. He had told the commander in chief that he would be happy to take extended sick leave or resign. MacArthur would not accept either. In truth, there was no one else MacArthur could substitute for Sutherland at this very important juncture. No one else had a complete grasp of the entire situation. Sutherland said that his blood pressure had shot up alarmingly and that as soon as MacArthur had departed for Brisbane he was going to rest for a few days, even though GHQ would be busier than ever changing plans to accomplish the Leyte operation. He was in a surprisingly good mood, as though the confrontation had relieved him of a great burden. Sutherland told me he believed it desirable to send the Australian WAC captain back to Australia for a time, to allow things to cool down. He said he would like to send her with me on *Bataan I* when I took MacArthur there, but under the circumstances that was not possible. He asked me to schedule a separate trip for one of my flight crews to take her later.]

Hollandia, Dutch New Guinea, Sept. 18, 1944   2100

I've spent most of today in seeing that everything was in readiness for my trip with General MacArthur to Brisbane, starting early tomorrow. Can't afford to have anything go wrong at the last minute.

Late this afternoon General Sutherland called me in to discuss various things relative to our air operations here. He told me of the speedup of all plans in this theater and he was in very good humor, since he was now virtually in command of all operations. Apparently he had decided not to allow his confrontation with General MacArthur to affect his outlook. He told me of the plans for entering the Philippines, and I asked

On duty in New Guinea.

him point-blank if I couldn't accompany General MacArthur and him when they made the first landing there. To my surprise he said he would take me with him as an assistant if necessary. I'm naturally more thrilled about that than about anything else that has happened to me during this war. The day that MacArthur sets foot upon Philippine soil again, he will have made good his famous promise of "I leave you now, but I shall return." For me to take part in this historic landing will be a treat far beyond my greatest expectations. I had resigned myself to remaining in Hollandia to bring the airplanes forward when it was safe to do so.

Port Moresby, New Guinea, Sept. 19, 1944   2100

General MacArthur arrived at the airplane at 8:20 A.M. and said he would like to remain overnight at Port Moresby. We made an easy flight down from Hollandia this morning and arrived here in time for lunch. We were delayed a half hour at takeoff, due to the fact that an official flash came in over the radio that Germany had surrendered. Naturally, General MacArthur did not wish to leave until he could confirm the report. When he talked to Washington directly, he learned that it was only a false rumor.

I am staying in the governor's mansion here with the general, and he amused us for hours with anecdotes from his colorful career. He is truly a great character because he possesses the highest of ideals and the strength to live up to them, regardless of opposition.

One incident he related is worth telling here because it reveals his moral fiber. In 1925 he was given command of the IV Corps Area, with headquarters at Atlanta, Georgia. At the time this was quite a promotion for him. His father had made a name for himself with the Union army in the Civil War, but his mother had had six brothers in the Confederate army. So the general took up his duties in the Deep South, anxious to make good in this land where narrow prejudices prefixed the name of MacArthur with the usual "damn Yankee." His first Sunday there, he took his staff with him, and all attended church. They entered the crowded church and proceeded to their allotted seats. When they were seated, three-quarters of the congregation arose and walked out. And this happened sixty years after the Civil War had ended! MacArthur said nothing to anyone about the incident, but he quietly telegraphed the War Department and asked to be relieved of his command, which had been such a promotion for him. His request was granted, and he departed with rancor in his heart but with no words of denunciation for the small people who had treated him so shabbily. Any lesser character would have been so bitter at this treatment that he would have hit back at his persecutors with ill-advised condemnation of their narrow prejudices.

Brisbane, Australia, Sept. 20, 1944   2000

[We departed Port Moresby at 0810 with a stop scheduled for lunch at Townsville. On the way General MacArthur spent a good deal of the time in the cockpit and once more wanted to see some of the Great Barrier Reef, so we deviated to the east to fly over a portion of it. We had a very jolly lunch at Townsville and the general was literally bubbling with enthusiasm. At last the way was clear for him to proceed to the Philippines.

On our flight from Townsville to Brisbane I had an opportunity to tell the general, half jokingly, that he would need a bodyguard when he stepped ashore at Leyte and that I could handle an army .45 automatic quite effectively. He smiled and said, "Would you like to go along?" He was no more committal than that. (Later, when the list of army personnel who would proceed to Leyte aboard *Nashville* was published, my name was fifth among nineteen individuals.)]

Brisbane, Australia, Sept. 21, 1944   2030

Spent a lazy day today, writing letters, walking, etc. Practically all of GHQ has moved to Hollandia, so there's nothing for me to do except to wait until General MacArthur is ready to take the trip to Canberra to say farewell to Prime Minister Curtin. Late today he decided to allow General Sverdrup to go in *Bataan* to Canberra tomorrow to see the prime minister. So we will be departing early in the morning. That will be much more fun than remaining in Brisbane.

Melbourne, Australia, Sept. 22, 1944   2330

We arrived in Canberra at 1030 hours this morning and remained there until 1430. I was pleased to have the opportunity to see Canberra at close range.

[The city itself was an experiment in long-range planning when it was first conceived in 1908, primarily as a central location for the seat of government for Australia.

It is a strange sight to see large, multistoried structures alone in the center of a pasture with sheep grazing peacefully around them. Large buildings appear very lonely when unsupported by other surrounding structures.

We departed Canberra at 2:00 P.M. and flew to Melbourne, where we spent the night.]

Brisbane, Australia, Sept. 23, 1944   2330

After breakfast in Melbourne this morning I took a two-hour walk along the beach. The air was crisp and invigorating, and I had much splendid exercise under ideal conditions. There is a fine natural collection of bird life along the seashore there, where existence is made easy by virtue of an abundant supply of mollusks and other marine life.

We departed at noon and had a fine four-hour trip to Brisbane.

[On the way General Sverdrup offered me the use of his beach house at Surfer's Paradise on the ocean south of Brisbane. Contingent upon General MacArthur's plans, I accepted.]

Brisbane, Australia, Sept. 24, 1944 2000

The usual Sunday atmosphere in Brisbane today—good weather, everything closed up, and no excitement. I accomplished little in a useful way. Wrote letters this morning and walked an hour this afternoon. I have absolutely no duties here outside of such little flying as I have to do. General Sutherland is not here to crack the whip, and General MacArthur is doing the unheard-of thing of taking a rest. When I contacted him he said he actually had been going for a drive each afternoon with Mrs. MacArthur and Arthur.

Brisbane, Australia, Sept. 25, 1944 2300

Walked to Eagle Farm this morning, flew *Bataan* for an hour, and then walked back. That's an eleven-mile hike, so that I now have that pleasantly tired feeling.

Brisbane, Australia, Sept. 26, 1944 2315

I did nothing useful today. Remained around the office for several hours and then came to my room to read a late novel, *Colcorton*, which is a good sociological study.

Tonight I played poker at Gregory Terrace and won thirty-five dollars.

Brisbane, Australia, Sept. 27, 1944 2300

The Raven out my window croaks
(And I'm surprised as Poe)
Those fellows at Dumbarton Oaks,
They really knead our dough.

Queer what reactions we have from the bits of news from back home. No doubt it's a good thing to be able to attempt to keep one's sense of humor when reading of the schemes of our bureaucrats. I think we who are now in the military service are going to take considerable interest in political affairs when this war is over.

This morning I walked to Eagle Farm, flew *Bataan* for an hour, and then walked back. The eleven-mile hike has pepped up my circulation a bit. When I set foot on Philippine soil alongside General MacArthur, I hope to be in perfect physical condition.

Tonight I played poker. Won thirty-five dollars.

Brisbane, Australia, Sept. 28, 1944   2315

This has been an idle day for me. There's been nothing to do except to write letters and read.

Brisbane, Australia, Sept. 29, 1944   1930

Walked to the airport this morning, flew *Bataan* for an hour in formation with Major Beezley, and then walked back to town.

General MacArthur telephoned me to say that he wants to depart for Canberra at 0700 hours tomorrow to pay his respects to Prime Minister Curtin. This means a very early call for me in the morning. Will be returning tomorrow afternoon, and then I will have to take *Bataan* to Townsville for an engine change.

No letters for three days now. I depend on them so much that it's most depressing when I receive none.

Brisbane, Australia, Sept. 30, 1944   2100

[It was a routine but pleasant trip to Canberra, where we spent four hours. I had the pleasure of meeting Mr. Curtin as well as the United States ambassador and his wife, Mr. and Mrs. Nelson Johnson. General MacArthur said his final farewell to Mr. Curtin at the airplane, and it was an emotional parting. At the time I wondered why the open display of sentiment. On the return flight the general told me Mr. Curtin had disclosed that he was suffering from an incurable disease and doubtless the two would not meet again. The two men had worked very closely together during a war situation, and many times conflicts had arisen between U.S. military personnel and local civilian authorities. These had to be resolved diplomatically. The confrontations could have been very difficult, even unpleasant, if either of the men had failed to cooperate and compromise between themselves.

When I inquired of General MacArthur regarding his need for *Bataan I,* he said he had no plans for its use for a few days. I would have an opportunity to fly the plane to Townsville to our large repair base there to have the engines replaced and various other types of repair work performed.]

General MacArthur confers in Canberra with Prime Minister Curtin and U.S. Ambassador Nelson Johnson. Courtesy U.S. Army.

Upon my arrival home I had a number of nice letters, answering all of which will give me something to do. Grace and the boys are getting along nicely, and Jimmy will be starting back to school the day after tomorrow.

Brisbane, Australia, Oct. 1, 1944 through Oct. 10, 1944

I kept in contact with General MacArthur almost daily during this period to make sure he did not need me. I had the B-17 worked on at Townsville, spent time relaxing at General Sverdrup's cottage at Surfer's Paradise, and exercised strenuously.

Although I made daily entries into this diary, I have condensed them into these paragraphs in the interest of brevity.

Brisbane, Australia, Oct. 11, 1944   2115

This morning Colonel Egeberg and I went out to Camp Columbia and practiced rifle firing on the range. We spent about three hours there, during which time I fired 135 rounds. This, coupled with some inoculations I had yesterday, has left the old body sore and creaking.

[That evening Roger and I spent many hours philosophizing about life in general and our own tiny part in the larger picture. I had arrived in Australia just nine months before to the day. That arrival day seemed very far away. Roger had been in the theater longer, but we had both joined MacArthur about the same time. We both had spent many hours alone here during inactive periods, sometimes with little to do but think and dream. And there would be countless other similar hours ahead—of physical discomfort, of loneliness among many, of fatigue, of self-pity, and of frustration. Roger and I vowed that after the war was over we would find some way of simplifying our lives.]

Brisbane, Australia, Oct. 12, 1944   1930

Today I flew *Bataan* for an hour. Did nothing else useful. No mail today.

Brisbane, Australia, Oct. 13, 1944   2200

The first thing this morning I had two fine letters from Grace. With this good start I went to the airport and flew *Bataan* to Amberley Field on business. I returned to town for lunch and then spent most of the afternoon packing, etc. Our departure with General MacArthur is at 0800 hours tomorrow, and we are on our way to the Philippines!

Port Moresby, New Guinea, Oct. 14, 1944   2100

[This morning we departed from Brisbane with General MacArthur and made a short stop at Townsville on the way to Port Moresby, where we are remaining overnight. Shortly after we arrived here General Sir Thomas Blamey, commander in chief of the Australian military forces and commander of the Allied land forces in New Guinea, stopped by to pay his respects to General MacArthur. I was privileged to listen to their discussions, which for the most part involved the further use of Australian troops.

(In retrospect, I remember distinctly hearing MacArthur tell Blamey that he would issue orders that no women in the Australian armed forces would be used north of the equator. Whether such a written order was ever actually issued I do not know. And, if it was, I do not know whether such an order applied equally to Australian women in the *American* army.)

This evening General MacArthur lingered over dinner, keeping us entertained and amused with stories of his past experiences. These monologues, in which he seems to indulge himself only when surrounded by a small group of trusted friends, are fascinating experiences for me. They show the general at his oratorical best in that he chooses the subject matter and the pace at which he expounds.]

Hollandia, Dutch New Guinea, Oct. 15, 1944   2000

[Today we departed Port Moresby for Hollandia. I was not feeling well at all and suspected I had a fever. Additionally, I felt an almost depressing sense of responsibility on the four-hour flight, which I had always enjoyed in the past because of the spectacularly beautiful scenery. General MacArthur's dominant aim in life now is to return to the Philippines. It is almost an obsession with him. All these years he has worked and planned for it. If I should in any way be responsible for delaying or preventing the attainment of his goal, I would never recover from the sense of inadequacy.

As we approached Hollandia I became more ill by the moment, but my copilot, 2nd Lt. John Shoemaker, was not sufficiently experienced to make the landing. My approach to the airstrip was satisfactory; my landing was unusually bad. My depth perception seemed to be greatly affected. As I left the cockpit to assist the general in deplaning, he asked me what had happened on the landing. I told him I had merely blown it. I did not want him to suspect that I was ill, because he might suggest that I turn in to the hospital instead of boarding the *Nashville* tomorrow morning en route to the Leyte landing. A great burden was lifted from me when the general deplaned. I had successfully completed the first leg of his return to the Philippines.

Generals Sutherland and Kenney met us at the airstrip, and there was no external evidence of the friction that had occurred earlier.

As soon as I had the opportunity I asked General Sutherland if I was still on the passenger list for the *Nashville,* and he assured me that I was. He kept me for an hour, questioning me about what had happened in Australia and discussing the detailed plans for the pending operation. All this time I was feeling too ill to care much about what he said.

I managed to pack some belongings this afternoon in preparation for an extended absence from Hollandia. I am now going to bed to try to gain as much strength as possible for tomorrow.]

Aboard U.S.S. *Nashville,* Oct. 16, 1944   2100

This has been one of the happiest and yet one of the grimmest days I've ever spent. This morning we were up quite early, and amid much confusion in a pouring rain we finally went aboard the *Nashville* at 1000 hours. I felt most miserable from the effects of what I thought was an approaching cold. However, I hid my condition from everyone for fear that I might be left behind. General MacArthur, Lieutenant General Sutherland, and Lieutenant General Kenney came aboard just before noon, and we were on our way. Lieutenant Thornton, one of the *Nashville's* officers, showed me about the ship. It is a 13,000-ton light cruiser built in 1937 and is one of the most up-to-date in our fleet. It carries fifteen six-inch rifles along with much antiaircraft armament, varying from twenty-mm to five-inch.

After lunch I had a long informal visit with General Sutherland. And then General Kenney came up on deck and talked to me for about three hours—all about plans and flying and personalities. It was the first time I'd had a long talk with him, and I'm proud of the fact that I've been permitted these intimate glimpses of so remarkable a man.

During our pacing of the deck I could feel myself growing steadily more ill at ease, and I was glad when he finally terminated his conversation. I went down to dinner, but suddenly became quite ill at the table and had to excuse myself. Soon I called Doc Egeberg, General MacArthur's aide, to my room, and he gave me a thorough examination. He finally said it probably was dengue fever, and now I feel perfectly miserable. My temperature is 101 degrees, and I'm having alternate chills and fever. Not only am I physically a sick man, but I'm mentally tortured by the fact that I have waited until the very eve of the most exciting point in my career to be incapacitated by one of the very few illnesses of my life. However, Doc says that in my excellent condition the fever may run its course in a couple of days, and that I may be quite able to go ashore at the landing. Right now I'm thoroughtly disgusted and thoroughly exhausted—

Above: General MacArthur confers with Generals Whitehead and Blamey. Courtesy U.S. Army. *Below:* General Kenney, Major Burton, and I on the deck of the *Nashville.*

Aboard U.S.S. *Nashville*, Oct. 17, 1944   2100

Well, this has been a bad day for me. My temperature has gone down considerably, but I'm still quite weak. My stateroom is very hot and the fever makes it appear more so, and I'm so sweaty and dirty that I stink. Still Doc Egeberg will not allow me to take a bath because of its weakening effect. Then I'm disappointed over the fact that I'm missing so many interesting things, such as torpedo drills, aircraft catapulting, etc. Doc tells me that if I'm a good boy today, tomorrow he *may* allow me to go up on deck and lie quietly in the open air.

Aboard U.S.S. *Nashville*, Oct. 18, 1944   2115

Was up early this morning and had a nice shave and bath, and although I'm still very weak and have some temperature, I've managed to remain out of bed all day.

It has been a most interesting day. Among other things I've watched three airplane catapultings and pickups and have bothered the navigation officer all day. He navigates very much the same as we do in aerial navigation, but in addition to the facilities we have, he has access to many other reliable aids, such as radar, accurate ocean current charts, accurate speed indicators, etc.

After lunch we joined up with the main convoy. It consists of some 280 additional ships of all types, and its size is almost beyond comprehension. This convoy is only one of the two which are to be involved. Including the other portion of the convoy which joined us from Seeadler Harbor, nearly 750 ships are involved. Late this afternoon we came alongside a tanker and refueled to our capacity. This ship holds 650,000 gallons.

From this point on, the excitement is going to increase rapidly. The softening-up process on Leyte Island has started, and we have made three unopposed landings on small outlying islands. Our guerrillas have succeeded in getting the civilian Filipinos evacuated from our landing points except in the the town of Tacloban, and there the Japs will not allow them to evacuate. Unfortunately, many of them may be killed and injured in the necessary shelling and bombing.

We had been making about twenty-five knots until we reached the convoy, but then we slowed and now are cruising at about twelve knots.

We are running under total blackout, and I have considerable difficulty in finding my way about this unfamiliar ship. This evening I watched the navigator take another celestial fix. I feel quite sure that I could handle the complete navigation of the ship.

Tonight I remained on deck for three hours, watching the activities on the darkened ship. The most pleasant part was watching the water from high up on the bow. The ship glided through the water with hardly a whisper, under a clear, starlit sky with the soft night breeze slipping along the deck. The water was aglow with phosphorescence. I reluctantly have come below for a few hours of sleep in my hot room.

Aboard U.S.S. *Nashville*, Oct. 19, 1944   2230

Was up before daylight this morning to watch the antisubmarine precautions, which are taken at dawn and dusk, as those are the most propitious times for the submarines. It was a beautiful dawn, and the convoy, stretched as far as one could see, was truly an impressive sight. Last night we had two alarms as the radar picked up two floating mines off our port side. Evidently there were subs ahead of us dropping those mines in the hope that a ship would collide with them in the dark. But for good old radar, we might have done so.

We have been going about ten knots all day, as we have to stay back to help protect the convoy. We are approximately 100 miles off the coast of the Philippine Islands now, and are running parallel to them. We are subject to Jap air and submarine attack at any time, and the ship is on constant alert. I have been fascinated all day at the operation. Paravanes, minesweepers, catapults, turret loading practice, and all the rest.

Tomorrow is D day, and I expect to be up at least by 0200 hours so that I will not miss any of the excitement. The naval shelling and dive-bombing will occur just before daybreak. The Japs now know that we are coming, and our intelligence reports they are dug in on the beach awaiting us. It's probably going to be a bloody scrap, and we can fully expect him (the Jap) to make an all-out air attack on this convoy. If he is smart, however, he will attack at night, as we will be able to give ourselves plenty of protection during daylight.

Aboard U.S.S. *Nashville*, Oct. 20, 1944   2115

What a wonderful day this turned out to be! I was up very early expecting things to start happening, but they were slow in getting under way. Just before 1000 hours the shelling of the beaches started, but we were too far away to see much of it. The rocket ships poured their short-range rockets into the beaches and then withdrew. This ship did not take part in the shelling. Finally about 1200 hours we started in to the beach in an LCM. There were ten officers in our party including Generals MacArthur, Sutherland, and Kenney, President Osmeña, Colonels Egeberg, Lehrbas, Whitney, and Wheeler, and myself. We could not get the LCM all the way on the beach, but had to wade ashore in water about knee deep. Dive bombers were making a beautiful show of taking out some gun emplacements on the hills back of the beach, and there was much firing from our guns on the beach. Everything from rifles to 155-mm was being used. There was, of course, much picture taking, and General Mac-Arthur and President Osmeña made radio broadcasts to their respective peoples. Then we plunged into the jungle and were hard pressed to keep up with the general as he visited several command posts in the front lines. Our losses so far have been relatively small. I saw quite a number of dead Japs, but only one wounded American.

[At one point, when the general paused for a few minutes, I edged up to the friendly trunk of a large palm tree, just in case. He noticed my movement, came over, and said, "What's the matter, Dusty, are you worried?"

I replied that I felt more comfortable when near the tree trunk. He volunteered, "Well, the Almighty has given me a job to do, and I expect to be able to finish it."

I replied that I was not sure the Almighty was equally interested in my survival, and the general walked on, smiling.

A very heavy tropical rain descended on us at this point. Otherwise I do not know how much farther the general would have proceeded into the combat area. At any rate, we withdrew to the beach and returned to the *Nashville* thoroughly soaked. En route to our ship we saw a lone enemy bomber come out of the clouds and attack the cruiser *Honolulu*, which took a direct hit and was badly damaged. Two tugs quickly came to her aid.

Back aboard the *Nashville*, things were relatively quiet until shortly after dinner, when the air raid alarm sounded. We all rushed to the deck to watch the excitement. Soon a Japanese bomber came over, quite high and above some scattered clouds. The *Nashville*, as well as all other combat vessels in the area, opened fire with antiaircraft guns of all sizes. I have never seen a more awesomely beautiful display of fireworks. The amount of shrapnel thrown into the air was incalculable, and the din aboard our firing ship indescribably impressive to an amateur like me. I had not stopped to realized that on our steel ship the firing noise of our guns would reverberate back and forth from the many flat surfaces until the sound became deafening. The Japanese airman decided to turn away and perhaps return another night.

Regarding the picture taking during MacArthur's landing on the beach, fulfilling his long-promised "return," there occurred some events, which, coupled with substitutions of photographs later, illustrate how the true records of historical events can be distorted. The picture of the real landing was published in *Life* magazine on November 13, 1944. In the foreground were General Sutherland (on MacArthur's left), General MacArthur, and Sergeant Abug. Just behind were General Kenney, Major Burton, and I. This picture was not to the liking of Colonel Whitney because he was not in it. Also, Carl Mydans, a photographer whose wife had been im-

Above: General MacArthur at ease on the deck of the *Nashville. Below:* General MacArthur talks with General Krueger and Admiral Kinkaid aboard the *Nashville.* Photographs courtesy U.S. Navy.

The landing at Leyte on October 20, 1944. Wading ashore are (*left to right*) myself, Major Burton, General Kenney, Sergeant Abug, General MacArthur, and General Sutherland. Courtesy UPI–Bettmann Photos.

prisoned by the Japanese in Manila and who was a friend of General Mac-Arthur's, some three months later arranged to stage a simulated picture on Luzon that he could take. That photograph shows General Sutherland on General MacArthur's right and Colonel Lehrbas positioned in the picture where General Kenney was in the true photograph. Still another picture shows Colonel Whitney just to the rear of General MacArthur. He was not in the original photo. All three pictures are at times captioned as having been taken upon MacArthur's initial return to the Philippines.]

I forgot to mention that a destroyer off our port side ran into two mines this morning just before daylight. She was badly hurt but managed to beach herself.

Aboard U.S.S. *Nashville*, Oct. 21, 1944   2000

There was an air alert at 0430 hours this morning, which aroused me from a fitful, hot sleep. We all hit the deck, but no enemy planes came within reach of us. They did some bombing on shore.

We had news this morning that the cruiser *Australia* took a hit on her bridge when a Jap suicide pilot flew his airplane directly into her. All ranking officers aboard were killed. Both the *Australia* and the *Honolulu*, now crippled, are on the way back for repairs.

[At 9:30 A.M. I accompanied General MacArthur to a landing on the beach below Tacloban. There we obtained jeeps and drove over much of the area we had captured to date. We visited the airstrip, which by our standards was not much of a landing area. The underlying soil was not compacted, and the Japanese had laid down a steel mat of sorts. The matting was very light, about the equivalent of our cyclone fencing material; it served the purpose for the lightweight fighter aircraft they flew but was entirely inadequate for use by our much heavier airplanes. Our engineers were in the process of rebuilding the airstrip from the foundation up.

We proceeded up the road toward the town of Tacloban but did not get far before being blocked by our heavy tanks, which were moving in to mop up any of the enemy remaining in the area. By 2:00 P.M. the town had been secured. It was heartrending to see the poor Filipinos who had survived our shelling. They were predominantly children under ten and older men and women; the ablebodied adults had been pressed into labor service and moved elsewhere. Some of the old men still had their *carabao* (water buffalo), some of which had miraculously survived our shelling, and already they were working in the fields. Our troops had captured a great deal of food that the Japanese had stored in Tacloban. This was given to the Filipinos, who were then well provisioned for some time to come.]

General MacArthur confers behind Leyte Beach with Generals Sutherland, Mudge, and Kenney. Courtesy U.S. Army.

We returned to the *Nashville* at 1300 hours. During lunch we were interrupted by another air alarm, but no aircraft appeared. Things remained quiet for the afternoon. We got under way about 1700 hours. We cruise about every night, so that we are less subject to night air attack. All of the Jap bombing has occurred in near the beach. Through an inadvertent news release, it was broadcast that General MacArthur was aboard the *Nashville*, and today Tokyo Rose announced that the *Nashville* would never depart from Philippine waters. Naturally they are making every effort to sink us and to destroy General MacArthur.

Tonight just at dusk we had another air alert. There was much anti-aircraft firing from ships near the beach, but no enemy aircraft came near us. We will, no doubt, have an alert tonight. Tomorrow will be a busy day, as we will go ashore at Dulag to see the airstrip there, which will probably be our main bombing strip in this area. We also will scout around for a location for installing an advance echelon of GHQ.

Aboard U.S.S. *Nashville*, Oct. 22, 1944   2000

Had our usual air alert this morning to disturb our sleep, but nothing happened. Ships in near the beaches shot down four "bogies" last night. This morning we went ashore at Dulag to visit General Krueger and the Sixth Army. He has made excellent progress in his landing. The village of Dulag must have contained about 10,000 Filipinos prior to the invasion, but after our shelling and bombing there now isn't a single house standing intact. Most of the natives got out before our attack, but quite a number were killed. We visited some of our wounded in a bombed-out old church and also contacted three wounded Jap prisoners. We then visited the airstrip, which shows good possibilities for development. Saw many *carabao* which had been killed in the shelling, as well as many that had not. We then went up to the front lines to watch our forces shelling a hill where the Japs were cut off and entrenched. There was a tank trap across the road that was about as effective as a telephone line would have been. Our tanks went through it as though it wasn't there. We returned to the *Nashville* for a late lunch and had a quiet afternoon. But soon after dinner the Japs, true to their unchanging tactics, came in on an air attack. They were obviously looking for our cruiser, as they came in low with torpedo planes. I saw our accompanying destroyers shoot down two of them before they came within range of our guns. We weren't given an opportunity to fire a single round.

The guerrilla chief, Kangleon, now a colonel in our army, came aboard with us. He is a most interesting little man, and for two and a half years has kept his forces well organized and fighting against hopeless odds. He is now doing invaluable service with harassing attacks at the Japs' rear.

I have an enormous appetite and can't get enough sleep these days. I suppose that is natural in view of my activity and the accompanying excitement.

General Sutherland told me tonight that he was planning on arranging for some kind of air transportation for the two of us back to Hollandia in a few days. It will probably have to be by seaplane as the airstrips will not be suitable for large aircraft for some time yet.

[During our stay aboard *Nashville* and on our various trips ashore it was interesting for me to observe the relationship between Generals MacArthur and Sutherland. They were most affable when together, and I could detect no rancor remaining from their confrontation at Hollandia. They did not, however, appear to consult as frequently as had been their habit in the past. But then there were not as many current problems to be discussed as during the protracted planning period.

This evening General Sutherland and I had a two-hour session about moving many of the critical elements of GHQ from Hollandia to Tacloban. The files and certain personnel are badly needed, and we will move them by air. The less critical items can come by ship. We will need more large aircraft to accomplish this. There is an ample supply of idle B-24s at Nadzab. We will requisition two of these, and as I have flown this type of airplane previously I will have to check out two or more of my flight crews on them.]

Aboard U.S.S. *Nashville*, Oct. 23, 1944   1845

At midmorning we left the *Nashville* via PT boat and went to the town of Tacloban. This place of about 15,000 natives has suffered very little damage from our attacks, as our tanks have driven the Japs out by an attack from the flank. The city is particularly dirty, almost filthy. Even in peacetime I doubt if it was much better, but now, with the Japs' having occupied it so long, it is almost uninhabitable for us. The American soldiers are as usual quite lavish with their ample money, using it largely for trading in Jap souvenirs, since there is nothing else to buy.

At noon there was a grand ceremony in which the American and Philippine flags were at last raised over liberated territory. The provisional government was established, with President Osmeña at its head. It was an impressive and moving ceremony which was broadcast throughout the world by radio. General MacArthur did himself proud with the fine speech he made.

We returned to the *Nashville* at 1400 hours and enjoyed a quiet but sultry afternoon. We did not have our usual air raid early this morning, and it was beginning to look like a quiet evening, too. But tonight, just before dark, they were overhead. There has been much antiaircraft firing in near shore, but no planes have yet come over us. However, the alert is still on.

It now appears that we may be able to land *Bataan* on the Tacloban strip within three days. If so, we will probably have Major Oviatt come after us soon and take us back to Hollandia. I'm anxious to get some mail from home.

Aboard U.S.S. *Nashville*, Leyte Gulf, Oct. 24, 1944   2030

This has indeed been a long and interesting day. We didn't have our usual daybreak attack by the Japs. Instead, they conveniently waited until 0800 hours, after we were well finished with breakfast. Then they really gave us a show. Fifty of them came over at once. Things were quite lively for a half hour, during which time the sky was literally filled with antiaircraft fire. I saw two Jap planes plunge straight into the water, burning, from about 10,000 feet. Altogether our forces shot down eight of them. Most of their bombs landed harmlessly in the water, but one burning Jap plane flew himself into an LCT and sank it. We also had a few casualties on the beach from the strafing.

About 1030 hours I went ashore with Generals Sutherland and Kenney. We first visited the Tacloban airstrip and then had lunch at Air Force Headquarters. After lunch General Kenney went back to the airstrip and General Sutherland and I drove into Tacloban to see what progress was being made on the construction of housing facilities for GHQ. We found things to be well advanced, and it now appears that General MacArthur will be able to move ashore in a couple of days.

In returning to the airstrip, we became hopelessly entangled in a traffic jam and were directed by the MPs to take a detour around it. Somehow our driver became confused and we suddenly found ourselves in the front lines. Sniping was going on all around, with plenty of artillery fire to support it. I saw about twenty-five well-bloated dead Japs. We got out of there as soon as possible but never found a road to lead us back to the airstrip. Finally we reached the beach, where General Sutherland, by virtue of his three stars, commandeered an LCM and we went to the airstrip by water. We finally got back to the *Nashville* just in time for another Jap air raid. A lone Zero came in just out of range of our guns, and, although we opened up with all we had, we missed him. However, a destroyer on down the bay shot him down.

On board we were immediately advised that a big naval battle was rapidly shaping up just southeast of us. The Japs were approaching with four battleships and an accompanying screen of cruisers and destroyers. The

Nashville wanted to join the fight, but Admiral Kinkaid would not permit this so long as we had General MacArthur aboard. Denied participation in the battle, we now must wait safely here in Leyte Gulf.

Starting about 1700 hours we had continuous air alerts until 2000 hours. Much shooting occurred in the distance, but no enemy planes came over us.

Tacloban, P.I., Oct. 25, 1944   2000

[At 6:00 A.M. the fireworks began in earnest. The day turned out to be a confused and confusing one. The early Japanese aerial attack was very intense. There was heavy antiaircraft firing all over the bay. I saw two enemy Bettys go down in flames into the sea. The attack was still in progress when we received an urgent message that a strong enemy fleet was converging on us from a position sixty miles away, and that the *Nashville* was sorely needed to join our forces in repulsing the impending attack. General MacArthur and the other eighteen of us aboard from the army packed our meager belongings and moved ashore to Tacloban.

On our way in we watched large numbers of our own carrier-based aircraft come in to the Tacloban airstrip to land. The small escort carriers from which these planes had been launched had been sunk or badly damaged by the Japanese battleships and cruisers. The unfortunate pilots were running low on fuel and had no place to go. Although the airstrip had been torn up for the purpose of permanent reconstruction, nevertheless, the planes had to use it. Many of them were completely demolished on landing and our bulldozers shoved them into the bay to make room for the others. Thus, many of the aircraft were lost, although most of the pilots survived. Some of our own antiaircraft batteries mistook our airplanes for "bogies" and fired at them as they approached.

We arrived at Tacloban about four days earlier than the construction crews had expected us. The filth left behind by the fleeing Japanese soldiers was strewn everywhere. Before we had an opportunity to find a place to leave our belongings, twelve Japanese planes came over on a strafing and bombing run. It was my first experience of being under direct bombing from the air. Two 250-pound bombs landed about 100 yards from me, but I received nothing more than a good scare.

Our communication facilities are not yet fully operative in Tacloban. This afternoon General MacArthur asked me to go to the airstrip to talk to some of the carrier pilots to see if I could gather some information regarding the naval situation. I found these pilots to be a discouraged group. There were no carriers to return to, they were out of fuel, they had been shot at by friendly forces while in the air, and they had no one on the ground to report to or provide them with food and lodging. And they knew very little about the tactical situation. By the time I got back to Tacloban our communication links had been established, and the general knew infinitely more about what was happening currently than I had been able to learn.

Tonight, had the Japanese known it, they could have inflicted real damage by staging a bombing raid on Tacloban. Fortunately for us it started raining steadily after dark. This has prevented a low-level attack due to cloud cover. The best place I could find to sleep was a filthy garage building. The roof has kept the rain off but the mosquitoes are plentiful and hungry.]

Tacloban, P.I., Oct. 26, 1944   1930

This day started out with a bang. Just before daybreak, a single Jap airplane came gliding in and dropped two 100-pound bombs in the block where I was. Debris fell all around me, and one large bomb fragment came through the roof of the garage where I was sleeping. Seventeen people were killed, including two newspaper correspondents. We had intermittent raids all during the early part of the morning, and two or three Nips were shot down.

General Sutherland and I went to the airstrip to see what we could learn there. We contacted some of the navy pilots, who are now without carriers. They are providing us with what little fighter cover we possess. But the best news is that by 1300 hours tomorrow we will have a group of our own P-38s here and a squadron of P-61 night fighters. They will be able to take to the air about 1630 hours tomorrow and can give us practically continuous cover. Then these Jap raiders are not going to find things quite so much to their liking.

While we were on the airstrip eight Jap planes came over to strike at the parking area, where about fifty of our navy planes were stationed. When our antiaircraft opened fire the Nips lost their nerve and swung wide of the strip, harmlessly dropping their bombs about 100 yards out in the bay. One of our navy fighters was just approaching for a landing when the attack started. He suddenly realized what was happening, raised his landing gear, and took out in pursuit of the last Jap aircraft in the column. He caught him and shot him down in flames, to the accompaniment of applause from thousands of our troops. General Sutherland and I hit the dirt behind a bulldozer, a comparatively safe vantage point from which we watched proceedings.

After visiting Lieutenant General Krueger at Sixth Army Headquarters, we returned for a late lunch, during which we were twice raided by Japs. No reported casualties from these sporadic raids. The afternoon was quiet.

The reports coming through from the navy are more encouraging. We definitely have sunk one Jap battleship and two heavy cruisers, and several cruisers have been badly hit.

[General MacArthur is now well settled in the "Big House," originally known as the Walter Price residence, a frame building in the center of the town that evidently served as the home of the leading town authority. The Price house is encircled by a veranda that is under the same roof. The rest of us are billeted in warehouse-type corrugated metal buildings nearby. The house also serves as the general's office, as well as that of General Sutherland. The Japanese airmen apparently know its location, as almost all of their bombing and strafing attacks are centered on it.

General MacArthur is in rare good humor. He enjoyed the various excursions we took while living aboard *Nashville*. He is now sixty-four years old but has the energy of a much younger man.]

We have had continuous air attacks through dinner and they are still occurring. I'm tired of hitting the foxholes each time a Jap plane appears, so I'm going to go to bed now, regardless of the noise. Probably will do little sleeping as our antiaircraft is throwing up an almost continuous barrage from a battery of 90-mm guns just outside my window.

Tacloban, P.I., Oct. 27, 1944   2000

Sure enough, the Japs were overhead all night long, and the moonlight assisted them materially. Fortunately for us they concentrated on the airstrip, and few bombs fell on the town. Preliminary reports from our navy are good, and it would now appear that we have inflicted considerable additional losses on their heavier units. Radio Tokyo is telling some tall tales this morning concerning the damage the Jap fleet has done to us. Our only bit of amusement here is the daily broadcast of Tokyo Rose. When there are no Nips overhead and I can think clearly, I'm amused at my reactions during the time when a raid is in progress.

[The nuisance air raids we are having arouse long-dormant instinctive reactions in me. I have never before been subjected to such direct physical assaults upon my person. The very randomness in timing and imprecise impact location are indignities which demand retribution in kind, but one is helpless to deliver such return punishment. My own logic tells me that when one or two enemy aircraft come over, the probability that a bomb or bullet will land on the exact spot on which I am standing is perhaps one in a million: in other words, insignificant. But somehow logic does not always prevail. To me at least, attacks from the air have more psychological impact than those made by ground fire. Perhaps this is because of a feeling of helplessness, an inability to fight back, to retaliate in kind. Logic gets mixed up with emotion, and the first reaction is to run or dodge or get behind some shield. A mathematics major in probabilities, I have to take myself firmly in hand in order to bring reason back into control. It is interesting to analyze one's reactions such new experiences. It is not quite as simple as telling oneself not to be afraid and expecting an immediate affirmative response.

This morning was quiet, and in the afternoon General Sutherland and I went to the airstrip to see the Fifth Air Force fighters arrive. Fifty-eight of them came in exactly on schedule, landing on the newly completed strip with only one minor mishap—a blown tire with no other damage. Major Bong, our top American ace, was among them. Now at last we will have some effective air cover. When the usual Jap bomber formation came over, it was raining very hard, and our fighters did not get off in time to repel them. Fortunately, the bombers dropped their explosives well out into the bay, with no resulting damage. Later, a number of our fighters took off and reported shooting down eight of the enemy, who were totally unprepared for such reponse.

Back at headquarters we learned that General Kenney's B-17 would arrive at 7:00 A.M. tomorrow. Generals Sutherland and Kenney and I will go as passengers back to Hollandia, with a stopover at Owi Island on the way.

General MacArthur has told me that for the next two months he does not intend to do any flying. He will remain at Tacloban until the campaign is launched against Luzon, the principal Philippine island. He will therefore have no need for my services. On the other hand the bulk of GHQ still is in Hollandia, and General Sutherland will operate most of the functions from that location. As soon as facilities can be completed at Leyte to accommodate all of GHQ, it will be moved, but in the interim it will be my task to fly various elements of the organization to the new location in a segmented fashion whenever the necessary housing can accept them.]

16

Withering on the Vine

OCTOBER, 1944–FEBRUARY, 1945

Hollandia, Dutch New Guinea, Oct. 28, 1944   2130

Sure enough the Japs were over all night last night, and there was no sleep for anyone. They did no damage in our immediate vicinity, but they effected considerable destruction around the airstrip.

General Kenney's B-17 arrived a bit late due to bad weather, and he, General Sutherland, and I departed for Hollandia about 1000 hours. Although we saw some Jap aircraft en route, we were unmolested. We landed at Owi Island to confer with Generals Whitehead and Wurtsmith, and then continued on to Hollandia, arriving shortly after nightfall.

I had four nice letters from Gracie awaiting me, along with three packages of goodies she had sent over by the ATC. I've read my letters, had some beer to drink, and am now ready to fall into bed for my first night of sound sleep in many days.

Hollandia, Dutch New Guinea, Oct. 29, 1944   2100

I've had a busy day catching up with all the work which has accumulated during my absence.

[The "point" system, under which personnel who have spent a certain minimum period of duty overseas can elect to be returned to the states, means that I either am losing or soon will lose some of my key flight crew members. There are interviews with prospective replacements, paperwork, farewells to be said, medals to be presented, etc. I will have to check out the new flight crews on each of the types of aircraft my group operates.]

Early tomorrow I'm departing for Nadzab to accept delivery on our B-24, which is ready to be flown away. It will be fun to fly a boxcar once more, as it's been nearly a year since I've been in one.

Hollandia, Dutch New Guinea, Oct. 30, 1944   2115

[I flew a B-25 to Nadzab and took an extra crew along to take the B-25 back to Hollandia. There awaiting me was a new B-24, which we added to our fleet. It was fully armed and capable of combat, but had had the interior modified to carry a small number of passengers and/or cargo. Since I had not flown this type of airplane for a year, I spent considerable time in the cockpit on the ground relearning the control and instrument systems, then made a few short flights to reacquaint myself with the takeoff and landing characteristics. It was after 4:00 P.M. before we departed for Hollandia. Arriving there after dark, we found the weather uncooperative, and I had to make several approach procedures before we finally were able to land.]

When I arrived at the office I found six letters from Gracie. That was indeed a treat.

Hollandia, Dutch New Guinea, Oct. 31, 1944   1900

This is my thirty-eighth birthday. I've had so much to do, however, that I haven't had many free moments during which to contemplate the results of my increasing years.

My day has been well filled with many details to check prior to my trip tomorrow. I'm taking off at 0630 hours for the Philippines in the fully armed B-24. I'll have a very heavy load to carry, including ten passengers and three general officers.

Wakde Island, Nov. 1, 1944   2345

Have just landed after eighteen hours of flying to complete a round-trip to the Philippines in bad weather. Couldn't get into Hollandia so had to land here at this emergency airport. So tired now I can't hold my eyes open, so will tell about my trip later.

Hollandia, Dutch New Guinea, Nov. 2, 1944   2100

Yesterday we departed from Hollandia in the B-24 with a load of 61,000 pounds. The aircraft was slow and the weather bad, but we got along all right, passing south of Palau (where we could land in event of trouble) in midmorning. About two hours out of the Philippines we set a watch at all gun stations, but we didn't sight any Jap aircraft until we were over Leyte Gulf. Then twelve raiders came over high alongside us and made a dive-bombing attack on a ship convoy in easy range of our vision. One bomb struck one of our tankers almost below us, and the ship blew up with a terrific blast of black smoke, it was still burning when we passed it on our outbound trip two hours later. Our navy threw up an ineffective antiaircraft barrage, and the Jap planes escaped untouched. None of our fighters was in striking distance at the time. The Jap planes didn't bother us as they were intent on making their escape after their successful attack.

We continued on to the Tacloban airstrip and landed safely, and my three generals were duly appreciative. The airstrip had been torn up by five well-spaced bombs only a short time before, but it had been hurriedly repaired and was in good shape for our landing. We remained on the ground only one hour to unload our cargo and to refuel. We were much in the way on the overcrowded field, from which our fighters were operating continuously in an attempt to ward off as many of the Jap air attacks as possible. Our large aircraft required the room and attention of a half dozen fighters.

Air superiority at this time is very much undecided, as both the Jap forces and our own are about equally divided. They have the advantage in that they are able to operate from many small, well-dispersed fields, while all of our operation comes from this one strip. It will be about November 10 before we will have in operation another strip, from which we can use medium bombers. Shortly thereafter we will be able to neutralize many of the enemy's present operational airdromes in the Philippines area. In the meantime, we are being raided constantly and are losing many aircraft and surface vessels. They strafe and bomb our airstrip at night almost constantly, and in view of our congestion the Japs cannot fail to do much damage.

[We departed Tacloban for Hollandia at 4:00 P.M. and saw no enemy aircraft on our way outbound. The return trip was anything but mentally comforting. We encountered steady rain at about dusk and for the next six hours were unable to get a single celestial fix to establish our position. Our radios were useless due to precipitation static. So we flew only by compass heading. I was not convinced of the accuracy of the compass in this new airplane since I had not had the opportunity to check it out on all headings. Furthermore, the persistent rough air made it difficult to establish a stable and satisfactory compass heading. A compass error of one degree could make a compounded error of as much as plus or minus twenty-five miles by the time we arrived at the New Guinea coastline, and a greater compass error could mean correspondingly increased distortions. I had taken a Benzedrine capsule in order to remain awake and alert, and this did not increase my tranquillity.

Finally, by means of calculating the elapsed time since takeoff, we arrived at what should have been the north New Guinea coastline, but clouds, rain, and darkness prevented us from seeing anything. We could not receive any radio signals. I was not about to risk a thrust into the mountain-rimmed Hollandia Valley without either visual or radio guidance, so decided to go westward to Wakde Island, where I could descend over the ocean and establish visual contact over the water. There I could make a flat approach to the runway. We landed safely at Wakde after midnight and after having flown nineteen hours and been awake for twenty-three hours. I took a Seconal capsule to counteract the effects of the Benzedrine, lay down on the sharp coral surface under the wing of the airplane, and slept for three hours. It was much too warm to sleep in the airplane.

(This experience caused me to reschedule most future trips between Hollandia and Tacloban. By departing from Hollandia about midnight we would have the stars to afford better celestial navigation northbound, thus better avoiding enemy-held territory, and additionally we could refuel at Tacloban and arrive back at Hollandia before dark. Also, if the weather was bad at Hollandia we would not have to make a hazardous night approach through the mountains into this valley under adverse conditions.]

We were up before dawn this morning and flew the hundred plus miles into Hollandia, where I reported in to General Sutherland, dirty, tired, and unshaven. He had been sending messages to all stations to try to locate me, and Wakde had just reported my departure from there. He said he was worried we might be down in the ocean somewhere. I chidingly asked him if he didn't have more confidence in me than that, to which he replied with a smile that he had unlimited confidence in my abilities as pilot and navigator but, after all, I did not control the elements.]

Hollandia, Dutch New Guinea, Nov. 3, 1944   2000

Had many troubles today. Two tires on my new B-24 were flat this morning and I had to send an airplane to Finschhafen to get new ones. I can only be thankful that they did not blow out on one of the landings on the trip to the Philippines.

I have still felt rather groggy today. Had a couple of drinks last night to relax a bit before going to bed, but they disagreed with me and the Seconal so I've had an irritating day. I think I may also be suffering from some of the aftereffects of my recent dengue fever infection.

No letters from home today.

Hollandia, Dutch New Guinea, Nov. 4, 1944   2330

This morning I flew *Bataan* for an hour to exercise it. Then the B-24 was finally ready to fly this afternoon at 1430 hours, and I gave Major Oviatt six landings in it before dark. He is not yet complete master of it, but I believe he will have no serious difficulties in handling it. So I'm going to send him to the Philippines in it tomorrow with a load of cargo. No mail today.

Owi Island, Nov. 5, 1944   2230

Early this morning General Sutherland called me in to tell me he wanted me to take this trip into the Philippines rather than to have Major Oviatt take it, as he wanted to send Admiral Sherman along. So I made rapid preparations and finally departed in the B-24 at 1500 hours for Owi Island. We are remaining here until 0200 hours tomorrow, when we shall take off for the Philippines, arriving there at about 0900 hours.

We have found much confusion here tonight. The field is being operated by the navy, and many Fifth Air Force units are in the process of moving out. Also a heavy bombing strike was taking off tonight. We had difficulty in getting fuel and other service.

Hollandia, Dutch New Guinea, Nov. 6, 1944   2100

We were out of Owi on schedule last night, and had a long, miserable trip up to Tacloban. There was rain and rough air most of the way, and strong headwinds. We finally reached the field at 0915 hours, which was an hour later than we had anticipated, but we saw no Jap aircraft en route. There was the usual confusion at the airstrip, what with all of the fighters operating, etc.

[I made a hurried trip into Tacloban to see General MacArthur for a few minutes while the airplane was being refueled. He said the ground operation on Leyte was not progressing as rapidly as he had hoped, "partly due to heavy rain, but there were also other reasons." He did not explain the latter remark.]

We still had bad weather most of the way back, but, after an interminable time, arrived here just at nightfall.

Things have quieted considerably at Tacloban, especially as to Jap air activity. Last night not a single Jap plane came over, and as our antiaircraft was silent our boys got their first night of sleep since the invasion. Our operational activity is still proceeding at fever heat, and soon all Jap raids will be a thing of the past.

Hollandia, Dutch New Guinea, Nov. 7, 1944   2000

I slept late this morning and feel considerably refreshed, although it will require another day before I'm ready to fight wildcats. The Benzedrine-

Seconal routine makes me irritable. Spent a large part of the day at the airstrip checking on the condition of the airplanes, etc. Then this afternoon General Sutherland called me in to arrange another trip to the Philippines, on which he will go. I talked him into going in a C-54 instead of the slower, uncomfortable B-24. I hope I'm not wrong in estimating the Jap air activities over the Leyte Gulf area, as we would be easy prey for their fighters.

This afternoon General Sutherland and I went for a local flight in a C-47, and remained aloft until dark. We had a fine bull session and discussed many questions concerning the war and otherwise.

[I am beginning to learn how a large-scale war is fought when reasonable resources are available. I used to have a more romantic concept—that commando-type raids such as hit-and-run tactics were usual procedure. In this theater at least the strategy used is to sit tight in position and build up and train massive forces. When the assault is ready the move is made with sufficient momentum to overwhelm the enemy and minimize our losses. But enough strength is held in reserve to maintain the momentum and keep rolling when the enemy becomes demoralized and before he can regroup his defenses. As a consequence, we have long periods of buildup during which planning and training are the principal activities. These periods of relative calm are followed by much shorter periods during which the frenzied action of the battles themselves occurs. These two violently dissimilar types of activity no doubt have led to the soldier's description of army life as one of "hurry up and wait."

General MacArthur is most concerned about the morale of the soldiers during the inactive planning and buildup stages. On several occasions I have heard him make inquiries about the morale of the troops. He does not appear to worry about this factor once an operation is under way.]

Hollandia, Dutch New Guinea, Nov. 8, 1944   1830

Today has been completely taken up by preparations for my trip tonight. Among other passengers, I'll have General Sutherland, General Kenney, General Willoughby, and General Fitch aboard. And, to complicate matters, there is a typhoon headed for Leyte Gulf, in such a position that it's somewhat questionable whether or not we will arrive there ahead of it. Oh well, if life were easy it wouldn't be much fun. The C-54 will make the trip much easier on me. Will be departing at 0100 hours tomorrow and, if all goes well, will be back here in Hollandia tomorrow night.

We now have elected another president of the United States. Out here we still do not know whether it is Roosevelt or Dewey, although election returns are coming in. As I have to get up at 2315 hours tonight to start my trip, I'm not wasting any precious moments listening to the radio.

Hollandia, Dutch New Guinea, Nov. 9, 1944   2100

I've had a most distressing day today. To start off with, when I arrived at the airplane this morning after midnight it was pouring, and there awaiting me in the dark were the two lieutenant generals and two brigadier generals. But, lo and behold, there was no crew about the airplane anywhere, and I had no explanation to make of it. A guard finally informed us that the flight had been canceled, but no one knew who had canceled it, and I was in a most distressing situation. I had left it up to two first pilots to get the airplane ready while I devoted my time to the weather, etc., but when mechanical troubles developed on the airplane, they took off without notifying anyone. For the first time since I've been associated with him General Sutherland is a bit disappointed in me. And I don't blame him, as it was entirely my responsibility. I had made the mistake of delegating that responsibility to someone who was not to be relied upon.

At any rate, we didn't depart, and I've never spent a more miserable night. The rain was torrential all night long, and my quarters were completely soaked, including my bed, which was a pool of water. And, after the most uncomfortable night, I had to face the wrath of General Sutherland this morning. He asked me to get a written report from the Air Transport Command as to what happened last night to prevent the departure of our trip, since it was their airplane we were to use. I've spent the day accomplishing this and setting up my trip for tonight. Now I believe all is in readiness, but I have to go to the airstrip immediately to check upon all details.

Hollandia, Dutch New Guinea, Nov. 10, 1944   2000

I departed from here at 0045 hours this morning in a C-54 with Generals Sutherland, Kenney, Willoughby, and Fitch. We had a fine trip to Tacloban, arriving there at 0800 hours. Then I departed at 1030 hours and returned here at 1730 hours this afternoon. Have to go back to the Philippines tomorrow night, so must have my sleep.

Hollandia, Dutch New Guinea, Nov. 11, 1944   1900

Up early this morning after eight hours of exhausted sleep. But I had so much to do today that I couldn't afford the luxury of any more rest.

I've now got three C-54s and one B-24 scheduled out for the Philippines in the next two days, and I will fly one of them tonight myself.

The old man is getting older rapidly under the pressure of all of this flying and desk work. Well, I asked for it.

My promotion is in the mill and unless something unforeseen happens will become effective tomorrow. That will be a happy day for me, as the added prestige of the promotion will enable me to get things done somewhat easier.

Finally received a letter from Gracie, written October 26. All was well at home as of that date.

I've made two more modest "firsts" in aviation history. I have taken into the Philippines the first B-24 that has ever landed there, and also the first C-54.

Hollandia, Dutch New Guinea, Nov. 12, 1944   2000

Again I'm a weary man. This morning at 0030 hours I departed from Hollandia in a C-54 for the Philippines with Generals Swift, Casey, Sverdrup, MacNider, French, and Baker, along with a number of colonels. The seven-hour trip northbound was uneventful. At Tacloban I took aboard Generals Sutherland, Kenney, and Willoughby and returned to Hollandia, also without incident, arriving here at dusk.

General Sutherland extended to me today an idea which has me up in the air. The War Department has at last approved the assignment to this headquarters of a deluxe-model C-54 for the transportation of high-ranking personnel here. The airplane will be fitted out in the States and be ready in about thirty days. I suggested to him that it would be a good idea for me to go back to San Francisco to give it a thorough inspection before bringing it back. He grinned, but didn't commit himself that I could go. He suggested jokingly that to do so would run my flying time well over 100 hours in that month, but I countered with the suggestion that my two sons should be permitted to see me, so as to be reassured that I'm not an entirely legendary character.

Hollandia, Dutch New Guinea, Nov. 13, 1944   2230

This has been another day of relaxation for me. I had many small chores to do in the office, and then this afternoon General Bertrandias and I spent an hour developing plans for the layout of our new C-54. He is going back to the States in a few days and will see that the aircraft is fitted to meet our exacting specifications. I believe, but I'm not certain, that I have convinced General Sutherland that I should go back to the States to give the airplane a thorough check and then ferry it over here myself. If only he will consent, it will be a great day for me. I can hardly believe that there is now an immediate possibility that I may see my dear family again.

Had two fine letters from Gracie, telling me all about how they celebrated Jimmy's and my birthday.

Hollandia, Dutch New Guinea, Nov. 14, 1944   2345

What a day this has been! I worked on specifications for the new C-54 and then went to the airstrip to accomplish various errands. This afternoon I flew for a couple of hours with General Sutherland.

[Colonel Phil LaFollette, the former governor of Wisconsin, rooms next door to me in the senior officers' quarters. We became very good friends during our sojourns in Brisbane, Port Moresby, and Hollandia. He has often accompanied me on local flights, and has undertaken to coach me, a not very promising student, in the subtleties of the political profession. This evening, after dinner, Phil came by my room and said General Sutherland wanted to see me immediately. He said the general appeared to be quite upset and even angry. That seemed strange to me, since when I had seen the general two or three hours before he was in excellent spirits.
At any rate I cooled my heels in Sutherland's outer office for what seemed to be an interminable period, trying to think of where I might have "slipped up." Finally he called for me to come in. There gathered in his office were most of the general officers of GHQ. General Sutherland, in front of the assemblage, removed my gold leaf, insignia of a major, and pinned on a silver leaf, making me a lieutenant colonel! All members of this group had flown with me and some of the flights had been under harrowing circumstances.
We proceeded to have several drinks. Then when I returned to my room I found another crowd waiting to have a promotion party. This lasted until well into the late evening. I sent my wife a cablegram saying, "Pappy got promoted."]

Hollandia, Dutch New Guinea, Nov. 15, 1944   2300

Early this morning we were greeted with the news that our C-54 had been bombed on the Tacloban airstrip yesterday. So I went down to investigate, as I hadn't flown the trip up due to fatigue. I learned that the Japs had come over on a bombing raid soon after the C-54 had landed at Tacloban and while it was being refueled. One fragmentation bomb which landed nearby put twelve shrapnel holes in the ship and wounded three of the crew. The crew chief was on top of the wing, refueling the aircraft, when the attack came. In attempting to get away, he fell from the wing and broke his hip. The fortunate part, however, was that another bomb landed between the fuel truck and the aircraft but failed to detonate!
This afternoon I flew a C-47 locally to get some much-needed practice.

Above: Col. Phil LaFollette (a three-term governor of Wisconsin) and I relax at Hollandia, Dutch New Guinea, where GHQ overlooks Lake Sentani. *Below:* The GHQ installation at Hollandia. Courtesy U.S. Army.

I'm feeling fine once more, having become thoroughly rested. I'm ready to tackle most any job. Starting about November 21, I'm to be faced with much flying, as we will then start moving GHQ to the Philippines. I expect to take General Sutherland up soon in the B-17 and will probably keep that airplane there for some time.

Hollandia, Dutch New Guinea, Nov. 16, 1944   2030

Had a fine letter from Grace this morning to start the day right. All morning I remained in the office, trying fairly to grade my officers on their efficiency. It's an important thing for the men concerned and requires much thought.

This afternoon I went to the airstrip and flew the B-17 for an hour, and a C-47 for a half hour. Then General Sutherland came down to fly around for an hour, after which the day was over. The general told me that I am to take him to Tacloban in the B-17 on November 22 and that I will return here to Hollandia to await further orders.

I feel a bit lonely and homesick tonight. Perhaps the possibility of seeing my family soon has stimulated the realization of how very much I miss them.

Hollandia, Dutch New Guinea, Nov. 17, 1944   2300

Spent the morning with officers of the Air Transport Command in an attempt to get some promotions for our crews on the C-54s. It's a difficult matter, and I'm afraid I made myself a bit unpopular, but someone has to look after the welfare of these men, who have given us so much loyalty and hard work.

This afternoon I worked in the office until 1600 hours and then General Sutherland and I went for a flight and remained aloft until dark.

Hollandia, Dutch New Guinea, Nov. 18, 1944   2115

I dispatched Captain Skov on a trip to Brisbane, Sydney, and Melbourne this morning. I would have enjoyed taking the trip, but the general is holding me here to take him to the Philippines on November 22.

It has poured rain here all day, and the fog is so thick one cannot see across the road. It's been the kind of day on which we would eat popcorn and lie about on the rug in front of the fireplace at home.

Hollandia, Dutch New Guinea, Nov. 19, 1944   2245

Was up early this morning to take jolly General Marquart to Finschhafen. It was a fine trip down and back, and I was aloft almost seven hours.

Hollandia, Dutch New Guinea, Nov. 20, 1944   2045

Spent considerable time in the office this morning, and then went to the airstrip and flew both the B-24 and the C-47. General Sutherland was going to fly, but rain started in midafternoon so he canceled his flight. I've spent some time planning my trip to the Philippines tomorrow night, as it will be a very important and responsible one. It now appears that another typhoon is forming directly on our course, and I'm of the opinion we may have to delay our trip for a day or two. Will be able to make a better decision on it when I have further reports tomorrow morning.

Hollandia, Dutch New Guinea, Nov. 21, 1944   2000

Sure enough the morning weather reports indicated a strong tropical disturbance moving into Leyte, and when I reported to General Sutherland he decided to delay not only our flight tonight, but also the entire movement of GHQ to the Philippines. Everything will be delayed a minimum of two days.

In the mail this morning was a copy of the October issue of the *United Air Lines News*. In addition to other things, there was the following very nice article about me:

> Capt. W. E. "Dusty" Rhoades, now a lieutenant colonel in the Air Forces flying General Douglas MacArthur to the war zones at the general's request, was pilot for 'Philbert No. 2.,' a C-54 which left San Francisco for Washington under special sealed orders. With him were first officer W. H. Gehlaar, navigator R. E. Walker, flight engineers H. A. Strzelecki and R. A. Carroll, radio engineer Raymond Wolff and flight purser R. A. Schmidt.
>
> Picking up important military leaders at Washington bound for the Cairo conference, they were to fly 31,380 miles in 150 flying hours and make 20 landings in almost as many countries before returning to San Francisco again via India and the South Pacific.

Having nothing else of an urgent nature to do today, I took the B-25 and went to Biak to visit with the UAL trans-Pacific crews and to get a Christmas package which Grace had sent me.

Hollandia, Dutch New Guinea, Nov. 22, 1944   2100

This has been one of the warmest days we've had here. I've felt particularly unambitious, so accomplished very little this morning. This afternoon General Sutherland and I took a two-hour flight into the interior of New Guinea to see some of this unknown, awe-inspiring land. The weather was good, and we flew up the saddle which forms the water-flow divide between the enormous Sepik and Idenburg rivers. We went on to the unbelievably rugged Oranje Mountains, played around the 17,000-foot peaks, and observed many of the native villages, some located on the knife-edged ridges as high as 12,000 feet. No white man has ever been in this country, and the natives are reputed to be fierce headhunting cannibals who allow no strangers to cross their frontiers. For that matter, no white man possessing normal good sense would want to enter into this forbidding wilderness, although it is universally held that its precious mineral deposits are tremendous.

Hollandia, Dutch New Guinea, Nov. 23, 1944   2030

This is Thanksgiving Day. I pause long enough to review the many things for which I am unreservedly grateful. My beautiful, loyal, devoted wife, my two fine sons, my position in life, my adequate allotment of worldly goods—what man in this world possesses more than I of the valuable things of life? And I cannot delude myself that I have obtained all of these through my own efforts. There must be a Power which has consistently looked after my welfare. And I have every confidence that this same Power will assure me a happy future which will be finer than that which any man has the right to expect. I look forward to many long years of beautiful life with my family and friends.

Today Uncle Sam gave us a fine turkey. It was the best he could do under the circumstances, but somehow it fell short of the mark. Materially it was of the best, but spiritually much was missing. I'm not so sure that the final disappointment wasn't the lack of emphasis on the spiritual side of the occasion, which necessarily was denied us.

I flew the B-24 over to the Hollandia strip for the loaded takeoff tonight at midnight. It will be an important trip as I'm taking General Sutherland and General Chamberlin to the Philippines. My afternoon has been occupied with the many pertinent chores such as checking weather and checking the airplane and its armament and equipment.

[Yesterday General Sutherland told me I was to take him and his friend, the Australian WAC captain, to Tacloban. When I learned that he was taking her north of the equator I was sorely tempted to remind him of the commitment that I had heard General MacArthur make to Sir Thomas Blamey at Port Moresby on October 14. This was to the effect that no female Australian military personnel would be taken north of the equator. Although she was Australian, she was a member of the American military establishment and thus might not be covered by the general's commitment. I thought perhaps General MacArthur had failed to follow up with a written order so that all involved personnel in the command would know of the ruling. I immediately searched the files to see if I could find such an order but could not locate one. Then I could conclude only that General Blamey might have issued such an order to all Australian personnel and we would not have a copy of it. At any rate I decided not to broach the subject to General Sutherland, since it was a highly personal matter and I try hard not to intrude into the personal affairs of others unless they invite such intrusion. I do not believe Sutherland was informed of the commitment; it is entirely out of character for him to disobey blatantly an order of his commander.]

Hollandia, Dutch New Guinea, Nov. 24, 1944   2100

This developed into one of the most exciting days yet. To start the day, we departed from Hollandia in a fully armed B-24 at midnight. On the takeoff the landing lights on the airplane burned out, and it was no easy stunt to get the heavily loaded aircraft airborne and climb out of these mountains here in pitch darkness. However, we got under way safely and had a good but slow trip to Tacloban. Things began to happen then. We arrived over the airstrip simultaneously with twenty Jap airplanes, and the fun began. The Japs had come on a bombing raid on the airstrip, and they had jammed our radio circuit so that I had no warning of the approaching raid. The first I knew I saw the enemy aircraft over the field and saw the bombs begin to explode. There was little I could do except to keep my guns manned and circle the airstrip, where there was the maximum fighter cover. So we had a bird's-eye view of the complete raid. On the first bombing run the Japs released their bombs a bit early, and about half of them landed harmlessly in the water short of the strip, but the remainder landed directly on the airplane parking strip. Three made direct hits on P-38s, and they went up in flames. Bomb shrapnel damaged many more of our parked airplanes. I saw one bomb hit a ship in the harbor, and it exploded. Fortunately for us no bombs landed on the landing mat, or we would have been unable to land and would have had to return to Palau. One navy B-24 pilot, in too big a hurry to land ahead of us and under the stress of the situation, ground-looped on landing and crashed into three of our parked P-38s, demolishing them as well as his own airplane.

After most of the Jap planes had departed or were engaged in dogfights with our own fighters, I decided to land. I rolled to a stop, cut the engines, and vacated the airplane in favor of a dugout immediately as two more Jap planes came over again. After the excitement subsided, we refueled as rapidly as possible and took off for Hollandia. The eight-hour trip seemed interminable, as it was a close race with darkness. I had no landing lights, and a night landing at Hollandia with no landing lights in a B-24 is something no one in his right mind would choose to undertake. As it was, we landed just at dusk and without incident.

[Incidentally, the Australian WAC captain did not go with us today, perhaps because General Chamberlin went along.]

Seventeen hours in the air today, and awake for thirty-six hours, so the old body is about to cry quits.

Incidentally, I qualified for the air medal today, as I completed over 100 combat hours.

Hollandia, Dutch New Guinea, Nov. 25, 1944   2100

This has been an inactive day. I've done little except rest and write letters.

General Beightler, Thirty-seventh Division commander, came into the office this afternoon and requested that I take him to Bougainville tomorrow. Having no other pressing work to do, I'm departing at 0630 hours, so will need my sleep now.

Bougainville, Northern Solomons, Nov. 26, 1944   2030

We came over here in *CXE*, our deluxe C-47, with the general and his party. Latoszewski came as my copilot, and we had an excellent trip with a stop at Nadzab for fuel.

Bougainville is about the most beautiful base in all the South Pacific. A ridge of sheer jungle-covered mountains rises just back of the beach, and one of the highest peaks is a volcano which erupts almost continuously. The soil is pure volcanic ash and, although it rains quite frequently, there is almost no mud. The base is old and well organized. General Lester treated us to all of the cold beer we could drink, and our dinner was a surprising affair. I actually had, among other things, two large tenderloin steaks and three dishes of ice cream. I didn't know such food existed in this area.

We are departing for Hollandia early tomorrow and will take more passengers with us.

Hollandia, Dutch New Guinea, Nov. 27, 1944   2130

The trip back from Bougainville was most pleasant. We stopped at Finschhafen, where, after much red tape, I drew an air mattress and a .38-caliber revolver for carrying into forward areas. We arrived here at Hollandia at 1300 hours.

Hollandia, Dutch New Guinea, Nov. 28, 1944   2100

A lazy, uncomfortable day. It's very hot and rainy, and I didn't have any flying to do so I spent most of the day in the office. Wrote some letters, read the communiqués, and have been generally lazy.

There were two fine letters from Grace today. She had seen a news-reel in which I was pictured going ashore with General MacArthur in the Philippine invasion. She went to see it twice and then the next day she saw practically the same picture in *Life* magazine. On top of that she received my radiogram telling of my promotion. So, all in all, she was quite elated. She also reports the boys are doing well except for the usual colds, etc.

Hollandia, Dutch New Guinea, Nov. 29, 1944   2000

Phil LaFollette and I went down to the Twenty-Seventh General Hospital this morning to have our teeth examined. Mine were in good condition, and the X-rays showed no work to be immediately necessary.

This afternoon I was busy preparing for another trip to the Philippines. Will depart tonight at 2330 hours in *Bataan*, with Generals Akin and Lumsden. (General Lumsden is the British liaison officer here.) The weather is not good, so we will have some fun. I ferried the airplane over to the Hollandia airstrip to afford a longer takeoff area.

Hollandia, Dutch New Guinea, Nov. 30, 1944   2030

After seventeen hours in the air today I'm much too weary to be spending my time writing this. Departed from Hollandia at 2330 hours last night in *Bataan* and had fair weather most of the way. It was raining in the Philippines, but we had no difficulty in landing there.

[General Sutherland had sent a radiogram to me asking that I bring the Australian WAC captain along.]

Saw no Jap aircraft but we did have an air alert while we were refueling on the ground. The return trip was long and without incident, and we arrived here at 1700 hours. After a good dinner, I'm now ready for my first sleep in thirty-six hours.

Hollandia, Dutch New Guinea, Dec. 1, 1944   2300

I took life easy this morning, wrote letters and such. As usual I still feel a bit dull from the effects of my long trip. This afternoon it started to rain early and I've never seen it rain harder or longer. A strong wind accompanied it, and as usual all of my belongings are thoroughly soaked. This has happened so often that it doesn't bother me now.

Had a most pleasant evening. I managed to pop some popcorn, which Grace sent me months ago, by sneaking into the general officers' kitchen and doing it myself. I used their butter and trimmings, and some of their beer, and then we spent the evening eating popcorn and playing poker while the rain beat down on us. Now to bed.

Hollandia, Dutch New Guinea, Dec. 2, 1944   2230

The campaign on Leyte is almost at a standstill.

[Since we lack sufficient air cover over western Leyte, the enemy has been able to resupply his forces there almost at will, usually at night, using men and equipment from adjacent islands. Consequently it is necessary for us to mount an expedition to land another attack force at Ormoc on the west coast of Leyte. General Chamberlin, our respected and overworked planning director who does much of the detailed work but who has had few opportunities to see any action, finally will get to accompany this landing.

The need to make the landing has delayed the planned operation against the island of Mindoro, where we badly need to establish a large installation for use by the Air Force. While this planning is in progress at Tacloban, Generals MacArthur and Sutherland are heavily committed. I am becoming bored with inactivity, waiting in Hollandia.]

Took a sightseeing trip this morning. I rounded up a load of generals and colonels and flew over to the little-known "lost Valley" of New Guinea. This valley is on the Baliem River near the foot of 17,000-foot Mount Wilhelmina, about 150 miles southwest of Hollandia, and is entirely inaccessible from the ground. I had first noticed this valley on a flight some months previously which I made from Merauke to Hollandia.

[Whenever the cloud cover allows us to get into the valley we have a visual treat, but an experience that provokes more questions than it answers. The valley is about forty miles long by ten miles wide, flanked on three sides by precipitous jungle-clad mountains. A vertical gorge blocks the other side. A river plunges through this gorge, goes underground in several places, and reemerges out into the lower mountains and hills toward southwestern New Guinea. The valley itself presents many intriguing aspects. It is densely populated (I estimate 50,000) by natives, who carry out extensive cultivation and irrigation of every available suitable area. A system of irrigation canals has been constructed in intricate and nearly perfect geometric patterns. The steep surrounding

mountainsides have been terraced far up into the cloud layers and perhaps higher still. Many of the crops appear to be some type of vine, and
today I thought I could detect a kind of small melon or squash on them.
The other plants could be yams or taro. Most of the fields are enclosed
by rock walls or fences. The terracing up to the higher levels could have
been done only by the expenditure of considerable labor, particularly
since the terrace walls appear to occupy more area than the usable surfaces they have reclaimed. There are numerous hogs, many of large size,
penned up in rock-walled enclosures separate from those around the cultivated crops.

The natives are dark-skinned and wear little if any clothing. In order
to get a good view of the people, I flew as low as seventy-five feet above
the flat areas, and naturally the natives were terrorized by the size of the
airplane and the noise of the propellers and engines. Some tried to hide,
even under the short vines, while others ran at top speed as if to escape
from this roaring airborne behemoth. From their behavior it was evident
that few if any of them had seen an airplane before. Some of the braver
individuals stood up and actually threw their spears at us, and others shot
arrows. Judging from the number of spears and arrows they possessed,
they probably do not always live at peace with their neighbors.

There are many villages, each surrounded by rock or log walls. The
houses within these stockades are of two types. Those of the round variety look like giant mushrooms, are of thatched construction, and generally seem to be larger than similar types I have seen built by other
natives. The other type of house is rectangular, considerably larger, but
uses the same thatching material in its construction. There are open fires
smoking in the areas between the houses. Most of the larger villages
have a large pole or truncated tree located inside the compound or just
outside. Some of these poles are forty to fifty feet in height, with platforms mounted on top.

There were men on many of these platforms. Probably they were
lookout towers. As we came by the natives hastily abandoned their platforms. In one case I saw a man either fall or jump to the ground.

The villages are much smaller in the terraced areas on the steep mountainsides. Some contain only two or three houses, and many have no protective rock walls.

We made several sweeps across the valley, taking pictures and speculating about the inhabitants, and then returned to Hollandia.

[The record is not clear whether this valley is the same one that the
Archbold expedition of 1938 reported to have discovered. In any event,
judged solely from a cursory inspection from the air, these natives appear
to have developed a social structure, an economic system, and perhaps
a moral philosophy under which they thrive without commerce with the
outside world. It is my fervent hope that in the future no well-intentioned
but zealous outsider will attempt to "civilize" them or "save" them, as
has happened so often in the past.]]

Hollandia, Dutch New Guinea, Dec. 3, 1944   2030

About midnight it started raining here. I imagine we have had at least ten inches of rain today. As a result, there has been little activity of any kind. This afternoon I went to the airstrip and flew for a couple of hours during a lull in the weather.

Had another letter from Grace today, but it was a disappointment since it was written on November 8 and I've already had one from her written November 24.

I walked the five miles up the hill from the airstrip. Tonight I played poker a short while and won thirteen dollars. Much fun.

Major Oviatt was to take one of our airplanes on a trip to the Philippines tonight, but in taxiing out for takeoff he ran into a parked airplane and damaged both aircraft. Tomorrow I will have to make an investigation.

Hollandia, Dutch New Guinea, Dec. 4, 1944   2300

Went to the airstrip to investigate Major Oviatt's mishap, which I found to be due to his carelessness, but the damage was not great. While I was there I saw an A-20 crash and burn on takeoff, but all of the crew managed to escape.

Today has been very quiet and I have accomplished little. I did manage to get some Christmas letters written as there are no cards available here to send.

Mr. Sulzberger, publisher of the *New York Times*, passed through here, and I had a short talk with him.

Hollandia, Dutch New Guinea, Dec. 5, 1944   2130

This morning I took another load of passengers over to see the "Lost Valley," but the flight didn't go as planned. When we reached the summit of the Oranje Mountains, clouds were obscuring their 17,000-foot tops, but I found a break through a canyon and got on the south side of them. There were so many clouds that I was unable to locate the valley.

This afternoon was an inactive one for me. Had a short letter from Grace but not much news.

One of the soldiers here gave me the following clipping from a recent *Palo Alto* (Calif.) *Times:*

WIFE OF DUSTY RHOADES SPOTS HIM IN MOVIE OF LEYTE LANDING
    The landing barge nosed into shore, dropped its ramp, and onto the beach at Leyte strode General MacArthur and behind him his staff. Cameramen rolled their cameras to record this historic occasion, and this week the news reel shots came to the Fox Stanford Theatre.

Mrs. Grace Rhoades of Green Oaks Drive, Atherton, went to see the show Monday night and was interested to see the general come ashore. Suddenly she sat upright in her seat, for there, behind the general, was her husband "Dusty"—known officially as Maj. Weldon E. Rhoades.

He appeared again in another shot of the general's party, this time apparently farther inland.

This morning another pleasant surprise occurred for Mrs. Rhoades. A cable came from the major telling her that he has been promoted to lieutenant colonel.

The new colonel is a pilot on MacArthur's staff. He was given this assignment last January when he became a member of the air corps. Prior to that time Colonel Rhoades was with United Air Lines and for two years flew under contract for the Air Transport Command.

In that time his duties took him to Alaska, Newfoundland, Greenland, Iceland, and later to the Pacific, where he had two assignments with MacArthur's staff, one of which was to ferry them to the Cairo conference, after which he continued on and made a complete circuit of the globe.

It is 11 months since "Dusty" has been home, Mrs. Rhoades says. . . .

Colonel and Mrs. Rhoades have two children—Jimmy, age 4, and Johnny, age 2. Mrs. Rhoades said she didn't dare take Jimmy to the theatre, for fear of the racket he would make on seeing his dad, and, she said, there was no use taking Johnny for he wouldn't recognize him.

Hollandia, Dutch New Guinea, Dec. 6, 1944   2030

Had to test the B-24 this morning so I went over to the fascinating "Lost Valley" again. The weather was good, and I flew down to the south end of the gorge, where rumor has it that the river disappears underground and never comes to the surface again. This is not true, however, as the river empties through a tremendous gorge out onto the swampy plains of southwestern New Guinea. There is a magnificent waterfall which tumbles down from the face of Mount Wilhelmina and spreads itself over a large part of the mountain. It was a beautiful trip.

Have been standing by all day for a message from General Sutherland in the Philippines as to whether or not he wants me to fly a trip north tonight.

Hollandia, Dutch New Guinea, Dec. 7, 1944   2100

Took another trip with sightseers over to the "Lost Valley" this morning. The weather was very good, and I did some exploring on beyond the valley. This was even more amazing and fascinating than the valley itself. There is some of the most rugged country in this area that I've ever seen, not excluding the wildest parts of Alaska. The natives have clean, well-developed villages and farms on the very sides of the sheer mountains at elevations up to 9,000 feet.

Had two fine letters from Grace today, but one of them brought rather bad news. Grace had to dismiss Elva, who had been our maid for two years. The reason was a complete breakdown of Elva's morals — a situation which could not be tolerated in our home, of course. It's too bad because now I'll be quite concerned about having Grace there alone with so much work to do, a shortage of supplies due to rationing, the boys to care for, and no relief of any kind. If she should become ill I don't know what the boys would do.

I made the five-mile climb up the mountain from the airstrip today for exercise. Then I had some ice-cold beer from the generals' icebox.

Hollandia, Dutch New Guinea, Dec. 8, 1944   2300

It was rainy most of the day and I did very little. There is no trip tonight so I have nothing to prepare for. This waiting is growing monotonous, especially that I'm now fully rested and anxious to go.

Played poker tonight and won a little. Something to pass the time.

When I finally am able to move to the Philippines, life will be much more interesting for me. General MacArthur and General Sutherland are both there, and I feel as though I'm almost out of the swing of things here.

Hollandia, Dutch New Guinea, Dec. 9, 1944   2100

Another sultry, rainy, useless day. I had absolutely nothing to do. Phil LaFollette and I drove down to Lake Sentani, and took a short hike into the jungle and talked to some of the natives.

Hollandia, Dutch New Guinea, Dec. 10, 1944   2100

Johnny is two years old today, and I expect he is having his first birthday party. It seems so long ago since the damp, dreary morning when I took Grace to Stanford Hospital and then Johnny arrived some hours later.

Read a very fine book today. It was *Kamongo* by Homer Smith, and, in short, it expresses my idea of life and evolution and religion in a way that I've never been able to put into words. It's a book I want my boys to read as soon as they have reached the age when they can properly understand it.

No mail today to dispel my depression from such prolonged inactivity.

Hollandia, Dutch New Guinea, Dec. 11, 1944   2300

Out of sheer desperation born of my enormous inactivity here, I commandeered a boat on Lake Sentani today and spent all day exploring the lake. Latoszewski, Borchert, and I took lunches and were gone most of the day. We stopped at each native village and chatted with the natives to the extent that our limited knowledge of Pidgin English would permit.

Our soldiers have given or traded the natives almost every conceivable piece of army equipment, and many of their articles of clothing are put to uses for which they were never intended. Some of the resulting costumes are sartorially original if somewhat ridiculous, according to our conventional standards.

No mail from home today, so I don't know how Grace is getting along without any help.

Hollandia, Dutch New Guinea, Dec. 12, 1944   2300

It has rained steadily all day today, and I've hardly stirred outside of shelter.

Hollandia, Dutch New Guinea, Dec. 13, 1944   2030

Test-flew *Bataan* this morning and landed it at Hollandia preparatory to a loaded takeoff tonight for the Philippines. Then I sat around all day waiting for a radio from General Sutherland to definitely confirm our departure tonight. At about 1800 hours the radio arrived, and now all is in readiness for the departure. It will be another of those seventeen-hour flights and as usual I'll be on the verge of collapse tomorrow night. Now for two hours of rest.

Hollandia, Dutch New Guinea, Dec. 14, 1944   2000

Departed for the Philippines at 2330 hours last night as scheduled. The trip up and back was routine, but very, very long, and, as usual, I've reached the extreme limit of my endurance.

I couldn't note much difference in conditions at Tacloban, other than a few dozen more airplanes cracked up on the airstrip. Most of them operational accidents. It has been raining heavily there and the place was a sea of mud. Our Air Force has at last obtained air control, so that only a few Japs come over now, and all of them at night only.

[I went into the town of Tacloban to see Generals MacArthur and Sutherland while the airplane was being refueled. General Sutherland said he was continuing to have trouble with his teeth and his blood pressure was still dangerously high. He said he was not feeling well.]

My tremendous exhaustion compels me to tumble into bed now after thirty-six hours awake and seventeen hours in the air.

Hollandia, Dutch New Guinea, Dec. 15, 1944   2100

I arose groggily this morning and went to my office late, but, lo and behold, I had no office. In my absence the new organization which replaces us here (United States Army Forces in the Far East, now largely a paper organization) had moved me out, even to the extent of removing the strong room in which I had locked some of my possessions. I went to General Alexander for an explanation, but, true to his reputation, he knew nothing. No one knows where my possessions are, and of course I'll never see them again. Since USAFFE moved in there have been many thefts of our officers' personal belongings, a trouble which we never experienced in the GHQ organization.

[For many of us it was a sobering bit of news when we learned that our good temporary home, the *Nashville,* had been hit by a suicide enemy pilot while she was participating in the Mindoro landing, suffering nearly 300 casualties, almost half of whom had been killed. Doubtless among those lost were some of the officers I had gotten to know during the Leyte assault.]

Had a most pleasant surprise today when I received a letter from Mr. Patterson, enclosing a check for $100 for a Christmas present. I haven't even worked for the company this year, but still they remember me in a very concrete manner.

Hollandia, Dutch New Guinea, Dec. 16, 1944   2130

Another rainy, useless day. I've done nothing but read and write letters. This afternoon, however, the weather cleared enough that we could play volleyball. Tonight is even worse. There is a bad movie which isn't even worth the effort of watching.

Hollandia, Dutch New Guinea, Dec. 17, 1944   2000

Received a radiogram from General Sutherland this morning instructing me to send Major Oviatt to Tacloban to get Mr. Bowles, who is an assistant secretary of war. Then I am to take him on down to Australia, departing here on the morning of the nineteenth, but I am to use a C-47 and *not Bataan I.*

Hollandia, Dutch New Guinea, Dec. 18, 1944 2000

[This morning two other radiograms arrived for me from General Sutherland, one of which referred to a personal letter which Sutherland was writing me and which was being handcarried by the pilot of the flight bringing Mr. Bowles to Hollandia. When the letter arrived it was a handwritten five-page document in Sutherland's peculiar angular scrawl. It contained agonizing news for me.

MacArthur and Sutherland had had a bitter confrontation in which MacArthur had temporarily relieved Sutherland of most of his official duties. Sutherland said the dispute had been building for a long time and involved many factors. However, it finally had been precipitated when MacArthur learned of the Australian WAC captain's presence in Leyte. Sutherland wrote that he had not known of MacArthur's commitment to Gen. Sir Thomas Blamey to the effect that no Australian female military personnel would be taken north of the equator. Sutherland went on to say that he had not yet made up his mind about his own future, that his health was deteriorating and he felt that he had to get out from under the pressure at least for a while. He said Gen. Richard Marshall had temporarily assumed some of his duties. He outlined specific instructions as to what I should do with and for his Australian WAC friend, who was a passenger on the flight with Mr. Bowles, and he said I should spend Christmas anywhere I chose between Melbourne and Hollandia. He ended by saying I was to destroy the letter as soon as I had read it. This I dutifully, but regretfully, did. It is most distressing for me to admit a serious flaw exists in the character of someone I respect and admire.

I met Mr. Bowles and my other charge at the airstrip, got them settled for a night of rest, then scheduled a departure for Brisbane tomorrow at 5:00 A.M.]

Brisbane, Australia, Dec. 19, 1944 2030

[The trip was routine but a long ten and a half hours' flying time, with fuel stops at Higgins Field (Port Moresby) and Townsville. The C-47 is not the most practical airplane for a flight of this distance. In Brisbane the female passenger was met by friends. I am relieved of my "emotional doctoring" chores for the evening and am billeted in my familiar room at the good, air-conditioned Lennon's Hotel, where I have spent a pleasant evening with my friend and shipmate from Leyte, Colonel Wheeler.

Brisbane has changed greatly. There is hardly an American uniform to be seen anywhere. It is a beautiful season of the year, with colorful flowers and flowering trees everywhere. The European and Pacific wars both are quite remote as far as these people are concerned, and life is settling back into the slow tempo the Australians seem to prefer.]

Brisbane, Australia, Dec. 20, 1944   2200

[I called on Mrs. MacArthur and spent several hours in her delightful company. When and if GHQ is to be established in Manila, she plans to go there by ship. I chided her gently about not allowing me to fly her there, but she said she would be taking her entire household effects. Moreover, on her flight out of the Philippines to Australia in 1942, the last leg of the trip by air had been anything but reassuring. I vowed to try to change her attitude toward flying.]

In the afternoon I went to the Forty-second General Hospital to see Pappy Gunn, who was badly wounded while I was in Tacloban. He is still in bad condition both physically and mentally and has lost the use of his left arm due to the severing of the main nerve trunk.

By late afternoon I had completed most of my chores, and then Colonel Wheeler and I got together for some drinks and some reminiscing about the Leyte invasion.

Sydney, Australia, Dec. 21, 1944   2200

When I awoke this morning I was not feeling as well as usual. I seem to have a light case of dysentery, which I no doubt contracted in the Philippines.

I spent the morning doing little except preparing for the trip to Sydney. We departed from Brisbane at 1330 hours, and although the weather was not good, we arrived here three hours later without any difficulty. I'm well billeted at the famous Australian Hotel, and had a fine, leisurely dinner.

Sydney, Australia, Dec. 22, 1944   2100

I relaxed today. After lunch I took a long walk across the Sydney Harbor Bridge and along the bay. This is really a beautiful location for a city, yet the Australians have done so little toward developing its aesthetic potentialities. The beautiful waterfront is everywhere obscured or cluttered with ugly factories or dumps, and there is no attempt made to properly zone the various areas into residential or business sections. Some day they will awaken to these needs and then it will have to be rebuilt.

This evening I had a terrible ordeal. [The Australian WAC captain was in a state of hysteria. I had no experience in handling this kind of situation. She appeared to be afraid to allow me to leave her there alone, I suppose because I am the last remaining link between her and General Sutherland. I tried to console her as best I could, but it was a horrible sight to watch a woman lose all of her dignity. It was almost the same as seeing a life being thrown away. In order to extricate myself, and entirely in her behalf, I agreed to forgo the holiday that I had expected to spend in civilized comfort. Instead I promised to return immediately to Leyte to make what I knew would be a useless plea for action that might result in the restoration of her self-respect.]

I plan to depart early tomorrow for Melbourne, and that will end my responsibilities toward my passengers on this trip, as I will discharge all of them there.

Sydney, Australia, Dec. 23, 1944   2115

Professionally this has been one of the most critical and hazardous days in my flying career. We departed on schedule for Melbourne, but on takeoff the airplane blew a cylinder head on one engine. This necessitated an immediate return to the airport to minimize the great potential fire hazard. I commandeered another airplane in the name of General MacArthur, loaded the assistant secretary of war and other passengers aboard, and again set out for Melbourne. This time I reached my destination without mishap through very foul weather, but on the return trip trouble again located me. An oil line broke in one of the engines, and I lost it entirely. I continued on into Sydney in bad weather, but again God was with me and no serious consequences resulted. To lose an engine on two different aircraft in one day is about enough. At any rate, I'm now stranded here in Sydney until I can effect the necessary repairs to my airplane.

[I received a radiogram from General MacArthur ordering me to be in Leyte at the earliest possible time. I got on the telephone and contacted just about every general south of New Guinea, pleading for a proper replacement cylinder to be sent. But the supply depots were closed for the Christmas holiday and the best I could do was to get a promise that the needed part would arrive Christmas Day. I am finally going to bed, frustrated and disgusted.]

Sydney, Australia, Dec. 24, 1944   2200

Christmas Eve and here I sit all alone in my hotel room with no one around to talk to and nothing to do exept to think. There'll be no St. Nick coming down my chimney tonight, the same as there'll be none for about ten million other American boys elsewhere, along with countless millions of other peoples. One cannot help but wonder just where our type of civilization is taking us when we are little better than frustrated slaves to its every whim. Many of us are developing a sincere skepticism concerning the values of life.

The cylinder for my airplane arrived today, and then we discovered that someone had made an error and it was the wrong part number. So we started all over and reordered the part. Only the Lord knows when it will arrive or when we can depart from here. There's little I can do except to twiddle my thumbs in impatience.

Sydney, Australia, Dec. 25, 1944   2045

I've never felt more frustrated in all my life. I had promises all day that the cylinder would arrive at any time by air, and I met every airplane that came in, but no cylinder. At dusk I left the airport in disgust, and just a few minutes ago Major Luedtke telephoned from Brisbane to say that the cylinder was coming in at 2230 hours tonight by commercial airplane. So I'll go to the airport soon to get physical possession of the article and not let it out of my sight until it is installed. The army has really folded up for the holiday. I radioed General Sutherland and asked him to start proceedings from that end to see if he couldn't get action.

What a way to spend a Christmas! I'll never forget this one as long as I live, and I may not live too long, considering the heights to which my blood pressure must have risen today. Of all of the faults of man, I think the most inexcusable is inefficiency, and when it comes in wholesale quantities I'm entirely unable to cope with it. My drive to the airport tonight may cool my fevered brow, especially if I get the coveted cylinder.

Wonder how my family spent the day. Whatever they did, it was more pleasant than the way I've spent it. I imagine the boys are so excited tonight that they will be unable to sleep. Santa Claus must have brought them many toys, none of which could fail to please their undiscriminating tastes. How simple and exciting life is for them!

Brisbane, Australia, Dec. 26, 1944   2000

We were up bright and early this morning to go to work on our airplane. As is usual in such cases, replacing the defective cylinder required considerably longer than one had calculated. We finally finished with the job and then flew up here to Brisbane, arriving about 1700 hours. I've had many little chores to accomplish here, all to be done in the very limited time before we take off at 0030 hours tonight for Hollandia.

Now I'm all set to go, so shall lie down for a bit of rest. At the rate the telephone has been ringing the past hour, I don't expect to get much sleep.

Hollandia, Dutch New Guinea, Dec. 27, 1944   1930

The trip up this morning was short and easy, but unpleasant, as are all trips which keep me up all night. At length, however, we arrived in time for lunch. Imagine my disappointment when there was only one letter for me, and that from Wayne and Marge. An hour later, though, I got two letters from Grace, but they were quite old, having been written on December 2. All is well at home, but Grace is having to work long and hard hours now that she has no household help.

A radiogram from General Sutherland asked that I bring another flight to Tacloban as soon as possible.

I slept for a couple of hours this afternoon but am still quite tired so will go to bed at once now.

Hollandia, Dutch New Guinea, Dec. 28, 1944   2015

Was busy most of the morning with chores having to do with my men, etc. One of them is in the hospital with dengue and I went down to visit him. Then I belatedly delivered to them my Xmas present of liquor, which they duly appreciated.

This afternoon I moved *Bataan* over to the Hollandia airstrip for the heavily-laden takeoff for the Philippines tonight. Will depart at 2300 hours and should have a fine trip providing the weather is as good as is forecasted. Will see General Sutherland and should be able to get an idea about the possible trip to the States, which has been delayed without any explanation to me.

Hollandia, Dutch New Guinea, Dec. 29, 1944   1930

Took off on schedule at 2300 hours last night and had a good trip up to the Philippines, arriving shortly after daylight this morning. I went at once into Tacloban. General Sutherland wanted answers to various questions, including many about the Australian WAC captain. My frank narrative about the situation certainly did not make him happy, but he appeared to appreciate my forthrightness. Then he talked about his relationship with General MacArthur. I stayed with him for a couple of hours.

[MacArthur's "grounding" of Sutherland had lasted only a very short time, was verbal only, and was not put into the form of a formal order.

Sutherland felt that although the dispute concerning the Australian WAC had triggered MacArthur's disciplinary action toward him, it was only one of several frustrations affecting the commander in chief. The Leyte cleanup operation was not proceeding well at the time of the confrontation and was behind the timetable that had been given the Joint Chiefs of Staff. The enemy had been able to resupply and supplement his forces on Leyte and we had seemed powerless to stop this reinforcement. Sutherland said MacArthur's mood was much like it had been in the early days of the New Guinea campaign, when progress had been slow and disappointing. But on that occasion we had lacked men and equipment, whereas now we were in a much more advantageous posture. MacArthur wanted to get on to Luzon and Manila, and these delays had been most distressing to him, increasing his impatience.

MacArthur is going to Luzon on board the cruiser *Boise* along with the Lingayen Gulf assault. I suppose I somewhat resent the other duties that prevent me from going with him on this landing. But until there is sufficient airdrome space in which our airplanes can be parked, I will have to remain in Hollandia. Sutherland wants me to fly him into Lingayen as soon as an airstrip there can accommodate us.

We discussed the new C-54 for General MacArthur. Sutherland said that it had been delayed at the factory and that the delivery date was now uncertain. He said that I would not be able to bring all my aircraft to Leyte for some time yet but that I should bring a B-25 and plan on remaining at Tacloban with one flight crew until we could move on to Manila. He kept talking and I finally told him I would like to leave so as to arrive back in Hollandia before dark if possible, since I expected the weather there to be unfavorable, thus making a night approach into that airport undesirable. We landed in Hollandia at dusk without incident.]

General MacArthur was not in his office.
I am to move to the Philippines on January 13 with the B-25.

Hollandia, Dutch New Guinea, Dec. 30, 1944   2030

Although I slept long and well last night, I've had the usual "letdown" feeling I always suffer after protracted wakefulness and long hours in the air. It always takes me a day to recover, particularly from the effects of the Benzedrine-Seconal regime.

This morning I had *three* letters from Grace, the last written on December 13. All is well at home and apparently Elva, our maid, is with us again. It's a relief to me to have this news. My outlook has improved decidedly overnight.

This afternoon I was confronted with a request from General Sutherland to operate two more airplanes to the Philippines tonight. I flipped a coin with Major Oviatt to determine which of us would go on one of them, as we were both tired from our trips yesterday. I was lucky and Oviatt drew the trip. I still may have to fly, however, as I've been unable to locate Captain Skov, who was to fly the other airplane. Will not know until the last minute.

My small detachment of men and officers is about the last of GHQ located in Hollandia now. We feel like lost souls here among the comparatively undisciplined USAFFE, but after experiencing the hip-deep mud of Tacloban yesterday I'm thankful for our comfortable living conditions here.

Hollandia, Dutch New Guinea, Dec. 31, 1944   2030

Captain Skov appeared last night in time, so I didn't have to fly the trip to the Philippines. Consequently, I've had a free day but haven't felt too well all day. To shake off my lethargy I took a five-mile mountain climb, but it didn't seem to have the desired effect.

Both Oviatt and Skov returned all right after successful trips north.

This is perhaps the quietest New Year's Eve I've ever spent. There's absolutely nothing to do—not even a movie. I'm retiring early to read a detective novel.

Hollandia, Dutch New Guinea, Jan. 1, 1945   2000

Although it was rainy and sultry this morning, I flew to Biak rather than tolerate a day of idleness here.

Upon returning to Hollandia, I had four letters from Grace, but a couple of them were quite old. When they were written she was thrilled with the anticipation of my prospective homecoming, but naturally by this time has suffered the same anguished disappointment that I've had to tolerate. I'm not relinquishing all hopes relative to the trip, however, as there may be a good chance of it yet as soon as I've played my part in this next operation in the Philippines. I will not be nearly as indispensable after that.

Hollandia, Dutch New Guinea, Jan. 2, 1945   1900

Did a bit of paperwork this morning and then caught up with some long-neglected correspondence. Had a letter from General Sutherland enclosing a letter and specifications from Douglas Aircraft Corporation of our new C-54. They are building innovations into it which even I had not considered possible. The letter answered the question in my mind as to why I had not gone back to the States to get it. Due to the fact that we could have a new C-54E rather than an old converted C-54 if we were willing to wait two more months for it, the Douglas Corporation assumed that we would prefer the delay. I'm pleased that they made this decision because we will have the very latest in equipment. Moreover, if the airplane were ready for delivery now, I would be unable to go get it because I will be needed in this forthcoming operation. But by mid-February we should be approaching Manila, and during the mopping-up interval my activities here should be minimal. The Douglas Corporation estimates that the aircraft will be ready for acceptance about February 25.

Tomorrow night I will go to Leyte again in the B-24. This likely will be my last trip prior to the time I move there on January 13 to stay.

Hollandia, Dutch New Guinea, Jan. 3, 1945   1900

Tested the B-25 this morning and went to look for my copilot, who crash-landed a borrowed airplane yesterday. Couldn't locate him, but I've had word that he is unhurt. Don't know any of the details of the accident.

I'm leaving tonight at 2300 hours for the Philippines on another of those long round-trip flights. So must get some rest now. Had a letter from Grace — still expecting me to arrive home in time for Christmas. Then there was a letter from Walt Addems and one from Wayne. The mail seems to be arriving a bit more on schedule recently.

Hollandia, Dutch New Guinea, Jan. 4, 1945   2000

Took off on schedule at 2300 hours last night in a driving rain and with low ceiling. If there's any more hazardous operation in flying than taking off a fully loaded B-24 in the darkness and rain, I don't know what it is. Each time I get by with it, I know God is looking after me. As usual, the trip to the Philippines was long. While in Tacloban I went in to headquarters to see Generals MacArthur and Sutherland. General MacArthur was embarking on the cruiser *Boise*, which would be helping to escort one of the huge convoys on the way to the Lingayen Gulf landing. The return portion on my trip was even longer. Had some weather to contend with upon arriving back here at Hollandia, and after seventeen hours in the air it isn't easy to do an accurate job of flying. To complicate matters, the gyro-horizon instrument was inoperative. It's all in the day's work. I sometimes wonder why I don't get myself a nice, safe, easy desk job.

Hollandia, Dutch New Guinea, Jan. 5, 1945   2000

As usual after one of these long trips, I've felt very unambitious and lazy today. Haven't done anything of a useful nature except to write some letters. It's rained nearly all day so I've remained indoors and read.

No mail today—another disappointing factor. So here I go to bed feeling just so-so.

Hollandia, Dutch New Guinea, Jan. 6, 1945   2030

It was one year ago today that I said good-bye to my family and departed for army duty overseas. It's been a very, very long year and a lonely one, but it has had its compensations. I've done more, seen more, and experienced more in this year than in any previous year of my life, and I've probably been more lonely and despondent at times than ever before. One can't have everything. In my case, it has been the separation from my family that has been my cross to bear. There have been many times when I've regretted coming into the army, since I could well have avoided it. Had I been another person, I could have found many justifications for remaining a civilian in an essential job, but, as it was before I entered the army, my conscience would have been prodding me all the time. Having had four brothers in World War I and having been reared in an atmosphere of service to one's country, I'm more mentally at ease now. I don't have to justify myself before man or God. My country is telling me what to do, and I'm obeying to the full extent of my ability. My motives and my actions cannot be construed to be selfish because they are all determined by someone else. I can get a good night's sleep.

It has rained most of the day, but I felt a bit more ambitious than was the case yesterday. So I flew another "Rhoades Tour" over to the "Lost Valley," taking General Alexander and other officers over to see that amazing place. The trip was duly appreciated by all.

Hollandia, Dutch New Guinea, Jan. 7, 1945   2000

Feeling a bit more ambitious and having nothing else to occupy my time, I've gone in for exercise quite heavily today. I walked down the mountain and back and then played four games of volleyball. Now I feel pleasantly tired. There was no mail and I'm becoming somewhat depressed, as I always do when I feel I'm being neglected.

Major Oviatt returned tonight after a successful trip, so I guess I made no mistake in sending him out in the bad weather last night.

Hollandia, Dutch New Guinea, Jan. 8, 1945   1900

It's a wonderful evening. Since dinner I've been sitting out in the late evening twilight, watching the stars and the lights from the airfields below and enjoying the luxury of the soft, cool breeze. Wonder why we fight wars when there are such fine, simple pleasures to be enjoyed everywhere? I wish the world and all its peoples could somehow return to a less complicated way of life. We have reached the ridiculous stage now where none of us quite knows where his allegiances lie amidst all of our complexities and selfish interests, which confront us at every turn. I'm afraid, however, that we've gone so far now in pursuit of technical advances and attempts to better our physical lives that it will be a long time indeed before we find the courage to turn back to a more wholesome way of life.

I flew the B-25 this morning and then made arrangements for an instrument-check ride tomorrow. My pilot instrument card is about to expire, and although I don't need one in this theater, when I do eventually go back to the States the possession of a current card will be mandatory.

Hollandia, Dutch New Guinea, Jan. 9, 1945   2015

Today was the day of the landing on Luzon. I haven't heard any details of its progress yet, but everyone expected it to be bloody. I have been carefully monitoring the dispatches that have been arriving in the communications center but there is only very meager information. A lot of fine young Americans probably died today. I wonder if their lives were well spent. I should have liked to take part in this operation, but I could not do so because I have to fly the first airplane into Luzon to bring the chief out after the first phases of the operation are completed.

Today I took an instrument-check ride to renew my instrument rating. I didn't do too badly. Upon returning to my quarters I had five letters, including two from Grace.

Hollandia, Dutch New Guinea, Jan. 10, 1945   2230

It's been one of the warmest days we've had here and, fortunately, I've had no work to do. I spent most of the day in my quarters in the nude. Packed most of my belongings in preparation for my move to the Philippines. This afternoon I played volleyball and tonight I played poker for a couple of hours. Won about seven gulden. Now to bed.

Hollandia, Dutch New Guinea, Jan. 11, 1945   1930

Went to the airstrip and gave the B-25 its final test flight this morning. It's all ready for the trip to Luzon on Saturday. Then I walked up the mountain for exercise in spite of the terrific heat. Don't think I've ever perspired more. This afternoon I played volleyball again.

Grace is just now resigning herself to the fact that I'm not coming back to visit for some time yet. From all reports the holiday season was a huge success as far as Jimmy and Johnny were concerned.

Hollandia, Dutch New Guinea, Jan. 12, 1945   2000

It's been another inactive day for me. Have finished packing and moved my belongings to the airplane. All is now ready for a 0500 takeoff for the Philippines tomorrow.

[Both MacArthur and Sutherland are now in Luzon and are proceeding down the great flat plain toward Manila with the Sixth Army.]

One year ago today I arrived in this theater and was called to duty in the army. Probably one-sixtieth of my life has been spent here, and all of my efforts, as everyone's efforts are in wartime, have been generally unconstructive. Such a waste of time and energy without many accompanying benefits! I imagine I'll still be in this theater one year from today, as I don't see how this bloody affair can be ended sooner than that.

Tacloban, P.I., Jan. 13, 1945   2100

Brought the B-25 up here in record time. Landed at Morotai for fuel and still arrived here at 1300 hours. Although I came up along Mindanao Island, I saw no Japs.

[There was a choice of billets—good quarters at Tolosa, about twenty miles down the coast, or terrible ones in Tacloban, where I could sleep in a large mud-floored garage along with about one hundred other officers. I have chosen the latter because I am among friends and will be close to the communications center as well as the Price house, so I can learn of developments as they occur. Also, I can receive orders almost immediately from General MacArthur or General Sutherland. The army is making very good progress sweeping down toward Manila. The arrangement is for General MacArthur to remain with the army and enter Manila, whereas General Sutherland will return to Tacloban. As soon as the airstrip at Lingayen Gulf can accept my B-25, Sutherland will order me forward to fly him back to Tacloban.]

It was good to get back among people of my own outfit again. I had a couple of bottles of whiskey remaining so we had a good session this evening.

Tacloban, P.I., Jan. 14, 1945   2300

Notwithstanding the rain and the hub-deep mud, I got a jeep and drove down to Tolosa today to obtain information about the new airstrips and approach procedures at Mindoro and Lingayen Gulf. Then I stopped at the Tacloban airstrip on the way back. The trip required four and a half hours of driving in the jeep. Among other things, I learned that the airstrip could not be made suitable for landing earlier than tomorrow afternoon, and possibly not by then.

Tonight I wistfully watched a poker game but did not engage. I have sent so much money home that I do not have enough remaining to protect myself adequately in a game of any size. Still it rains—

Tacloban, P.I., Jan. 15, 1945   2345

This has been another hot, rainy day, so I haven't done much. Obtained the necessary papers for two of my men, Sergeants Burden and Bone, to return to the States on rotation policy. Both of them have been overseas for thirty-seven months, and now certainly deserve some duty in the States. Tonight I played poker and won a few pesos. There were three letters— nice ones—from Grace today. Much news about the antics of those boys. I'm surely missing much of the interesting part of their development, and I'll never be able to recapture it.

Tacloban, P.I., Jan. 16, 1945   2200

This morning, accompanied by several of my friends, I took the B-25 up for a test flight and to make a reconnaissance trip through this area. Although I'd made many trips in and out of the area, I'd never had an opportunity to obtain a good perspective of the place. It was most interesting to fly over the places which have figured so greatly in recent war dispatches, and to view the devastation wrought by bitter land and naval battles. This afternoon was a sultry, muggy time and I was not busy.

Played poker for an hour tonight and tripled my money.

Tacloban, P.I., Jan. 17, 1945   2330

At dawn today we had an air raid by a lone Jap bomber, but he did manage to wound forty-two men with his one stick of bombs.

It's been another sultry day with little activity. Things are moving ahead with gratifying speed on Luzon, so that leaves us with little to do here. Before long now I expect we will be moving to Luzon. General Sutherland apparently is too involved with the operation there to be able to depart, as he radioed me to the effect that he would send for me "in a few days."

After dinner tonight we had another air raid but no reported damage. The Japs have very few airplanes remaining in the Philippines, and these are hidden away in the jungle. The most they can do is to pull an occasional sneak raid with two or three aircraft.

Tacloban, P.I., Jan. 18, 1945   2245

We started the day with the usual dawn air raid, but no airplanes came near our barracks. Today has been quite warm, with no great activity. The war is moving ahead well on Luzon, while all of us here mark time awaiting instructions.

I played poker for an hour after dinner tonight and won a bit. Certainly there must be better movies available than the ones they send us here. We have no other possible recreation since poor lights and blackouts make reading at night quite out of the question.

No mail today. It has started raining again now, and from all outward appearances it will continue all night. And then tomorrow the mud will be hip-deep again.

Tacloban, P.I., Jan. 19, 1945   2300

It has rained steadily all day today, and activity has been at a minimum. During a lull this afternoon I went to the airstrip to test-fly the B-25. I was all set for takeoff when the operations officer suddenly closed the field account weather. No mail today, and I'm still awaiting instructions from General Sutherland.

Tacloban, P.I., Jan. 20, 1945   2300

This has certainly been a long and tiring day. At a little after midnight I received a radiogram from General Sutherland to the effect that I was to arrive at Lingayen Gulf on Luzon at 1300 hours today. At that time of night it was most difficult to make the necessary arrangements, including informing the crew, etc., for a daylight takeoff.

Having no armament on the B-25, I elected to accompany an armed B-25 which was going partway up. He was considerably delayed, which finally resulted in a takeoff here at 0830 hours. We went to Mindoro and landed, and the other B-25 developed engine trouble, so I had no alternative but to go on to Luzon, unarmed. I landed at Lingayen Gulf at 1330 hours without seeing any Jap aircraft en route. General Sutherland and General Beebe were awaiting me there and we took off at 1400 hours for

Tacloban. We had three P-38s escorting us back as far as Mindoro, so I passed rather close in to Bataan, Corregidor, and Manila. Still saw no Japs and could notice little activity around these historic places. I imagine it will not be long now before we are in Manila again.

The trip back was short, and we arrived back at Tacloban at 1700 hours. The general indicated that he might want to go to Brisbane in a day or two.

Tacloban, P.I., Jan. 21, 1945   2030

Early this morning General Sutherland told me that he wanted to go to Brisbane, starting early tomorrow. He said his teeth had been bothering him and he wanted to have much dental work done. We will go in the B-25 as far as Hollandia and then take the B-17 on down. I've been busy today making the necessary arrangements, obtaining orders, etc. Will go by way of Palau for refueling. I had never expected to go to Australia again, but it will be good to have a hot bath and a few of the comforts of civilization after having lived under most primitive conditions here.

Today I had a field day on mail. Had seven letters, including six from Grace. Some of them were quite old, however, one having been written on November 18. They were filled with news of herself and the boys, so naturally were the best of reading material.

Hollandia, Dutch New Guinea, Jan. 22, 1945   1930

General Sutherland and I came down from Tacloban to Hollandia in record time today in the B-25. We stopped at Palau to refuel and had a most pleasant lunch with Colonel Dunn. Upon arriving here there was some confusion, because the B-17 in which we planned to continue to Brisbane developed engine trouble and it appeared that we would have to use a C-47 instead. However, the B-17 now seems repairable and we plan to continue on tonight at about 2100 hours.

Upon landing here at Hollandia, there were two packages for me which the UAL boys on trans-Pacific had brought over. One of them is a photograph, and although I haven't had time to open it, I just know it's a lovely photo of Grace.

Brisbane, Australia, Jan. 23, 1945   2200

Completely exhausted, I arrived in Brisbane at 0800 hours. There was the usual fanfare with General Sutherland and much delay before I could fall into bed between clean sheets. Imagine! A hot shower and all of the luxuries! But before I could go to bed I had to open the package of photographs. And there were *two* of the most beautiful pictures of Grace! They are truly wonderful and show to the best advantage all of her fine qualities of sweetness, poise, and friendliness. They are my most valuable possession now.

I slept until 1700 hours and when I awoke there was Grace, staring at me reprovingly from her photographs. They are so real that I feel as if I should talk to them.

I spent a most delightful evening with Mrs. MacArthur. She is one of the most charming, sincere women I've ever known, and her life is devoted to the general's welfare—a most worthy cause in my estimation. We had a stimulating visit and then listened to symphonic music for hours.

Now to bed, feeling washed-out from my long flight.

Brisbane, Australia, Jan. 24, 1945 2200

Was quite busy today with my errands. Made many telephone calls, delivered letters, collected liquor to take back, etc. And I've spent much time ogling the photographs of Gracie. This afternoon I reveled in the luxury of a hot bath, beer to drink, and radio music.

No information yet concerning the time of our departure for the Philippines.

Brisbane, Australia, Jan. 25, 1945 2200

I arose leisurely this morning and got a car to drive to the airstrip to check on the airplane. Then I went to the hospital to see Pappy Gunn, who is still recuperating from the bombing in which he lost an arm. I feel a bit guilty just now, enjoying myself so much during the war, when many other more deserving soldiers cannot have access to any form of recreation. However, I can see no reason why I should sit in my room when I can be enjoying these things.

Brisbane, Australia, Jan. 26, 1945 2130

After a quiet lunch, I went to the airport to load some supplies on the airplane, and then this afternoon I went for a drive with Mrs. MacArthur and Arthur. We stopped off at Gregory Terrace and I had a set of tennis. The weather was very warm indeed.

Today is Gracie's birthday. I hope the boys will throw a very fine party for their Mummy.

It now appears that we may return to Luzon, starting tomorrow night.

If so, this is my last night to enjoy having a hot bath and sleeping between clean sheets.

Before long now I should be receiving information concerning the C-54 which is being prepared for us in the States. I'm still hoping I'll get to go back to fly it over here.

Brisbane, Australia, Jan. 27, 1945   2230

I went out with little Arthur MacArthur for a lesson in horseback riding. Then tonight Gerald Graham and I had a delightful steak dinner together, after which Mrs. MacArthur invited us up to a private showing of a very good movie. A few more days of this life and I could easily fall into the Australian way of thinking that the war is over. In fact, at the rate progress is being made in Europe, it may not be too long now before the war does terminate. I can't be convinced that the Japs will pursue the war long after they find themselves fighting the entire world.

Still no news about the date of our return to the Philippines. I'd like to get back to collect mail which no doubt has accumulated there.

Brisbane, Australia, Jan. 28, 1945   2130

A Sunday in Australia is never an event to write home about, and today has been no exception. I couldn't get up a tennis or golf game, so I've vegetated. Took a walk this afternoon, but the extreme heat soon forced a restriction on so much activity. I wrote a letter and read magazines — at least it's physically comfortable to vegetate in an air-conditioned hotel room.

Still no information concerning the date of our return to the Philippines.

Brisbane, Australia, Jan. 29, 1945   2230

Another aimless day, with no real progress to report. No word from the general relative to our departure time, and I've managed to find very little to occupy my time. This was another of the myriad Australian holidays, so that everything was closed up. It was their Foundation Day, corresponding to our Independence Day. They, unfortunately, have not achieved and apparently do not want independence from Britain, a difficult thing for an American to understand.

Couldn't promote a tennis game, but tonight Mrs. MacArthur invited me to her apartment to see a private showing of a most amusing movie. She certainly goes far out of her way to look after my happiness and welfare.

Surely tomorrow will bring some information regarding the time of our departure for the Philippines.

Brisbane, Australia, Jan. 30, 1945 2200

[Early in the morning General Sutherland told me he wanted to depart about midnight tomorrow night. He has been having dental work done almost daily, and the fungus infection on his feet is much improved. The Australian WAC captain also has been in Brisbane during the general's stay there.

I am anxious to get back to the combat area, where things are happening. It has been several weeks since I have spent any significant amount of time with General MacArthur, having seen him briefly only during my turnaround fuel stops at Tacloban.]

I went to the airport to test-fly *Bataan* for a couple of hours to make certain that it was in good flying condition. The general wants to go through directly to Tacloban with only one stop at Hollandia for refueling. That means about eighteen hours in the air again.

Brisbane, Australia, Jan. 31, 1945 2000

This has been a busy day, getting all things ready for our trip tonight. We will take off at 2230 hours and the weather is not good. Have spent much of the time in company with Al Luedtke, Gerald Graham, or Mrs. MacArthur. Had my last big filet steak for dinner, and now I'm ready to go back on a diet of field rations and mud.

Tolosa, P.I., Feb. 1, 1945 2100

We departed from Brisbane as planned last night at 2230 hours. Naturally the trip was very long, and we didn't arrive in Hollandia until 0830 hours this morning and had much bad weather with which to contend throughout the night. We remained one and a half hours in Hollandia for refueling and then took off for Tanauan, arriving here at 1700 hours. (Tanauan is the name of the air strip located near Tolosa.)

Here I found everything in a state of great confusion. During my absence, GHQ had moved from Tacloban to Tolosa. It was dark before I got my new billet assignment, and then in the rain I set out to locate my belongings. I finally located my footlocker and barracks bag out in the rain, where they had been for some days. Everything I own is ruined beyond salvage. But, having been awake for forty hours, I'm now so tired

I don't care any longer. Have to be up at 0500 hours tomorrow to take General Sutherland on to Luzon.

Tolosa, P.I., Feb. 2, 1945   2100

We were somewhat delayed in our departure this morning, but we finally got away before noon, going in the B-25 directly up to Lingayen Gulf. We flew over Batangas, Cavite Naval Base, Corregidor, Manila, and then Clark Field. Cavite was burning and there were large fires on Corregidor, but there were no fires in Manila proper. About the time I went over Manila, General MacArthur was scheduled to make his entry into the city. As yet we haven't had official word confirming his entry. We went on up the valley and circled Clark Field for some time, trying unsuccessfully to find a strip suitable for landing. All of the strips are still pock-marked with bomb craters, and the engineers haven't yet had time to rebuild them. There are perhaps 200 wrecked Jap aircraft on the field, and Fort Stotsenburg nearby is completely demolished.

We continued on up the valley at low altitude to Lingayen Gulf, where we landed and discharged General Sutherland. After a quick refueling, we took off and returned over Manila but could see no evidence of unusual activity. At Lingyen Gulf we learned that our entry into Manila had been delayed by the fact the Japanese had destroyed bridges across the rivers. Arrived here before dark with engine trouble. Needless to say, I am utterly exhausted after my three days of almost continuous flying. Had six letters from Grace, as well as others, but I'm much too tired to appreciate them.

Tolosa, P.I., Feb. 3, 1945   2000

Today I've been quite busy with personal chores—trying to arrange to sleep a bit more comfortably, etc. I've had to outfit myself with new clothing. It has rained much of the time, so I haven't been able to dry my laundry, but I've managed to get my personal effects into a dry place.

Tolosa, P.I., Feb. 4, 1945   2130

Sure enough I was asked to go to Luzon this morning to take Generals Chamberlin and Marquart. We got away at a reasonable hour and went up over Manila to see what progress our troops were making in the city. The spectacle was an appalling sight. The entire downtown section of the city was a mass of flames—the Japs having dynamited and set fire to the whole business section of the city before being forced out of it.

A deathly pall of smoke obscured the bay and the countryside for miles around, and flames were rising 200 feet in the air from the center of the city. The residential section of the area indicated no fires, however, and the piers appeared to be intact, although doubtless they had been damaged to a great extent. One compensating feature was about thirty hulks of Jap ships sunk in the harbor. We continued on to Lingayen Gulf, where the generals deplaned, and then returned to Tolosa.

[At Lingayen I received a report that General Yamashita had declared Manila an open city and ordered his troops to withdraw before he fled to Baguio. Either this was a false report or he had lost control of his military forces. In any event, I imagine that General MacArthur, who is now in the outskirts of the city, must be shocked and grossly angered by this senseless destruction of Manila, which for many years was his home. This being war, there was a feeling of retribution when we received this morning the report that our B-29s had dropped 200 tons of incendiary bombs on Tokyo.]

As we came over Manila this time, the fires were burning even more fiercely. Arrived back in time for dinner after having had no lunch, and I plan on an early retirement to fortify myself against another trip to Luzon which is scheduled for tomorrow.

Tolosa, P.I., Feb. 5, 1945   2000

Was out early to take off for Luzon again this morning but was delayed for over an hour. A bomb was unexpectedly dropped in the center of the runway, and some time was required to effect repairs in the runway surface matting. We had excellent weather, and when we arrived over Manila, we found that even more of the city was burning fiercely. The Japs are destroying all of it they can, but they are hopelessly trapped now and death to them is certain. Manila is the last city of ours that they can destroy, but there are plenty of Japanese cities left for us to burn.

We landed at Lingayen Gulf, where we discharged Generals Stivers, Willoughby, and Whitlock, and then we departed for Tolosa as soon as possible. Arrived here only in time for dinner. Haven't even had time for a bath for three days. Must get a note away to Grace tonight. Have to be up very early again tomorrow for another trip.

Tolosa, P.I., Feb. 6, 1945   2200

I had a most pleasant surprise this morning in the form of a radiogram from General MacArthur to the effect that I was not to make my scheduled trip to Luzon today as the official parade into Manila will not be made until all Japs are destroyed and the burned-out city partly cleaned up. So I've had a day of comparative freedom during which I've washed clothing, dried my equipment, written letters, etc. Tonight I even found time to play poker for an hour.

We have slowed down considerably in our conquest of Manila. The Japs in the city are practically surrounded, and since they will not surrender, our troops have to slowly and methodically slaughter them. It's difficult for us to understand the psychology of such people. It will be a considerable physical relief for us to get GHQ moved into Manila and out of the mud and rain of Leyte.

Tolosa, P.I., Feb. 7, 1945   2130

A further radiogram this morning advised me that I would not have to come to Luzon today either. This interlude in my flying activity enabled me to clear my desk of much accumulated paperwork today, as well as to close out all pressing correspondence.

Tolosa, P.I., Feb. 8, 1945   2200

Went to the airstrip and test-flew the B-25 for an hour. I didn't feel at all well and after lunch I suddenly took ill. I managed to get to the dispensary and Doc January discovered I had a high temperature, rapid pulse, and congested lungs. He filled me with sulfa and sent me to bed. The weather is hot, and I've been utterly miserable all day. It seems to be one of the unidentified tropical fevers along with a violent dysentery and should run its course in a day or two. Then, to add to my miseries, we had an air raid tonight, and in my attempt to hurriedly blow out my open oil lamp near my bed the boiling oil splashed back into my face, painfully burning it all over. The burns are not deep, but will keep me from my slumbers, and I'm now minus eyebrows and eyelashes.

Tolosa, P.I., Feb. 9, 1945   2100

After a most miserable night, my temperature broke early this morning amidst much perspiration. By the time Doc came around, my temperature and pulse were normal, but I'm very weak and still have much dysentery. Even my facial burns have stopped hurting, although I'm temporarily considerably disfigured. So life could be worse.

Today I had a fine letter from Grace but she too is having her troubles with boy illnesses, teeth, rent troubles, etc.

Tolosa, P.I., Feb. 10, 1945 2100

Was up this morning feeling well but still groggy from the sulfa. I went to the dispensary and then to the X-ray lab, where the picture indicated no TB. I went to the office and joy oh joy! There was a radiogram from General MacArthur directing me to proceed to Santa Monica, California, to get his new C-54 airplane. A little later a correction came through from General MacArthur stating that the airplane was in Dayton instead of Santa Monica. Needless to say I've been very busy getting everything ready to go. If it can possibly be arranged I'll take off at 0800 hours tomorrow and go to Guam, from which I'll continue on to San Francisco with United Air Lines. Tonight I'll get a final letter of instruction from General MacArthur. Hope I get to stay at home a few days. Oh boy!

17

Home and Back

FEBRUARY–MARCH, 1945

Guam, Mariana Islands, Feb. 11, 1945 2100

I was up long before daylight this morning and off on the long jeep ride to the Tacloban airstrip. Although I was told to be there at 0630 hours, we had the usual delays and didn't depart until 0900 hours. I was a passenger on the trip to Guam, which required over seven hours, and I was most miserable all the way. My dysentery and my burns, coupled with a bad cold and ear troubles, conspired to make me an unhappy boy. To add to my woes, I had to be courier officer, responsible for the safe delivery of about 1,000 pounds of top-secret documents.

For some unknown reason we have remained on the ground here for hours, and it now appears that we will not depart before midnight. I was hoping I could make a quick trip back as I'll have so little time to spend at home anyway.

Johnston Island, Feb. 11, 1945 2230

Making a midnight departure from Guam, we arrived at Kwajalein Island at midmorning. Unfortunately, I did not get on a United Air Lines airplane at Guam, so I will have to ride this bucket-seated, army-operated plane all the way to San Francisco. We had a four-hour wait for some unexplained reason at Kwajalein, and then made the seven-hour flight here to Johnston Island in time to finish dinner before midnight. This island is operated by the navy and is a very busy place.

We are almost ready to depart now, having had only a one-hour stop here. Although this has been an extra day, the date is still February 11 as we have crossed the international date line.

En route Honolulu–San Francisco, Feb. 12, 1945 2100

We arrived in Honolulu at daybreak and then had another of those interminable delays. I tried to sleep but was unsuccessful, since the noise and daylight conspired against me. Nothing can stop me now, and in only a few more hours I'll be seeing Grace and those two boys.

Atherton Calif., Feb. 13, 1945   2200

Upon arriving at Hamilton Field at 0330 hours this morning, there was much red tape to struggle through trying to dispose of the secret courier mail I had. I obtained a staff car and was driven into San Francisco. I telephoned Grace from the bus terminal, getting her out of bed at 0530 hours to ask her to meet me at the bus stop in Menlo Park. It seemed as though the trip would never end, but at length I stepped off the bus to find Grace and Jimmy awaiting me with outstretched arms in the cold twilight of the early dawn. It was a joyous moment indeed after an absence of almost fourteen months. I can't describe my emotions on the occasion except to say that it was easily the happiest moment of my life to date.

I found everything at home almost exactly as I had left it over a year ago. Grace is the same sweet, delightful person she has always been and of course the boys have grown a lot, but they also are finer and sturdier than I have any right to expect. Johnny didn't know me but he soon came to accept me. Jimmy is the same serious little dreamer.

Atherton, Calif., Feb. 14, 1945   2345

We were up reasonably early this morning and Grace and I took a bus into San Francisco. I had lunch with Jim Brenner and a group of San Francisco lawyers at the Bohemian Club while Grace and Patty had lunch at the Women's City Club. Afterwards Grace and I met at the St. Francis Hotel, from where we proceeded about town to do a lot of my official chores. I received a telegram advising me that the new airplane had been moved from Dayton to Santa Monica. Among other things we went to the United Air Lines office, where Ben Berry managed to get Grace a reservation on the early plane to Los Angeles tomorrow so that she could accompany me down to the Douglas Aircraft plant to get the new airplane.

Early tomorrow we leave for Los Angeles, so there will be little sleep tonight.

Santa Monica, Calif., Feb. 15, 1945   2015

After barely two hours of sleep last night we were awakened by a telephone call from UAL advising that Grace would be unable to accompany me to Santa Monica, as her reservation had been surrendered to a priority passenger. So I boarded a bus in the early-morning darkness and proceeded to the airport alone. Had an excellent trip down on United to Burbank, where the Douglas Aircraft Corporation sent a car to take me and crew to Santa Monica. I suspected that the airplane would not be ready for delivery, and sure enough it was not. However, this gave me an opportunity to check the equipment thoroughly and to become familiar with the new installations. It's a wonderful airplane in every respect, but of course, being new, will have many mechanical imperfections which will have to be corrected.

I met Mr. Donald Douglas and had a fine talk with him. Incidentally, he gave me a case of Scotch whiskey to distribute in GHQ.

I was very busy with ground details until dark and then Johnny Martin and I took the airplane up for a test flight. It performed perfectly except for one or two items which can be easily corrected tomorrow. With luck I should be able to leave by noon.

Atherton, Calif., Feb. 16, 1945   2200

Because of the usual unanticipated delays, we didn't get away from the plant with our new airplane until well after noon. We made a fast trip to San Francisco to land and allow Grace and Jimmy, as well as some of the UAL pilots, to see the new airplane. I'm quite proud of it and am glad to show it off. Jimmy in particular was well pleased.

After spending one and a half hours at the San Francisco airport, I took the airplane on over to Hamilton Field to park it and to place a guard on it until we are ready to take it across the Pacific. Now, even though I'll be technically AWOL, I'm going to spend a couple of days at home unless General MacArthur radios instructions to the contrary.

Atherton, Calif., Feb. 17, 1945   2200

Have remained at home all day today relaxing and enjoying my family. None of us have felt too ambitious, but I'm glad to have the opportunity for conversation. Our quiet day was interrupted three times, however, by newpapermen wanting interviews and pictures. There was little I could tell them and still remain within restrictions imposed for reasons of security.

It's a wonderfully gratifying sensation which all too few people experience to come home and find everything to be exactly the way you want it to be. Without a wife and mother like Grace, it couldn't possibly be that way.

Atherton, Calif., Feb. 18, 1945 2230

This has been one of the most pleasant days of all. It has been a fine, sunny Sunday with a good crisp breeze blowing—one of those rare days when everything is in tune and life seems eminently worthwhile.

After a leisurely breakfast we went for a drive up into the hills above Palo Alto. We came upon an open field which was so inviting with its clear brook and many oak trees that the boys and I took out on foot cross-country to "explore." Fun isn't the proper word to express my emotions under such conditions. At last it dawned upon me that here I was, doing the very things, living the very life which I had started out in my youth to try to attain for myself. Suddenly I realize that I have everything in life which any man could want. I have a fine beautiful wife who loves me as much as I do her, if that's possible, and I have two boys as fine and strong as any there are. I have more than my share of the material things of this world, and I've kept the respect of my fellow men even while attaining my present position. So what more could a man want?

Hamilton Field, Calif., Feb. 19, 1945 2130

We were up early so that I could tell Jim good-bye and send him off to "school." Then when I said good-bye to Johnny, he promised me he would take good care of Mommy and Jimmy until I return. I hated to leave those boys because I'll miss so much of the fun of watching their development. Grace and I then drove to San Francisco, where we met General and Mrs. Luedecke and had lunch with them. Then we drove on to Hamilton Field, where I spent a busy afternoon with details concerning my departure early tomorrow morning for Honolulu and points west. It was late afternoon before I could break away, and then I had to have six inoculations in my arms before they would clear me to leave the country. Queer how they worry so much over such things here in the States, while we who are out in the war zone where all of these diseases are to be found have little time to worry about them. At any rate, I now have two very sore arms.

Grace and I went to Galli's in Marin County to have one of their world-famous dinners but found that they were closed on Mondays. So we went on to the Chateau, where we enjoyed excellent drinks and a fine dinner. Then sadly we drove back to Hamilton Field to say good-bye for another indefinite period. But the parting was not so difficult this time. We realize now that the war isn't going to change either of us basically, and that our love will endure, regardless of what may happen before we again have an opportunity to meet and renew our vows.

Grace drove back to Atherton alone, and now I must get a few hours of sleep before my takeoff in the darkness of the early-morning hours for Honolulu.

Honolulu, T.H., Feb. 20, 1945   2100

We took off from Hamilton Field just before dawn this morning and flew the 2,400 miles over here in 11:45. The weather was excellent and the trip entirely routine. The Air Transport Command has provided me with an excellent navigator and crew chief, and that permits me to take my responsibilities somewhat less seriously.

Because we need to have some minor maintenance performed, I plan to remain here tomorrow and then continue on the following day.

Honolulu, T.H., Feb. 21, 1945   2000

After arising late, I had a very busy day. I went to see Lt. Col. Red Elkins, an old friend of mine, about some official items. Then I checked on the work being done on the airplane. I obtained a staff car to drive me into the city to do some bits of shopping I had overlooked while in San Francisco. All chores are done, the airplane is ready to go, and we depart at 0630 hours tomorrow for Kwajalein.

En route Honolulu–Kwajalein, Feb. 22, 1945   1200

This is the day that doesn't exist for us, since we are now crossing the international date line.

Kwajalein, Marshall Islands, Feb. 23, 1945   2030

We made our departure from Honolulu just before daybreak. The weather was perfect throughout the trip and with a helping wind we made the 2,400-mile trip in 10:45. We arrived here in midafternoon and will remain overnight.

There are eight UAL crews having layover here, and, of course, I know all of the pilots. Their consensus of opinion is that the company and the CAA will be quite lenient in taking us back in spite of many minor marks the war may leave on our health records. All of which is comforting.

Guam, Mariana Islands, Feb. 24, 1945   2030

We were out of Kwajalein on time this morning, and our flight over required only 7:45. Upon arriving here in the early afternoon I had a few details of airplane maintenance to see after, and then I looked up Red Clark, who is now commanding officer of the field. We started out on the North Atlantic operation together in June of 1942.

There was no radiogram of instructions from General MacArthur changing my itinerary, so we will have to go to Hollandia tomorrow to await further instructions there. It would be unwise to take this beautiful airplane to Leyte or Luzon and risk losing it when it is not needed there for the time being.

This island of Guam must have been a beautiful place before the war spoiled it. Now, with its covering of scars of military installations, it appears half naked as seen from the air.

Hollandia, Dutch New Guinea, Feb. 25, 1945   1930

As there was no answer to my radiogram to General Sutherland this morning, we took off at 0800 hours for Hollandia. The trip was uneventful and required only six hours, so that we arrived in early afternoon. I came up on the hill where I had lived before, but it was a changed place. It's almost completely deserted here, only a small garrison remaining, and there is no activity. The few men who are now here will be moved on to the Philippines before long, and unless the Dutch make some effort to take over, the jungle will soon reclaim all of our improvements at Hollandia. I hope it will not be too long before I can proceed on to the Philippines, because there's absolutely nothing to do here and I do not thrive on idleness.

Hollandia, Dutch New Guinea, Feb. 26, 1945   2100

There has been nothing for me to do today. It has been rainy, so I've remained in my quarters most of the time, reading, writing letters, etc. Of course I'll have no mail until I can get back to the Philippines so will grow lonesome on one-way correspondence.

This idleness is quite a letdown after so much recent excitement and the resultant stimulation of being home. The trip has done more for my morale than I can possible know. I feel as though I'm riding on the crest of a great wave.

Hollandia, Dutch New Guinea, Feb. 27, 1945   2030

Another idle day. Could find nothing to do except to read and write letters. I had a radiogram from General Sutherland saying he was glad I was back and that he hoped to be able to call me on to Manila with the new airplane in the "comparatively near future," whatever that means.

Hollandia, Dutch New Guinea, Feb. 28, 1945   2100

I arose before before dawn this morning, collected my crew, and flew to Biak to have a fifty-hour inspection done on the new airplane by the ATC there. I met many old acquaintances and thoroughly enjoyed myself. The inspection work required much longer than I had anticipated, so that we didn't get back here until well after dark. And it's too late to get any food to eat so I'm going to bed hungry.

It seems a shame that I can't be doing this waiting in San Francisco with my family instead of here. I felt all along that this would happen, but I had to follow my orders.

Hollandia, Dutch New Guinea, March 1, 1945   2130

With nothing useful confronting me at which to work, I continued to manufacture a task for myself today. I spent all day at the new airplane, cataloging all spare parts and equipment and adjusting the weight locations of different items in the airplane.

This base is rapidly being abandoned to the Dutch and Australians. In a few days we go back to field rations.

Hollandia, Dutch New Guinea, March 2, 1945   1930

Fortunately I brought back with me some detective stories, which are proving most useful in these long days of idleness. I believe I'm showing some promise as an amateur detective.

Had a small ration of beer today, and that will stimulate my flagging morale slightly for the next day or two.

Hollandia, Dutch New Guinea, March 3, 1945   1945

Had a pleasant surprise today in the form of a large bundle of letters which had accumulated in the Philippines during my absence. Although they were old—having been written before I made my visit to the States —nevertheless they were interesting. One letter contained photographs which I hadn't seen of the boys. Aside from reading and writing letters, I've done little else today.

Hope the general will call me forward soon as this life is growing most monotonous.

Hollandia, Dutch New Guinea, March 4, 1945   1900

Last night it rained in quantities which I never had believed to be possible. Early this morning, however, the weather was good, and I flew the airplane for almost three hours. Went over to the "Lost Valley" for one last good look at that incredible place.

This afternoon the rain resumed its unbelievable volume, so that nothing stirred outside, and in our crude shelters the wind made sure that the spray soaked everything I possess. To a certain extent I enjoy a good storm, though. This was a violent typhoon. I spent an interesting hour watching the furious downpour and its slow but inexorable eroding effects on our campsite here.

Tomorrow, if it is not raining, I plan to take a hike through the jungle to a beautiful waterfall which I've often found considerable delight in surveying from the air.

Hollandia, Dutch New Guinea, March 5, 1945   2330

The jungle hike was a thrilling and stimulating experience. In the company of my men, I started up the mountain at 0900 hours. The first portion of the trail was comparatively level and led through dense, damp jungle growth, through which very little sunlight entered. The thickets abounded in wildlife. There were wild pigs and cassowary birds, and many other strange, furtive, silent, brilliantly plumaged birds, the like of which I had never seen. As the trail approached the mountain it rapidly became steeper. The last mile was up a riverbed which was a veritable labyrinth of huge boulders. Finally, we came to the waterfall, beyond which we were unable to go. A gigantic boulder completely blocked the sheer 100-foot-wide gorge, and the waterfall poured over this rock. In the delightfully clear pool below the falls we had an invigorating swim, then rested for a time and returned down the trail.

Hollandia, Dutch New Guinea, March 6, 1945   2100

Another completely blank, useless day. I've finished *A Tree Grows in Brooklyn*, written a letter, played three games of cribbage, eaten three meals, and that's all.

Hollandia, Dutch New Guinea, March 7, 1945   2315

After a leisurely breakfast this morning, eight of us went to Lake Sentani, where we had obtained permission to use a cabin cruiser for the day. We took our lunches along and cruised all day on the beautiful lake. We swam for a time in the clear water in the center of the lake, then we went down to the remote end of the navigable water to the most inaccessible village we could locate in order that some of the boys could trade more effectively for some of the crude native souvenirs.

Hollandia, Dutch New Guinea, March 8, 1945   1930

Had to fly to Biak this morning to take Sergeant Yacher so that he could board the San Francisco–bound airplane to return home. I had used him temporarily to help us to bring the new C-54 across the Pacific. I accomplished several missions at the depot and had some minor repairs made on the aircraft.

Hollandia, Dutch New Guinea, March 9, 1945   2300

Today was another rainy day. After spending most all day tearing my hair and biting my nails, I played poker tonight.

Hollandia, Dutch New Guinea, March 10, 1945   2330

I spent most of the morning at the airplane practicing celestial navigation so that I would not lose my proficiency at it. I had a new octant which I wished to calibrate also. After I was satisfied with my technique, I walked up the hill from the airstrip and had good exercise, although it rained on me in great quantities.

No mail and no word from Manila about moving the airplane forward. I've practically resigned myself to my fate here.

Hollandia, Dutch New Guinea, March 11, 1945   2200

It rained again most of the day. The few officers remaining here have absolutely no duties, so time hangs heavily on everyone. Fortunately, I have a fair supply of magazines to read and just now am reading Walton's *The Compleat Angler*, which I should have read years ago, since I'm a member of the Isaac Walton League of America.

Hollandia, Dutch New Guinea, March 12, 1945   2315

I had promised to take several of the officers over to the "Lost Valley" this morning on a sightseeing tour. However, it poured rain last night and throughout the morning, and since we would have been unable to get into the high valley because of cloudiness, I had to postpone the trip.

Still no mail and no orders to move north.

Hollandia, Dutch New Guinea, March 13, 1945   2015

The weather was fine this morning so we made the flight to the "Lost Valley." The trip was uneventful but fascinating as usual. The passengers were enthusiastic and quite pleased with this opportunity of glimpsing a strange, unknown civilization.

This afternoon there was no activity. I played rummy for a time and won a few dollars. Tonight I'll try to finish *The Compleat Angler* before Morpheus arrives for the knockout blow.

Hollandia, Dutch New Guinea, March 14, 1945   2245

A tropical typhoon is forming just off the north coast of New Guinea. During the past twenty-four hours we have had the longest and most severe storm I've witnessed. It has rained steadily in sheets of rain, carried along by a wind whose gusts have often attained a velocity of 75 MPH. This horizontal rain has soaked quite thoroughly our every possession, and it's miraculous that the tin roof has remained on our shack. From local appearances, the storm will not abate within the next twenty-four hours.

To make the time pass quickly in these uncomfortable circumstances, I played poker and rummy and won a few dollars. Today I had three letters from Grace, written after I had departed from home subsequent to my short visit.

Hollandia, Dutch New Guinea, March 15, 1945   2300

Although the storm has continued almost unabated, I went to the airstrip this morning to determine whether or not any damage had been done to the airplane. Fortunately, everything seemed to be in order. Then I made the five-mile hike up the hill to get my exercise. This afternoon I spent sleeping and writing letters. The very mechanics of living become unpleasant chores during times such as these.

Played poker for three hours tonight and won a few dollars. I don't like, particularly, the type of game we play, but it does serve to make the almost interminable evenings pass more quickly.

Hollandia, Dutch New Guinea, March 16, 1945   2330

Our big storm has ended. The day was fine and clear. It almost was worth enduring forty-eight hours of wind and rain to be compensated with such a fine reward.

Hollandia, Dutch New Guinea, March 17, 1945   2300

Went to the airstrip early this morning to fly the airplane locally, but we burned out a generator and were unable to fly. I walked up the hill for exercise and then played cribbage for a while this afternoon. Tonight we had a movie, *Pride of the Yankees,* and now to bed. No mail today.

Hollandia, Dutch New Guinea, March 18, 1945   2000

Just received a radiogram from General MacArthur instructing me to proceed to Leyte at once. I'm so pleased I can hardly contain myself. Now I plan to take off at 0700 hours tomorrow, to arrive there at midafternoon.

This morning I flew the airplane locally for an hour and a half and then walked up the hill again. This evening I've spent in packing up and preparing for the trip. I had no mail today but now will be getting to a place where I can receive it regularly. I hope I'll be able to proceed on to Manila in a very short time. Once more I'll be back into the war and will know what is going on.

Tolosa, P.I., March 19, 1945   2000

We departed from Hollandia on time (for the last time, I hope) and had a splendid trip here to the Philippines. I did my own navigating and even my modesty permits me to say that I was never more than five miles off course, and that I arrived within three minutes of my estimated time of arrival. Was unable to land on the Tanauan airstrip as it's a one-way strip and a strong tailwind was blowing. So we parked the airplane at Tacloban and will ferry it down from Tacloban tomorrow.

It was good to get back among my friends once more. They welcomed me with a most gratifying sincerity which gave me much pleasure. They had a small party with drinks, etc.

The only disappointing note was that there was no mail. I suppose some of it has been forwarded on to me at Hollandia and will be weeks in returning.

Tolosa, P.I., March 20, 1945   2100

My day has been a busy one. I drove the dusty road to Tacloban for the purpose of ferrying the airplane back to Tanauan, but a strong tailwind sprang up suddenly, so that I was unable to do so. This afternoon, however, the wind abated and once more I went to Tacloban. This time we brought the airplane back safely. Then there was a great accumulation of paperwork, which I tackled industriously and much of which I disposed of. It will require at least two more days to finish with it. Tonight I received a letter from General Sutherland requesting that I check Major Oviatt out on the C-54 at the earliest possible date in order that he can look after the airplane while I am away. Upon the completion of this task I am to proceed directly to Manila to assume additional duties. I suppose I am again wanted in the general's office to assist during such times as my flying does not require my presence elsewhere. It will be fine to get back into action.

Tolosa, P.I., March 21, 1945   2100

This day has been spent in doing many chores. All morning I spent with Major Oviatt at the airplane, going over every bit of equipment and explaining the operation of all accessories. Flying a C-54 is as much an engineering job as it is one of piloting. We were unable to fly as the wind was adverse on this one-way field.

Tonight I was intending playing poker but I'm much too sleepy. So I shall retire and sleep to the drumming of the rain on my tent.

Tolosa, P.I., March 22, 1945   2115

I flew for an hour and a half with Major Oviatt in the C-54 this morning. It is going to require a bit longer to check him out than I predicted, so I'll probably not be ready to move to Manila before March 25.

All afternoon I was busy at the office with personnel problems, and it poured rain all the time. I was invited to the navy officers' club for drinks, but the rain prevented me from reaching the designated rendezvous point in time.

Tonight General Sutherland sent me a radiogram inquiring about the possibility of sending the B-25 on a trip to Melbourne. Unfortunately, although it has been repaired since it was damaged on the ground here a month ago, I still consider it unsafe and am reluctant even to test-fly it. So I had to advise him that, if the trip to Melbourne must be made, we should use the B-17, which is still at the depot at Biak. I am awaiting his decision.

Tolosa, P.I., March 23, 1945   2100

I flew with Major Oviatt for an hour and a half this morning and he did considerably better. I worked at the office this afternoon and I received a note from General Sutherland to the effect that he is coming to Tolosa for a few days and wants me to come up after him on March 24. This probably means that I will not be moving to Manila for some time, as he no doubt will keep me here with him as long as he remains.

Another letter from Grace today and all is well at home. I can breathe a sigh of relief as I have now brought most of my paperwork up to date.

Tolosa, P.I., March 24, 1945   2100

Was up before daylight this morning to go to Manila to get General Sutherland. At 0730 hours, as I was ready to take off, a PBY crashed on the airstrip ahead of me, tearing large holes in the steel planking. The strip had to be closed temporarily for repairs and, as a result, I didn't depart until 1030 hours. I had to advise General Sutherland by radio that I would be delayed, and eventually I arrived at Nichols Field at 1245 hours. The general was waiting and we took off at once, arriving back here at Tolosa at 1545 hours. I spent some time showing him through the new C-54. He will spend a few days here, during which time he will not only fly locally but also try to take side trips to Zamboanga, Iloilo, etc.

Tolosa, P.I., March 25, 1945   2130

This day has been devoted to paperwork. All of it is finished now, for which I am most thankful. Now I'm free to do more flying.

Several of my key men are being rotated back to the States and properly motivated replacements are hard to find.

Tonight General Sutherland called me to his house to plan a trip for tomorrow. Over a couple of drinks we planned the trip. We are going to Mindanao by way of Cebu City. It should be most interesting, since we will see some real action both from the air and from the ground.

Tolosa, P.I., March 26, 1945   2000

I was up early this morning and off to the airstrip to depart on a most interesting trip. General Sutherland and I flew to Cebu to witness our amphibious landing there in which we were to take Cebu City, the second largest city in the Philippines. We arrived over the beach in time to witness the naval bombardment, which literally leveled the ground. We remained to watch the first assault wave land on the beach and then the second and third waves. From an altitude of only 1,000 feet we had a ringside seat. The landing went off very successfully, but not without losses. I saw two Jap mortar shells land in the midst of our first assault wave at the instant the men waded out of the water. All of the soldiers hit the ground and several of them remained there, never to rise again, while their comrades jumped up to rush forward and seek shelter in the jungle. At the end of ten minutes our amphibious tanks had gone inland a half mile, and then a squadron of B-24s came over and dropped fifty 1,000-pound bombs on some objective immediately ahead of the infantry. I couldn't determine what the target had been nor what it was after it disintegrated as if by magic in the terrific explosions. Then the A-20s came in, strafing every square foot ahead of the infantry. If any Japs were left alive, they were certainly groggy.

After we had witnessed most of the action in this operation, we flew on down over the Mohammedan Moro country of the Zamboanga Peninsula, then over the Sulu Sea, to land on a muddy airstrip outside the town of Zamboanga. On the way across western Mindanao I tried unsuccessfully to locate the village and dirt airstrip where I had once intended to land with a cargo of medicines and counterfeit money for the guerrillas before we started the Philippine invasion.

One of our divisions landed here near Zamboanga in the face of 8,500 Japs on March 10. The Jap had made most extensive preparations and installations here, and could have held us off for weeks. However, for some reason understandable only to the Jap mentality, he chose not to defend himself from his laboriously hand-constructed trenches and pillboxes. Instead, he abandoned them and took up a defensive position, poorly prepared, in the foothills. This permitted our forces to come ashore with very little loss and to establish themselves well before beginning a methodical mopping-up campaign.

We went up the hill to the front lines and watched our artillery and mortar fire tear into the pitiful Jap positions. We saw some captured Jap artillery pieces which were made in the United States and England. After a good lunch, we prepared to depart for Leyte.

Although everything there is utter devastation at present, I had a very good impression of Zamboanga. The setting is beautiful and the climate very good. It's the best spot I've seen thus far in the Philippines and wouldn't be a bad place to settle down with a select crowd to vegetate. Of course that's one thing I dream about but will never do.

I can vouch for one fact which is generally obscured because of the misleading words of a certain well-known song. The monkeys *do* have tails in Zamboanga. I saw them.

I called on General Sutherland after dinner to make plans for our activities tomorrow. He will be unable to depart for Manila until March 28, so I'll have ample time to close up my affairs here tomorrow.

[During a long evening of conversation General Sutherland abruptly asked me my opinion of why General MacArthur no longer was friendly toward him and no longer seemed to seek out his opinions. Somewhat apprehensive of his reaction toward me, but sensing that he wanted me to be frank and direct with him, I told him what I believed. I told him that in the first place MacArthur was incensed by his relationship with the Australian WAC, and particularly by his near flaunting of the woman publicly around GHQ. Her temperament was such that she created friction in her relationships and made others feel that since she was Sutherland's friend she could do about as she chose in ordering others about.

She was not at all diplomatic. And when Sutherland left the combat zone on Leyte to go to Brisbane to have his teeth repaired, MacArthur knew that another purpose of the long trip was to see the woman again. Mac-Arthur knew very well that there were dentists in GHQ equally as quali-fied as their counterparts in Australia.

General Sutherland accepted this much of my unpleasant discourse without any outward reaction. He then asked me if I thought there might be other reasons. I told him I thought MacArthur felt that he did not need Sutherland as much now as he had previously, when the war was not going well. MacArthur felt much more self-sufficient with each suc-cessful campaign. He had two complete armies now—the Sixth and the Eighth—and the Japanese air and naval forces in the theater had at the very least been neutralized. Sutherland had built up a very effective staff in GHQ that could carry on without much supervision. The army com-manders, Krueger and Eichelberger, were completely different in their dispositions and methods, the one cautious and probing, the other im-petuous and aggressive, but they complemented each other. This permit-ted the commanding general to select whichever army he chose, depend-ing on the type of mission to be accomplished. MacArthur had developed the habit of dealing directly with his air, naval, and army commanders, sometimes failing to keep Sutherland informed of his decisions. This not only was embarrassing to the chief of staff but undermined his authority. We talked for several hours about these and other matters, and when we said good night he appeared to harbor no resentment toward me because of my frank comments.]

Tolosa, P.I., March 27, 1945   2100

Went aloft in the C-54 early this morning to finish checking Major Oviatt out. Then our B-25 was ready to test after having been rebuilt from its badly damaged condition. The repair group were very reluctant to test-fly it, and I didn't want to assign one of my pilots to do it, since there was some doubt concerning its airworthiness. So I took it up and put it through a rough workout. No mishap occurred, so I pronounced it satis-factory for routine use.

All afternoon I was busy packing my personal belongings. I'm now ready for an early-morning departure, and this will be, probably, my last permanent change of station for some weeks to come.

18

End Game

MARCH–MAY, 1945

Manila, P.I., March 28, 1945 2000

I arose early this morning at Leyte and took off in due time with General Sutherland for Manila. Our trip up was routine, and we landed at Nichols Field in midmorning. I was busy until 1300 hours getting my billet, moving my possessions in, and unpacking. I'm quite comfortably situated in the Admiral Apartments, which in prewar days were almost luxurious. The building escaped complete destruction and is one of the very few buildings which did. It is very badly damaged, however, since the Japs set off a large demolition charge in the basement and then fired cannon shells at point-blank range through all its walls. The plaster is off, the windows are out, and there are shrapnel holes in it so that it resembles a piece of Swiss cheese. However, the substantial walls are still standing, and it can be reclaimed in due time and with much labor.

After I was settled, I went down to headquarters to report in to General MacArthur. I received a most cordial, entirely informal greeting, which was gratifying. I'll have to admit that I'm a complete hero worshiper when it comes to the general, and I admire him more with each talk I have with him. Our country will never bring forth a more sincere, more idealistic American. General MacArthur told me he had chosen to make "Casa Blanca" his home in Manila, and that as soon as the house next door could be refurbished, I was to live there.

[Although the Japanese had occupied Malacañan Palace, General MacArthur refused to do likewise, leaving it to be taken over by the new Philippine government. He had hoped to reoccupy his old penthouse atop the Manila Hotel, but at the last moment the enemy had set fire to it, destroying his library and most of the other articles he had left behind. "Casa Blanca" is luxurious but not pretentious. It is located a few blocks from Malacañan. Mrs. MacArthur had arrived by ship with the family and belongings, and they were well settled in their new home.

He said that I would be assigned a desk in his outer office. Once again I am to be in a position where I can hear and read all of the important information that comes into this nerve center.

My jeep driver took me for a drive through the ruined city to witness from the ground the almost total destruction that I had seen from the air being enacted only a few short weeks before. Manila, the gem of the Far East, is no more. Hardly a major building in the city is left intact. Very few of the walls are even standing. Debris is everywhere. Filth is beyond imagination and disease is rampant. The pitiful, dazed, homeless people aimlessly roam the streets, picking in the rubble of their burned and demolished homes in a near futile attempt to salvage every scrap of usable material. Their clothing is in tatters, and they can hardly hide the nakedness of their emaciated, disease-racked bodies. It is sickening to us, who have never known want and hopelessness and black despair. I wanted quickly to forget many of the tragic scenes but knew I never would. If ever again war and destruction and misery walk the face of the earth as they have during the past few years, mankind must forever admit that it can do practically every reasonable thing for itself except to find a sane, simple, workable method of governing itself. After having advanced civilization to its present state, I wonder if we are going to fail in this one all-important objective.]

Manila, P.I., March 29, 1945　2015

[I had a number of errands that took me around much of the city. The ruthless destruction was evident everywhere. It was sickening to see the deliberate damage the Japs had inflicted after Manila had been declared an "open city" by Yamashita. We had been fighting a savage military machine that was not being governed by normal standards of civilization.]

Manila, P.I., March 30, 1945　2015

After a good morning to General MacArthur and a long and informal visit with General Sutherland, MacArthur discussed our future plans at some length.

[We are starting another interval of buildup for the next large operation. There remains some further mopping up to do in the outer Philippines, most of which is being done by the Eighth Army. Some decisions have to be made by the Joint Chiefs of Staff, but it is presumed that the next major move by General MacArthur's forces will be against the Japanese mainland. There will be considerable direct liaison required between MacArthur's staff and that of Admiral Nimitz in Guam. Admiral Nimitz has been given the go-ahead for the assault on Okinawa using the Tenth Army.

I am grateful for once again being in a position where I can monitor most of the information coming into GHQ. As soon as I can move into the aides' house and be physically more comfortable, life will improve for me. For example, I have no electricity for lights and only a gallon of water daily with which to shave, try to bathe, and keep odorless. Almost an impossibility.]

I fell to my routine desk work and completed it in short order.

[This afternoon I decided to walk to my quarters from GHQ. There was a promise of a beautiful sunset. Although there is a great deal of beauty in nature in this country, there is also much ugliness in that which "man has wrought." The foreground of blasted walls and blasted human hopes could not, however, completely eclipse the beautiful spectacle of a colorful sunset about to unfold for all of us. Sometimes I have an almost overwhelming desire to return to nature and a simple life to escape the tribulations induced by the peaks and chasms of emotional experiences that apparently are inexorable claims upon a gregarious society.

Halfway home, lost in my thoughts, I sensed the patter of small feet behind me. Turning, I beheld the figure of a dignified but emaciated little chap of perhaps six years. He looked up at me and spoke one simple word, "Bread." Neither of us spoke the other's language, literally or figuratively. We were poles apart, yet in that simple word we had a complete understanding. I took him by the hand and led him to a humble little shop in a nearby shed. For a few centavos I bought a loaf of bread. When I placed the bread in his outstretched arms his hungry brown eyes became alight with incredible gratitude. But the lion's share of the pleasure was mine. I was selfish in my paltry gift because it gave me the unique pleasure that comes with giving. At any rate, when I continued my walk the beauty of the sun falling into the restless sea beyond Manila Bay was infinitely greater than the same spectacle which had afforded me so much pleasure only a few minutes before.]

Manila, P.I., March 31, 1945   1930

[Starting today I will be occupied for the next two days in the vicinity of Manila. We are using Nichols Field as a temporary base for some of our aircraft, but the field is much too small to provide safe operation under all conditions. For example, our C-54, *Bataan II*, is the only four-engined airplane permitted to use this airdrome, and it can be safely operated there only by considerably limiting its weight, consequently its fuel load, and by restricting it to daylight hours. It has been decided to develop nearby Neilson Field as a main base of operations, but that field requires extensive repair and enlargement. In a meeting with Generals MacArthur, Sutherland, Kenney, and Sverdrup, I was given the task of locating the points where the radio navigation aids should be installed to best serve the area. This requires extensive local flying to determine optimum approach paths, letdown procedures, etc. This is interesting work but takes more desk and ground work than flying.

The war in Europe appears to be nearing a climax, and we hopefully scan each incoming message. Additionally, the Central Pacific forces are starting the assault on Okinawa tomorrow, but we receive little news of developments there. General MacArthur is particularly interested in that operation. He says he believes it is the first time the navy has ever had overall command of a complete army, the Tenth Army commanded by General Buckner. On the other hand, the army has frequently had overall command of navy fleets.

To make the Okinawa operation even more interesting to me, I have been privileged to listen to two long discussions between Generals Mac-Arthur and Sutherland regarding the various tactics that might be employed against this island, which is about fifty miles long and ten miles wide. The enemy is known to have strongly fortified it, and at least 60,000 troops are thought to be deployed there. The Japanese have numerous air bases on Formosa as well as on other islands on the Ryukyu chain. Also, mainland China as well as the Japanese home island of Kyushu are well within kamikaze range. General MacArthur developed great respect for the kamikaze when he witnessed the severe damage a relative few of them inflicted on our convoy that he was accompanying on its way to the Lingayen Gulf landing. Moreover, his beloved cruiser *Nashville* and its crew suffered great damage from one enemy aircraft.

General MacArthur said he had not studied the Okinawa situation in depth but he would not want to accept the losses that inevitably would result from facing this large, well-entrenched enemy force in a head-on confrontation. He had learned that it was characteristic of the Japanese that if given a retreat route, or if cut off but not pushed, they were much less inclined to resist viciously. On the other hand, if there was no possibility of retreat or stalemate, they would fight almost to the last man. He speculated that possibly the best strategy would be to land on a selected portion of the elongated island, secure an impregnable perimeter large enough to enable us to operate ground-based aircraft for neutralizing enemy air bases within reach, and leave the other end of the island open as a haven into which the enemy could withdraw. Kamikazes originating in Japan or mainland China could be more effectively intercepted en route by ground-based aircraft. He doubted that carrier-based airplanes, with their innate endurance limitations, could remain effective long enough to permit the Tenth Army and the marines to completely secure the entire island in one prolonged assault.

(It was an interesting hypothesis. No one will ever know for certain whether the navy's actual campaign as waged or the general's hypothetical one would have proved the less costly. No one ever knows for sure in war whether some alternate plan might have been preferable. There are no practice sessions.)]

Manila, P.I., April 1, 1945   2000

My cold very nearly got the best of me during the night last night, and I had practically no rest. Today I've felt quite unambitious. However, there was a certain amount of work to be done and I've managed to drag through the day. Now, surprisingly enough, I feel quite good.

Since it's been a dull day, I've been quite oblivious of things around me. Had a short talk with General MacArthur and a longer one with General Sutherland. Nothing exciting. We received no report as to the progress of the new landing by CINCPAC (Admiral Nimitz) today, beyond the fact that it started off on schedule. It would appear that the war in Europe has reached its climax and that the end must be very near.

Manila, P.I., April 2, 1945   1930

It has been a rather dull day. I created a bit of diversion for myself this morning by flying over to San Marcelino to pay a call on Maury Wiley. Unfortunately his group had moved to Mindoro.

Tomorrow I have a more cheerful prospect. General MacArthur asked me to go to Clark Field to greet General Wedemeyer and the China-Burma-India Theater crowd and bring them down to Manila. I know General Wedemeyer and look forward to a pleasant hour with him. Additionally, he might be bearing the good news all of us have been anticipating—namely that General MacArthur has been made supreme commander of all army forces in the Pacific.

Manila, P.I., April 3, 1945   2015

Each morning I go to the office with two items to be hopeful for. One is that I'll have some mail and the other is that the war in Europe will have ended. To date my disappointment has been as consistently regular on the one count as on the other.

This afternoon I flew to Clark Field to greet General Wedemeyer and bring him down to Manila. I waited all afternoon without success. His airplane didn't arrive, and there was no record of it. Just before dusk I departed for Nichols Field in order to land before dark, as the field is unlighted. I suspect that General Wedemeyer went into Leyte for the night.

Manila, P.I., April 4, 1945   2130

Many things have been exasperating today. To start off I was awake most of the night reading radiograms from too many different and poorly informed sources concerning the probable arrival of General Wedemeyer. Not being able to decide just what was going to happen, I flew to Clark Field quite early in order to be sure to welcome him if he did land there. I waited until 1100 hours and finally he arrived. I brought him down for a short conference with General MacArthur and then returned him to Clark this afternoon so that he could depart for Chungking. Unfortunately, as I was ready to depart from Clark Field, it started raining, and at the same time a group of B-24s returned from a long strike on the China coast today. The poor kids had a very difficult time landing in the rain, and it required over two hours to safely land the group. I wasn't allowed to take off during this time, which resulted in a late landing for me back here at Manila.

Manila, P.I., April 5, 1945   2000

No letter today; not a trace of news from home about all that is dear to me. I'm thoroughly discouraged and depressed, and I don't care much about anything. It's queer, isn't it, that things that others consider so trivial can mean so much to me. I'm having a genuine siege of self-pity. What have I done or what have I failed to do to deserve being completely ignored?

Manila, P.I., April 6, 1945   2000

I was up early this morning for a dawn takeoff to fly Generals Akin and Chamberlin to Leyte. The trip was uneventful as usual, and I spent a few hours in Leyte, arranging to move my organization and airplanes here to Luzon as soon as Nielson Field can accept them. Returned here this afternoon and received all the good news. General MacArthur has finally been announced as the supreme commander of all army forces in the Pacific Ocean, and this is the news we've all been hoping for. It now means that we can get on with the war with no uncertainty as to the part we will play in it.

[One disappointing side effect for me could be that in his elevated command responsibilities the general will have to spend more time in his headquarters and that, consequently, I will not be flying him to other locations as often to visit units of his command. His field commanders will have to come to him instead.]

Also, there was the gratifying news of the fall of the Japanese cabinet, and the announcement that Russia would not renew her neutrality pact with Japan.

Manila, P.I., April 7, 1945   2000

I was desperately sick last night and today. I was vomiting and retching almost continuously and am now so weak I can hardly raise my head. The doctor doesn't know just what it is but thinks with good reason that it is some germ resulting from the general unsanitary conditions of our surroundings here. There are still many unburied dead, and flies and mosquitoes swarm everywhere. I feel somewhat improved tonight.

Still no mail today.

Manila, P.I., April 8, 1945   2030

I managed to drag myself out of my hospital bed this morning, but I've been quite weak and unambitious all day. Fortunately I've had nothing much to do today. I managed to have my belongings moved over to another building and now I have no lights or water. These facilities will doubtless be available very soon now, however.

Saw Mrs. MacArthur for a while. Still no mail from home.

Manila, P.I., April 9, 1945   2200

I had a dull and long day today. Didn't feel at all well, but I managed to stay on my feet. Did some business with the ATC and then studied the new command setup which has evolved here, now that General MacArthur has been given the bigger command. Tonight we had an invitation to Irving Berlin's *This Is the Army* at a special showing. It was an excellent show and made me proud of the army in many ways.

No mail today except for an Easter card from Jimmy.

Manila, P.I., April 10, 1945   2200

I've had a busy day and have felt better, or else I've felt better and have had a busy day as a consequence. General Sutherland and I flew up to Clark Field to have lunch with Generals Whitehead and Beebe. There was much discussion concerning the new organization of General MacArthur's command, and the manner in which the air forces would function in relation to the other elements. It was all most interesting to me.

On April 13 I am to fly this headquarters over to Guam for the first general conference with Admiral Nimitz about the former Pacific Ocean Areas, which we are absorbing. I'll have to bring the C-54 up here from Leyte and arrange many of the details so that the trip will be successful.

At last I had a short note from Grace today but with very little news.

Apparently all is well at home, although she didn't mention the boys or any of her activities.

Manila, P.I., April 11, 1945   1930

I've been running about all day in an effort to get ready for the Guam trip. It would be quite simple if our fields were suitable and fuel were available here, etc. As it is, the trip is rather complicated.

Early tomorrow morning I am going to Tolosa to get the C-54 and to fly it empty here to Nichols Field. We will then depart before daybreak the following morning, refuel at Tolosa, and proceed on to Guam.

Had two nice letters from Grace today. They were written on March 17, and at that time all was going well at home. I guess the disappointments I suffer are due to the fact that she doesn't write as often as I'd like.

Have practically recovered from my attack of amoebic dysentery and the jaundice.

Manila, P.I., April 12, 1945   2130

It has been a hectic day. There have been many chores relative to the trip tomorrow. Tonight I was invited out to "Casa Blanca," and was to be there at 1900 hours. At 1830 hours, General Sutherland instructed me to go out to see General Alexander on an urgent mission, so of course I had to go. As a result I was late and didn't get to see Mrs. MacArthur, although she well understood the reasons for my absence, and I was forgiven.

All preparations are now ready for our departure from Nichols Field at 0530 hours. Practically all of the generals on the staff are going except General MacArthur himself, so it is a very important and responsible trip. Now for a few hours of rest.

Guam, Mariana Islands, April 13, 1945   2200

I could not take off from Nichols Field with sufficient fuel to fly to Guam, so we had to land at Leyte for refueling. General Kenney came aboard there. With little delay, we departed for Guam and had a most pleasant trip over, albeit rather slow due to headwinds. Among others, the passengers included General Kenney; Lieutenant General Sutherland; and Major Generals Chamberlin, Akin, and Whitlock. We arrived here in late afternoon, and I was quite busy for a couple of hours, arranging for some much-needed work on the airplane.

It would be a relief to know what reaction is occurring in the States to President Roosevelt's death.

Guam, Mariana Islands, April 14, 1945   2145

I had a lazy morning on this pleasant island, where the climate and the scenery are almost ideal. This afternoon *Bataan II*, our new C-54, was ready for a test flight after the considerable maintenance work that was performed. I flew it for half an hour and found only some minor work still to be completed.

We were entirely ready for a tentatively scheduled departure at 2000 hours tonight, but General Sutherland telephoned at 1800 hours to advise that we would not depart earlier than tomorrow night. I'm glad to have the extra rest as well as to be able to enjoy the comforts of navy-type civilization for at least another twenty-four hours.

Guam, Mariana Islands, April 15, 1945   2300

Had another leisurely day here on this lovely island, with little to do except to visit with the UAL crews who are here. I checked our airplane and found that it was now completely ready for flight, and there was nothing more to be done except to wait for instructions from General Kenney or General Sutherland regarding the return to Manila.

About 2230 General Sutherland called to advise that we would be departing at 0830 hours tomorrow. At this late hour, I had to get out of bed and make all the necessary arrangements for the departure. Generals aren't always as considerate as they might be. Now for a few hours of sleep and an early call.

Manila, P.I., April 16, 1945   1930

We took off from Guam on schedule this morning and had a beautiful trip back. The weather was perfect and we had a helping wind which enabled us to arrive here at midafternoon.

There were many letters awaiting me and everything is well at home. All my fears are allayed, and I'm assured that I still possess everything that a man might ask for.

Manila, P.I., April 17, 1945   2000

Today was a busy one for me. I had to check in at the office early to see what had accumulated on my desk in my absence. I saw General Kenney, and he stated that he desired to take off for Tolosa at 1000 hours. I awaited at the airplane until 1100 hours, when General Whitehead arrived to see General Kenney for a few minutes. Finally, at noon, he was ready to depart. Alas, one of the engines of the C-54 would not function properly and I had to call out old reliable *CXE*, a C-47, to fly the general to Tolosa. As a result I didn't return until almost dusk tonight.

Our living conditions haven't improved much, so that considerable time still is consumed in doing personal chores. We still have only one gallon of water a day, and it's quite difficult to keep presentable and odorless on that limited quantity.

Manila, P.I., April 18, 1945   2000

Many administrative troubles beset me today. There is a jurisdictional dispute between Air Forces and GHQ concerning which organization shall control my airplanes and my personnel. Eventually the argument will reach General MacArthur, and he will rule in my favor, I'm sure.

General Sutherland asked me to bring the B-17 up from Biak, so I must send Major Oviatt and Major Skov down for it. The C-54 engine refuses to run properly and requires a carburetor change. There is some electrical trouble in the B-25. I find it most difficult to operate my group from Nichols Field here, on which there is no fuel, no tools or equipment, and no mechanical help.

This afternoon, after I had the C-54 torn down, ready for the performance of much work, Mrs. MacArthur advised that she would like to be shown through the airplane tomorrow morning and that possibly the general would also accompany her. This, of course, necessitates a complete cleaning and polishing of the airplane in lieu of the mechanical repairs which I should like to complete. However, the general's or Mrs. MacArthur's requests are commands to me, and of course I'll have the airplane ready for their inspection.

Manila, P.I., April 19, 1945   2130

This morning I went to General MacArthur's home to accompany him and Mrs. MacArthur to the airfield so that they could inspect the new C-54, *Bataan II*. As usual, Mrs. MacArthur was much more enthusiastic than the general.

[They spent an hour looking it over inside and out and were very pleased with it. Perhaps I have convinced Mrs. MacArthur that a flight in this new machine would be infinitely more pleasant than the last, unfortunate flights she made, from Mindanao to Darwin and Alice Springs in

Above: I test-fly the new C-54 *Bataan II* at Santa Monica. Courtesy McDonnell Douglas Co. *Below:* General and Mrs. MacArthur and I inspect *Bataan II* at Nichols Field.

Australia when escaping from the Philippines more than three years ago. After the inspection, General MacArthur stopped off at the office and I accompanied Mrs. MacArthur on to her home.]

In her feminine way she is quite as wonderful a person as is the general. Tomorrow I'm hoping she will go with me to do some shopping for some beautiful articles which some of her friends here find it necessary to dispose of. It looks as though I might get a trip to the States in a few weeks, in which case I could take home any articles which I might be able to purchase.

Had two fine letters from Grace, written April 9.

Manila, P.I., April 20, 1945   2230

Two of my crews departed for Biak before dawn this morning to ferry the B-17 to Manila. It has been in the depot for repairs for some time, and now we propose to use it regularly between Manila and Guam.

I moved our airplanes from Nichols Field to Neilson Field this morning. That will be our new operating base for all aircraft except the C-54.

At noon General MacArthur instructed me to go to Clark Field to meet Lieutenant General Richardson, who was arriving there from Honolulu. The time of his arrival was uncertain and I awaited him until 1600 hours, when he finally landed. I flew him and his staff to Manila, where we were met and greeted. Now there will be a series of conferences here which will last several days.

Another fine letter from Grace today.

Manila, P.I., April 21, 1945   2100

This developed into another busy day for me after I had expected to have a leisurely one. I was occupied in the office all morning, then this afternoon I had a conference with the operations section of Air Transport Command about navigational facilities, airports, etc.

Major Oviatt and Major Skov, who flew the B-25 down to Biak to ferry the B-17 back, both arrived here before dark tonight. Now we have all of our aircraft here and all in flying condition, so that we can take trips to almost any part of the world. I'm hoping a long trip develops soon, as I'm growing impatient.

Manila, P.I., April 22, 1945   2130

Had another conference with the ATC this morning concerning navigational facilities. It appears that we must necessarily compromise on something less than the ideal installation I wanted, due to terrain difficulties and other factors. It seems that everything one does in aviation must be a compromise.

Manila, P.I., April 23, 1945 2300

My day at the office was routine until midafternoon.

Gerald Graham, who oversees the operation of the MacArthur household, Mrs. MacArthur, and I then went for a long drive out on the highway toward Clark Field in the late afternoon, and I had dinner with Colonel Lehrbas, Colonel Egeberg, and Gerald, after which we attended a movie at a private showing with General and Mrs. MacArthur. It's now late and so to bed.

Manila, P.I., April 24, 1945 2100

Nine years ago today there occurred the most important, deliberately considered, event in my life. Grace and I were married. It was indeed a fortunate day for me when she accepted me for better or for worse. No doubt I have failed on many occasions to live up to her expectations. Many times our sharp differences of opinion have culminated in temporary unhappiness, but we've always managed to compromise on a mutually acceptable solution. From my viewpoint, our life together has proved to be the most fortunate, the most successful partnership that is possible between two individuals. Born of respect, nurtured in understanding, and reaching its climax in true love, our relationship will continue until death, to be the most beautiful thing in all of life.

Today I have planned three trips for our airplanes. One is to go to Clark Field, one to Tacloban, and one to Melbourne. I wanted to fly the one to Melbourne, but General MacArthur quickly decided I should remain in Manila.

A very despondent letter from Grace today. She has her moods of depression much the same as the rest of us. I suppose it is another one of those many things attributable to the war. There is a sense of frustration and futility which it is quite impossible to escape.

Manila, P.I., April 25, 1945 2030

Up at 0500 hours this morning to fly General Richardson and party to Clark Field, from which they departed for Honolulu. Guess I'm growing too old to relish the idea of such an early rising. I'm afraid I'll get into a habit of awakening early and I won't be able to enjoy sleeping late.

Manila, P.I., April 26, 1945   2100

I flew all morning with officers from the AACS and ATC in an effort to decide upon the final installations for the radio range and other navigational aids to be installed here at Manila. It now appears that we have arrived at the best solution to our problem. This afternoon I flew the C-54 on an exercise flight and took along a number of GHQ officers in order that they could inspect Corregidor, Bataan, Subic Bay, and other points of interest. Most of them had not seen ruined Manila from the air, and the trip proved to be of considerable interest to them.

Manila, P.I., April 27, 1945   2100

There hasn't been much to keep me occupied today. I was thrilled when General MacArthur informed me that he would be pleased to have me live at his establishment. I will be living directly with Colonel Egeberg, Colonel Lehrbas and Major Graham, all of whom are aides or assistants, and Mrs. MacArthur and will be constantly available to him at his home. Aside from all this, my living conditions will be much better, and I'll have baths and all the other luxuries available, along with good food.

Spent a quiet evening, reading and being lazy. Passed up a chance to play poker because I didn't feel lucky.

Manila, P.I., April 28, 1945   2200

Went out to the "Big House" this morning to inspect my new billet. I will be very comfortably situated there with a screened private room and bath and all my physical needs provided for by competent Filipino boys. There will be late movies privately shown on four nights each week at Casa Blanca, a complete selection of excellent recordings, plenty of good books—in short, everything I could ask for except my family. I plan on moving there next Tuesday.

This afternoon has been dull. Nothing happening, no mail, no flying. At present there's no promise of excitement tomorrow either. It's another one of those dull waiting periods.

Manila, P.I., April 29, 1945   2330

There was much excitement this morning when the false rumor of the termination of the war in Europe swept through headquarters here, as it did all of the remainder of the world. The feeling persists here that the war is probably ended, but that a few days will be required for the complete announcement to be made. We are of course wondering what reaction Japan will indicate immediately following the termination of the fighting in Europe. Japan's lot is certainly not a happy one just at this moment. In the meantime, our Strategic Air Force B-29s are taking an ever-increasing toll of burned-out cities in the Japanese homeland.

This afternoon I flew the C-54 for an hour, visiting many places throughout Luzon. This is a beautiful country when seen from the air and when one cannot see the rubble and destruction of war.

Manila, P.I., April 30, 1945 2100

I've not been at all busy today. In fact, I've had practically nothing to do except to visit with my men, write letters, and be lazy. I've finished packing in preparation for my move to my new abode tomorrow. It will be great to be able to act civilized and have a bath whenever I want it.

Not much news from Grace. However, Al Luedecke is able to send me daily a copy of the *New York Times*, and it reaches me when only about a week old. Thus I am able to keep abreast of home news. Heretofore, I've suffered more from not having a daily newspaper perhaps than from any of the other minor inconveniences.

Manila, P.I., May 1, 1945 2200

Spent the morning moving and then for an hour this afternoon went shopping in Chinatown.

Tonight we had most pleasant dinner, with much conversation, and then we went to a private showing of a good movie to General and Mrs. MacArthur. I'm flying at 0700 hours tomorrow so must go to bed.

Manila, P.I., May 2, 1945 2230

After a rather dull morning, I flew the C-54 this afternoon. Took several officers up for a sightseeing trip while I exercised the aircraft. Guy Cain came in from Kunming with General Wood, and we had him out for lunch and then took him around to inspect devastated Manila.

Another good movie for General MacArthur tonight. This high living is rapidly spoiling me. Another awakening at 0500 hours tomorrow will bring me back to reality.

Manila, P.I., May 3, 1945 2115

It's been a long and tiring day. Was up early to fly with General Sutherland and then I spent all morning and much of the afternoon in a conference with Far East Air Force and Air Transport Command relative to establishing an effective air traffic control for this theater. No real effort has been made toward devising and effecting a system whereby all aircraft in flight can be accounted for and aided when in distress. I feel that many aircraft are lost here merely because rescue procedures are not initiated soon enough after some airplane is overdue at its destination. Our new plan may not be too effective because of poor administration, but I feel that the start we have made is in the right direction.

Had a fine descriptive letter from Grace today, outlining a very happy day she and the boys had had at home. Grace had a cold and both boys were recuperating from whooping cough; nevertheless they seemed to be convalescing well and happily together.

Another 0500 call tomorrow.

Manila, P.I., May 4, 1945   2030

Since sleepily deserting my fine bed at 0500 hours this morning, I've been on the move constantly for fourteen hours. It began with an early flight with General Sutherland, then a long, tiring flight during which I made a complete technical check of the newly installed direction finding station for aircraft here at Manila. It was a tedious task, involving much precision flying. I had hardly finished with that when I had to go to Clark Field to greet Gen. Sir Thomas Blamey, the ranking Australian general officer. As usual, he was late, and I didn't return to Manila until late afternoon. Some work at the office kept me there, necessitating a late dinner. In spite of the resulting fatigue, I love these busy days.

I'm gazing at the beautiful picture of Gracie now, and dreaming. I'm such a fortunate person to have her love me. How incomplete life would be without her care and confidence and affection!

Manila, P.I., May 5, 1945   2045

A fine letter from Grace to start the day cheerfully. The boys have recovered from the whooping cough, and Jimmy is getting freckles on his nose and thinks our wedding anniversary is the day on which Mommy is *going* to be married. So things at home are developing quite normally.

I have another early call tomorrow. General Blamey is returning to Australia and I must be up to see him away. He is an almost exact, life-sized replica of the famous English cartoon character, Colonel Blimp.

Manila, P.I., May 6, 1945   2130

Up before dawn and off to Clark Field with General Blamey. The trip was without incident, and after he was safely on his way I returned to

Manila, where I was engaged for some time in sending a trip to Tolosa to accomplish some errands there. After that, I returned to the office, where there was little to keep me occupied during the remainder of the day. It's always most interesting to stay in the office, reading the communiqués and listening to discussions and watching the situation maps, even though I don't play an active part in all of it.

[I'm sure General Eichelberger feels that General MacArthur doesn't grant him the credit he should have as the commander of an army. His actions and his speech occasionally betray him.

(I heard General MacArthur give General Eichelberger a classic come-uppance, but Eichelberger failed completely to recognize it as such. I was in MacArthur's office when Eichelberger was there. I don't know what preliminary conversation had led up to it, but I heard MacArthur say, "Bob, I've observed during my long career that when a man can put aside his own selfish interests and can place the welfare of his country and his troops foremost in his thoughts, he can really accomplish much in life. On the other hand, the man who is wrapped up in himself makes a very small package indeed.")]

Tonight we had much pleasant and stimulating conversation at dinner, when Dave Chambers, Ben Whipple, and Joe Werren were guests of Roger Egeberg.

Manila, P.I., May 7, 1945   2100

A hot, indefinite sort of day today. Not too dull, and yet nothing exciting. I spent all morning in the office and most of the afternoon at Neilson Field outlining and checking on maintenance conditions for our aircraft. There are many procedures which don't produce the results I desire, yet to get the work done properly resolves itself into the problem of maintaining constant pressure.

Manila, P.I., May 8, 1945   2045

[It all started at midnight last night, when I was awakened by a telephone call from General Sutherland. He said a radiogram had just arrived advising that Germany had surrendered unconditionally. At the same time he suggested we should not get too excited as we had received similar reports before that had proved to be false. I went down to the GHQ building and spent a few hours on the telephone answering the various general officers who were calling in to Generals MacArthur and Sutherland seeking verification of the surrender. A sense of excitement rapidly spread throughout the command, as everyone knew that the task that lay ahead for us would become infinitely easier when Europe no longer absorbed the men and equipment that we desperately needed to complete the job in our theater. By evening we had received much more information, and the end of the European war was verified.

General MacArthur and General Sutherland are still having many long discussions regarding the planning for the invasion of Japan proper. The Joint Chiefs of Staff have given tentative approval to a two-step plan. The first phase is to be a gigantic landing on the island of Kyushu, followed some months later by an assault on the main island of Honshu. Plans necessarily have to be preliminary in nature as it is not known what additional units from all services will be available from Europe and Africa. Yet planning has to continue because the first operation has been scheduled for November 1, 1945. MacArthur frequently voices his opinion that a direct campaign against Japan will never be required, since he believes the emperor of Japan will sue for peace before long. He bases his opinion on two facts, namely that Russia will declare war on Japan (which MacArthur opposes) in order to have a voice in the peace negotiations, and that General LeMay's airplanes are steadily but surely inflicting enormous wounds on the already raw-material-starved enemy nation. He has become a real believer in the effectiveness of air power, and he expresses surprise that the Joint Chiefs of Staff in Washington still do not appear to totally comprehend its real value. He says that the emperor is an intelligent man and that as soon as Tojo and the other warlords have been completely discredited at home the emperor will again assume power. He does not believe the emperor wants to see his country and most of his people destroyed in this potential three-way pincers movement.

On one occasion I distinctly remember hearing him say to Sutherland, "Dick, don't spend too much time in planning for operations Olympic and Coronet (the code names for the massive assaults to be made on Japan). If you can find a way to drag your feet, do so, because we are never going to have to invade Japan."]

It is my personal opinion that Japan will start introducing peace overtures very soon now, and I also believe that Russia will intervene in a military way as soon as she can marshal her forces in the Asiatic theater. There are many, however, who believe that we will have to continue on and crush Japan completely.

Manila is slowly but surely digging itself out of the rubble and ruin. I must say that it is largely American effort which is responsible, for the Filipinos seem incapable of sustained effort without much American supervision. Each day that passes, many people lose their lives in this inert city as they dig into unexploded mines and shells while removing the debris. And each day many Japs are dug out both dead and alive, and there are thrilling local episodes as these starving Japs attempt to fight it out with our soldiers. The dead bodies are collected and burned by squads of Japanese prisoners of war, and there is always a smoke pall and the unforgettable stench of decomposed and burning human flesh. The Japs may have regarded themselves as glorious and invincible in war, but there isn't much glory apparent in the stinking flesh which drips from the bones of their very mortal, broken skeletons.

Manila, P.I., May 9, 1945   2130

This was another one of those days with nothing to do which was urgent. I went to the airstrip twice to press through some maintenance difficulties on the airplanes, but did no flying.

[We are settled in for the first time since leaving Brisbane, into what we expect to be a period of many months while planning proceeds for the ultimate attack on the Japanese mainland *if necessary*. Due to many factors the pending campaign will be far different and much more difficult than those of the past few years. We cannot get accurate information regarding the enemy's strength or defense distribution, and we will not be able to neutralize completely his air defenses from our distant bases. Moreover, he will be defending his homeland, which he can be expected to do with even more fanaticism. Plans have to be made, coordinated with the three military commands, then cleared with the Joint Chiefs of Staff. General MacArthur and General Sutherland spend many hours together poring over maps and aerial photographs. I have been privileged to sit in on some of their discussions. MacArthur is doing a great deal of reading about Japan, endeavoring to gain any bits of information that might be helpful.]

Manila, P.I., May 10, 1945   2045

All day in the office today with no activity. Had a very fine letter from Grace and another from Wayne and Marge. Everything is progressing at home except that Grace has as yet not located a house into which to move after the lease expires on our present house in September. The problem may become very acute.

I want to take a long flying trip somewhere. There is the possibility of a trip to Guam in a few days. I'm sending a nice trip out tomorrow to Mindanao and Borneo, but I'm unable to take it because of this possible one to Guam in the C-54. My pilots usually get the better trips because I have to stand by to take General MacArthur in case he wishes to travel, which he practically never does now of course. He has reached the stage where his command is so large that his men have to come to him and he has little time or opportunity to go afield. All of which is unfortunate for me.

[As there is not to be much long-distance flying in the near future and since I now have sufficient well-qualified flight crews to do any required flying within the Philippines, General Sutherland has asked me if I would like to do work within his and General MacArthur's offices. Heretofore, I have had my desk in their area, but I actually have not done any work directly for them in the office. I have readily agreed since inactivity is abhorrent to me. Colonel Wheeler and I are thus established as "office flunkies," a job without title but a most interesting one. We receive and route all important incoming correspondence, make appointments, meet visitors, etc. Colonel Wheeler carries the main burden of in-office continuity, as I have to be away a part of the time to operate the headquarters flight detachment and to be the official "greeter."

It is pleasing to me to note that somehow MacArthur and Sutherland have managed to repair the almost abrasive relationship between them that reached a climax at Tacloban. There does not appear to be quite the same warmth of feeling that once was present, but they are again freely discussing the progress of the war effort and its problems.]

Manila, P.I., May 11, 1945   2145

I spent the major portion of this day at Neilson and Nichols fields on business having to do with airplanes. At last our maintenance program is shaping up, and I hope to have all our aircraft in top condition within a few days.

This afternoon I flew the C-54 for an hour and practiced some instrument flying, of which I get entirely too little here with all of this fine weather. The approaching rainy season will, no doubt, help to remedy that situation. Tonight I attended a very fine movie at General MacArthur's house. It's really fine to have access to so many of the luxuries and pleasures of good living. The general's only real recreation is in movies, and of course he is shown only the finest.

Manila, P.I., May 12, 1945   2200

Another day spent largely on aircraft affairs. Our B-17 (*Bataan I*) is too old and war-weary to give us much more service. Today I suggested to General Sutherland that we try to exchange it for a late-model B-17.

Tonight we had a different and delightful dinner here at the house. Colonel Egeberg and Major Graham each brought a WAC officer for dinner, and the resulting changed atmosphere afforded by the girls was a welcome, civilizing experience. I'm afraid we forget to practice many of the normal courtesies when we spend so much time with purely masculine companionship.

I had a bit of practice in the art of being an aide de camp a few minutes ago. Both Colonel Egeberg and Major Graham took their guests to a dance, and I was here alone writing a letter to Grace when we had a sudden failure of the electric power system. Mrs. MacArthur telephoned frantically to see if I could do something about it, as they had guests and were left in total darkness. Fortunately, I was able to set the wheels turning and to get the power back on in a very few minutes. I'm sure I wouldn't care to be one of the regular aides.

Manila, P.I., May 13, 1945 2215

This morning we moved our office over to the rebuilt Manila City Hall, so that now GHQ is practically all under one roof again. There was much confusion accompanying the move. General MacArthur was well pleased with his new office, but many things did not please General Sutherland.

To my delight, I was assigned a desk just outside General MacArthur's office. Soon after I moved in, he stopped at my desk to tell me once more that I was to read any and all of the official letters, radiograms, and telemeters which came in. If I am absent for flying, the correspondence will merely bypass my desk. Obviously, I am flattered by this assignment.

Have to be in bed earlier now, as I'll spend much more time in the office. Usually work until 1930 hours there.

Manila, P.I., May 14, 1945 2215

After a busy morning spent with my nose buried in many papers, I was a bit weary of regiments and divisions and combat teams and air forces. So this afternoon I flew the C-54 for an hour and completed arrangements for greeting Admiral Nimitz tomorrow.

Had *four* letters from Gracie today and they made me very homesick. My, how I love that gal!

Tonight we attended a movie at General MacArthur's house. It was an old story, newly filmed—a modern version of *Brewster's Millions*. It was light but entertaining.

The rainy season has started early and lustily. Already it is raining at almost all hours of the day, although not in great quantities as yet.

Manila, P.I., May 15, 1945 2230

The day started with a steady rain, and it has continued almost without intermission. It was not a good day for flying, but my flight today was one of importance. I took the C-54 to Clark Field and met Admiral Nimitz and flew him to Manila. General MacArthur was at Nichols Field to greet the admiral, so of course the timing, etc., had to be figured exactly. Everything went off perfectly; it even stopped raining just as I landed here.

[General MacArthur wanted to meet the admiral at the airport but of course did not want to wait too long in the rain. I gave him an "exact" estimated time of arrival back at Nichols Field and managed to land at the "exact" time. He met us in the rain and with a twinkle in his eye said to me: "You're pretty good, aren't you?" I did not tell him that I had given him a time of arrival that I knew could be made quite easily and that I had had to fly a longer-than-direct route from Clark Field in order not to arrive ahead of my promised time.]

Although the navy may criticize us about many things, I don't believe Admiral Nimitz can possibly find fault with the way I've handled him thus far. He is departing on Thursday morning, and I have my fingers crossed that we will see him off without any unfortunate incident.

Had a private movie here at the house tonight—*God Is My Co-Pilot*, the story of which was written by Robert Scott, a contemporary pilot and acquaintance of mine.

Manila, P.I., May 16, 1945   2210

Another rainy, sultry, nasty day, but fortunately I avoided most of its unpleasant aspects by working in the office all day. Many interesting things are coming over the desk, and I am frank to admit that I find my work inside to be most intriguing.

Early tomorrow I have to arise to take Admiral Nimitz to Clark Field, from which point he will depart for Guam. There have been continuous conferences here between him and our staff officers since his arrival. I'd like to have been able to listen in on some of the conversations between General MacArthur and Admiral Nimitz. On the surface there seemed to be ample cordiality.

Manila, P.I., May 17, 1945   2350

Was up long before daybreak this morning to complete all preparations for taking Admiral Nimitz to Clark Field. Everything went off without a hitch, and even General MacArthur went out at that early hour to see the admiral off. It was raining, but not enough to interfere with the flight. Naturally I was relieved to deliver the admiral safely, and in a manner which he could not possibly criticize.

The remainder of my day I spent with routine affairs at the office.

Tonight I received a letter from Grace and opened it with the thrill of anticipation, only to find that it had been written on March 30. It's strange the things that happen in such cases. That letter, sent by air mail, had been forty-eight days en route.

Manila, P.I., May 18, 1945 2230

Spent the morning in the office and then General Sutherland wanted to fly after lunch. I went to Neilson Field and test-flew the C-47 for a few minutes to make certain that it had not been molested by saboteurs, a precaution which I always take before allowing a high-ranking officer to ride. While we were awaiting the general, he sent his driver out to tell me that he couldn't get away from the office long enough to fly. So I took the B-17 up for a much-needed two-hour test run and found many troubles with it. Upon returning to the office, I found five letters, including three from Grace. All of them were cheerful and filled with news except for one, and it carried some truly sad information. Harvey Berger, a Kelly Field classmate of mine, was killed over Germany just before the end of hostilities there.

Manila, P.I., May 19, 1945 2000

I spent the entire day at the office. Many interesting things came across my desk, so the day went fast.

I feel quite depressed today. No particular reason, but I can't seem to throw off a feeling of futility and impending disappointment. Normally I scoff at the usual hunches and premonitions, but for some reason this feeling seems quite real. I can only hope it is unfounded and perhaps it was occasioned by the sad news of Harvey's death. The bright spot of the day was the rereading of Grace's cheerful letters.

Manila, P.I., May 20, 1945 2100

Nothing of a serious nature has occurred today, so I can assume that my premonition was unfounded unless I later learn that something at home is amiss. Yet I am depressed and homesick to an extent unusual for me. Among other things I have an idea that there will be an explosion of tempers in our office soon which will have unpleasant repercussions for all of us nearby. I am afraid that the subdued war between the C in C and the C of S is going to break out into the open again in a couple of weeks, and although I am an innocent bystander, it will necessarily affect me to some extent. It's becoming increasingly more difficult for me to understand why people have to be unpleasant. Perhaps it's the heat and the homesickness and the boredom, which are getting on the nerves of all of us.

This afternoon I flew the C-54 for an hour. Already it's a relief for me to get away from the office and up in the fine, rain-swept air, where no one is playing politics and where a man can think his own thoughts, react to his own emotions, without concern over consequences. If there's anything I desire after this war it is a simple, straightforward, tolerant attitude toward life and people. In my own mind, I feel that the best way to achieve this ambition is as a gentleman farmer and pilot in California.

Manila, P.I., May 21, 1945   2345

This morning I had some routine work in the office and then this afternoon I went to Tacloban to take General Mudge to ATC's terminal in order that he could enplane for San Francisco for recuperation. He was badly wounded by a Jap grenade about six weeks ago, and but for a very tough constitution would have died. Now he will stay a couple of months in the States and if he recovers sufficiently will return to command one of our best divisions, the First Cavalry. It's never possible to predict with absolute certainty whether a badly wounded soldier will recover his aggressiveness, even though his physical wounds heal.

Manila, P.I., May 22, 1945   2030

A rather dull day at the office today. There isn't much of interest coming across the desk, and General Sutherland is a very sick man. I haven't been too ambitious due to a short ration of sleep last night.

Had two fine letters from Grace today, filled with accounts of amusing episodes concerning the boys. One was describing Johnny on his first day at nursery school, and the other was a colorful description of an adventure of both Jimmy and Johnny and a large puddle of mud. Of course with their best clothes on.

Manila, P.I., May 23, 1945   2130

What a day! I spent the morning in the office at routine affairs. General Sutherland is quite ill, and naturally since he can't come to the office there is more to be done by the rest of us. Then this afternoon President Osmeña and his party arrived at Clark Field from Washington, almost simultaneously with Senator Tydings and his committee for investigating Philippine rehabilitation. Of course it fell to my duty to meet them there and welcome them, as well as to bring them on here to Manila. About eight Filipino women accompanied Osmeña, and I had a wild time trying to quiet these animated females and to get them and their baggage on the proper airplanes bound for Manila. Poor Senator Tydings took a rather dim view of all of the furor, but we finally got the entire party safely into Nichols Field, where they were met by 2,000 or 3,000 political climbers and other fans. General MacArthur was also out to welcome Tydings, and all in all we had a merry picnic—well attended, of course, by press photographers and army brass hats. As a result of it all, I'm well ready to relax tonight.

Manila, P.I., May 24, 1945   2045

General Sutherland was too ill to come to the office today, and I was quite busy this morning. But this afternoon I had to exercise the C-54, so I set out to find Maury Wiley. I finally located him at the new Florida Blanca airstrip, where he had only recently moved, but I was unable to land the C-54 there. So I landed at Porac strip about five miles away, commandeered a command car, and drove on to see him. By that time it was so late that I could spend only a half hour with him. He is quite anxious to get home and get out of the army, as he has had over two years overseas.

Tonight I received a letter from Grace written on April 13, just forty-one days ago! It was sent air mail, too!

Manila, P.I., May 25, 1945   2300

Spent all day at the office today except for a visit to General Sutherland at his home. He has recovered somewhat but is still a sick man.

There wasn't much of interest going on. The war is definitely in a re-staging period, necessitated by the time required to move and regroup the units from the European theater of war. It will be three months yet before we will be in any position to open a major offensive except by air. By that time, however, there will be few of Japan's cities still standing.

Tonight I went to a movie at General MacArthur's and spent a pleasant evening.

Manila, P.I., May 26, 1945   2300

Well, I have another attack of jaundice, with all of its unpleasantness. I spent an uneasy night last night and then today I've been constantly torn between a desire to vomit and a desire to remain seated on the johnny. However, I've kept dragging myself along all day—in the office this morning and flying this afternoon. I missed a pleasant boat trip on Manila Bay this afternoon. General Sutherland, who is recuperating rapidly, sent for me to go out with him, but I was already flying and could not be reached.

Manila, P.I., May 27, 1945   2030

The last eighteen hours have been a nightmare. What with trips to the bathroom for evacuations from both extremities, I got no sleep last night. Today I've kept going in spite of my misery, and I imagine I've suffered no more than if I had remained in the hot bed. But it's an extremely uncomfortable, inescapable feeling.

The radiograms at the office this morning were most interesting. However, by midafternoon I needed a bit of escape, so I went out to fly the C-54 for an hour. Went up to 10,000 feet, and it didn't do my bloated stomach any good. I've suffered from severe gas pains since.

There was a nice letter from Grace only seven days old. Things are fine at home and, along with my self-pity, I'm afraid I'm indulging in a bit of nostalgia.

Manila, P.I., May 28, 1945   2000

My business day included a long morning in the office, lunch with Karl Oviatt, and a trip to the ATC, where I had a long talk with Lloyd Treece and Slim Hammond. More duty at the office late this afternoon, and then home to a bottle of cold beer.

Had a discouraging letter from Wayne and Marge. It is raining and cold on the farm, and the crops are not in. Noble is ill, Barbara just had a miscarriage of a six-month baby, her husband was drafted, and her landlord made them move out. And sometimes I think I have troubles!

I will be going to Guam on Thursday, to take our general staff over for another conference with Admiral Nimitz. Have to get Senator Tydings and General Stilwell off tomorrow.

It's raining tonight, and consequently pleasantly cool. A distinct relief from the heat of the last few days, and something we can anticipate during the coming rainy season.

Manila is slowly but surely digging itself out of its rubble. Or rather the American army bulldozers are digging it out. Decided progress has been made, yet there's still so much to be done. The people here have taken their tragedies with good grace. They are by nature cheerful, emotional, friendly. Although their suffering was great, they are forgetting it quickly. Not so with the white people who remained here during the Jap occupation. Those people are still semihysterical and suspicious.

Manila, P.I., May 29, 1945   2230

Spent a full day at the office today, with many interesting things to note. General Sutherland isn't back from the hospital as yet, so I still have much to do there. And then I had several callers at the office who wanted to visit.

I had a fine letter from Mr. Patterson today. He has been president of United since my earliest connection with the company.

I went to a very good movie at General MacArthur's tonight. It was *Catherine the Great* and was excellent comedy.

Manila, P.I., May 30, 1945   2130

All day in the office today, but very interesting, notwithstanding. There were many radiograms and communiqués to be studied, and then I had to direct the preparations for the trip to Guam tomorrow. I'm now ready for a takeoff at 0630 hours tomorrow.

19

Triumph

MAY–AUGUST, 1945

Guam, Mariana Islands, May 31, 1945   2100

We departed from Manila at 0630 hours and arrived here at Guam just nine hours later. I had aboard most of the general staff and we had an excellent trip. They are a good gang and I always have an enjoyable trip when flying them around. Skov, Hinckley, and Shoemaker came over as part of the crew, and one of my enlisted men became quite ill on the way over.

This place is even busier than before, what with the accelerated pace of bombing of the Japanese mainland with B-29s. We will be here for a couple of days, during which I hope to swim a bit and rest. I'm sure the change of scenery will improve my jaundiced condition. The climate is delightful, and almost everything presents a favorable contrast with Manila.

Guam, Mariana Islands, June 1, 1945   2200

Much of today I spent visiting with UAL pilots who lay over here. I now feel almost up to date on all news concerning United and many of my acquaintances.

Three years ago today I started keeping this diary. Then I was on my way to the North Atlantic. I've planned to discontinue it when the war ends. Wonder how much longer that will be. I don't know as it has any value, practical or otherwise, but I make my entries with religious regularity, thinking that years hence it may be interesting to me or to my family. Perhaps it's a bit egotistical for me to assume as much.

Guam, Mariana Islands, June 2, 1945   2230

This has been a thoroughly fine day. A late breakfast, then a trip to Admiral Nimitz's headquarters, and finally a long drive about the island to inspect the tremendous navy installations required all of the morning hours. Directly after lunch we went swimming for a couple of hours of splendid recreation.

Tonight Kip Chase and I again played gin rummy for a couple of hours and I won twenty-one dollars. I had a phenomenal streak of luck. Now I must write a letter to Gracie. If possible, my love is increasing rapidly with my returning good health.

Guam, Mariana Islands, June 3, 1945   2345

I started the day with a late and lazy breakfast at which I met and conversed with some more UAL pilots. The relaxation of the past two days has completely changed my attitude and morale, and once more life is a mighty pleasant episode. Today hasn't dulled my receptive senses either. After lunch a number of us went for a swim again on the beautiful beach. Spurred on by the bug of ambition, we attempted to swim out to a small island about a half a mile offshore. Just before reaching our goal, we were blocked by a reef of very jagged coral, and we had to swim back without benefit of rest. Of course we were delightfully exhausted, so that we had to return to the officers' club immediately and recuperate over much iced beer.

Manila, P.I., June 4, 1945   2030

We made the eight-hour-and-twenty-minute flight from Guam to Manila under almost ideal conditions. There were five congenial generals aboard, and all factors united to make the trip a pleasant one indeed. We arrived here at midafternoon, and a short stop at the office yielded four letters from Gracie and one from Wayne and Marge. All of which gives a good boost to my already soaring morale. These three days of rest have been more beneficial than I could have imagined possible.

Manila, P.I., June 5, 1945   2045

It has been a most interesting day at the office. There were many radiograms of interest and then there was the completed outline plan for the next two major operations, which I spent much of the day studying. It is fascinating to see how all of the hundreds of various elements are considered and fitted into the plan so perfectly. It can hardly fail to work, and if the Japs don't surrender before these operations materialize, there will be little remaining for them to surrender.

Now I'm confronted with another, more immediate problem. Under the recently announced army discharge plan, two-thirds of my men are to be released from the army. That means that I must obtain replacements as soon as possible, and men possessing the requirements necessary to suit me are indeed difficult to locate.

Manila, P.I., June 6, 1945   2040

It was another routine day for me. I spent all morning at the office, and this afternoon I set out on a local expedition to locate replacements for my enlisted men whom the army is releasing. I obtained about half the necessary men and will pursue this objective further tomorrow.

There is a movie tonight at General MacArthur's, but I decided not to go, since I had a letter to write to Wayne and another to Grace. Besides, I'll see another movie tomorrow night if I get back from Leyte in sufficient time.

Manila, P.I., June 7, 1945   2300

I flew the C-54 this morning then proceeded to find two additional enlisted men to serve as replacements. I decided against flying the trip to Leyte, so sent Vic Skov down instead. I had some guests coming for dinner and wanted to be home in time to welcome them.

It was indeed a pleasant evening. My guests were Red Boland, Karl Oviatt, and Harry Harrison. Harry I have known for years. He was chief meteorologist for United Air Lines, and a very good one at that. He is now a lieutenant colonel in the army and has just arrived in this theater from Washington to enter the Theater Weather Central. He will play a most responsible role in our coming operations.

Following an excellent dinner, we had a private showing of an entertaining movie, so a good time was had by all.

There were two fine letters from Gracie today. Things are well at home as usual under her efficient care. There is really so little for me to worry about, but yet I'm always just a bit apprehensive.

Manila, P.I., June 8, 1945   2015

There were three trips to be arranged today in addition to other details at the office. Generals Sutherland and MacArthur will not permit me to take trips which keep me away from GHQ. It was a busy, bickering chore, so this afternoon I got away from it all, took the B-25, and soared away into the rain and the clouds for two hours alone with myself and God. After almost sixteen years of flying, I still gain a great, indescribable lift in my soul when I find myself free in an airplane, away from the tired old earth and her cares. Life is so clean and pure—completely undefiled by squalor and misery and intolerance. There is an empty vastness which nevertheless is pregnant with a substantial feeling of freedom and an awareness of something greater than the puny soul of man. Nature is so tremendous and awesome that a philosophic airman should never be a small man. Distances and perspectives and feelings are too great in scope to permit of pettiness.

After my stimulating surge aloft I had some difficulty in returning to the field due to rain and low clouds. Yet it's also stimulating to tax one's skill and to find oneself still not lacking. It was a fine and exhilarating afternoon. Back through the mud and the rain to the office, where I found two delightful letters from Gracie and one from Marge. Gracie's were filled with descriptions of "a day at the circus" with Jimmy.

Our rainy season has beset us with a vengeance. It pours and then it rains, but it never stops.

Manila, P.I., June 9, 1945 2300

I spent all day in the office, largely to avoid the rain, which fell almost incessantly. There were several very interesting radiograms and communiqués to study, and there was General Stilwell's welfare to be looked after. This proved to be no chore at all. He is a most elusive person, and difficult to find when wanted. I can now understand why he was relieved of his command in China. He was doubtless a fighting general but not at all politic in his dealings with others.

Manila, P.I., June 10, 1945 2100

[General MacArthur is away from GHQ for several days. He has gone on to the Brunei Bay amphibious landing in Borneo aboard the cruiser *Boise*, to land there where Australian ground forces are making the assault. Roger Egeberg, his aide and doctor, is accompanying him. I will use some of this time to familiarize myself with the various airfields.]

Although it has rained all day, I've had much flying and much fun. I exercised the C-54 this morning, and then this afternoon I had my first flight in an L-5, commonly known as a "Cub." For one who had never flown anything except large, heavy aircraft, it was indeed a thrill. The airplane was so small and sensitive that I quite naturally inclined toward overcontrolling, but I did manage to make four decent landings. Thus in one day I flew both the largest ship and the smallest one in the theater. Some fun!

Manila, P.I., June 11, 1945   2245

Went for a four-hour exploratory flight around Luzon this morning. Flew up over Baguio, which must have been a beautiful place before the Japs destroyed it, and then I went up to Laoag at the northwest tip of the island to investigate its condition in case I wish to refuel there on the way to Okinawa. I returned down the west coast over Lingayen Gulf, San Marcelino, Subic Bay, and Bataan. This afternoon there was little activity, and since it was raining I remained indoors.

Manila, P.I., June 12, 1945   2045

A very humdrum day. There were many things of interest at the office, and I never went to the airport. Judging from all of the many developments, I can't help but believe that the war will end before many more months.

[There are many wagers being made between officers in the command as to when the war will end. Planning is still going forward but with little enthusiasm, and the office is being besieged with calls seeking the latest news.]

No letters from home today. I've had some idle time which I've put to use making some studies of the stock market. Wish I were able to watch it more closely, and then I believe I could make some money. The war seems to offer many disadvantages to those of us who are directly in it. But there are compensations of an intangible nature too, from which we will derive later benefits denied to nonmilitary people. I wouldn't willingly exchange places.

Manila, P.I., June 13, 1945   2000

I flew the C-54 for an hour this morning, and then spent the remainder of the day in the office. General MacArthur has not returned from the Brunei Bay landing on Borneo, and things are rather quiet here.

There were two fine letters from Grace today. Things at home are thriving under her usual excellent control. In one letter she outlined for me some of her ideas concerning our personal lives after the war. I am heartily in accord with most of her ideas of more tennis, more entertaining, more sociability. In the past we've always been just a bit too busy to allow ourselves to *live*. And I think that of all the things I've learned from this war a finer appreciation of the intangibles in life will remain with me longest. From this point on, I hope the major emphasis can be changed from the material to the social objective.

Following is a clipping from the *Free Philippines:*

Manila, Tuesday, June 12, 1945

MacArthur Uses New C-54 as 'Flying Headquarters'

SANTA MONICA, Calif.—Gen. Douglas MacArthur is using a giant four-engined C-54 Skymaster as a 'flying headquarters' to direct his operation in the accelerated Pacific war drive, the Douglas Aircraft Company announced yesterday.

The big plane, named Bataan, was flown from California by Lt. Col. W. E. Rhoades, MacArthur's personal pilot.

The interior provides desk space, meals and sleeping accommodations for the General and staff members.

Manila, P.I., June 14, 1945   2000

A routine morning at the office and then this afternoon I flew the L-5. Went sightseeing entirely around Manila Bay. First I visited Corregidor and spent some time observing it from my slow vantage point a hundred feet above it. The Cub airplane is ideal for such uses. The destruction on Corregidor is complete. There isn't a single square yard that hasn't been hit directly by a bomb or a shell. Our ideas of war were truly archaic prior to the present conflict. There lies Corregidor, once one of the "impregnable" fortresses of the world. The Japs captured it in weeks, and we recaptured it in days. Now it's a dead, desolate, useless rock. Its many great artillery rifles lie broken and useless in their emplacements, never having fired a shot at their enemies. How smug the world was before it realized the possibilities of the airplane! The coastal artillery must helplessly wait in its bed of concrete for some ship to come within its range, but the modern way is for the ship to unload its cargo of troops just out of range of the immobile giants. How different the airplane, which carries its weapon 2,000 miles to meet the enemy even before he leaves his base.

I flew on to inspect closely the bloody battlefield of Bataan, thence on to the central plain of Luzon. With the L-5 I could sit over the native villages and observe carefully their way of life. Many of these villages located in the marshes and fishponds of the valley are practically inaccessible to the average white man, and the people lead a life which is entirely different from that we observe in Manila. Apparently they live almost completely on fish and rice, both of which they cultivate in their marshes. Everywhere there is unbelievable filth. Really not all of the Filipinos are quite the wonderful people we've often been led to believe they are.

I returned to the field and then to the office, hoping to have some mail. No such luck, however. Tomorrow General MacArthur and Doc Egeberg return from the Brunei Bay landing operation, and perhaps activity will increase around headquarters.

Manila, P.I., June 15, 1945   2330

General MacArthur, Doc Egeberg, et al. returned this morning, and sure enough things started popping at the office. One thing the general fails to realize is that he has a very tired staff. Many of the officers have dragged through this war for three and a half years now, and very few of them have had any rest. There is no effective relaxation for any of them. The general has his family with him and leads an entirely normal life. None of his officers do. As a result, when the general is away everyone unconsciously lets down a bit, and this attitude is reflected right down through the ranks.

This afternoon I took Lieutenant Rogers, the GHQ office manager, in the L-5 and went out to look at Corregidor again. He was on "The Rock" all during the Jap attack, and was anxious to view all of the destruction which had been wrought during two successive sieges of the island.

At the office there were two letters from Gracie. She is so sweet and considerate, and her letters are wonderfully stimulating to me.

Manila, P.I., June 16, 1945   2115

I gave Major Skov an hour of practice time in the C-54 this morning. He flies it very well. I had some disciplinary problems with my men, which required considerable time. Then I spent all afternoon at the office, during which time the sky literally poured down upon us. I very nearly drowned en route home.

Manila, P.I., June 17, 1945   2015

Had a busy morning in the office this morning. General Arnold and many other stars were in, and I had a number of other chores which had to be finished. Then I got notice from General MacArthur of a trip to Okinawa tomorrow, which of course I want to take myself. The purpose of the trip is to take Commodore Flannagan and his party to Okinawa. This bloody island will live long in our history, and I want to have a part in it before the fighting is over.

Manila, P.I., June 18, 1945   2000

Up at 0300 hours this morning in order to prepare for a takeoff at 0500 hours. The fast B-25 got us off in good shape, and an hour later we watched a beautiful sunrise from our vantage point high above the wild, jungle-covered mountains of northern Luzon. As we flew high across our front lines east of Baguio, down below us in the still-dark valleys, our predawn artillery barrage was opening up on the luckless Japs, now hopelessly pinned in the gorges. I couldn't fail to be impressed by the contrast between the man-made pinpricks of heavy-artillery fire and the God-made, all-encompassing sunlight reflected from the surface of the clouds. We are a rather puny lot, after all.

The weather en route was good, and we arrived at Okinawa just four hours after takeoff. This bloody island was indeed a spectacle to behold. First we flew along the southern tip to see the activity there, where our forces have at last compressed the remaining 15,000 Japs into a five-square-mile area and are methodically slaughtering them. Naval vessels, including battleships, are shelling them from three sides, and army artillery lined axle to axle is shelling from the land side. There's hardly a square yard of land that is not under a perpetual pall of smoke and explosions and dust. The ceaseless explosions of shells and bombs must have driven the sleepless Japs mad long before this. They are holed up in subterranean dugouts which are practically impervious to shellfire; firebombs and flamethrowers are the keys which unlock these vaults. The entire island is pocked with an unbelievable mass of fortifications. Some of these I examined at close range, and without doubt they were years in the building. Judging from the ones I saw, most of these fortifications must have been started if not completed many years prior to the outbreak of the present war. It's truly remarkable that we have been able to make the progress we have made in capturing this island. It is all finished now except for the necessary slaughtering of the hopeless remnants of the "invincible" Jap army.

We landed on the excellent Yontan airstrip, which was the first one we captured from the Japs. The aerial activity is naturally great there, and many sorties are made purely in defensive action against the suicide bombers so effectively used at Okinawa by the Japs. We remained on the field two hours, during which time we said good-bye to Commodore Flannagan and his party, then did what limited sightseeing we could without transportation.

After takeoff we had one last look at the ruins of Naha, once a thriving capital city of 30,000. Then once more there passed beneath us the awesome spectacle of mass extermination, which is moving slowly but inexorably toward a conclusion in complete death.

Out into the clear, cool air, we could soon forget the stench and the destruction of warfare. Four hours later we were back in Manila and its heat and rain. Here at least there is a slowly growing promise that something new and clean will rise out of the ruins. Progress already has started amidst physical and moral chaos.

The tragic note of the day was the death of Lt. Gen. Simon Bolivar Buckner. He was killed by Jap artillery fire at Okinawa while we were there. He was a great soldier who had fought a bloody but successful campaign, and it's hard luck that he couldn't see its conclusion.

Manila, P.I., June 19, 1945   2100

Even after a fine night of sleep, I've still not recovered completely from my trip yesterday. Eight and a half hours in the extremely noisy B-25 at high altitude is conducive to lingering fatigue.

I've had an easy day at the office. There were many radiograms of interest but not much for me to do. The pleasant part of the day was the arrival of five letters, three of them from Gracie. All of them were cheerful and gay—which makes me feel that although I'm naturally missed at home, things are under control there.

These past eighteen months in the army, my reactions toward people high up in our military establishment have gone through complete metamorphoses. On first seeing the "inside" of higher-up policy and politics and personalities, I was amazed. The next stage was shock at the idea of some things which go on. Now I've reached the final and worst stage of disgust. I think this must be the last stage, because I can't be any more disappointed than I have been at the realization that many officers really have feet of clay. The intelligence displayed in the constant petty bickerings wouldn't be at all complimentary to my men.

Manila, P.I., June 20, 1945   2350

For me it has been a day indoors. The only time I left the office was to go to the airport to tell my men good-bye just before they departed for the States and for civilian life. They were a happy lot after three and a half years of unpleasant army duty.

There were many interesting dispatches at the office this afternoon.

Manila, P.I., June 21, 1945   2115

At an early conference with General Sutherland this morning, he gave me enough work to keep me occupied at my desk all day. Among other things I had to set up a trip and make preliminary plans for General Sutherland to return to the States on leave. He also will go to Walter Reed Hospital for a complete medical checkup. I'm sending the B-17 back, but unfortunately I'll be unable to go because General MacArthur will not permit me to. I'll send Major Oviatt and Major Skov, and they will be in the States at least for thirty days. What a break!

General MacArthur asked me to plan another long, secret trip, but he said I couldn't go on this one either.

Then I had a long radiogram to prepare to go to Wright Field, relating to much work to be performed on the B-17 while it is there. After that, there was a trip to Chungking to be planned for tomorrow night. I didn't get away until 1845 hours, but I'm very happy to be busy. A quiet evening now, in which to do my personal chores.

Manila, P.I., June 22, 1945   2230

Another morning at the office and then this afternoon was spent at Neilson Field, solving problems relative to airplanes and crews. Although the office work is stimulating, and I enjoy it immensely, I'm still thankful that when I feel stale I have sufficient opportunity to leave the office and get outside without having to explain.

Manila, P.I., June 23, 1945   2015

All day today we enjoyed a good sample of Manila's rainy season. It started at about midnight and is still continuing. At times last night it rained so hard that the noise kept me awake. There have been periods during the day when the weather has cleared for a short time, but for all practical purposes the rain has been continuous.

It was a busy morning at the office.

[There seems to be a constant stream of visitors. Now that the command has been expanded greatly I cannot help but notice the parade of unfamiliar officers, mostly one- and two-star generals from the European theater, coming by, seeking an audience with General MacArthur. I suppose some of them want to show him that he needs them in his command. (The same thing happened when the Eighth Army was being activated.) However, for his top jobs at least, the general prefers to keep his own tried and true officers, who have been with him through the hardships of the past three and a half years. I notice that particularly in wartime the ambitions of many men who receive their first star sometimes override their normally restraining scruples and their personal dignity and pride. There is a certain amount of backbiting and failure to follow command channels.]

This afternoon, in spite of the rain, I decided to go out to fly in order to do some real instrument practice. I spent an hour and a half in a C-47, high up in the clouds and rain, practicing every maneuver possible in a C-47. Then, after I had myself completely lost, I worked an instrument letdown procedure, which resulted in a good approach, much to my satisfaction. I guess I haven't lost much of my technique, although I am a bit rough in doing some exercises.

Manila, P.I., June 24, 1945   2015

In the rain this morning I flew the C-54 for an hour. Then there were many interesting developments at the office when I returned. Spent all afternoon there, and at 1730 hours, just as I was ready to leave the office, General Sutherland asked me to get a radiogram off to the War Department. It required considerable effort to collect the necessary facts in order to write it. As a result I was very late in getting away.

[The plans for the attack on Japan proper are shaping up, and I have heard some interesting discussions between the commander in chief and General Sutherland on whether or not Russia will enter the war against Japan. MacArthur feels that Japan would much prefer to come to terms with us rather than with the Soviets. Once she is completely convinced that she will lose the war, he believes, Japan will hurry into peace overtures before Russia can enter the conflict. On the other hand, Russia doubtless will want to have more than a token voice in the peace terms. To do so she will have to make every effort to redispose her Asiatic forces so that she can enter the war before Japan collapses. Two conflicting motives are thus working against time, so that almost any development can occur at any moment.]

I personally am convinced that the Japs will try to get out of the war soon after we land on their homeland. By that time there will be practically nothing left there except their army and the homeless people. Of course they can continue to resist, but they will have some self-justification upon which to base their reasons for quitting. Any faction which is now in power could not long survive if it offered peace terms, because the effective propaganda to which the people have so long been subjected has convinced them that even now they are winning the conflict. However, once we put troops ashore, the people who see the invaders can no longer be convinced by propaganda.

Manila, P.I., June 25, 1945   2330

This morning at the office was not too stimulating, so I decided to take the afternoon off. I filled my jeep tank with gas, took Commander Borchert, and away we went on a drive to Tagaytay. Although I've seen much of the Philippines from the air, I haven't driven through the countryside to any extent. It was a beautiful drive, extending from the sea-level sultry land of the rice paddies around Manila up a gradual ascent to a plateau about 2,000 feet high. After the first few miles out of Manila, the character of the land and its vegetation change rapidly. The air is cool and windy, and the monotonous paddies give way to small farms of considerable variety. There are plots of corn and beans and peanuts, and then groves of coconuts, avocados, papayas, and bananas, as well as mangoes, rubber, and kapok. The people change too, from the dirty, slovenly, lazy racial mixtures to pure Filipinos, dignified, simple, and proud. They are entirely agrarian and in almost every respect appear superior to the inbred people of Manila. In fact, I've reached the conclusion that Manila, being the only large city in the Philippines, is the curse of the country. These people are suited best to a simple country life, and they simply are not capable of solving the complex problems of the type of civilization to which we have introduced them.

Tagaytay is a beautiful spot. It is located atop a cliff which falls away precipitously to beautiful Lake Taal. The air is cool and revivifying. One sees a different facet of the country—one which could be very pleasant under other circumstances.

Manila, P.I., June 26, 1945   2100

This morning I talked for an hour and a half with General Sutherland about various problems. The Air Transport Command, air operations, and many other topics were covered. He outlined our future military operations and confirmed to me the fact that Russia had committed herself to enter the war against Japan between August 1 and August 15. Although I'd heard this rumor for some time, it was the first official commitment I'd heard. Then he told me that if the war extended into next year and I wanted to remain in the army, he would send me back to any army school which I might wish to attend. That was indeed flattering.

Manila, P.I., June 27, 1945   2000

An early departure for Laoag with Generals Styer and Sverdrup required me to be up at 0600 hours. I'm afraid I'll have to admit that I'm getting a bit soft. As boss of my own organization I often find myself assigning the less desirable and more uncomfortable trips to my other pilots rather than to myself.

An indicated delay beyond the estimated stay in Laoag permitted me to go for a walk lasting an hour and a half, and covering many things of interest. I walked along the beach, talked to many natives, and became unbelievably sweaty, after which we had an excellent trip back to Manila. Since I had missed my lunch, I went directly home, thumbing my nose at my duties at the office.

General Fellers, Doc Egeberg, Colonel Soriano, and Gerald Graham departed late this afternoon to accompany General MacArthur on the cruiser *Cleveland* to the landing at Balikpapan, Borneo.

Manila, P.I., June 28, 1945   2230

After a long morning in the office, I flew the C-54 for an hour this afternoon. I took along four nurses, who were friends of Colonel Wheeler's but whom I didn't know, and gave them a fine sightseeing tour of most of the points of war interest in this area. Apparently the trip was duly appreciated.

Manila, P.I., June 29, 1945   2230

It was an ordinary morning at the office, with no particular things of interest nor any mail to enliven the scene. With General MacArthur away for a few days, the tempo has slowed down at GHQ. Oboe II (the code name for the landing at Balikpapan) is to occur in a couple of days, but no one is much worried about its success. It is to be done with Australian troops, and no great difficulty is anticipated. This is the last of our operations in the rear area and not pointed directly at Japan.

This afternoon I took the B-17 and went sightseeing. Went as far down as Legaspi on the southeast tip of Luzon, and explored from the air much of this most beautiful country. If someone could devise a scheme to reduce the temperature about fifteen degrees, it would be a wonderful place indeed.

I went to a movie with Mrs. MacArthur tonight.

Legaspi, Bicol Peninsula, P.I., June 30, 1945   2300

After a normal morning at the office, I took off early this afternoon with Major Generals Chamberlin, Whitlock, and Brigadier General Sverdrup for a tour of southern Luzon. First we landed at Lipa in Batangas Province. We were met by cars and drove throughout the Batangas Bay area on an inspection of the base being constructed there. The project is an enormous undertaking, as we will stage two corps through there —almost a complete army.

The countryside around Batangas is not at all similar to that in the Manila area. The terrain is quite broken and the farming very diversified. It was here that the Japs anticipated we would make our major landing on Luzon, and consequently they expended much effort in preparation. As it developed, we landed no troops at Batangas, but rather went overland and attacked them from the rear. Among other measures which they effected in preparation was the disposal of 25,000 of the male population. A serious aftermath of all of the mistreatment of the people is a real crime wave now in full progress. There have been some seventy murders committed during the past two months. All in all, however, the people, being agrarian and unspoiled, seem infinitely happier and more prosperous than those in Manila.

At about 1600 hours we departed from Lipa and landed an hour later on a small, rough sod airstrip at Legaspi in the extreme southeastern portion of Luzon. The town is located on a picturesque bay at the foot of towering, symmetric Mayon volcano, from whose summit a column of vapor rises continuously.

We were met by one of my favorite generals, MacNider, who is tops in any man's army and who has a brilliant record in two wars as well as in civilian life. We are billeted at the headquarters of the regimental combat team in Legaspi, which, incidentally, was completely demolished during the fighting here. Tonight Major Murphy and the other officers outdid themselves to be sure that I had a good time.

Manila, P.I., July 1, 1945   2030

After a fine combat breakfast, Major Murphy took me on an extended jeep ride through the province. We drove for miles along a good road which led us through the colorful, varied country. Agriculture is the only major activity, but that comprises the growing of almost every crop, from rice to hemp. The soil is remarkably productive so that almost no effort is required to grow rice, vegetables, corn, bananas, coconuts, and any other crop the people may desire. The finest hemp in the world is grown here, and in normal channels of commerce it is shipped to Manila to be made into manila rope. Of course, now that all transportation is interrupted, the people are suffering from a depression brought about by the total absence of a market for their principal product.

We departed for Manila in the late afternoon and arrived here amid much rain, but without incident. Two fine letters from Gracie served to reassure me, and now I'm ready to retire after the happy experience of a most pleasant weekend.

Manila, P.I., July 2, 1945   2000

What a day I had. It seemed that everyone in GHQ wanted something of me, accumulated requests built up during my short absence. Many things complicated matters, such as poor telephone service, no gasoline for aircraft at either airstrip, etc. But the day finally ended, and now I'm home and rapidly forgetting my troubles. Tomorrow promises to be more of the same, and in addition I have some flying to do.

General MacArthur and the aides will return from the Balikpapan landing tomorrow. Everything went off very well, and there was little opposition on the beach. Once more the "old man" has fooled the Japs. This is the last major effort in the Southwest Pacific. The cleanup task will now accrue to the Australians and Dutch, while our effort will be toward Japan proper.

After lunch today General Sutherland advised me that he will now delay his trip to the States until about August 1. Major Oviatt, who originally intended to fly him back, now wishes to take leave and go back immediately, since his wife already has arrived on the West Coast to meet him. If he does this, it's just possible I might fly the general back in August, providing Oviatt returns in time to stand by as General MacArthur's pilot in my absence. That would be a good break all the way around. It might happen that way, because fortune seems to smile upon me.

Manila, P.I., July 3, 1945   2215

I flew the radio range for a couple of hours this morning in pouring rain, in order to run a final check on it. It is very much to my liking, but Far East Air Force doesn't seem to care for it, although they seldom appear to approve of anything which others do.

This afternoon I flew with General Sutherland for an hour and a half. Due to illness, this was the first time he had flown in two months. We had a good visit, much like old times, and I'm glad to see that he is again feeling himself.

General MacArthur arrived back this afternoon. Tonight I saw a very fine movie there. The general has developed a fondness for movies to the extent that he sees one almost every night.

Manila, P.I., July 4, 1945   2300

There were two letters from Gracie today, and one of them was quite the best one I've ever had from her. It was filled with news, and the occasional bits of comedy were quite original. She must have been in rare good humor when she wrote it, although she was very busy and very sore from dental work. Perhaps the port wine which she mentioned was partly responsible for her wit.

It poured rain the entire day, so I remained in the office all day. There were many things of interest coming in, so the day passed quickly.

Although this is a holiday, there are not and never have been any

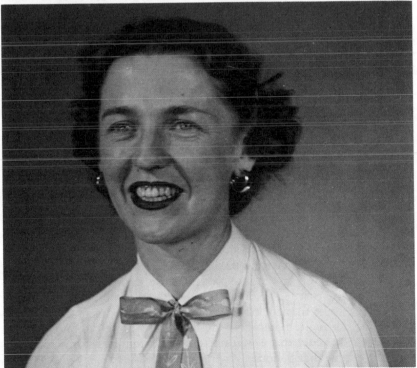

Above left: Jimmy, and *right,* Johnny. *Below:* Grace.

holidays or weekend breaks for us. We work 365 days a year and this includes General MacArthur.

Manila, P.I., July 5, 1945   2115

I was rather upset this morning when General Sutherland hit the ceiling over a radiogram which G-1 had written. Yesterday I had relayed the necessary information from General Sutherland to General Gunner for proper preparation of the radio. But General Gunner, carelessly or otherwise, managed to write the radio with a meaning exactly the reverse of that intended. Consequently, General Sutherland had to decide whether I had failed to relay the information properly or whether General Gunner had been careless in handling the matter. Which alternative he finally accepted in his own mind to be the factual one I do not know, but usually in such cases the junior officer is adjudged to be wrong.

Manila, P.I., July 6, 1945   2000

There has been no excitement today. Things at the office were quiet, with no startling war developments. I'm afraid the public back home may grow a bit impatient before the next operation develops. There will be a dearth of news for quite some time to come because the next show, being of tremendous scope, will be much larger in preparation.

I'm going to spend a quiet evening now. I have a humorous book to read and fully expect to be asleep by ten o'clock.

Manila, P.I., July 7, 1945   2100

I spent an interesting morning in the office and then was further rewarded with a fine letter from Gracie. To add to the sense of well-being, it seemed that the boss was not as irritated over the radio episode as I had feared that he was. All of which goes to confirm the idea that worry is a useless pastime.

This afternoon General Sutherland and I flew for one and a half hours over southern Luzon, visiting Batangas and Lipa. During the flight we had a fine visit—very much like old times. He has been too busy or too sick during the past two months to relax the way he once did.

Tonight I went to a cocktail party, but it was my week for not taking a drink. Each alternate week I do not permit myself to have an alcoholic drink, in order that I will not develop a fondness for alcohol beyond the extent that I should. At the party of course everyone else was a bit silly, since I was drinking fruit juice. But I had an hour of most pleasant conversation.

Manila, P.I., July 8, 1945   2100

The only reason I ever know that it is Sunday is that the predawn church bells awaken me, and there's no daily news sheet to peruse during breakfast. My hours of work go on day in and day out—always the same. The greatest penalty derived from such a schedule is not the monotony, but rather the indelible habits one forms. Right now it would be virtually impossible for me to sleep beyond seven o'clock, or to remain at home all day.

I worked at the office during the morning and then flew the C-54 this afternoon. I took Dave Chambers and Ben Whipple up to see the sights around Manila.

No mail from home today has tinged the hours with a dull hue. My happy reaction to frequent letters still amazes me. They mean so very much.

Manila, P.I., July 9, 1945   2330

This morning I gave Vic Skov an hour and a half of flying time in the C-54. I'm checking him out on it so that he can fly it himself, although the occasion probably will never arrive when I will have to use him. Officially it flies so little that I can well handle it myself. We haven't had too much flying to do in any of our airplanes during the last two months.

I spent the afternoon in the office. There was a letter from Gracie telling of Mrs. Oviatt's arrival on the West Coast to meet Karl, who will not be there.

Tonight I went with Latoszewski to dinner, and then we had a poker game afterwards. Many things which once were fun are now losing their appeal—I suppose because of the war and its attendant monotony.

Manila, P.I., July 10, 1945   2215

Early this morning I invited some of my friends to go with me on a sightseeing tour of the Philippines. I took a C-47, and we were aloft for seven hours. We flew down over the Visayans to Mindanao, inspecting such places as Iloilo on Panay, Bacolod on Negros, and Cebu City on Cebu. On across Bohol, we progressed to wild and unexplored Mindanao. We went over Gingoog Bay, Del Monte, Lake Lanao, and on down to inspect the guerrilla airstrip on which I had planned last year to land a C-54 in the very midst of the Japs, whose occupation of Mindanao and the remainder of the Philippines was at that time still unchallenged.

This strip is located in the wildest part of the Moro country, and after seeing the place I'm just as glad I never made the flight. In the first place,

I'd most likely never have located the airstrip among the jungle-covered mountains in the poor light of the dawn, and in the second place, I don't believe I could have gone into and out of the field without an accident. In that case it is almost certain that I would have become a prisoner of the Japs, even if I had survived an accident. God and General MacArthur really seem to take care of me.

We returned to Manila in the late afternoon, and upon arriving home I learned that Mrs. MacArthur wished to have me escort the general to a public movie tonight. This was indeed a pleasure, as it gratifies my ego to sit beside the general in public. I'm one of his greatest admirers, not only professionally but also personally.

Manila, P.I., July 11, 1945   2230

After a quiet morning in the office, General Sutherland wanted to fly this afternoon. Much like me, he seems to like to get away from the office and not having to keep up appearances. There are few if any people here in whom he can confide without being quoted or without starting rumors. He always seems to be at ease with me, even to the extent of relating some incidents that are almost embarrassing to me. We spent an hour flying and gossiping, and when I returned to the office there was a call to the effect that Fred Angstad and Norve Rader, both friends of mine in the Marine Corps and formerly with me at United Air Lines, were in town. I finally got in touch with them, and they came out to dinner. We had a very fine evening of conversation, reliving all the old days with United Air Lines and discussing our mutual acquaintances. I took them to the movie at General MacArthur's and they were quite awed at the situation. They are both fine men. Both of them are much quieter and more subdued than they were formerly. They have been in the war almost from the start, and are naturally tired, both mentally and physically.

Manila, P.I., July 12, 1945   2300

Another quiet day at the office, with only one break in the monotony. This afternoon I flew with Major Skov for an hour and a half in the C-54, giving him additional time toward a checkout.

Tonight I went out with Ben Whipple and Dave Chambers for drinks and dinner, and had one of the finest steaks I've ever eaten. There was much good conversation throughout the evening. Tonight I can imagine I am home.

Manila, P.I., July 13, 1945 2230

On this Friday the thirteenth I'm a very unhappy man. The jaundice or the dysentery again has me in its grasp, and I've been most miserable all day. I'm still able to drag about, and I think it best not to go to bed during an attack such as this unless it is necessary because of weakness. I remained at the office all day. Lord Mountbatten with his entourage is visiting us — in fact living in our house. Necessarily we have to be on our best behavior.

There was an excellent ballet, featuring many of the Filipino folk dances. Tonight was the last showing, so I took a chance and attended it. It was the finest thing of its kind I've ever seen — colorful, unusual, and it effectively depicted many of the normal phases of life in the provinces of the Philippines. The costumes were unusually beautiful, and one wonders how they managed to preserve these beautiful, fragile things during the long, destructive years of Japanese occupation.

Manila, P.I., July 14, 1945 2100

It has been a miserable day for me. My dysentery has kept me on the toilet or in abject fear of not being there all the time. I didn't want to stay at home as there was much to be done. This afternoon I went to Clark Field to fly Lord Mountbatten back to Manila. From all reports, he has no great military brain, but he certainly has plenty of personal charm and good looks.

Doc Egeberg is doctoring me up with many near-lethal potions tonight, and I'm going to sleep with a complete faith that tomorrow I will be a well man.

Manila, P.I., July 15, 1945 2015

It was another rotten morning. Upon awakening, I felt so bad that I didn't want to get out of bed. I struggled out for a cup of coffee and then went back to bed. After noon, however, I felt better but guilty, so I went to Nichols Field and flew the C-54 for an hour. This didn't seem to have the desired salubrious effect which I had felt it would, and upon returning to the office I felt distinctly unwell.

General Sutherland invited me to a party which is for Lord Mountbatten, but I begged off due to too much rank to be at the party and due to my physical condition.

Manila, P.I., July 16, 1945 2345

For me this has been a very full day in spite of the fact I'm still not feeling too well. First I had a dental appointment and was in the chair

Lord Louis Mountbatten visits General MacArthur in Manila. Courtesy U.S. Army.

over two hours. That of course was unpleasant but necessary. Then after lunch I went up with Colonel Beezley, General Kenney's pilot, for an instrument-check ride. I'm going to fly with him again before I give him an instrument card. All of the flying was done during a heavy rainstorm, resulting from a typhoon which missed Manila by only a hundred miles.

[Tonight upon my arriving home Mrs. MacArthur called to say that she was still not feeling well and requested that I represent her at the first postliberation concert of the Manila Symphony Orchestra, some 75 percent of the musicians having been in the organization prior to the war. After the concert I was to go to a supper at the elegant home of the Lagardos. The supper was elaborate and luxurious. The other guests were the elite of Philippine society, beautifully dressed and mannered. Their homes and possessions had somehow been spared by the occupying Japanese forces, while most of their less-affluent countrymen had suffered great loss and deprivation. This contrast in treatment by the enemy bothered me. (Some days later I had an opportunity to ask General MacArthur if there had been extensive collaboration with the Japanese by these business and society leaders. He said that from our safe and unthreatened vantage point it was hardly fair for us to judge or criticize people for employing almost any means to save the lives of their families and themselves, particularly when relief from their oppressors was nowhere in sight. He said the French had coined a definition of a collaborationist as "one who collaborates more than you do." He did not elaborate.)]

Manila, P.I., July 17, 1945   2345

I spent a busy morning at the office, also managing to remain dry during this veritable monsoon we are having. Many interesting messages came over, having to do with the present dire straits in which Japan now finds herself. In my humble opinion the war may be over before any of us realizes it. By August 15, when Russia enters the war, Japan will practically have lost her will and her resources with which to resist. I believe that Russia's declaration of war will be the final straw which will precipitate Japan's capitulation.

Manila, P.I., July 18, 1945   2000

Spent the morning preparing for the trip to Guam, which I will be making on Friday. In addition to having a nice trip with its accompanying escape from Manila, I hope to be able to catch up on many technical developments. Pete Sandretto, formerly with United Air Lines, is there in charge of all radar installations, which the Twentieth Air Force has found so necessary in its operations against Japan. I expect to prevail upon him to teach me a bit about this equipment, which has been so neglected in our theater.

There were four fine letters from Gracie today. A real field day for me.

Manila, P.I., July 19, 1945   2000

I was up at 0500 hours this morning to go flying with General Sutherland. We went to Florida Blanca, where he had his first instruction in flying a B-17. He did remarkably well. In fact his takeoffs and landings were, with a little advice and help from me, even better than are my own normal ones.

After the flight I spent some time checking on preparations for the flight to Guam tomorrow. At the last minute there were many changes in plan, including the addition of four major generals to the party.

There were many interesting radios at the office this afternoon. The complete Ryukyus are being turned over to us, so that now we have direct command of all army forces in the Pacific. And the tempo of the air and sea attacks against Japan is increasing with every passing day. When the conference in Berlin is over, even the Japs will not have much left over which to be optimistic.

Guam, Mariana Islands, July 20, 1945   2300

It has been a long day. After arising at 0400 hours, we took off at 0630 and had a nine-hour flight over. Generals Chamberlin, Casey, and Whitlock decided to come at the last minute, and this complicated matters a bit. Upon arriving here I immediately contacted a number of UAL men. We sat up for hours this night, talking about mutual friends, the company, and other topics of interest. It will be wonderful to be back with the airline once more. I believe it will be a long time before I can become too concerned with the petty problems about which I once worried and gained increased blood pressure.

Guam, Mariana Islands, July 21, 1945   2230

I spent the morning checking on the airplane, talking to UAL people, and generally relaxing. Got a letter off to Grace after having neglected writing her yesterday.

This afternoon Pete Sandretto took me to his office and outlined some of the late developments in radar equipment. He arranged that we go up in a B-29 tomorrow morning for a practical demonstration of some of the things radar can actually do. That will be much fun for me, as I've never even ridden in a B-29.

I had dinner at the senior officers' mess, where I met two officers I knew when I was in the army years ago, namely Nick Carter and Pete Goerz, both of whom are now colonels. This is my week of self-denial, so I had to pass up some very fine drinks.

Guam, Mariana Islands, July 22, 1945   2000

This has been a long and exciting day for me. This morning Pete Sandretto arranged for me to ride along in a B-29 for a demonstration of the radar and instrument-landing equipment. The instrument-landing equipment is almost unhuman in the way it takes over the airplane, orients itself, and flies the airplane down onto the end of the runway with no effort from the pilot except to keep proper flying speed with the use of the throttles.

This afternoon Pete took me on a long drive on which we went almost around the island. It was quite interesting, as we visited some native villages. We had to carry arms in order to go into the southern part of the island, because many Japs still roam the jungle there.

Incidentally, I forgot to mention that due to pilot error and misunderstanding in the cockpit we actually made the first real instrument landing ever made with a B-29. We didn't intend to land, but when we got down to about ten feet above the runway the pilot got confused and forgot to release the automatic device, so that the airplane went on in and landed itself.

Guam, Mariana Islands, July 23, 1945   1930

This has been a quiet day. Late last night I learned that we were not to return to Manila today. So I got up late, had a leisurely breakfast with Dick Fregulia, and then wrote a letter home. This afternoon I went down to Admiral Nimitz's headquarters to pick up three bottles of liquor which Colonel Larr had gotten for me from the navy. After that I definitely set up our trip for a takeoff at 0800 hours tomorrow and since then have spent the balance of my time reading.

Manila, P.I., July 24, 1945   2000

Our return trip to Manila today was fast and pleasant. We departed at 0800 hours and took only 7¾ hours en route. There was hardly a cloud in the sky, and we benefited from a good helping wind.

There was considerable mail awaiting me, including two fine letters from Grace. All is well on the home front, so I have no complaints to make.

I'm rather tired tonight, but General Sutherland just telephoned to say he would like to fly the B-17 at 0700 hours tomorrow. He also wanted me to come to his quarters for a drink and some conversation.

Doc Egeberg informed me that the general had just informed him he could go home upon his own request. He certainly deserves it, having been out here almost four years, but for purely selfish reasons I hate to see him go. He is one of my best friends.

Manila, P.I., July 25, 1945   2130

General Sutherland wanted to fly at 0700 hours, so as usual I was up at 0500 hours after a night of fitful sleep. I can never rest well when I know that I have to get up early. Anyway, we spent two and a half hours flying in the rain in a B-17, practicing landings and radio range procedures.

There were many interesting things to be scanned at the office, and then this afternoon General Sutherland again got me in his office and kept me there for two hours, discussing various things, especially flying. He wants very much to take thirty days of leave, return to the States, and have a thorough physical examination.

I am going to Okinawa in the C-54 the day after tomorrow. Will take Mr. Howard of the Scripps-Howard newspapers and will remain there overnight. Then in about a week General MacArthur expects to go there to spend a few days.

Manila, P.I., July 26, 1945   2000

I had to go to Nichols Field this morning to set up the Okinawa trip for tomorrow. It was a glorious, cool, rain-free day, and I enjoyed being outside a bit. This afternoon I remained inside the office reading some interesting communiqués. Among them was one outlining the boundary between ourselves and Russia, when and if Russia enters the war. Certainly no one would have wasted time in meeting with the Russians to determine our respective zones of operation, unless the Russians had committed themselves on entering the war. I really believe that there is a possibility, though not a probability, that Russia will enter the war and Japan will sue for peace before August 15.

No mail today. Grace is quite busy, no doubt, but I would like to have more frequent letters. One can't have everything, however. Now I must have sleep in order to be able to get up at 0500 hours.

Okinawa, Ryukyu Islands, July 27, 1945   2200

This has been the most fascinating day I've enjoyed in a very long time. We departed from Manila at 0700 hours and, after a fine trip, delivered

Mr. Howard and his party here in good condition. Then the interesting things started to happen.

First we got a weapons carrier and delivered Ben Whipple to Tenth Army Headquarters after a long drive through this unusual country. Upon returning to Yontan airstrip, I set upon a walk which lasted until dark.

The terrain of the island is low, but very broken and rugged. The climate is semitropical, so that the vegetation varies from bananas and palms to corn and soybeans. There is little level ground, and since the soil must support a large population, the limited space is intensely cultivated. Most of the numerous villages have been destroyed as a result of the war, and all the natives, except for a few now employed as laborers for our army, are impounded in huge camps and clothed and fed by us. There are still about 20,000 Japs at large, mostly in the northern part of the island.

The Okinawans are a strange mixture, and not too much is known concerning their origin or history. Originally the island was inhabited by the now almost-extinct, hairy Ainu people. Then about a thousand years ago the Chinese invaded the island and forced the natives under their rule. A mixing of races resulted, and the Chinese dominated the island for several centuries. At length the Japanese made their way into the place and started exerting the major influence about 300 years ago. Little is known about the island since the invasion by the Japanese. However, Admiral Perry landed here on the same voyage on which he opened the doors of Japan to the rest of the world. In fact, he was so impressed with Okinawa that he recommended that it be acquired by the United States. At any rate, it remained under the domination of the Japs, and in recent years they excluded all white peoples therefrom. Apparently they began their program of fortification of the place many years ago. However, the Okinawans do not seem to have accepted the culture or ideas of the Japs. In appearance they are distinctly Mongolian, small and almost childlike, and even now readily betray any Jap soldiers whom they know to be hiding from our forces.

The people are very sincere in their religion of pure ancestor worship. They have no churches or temples, but worship entirely at the tombs of their ancestors. They construct, or have constructed for them, these massive tombs for each clan or family. They are cavelike affairs dug into the sides of hills or cliffs and walled with concrete or hewn stone. The entrance or portal is often sixty feet in diameter and has an odd circular shape. They believe that, upon death, the human body returns to the womb from which it came. Thus they construct the tomb to resemble, as far as possible, the womb. The labor required to build with their crude tools these enormous burial places is incalculable. The moneylenders of the land construct the tombs and then keep the poor people in debt to them for generations. It is a most effective feudal system, perpetuated by exploitation of religion, superstition, and ancestor worship.

Upon death, the body is folded up into a fetal position, exactly the way it issued from its mother's womb. It is placed in a very small box and then sealed in the family tomb for a year. Then the tomb is opened and the bones are cleaned thoroughly and placed into earthen urns. As the bones slowly turn to dust, more bones of later-demised family members are added to the urns until they are filled with human dust. Then the urns are placed neatly along stone shelves—there to remain as silent reminders of the countless family members who have preceded the present living ones. The lavishness of the tomb of course is in direct ratio to the economic level of the family. They vary from pitifully crude little structures to most elaborately decorated stone edifices. Likewise the urns are very simple and crude in the poorer tombs, while those containing the dust of the wealthier families are magnificent, colorful baked porcelain containers.

Whether this information is factual or not, I cannot say. It was told to me by an elderly Okinawan who spoke barely adequate English but appeared to be well informed. He guided me through several of the tombs where the huge slabs of rock which sealed the small entrances had been moved aside.

There are many cedar and pine trees on the island—rather scrawny and windblown, but somehow majestic, in the manner of the cypress of Carmel. They are just a bit incongruous in this semitropical setting.

I spent so much time exploring the tombs, where I found human bodies in all stages of disintegration, that it was almost nightfall before I realized it. There was an ancient castle on top of a hill a mile or so in the distance, and I wanted to visit it before dark. I made my way up to it at sundown, and it was an interesting place indeed. Of course recent battles had destroyed most of it, but the walls were still there. These walls were built of hewn or broken stone, carried laboriously to the top of the hill probably by manpower alone. They were started perhaps a thousand years ago, and the stones were in all stages of decay. Forty feet thick at the base, the walls appeared to have been continuously strengthened and repaired throughout the centuries, and in the process had lost much of their original symmetry. There was only one entrance through the walls to the castle proper. This was an archway of unique construction. Apparently the builders at that time knew nothing of the use of a keystone, so the archway was built with cantilever constructions, and the two stones forming the top of the arch met in the center and were prevented from slipping apart by carefully doweled fittings at the anchor ends. The strength of the archway was attested by the length of time it had stood. One could note the anachronistic impression given by our 40-mm antiaircraft guns mounted upon these ancient walls.

I got back to camp after dark, exhausted but happy on this fresh, moonlit night.

We had an air raid during the early-morning hours when a single Jap aircraft came over and dropped a single 1,000-pound bomb about 100 yards from our airplane. Miraculously, no damage was done, although there were 500 airplanes parked on the one airstrip.

I was up early and off to observe more of this strange land. Most of the villages have been demolished by the war, but in many places individual houses have been left standing. These are, by our standards, unusual buildings. The construction details of most of them are essentially similar. First, an elaborate stone wall is built around each house, and then the main structural members of the house are made, either of stone or of massive stringers of hardwood. To these are attached flimsy walls of very thin boards, but the roof is of handmade tile of heavy gauge. Not content with this great weight on the roof, they fill all the curved interstices between the tiles with clay. As a result, each building is well weighted down with its own roof. This is a deliberate measure, calculated to prevent the usual damage inflicted by typhoons, which strike the island with severity and regularity. The most elaborate part of each house is its pigpen. It is built with almost lavish abandonment. It is of stone, cradle shaped, and about four feet by eight feet. Pigs are placed in it at birth and are fed through a convenient trough which leads directly from the house. All excesses from the house, including human waste, come down this trough to nourish the pigs.

The people themselves are small, swarthy, childlike. In their personal habits and in their persons they are quite clean, but unsanitary to an absurd degree—I saw women bathing themselves by dipping many buckets full of water from a stagnant pool and pouring it over themselves, only to allow the water to flow back into the pool so that they could dip it out and pour it over themselves again. Their utensils are of the crudest clay and their clothing of shoddy, coarse cotton, doubtless sold to them by the Japanese.

We departed from this strange island and had a quick, pleasant trip back to Manila. It's always good to get back to one's temporary abode, however humble it may be. There was a fine letter from Grace to reassure me.

Manila, P.I., July 29, 1945   2145

Up early this morning and off to the airport to give a couple of instrument-flight checks. Neither of the examinees did at all well with his flying, and I was particularly disappointed with Major Oviatt's performance, as well as with his attitude. I am making him fly his test again tomorrow before I issue his instrument card.

There were many interesting radiograms at the office late this afternoon, but I didn't have sufficient time to study them properly. However, everything was optimistic, and now it's an established fact that Japan is seeking a way out of the war.

Tonight Doc Egeberg and I had some very serious discussions. He is departing for the States soon, and now that he has received permission, he is naturally somewhat sad at leaving friends and a way of life he has known for almost four years. He is debating with himself whether or not to stay with us until we reach Japan.

Manila, P.I., July 30, 1945   2045

Up early this morning in time to give an instrument flight test to Major Oviatt and then to give oral examinations to both him and Colonel Beezley. This afternoon I spent two hours in the dentist's chair. Besides being tired and sleepy, I'm not feeling too comfortable. No mail to stifle my self-pity, so I'll try to sleep off this mood.

Manila, P.I., July 31, 1945   2315

I flew for three hours this morning, practicing instrument flying myself and giving Major Skov an instrument-flight test. I had decided that since the pilots I'd been testing had not done well, the flying perhaps might not be as simple as I had thought it to be. However, I found it quite easy to do the exercises I required of them. Consequently, I shall not relax my standards.

There were several interesting radiograms at the office this afternoon. Also a couple of very nice letters.

Tonight I had dinner at the old Manila Hotel (rebuilt) and then played poker afterward. Had fair luck and won sixty-five pesos. Tomorrow is payday too.

Manila, P.I., Aug. 1, 1945   2000

Much excitement this morning. I went out to fly the C-54, and just before we were ready to take off a fire developed in one of the cargo pits.

The exhaust from the auxiliary power unit had ignited some packages of spare parts, and in short time we had a good blaze under way. With the assistance of the airport fire-fighting equipment, we soon had the fire under control, and before it did any serious damage, I hope. Some wiring will have to be replaced, and I'm having an inspector examine the plane for traces of structural damage which might have resulted. A nearby fuel line could easily have been ruptured, and then we would have lost the entire airplane in a very short time. This excitement had not yet subsided when a B-24 started a takeoff nearby, lost an engine, crashed, and burned. Several of the occupants didn't get out.

I'll tell a little secret. General Sverdrup (Jack to me) has just been offered the position of secretary of war by President Truman. Very hush-hush, and he is not certain that he will accept it, although he is now on his way back to Washington to talk it over with the president. I've flown him all over the Pacific, and we have the greatest respect for each other. He would be a most capable man in the job and would do much good for the War Department.

Manila, P.I., Aug. 2, 1945   2000

The aircraft inspector's reports and a thorough test flight revealed no apparent damage to the C-54 from the fire which occurred yesterday. That was a great relief, as it would have broken my heart to have lost the beautiful aircraft.

General Sutherland is winding up loose ends in preparation for his trip to the States the day after tomorrow. While he is absent during the following thirty days, I'll be busy flying but will not be tied down at the office.

Manila, P.I., Aug. 3, 1945   2300

Today I had no outside activities on my schedule, so I managed to catch up with all the odds and ends which had been moving in on me. There were also certain final arrangements to be made relative to General Sutherland's trip to Washington.

[Today I was privileged and fascinated to listen to probably the most interesting dialogue I have heard between Generals MacArthur and Sutherland. General MacArthur had asked me to come into his office to tell him the details of the cargo pit fire that had occurred on *Bataan II* a few days ago. While I was describing the event, General Sutherland entered.

General MacArthur said: "Dick, before you leave for the States I want to have your ideas about a problem that certainly will surface shortly. That is what to do about General Homma and General Yamashita. Both will be prisoners of war when the hostilities end, and there will be many other high-ranking officers who may fit the definition of war criminals."

Naturally I cannot quote verbatim the conversation between the two men, but the following is an accurate condensation and paraphrase of what was said during the half-hour discussion.

MacArthur: I worry about problems like this and try to forecast such troublesome things in order to think them through deliberately and not be surprised later. Sometimes one can rely on history to provide guidance, but in this case history provides too much guidance. Sometimes in the past a general who bested an opposing commander killed him on sight. At other times he fêted his defeated opponent and sent him on his way. So one could choose from history almost any action he decided to take and find a precedent for it.

Sutherland: When only professionals were involved in war and civilians were not frequent casualties there developed a rather bizarre type of sportsmanship, a Marquis of Queensberry set of rules, by which conduct could be determined. That idea has generally prevailed during the major wars in which the United States has been involved, such as the Revolution, the Civil War, and even World War I.

MacArthur: But events have been different here in the Philippines. The treatment of our defeated, defenseless, weak, and sick men by Homma's forces during the Bataan Death March certainly violates the intent and terms of the Potsdam Declaration of this past July 26. That document specifically states that uncompromised justice shall befall all war criminals who have mistreated our prisoners. Yamashita's failure to enforce his open city declaration in Manila, and the resulting ruthless slaughter of hundreds of innocent civilians by troops under his command, constituted a crime against all civilization.

Sutherland: I agree. I believe both Homma and Yamashita should be tried as war criminals, and they should be tried by a military court that would understand their crimes. There has been talk of establishing an international tribunal to try war criminals both in Europe and here. Perhaps such an organization will handle the trials here and you will be spared the responsibility for such a distasteful proceeding.

MacArthur: Don't be too sure of that. There are those in Washington who delight in washing their hands of any unpleasant events in this part of the world. But regardless of who conducts the trials, I hope they understand clearly that a commanding officer has two sacred responsibilities when he conducts a war. His prime responsibility is to win the final battle, but along with that is his equally hallowed duty of protecting the weak and the defenseless. These two captured generals have in my opinion failed completely in enforcing this latter duty.

General MacArthur terminated the discussion by saying, "Dick, see what you can learn in Washington, but in the meantime be thinking about the composition of a military tribunal, because I feel certain that it is coming down to that. And if these enemy commanders should be found guilty, it will be most revealing to see if President Truman or the Supreme Court intervenes after a sentence is imposed."

General Sutherland departed, and I finished my report to General MacArthur concerning the fire on *Bataan II*. It seemed such a trivial matter after what I had just heard.]

Manila, P.I., Aug. 4, 1945 2200

I had to get up before dawn this morning in order to take a trip down to Iloilo on Panay Island. It's a two-hour flight each way, and the island of Panay is a beautiful place when seen from the air. However, we found it to be one of the most intolerably hot places we had ever been. I arrived at Manila at noon.

Tonight I went to the airport to see General Sutherland off to the States. Karl Oviatt is the lucky pilot who is flying him back, while I have to remain here with General MacArthur. Everything was in readiness, and he got away exactly on schedule at 2000 hours. There is more than a good possibility that he will be unable to remain in the States the full thirty days as he now expects to do. If the war ends suddenly, he will have no choice except to return immediately.

Manila, P.I., Aug. 5, 1945 2345

At Nichols Field this morning my inquiries disclosed that General Sutherland had arrived in Guam safely but was an hour behind his tentative schedule.

I flew the C-54 for an hour, then returned to the office. The afternoon there was rather dull for all.

Another typhoon is upon us and the water is coming down in sheets. The little tree frogs which seem to hibernate between showers are now in full voice.

Manila, P.I., Aug. 6, 1945 2200

General MacArthur had indicated that he might wish to fly to Okinawa on Wednesday, so I spent most of today in making preparations for the trip. It was a rainy, nasty day so that I worked under a handicap. Also, General Hodges just arrived from Europe and will command our First Army under General MacArthur. It was my duty to look after his aides and give them such help as I was able to do.

Dr. Karl T. Compton of MIT, chairman of the National Research Bureau, and Dr. Moreland arrived and were closeted with General Mac-

Arthur behind closed doors for a couple of hours. This was somewhat unusual, and Colonel Wheeler and I speculated about the reasons for so much secrecy.

I went to a movie with the MacArthurs. Rather a poor show, and I'd have preferred to remain home with a good book. However, I have developed what is perhaps an undesirable habit of withdrawing into a shell and excluding too much of the outside world. So I feel that I should make a distinct effort to associate with people more frequently.

Manila, P.I., Aug. 7, 1945   2100

Now that it has happened, we can speculate a bit about the atomic bomb, and its impact not only upon the physical world but also upon the social world. This project has been the most carefully guarded secret of the war, but now that the first one of them has been loosed, many details have been released to the public. Even I did not know just what to expect, but I knew that some project of the greatest importance was to be tried on Japan during the first week of August.

After the release of the publicity on the bomb, I was fortunate to be able to discuss some of its aspects with Dr. Compton and Dr. Moreland. The bomb is not a true atomic bomb in the sense that it derives its power from the explosion of atoms. It uses groups of atoms as a storehouse of external energy. A tremendous amount of energy can be stored in the atomic structure of a relatively small mass, namely the bomb, and when this energy is released suddenly the destructive power is beyond comprehension. It is detonated above the ground at considerable height and definitely destroys all man-made structures and all life in an area variously estimated from five to fifteen miles in diameter. In the only test of one made to date, at White Sands, New Mexico, observers at a distance of six miles from the scene were blinded by the flash of light, estimated to be ten times as bright as sunlight at a distance of six miles. Two billion dollars was spent on the scientific work on the bomb, and each unit costs thirty million dollars. We now have three of the units available, and the production rate is three per month. Unless Japan capitulates, we apparently will systematically depopulate the entire nation. It seems barbaric, but it spares American lives. I now believe the war will end not later than August 31.

Although I do not know it to be a fact, I believe Dr. Compton briefed General MacArthur about the bomb the day before it was exploded. I didn't hear the general make any statement concerning such a briefing, but he did say the war would end within a week.

We have only meager reports of the results of the bomb, but expect more tomorrow. The airplane that dropped it was not destroyed, as was feared. Debris was hurled 40,000 feet into the air, and metal structures on the ground were seen to vanish completely. It was used on the naval base at Hiroshima, where no known prisoners of war were being held. Tomorrow we will have more details.

The physical effects of the bomb are practically predictable, but its impact upon the social structure of the world is at present imponderable. Man at last has a weapon with which he can quickly and totally destroy himself. This immediately means that mankind will have to develop a method of living together in peace. This in turn means that a workable world-state is a must on the agenda of society, and I'm afraid we haven't yet reached the state where all races and nationalities can live together without quarreling. It is useless to argue that we can, when even we in America are unable to find a solution to the Negro problem. To introduce the Chinese, Japanese, Indians, British, Russians, etc., into a world-state overnight and expect harmony therefrom is ridiculous. Yet man can never survive another war with such weapons. Perhaps it were better had we never developed this monster.

General MacArthur definitely is appalled and depressed by this Frankenstein monster. I had a long talk with him today, necessitated by the impending trip to Okinawa. He wants time to think this thing out, so he has postponed the trip to some future date to be decided later. He wants to remain in immediate contact with the communications network in order to be ready for any duties assigned him when the Japanese are ready to surrender.

I flew the C-54 to make certain of its condition.

Manila, P.I., Aug. 8, 1945   2130

This day has been one of anxious waiting. We have watched the communiqués closely to seek indications of the manner in which Japan is reacting to the appalling implications of the atomic bomb. Also another interesting speculation has been its effect upon Russia's entry into the war. Russia is due to declare war on August 12, but now, faced with the possibility of an immediate capitulation by Japan and wanting to have a definite voice in the peace to follow, she may hasten her declaration of war. The next few days may be thrilling indeed.

I remained near the office all day, and then late this afternoon the Philippine governmental authorities asked me to attend a conference. They are soon going to reestablish a civil airways system throughout the islands and wished to ask me for my advice and opinions on some matters of policy.

[[Among my friends at GHQ the reactions ran the gamut from elation that the war was all but over to horror at the potential use of this weapon in future conflicts. Some thought it might make all future wars unthinkable. Others felt that any nation that possessed the bomb would never accept defeat before employing it in one last effort to survive. In a long talk with General MacArthur late in the day he said that at the moment the only thing he knew for certain was that its use had spared us tens of thousands of casualties that otherwise would have resulted from an assault on Japan. He spent most of his time pacing back and forth in his office, pausing only to read the pertinent communiqués as they arrived.]]

Manila, P.I., Aug. 9, 1945   2230

At 0400 hours this morning I was awakened by the telephone to be informed that Russia had declared war upon Japan. So she really did jump the gun in order to be in on the kill after all. We had given Japan an ultimatum to capitulate within forty-eight hours, and at 0900 hours the time limit expired, so we apparently are now proceeding with the systematic destruction and depopulation of Japan. The second bomb was dropped over Nagasaki this morning. Preliminary reports indicate that 100,000 people were killed or injured by the bomb at Hiroshima.

[We had a reorganization in our office today. General Fellers, who was military secretary to General MacArthur, is to be provisionally ordered to Siberia to head a military liaison group with the Russian army. He has invited me to accompany him, but I have declined. He obviously does not want to be in Siberia without an airplane and pilot. Actually the liaison group may never be activated.

I like General Fellers personally but am pleased to see him depart from the office. I feel he is a negative influence on General MacArthur. He is a man of considerable talent but one with great personal ambition. It is my opinion that at times his ambition obscures his ethics, to the point where he avoids advising General MacArthur of some of the unpleasant things and tends to relay only the more agreeable items. The general already is too carefully shielded and should be apprised of events in a more realistic manner.

Colonel Wheeler becomes the military secretary, and Colonel Whipple replaces Colonel Wheeler. He will be placed in charge of the surrender activities that are sure to develop. These gentlemen are two of my closest friends and we now have a most pleasant working organization.

There has now developed a situation in the GHQ building that almost all officers who are familiar with the inner workings of the command are appalled to see. Colonel Courtney Whitney, who has known General MacArthur since prewar Manila, is increasingly finding reasons to work his way into the general's office. He is so patently seeking publicity and recognition that his motives are distrusted by many officers. We are apprehensive that in his meetings with the commander in chief he will relate only the pleasant things that might elevate his own stature. Perhaps we are wrong.]

Tonight Col. Bill Creasy of the China theater was in town and he came out to dinner with me, after which we saw a movie at the MacArthurs'. We were in the army together in Hawaii in 1932.

Manila, P.I., Aug. 10, 1945   2115

[All day GHQ was in a state of suppressed excitement. There were many rumors and denials of these rumors. I made a hurried trip to Nichols Field to make certain *Bataan II* would be ready at any moment to take General MacArthur to Tokyo if necessary. In the afternoon we sat around expectantly waiting for developments. Finally we received a flash radio intercept to the effect that Radio Tokyo had announced that on Monday, August 13, a proclamation would be made to all the Japanese people, and that it would be what the war-weary world had been waiting to hear.

At about 5:00 P.M. Dr. Compton again came by the office and made himself available for answering questions concerning the bomb, insofar as security limitations would permit him to answer. After dinner General Diller called our house to say that Japan had just accepted the Potsdam ultimatum of unconditional surrender, provided the emperor of Japan would not be molested. A few minutes later, however, Diller called back to relay a message that both Washington and London had denied they had received acceptance of the surrender conditions by Japan. Although we could only conjecture what had actually happened, we felt that aside from some remaining diplomatic sparring, the war really was over.

(When we finally comprehended the full meaning of the end of this long struggle, that realization came as something of an anticlimax. Heretofore, we had given little thought to what would confront us both personally and as a nation after the war, since our objective in winning the struggle had been almost exclusionary of other matters. My first thoughts turned toward home and my wife and two sons. Suddenly I wanted to be there and celebrate the release from the strain all of us had endured for so long. But I also realized that my return home could not happen immediately, since there still lay ahead the occupation of Japan and its dearming process. Many weeks would be required to return enormous quantities of our own men and equipment to the States, and I probably would be caught up in helping in this return movement. My more immediate task I hoped would be to fly General MacArthur to Tokyo to inaugurate the occupation process, then perhaps a short time later fly him back to Washington. He might, however, decide to return to the States by battleship or carrier.)]

Of course it's been another hectic day. All night last night the telephone rang to advise of reports and rumors, but nothing really official ever came through. This morning, however, we did get the official announcement that the United States had received a peace proposal. All day long we've had frantic activity at the office, as a hastily prepared plan for aerial occupation has been decided upon, and much work has had to be done to alert everyone concerned for action as soon as peace is declared. It will be the first aerial-climaxed war and the first aerial occupation in history. It is particularly fitting that General MacArthur, the country's oldest and most experienced soldier, should wind up his illustrious career with this most modern ending that war has ever had.

[[When General MacArthur arrived at the office that morning, the first thing he said was: "Get Dick Sutherland back here." That was easier said than done. I had authorized leave of absence for the two pilots, Major Oviatt and Major Skov, who had flown him to the States. They had to be located, along with the remainder of General Sutherland's crew. Also, the old faithful B-17, *Bataan I*, was undergoing extensive repairs at Wright Field, and its flight status was unknown. But at length we had them all on their way back, and Sutherland had had only five days at home. I am certain he did not have time for the medical checkup he so badly wanted.]]

My part from here will be insignificant but important. I will fly MacArthur to Tokyo and land him there in order that he may accept officially the surrender of Emperor Hirohito. I've been busy with elaborate plans to ensure the safest, surest possible flight to Japan. The general hasn't decided how long he will remain or just what his plans will be after he receives the surrender, but I imagine we will remain in Japan for a month or more.

Then tonight we received a report that the Allied Powers had refused the offer of surrender on the grounds that Hirohito could not be assured future sovereignty even though Japan had agreed to the Potsdam ultimatum. So the war isn't really over after all. But none of us believe it can last more than a few more days at most. There is a bit of diplomatic bickering under way now, but it cannot change the inevitable course of events.

[August 12 has been another day of feverish activity. Plans were changed a number of times. It became known that President Truman wanted the surrender ceremony to be conducted aboard the battleship *Missouri*, which had been named for his home state. In that case, I would fly General MacArthur to Okinawa and Japanese emissaries would be taken there, where the *Missouri* could be used to stage the event. Then the battleship would steam triumphantly with the general on to Tokyo, where he would establish his Supreme Headquarters. I personally do not like this plan because I will have little reason to proceed on to Tokyo on the *Missouri*. Every general officer and politician in the theater also will want to make the trip, and there will not be much room for a lieutenant colonel. However, I have made up my mind that if necessary I will ask the general for permission to go.

In the afternoon the good news we were all waiting for finally arrived. General MacArthur has been named Supreme Commander, Allied Powers (SCAP), for all military forces that are to occupy the Japanese Empire. This brings the Russian, Chinese, British, American, Canadian, Australian, New Zealand forces under his command. Admiral Nimitz has been named commander of the American forces only, and at long last that settles the argument that has persisted in some quarters as to which of the two men really exercises command in the Pacific.]

This afternoon I made a test flight in the C-54. There were a few small defects, which my men are now correcting. It will be in top shape tomorrow. Of course we do not know just when the war will end, but we expect to depart from Manila a few hours after the news reaches us.

Manila, P.I., Aug. 13, 1945 2000

[This day was a relatively quiet day. I had the opportunity to spend a few minutes with General MacArthur, and I tried as effectively as I could to persuade him that he should make a triumphant entry into Japan by air. Japan's final agony that ultimately led to capitulation had been inflicted by air power, and without invasion of the homeland. It was no more than fitting that he, the conquering commander, should enter the conquered land by air. He merely smiled and said: "We'll see." (This talk started a jocular private verbal skirmish between the general and me. For several days following, each time I saw him he would ask me some small question, such as "Do you think you could find an airport at Tokyo?" or "How do I know you could land me there at the precise time I want to arrive?" I would usually answer with something like "If you enter Tokyo Bay with the navy on a carrier or battleship you might hit a mine and really be delayed." He would come back with something like "What will you do if the weather is bad?" But he always had a twinkle in his eyes, and I felt reassured that he already had made the decision to stage a grand entry by air.)

I gave up my desk this day to Ben Whipple, who will be in charge of planning the surrender ceremony in all detail. Until we depart for Japan I will have little need to be in the office. My job will be to plan and execute the perfect flight from Manila to Tokyo. To this end I will test-fly

Bataan II every day to keep it in perfect condition. When I left the office tonight, Admiral Sherman and Generals Stilwell and Kenney were in conference with General MacArthur, discussing the overall aspects of the surrender and occupation, which had been given the code name Blacklist.]

Manila, P.I., Aug. 14, 1945   2230

Believing that I would not be in Manila much longer, I spent much of the morning winding up such of my personal affairs as are invariably necessary before each move. There was disappointingly little news concerning the progress of peace negotiations, but it's probably quite as well that we are having a bit of time available before putting Blacklist into operation. We thought we were ready, but there are a surprising number of changes to be made.

This afternoon I went to Nichols Field but did not fly the C-54 because there was a strong, gusty crosswind, and at this late date I don't want to run the slightest risk with the airplane.

Although late this afternoon we received reports which lead us to believe the war is over, we have nothing official on it. I went to a movie at the MacArthurs' tonight. He refuses to get too excited until official reports arrive.

Manila, P.I., Aug. 15, 1945   2115

At breakfast this morning we received the final, official news that the war with Japan was over. No one got too excited over it because of the events of the past few days, but I'll have to admit it was a tremendous relief. At the office the ponderous machinery was set in motion for accepting the surrender and for redeploying our forces for the occupation of Japan. This of course isn't as easy as it might seem, and even now we have not yet established any satisfactory radio contact with Japan. General MacArthur, having been named Supreme Commander, Allied Powers, will personally accept the surrender. But before this can take place, we have to receive some envoys out of Japan in order to instruct them as to how we will enter their country, where the emperor will report for surrender, etc. As of late this afternoon, the Japs were still shooting at us on land and sea, and we can't order our forces to cease fire until we are assured that Japan has so instructed her forces. I estimate it will be a week before we can fly into Tokyo.

General Sutherland is on his way back from the States, having had only five days at home. He will be completely exhausted when he reaches Manila, but will have to plunge immediately into this intricate business of occupation. Oviatt and Skov will be most discouraged after their very short stay in the States.

I flew the C-54 again this afternoon in order to keep it in perfect condition. I pray that God, skill, and knowledge will once more enable me to complete this trip to Tokyo successfully. This will be, by all odds, the most important flight of my life. It *must* go through successfully.

I managed to obtain a copy of the emperor's statement to his people concerning the capitulation of Japan. It is certainly a masterpiece of vague implications and misstatements designed to save the all-important Japanese face.

Manila, P.I., Aug. 16, 1945   2030

In comparison with recent days, this has been a very dull one. Nothing at all exciting has happened. We established direct radio communication with Tokyo, but there has been no indication that they are going to comply with our request to send out envoys to start negotiations. They did announce that they had issued cease-fire orders but that it would require some time for these orders to reach all the widely scattered forces.

All of our mail from the States has been discontinued due to the pending requirement of the use of all C-54s for our airborne occupation of Japan. It will be weeks now before the backlog of mail can be cleared. I wrote Grace today that it's possible I will be home by Thanksgiving, but that it is more likely to be Christmas.

I flew the C-54 again this afternoon and found it to be in good condition. I now estimate it will be August 21 at the earliest before we can leave for Tokyo.

20

Eyewitness to History

AUGUST–SEPTEMBER, 1945

Manila, P.I., Aug. 17, 1945   2100

[This was a day of momentous happenings in our part of the world. Our office, always a fascinating place, now has suddenly changed from the nerve center of a war theater to the nerve center of half a world. Britain's decision to occupy Hong Kong, regardless of China's desires in the matter and regardless of previous pledges made, is the type of problem that impinges upon General MacArthur's efforts to get an effective peace agreement into being. Russia's refusal to stop fighting in Manchuria in spite of the surrender of Japan is another annoying reality. But Japan's delay in starting the machinery for peace negotiations is the item that appears to be troubling General MacArthur the most.]

General Sutherland returns tomorrow. I expect to have to get up very early in the morning to meet him, and no doubt he will be very tired. I'm glad he is to be with us now during these decisive times.

Had lunch with Kay Kyser today. He is quite as entertaining off the stage as on, and has a most charming personality.

Manila, P.I., Aug. 18, 1945   2245

Four o'clock is much too early to be called, but it had to be done this morning. General Sutherland arrived from the States at 0615 hours, tired but ready to plunge into this tremendously complicated job here. In spite of his three-day trip, he was in the office within an hour of his arrival time, and then was still there at 2000 hours tonight. There were conferences all day.

The Japanese envoys didn't arrive today as scheduled. I heard General MacArthur make the remark that if they did not arrive tomorrow, we might have to go after them. The Chinese delegation arrived in full dress this morning, but the Russian and British delegations haven't yet made an appearance.

I flew the B-17 that General Sutherland brought back. (He abandoned tired, old *Bataan I* in the States.) Then I flew the C-54 this afternoon. Tonight Shelly Mydans had dinner with us, and much interesting conversation afterward. She is the wife of Carl Mydans, the *Life* magazine photographer who became famous in the recent Spanish Civil War. She was imprisoned here in Manila all during the Japanese occupation and was freed by us last February. She is a Stanford girl and a resident of Palo Alto and had fascinating stories to tell.

Manila, P.I., Aug. 19, 1945   2115

[Late this afternoon the Japanese envoys finally arrived at Nichols Field from Tokyo. At Ie Shima they had been transferred to one of our transport planes and brought on to Manila. Roger Egeberg, Ben Whipple, and I deserted our desks and went to the airport. There we literally pushed our way into the reception line of military police. Doubtless someone had chosen these MPs for their size. I do not believe any of our soldiers there were less than six feet five inches in height, whereas the envoys perhaps averaged five feet, two inches. The humiliated, myopic little men, sixteen of them, in their ill-fitting, ribbon-bedecked uniforms came humbly down the steps of the large American aircraft, their sabres rattling on the airplane's steps, to confront the dignified, giant Americans. They were treated with coldly correct formality. Their proffered handshakes were politely but unostentatiously ignored. Their swords and hara-kiri knives seemed so completely out of order. Quite firmly they were ushered into waiting automobiles and sped on their way to dinner and then to an all-night conference with tough, fair-minded General Sutherland. This time they will be doing the listening and not the talking.

There must have been a thousand American military men at the airport, ranging from privates to three-star generals. One had to be proud of the exemplary behavior of all our troops. There was no display of base emotions to rob the occasion of its dignity and seriousness and no discernible retributive comments or actions from any of those who witnessed the occasion. Many of these men had the strongest of personal reasons for blind hatred of everything Japanese, yet the reaction was one of typical American curiosity, perhaps flavored a bit by typical American contempt. I have to admit that my emotions were a bit disorganized.

Late in the day I was given an impressive assignment. I was handed a United States flag and instructed to see that it was flown over Tokyo at the earliest appropriate moment. It was the flag that was flying over our Capitol in Washington the day war was declared. Since that time it has been flown over Rome, Paris, and Berlin. After it has flown over Tokyo, it will be returned to Washington and placed in the National Archives.]

I'm still dreaming of a Christmas with my family.

Manila, P.I., Aug. 20, 1945   2015

It has been a long but interesting day. There were many little episodes in connection with the Japanese envoys.

On one occasion General Willoughby half-jokingly apologized for the relatively poor living accommodations we were able to provide them, explaining that they were quite the best quarters the Japs had left undestroyed in Manila. Wereupon the Japanese lieutenant general said, "But you should see what you Americans have done to Tokyo."

[This evening General Sutherland called and invited me to his quarters. Although he was physically exhausted from his long flight from the States and from three days of frantic activity involving the surrender arrangements, he said he could not sleep and obviously wanted to talk. He related the following episodes involving the Japanese envoys.

They had departed from Japan in two Japanese Betty-type bombers, which had been painted white with green crosses on the wings and fuselage in accordance with instructions from our headquarters. They had landed at Ie Shima, an island off the north shore of Okinawa, where they were escorted to one of our C-54s for the trip to Manila.

They had come to Manila expecting to be sacrificial offerings. They came as a thoroughly beaten foe, full of humility and fully expecting to be tortured or killed. After the dignified, courteous, and proper treatment they received, they were embarrassed by their earlier fears, and some of them talked quite freely in excellent English. They left Japan within twenty-four hours after they were chosen and thus were not fully informed concerning all aspects of their mission. The kamikaze forces in the Tokyo area had refused to surrender and had vowed to fight to the finish. The envoys fully expected to be shot down by the kamikazes after their departure, which had been kept secret.

After leaving Ie Shima aboard the American C-54 on the final leg of their journey to Manila, they threw what they thought was to be their last party. Upon deplaning at Manila they each carried two pistols, a sword, and a hara-kiri knife. When it was pointed out to them that none of the Americans carried arms of any kind they were quite embarrassed and admitted that they had come with the resigned resolve to fight to the end and die as good soldiers. They quickly removed their arms and apologized profusely. They did request that they be permitted to wear their swords when out of doors because they were part of their normal uniform and they would lose face without them. However, before entering the conference room they carefully removed the swords and knives and placed many of them on my desk. (I managed to get a photograph of some of them.) They admitted that all of them except for Lieutenant General Kawabe, who was in charge of the party, were men who had failed the emperor in their previous respective assignments. Thus they were in disfavor. If the Americans did not kill them on this "dangerous" mission

Japanese envoys leave swords, hara-kiri knives, briefcases, caps, and pistols on my desk before meeting with General Sutherland to be told the details of surrender. Courtesy U.S. Army.

they said they would be obliged to destroy themselves upon their return to Japan. I doubt if they did so.

General MacArthur did not meet with any of the envoys. He left all arrangements regarding the mechanics of the pending surrender ceremony up to General Sutherland.

General Sutherland also told me a little about his very short trip to the States. Although he had planned to have a stay of thirty days, he was there only five. He did not have time for his medical checkup, which was one of the primary reasons for the trip.

After talking for about an hour, the general was ready to retire. He said the preliminary schedule was to fly to Tokyo on August 26 and 27 and conduct the surrender ceremony on August 31.]

I had two letters from Grace today, both of them quite old. They contain the very bad news that our landlady fully expects us to move out of our house upon the expiration of our lease on September 15. It may be that, by resorting to one of the emergency regulations dealing with wartime rentals, Grace may be able to remain there for three additional months. I don't know how she will possibly be able to find a place to live, what with the crowded conditions of housing on the West Coast.

Manila, P.I., Aug. 21, 1945   2100

Another one of those days of intense activity. In addition to much to be done in the office, at midmorning Maury Wiley came in and reported that after twenty-seven months here he was on his way back to the States to be released from the army. Unfortunately, just now all transportation to the States is tied up waiting our move to Tokyo. We called on air and water divisions to try to get him passage back, but two weeks' delay before departure was the earliest possible by normal means. Finally I located a new War Department directive, buried deep in the AG files, which called for number-one priority for airline pilots being released from the army. By invoking this directive, I think I have obtained passage for him on the first airplane as soon as he has his orders cut. He came out to lunch with me and Kay Kyser and Ish Kabibble the comedian were also here, so everyone had much fun.

Among other things, I had the privilege of seeing and handling Emperor Hirohito's signature today. It was on the letter of credentials which the Japanese delegation presented to us upon their arrival. It also contained the official seal of the Empire of Japan.

Manila, P.I., Aug. 22, 1945   2030

I flew to Clark Field in the C-54 this morning to get Maury Wiley and bring him to Manila. Guy Cain and Dwight Hansen went along with me, and on the return trip I flew them over Bataan and Corregidor so that they could inspect these historic places.

Things of interest piled up on me at the office. I spent a busy, interesting afternoon there. I managed to obtain photostatic copies of the credentials which the Japanese envoys presented. Although they fail to bring out the beauty and quality of material in the original document, nevertheless they show the Imperial Seal and the signature of Hirohito.

Manila, P.I., Aug. 23, 1945   2000

The morning was routine but interesting, with many radiograms arriving concerning the situation in Russia and China. It's maddening to watch Britain falling back into her old regime of empire building. Against all protests from us and China and Russia, she insists on moving back into Hong Kong with a great show of force, thus giving any other power a precedent for taking aggressive action against almost any other weaker nation. She can't very well protest against the Russian expansion as long as she insists on "once British, always British," even though her claim is tenuous at best.

Manila, P.I., Aug. 24, 1945   2100

I went on a test flight in the C-54 this morning. That and a lot of planning for the Tokyo trip consumed most of the morning.

The mail has been quite spasmodic of late. I've had very few letters from Grace, and now during this period of uncertainty I miss them.

Manila, P.I., Aug. 25, 1945   2115

Again I flew the C-54 to assure myself of its condition. I had had some changes made in the carburetors, and they appeared to function even better than usual.

Back at the office, things were on an even keel when I went to lunch, but most certainly that condition did not prevail immediately after the lunch hour. General MacArthur had decided to postpone our occupation of the Tokyo area by forty-eight hours. The decision, doubtless a bitter one for him to make, was quite soundly supported by several developments. An active typhoon lies directly athwart the route from Okinawa to Tokyo. An additional factor was the heavy rainfall during the past few days at Tokyo. The Japanese reported that the airstrips were quite soft and muddy off the runways so that we would be unable to park our heavy aircraft over any considerable part of the field. Also, the rain had disrupted communications to the extent that they had been unable to clear the population from the areas we had specified. Of course this information may be based on a desire to delay our occupation as long as possible. On the other hand, any rash acts at this late date might cost us additional American lives. So now we are waiting patiently for next Wednesday morning, when we expect to be on our way to Tokyo.

Manila, P.I., Aug. 26, 1945   2030

Although I had intended to fly this morning, I postponed it until tomorrow. Even if it has been a most exciting day at the office, I haven't been able to shake off a sense of depression.

I completed my packing tonight and will load most of my belongings on the airplane tomorrow. This may be the last time I'll ever see Manila, but then that might not be too regrettable. I've been well cared for here, yet not too happy.

Manila, P.I., Aug. 27, 1945   2000

News both thrilling and depressing came to me in that order today. General Sutherland called me into his office this morning and showed me a radiogram which was from Washington and which directed that I be returned to the States immediately by highest air priority to be released from the army for return to the airlines. General MacArthur came into Sutherland's office and both asked that I stay with them until the move to Tokyo was over and until I could find some good replacement for myself. General Sutherland said he wanted to promote me to full colonel before I left, but I cannot possibly be promoted unless I'm still in the army on November 12.

[This request provoked strongly conflicting emotions within me. I wanted to complete my small part of the war effort but at the same time I wanted to go home, where I knew my family badly needed me. General Sutherland said he thought I should remain in my present assignment at least until GHQ was established in Tokyo and was functioning smoothly. I told him I would like to think it over for an hour, then if possible would like to discuss it with him and General MacArthur. This the three of us did later this afternoon. It was agreed that a three-month extension of my active duty assignment would be requested. General MacArthur volunteered a guess that such an extension would be approved.]

So I have agreed to remain another three months, during which time I'll earn a command pilot rating and will also get a promotion if General Sutherland makes good his promise. He has never failed yet.

I was all thrilled with this news—certainty of going home, a promotion in the offing, seeing Tokyo, etc.—so General Sutherland sent a radiogram to Washington requesting that I be allowed to remain for an additional three months. Then this afternoon I received a letter from Grace containing disconcerting news relative to the expiration of the lease on our house and the imminent possibility of being forced to move with no place to go. So I'm most unhappy about my decision, now irrevocable, to remain another three months when I had a certain opportunity of going home. It may well develop that I have allowed my personal ambitions to forge ahead of the welfare of my family, a thing I've always sworn I'd never do.

I flew the C-54 early today. According to present plans, I'll take General MacArthur to Tokyo, starting on Wednesday morning and remaining overnight at Okinawa. The triumphant landing at Tokyo will occur on Thursday morning. I probably will not return to Manila at all and expect to be rather busy in Tokyo for some time to come. It will be an interesting place to explore.

[Up until this pending flight to Okinawa and Tokyo I have never permitted Generals MacArthur and Sutherland to be on the same airplane on any flight in the theater, the reason being that in the unlikely event of a major accident there would be no one remaining in the command who was sufficiently familiar with the total operation to assume immediate control and continue to prosecute the war effort. But for this flight General MacArthur called me into his office and told me to overlook this restriction because he wanted General Sutherland to be with him. Including the general, there are a total of sixteen men to be transported by air on this mission. My two concerns are weather and aircraft mechanical problems en route. To minimize the latter problem, I will dispatch a standby C-54 to Okinawa the day preceding our departure, to remain there until after we have taken off from Okinawa on the final flight to Tokyo. Another C-54 will be ready for flight but will remain in Manila until it receives confirmation that we have landed at Okinawa. The standby airplane at Okinawa will carry half of the passengers along with many spare airplane parts and some highly skilled mechanics.]

Manila, P.I., Aug. 28, 1945   2045

I went to the airport early this morning, and while there I had a man die in my arms. I was standing near the runway when an officer started to run across the runway just as an L-5 was taking off. The propeller cut him half in two and threw him at my feet. I held him until he bled to death, which mercifully took only about three minutes. Such things are so needless. Both the pilot and the victim were at fault because if either of them had been obeying rules, it certainly could have been prevented. Now one of them is alive and the other is dead. I don't quite know which I'd rather be.

It's been a hectic day. There was so much confusion in arranging the last-minute details — so many people to notify and so many things to check on. At last I think we are ready to depart at 0800 hours tomorrow morning. I can only pray that everything goes well, because *nothing* must happen now. Only God can help from now on.

To bed to get what sleep my nervous tension will allow me. I'll be up at 0500 hours, with a long day ahead. The high point of the day arrived when I called on Mrs. MacArthur to bid her good-bye. Undoubtedly she is one of the most charming ladies I've ever known, and probably I'll never again have personal contact with her. It will be a loss from my life.

Okinawa, Ryukyu Islands, Aug. 29, 1945   2100

The trip is half over and all has gone well. I was up at 0500 hours this morning and off to the airport. Due to business at the office, General MacArthur didn't reach the airport until 0900 hours, so that I had everything in readiness long before departure time. There were more delays due to much picture taking, but at length we were under way for one of the finest trips I've ever flown.

The general wanted to see Balete Pass, the Cagayan Valley, and Aparri, where so much bitter fighting occurred. Fortunately, the weather was perfect, so he had an excellent view of all of these places which have figured so prominently in his communiqués of recent months. The trip to Okinawa required only 4¾ hours, and we were not in a cloud the entire distance. The general was pleased as a little boy with his new airplane, and he spent much of the time up in the cockpit.

Here at Okinawa there was much more photographing and confusion. Now, however, I'm comfortably billeted in a general officers' billet along with Generals Wurtsmith, Fellers, Whitney, and Hutchinson, and my good friends Egeberg and Whipple. Thus I'm not faring badly. Our departure tomorrow is set for 0900 hours.

Yokohama, Japan, Aug. 30, 1945   2045

First let me say that I have safely delivered General MacArthur to Japan, and the terrific tension under which I've been laboring during the past few days has suddenly lifted. I'm tired and I want to sleep, but I feel that I should record some of my impressions of this historic day before they escape me. So I'll do so in chronological order.

Up before dawn this morning, I found that the transportation for my-

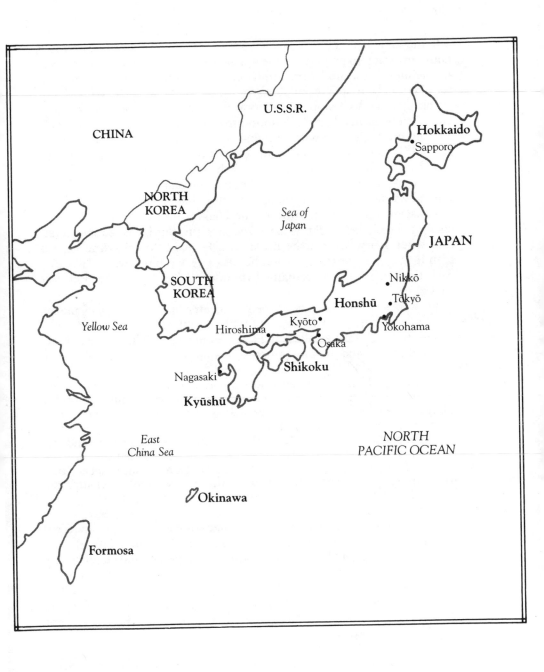

CHINA

U.S.S.R.

Hokkaido

Sapporo

NORTH
KOREA

Sea of
Japan

JAPAN

SOUTH
KOREA

Nikkō

Honshū

Tōkyō

Yellow Sea

Kyōto

Hiroshima

Yokohama

Osaka

Shikoku

Nagasaki

Kyūshū

East
China Sea

NORTH
PACIFIC OCEAN

Okinawa

Formosa

FLYING MacARTHUR TO VICTORY

self and crew had not arrived. We finally reached the airstrip with two hours in which to prepare for the departure at 0900 hours. After all was in readiness, I was under the airplane, changing into a fresh uniform so that I could be more presentable when the general arrived. Just as I had stripped to the bare skin, the general drove up with a flourish and the crowd gathered in a hurry, all around me, with my pants literally down. At dinner tonight I sat with him and in front of the dinner table full of generals he told the story of having caught me with my pants down, but in his own inimitable way he embellished the episode considerably.

We took off from Okinawa on schedule and had a wonderful trip. The general was nervous with anticipation but as happy as I've ever seen him.

He spent much of the time in the cockpit on this trip. He left the cockpit shortly before Fujiyama came in sight, but he asked me to tell him when I first sighted the mountain. He said the last time he had seen it was many years ago when he was a very junior officer. He came back to the cockpit and remained there until just before we landed at Atsugi.

We were scheduled to land at the Atsugi airstrip at 1400, and by means of a wide turn over Tokyo Bay, I touched down exactly on schedule. It was with the greatest sigh of relief I've ever breathed. The boss was here, safe and sound, and my most important mission of the war had ended.

[Obviously the Japanese were uncertain as to what we would do. A military jeep led us off the runway to a parking area, where quite strangely a large sofa and two chairs of the grossly overstuffed variety were drawn up on the grass facing a small dais.

A group of perhaps 150 men, predominantly American troops and correspondents but with a few Japanese included, surrounded the airplane exit as General MacArthur descended. He delivered a short speech and then entered a staff car to be driven to the New Grand Hotel in Yokohama. The overstuffed furniture remained unused.]

At length, after the confusion diminished somewhat, I commandeered a Jap truck and a Jap car with Jap drivers and an interpreter, to take me and the General's baggage into Yokohama to the New Grand Hotel, where we are now billeted. It was a memorable experience, driving through a strange land in these strange old vehicles, with Jap civilians as well as soldiers everywhere trying to be polite and friendly. There have been no shootings, and many of the Jap soldiers with rifles and other equipment guard the highways we use.

[Along the road into the city, spaced at regular, short intervals, were many Japanese soldiers carrying rifles. Invariably, as we approached they turned, facing away from the road, their rifles held at "present arms" posi-

Above: General MacArthur gives me final instructions regarding the flight from Manila to Tokyo. Generals Byers, Marquart, and Eichelberger are looking on. *Below:* General MacArthur sets foot on Japanese soil after we land at Atsugi. Courtesy U.S. Army.

tion. We were told two different versions of why they did this. One was that they were protecting us from any attack that might come from off the roadside. The other version was that this was a method of showing contempt for us. I did not learn which was the correct answer.

The Atsugi airdrome is located well out in the countryside away from Yokohama. The first part of the drive took us through small villages and farmland. Having been brought up on a large midwestern farm, I am amazed at the Lilliputian aspect of the farms in Japan. They are miniature plots of ground, intensely cultivated and tended to perfection. Even the trees seem dwarfed and the buildings are almost like dollhouses. As we passed, the farmers stopped their toils, some smiled and waved, but most seemed merely curious about these strange big Americans.

Abruptly we came to the outskirts of Yokohama, and the contrast was stark indeed. The devastation is almost unimaginable and was caused by one firebomb raid we made on the city in May. For mile after mile everything has burned, and there are no houses standing. Apparently most of the original houses had tin roofs. Now the people have collected these strips of scorched, buckled metal and constructed small lean-tos atop the rubble and are living there by the thousands.

My first impression of the people is that they are to be pitied. The children, of whom there are great numbers, were crying from hunger, the same as they would do anywhere in the world. I could not detect any look of resentment in the faces of the people. Rather, they seemed to be amazed and curious. Seeing the ignorant, tattered masses here with their pitifully inadequate equipment and resources, one could not but be amazed at the quality of reasoning that led them to believe they could conquer the Pacific world. Surely even the leaders could not have believed it. It is more likely that even from the beginning the warlords were trying a tremendous bluff, hoping it would succeed or else win a compromise beneficial to them.

We are all temporarily billeted in the best hotel in Yokohama, the New Grand. It catered to Americans before the war and is about equivalent to a third-class hotel in the States. I had dinner with General MacArthur and the other general officers in the main dining room tonight. Although somewhat weary, the general was in rare good humor. Not only did he tease me about catching me with my pants down, but he made many other typical observations. Once, when someone remarked that the Japanese probably did not particularly like to have him here, he said, "Well, I'm not exactly here by invitation." Then later, when it was mentioned that a suitable undamaged house for his occupancy was going to be difficult to find, he replied, "It would be too bad if we have to make the emperor move out of the Imperial Palace in order to have adequate housing."

The food at dinner consisted of only two items: fresh grapes and fish fried in very rancid fish oil. Although the fish was almost repulsive, the general asked us to eat as much as we could in order to demonstrate good faith because this was doubtless the only food they had to offer us.]

Yokohama, Japan, Aug. 31, 1945   2300

If I didn't have a sense of humor and a bit of tolerance for human weakness, I'd be in a straitjacket right now. But perhaps I'd better start at the beginning.

[Today was a day to remember. I was up early and went to our temporary offices in the Japanese customhouse. It poured rain all day. Since there was no excitement at the office I went back to the hotel, where I found General Sutherland standing in the rain, trying to hail some type of transportation to get him to the office. He had not yet mastered the technique of stepping in front of any oncoming auto that did not contain passengers, stopping it, and then ordering the driver to take him to his destination. I took him to the office in this manner, then returned to the hotel, where my good friend Ben Whipple, in charge of the surrender program, asked me to help him. Foreign military dignitaries from all over the Pacific Basin were to arrive at Atsugi airport in two different airplanes for the purpose of attending the surrender ceremony aboard the battleship *Missouri*. Colonel Whipple asked me to meet each of the two arriving aircraft and see that ground transportation was available for the dignitaries and their baggage. This certainly was not in my line of duty, but he begged me and, as I had no good excuse not to do so, I reluctantly agreed to take on the chore.

When I arrived at the airport in the driving rain, everything was in a state of confusion. No one knew when the planes would arrive or where they would be parked. There would be about forty passengers requiring transportation into Yokohama, and there was no transportation. Finally, by all means possible, including physical intimidation, I commandeered three old buses and two sedans, all with Japanese drivers. During the day about 200 airplanes landed at the field, and, not knowing which two would be the ones I was looking for, I met as many as I could. About midafternoon a General Duff arrived in his own airplane, pulled his rank on me, and literally took one of my buses from me despite the fact I told him it was specifically allocated for General MacArthur's guests. But he was not alone in his rude behavior, as I was soon to learn.

About 5:00 P.M. both airplanes I was seeking arrived at the same time. Through some misunderstanding of my instructions to the control tower one of them was told to park on one side of the field, and the other one parked about a mile away on the other side of the airport. By luck I chose to meet the more important one, whose passengers included Generals Wainwright, Percival, Krueger, Blamey, and Gardiner. General Krueger, in my opinion, made something of an ass of himself by demanding and taking for himself the better of the two cars, then complained sarcastically in front of the others about the poor arrangements that had been made for his arrival. He took off on his own, and I hoped secretly that he would get lost in the rain on the way into the city. I got the other generals on the remaining bus and sent them on their way.

Back at the control tower I commandeered two more buses and went to the other airplane. Here were the Russians, the French, and the Dutch, in a state of great confusion and anger. After an hour of communicating largely by sign language and with no help except the two Japanese bus drivers to aid with the baggage, I finally had everything aboard, including two large uncrated glass containers, each holding about five gallons of vodka, that the Russians had brought along. Then they were on their way into the city.

About this time General Willoughby, who was supposed to have met the foreign delegation, but had not done so, came along and wanted to ride with me behind the convoy. By this time it was completely dark and raining hard. A mile from the airport my Japanese driver ran off the road into a ditch, and we were hopelessly stuck. My driver disappeared in the dark. I went into a nearby Japanese army barracks and by gestures alone succeeded in persuading a number of troops to follow me to the automobile. These strange little men surrounded the vehicle and to the accompaniment of much jabbering and gesticulating, lifted the small car back on the road. The driver reappeared, and I decided to go back to the airport to get better transportation. On the way back our headlights burned out. Fortunately a Japanese truck came along, driven by an American soldier, so General Willoughby and I climbed aboard, turned around, and started for Yokohama again.

A third of the way into the city we caught up with our two buses, stalled along the narrow road. They were powered by charcoal burners, and one of them had run out of fuel. A roadblock rapidly developed, but with the help of some American soldiers caught in the roadblock, I soon had this problem cleared. We transferred the passengers and baggage into our truck and proceeded onward. Russian General Derevyanko removed his jacket and worked alongside us in the mud and rain, helping to transfer the baggage, and he was particularly solicitous of his precious vodka.

Upon arriving at the hotel I discovered the first busload of passengers had not yet arrived, although more than four hours had elapsed since they had departed from the airport. We were preparing to send out search parties when they finally arrived and reported that their driver, who spoke no English, got lost and had taken them almost to Tokyo.

As I entered the hotel, General Sutherland was standing in the lobby. I was muddy from the waist down and thoroughly drenched. He said, "What the hell have you been up to?" Of course I had to explain to him that I had been stupid enough to volunteer to be his headquarters commandant and chief of military police. I could have remained dry and warm in the hotel.

Colonel Wheeler told me that a radiogram had been received advising that both the War Department and United Air Lines had agreed to General MacArthur's request for a ninety-day extension to my military assignment to general headquarters.

General MacArthur greeted General Wainwright upon his arrival at the hotel. I was not present, but Roger Egeberg said it was a most touch-

Above: General Akin, myself (in flight cap), and Generals Sutherland, Byers, MacArthur, and Eichelberger after landing at Atsugi, Japan. *Below:* General MacArthur greets two prisoners of war, the British general Percival and General Wainwright, in Yokohama. Photographs courtesy U.S. Army.

ing affair. Both of them almost lost control of their emotions but soon started reminiscing. His long suffering as a prisoner of the Japanese had left its mark on General Wainwright.]

Yokohama, Japan, Sept. 1, 1945   1930

This day has been much quieter. I was tired from all of the activity and excitement of the past few days, so I slept as late as I could and then played hookey from the office. It rained all morning, so I didn't stir outside. There was much correspondence to bring up to date, and then I felt lazy.

With the exception of the first meal we had here, we've had only stale fish, soybean bread, and grapes to eat three times daily. I can no longer eat the fish, and Doc advises against the grapes, so I've eaten only hard bread and water today.

Tomorrow morning at 0700 hours we depart in the destroyer *Buchanan* for the battleship *Missouri*, which is anchored in Tokyo Bay. There the surrender of Japan will take place officially at about 0930 hours. It still appears that I will go, and if so, I'll be about the most junior officer there.

Yokohama, Japan, Sept. 2, 1945   2100

We were up at 0430 hours this morning after very little sleep last night. Our room was headquarters for all the last-minute preparations for the ceremony. Ben Whipple herded all of our rank and the foreign dignitaries aboard the destroyer, and we departed from the Yokohama pier at 0700 hours. We arrived alongside the *Missouri*, which was anchored eighteen miles out into Tokyo Bay, and went aboard about 0800 hours to prepare everything for the big show. At 0840, General MacArthur came aboard and went to the captain's cabin.

[After a while, he emerged on deck and started talking to many of his friends and acquaintances.

Shortly thereafter the general saw me, motioned to me, and asked that I accompany him. He went back into the captain's cabin and then directly into the "head" or bathroom. I could hear him retching, and I asked him if he wanted me to get a doctor. He replied that he would be all right in a moment. Soon afterward he emerged, went on deck, and staged the ceremony without a quiver in his voice. I believe his momentary problem was merely an emotional reaction to his realization that this occasion could be his final significant action in a long and illustrious military career.

At 8:55 A.M. the eleven Japanese envoys came aboard and lined up along the rail of the ship. The Allied participating dignitaries were standing

Above: The Japanese delegation stands at attention for the surrender ceremonies aboard the *Missouri* while General MacArthur delivers his speech and instructions. *Below:* General MacArthur signs as supreme commander of the Allied Powers. Photographs courtesy U.S. Army.

in a square formation, facing a table on which the surrender documents and a microphone were placed. The remainder of us were lined up according to grade, and naturally I was in the rear row. At nine o'clock sharp General MacArthur came forward and started the proceedings. He made a short, moving speech, then called the Japanese delegation forward to sign the instrument of surrender. The Japanese copy of the document was appropriately bound in black, whereas ours was bound in green. Foreign Minister Shigemitsu signed for the emperor, then General Umezu signed for the Japanese Imperial General Headquarters staff. Immediately afterward General MacArthur affixed his signature to both copies of the document as Supreme Commander, Allied Powers, and thus started the "incident of the pens." He used six fountain pens. The first two were to be presented to Generals Wainwright and Percival, both former Japanese prisoners of war. The third was to go to West Point, the fourth to the Naval Academy at Annapolis, the fifth to the National Archives, and the sixth was Mrs. MacArthur's personal pen. That one he kept for her. The other five pens he left each beside the others lying on the table, then called the various national representatives forward one at a time to sign on behalf of their respective countries. When Adm. Sir Bruce Fraser signed for the British Empire, he picked up two of the pens and presented them to two of his aides in a gesture poorly imitative of General MacArthur, thus hoping to obtain two of these historic pens. Immediately after the ceremony General MacArthur told Ben Whipple and me to "get those pens back." We did so, but only after considerable trouble and embarrassment requiring a half day of detective work.

The only other untoward incident occurred when Colonel Cosgrave, the Canadian representative, came forward to sign for his country. He staggered as he walked, and many of us thought he might have imbibed too freely. He signed the Japanese copy on the wrong line, thus throwing all subsequent signatures out of order. Mr. Shigemitsu, representing the emperor, objected vociferously, and it appeared for a moment that the proceedings had reached an impasse. However, General Sutherland stepped forward, drew lines through the printed national names, and wrote in the proper names for each country, and Shigemitsu agreed to continue. (Later General Sutherland told me that even though the Japanese copy was slightly blemished, he suspected that very few people ever would see it anyway, since it probably would be buried in the deepest recesses of their most secret archives.)

The entire ceremony required only about twelve minutes, after which we roamed around the *Missouri* for half an hour. The ship was a wonderful piece of the most modern machinery, but she has already been rendered hopelessly obsolete by the airplane and the atomic bomb.

We were back in Yokohama by 11:00 A.M. and could hardly believe we had just witnessed one of the very historic events in the long and colorful history of our nation. It is a privilege that we will cherish throughout our lives.]

My reaction just now is one of tremendous tiredness. Poor, unsustaining food, nervous tension, and lack of sleep have very suddenly conspired to let me down completely. I slept an hour this afternoon, took a three-mile hike, and then went to the office late.

21

In Japan

Yokohama, Japan, Sept. 3, 1945   2330

After going to the office this morning, I drove to the airstrip to see how my men and the airplane were getting along. I found that they were living better than I was. So I stopped worrying about them and returned to Yokohama. This afternoon I had a leisurely time during which I wrote one letter to Grace and one to Mrs. MacArthur. There were a few interesting radiograms.

Tonight after I returned to the hotel, Gen. Richard Marshall telephoned to advise me that General MacArthur had authorized him to use the C-54 to return to Manila tomorrow. I advised him that I could not be certain of a departure before 1100 hours tomorrow but that I would do my best to make it earlier.

Ben Whipple has received permission to go to the States for forty-five days' leave, which means that he will never return to this theater. So all evening, while I've been hopeful of getting some rest in preparation for my trip tomorrow, Generals Casey, Marshall, and Sverdrup, Ben, and I have been having a very loud party here in my room. All of them have been quite high, except for me, who cannot imbibe because of the flight tomorrow.

Manila, P.I., Sept. 4, 1945   2230

I got out to Atsugi airstrip and was ready for takeoff at 0830 hours. But, as I had expected, General Marshall did not arrive until two hours later. Once under way, however, we had a fine, fast trip to Manila, arriving here after nine hours and ten minutes of flying.

Manila, P.I., Sept. 5, 1945   2100

I've spent one of the laziest days in my recent life. I didn't get out of bed until 0800 hours, had breakfast an hour later, and then went over to spend an hour with Mrs. MacArthur to tell her as much as I could about the events that had transpired since the general had departed from Manila for Japan. She is a splendid audience for a monologue, and it pleased me greatly that I could tell her so many nice things about the general which she wanted to hear.

This afternoon I read and drowsed and did nothing except to write one letter to Grace.

Manila, P.I., Sept. 6, 1945   2200

Ben Whipple departed today by air for the States. Although he is going on leave, he will probably not return to this theater, as he will endeavor to get some of his friends in the army to ask for him so that he can remain at home. As soon as he can do so, he intends to resign from the army to become a civilian and make his home in San Francisco.

I went with Ben to the airport, and on the way back I accomplished a number of errands in town.

Manila, P.I., Sept. 7, 1945   2330

It has rained continuously today. That plus another attack of dysentery has kept me rather closely confined, although I did venture down to my old deserted office to mail some letters.

I had a talk with General Gunner, the G-1 of AFPAC. He reminded me that I was due to receive my command pilot's wings on October 11 and that my promotion would be possible on November 15. So I imagine he must have been prompted by General Sutherland, since I know he never would have remembered these dates by himself.

Tonight Mrs. MacArthur, Jerry Graham, and I heard transcriptions of the surrender ceremonies of Japan and also of General Yamashita here on Luzon. Afterwards, the rather dull movie which we saw kept me awake much past my bedtime.

Manila, P.I., Sept. 8, 1945   2100

Feeling somewhat more energetic this morning, I sallied forth on an expedition to accomplish a number of small personal errands. My momentum carried me along for a couple of hours, and then I suddenly ran low on energy. So this afternoon I remained in bed, taking paregoric and praying to be rid of this lingering, debilitating dysentery, which seems to be a new type I contracted from the Japs. I feel better now and believe I'll be able to go with Mrs. MacArthur to Corregidor early tomorrow.

I'm praying that Mrs. MacArthur will decide to go on to Tokyo within a week or ten days. At this critical time when I wish to hear from Grace concerning her progress with the housing situation, my mail is all being delayed because it goes to me at Tokyo first.

Manila, P.I., Sept. 9, 1945   2115

I was kept awake last night by the fact that Major Skov was unable to get off with General Chamberlin due to a runway collapse in which he broke through the surface of the runway with the B-17. I had to make other arrangements in the middle of the night.

This morning it was raining hard so that we were delayed in our departure for Corregidor. We got away, however, at about 1100 hours, Mrs. MacArthur, Jerry Graham, and I. We went over in a nicely furnished Q-boat, which took two hours to make the crossing. The bay was rough, but not so much so that we couldn't enjoy a splendid lunch aboard. At the north dock on Corregidor we were met by a staff car and a jeep, which took us first to Topside. Here we examined closely this shell of an old fort, and saw the house in which Mrs. MacArthur was living when it was bombed. The house was completely demolished. There's nothing living on the rock except the vegetation, which has at last grown up to cover many of the scars of battle. From Topside we went down to Middleside, then to the tunnels. Navy Tunnel has been sealed off by a rockslide, but Malinta Tunnel is still open, although completely wrecked. This fortress was built without due allowance for air power, and it quickly fell a victim twice in three years.

Then there were *twelve* letters awaiting me—seven of them from Gracie. Although she is trying hard to keep her chin up, I can tell from the tone of them that she is becoming tired of the endless monotony of her dull job at home. If she can only hang on for three more months, then I can take over and send her off on a good long vacation.

Among my other letters was one from Doc Egeberg, who reports missing my company in Tokyo. He also intimates that General MacArthur may be flying to Washington in October, although Doc says he will deny he started any such rumor. If that should be the case, I'm afraid I'd have to return with him to Tokyo before I could be released from the army.

Manila, P.I., Sept. 10, 1945   2030

I checked the weather carefully for Okinawa and Tokyo this morning and then made a test flight in the C-54. I'm set up now for a takeoff shortly after midnight tonight unless the weather turns definitely worse. I spent a quiet, restful afternoon and will now try to get two hours of sleep before departure.

Yokohama, Japan, Sept. 11, 1945   1900

We departed from Manila at the ungodly hour of one o'clock this morning in the midst of the rain and wind of a typhoon. I flew east for 400 miles before turning northward, in order to avoid the center of the disturbance. It was quite intense at its center. We arrived at daylight at Okinawa, where we refueled and then proceeded on here to the Atsugi airfield outside Yokohama. Although we landed at noon, it was late in the afternoon before I got all the notes and messages delivered to people here from friends in Manila.

I was quite surprised to find that GHQ is still located in Yokohama. I had understood that it already had moved into Tokyo. Now, from what short conversations I had this afternoon, I gather that we are to have two headquarters—one a very small, select one for the Supreme Commander, Allied Powers, the other, which will remain in Manila, a headquarters for military control only of occupational forces. Thus the GHQ located in Japan will be quite small in comparison with the enormous one with which we've been associated in the past.

On the way in today, I circled low over Tokyo for the first time. Indeed it is a city of contrasts. Thousands of city blocks are nothing more than ashes, but for some crazy reason there are countless other blocks in the midst of devastated areas which are entirely undamaged. I flew low over the emperor's palace and grounds, and I must say that it is one of the most magnificent pieces of man's handiwork that I've ever seen. I'll describe it in detail later after I've had an opportunity to examine it from the ground. As seen from the air, the most impressive thing is the wide moat which encircles the grounds completely, and then the intricate, perfect patterns of landscape gardening. If the emperor spends all of his time at this institution, he certainly has no firsthand knowledge of the sordid realities concerning his people.

Yokohama, Japan, Sept. 12, 1945   1930

This was an extremely interesting day. Roger Egeberg (now assuming his role as doctor rather than aide) came by my room and asked if I would like to accompany him to the hospital to check on the physical condition of former prime minister Tojo. Naturally I was thrilled at the idea, and we were on our way.

[(Yesterday our military patrols converged on the residence of Tojo in Tokyo to arrest him as a probable war criminal. He came to the window and asked them to wait a moment. This request was followed almost immediately by the sound of a gunshot. Our men broke into the house and found Tojo seated in an upholstered chair with a bullet hole in his chest just above the heart. He shot himself with an American .32-caliber pistol, of the type issued to our Air Corps pilots and, incidentally, bearing a serial number sufficiently high to attest to the fact it had been manufactured in the States since the start of the war. Likely it had been taken from one of our pilots who had come down somewhere over the Japanese homeland or occupied territory. At any rate the wound was not immediately fatal, and he failed in suicide as well as in war. He had drawn his hara-kiri knife but had not used it. Our soldiers administered emergency treatment on the spot, then brought him to Yokohama to one of the army hospitals. He apparently was given about an even chance of recovery.)

Doc Egeberg and I reached the hospital only to find a large crowd of other curious troops eager to find some excuse to see Tojo. Doc told the guards that General MacArthur was anxious to know Tojo's true condition, so we marched into his room like professionals.

There he lay, a small, pitiful wreck of a man who once had dreams of conquering the world! Because of American blood plasma and American antibiotics, he would survive. He supposedly told his captors at the time he was apprehended to "cooperate with the military authorities of Japan to create a greater nation."

With his bristling mustache and popeyes he looked exactly like his photographs and resembled the many cartoonists' unflattering caricatures of him. Doc Egeberg took Tojo's pulse for, as he said later, "purely professional reasons." I reminded him that, with Hitler dead, he had just counted the heartbeats of the most hated man in the world that day.

This afternoon General Sutherland called me into his office, apparently just to visit. In the midst of our conversation, General MacArthur entered. He walked over to me, grasped me by the arm, looked gravely into my eyes, and said he wanted me to make the most important flight of my military career as far as he was concerned. He wanted me to go to Manila and fly Jean MacArthur and his son, Arthur, to Tokyo about September 17 or 18. He talked at some length, cautioning me to exercise the greatest possible care, to use my best judgment about the weather, and make sure that the airplane was in perfect mechanical condition. He said these two people were his most treasured possessions and he could not carry on if he lost them. He said that I should take any delays necessary in the interest of safety, but that he wanted to meet the flight upon our arrival at Atsugi and that I should constantly keep him advised of the expected time. I gave him all the verbal assurance I could, and then he changed the subject. He said, "Dick, I'd like to discuss the perplexing question of war crimes, particularly as it applies to Tojo."

He went into a long discussion with Sutherland while I stood and listened. He said he had struggled through an intense consideration of pros and cons of the problem of Generals Homma and Yamashita and now clearly saw the path that should be taken. Admiral Yamamoto's earlier death in an airplane had eliminated him as a possible war criminal, and he said he was not too familiar with Yamamoto's activities anyway. But there might be others falling into the war crimes category. He said he was now quite content to allow a military tribunal to handle the problem as far as enemy military personnel were concerned. This had long been established by at least some precedent. He would abide by any just decision. He told Sutherland to proceed at once to instigate trials by military court of all others who properly could be tried by such means. He wanted to get the onerous task behind him as soon as practicable.

But both of them agreed that the case of Tojo presented a different aspect. The discussion became lively at times. Tojo, although previously having come from the military, had been head of a government that had permitted its military forces to commit unspeakable atrocities, at least as judged by most civilized nations. He was prime minister of Japan at the time of Pearl Harbor and remained in that position through most of the war. Yet it would be most difficult to prove that Tojo had ordered those things to be done. Condoned them? Yes. Ordered them? Perhaps. Certainly he had ordered an attack against one nation, the United States, without a declaration of war and while still on supposedly friendly terms with it. General Sutherland said he believed similar situations prevailed when Tojo had ordered attacks on at least some of the Asian nations also.

General MacArthur said he strongly believed our government itself should prefer the charges against the offending head of the Japanese government. In his opinion it was improper for him as a conquering *military* man to be asked to indict, try, and possibly convict the *political* head of a vanquished nation. However, if Washington sidestepped this responsibility and ordered him to institute a trial of Tojo, he would do so, charging him with "crimes against the world." General Sutherland noted that a new page in modern history would have to be written if a conquering general of a major power tried and executed the head of state of a defeated enemy in this day and age.

The discussion lasted for an hour and both generals were most eloquent. It was a privilege for me to be exposed to this dialogue. I came out of Sutherland's office feeling that I had witnessed one more bit of history in the making.]

It now appears that I will leave early tomorrow for Manila. After this pleasant weather, I hate to think of returning to that hot, dirty place. My stay there will be for only a few days, however.

Manila, P.I., Sept. 13, 1945   2200

Here we are again after a quick, pleasant nonstop trip down from Tokyo. Naturally I'm tired, but happy. Generals Marshall and Whitlock and Doc Egeberg came with me, along with a number of officers from the Judge Advocate General's Office who are going to start the trials of the Japanese war criminals. General Sutherland did not wait long to start the trial proceedings.

Now I'm tired, and there's a busy day ahead of me tomorrow.

Manila, P.I., Sept. 14, 1945   1930

It was fortunate that I left the house early this morning and accomplished most of my errands before lunch because this afternoon I had another violent attack of dysentery.

Weather permitting, I will depart for Okinawa and Tokyo with Mrs. MacArthur and Arthur on September 18. If she likes this trip by air, perhaps she can bring pressure to bear upon the general to fly to the States soon.

Among my other errands today was one to the Recovered Prisoners Bureau to determine the status of Lt. William Strangman, the friend of Nick Ball of Douglas Aircraft. I found that he was recovered on September 5 in good condition, and I radioed the information to Nick.

I had two fine cheerful letters from Grace today. She isn't too worried about the rent situation, so that in turn encourages me. I think she is getting about as much of a thrill from following my activities as I am in actually being present during such excitement.

Manila, P.I., Sept. 15, 1945   2030

Up early this rainy morning to go to Neilson Field to see General Kenney about quarters for Mrs. MacArthur for an overnight stop at Okinawa.

We have closed our mess here at the aides' house, so that Doc, Jerry, and I are now having our meals with Mrs. MacArthur until we all depart for Tokyo. This afternoon she asked me to go with her to do a number of errands—paying bills, etc.—so I proudly squired her around. And it was a most pleasant dinner with her tonight.

Had two more fine letters from Grace tonight, one of them containing some excellent snapshots of herself and the boys. She advises that, in accordance with a revision of OPA regulations, she may be able to continue living in our present house for at least six months, even after it is sold.

Manila, P.I., Sept. 16, 1945   2015

Although most Sundays in the Philippines are dull, this one has not been dull for me. I gave the C-54 a thorough test flight this morning, discussed replacements for my men who are leaving, made preliminary arrangements for my trip north with Mrs. MacArthur for the day after tomorrow, and got another C-54 dispatched with the MacArthur household belongings aboard.

Mrs. MacArthur is so nervous and excitable that the confusion of moving has her upset.

Manila, P.I., Sept. 17, 1945   1930

I earnestly hope that this is the last full day I'll ever spend in Manila. Although many phases of my stay here have been most pleasant and my relationships have been some of the best of my lifetime, none of these things were as fine as they could have been under better conditions of weather and environment.

Much of my day has been given over to last-minute preparations for the trip to Tokyo tomorrow. I'm hoping that everything goes well so that Mrs. MacArthur will be pleased and unafraid of airplanes in the future. Our entourage will be small, consisting of Mrs. MacArthur, Arthur, Colonel Soriano, Doc Egeberg, Major Graham, Ah Cheu, and Mrs. Gibbons (Arthur's tutor). We should take off at about 0830 hours, reach Okinawa in the early afternoon, and remain there overnight.

Okinawa, Sept. 18, 1945   2230

The trip went off as planned, and was about as perfect as any trip could be. Except for a bit of rain in the Manila area, the weather was excellent and there wasn't a bump in the air. Mrs. MacArthur enjoyed the trip thoroughly, as did Arthur. Due to poor communications, there was no transportation at the airstrip to meet us. It didn't take long to get it, however, and we are now comfortably housed in a Quonset hut set high on a cliff overlooking the placid China Sea. We all had a pleasant dinner tonight and then a long movie afterward.

Gen. Larry Carr was at the airstrip to meet us today. He was my flight instructor at Kelly Field in 1930 and is one fine man. We had much fun in a short time spent in discussing former friends.

Tokyo, Japan, Sept. 19, 1945   2130

Perfect weather, good luck, and God contrived a fine trip for us today. We flew from Okinawa to Tokyo in 4⅔ hours and were not in a cloud through the entire trip. Mrs. MacArthur was more than pleased, and we arrived here at exactly 1330 hours as we planned. General MacArthur had driven out from Tokyo to the airstrip, and the family reunion was an emotional, moving scene. Outside of his work, the general has only one interest in the world and that is his family. It was with a sigh of relief that I delivered them here safely.

The drive into Tokyo was interesting. The strip is about thirty-five miles out, and, except for the farming areas, the devastation along the entire way is complete. Mile after mile of the built-up area along the highway is in complete ruin, and only the metal portions of the houses remain as symbolic headstones of the graveyard of houses. One cannot believe that such complete destruction is possible.

I went directly to the American Embassy, where Doc Egeberg and I have an apartment together. The MacArthurs live in the residence and we have this apartment alongside. This place has long been famous as the showplace of the Far East, and to say that Doc and I are comfortably situated is to put it very mildly. We have separate bedrooms, a living room with fireplace, a dining room, a Japanese man and woman to cook for and care for us, a beautifully landscaped garden in which to stroll, a flag flying overhead, and the MacArthurs to look out for our welfare.

Tokyo, Japan, Sept. 20, 1945   2100

Being quite tired, I slept late this morning. I walked to the office a mile and a half away, and although the cool, fresh air was most stimulating, nevertheless the walk was depressing. The route I took was through a completely burned area, with only a few brick chimneys still standing.

[One young family living on the ground under a few sheets of tin caught my attention. The group consisted of a young couple with two small, handsome children. Although obviously destitute, they were smiling and almost too deferential in the typical Japanese manner. I tried to converse with them but found that impossible. I had some candy bars with me and gave them to the father. He took them with much bowing and scraping. (On a subsequent day I walked past the family again. This time the father saw me approaching, entered the lean-to, and came out with an egg, which he quite ceremoniously gave to me. Instinctively I realized this egg had been most difficult for him to obtain, but I also had been told that to refuse a present offered by a Japanese was an insult, so I accepted it. Thereafter each time I walked by I took two or three cans of army ration. He always accepted these gifts but also always gave me some trinket in return.)]

The office building taken over for the use of GHQ, now called the Dai Ichi ("Number One") Building, is entirely intact, and is indeed modern and convenient. Our offices are on the elaborate side, heavily carpeted and nicely furnished.

I had a long session with General Sutherland relative to plans for replacing the personnel I am losing because of their return to civilian life. I asked him if he expected to remain in Tokyo for any considerable time.

[He replied that General MacArthur had about decided that for the present, at least, he would not work through a chief of staff, but rather through various aides, each of whom would be accountable for a discrete aspect of the occupation task. Sutherland said he wanted to take some leave as soon as things settled down a bit but did not know as yet where he would go. He indicated he might want to do some flying around Japan to gain a better visual impression of the country.

I then went in to see General MacArthur briefly to inquire if he planned to do any flying in the near future. I knew he had received an invitation from President Truman to return to the States to receive his past-due acclaims from a grateful public. He said he expected to be much too busy during the coming weeks to be able to leave Tokyo for very long.]

On the way home from the office tonight I walked around the emperor's palace. As yet we are not allowed to go into the grounds. I walked along the moat which encircles it. It is indeed a magnificent estate. The moat is about 200 feet wide and is literally filled with carp. Once each year, on the emperor's birthday, the social elite are permitted to catch these fish in the moat. They put on their best clothes, including top hats and morning coats, and go fishing. I hope that day occurs while I am still here, as it must be quite a ridiculous sight for a westerner to behold.

Tokyo, Japan, Sept. 21, 1945   2215

A long and interesting day. Early this morning at the office I had a session with General Sutherland. Among other things he told me that whether or not General MacArthur goes back to the States in October, he would like for me to consider the possibilities of flying him back to Washington nonstop in a B-29. Naturally I was thrilled at this prospect, although the chances are ten to one I'll never have the opportunity. The Strategic Air Force has tried several times to make this spectacular flight, but they have always run out of fuel and have had to land short of Washington. I'm sure that if I'm given free rein I can do it.

[General Sutherland has very little to do and he is thoroughly bored doing it. He obviously does not intend to tolerate this inactivity for long. Each day he wants to talk to me more and more. He said that as events are progressing it appears less likely that there will be a suitable place for him in the organization of the United States occupation forces in Japan.]

I went to the Atsugi airstrip later in the morning, and the thirty-five-mile drive required one and a half hours. I found that my crew and airplane were faring well, so I returned to Tokyo in the early afternoon. Late this afternoon I took a five-mile hike, including an inspection tour of the Japanese Diet Building, the home of the prime minister, and a turn along the northwest side of the Imperial Palace. I even fed the royal carp in the royal moat around the palace.

Tokyo, Japan, Sept. 22, 1945   2045

There wasn't too much activity at the office early this morning, so Doc, Jerry, and I drove down to Yokohama on a shopping tour. We found some excellent silk, and I bought 150 yards of it for thirty-four dollars. I also contracted to buy a couple of very fine silk kimonos, which I haven't seen yet.

Back at the office we had a good example of dirty army politics working at its worst. The heads of a couple of our acquaintances figuratively fell on the block, all because they had been a bit too enthusiastic about their new jobs. I certainly don't know what the answer is, but the army hasn't found an entirely satisfactory solution for running its internal affairs.

It rained most of the afternoon, but when I left the office tonight I walked for four miles—almost encircled the emperor's palace. My project for conditioning myself for a return to civilian life is causing many physical creaks and groans. Perhaps fortunately for me, I haven't suffered many mental twists as yet.

Tokyo, Japan, Sept. 23, 1945   2300

In spite of the rain this morning I took the long drive out to Atsugi airstrip to fly the C-54 for an hour. It badly needed excercising. After an hour of trying to see down through rain and clouds I gave it up and landed. Most of my day of course was consumed by the long drive and the flight. I failed to take my usual late-afternoon walk because of the rain.

Tomorrow Doc Egeberg and I are going to set out on a long exploring trip. We will go in a jeep and expect to see Japan much as it was before the war.

Tokyo, Japan, Sept. 24, 1945   2350

At 0500 hours this morning, Doc and I were out of bed and off, after a quick breakfast, to the wilds of Japan. We started off for Kofu, which is on the northwest side of Fujiyama, and we didn't know whether or not we would be able to reach it in a jeep. The weather was perfect, with not a cloud in the sky, and Fujisan served as a landmark all of the way. The roadway was much poorer than we had expected, so that our rate of progress was disappointing. We got off the road a number of times and at the end of two and a half hours had covered less than half the distance.

The countryside was variable but uniformly beautiful. The miniature farms and the small plots of intense timber farming combine to utilize all the land effectively, and at the same time to make a beautiful landscape.

We crawled along through Hachioji, a town of 100,000 which was completely obliterated by firebombing. Then at Uenohara we started through mountainous country, through which the construction of railroads and highways had presented many engineering difficulties. Every mountain stream of any capacity has been harnessed for electric energy, thus making the communications system of the country particularly vulnerable to aerial attack. The railroads and highways frequently go through tunnels or over trestles to continue their precarious ways through the mountains.

At Otsuki we left the last American outpost and went on somewhat apprehensively into Japanese-held territory. The Japs were quite as curious as we were, because most of them had never before seen an American. As we got farther and farther into the country, their attitude of hatred and suspicion increased. At Fujioshida we turned northward around Fujiyama, which by now had become almost entirely concealed by rapidly developing cumulus. We started climbing, and a half hour later finally approached the summit of a ridge, under which we went in a long tunnel. We descended rapidly on a tortuous road into the Kofu Valley and, at length, reached Kofu about 1330 hours. This town of 100,000 population had been attacked in one single raid with 100 B-29s, and it was an example of complete destruction. Only two buildings remained standing in the city, and the chief of police said one thousand people had burned to death. Fear, suspicion, and hatred in the faces of the people was as evident as the ashes of the conflagration. They had been so thoroughly propagandized that they fully expected we would shoot them or loot their few remaining possessions or rape their women. Instead, we called on the chief of police, gave the children cigarettes and chewing gum, and before long had a big following. Kofu is the center of manufacture of some of the finest crystal in the world, so we were able to obtain a few crystal carvings which had been salvaged from the fire. The people expected us to rob them of it, but instead we paid fair prices to them.

We departed at about 1500 hours and started the long drive back. At the summit of the mountain pass we stopped at a teahouse and refreshed ourselves with army ration and Japanese tea. We made quite a hit with a family by giving the children bits from the ration. While we were having our tea, Fujiyama broke out of the clouds, and we had a most inspiring view of this beautiful peak.

We traveled on as rapidly as possible in order to get out of the mountainous terrain before dark. At Uenohara we stopped to call on the American garrison and to try to replenish our dwindling fuel supply. We asked where we could get some food, and the garrison commander, Lieutenant Webb suggested we go with him to the geisha house, the only place in town where food could be purchased. This proved to be a unique experience, and one which I wouldn't have missed for anything. We went into the dimly lit paper house and were ushered upstairs into a private room (shoes off, of course), where we made ourselves as comfortable as it is possible for an American to be while sitting on the floor. Soon three most homely girls came in, dressed in their native kimonos. They served us hot sake and tea and tried to be entertaining. After a time the local police chief and two of his friends came in uninvited. They had heard some high-ranking Americans were there, so had proceeded to get half drunk and had issued their own invitation to our party. We at first tried to be courteous to them, but soon they tried to become familiar with us. Thereupon, through our interpreter, we asked them to depart, as we were having a business conference with Lieutenant Webb. They refused and began to behave belligerently, so I quietly strapped on my pistol, called their attention to it, and again asked that they leave. Still they tried to refuse, so Doc and I took them by the seats of their pants and literally threw them out. Of course they immediately lost face in front of all the other Japs there, and within a very few minutes they sent word back that they would like to be permitted to apologize. We refused to see them, so they sent us presents of sugar and meat, items almost nonexistent in Japan. We were not bothered by them again and we issued orders that the police chief be relieved of his office and humiliated in the town. It's these petty government officials who have so much power who may cause us trouble.

The geisha girls brought out the charcoal stove and prepared our dinner of sukiyaki on the floor in front of us. The taste was excellent, but probably the food was not too clean. At any rate, we ate it, and then the girls brought out their long, inharmonious musical instruments and proceeded to sing those famously unusual songs. We endured those for about half an hour, then departed. It required two hours to drive back to Tokyo through Tachikawa. It has undoubtedly been one of the most varied and interesting days I've spent.

Tokyo, Japan, Sept. 25, 1945   2300

I hadn't been missed at the office yesterday, and there wasn't much to be done today. I did some correspondence, then went for two long walks around the Meiji Shrine and on an inspection tour of Frank Lloyd Wright's famous Imperial Hotel, which withstood the great earthquake in 1923. Tonight I was able to purchase a very fine kimono for Grace at a reasonable price.

Tokyo, Japan, Sept. 26, 1945   1930

Our long-delayed mail started coming in today. I got six letters. Two of them were from Grace and were rather old. I spent part of the day at the office in writing letters, since there was little else to do. I took two long hikes.

Tokyo, Japan, Sept. 27, 1945   2200

Up early this morning and away to Yokohama to do some trading for silk, and then on to Atsugi for a test and exploration flight in the C-54. We went up to Nikko, about 100 miles north of Tokyo and well back in the mountains. This is the religious center of Japan and contains the finest shrine. The town is located under a beautiful lake and at the base of a most symmetric volcanic mountain. Here is the place where all who can afford to do so go to meditate and to study. Here certain chosen children are schooled to carry on the culture and ideals of the Japanese, and in recent generations the area has served military clique as a school for superspies. There is also a huge copper smelting plant which utilizes the waterpower provided by the lake. It was a most interesting trip, and one which I now wish to take by jeep.

Was thinking today that I'm not really living on foreign soil. The American Embassy is actually American territory located in a foreign country.

Today Emperor Hirohito called on General MacArthur. I could have witnessed it had not my duties required my presence elsewhere. Doc Egeberg was there. He and Mrs. MacArthur hid behind the draperies in the balcony and watched. He said it was a moving scene indeed. In 2,500 years it was the first time the Japanese ruler had called on a foreigner, and Hirohito was properly humiliated that he was the one who had to break this tradition. He talked with General MacArthur for about thirty minutes.

Tokyo, Japan, Sept. 28, 1945   2300

It has been a dull, rainy day here today. I remained rather close to the office all day, and nothing very interesting happened there. There was no mail, and no interesting people came in.

Above left: At Okinawa General Larry Carr welcomes Arthur and Mrs. Mac-Arthur. *Above right:* Mrs. MacArthur, myself, Arthur, and his tutor Mrs. Gibbons prior to takeoff for Japan. *Below:* Emperor Hirohito calls on General MacArthur at the American Embassy in Tokyo. Courtesy U.S. Army.

Tokyo, Japan, Sept. 29, 1945   2030

Went to Atsugi early this morning to see Colonel Holmes of the ATC on airplane business. I reached there after driving one and a half hours, only to discover that Colonel Holmes and Colonel Langdon had driven into Tokyo to see me. So I rushed back in time to intercept them at the office. They came out to the embassy with me for lunch, and we got most of our business transacted at that time. A few more days and most of my problems will have been solved.

No mail today. I've had mail on only one day since returning from Manila. I'm very anxious to hear how Grace and those boys are thriving.

Tokyo, Japan, Sept. 30, 1945   2215

This day marks the end of the next to the last full month I expect to spend overseas. I've reached the stage now where I'm really counting off the days as they go by.

It's been a full day for me. After an hour at the office, I had to undertake another long trip to Atsugi on business. While there I decided to exercise the C-54, so Major Skov and I went up to pick out a better location for a "Cub" airplane strip.

I said good-bye to Generals Kenney and Wurtsmith, who are going back to the States. I'm always torn between happiness for them and sadness for myself when I see my many acquaintances going out of my life one by one.

New replacements are showing up daily, and GHQ is changing its character rapidly.

[It is still a place where decisions are made, but now the Japanese government is increasingly being held accountable for planning the implementation of these decisions. There no longer is the intricate, frantic planning, so necessary and complex, that once was required for coordination and deployment of large and diverse military units. Many more civilian advisors with economic, legal, and political expertise are being substituted for military personnel.]

Tokyo, Japan, Oct. 1, 1945   2230

[This has been a thoroughly fine day. Roger Egeberg, Major Anderton, and I took a jeep tour down the coast as far as Miyanoshita. We drove through Yokohama to Kamakura, where we visited the shrines. This city was one of the seats of Japanese culture during the time of the expansion of Buddhism. Early in the thirteenth century they erected here a cast bronze likeness of Buddha, which, considering the engineering difficulties involved at that time, was a marvelous accomplishment. The figure is about forty feet high and is estimated to weigh around one hundred tons. The intricate details of the face, hands, and features in general are remarkable, extending even to the many snails that crowded onto Buddha's brow to cool his head while he sat meditating in the sun. How the early Japanese molded these parts so perfectly and then managed to assemble the heavy sections is indeed a subject for conjecture.

We also visited the shrine of the god of war, who certainly must have lost face in recent months.

We then drove through Odawara to Miyanoshita, where one of the finest tourist hotels in Japan is located. It is set well back in a beautiful mountain area, with all the amenities of a modern hotel but with the added elements of oriental charm. A mountain stream flows through the building, forming numerous basins in which carp are raised. One of the fish was said to be over a hundred years old. Above the hotel are located a swimming pool and tennis courts. A number of foreign internees are billeted here pending possible indictments as war criminals. There are German, Filipino, Italian, and various Asiatic nationals, including both men and women. Among others we saw Pu Yi and his beautiful Mongolian wife, who had occupied the Japanese puppet throne of Manchuria. Their current environment is luxurious, but their future is cloudy.

We drove directly back to Tokyo and arrived in time for a late dinner at the embassy.]

Tokyo, Japan, Oct. 2, 1945   2115

It's been a dull and rainy day today so I haven't been too active. In fact, I remained in the office all day except for such time as was required to visit a very fine exhibit of Japanese art. I saw some of the most exquisite things I've ever been privileged to examine.

Tonight there was an excited and exiting letter from Gracie about building a house. It seems that she has a scheme suggested by a contractor she met, and it sounds too good to be true.

Tokyo, Japan, Oct. 3, 1945   2115

I made the long trek to Atsugi this morning to fly the C-54 for an hour. The weather wasn't good, but still not too bad. Had a long dull afternoon in the office, but came home early because I'd had no lunch. Then before dinner tonight Doc Egeberg and I called on Mrs. MacArthur to have a long visit. She showed me through the residency, and it was indeed a privilege to see the place and all its exquisite oriental furnishings. Many of them are really museum pieces, and most are the property of former ambassador Grew.

Tokyo, Japan, Oct. 4, 1945   2145

This was a day for the records. Doc and I were up at 0400 hours, prepared our own breakfast, and were off for Atsugi airstrip for an early take-off for Osaka. We cleared at 0700 hours in weather which did not appear too promising, but the meteorologist assured us it would clear by noon. We planned to land at Osaka and beat our way into Kyoto, thirty-five miles away, and spend enough time to see this ancient Japanese capital. Shortly after takeoff I suspected that something was wrong, because we were flying on instruments almost constantly. However, I continued on, and finally over Osaka there was a rift in the clouds. I tried to spiral down, but at length abandoned my plans to land when the visibility became so restricted that I could hardly see the ground from a few hundred feet. There were no radio navigational aids there. Still, unsuspectingly, I returned to Atsugi, only to discover that the field was completely closed in. I remained aloft over an hour in the vicinity, during which time I made six attempts at an instrument landing. At length I gave up and went to a nearby auxiliary field. As I was making a final approach there, that field closed in. Then I decided I had better get on the ground before it was too late, so I went to the Yokosuka Naval Base and landed in a forty-mile crosswind. There we learned for the first time that an unsuspected typhoon had suddenly struck the south coast of Japan, and that the bad weather would continue for a couple of days.

We are now in the midst of the worst typhoon of the season. So we had a fruitless day, yet one which everyone accepted as a new and different experience. Perhaps it was not wasted. Some other day we shall go to Kyoto.

Tokyo, Japan, Oct. 5, 1945   2200

Caught in the clutches of the typhoon, we have had continuous rain for the past twenty-four hours. I haven't thrust my head out of doors except to travel back and forth to the office. Still at this late hour the rain comes down in sheets, although there are now some rifts in the clouds.

There wasn't much excitement at the office today except for that created by the resignation of the Japanese cabinet. No one quite expected that to happen, although the order releasing all Japanese political prisoners was expected to create lesser repercussions. Late this afternoon former foreign minister Yoshida called on the general. I don't know just what was discussed during the conference, but when Yoshida departed he was most distressed. He must have been considering either creating a new cabinet or committing hara-kiri. I heard General MacArthur tell General Sutherland that perhaps one or two more cabinets had to fall before things ran smoothly, and that he hoped that the Japanese would save Prince Kanoye to form the last and permanent cabinet.

[Those few of us remaining from the old GHQ organization are becoming restive. There is little for us to do and no great urgency about the few things we do accomplish. Most of us have skills that were not only useful but highly essential in the war effort, and we felt we were needed then. But these same skills are certainly not so important to the less exciting or demanding chores of the occupational forces. And there is no sense of accomplishment derived from the few useful things we do. The making of a democracy out of an autocracy is an almost imperceptible, tedious process. Perhaps General MacArthur can detect some progress, but most of us cannot.]

Tokyo, Japan, Oct. 6, 1945   2015

The typhoon blew itself out during the night, and this morning the weather was clear and cold. I was stuck in the office all day, and this morning General Sutherland handed me a job which will require considerable time. I am to design the radio aids to navigation for the Tokyo area and choose appropriate ground locations for the radio ranges, etc. Colonel Rocky will work with me.

Early tomorrow Roger Egeberg, John Anderton, and I are starting out for Nikko in a jeep.

The typhoon has again interrupted our mail service. Have had no word from home now for several days.

Tokyo, Japan, Oct. 7, 1945   2100

We were up at 0400 hours again this morning and off before daylight to Nikko. The morning air was really cold, and we drove in a jeep with the top down. For the first time in a very long time I was quite numbed by the cold, a feeling which in Manila I had despaired of ever again experiencing. The highway for the first few miles out of Tokyo was excellent, and we were lulled into a false expectancy of continued comfort. After the first hour we were rudely jolted from this viewpoint by the abrupt deterioration of the road into an improved cow path. We kept on doggedly, however, and at Kanuma we entered the famous Avenue of Pines, which were planted along this road to Nikko by the builders of the great shrine of Tokugawa some 320 years ago. The trees are cryptomeria cedars and are beautiful specimens.

This cedar-lined highway extended about twenty miles to Nikko, and at times these splendid trees were so closely spaced that the double line of them made the highway quite gloomy. At about 0830 hours we reached Nikko, drove on through the town, and stopped at the Kanaya Hotel. Here we obtained hot water, provided our own K rations, and had a warming breakfast.

We obtained a guide and started on our tour of the shrines, of which there are about twenty in this one region. Although these are magnificent structures and contain the most intricate bits of carving and decorating, the physical condition of the edifices has suffered during the war years from a lack of maintenance.

The most elaborate shrine was built over 300 years ago by the grandson of Tokugawa for his grandfather, who was the first of the great Shoguns. Details of the shrine are of course common knowledge, but, elaborate as it is, to me it appears to lack something. The wooded setting is ideal, yet the overall effect is not too impressive. To me it seems that the tremendous efforts of 10,000 men working for twelve years to create the finest shrine of its type in the world have fallen short of their mark because of the lack of a central theme in the Shinto religion. There are literally hundreds of gods, and ancestor worship is the motivating force, but the shrines are built to any one of numerous gods. Buddha enters the religious picture to a considerable extent, yet no one can quite explain the exact role.

The Shinto torii is to my way of thinking architecturally beautiful, with its leaning pillars and its delicately curved crossbar. I like it much better than the Buddhist torii. It was most interesting to see the original scroll, carved on one of the buildings, depicting the now famous three monkeys of "see no evil, hear no evil, speak no evil," as well as the historic carved cat of Nikko, which was created by a famous artist with his left hand only, after his rival, fearing competition, had cut off his right hand.

The sheer top-heaviness of the shrine buildings detracts somewhat from their detail. This tends to give them an atmosphere of impermanence. The famous gateway of Yomeimon is a delicate showpiece, and the five-storied pagoda is as colorful and graceful as one might guess from its picture.

Tired from much walking, we returned to the hotel and had a late lunch. We had intended to drive on up to the lake, but the clouds had descended to obscure the mountains and to release a drizzling rain, so we dismissed the idea. We went shopping instead and purchased some interesting small items. At 1545 we started back to Tokyo, where we arrived at 1930 hours, tired but happy after a full day.

After having seen another phase of Japanese life today, I have formulated some conclusions regarding my overall concept of these strange people. Mentally and physically they are dignified, unsophisticated, ceremonious little people who occasionally have visions of grandeur but who usually fail to grasp the larger picture because of mental myopia. They are patient perfectionists of detail but hopelessly inadequate architects. They can see and they can do but they cannot perceive. In all their life, as in their religion, they have many gods but no God.

Tokyo, Japan, Oct. 8, 1945   2230

All day it has rained, and the wind has kicked up at a great rate. Another typhoon passed to the west of us, and although I expected to do some flying, that proved to be out of the question. I remained at the office all day.

Tokyo, Japan, Oct. 9, 1945   2300

One typhoon passed and another is on its way. In spite of a high wind and low, scurrying clouds, I flew for a couple of hours this morning in a C-47. Colonel Rocky and I made a survey of the Tokyo area for a layout of navigational aids to flying. The crew became ill from the extremely rough air, but we completed our mission in the roughest of flying conditions. The final plan encompasses radio ranges at Kisarazu, Atsugi, and Haneda, and various other miscellaneous facilities. Flying weather here is the worst we have had in this theater, and the lack of radio facilities is going to cause delays and losses which we are not conditioned to accept at this late stage. Consequently the great need for speed in getting the installations completed.

Tokyo, Japan, Oct. 10, 1945   2230

Rain, rain, rain. I traveled only between the American Embassy and the office today, and then merely because I had to do so. The typoon shows no signs of abating so we shall have to endure it.

I've accomplished little of value today. Things are quiet here while the Japs are forming a new cabinet. We had a short flurry of excitement this afternoon when the released Japanese political prisoners, whom we set free a few days ago, staged a political parade in the driving rain. It was the first free political demonstration in Japan in fifteen years, and it finally concluded with one tremendous shout of "Banzai MacArthur!" The pitiful people have been mistreated for so long that now they don't know how to behave.

Tokyo, Japan, Oct. 11, 1945   2200

The typhoon raged today until 1600 hours and then blew itself out. In spite of it I went shopping this morning and bought a couple of pieces of beautiful lacquer.

Today I became eligible for a rating as command pilot and General Sutherland sent in a radio request for it. That means the completion of fifteen years as a rated army pilot.

Tokyo, Japan, Oct. 12, 1945   2350

Bill Hogan and I staged a farewell party for Roger Egeberg tonight. About twenty of our choice acquaintances came, and even if I do say so myself, it was one of the nicest parties. Everyone got nicely high, the food was excellent, the songs were good, and the party broke up at a reasonable hour. Roger's replacement, Colonel Kendrick, arrived at a most appropriate time, just as the party was at its height.

The earlier part of the day was routine, with fine, crisp autumn weather which should bring us airplanes and mail. I was at the office all day.

[I sent a dispatch to the Air Transport Command in Washington asking for a replacement for me, to arrive in Tokyo by November 15 if possible. The job specification was quite restrictive, and I showed it to General MacArthur to see if such an individual would meet his desires. He inquired as to whether I could remain longer. I told him I believed my duty now lay with my family. He agreed.]

Vic Skov arrived from Manila with the B-17 and just before I left the office General Sutherland called me in to his office.

[He said he wanted me to take him to Australia in a B-17 about October 14, to be there for two weeks of rest and recreation. I tried to persuade him that Major Skov should be his pilot rather than I, but he would not agree. It is springtime in Australia, and although I will have nothing useful to do there, it can be a pleasant interlude. It is patently obvious to me that General Sutherland's primary motive in going to Australia is to renew his relationship with the WAC captain, who doubtless by now has returned to civilian life. It is also becoming obvious that he and General MacArthur are on the verge of severing their long military association. Of course MacArthur also is aware of the real reason for the trip, but Sutherland has earned some vacation time.]

Tokyo, Japan, Oct. 13, 1945   2200

Early this morning I was up and away to Tachikawa to ferry the B-17 over to Atsugi airstrip. Major Skov was given wrong advice and landed at Tachikawa last night instead of Atsugi. The field was very soft and congested, and I got the airplane stuck in the mud. It was 1500 hours before I got to Atsugi, and there were many minor faults with the airplane that had to be corrected. I hope now that all will be in readiness for the take-off for Guam tomorrow.

[When I returned to the apartment, a delegation of enlisted men from the quartermaster was waiting to talk to me. They were highly and justifiably incensed that one of the officers (so they claimed) attached to General MacArthur's household had been drawing excess supplies for the household and selling them on the black market. They mentioned that they had positive proof of their claim and that if this officer was not removed from his post they would prefer charges through channels. This was a most serious matter. I conferred with Roger Egeberg and we agreed we had better persuade this offender to depart immediately to avoid any adverse publicity that could reflect unfavorably on the MacArthur family. It fell to my lot to be the "tough guy" at the confrontation. The officer, although not directly admitting his guilt, said, "Everybody is doing it." (This certainly was not true. He agreed to leave the following day for the States. Mrs. MacArthur was startled by his sudden departure, and although she kept inquiring of us why he had gone so suddenly we did not tell her the real reason.)]

22

The Final Days

Guam, Mariana Islands, Oct. 14, 1945   2200

I was up early in Tokyo this morning, and drove out to Haneda airfield, a small field about eight miles from the embassy. There Capt. "Whisky" Still flew *CXE* up to pick me up and take me to Atsugi. This saved a two-hour drive over an all but impassable road. A little later he again flew to Haneda to get General Sutherland, and we took off from Atsugi about 1000 hours for Guam. We arrived here well after dark, and there was much work to do in order to get the B-17 ready for a continuation of our trip tomorrow.

I'm billeted with ATC, but there remain here none of the personnel I know. UAL no longer operates beyond Honolulu, and all of the military I once knew are either back in the States or out of the army. We plan to depart at 1400 hours tomorrow.

Los Negros, Admiralty Islands, Oct. 15, 1945   2115

It was a hectic morning at Guam, trying to complete all the necessary work on the airplane. The war is over, discipline has collapsed, and the only interest the men have is in getting home. Consequently, it is most difficult to get anyone to follow through on a task. At length we got away at 1500 hours and arrived here a few minutes ago. We are refueling and expect to be on our way shortly. The navy is taking good care of us.

Brisbane, Australia, Oct. 16, 1945   2030

A year ago I brought General MacArthur through here on the way to Canberra to bid farewell to Prime Minister Curtin. Then we stopped off here for several days while he took leave with Mrs. MacArthur and Arthur before we proceeded on to Hollandia to plunge into the Leyte landing and on into the Philippine campaign. At that time I thought that would be the last time I'd see Australia. However, I returned again last January with General Sutherland and now I'm here again. Certainly this will be my last trip, at least during this war.

The trip down was long and tiring, and I was weary in every bone. Flew twenty-five hours in the last forty-eight and I guess I'm getting too old for much of that.

I'll write a note to my long-neglected Gracie, listen for a while to the softly falling rain, then throw myself back into the care of Morpheus.

Brisbane, Australia, Oct. 17, 1945   2230

I slept through until 0700 hours this morning, having slept more than fifteen hours in the past twenty-four. That is a remarkable performance for me, and indicates just how tired I really was. I had a leisurely morning during which I walked the three miles out to Victoria Park, the sole remaining U.S. Army installation in Brisbane.

Brisbane has changed greatly since the Yanks departed. It's a quiet, provincial town now, and not nearly as crowded as formerly. It's a beautiful time of year here, with all the flowers in full bloom and the weather ideal. I'm afraid I'm going to enjoy my forced vacation.

Tonight I had a long talk with my old friend Col. Woody Wilson. He is chief of staff of Base Section here and is busy closing out U.S. interests in Australia. His office is actually in Sydney, but he came up here to meet General Sutherland.

Brisbane, Australia, Oct. 18, 1945   2215

It's been a glorious day here. I took my time about getting out of bed today, and then after a leisurely breakfast drove out to the airport to see how the work was progressing on the B-17. I walked back from there, getting a lot of good exercise and enjoying the scenery along the five-mile journey.

If only I could have Gracie here we could have a wonderful vacation together. As it is, I'm enjoying quite comfortably the passage of time, but I'm getting no particular thrill out of anything. Wonder how much longer General Sutherland will stay here.

Brisbane, Australia, Oct. 19, 1945   2000

It has been another beautiful day but after all a rather dull one. Early this morning I went to the airport to check on the progress of the work on the B-17, and then I took a circuitous walk back to the hotel and covered about eight miles in the process. Now my duties of the day are finished, so I shall lose myself in the intricacies of a detective story.

Brisbane, Australia, Oct. 20, 1945   1915

I was up at 0600 hours this morning and off to the airport to test-fly the B-17. I found it to be in good condition, and then General Sutherland came out at 0900 to fly it locally for one and a half hours. After landing, I walked back into Brisbane and have remained in the hotel the balance of the day as it has been raining.

I hope the general decides to return to Tokyo soon so I can get back into the stream of things again and can get my mail from Gracie. I can only eat so much and sleep so much and walk so much each day, and then there are always many hours left over, which have a way of passing exasperatingly slowly.

Brisbane, Australia, Oct. 21, 1945   2100

I was up at a reasonable time, went to Eagle Farm Airdrome, and flew for two hours with General Sutherland. After landing, I walked the five and a half miles back to the Lennon's Hotel, drinking three thin milkshakes on the way.

Brisbane, Australia, Oct. 22, 1945   1940

The B-17 was being worked on today, so I didn't even have any flying to do. This morning I did some paperwork on a possible pending trip in a B-29 nonstop from Japan to Washington late in December. After all my careful calculations, I believe it is impossible to accomplish safely unless more fuel can be provided, or unless one can be extremely fortunate in regard to winds. I always distrust leaving too much to good fortune.

Brisbane, Australia, Oct. 23, 1945   2015

Flew with General Sutherland for two hours again this morning. Then I came back into town and had lunch with John Anderton's wife. He is an American army major from SF and he asked me to look her up.

Tonight I've spent in my room, reading and dreaming of home. In just about a month I expect to be at home. Some untoward incident could, of course, intervene.

Brisbane, Australia, Oct. 24, 1945   1900

This day was rather much like other recent ones. Flew for two hours with General Sutherland this morning, walked into town, and then saw a movie this afternoon. It was *Gaslight* and rather good, yet most depressing.

I've felt rather depressed today. Been thinking about problems of the world and the stupid way in which we seem to be attempting to solve them. Already the United States has enough atomic bombs to all but de-populate the world of our enemies. A single bomb dropped to explode under the water in San Francisco Bay, it is said, would bury most cities on the perimeter of the bay under fifty feet of water. Yet our great brains at home seem to be crying out for more battleships, compulsory military training, etc. All this so soon after we've just witnessed the surrender of an army of 6 million Japanese, the great majority of whom never even fired one of their archaic weapons at an American nor even saw an Amer-ican to shoot at! And yet we would teach our sons to drill with rifles! The meaning of individual safety and security is a thing which perhaps we will not know again for a long, long time if ever. We certainly shall never again know them if we persist in putting our faith in things ob-solescent. Either we get along with the world or we build a force ready for *the immediate offensive* and so powerful that none can challenge us with any hopes of success. Judging from present progress, we aren't going to get along with the world too well, so we'd better prepare ourselves rap-idly for the other alternative.

Brisbane, Australia, Oct. 25, 1945   2030

This was a day which brought disappointing news. I flew with Gen-eral Sutherland again this morning, and at the end of the flight I went to his apartment and we had a long talk about war, peace, and lesser prob-lems. Then he broke the bad news that probably he would extend his visit here another week. That means we will not depart for Tokyo before November 6.

Brisbane, Australia, Oct. 26, 1945   2045

Flew for two hours with General Sutherland this morning. Lieuten-ant Harding, my navigator, and I decided to play tennis. We found a con-crete court at the officers' club at Eagle Farm and went at it. We played for three hours in the warm sun, and I'm frank to admit that I overdid myself. Tonight I'm a red, creaking old man who has certainly seen better tennis days.

Brisbane, Australia, Oct. 27, 1945 2000

This has been one of the dullest days yet. The aches and pains resulting from yesterday's tennis have had a most dampening effect upon any ambitions of physical activity, although I did take a three-mile limbering-up hike this morning.

Tomorrow we fly locally again, and then possibly on Monday we go to Sydney.

Brisbane, Australia, Oct. 28, 1945 1900

Another unusually dull Sunday in Brisbane. I flew with General Sutherland for a couple of hours this morning and then had my usual five-mile walk into town from the airport. I'm still quite stiff from my tennis contest of two days ago.

The local newspapers are filled with ominous news of happenings in America. According to them, inflation is now rampant, and the country is generally in a state of great disturbance. How I wish the next month would pass so that I could get back home, where I could see after the welfare of my family and my business affairs!

Brisbane, Australia, Oct. 29, 1945 2200

Late last evening General Sutherland telephoned to say that he was sending some mail to my room, as it had been forwarded along with some official stuff from Tokyo. Imagine my pleasant surprise when, a few minutes later, here arrived ten letters and one radiogram! All but one were from Gracie, so I stayed up hours reading and rereading them to be sure that I hadn't missed any single shred of information about things at home. The last letter was written on October 7, but the radiogram was sent on October 11. Thus my latest news isn't at all recent, but it makes me feel infinitely better.

Today has been more of the usual routine here. Flew with General Sutherland for a couple of hours this morning and then played tennis until my sunburn drove me from the courts.

Brisbane, Australia, Oct. 30, 1945 2215

This day's schedule has followed my usual routine very closely. Up early as is customary, and off to the airport to fly for a couple of hours with General Sutherland. One would think that at last he might grow tired of flying round and round, up and down, day in and day out.

I walked into town, had a quiet afternoon, then dinner. Tomorrow is

484   FLYING MacARTHUR TO VICTORY

my birthday, I'm sick of idleness, and those are all of my thoughts at present.

Brisbane, Australia, Oct. 31, 1945   2015

Today I have reached the good age of thirty-nine years. About the first half of my life has passed. It has been a good half, and regrets and remorse for any part of it occupy no place in my curriculum. Wonder if the last half will be as good and as interesting. I face it with much optimism, because I'm now well able to assess the true values of most of the elements which go into living. There may be many changes to be faced and dealt with, but I'm sure that with the fine guidance and understanding which Grace will provide, we'll get along.

Jimmy probably had a birthday party today. Next year we'll have one together. I've done no celebrating—in fact my day has been decidedly routine. Flew for over two hours with General Sutherland and then played four fine sets of tennis with Lieutenant Harding. I beat him easily, which pleased me greatly, because he had beaten me badly during our last match.

Brisbane, Australia, Nov. 1, 1945   2000

This day was routine—in fact, depressingly routine. Was up early as usual and flew two hours with General Sutherland, and then I played four sets of poor tennis.

This afternoon I placed a trans-Pacific telephone call to Gracie, and it is estimated that I'll get the connection through about noon tomorrow. It will be a thrill indeed to hear her voice once more. Have nothing important about which to talk, but it will be most reassuring to know that she and the boys are all right. As a matter of record, the cost is $4.10 per minute.

Brisbane, Australia, Nov. 2, 1945   2000

The highlight of today of course was my telephone conversation with Gracie. Her voice came through quite distinctly and it was indeed a thrill to hear her once more. She reassured me that everything at home was running smoothly, and all were anxiously awaiting my return. Time was so limited that we couldn't exchange many thoughts. She told me one bit of interesting and tantalizing news. It seems that a number of the airline pilots on United have gotten together on an idea of starting an airline in Japan. They have written letters to me in Tokyo and are sending someone there to see me about using my influence to obtain a franchise for airline operation in Japan. Naturally I don't possess enough facts to consider the proposition seriously. I have no idea whether General Mac-Arthur will consider allowing ordinary U.S. commercial companies to come into Japan at present. If he does, then I have an idea that I may have a fair chance of doing something for these boys. They are, apparently, offering me a share in the enterprise, but I don't know whether or not that means I would be expected to remain in Japan to operate the company. I'll feel out General Sutherland on the idea in the next few days, and he can give me details of the general policy. We shall see—

This morning I flew as usual with General Sutherland. Afterward I returned to town to receive my telephone call from Gracie, sent some official radiograms to Tokyo, got a haircut, and then started taking life easy. Haven't bothered to go down for dinner tonight.

Brisbane, Australia, Nov. 3, 1945   2000

No flying today.

This afternoon and evening I've been most un-busy. I haven't left my room, in fact. Have been reading since this afternoon, so there's nothing about which to write. I'll have to admit I've been considering the idea of starting an airline in Japan since Grace planted the seed in my mind. My reactions to the idea are mixed. I'm going to fly with General Sutherland tomorrow morning so I shall discuss the idea with him.

Brisbane, Australia, Nov. 4, 1945   1900

An ordinary, dull Sunday in Australia. Flew with General Sutherland this morning for a couple of hours, during which I discussed the possible formation of an airline in Japan. He was somewhat noncommittal, but seemed to think it would be a good idea. He says the military government will not permit Japan to own or operate aircraft of any type for any purpose, and that some type of American air service could and should be inaugurated soon.

General Sutherland invited me to his apartment for dinner tonight.

[(He was in an expansive mood and launched forth into some interesting sidelights and behind-the-scenes aspects of recent world events. For example, it was generally conceded at the highest level at GHQ that the Japanese would have surrendered in another six weeks or so, even without the use of the atomic bomb. At the same time it was known that Russia had definite plans to keep right on advancing in eastern Asia, once she had decided to declare war on Japan. Then she might have an opportunity to fulfill her long-standing dream of a practical, ice-free port on the Pacific Ocean. There was no one to effectively challenge her—no one to stop her. But when we dropped the perhaps (controversial) unnecessary atomic bomb, it accomplished two purposes, the second of which may have been the more important of the two. It hastened Japan's decision to surrender but it also forced Russia to stop and reconsider. Whereas before that event no enemy could challenge her ambitions to advance in Asia, here suddenly appeared a weapon of unpredictable potential and the least she could do was to sit up and take notice, reassessing her plans. So, those who even now condemn our use of the bomb to shorten the war and who say it would have been better never to have used the bomb must also answer another question. Would it have been better for the world if a ruthless, aggressive, ambitious Russia, without any real opposition, had been allowed to overrun Manchuria, Korea, and as much of China as she chose and at her own pace?)]

Brisbane, Australia, Nov. 5, 1945   1900

Some maintenance work to be done on the B-17 this morning prevented General Sutherland from flying as is customary. So Harding, Shoemaker, and I got a car and drove to Southport. First we visited the small zoo at Surfer's Paradise, where I saw my first Tasmanian wombat. Then we went to the beach and battled the breakers and baked in the sun for about four hours.

Brisbane, Australia, Nov. 6, 1945   1900

Another day without a single highlight. This morning I flew with General Sutherland for a couple of hours, during which time we went out over west Queensland to see what the sheep station country looked like.

Each day that passes I become a little more anxious to get back to Tokyo, even though I've resigned myself to another full week here. My biggest worry right now is that General MacArthur will grow disgusted with General Sutherland and relieve him of his job of chief of staff.

Brisbane, Australia, Nov. 7, 1945   2000

The only difference between today and most of the other days we've spent here is that the weather was much hotter. The routine of the day was exactly the same. I flew two hours with the general, took a sunbath for one and a half hours, then walked the five miles in to town.

In talking to General Sutherland this morning, he dropped a hint that he might extend his leave here to forty-five days, meaning we wouldn't go back until near December 1. If he does that, I think I'll go nuts or hand in my resignation. Certainly it will upset all my personal plans, yet I'm entirely helpless to do anything about it if he so decides.

Brisbane, Australia, Nov. 8, 1945   1900

Today has been routine except for the information I received from General Sutherland. I flew with him a couple of hours this morning and during the flight he told me that we would be going to Sydney and Melbourne on Saturday, returning here on Sunday, and departing for Biak and Manila on Tuesday, November 13. This was indeed good news for me. I have so much to do in Tokyo upon my return there. Also General Sutherland told me he hoped to change my insignia from silver leaves to eagles at Manila if it was still legally possible to do so. Naturally I'm hoping my luck still lasts for the next few days.

Brisbane, Australia, Nov. 9, 1945   1900

We flew as usual this morning and then I walked into town. Plans are complete for our trip to Sydney and Melbourne. The only change now is that we will depart for Manila and Tokyo on November 14 instead of November 13. Also we will stay a day in Manila, thus arriving in Tokyo about November 17. Prospects of being home for Thanksgiving are fading rapidly, but Christmas is a sure bet.

Melbourne, Australia, Nov. 10, 1945   1930

We departed from Brisbane at 0745 hours this morning and landed at Sydney two and a half hours later. We remained there only long enough to clear for Melbourne, and then came here through some nasty weather.

Tomorrow we will depart at 0830 hours for Brisbane, with a stop at Sydney for the purpose of returning Colonel Wilson to his base.

Brisbane, Australia, Nov. 11, 1945   1900

It was a rough, nasty, uncomfortable trip we had back from Melbourne today. It was cold and rainy at Melbourne, and after I was all ready to go, General Sutherland decided he would come directly to Brisbane without stopping at Sydney. I felt that I had enough fuel to do this, but after we were aloft an hour and encountered strong winds, it appeared that we might run dangerously low on gas. So I stopped in at Sydney anyway. Almost all the way from Sydney to Brisbane we were in a "front," and there was much rain, ice, and turbulence. Everyone was airsick except General Sutherland and me. At length we arrived here in midafternoon.

A package of mail which had been forwarded to me from Tokyo was here in Brisbane, but I was unable to locate it until a few minutes ago.

Now I'm head over heels opening all of my fifteen letters, most of them from Grace.

Brisbane, Australia, Nov. 12, 1945   2200

I read and reread my letters until a late hour last night and had much fun daydreaming. Then I got up this morning in a leisurely style and went to the airport, after which I played five sets of poor tennis. All of the time, however, I felt quite elated over the prospects of a quick return to Tokyo, then a trip to the States and a release from the army. However, any such illusions I had were rudely shattered this afternoon when General Sutherland told me we would not be departing for Tokyo before this weekend (November 17) at the earliest. He went to the doctor this morning for a physical exam for his promotion to permanent brigadier general (on the regular promotion list) and his blood pressure was above 200. So he is now under observation and cannot travel at least for a few days. Now once more my plans are all upset. I can't return home until I get back to Tokyo and I can't get back to Tokyo until he decides to go. Really I'm a jailbird, even though I may be free to move about in Australia. I'm sick of the whole deal. The real reason why we do not return is most evident to me, yet just now I don't dare write the whole truth. The high-level dispute which I've so long feared would come to a head between Generals MacArthur and Sutherland has at last erupted, and I'm caught between the two.

In one of her letters, Grace gave a bare outline of the proposal for the establishment of an airline in Japan. Unless there's more behind the proposition than she indicates, I'm afraid it doesn't sound too promising.

Brisbane, Australia, Nov. 13, 1945   2000

I've suffered from a depressing feeling of frustration today. I so much want to get started home, yet am powerless to do anything except to sit here and wait. It's like having a foe to fight and not being able to get to him.

Went to the airport this morning and canceled all plans for a departure tomorrow.

Brisbane, Australia, Nov. 14, 1945   1945

This idle, useless day has done absolutely nothing to bolster my flagging morale. General Sutherland was much too scared and considerate of his flare-up in blood pressure to want to fly today. So I went to the airport anyway. I walked into town this afternoon, and then did nothing more interesting than read *Reader's Digest*. I haven't talked to General Sutherland today, so I haven't received any word of any new "tentative" plans. I still have hopes that we may depart for Tokyo this weekend but I wouldn't risk a bet on it.

Brisbane, Australia, Nov. 15, 1945 2030

Last night after I was well in bed, General Sutherland telephoned to inform me that I was then a full-fledged colonel in the army. It was the one piece of news I most wanted to hear, and he had received it through a radiogram from Tokyo. I didn't do any celebrating, but I did get up and replace the oak leaves on my uniform with the eagles which I had purchased for the event. So now the army has done about everything for me which it can do. I am a colonel and a command pilot, and I can't hope for more, because that's as high as I can go. The next promotion is to civilian. Whoopee!

I flew for an hour with the general early this morning. He wished to see whether or not flying affected his already-high blood pressure. I sent a cablegram to Gracie, telling her of my promotion and giving her instructions relative to preparation for our vacation when I arrive home. The general said that probably we would leave for Tokyo about November 21, so based on that estimate I predict that I will be able to arrive in San Francisco about December 5.

Brisbane, Australia, Nov. 16, 1945 1915

There was no flying today, and since it was a cloudy, threatening day, I didn't even go to the airport for my usual sunbath.

I've resigned myself to the cruel punishment of fate. I'll simply have to remain here until General Sutherland is ready to return to Tokyo. I derive some satisfaction from my promotion, which I no longer have to "sweat out" and which is no longer dependent upon congeniality between Generals MacArthur and Sutherland.

Brisbane, Australia, Nov. 17, 1945 2015

Another cloudy, rainy, useless day. I'm completely convinced that I'll never want to retire voluntarily. Trying to make time pass without having any work to take up a part of it is indeed a difficult task.

No flying today, but I went out to the airport this morning in order to walk back to town and get some exercise. I got rained on in the process.

Brisbane, Australia, Nov. 18, 1945   2230

I forgot to obtain a sufficient supply of reading material to occupy my-self all weekend, so on this dull Sunday I've had to twiddle my thumbs much of the day. One can't buy even a magazine here on Sundays.

I did go to the airport as usual and then walk back to town. It was a bit too cloudy for good sunbathing.

I had arranged for a car to take us down to the beach at Southport to-morrow, and just now the general called to say he would fly tomorrow morning. Consequently, I've had to call off the trip. I pray that tomorrow I'll get the good news that we are leaving for Tokyo Wednesday.

Brisbane, Australia, Nov. 19, 1945   1930

Today hasn't been an auspicious day for me. I had to cancel the flight of General Sutherland because of oil pressure troubles on two of the engines.

It has been a cloudy, sultry day, and tonight it's raining. Perhaps General Sutherland will not want to fly tomorrow. Wistful thinking, no doubt.

Brisbane, Australia, Nov. 20, 1945   2300

Last night, after I was in bed, General Sutherland called to say he would like for me to come to his apartment. I dressed hurriedly and went there, to find him all prepared, with elaborate lighting arrangements, to take some photographs of me. I posed for a number of shots. He told me he would like to fly this morning.

In spite of the drizzling rain and low ceilings, we spent almost two hours aloft. Didn't make my usual walk into town because I was thor-oughly angry and disgusted. The general had just told me that we wouldn't depart for Tokyo before the first of next week. Right now I'm so depressed I don't care much what happens.

Brisbane, Australia, Nov. 21, 1945   1930

Flew with the general again and had a long discussion with him. He said definitely that he would return to Tokyo not later than November 27. Then he said that it was more than probable that he would go back to the States after spending only a week in Tokyo, and that if it was pos-sible to do so he would borrow General MacArthur's C-54 to make the trip. If so, I could fly him back and pick up Grace (illegally) at San Fran-cisco and take her along to Washington. If such a plan doesn't delay me,

I'd much prefer it to simply flying back via ATC. I could take all of my belongings along and wouldn't run the risk of losing any of them. Besides, I'd be sure of getting Grace to the East Coast with a minimum of delay, and she would enjoy the nonstop trip across the United States. All of this is tentative, of course, but I've written Grace to be prepared for anything.

Brisbane, Australia, Nov. 22, 1945   1915

It was a usual Brisbane day for me. I flew with General Sutherland this morning, had lunch at Eagle Farm, and then walked into town. General Sutherland reiterated his statement that we would depart for Tokyo not later than Tuesday next.

Brisbane, Australia, Nov. 23, 1945   1915

Nothing new to disclose tonight. Flew with the general this morning, played five sets of tennis with Lieutenant Harding after lunch, and then vegetated.

I've arranged for a car to take myself and all of my crew to Coolongatta to the beach tomorrow.

Brisbane, Australia, Nov. 24, 1945   1930

Our day on the beach could not have been more perfect. We went first to Coolongatta and then back to Southport, and I spent a full three hours playing in the surf and baking in the sun. The other members of the crew tired of it sooner than I, so I remained on the beach while they drove away and had lunch. We returned to Brisbane late this afternoon, and I've luxuriated in my comfortable, air-conditioned room at Lennon's Hotel.

Brisbane, Australia, Nov. 25, 1945   1900

It has been the usual Australian Sunday. Beautiful, clear weather and nothing to do. Except for a thirty-minute walk, I've hardly stirred out of my room. Tried to buy some reading material but was unable to do so. Called General Sutherland to see if he wanted to fly, and he didn't. Then I wrote a letter to Gracie telling her all the latest news, which was exactly none.

Brisbane, Australia, Nov. 26, 1945   1930

Flew with the general this morning, had lunch with Maj. John Anderton and his wife, spent the afternoon in preparing for the trip to Biak to-

492 FLYING MacARTHUR TO VICTORY

morrow, and that is about all. Now everything is in readiness for a departure at 0500 hours.

To bed now, because I must be up at 0300 hours.

Biak Island, Nov. 27, 1945   2015

We left Brisbane at sunrise and got in here after 11¼ hours of good flying. We are now making ready to depart for Manila in a couple of hours.

The trip up couldn't have been better, except we did have a bit of local rain to make our landing here at Biak a bit interesting. It has cleared now, however, and we have had one of the most colorful sunsets I've ever witnessed. This island, which cost many American lives to capture and which once was a beehive of activity, is now practically deserted. Dozens of buildings stand unoccupied, and the jungle is rapidly edging up to the roads and the fine airstrips. In a very few years, I dare say, it will be difficult to find traces of this once tremendous air base. However, if one digs into the vines, he will certainly locate the acres-wide expanses of airplane graveyards where hundreds of torn and twisted hulks of once-proud airplanes now bear mute witness to many past tragedies.

Must be on my way now—to see that all is in readiness for our departure.

Manila, P.I., Nov. 28, 1945   1900

We arrived here at daylight this morning and I'll have to confess that I was just about at the end of my endurance. Twenty hours in the air at one time is just a little too much for the old man.

It is hot and humid and uncomfortable here in Manila, as it always seems to be. It rained most of the afternoon. After getting my crew properly billeted, I had breakfast and then collapsed into bed.

Manila, P.I., Nov. 29, 1945   1900

Late this afternoon, after all preparations had been made for our takeoff for Tokyo early tomorrow morning, General Sutherland informed me that we would delay our departure for twenty-four hours. Sometimes generals can be exasperatingly inconsiderate. It would appear that I never will get back to Tokyo, in spite of the fact that it would be so very easy to do if only I were not stopped at every turn by the general's change in plans. But just about the time I reach the exploding stage, I recall all of the consideration and opportunities he has given me in this war and I can't be angry with him. Especially now that he is a sick man and needs my help and loyalty. Another day wasted here cannot make too much difference to me now anyway.

I sent a long radiogram to Gracie, went to the airport to inspect the work being performed on the airplane, did some shopping at the post exchange and the quartermaster, and then spent the balance of the day in my room. Tomorrow promises to be another long, dull day.

Manila, P.I., Nov. 30, 1945   1900

True enough, it has been a dull day. I went to Nichols Field to see that the necessary work had been completed on the airplane. I couldn't dispose of much of the day this way, so I finally went back to the apartment, where I've vegetated all the remainder of the day. It has been very hot.

The *latest* plan calls for a departure at 0300 hours tomorrow. The weather at Tokyo is not good, but with luck we should be able to get in.

Tokyo, Japan, Dec. 1, 1945   2130

The weather for the trip up turned out to be very good indeed, in spite of early pessimistic predictions. We landed at Okinawa for fuel which we didn't need, then came on to Tokyo. Fujiyama, snow-covered and beautiful, was thrusting itself into the blue sky quite invitingly, so we went alongside to admire it and take some photographs. Upon landing at Atsugi we transferred to a C-47, and Major Skov flew us to Haneda, where staff cars were waiting to drive us to our homes.

I went by the office and was rewarded by ten letters from Gracie. She still awaits patiently my return and everything seems to be progressing well at home. Before long now I'll be seeing her.

It was good to get back home. Although there aren't many people left here whom I know, still the ones who are seemed glad to see me. Even my little Japanese maid, Nakagawa, threw her arms around me and cried. She had thought I had been killed.

The American Embassy is quite as comfortable as ever, in spite of the cool, pleasant weather. I had some drinks and a fine dinner, and now am going to retire early to regain the sleep I lost last night.

Tokyo, Japan, Dec. 2, 1945   2300

It's been a busy day of odd jobs for me. Such things as pay vouchers, per diem vouchers, influenza inoculations, etc., have kept me running all day. Late this afternoon I saw General Sutherland, hoping he had definitely formulated his plans relative to flying back to the States. However, he had not yet talked to General MacArthur concerning his release, so he had no news for me. He did say that he would get me home by Christmas in any case.

Tonight all my officers came out to the embassy to have dinner with me—sort of a farewell party for Vic Skov, who will be leaving for the States in a few days. A very quiet party with drinks and much conversation. Tomorrow I'll start my big job of packing.

Tokyo, Japan, Dec. 3, 1945   2230

I remained in the embassy apartment all morning, separating my belongings into appropriate allotments and packing them for shipment home. I'm afraid I didn't accomplish too much, but at least I got a good start.

At the office this afternoon General Sutherland still could not tell me definitely whether or not I would fly him back to the States. He hasn't approached General MacArthur on the subject yet. Consequently I can't formulate any plans, and I can't predict when I'll be leaving for home.

Tokyo, Japan, Dec. 4, 1945   2130

Most of today I spent in making more preparations for going home. The adjutant general has not kept my records properly, so now I'm spending hours going through my files to bring them up to date.

This afternoon I met with five Japanese men who were high up in airline operations or civil aeronautics here in Japan prior to and during the war. I've ordered them to collate such data as might be useful in case some of us wish to come out here to initiate an airline project of our own. It was interesting to talk with them, but I'm not too sure the information they are going to provide me can be too well translated into terms applicable to the type of operation we would inaugurate.

The highlight of the day was when my replacement reported in. He is Maj. Anthony Story, and he is highly experienced and qualified, so that there is very little I have to do in instructing him to assume my duties here.

Tokyo, Japan, Dec. 5, 1945   2000

The good news for which I'd been waiting finally came this morning. I took Major Story in to introduce him to General Sutherland and General MacArthur. Whereupon General Sutherland announced that we should prepare to depart early next week for the States in General MacArthur's C-54! So I'm sending Skov to Guam tomorrow to have some work done on the airplane, and then he will bring it back here so that we can depart for Manila about December 11. If we spend a little time there, we should still be able to reach San Francisco by December 16, and Washington by December 18. I *do* hope that Grace will be able to find someone to stay with the boys. Then we can take her right on to Washington with us and she will have no transportation difficulties eastbound at least.

I've spent most of the day working on my personnel and pay records. In another day or two I will have reached the point where I can be ready to depart at only a moment's notice.

Tokyo, Japan, Dec. 6, 1945   2000

This hasn't been an entirely satisfactory day. In the first place, Major Skov wasn't able to depart for Guam with the C-54. He made three starts and had to return each time because of trouble with the No. 4 engine. Tonight they are changing a carburetor with the hope that this will correct the difficulty and they will be able to depart early tomorrow morning. At best our trip to the States will now be delayed a day because of this.

Tokyo, Japan, Dec. 7, 1945   1930

I was up early this morning and off on the two-hour drive to Atsugi to do some flying in a C-47. I wanted to fly one in order to extend my qualification for another ninety days. It was fun, all right, but I'll have to admit that the cockpit was a bit strange to me.

Major Skov got away, headed for Guam with the C-54 this morning. With luck, he still may return on December 10, in which case we should be able to depart for Manila and the U.S. on December 12.

Haven't received any mail from home, as all are expecting me back there and of course have stopped writing. With any kind of good breaks, I should be in San Francisco within ten days.

Tokyo, Japan, Dec. 8, 1945   2350

The day was rather dull as I couldn't find much to do to keep myself occupied. The office is closed as far as I am concerned. There are some pay difficulties to be straightened out among my men, then I have to get my personnel records to take home with me. All else is in readiness for immediate departure.

Tonight Bill Hogan and Doug Kendrick gave a very nice party for me here at the embassy. There were only about a dozen guests, as practically all of my friends and even my acquaintances have gone back to the States. It makes me feel that I'm really going home when they give a farewell party in my honor.

Tokyo, Japan, Dec. 9, 1945   2230

It was a dull Sunday in Tokyo. Although GHQ is still working seven days a week, on Sundays there is a distinct tendency to let down. People get to work a little later and leave a little earlier. I had nothing of consequence to do today so managed to take it easy all day. Tonight Lieutenant Silver came to have dinner with me. He worked for the Japanese airlines prior to the war, and had many things of interest to tell me. The problem of starting an airline here becomes increasingly involved.

Tokyo, Japan, Dec. 10, 1945   2200

[Today General Sutherland and I took off on a six-hour flight in a C-47 for a sightseeing jaunt southwestward over Japan to Hiroshima. We took off from Tachikawa and proceeded past towering Mount Fuji on over Nagoya, Kyoto, Osaka, Kobe, and Kure to Hiroshima. These cities, except for Kyoto, were all but completely demolished by our air attacks. Kyoto was spared because it was militarily unimportant and because it had been the ancient capital of Japan. It is still a seat of their culture.

The degree of destruction reached its maximum at Hiroshima. We flew low over the area for several minutes, noting some of the peculiarities of the havoc produced by the atomic bomb. Almost no buildings were standing. There were a few bridges, damaged but visible, across the numerous canals or lowlands. Building materials in any normal shape were absent, and it appeared that most such material had been reduced to dust or had melted. We saw a number of small plots that seemed to contain grave markers, most of which looked to be erect and undamaged. (Later I discussed this strange phenomenon with a physicist and he said those markers probably were slabs of granite. He further explained that most materials contained moisture and that the nearly instantaneous rise to very high temperatures concurrent with the explosion of the bomb had caused high-pressure steam to be formed inside these materials. This extreme pressure had exploded from within and pulverized the materials. Granite, containing very little moisture, was not so easily disintegrated, and those slabs that we saw could very well have been some type of granite markers.)

We did not linger too long over the atomic bomb site because of residual radiation. We returned directly to Tachikawa.

Back at the office General Sutherland gave me copies of travel orders that allowed us to proceed to Shanghai and on westward around the world to Washington. He said he had not yet decided which way we would travel but would have orders covering either contingency.]

Tokyo, Japan, Dec. 11, 1945   2030

Everything is now in readiness for our departure tomorrow morning. I think I have completed all of the little chores which are so necessary for the trip as well as for the process of getting out of the army. I will proceed to Washington, then to New York for a few days, then to Camp Beale (near Sacramento) for separation from the army. As I understand it, I then go on terminal leave, and when that is over I go back to Camp Beale, where all of my papers will have been collected and made ready for my final release. That will occur about March 1.

[Today I spent much of the day saying good-bye to friends. When I was in General Sutherland's office, General MacArthur came in and launched into an exchange of opinions with Sutherland, much as had happened on many previous occasions. He had received information or rumors that a great deal of the hundreds of millions of dollars' worth of military equipment remaining in the Pacific area was not to be returned to the United States. This included trucks, tanks, airplanes, earthmovers, and numerous other categories of equipment. Some of this material was new, some slightly used or slightly damaged. Authorities at home had concluded that a recession with high unemployment was likely to develop after a great many men had been released from military service and that if these supplies were released to the consumer market factories would be idled and economic conditions would deteriorate. MacArthur's innate conservative nature rebelled against such waste. He concluded by saying he supposed it was just another one of the penalties of war, and then philosophically added that he no longer had sufficient ships or manpower to efficiently move all of the equipment back to the States anyway.

I followed General MacArthur back to his office to say my farewells. He was warm and flattering. Among other things, he said, "Dusty, through the confidence which we gained in you personally and which we gained through observing your self-assurance around airplanes, we learned to have greater confidence in airplanes than we had in the beginning. That, in turn, contributed immeasurably to our reliance on the use of aircraft in combat operations in this theater."

I asked for, and he gave me, an autographed picture of himself. I saluted sharply, turned, and departed with tears in my eyes. I didn't expect to be associating with him again. My next stop was at the residency, where I said good-bye to Mrs. MacArthur. I will miss this charming lady, but my memories of her always will be with me.

This evening I feel a bit sad. It is the eve of the closing of another episode in my life. I have been overseas and away from my family much too long, serving in the army that of necessity violates many of my personal concepts of democracy. But through pluralistic effort and fine leadership we have been able to help accomplish the national objective.]

Tomorrow will be a long day, due partly to the two-hour drive necessary to reach the airfield. The flight to Manila should require less than ten hours, but I'll have to be up not later than 0500 hours.

General MacArthur presented this picture to me upon my departure from Tokyo in December, 1945.

Manila, P.I., Dec. 12, 1945   2030

Except for very strong winds which delayed us considerably, the trip down was routine until we reached Manila. But here we arrived simultaneously with one of the very few rainstorms which they ever have during the dry season.

I hope we will be able to depart for "Amerika-Shima" on the night of December 14. However, General Sutherland hasn't been very specific about it as yet, and I'm very much afraid he doesn't plan to depart until some time later than that.

Manila, P.I., Dec. 13, 1945   2000

This hot, sultry, rainy day saw many small missions accomplished. I made two trips to Nichols Field, did several chores in Manila, and had arrived at the conclusion that I was ready to depart for home. This afternoon, however, the general asked me to scout around and try to borrow a C-47 for a flight down to Cebu City tomorrow. I hoped I would be unable to obtain one, but the ATC, as usual, found it convenient to lend one to us. Now it is planned that we leave for Cebu at 0800 hours and return tomorrow afternoon. This, of course, means that we will not depart for the U.S. tomorrow night as I had hoped.

Manila, P.I., Dec. 14, 1945   1930

Was up early this morning and away to Cebu City in a C-47 with General Sutherland. The weather was excellent and the flight was routine as usual. At Cebu we had lunch with President Osmeña's son and Governor Cabahug. After a drive through this badly damaged city, the second largest in the Philippines, we returned to the airport and had a good return flight to Manila.

But tonight the bad news came. General Sutherland told me that we would leave for *Brisbane*, not Guam, tomorrow night. He is going there, of course, to see the WAC captain. I'm so angry and frustrated that I can hardly talk. All because of that woman, he'll have us fly another 6,000 miles, and I *know* that once we get to Brisbane we will be there for days. There's not the slightest chance of getting home for Christmas. He wasn't honest with me, because all the time he knew he was going to do this. If General MacArthur knew Sutherland was using his airplane for this purpose, he would recall the airplane immediately. There's absolutely nothing I can do about it all because I'm still in the army and have to take orders from my superior. I've seen old men go nuts over women before, but never to this extent. There ought to be a law providing for the castration of every man at the age of fifty.

Now, because the general hasn't played fair with us, all of my crew members are in uncomfortable circumstances. We haven't enough tropical clothing for the hot weather of Brisbane, all of our travel orders have to be reissued, and all of our families will be expecting us long before we can possibly be home. The worst part is that once we get in Brisbane we'll never get away again, the same way as it happened before. I'm sorely tempted to radio General MacArthur, yet I can't quite bring myself around to the point of being a stool pigeon.

Manila, P.I., Dec. 15, 1945   1800

It has been a day of frantic rushing here and there, changing orders, revising plans, sending another disappointing radiogram to Gracie, etc. My disgust with the whole affair is even greater than it was last night, and all day I've been debating the possibility or desirability of having a showdown with General Sutherland about it. I feel that if General Mac-Arthur is advised of our presence in Australia he will order his airplane back to Tokyo, and none of us will get to the States. I've decided that if General Sutherland stays in Brisbane longer than he has said he will, I will tell him I feel duty bound to inform General MacArthur by radiogram that I will be unable to accomplish his pre-Xmas missions in the States because I cannot get away from Australia. This may have some effect upon General Sutherland.

We are still scheduled to depart for Biak at 2100 hours tonight. As far as I know, all is in readiness, but my heart isn't in it.

Brisbane, Australia, Dec. 16, 1945   2300

This is the end of one of the longest and most tiring days within my memory. We departed from Manila at 2100 hours last night and, after flying all night, reached Biak shortly after dawn this morning. Here we had bad luck. I made an excellent landing, but while we were taxiing to the parking area the nose wheel tire suddenly blew out. We were moving at only five miles per hour, and I was able to stop the airplane immediately, so no damage resulted to any other part of the airplane. However, three hours was required to effect the repairs, and then we departed at 1000 hours for Brisbane. The weather across the Oranje Mountains of New Guinea appeared good, so I decided to go directly across them. When I reached the summit of the mountain range, though, I found that my heavily laden aircraft was reluctant to climb to sufficient altitude to clear the

17,000-foot peaks. I had to do some circling, but finally got across. The remainder of the trip was very slow due to thirty-knot headwinds, and the trip required over twelve hours. We encountered some mechanical difficulties on landing here, but I finally staggered from the airplane, still able to make the hotel.

On the way down, the general presented me with the Legion of Merit and a very nice citation with it. During the landing when things went wrong, I made two or three sharp, sarcastic statements to him which were probably not exactly in order and which were caused by my enormous fatigue after thirty-six hours of sleeplessness. I hope he didn't take offense at them.

Now for the good bed. Hope I can sleep until noon tomorrow.

Brisbane, Australia, Dec. 17, 1945   2015

Although I had hoped to be able to sleep late today, I was wide awake at 0700 hours. Habit is a strong force. I've rested all day, although I've been unable to sleep.

The airplane was worked upon and test-flown today, although as yet I've had no report upon its condition. Tonight I'll catch up on lost sleep, and tomorrow I'll be ill at ease, fearing a telephone call from the general advising me of a change of plan again.

Brisbane, Australia, Dec. 18, 1945   2000

I journeyed to Eagle Farm twice today to see that all was in readiness for our departure early tomorrow. Now, to the best of my belief, there's no reason why we shouldn't be able to take off at 0600 hours. It rained all afternoon and that did not make the errands any more pleasant to perform.

So once more I'm saying good-bye to Australia. The country has been good to me, and I've enjoyed it as much as I could have enjoyed any country away from my family. In fact, I should have no great objections to living here permanently.

En route Fiji–Canton, Dec. 19, 1945   2030

We departed from Brisbane on schedule this morning and had a fine, fast nine-hour flight to Nandi, Fiji Islands. We were there one and one-half hours for refueling and an early dinner, and then were off before sunset for this beautiful, moonlit flight to Canton. We are favored with excellent weather and helpful winds, so that we should reach Canton shortly after midnight.

It's very difficult for me to believe that at long last I'm on my way home! Please, God, may there be no accidents or delays at this late date.

Each hour that passes I feel just a little closer to Gracie and all the other things that home means to me. Yet each succeeding hour is infinitely longer than the one that preceded it.

23

Going Home

Honolulu, T.H., Dec. 19, 1945   2000

After twenty-five hours of continuous flying, we reached Honolulu at a bit past noon today. Needless to day, we were all desperately tired, but there were many chores to be done before we could relax. More than two hours was required for clearing customs. Then there were arrangements to be made for maintenance work on the airplane, operations reports to be turned in, etc. Then I sent a radiogram to Gracie, telling her I would arrive in Hamilton Field on Friday morning.

At 1700 hours I collapsed on my bunk and was oblivious to everything until hunger aroused me in time for a late dinner. It's the bed for me again in a very few minutes now.

On the calendar this is the same date as yesterday, because we crossed the date line. So I actually get two days for the cost of one in my life.

Honolulu, T.H., Dec. 20, 1945   1900

This day has been a lazy one, spent for the most part in waiting for departure time tonight.

We are scheduled to depart at 2000 hours tonight for San Francisco. The weather is not good on the coast, but I'm hoping we'll have no trouble in getting into Hamilton Field.

Atherton, Calif., Dec. 21, 1945   2100

This has been a long and trying day indeed. We departed from Honolulu last night according to plan, and had a fine, fast flight to California. But upon approaching the coast we ran into bad weather and encountered many vexing difficulties. There was much traffic in the Bay Area, but at length we received traffic control clearance to descend to Hamilton

Field. I managed to get contact off the bay shoreline at Hamilton, but low clouds, high winds, and fog prevented me from making a landing there. Eventually I was recleared to Fairfield, but that too was closing in rapidly. En route to Fairfield, I broke out in clear weather over a fine but deserted field with nice long concrete runways. I didn't know the name of the field but elected to land there anyway. After landing I learned that it was the Napa County airport, and I soon obtained army staff cars from Fairfield to take General Sutherland and me into Hamilton Field.

Gracie and Al Luedke still were waiting for me at Hamilton, but she soon broke the sad news to me that our car had quit running on the way up to meet me this morning, and was at that time parked along the highway south of San Francisco. However, United Air Lines had graciously provided her with a station wagon and driver, and we were able to be on our way home with all my baggage with only a minimum of delay. On our way down, we were able to push our car and start it with no difficulty, so we got it home safely.

There was a grand reunion at home with the boys. There is so much to discuss and to do that it's most difficult to break away and get the sleep which I need so badly. However, I'm now giving up because tomorrow will be a day crowded with activity.

Atherton, Calif., Dec. 22, 1945   2300

This morning Vic Skov managed to ferry the airplane over to Mills Field for our proposed takeoff for Washington at 1200 hours tonight. The weather was not good, and I went to the airport at noon to study it with United's facilities in time to give General Sutherland a decision as to the departure probabilities. I decided that, although the weather was flyable, it would be somewhat hazardous for us since we had no deicing equipment on the airplane. Therefore, I postponed the departure time to 0600 hours tomorrow morning. Having made this decision, I tried to notify the general accordingly, but was unable to contact him by telephone. Therefore, I had to go back to the airport tonight in order to be there in case he didn't get the message I had left for him regarding the postponement.

Now we definitely are set for a takeoff at 0600 hours tomorrow morning, with one stop somewhere in the Middle West to allow Vic Skov to deplane. We'll be in Washington after dark. I have to get up at 0330 hours.

Washington, D.C., Dec. 23, 1945   2330

The trip came off with only minor deviations from the plan. I've now flown my last airplane for the army during the present war emergency.

Although the weather was bad over the western part of the country, we made excellent speed, thanks to a favorable wind. We had intended to land at Kansas City or Saint Louis to discharge Vic Skov and Colonel Luedtke, but a sudden deterioration of the weather in the Middle West brought freezing rain to those places. So we proceeded on to Chicago and made a landing at dusk. It was snowing and very, very cold, so we remained on the ground only sufficiently long to refuel.

Gracie was snugly but illegally stowed away on the airplane and survived the trip in good condition, although flying for five hours at 13,000 feet gave her a headache. General Sutherland had agreed that I could take her along. We arrived at Bolling in Washington at 2330 hours.

[[General Sutherland and I said our farewells on that frigid, lonely tarmac, and it was an emotional occasion. We both had tears in our eyes, one of the few times I ever saw the general display any tender emotions. Our relationship had been a unique one from which both of us had benefited. Although we corresponded at varying intervals until his death on June 25, 1966, I saw him on only two occasions after that evening.]]

Our airplane, *Bataan II*, will be ferried back to Tokyo for General MacArthur for his future use.

We have a fine room at the New Statler Hotel, which is perhaps the world's most modern building. Now for a long sleep, and we will allow tomorrow to take care of itself.

New York, N.Y., Dec. 24, 1945   2330

Luck was with us this morning. In spite of the fact it was Christmas Eve, the first telephone call to American Air Lines in Washington produced space for Grace and me to come by air to New York today. I scurried around and went to the Pentagon for a transportation request, and we got to Washington National Airport just in time to catch the 5:15 airplane to New York. Upon arriving, however, we found that the airline had left our baggage in Washington and that it would not arrive here in New York until tomorrow.

We had a late dinner at a small Swiss restaurant on Fifty-third Street, then went up Riverside Drive to spend a couple of hours with Gracie's family. Thus passes Christmas Eve, far from our two boys who are at the other side of the continent, no doubt impatiently awaiting the arrival of Santa Claus.

New York, N.Y., Dec. 25, 1945   2330

Gracie and I rolled out of our very comfortable beds at the hotel all too early this morning in order to go to the Halls' (Grace's brother's)

apartment in time to be off on an automobile drive to Waterbury, Con-
necticut.

The snow-covered countryside was beautiful today. For me it was the
first old-fashioned Christmas I'd had in years, and it came with all the
trimmings. Wish our two boys could have been with us.

New York, N.Y., Dec. 26, 1945   2345

Didn't get up until almost noon today, and then we went down to
United to start the wheels rolling in the project of getting ourselves air
travel reservations within the travel priority system to get back to California. This will not be easy to do, but at present we are cleared as far
as Cleveland.

I'm really enjoying my lazy life here. Nothing to do except to eat and
sleep and shop and see shows. A few more days of this and I should be
completely rested.

New York, N.Y., Dec. 27, 1945   2345

Today we slept very late and then did much walking about town,
window-shopping. We tried to purchase some things for the boys but
were unable to get what we wanted. Prices of everything are much, much
too high, so I guess we will simply go without many things we need.

New York, N.Y., Dec. 28, 1945   2130

This was another day of lazy shopping and good living. We had tickets
to *Hats Off to Ice* at the Center Theater for the matinee, so we had a
most entertaining afternoon watching this breathtaking spectacle.

New York, N.Y., Dec. 29, 1945   2245

I was up early this morning and off to town to buy some tickets to
the Radio City Music Hall. Being in uniform I was able to get excellent
seats for the performance this evening. All during the day Gracie and I
walked the streets and generally practiced being lazy. The show tonight
was *The Bells of St. Mary's* and was a well-acted Catholic church propaganda picture.

We are having a lot of fun, and it's exactly what both of us need. I
wish we could have our boys with us, yet if we did have we'd be less
free to enjoy each other. There will be plenty of time to spend with them
later.

New York, N.Y., Dec. 30, 1945 2245

We had no definite schedule to follow today, so most of the day we did nothing. It was rainy and unpleasant outside, so we read the Sunday newspapers over a late breakfast, then at midafternoon we went out to the Halls' for drinks and conversation.

Last night we telephoned Palo Alto to learn how things were going at home. All is well, and Jimmy was still awake and talked to us. So our vacation to date has been perfect, and no uncertainties have developed to detract from the fun we are having.

New York, N.Y., Dec. 31, 1945 2400

After a quiet day, part of which I spent at the broker's office, we went out to some friends' apartment on Riverside Drive to see the old year out and the New Year in. The old year finally came to a close, and a critical, historic year it was!

On our way home in the subway we saw many revelers still trying desperately to make merry, but the crowd was generally well behaved.

New York, N.Y., Jan. 1, 1946 2330

The city was closed up tightly today, as though all the celebrants of last night were sleeping off their respective headaches. It was very cold and windy, and in the afternoon Grace and I took a walk. We purchased two miniature pet turtles for the boys, and then we went to Victor Herbert's *Red Mill*, which was quite well presented and very entertaining.

We have only one more day in the City and then we start our long trek back to California. It appears that we may encounter some difficulty in getting there by air, as much of our space has not yet been confirmed.

New York, N.Y., Jan. 2, 1946 2100

Today we've rushed about almost frantically, doing all of our last-minute shopping and preparing for our departure tomorrow. It's been a fine vacation, yet I'm quite pleased that it's now over. Perhaps my desire to see those boys is partly responsible for my feelings. At any rate, we start for California at 1300 hours, although at the present time we do not hold air space beyond Cleveland. I'm depending on good old United Air Lines to help me along.

This evening has been a quiet one. We are packed and ready to depart.

New York, N.Y., Jan. 3, 1946   2230

We went to the airport early today so that Grace could have an early lunch with two friends of hers before our departure. Imagine our disappointment when the passenger agent at the airport informed us that our flight and all succeeding ones for an indefinite period had been canceled because of weather! There was nothing for us to do but return to the City to await a change of weather. Fortunately, we were able to get our room back at the hotel.

Conditions do not appear favorable for our departure tomorrow, yet all I can do is to arise early and go to the airport to try for space.

It was a fine day here in New York, clear and cold, and Grace and I walked all afternoon, window-shopping and having fun.

New York, N.Y., Jan. 4, 1946   2100

I was up early to call the airport for information relative to possible departure. Was informed that no trips would fly today. Spent the morning at the broker's office, since I had placed orders to sell certain stocks short yesterday. There was little activity, however, so the morning was an uninteresting one.

Chicago, Ill., Jan. 5, 1946   2200

Again I was up early to call UAL at the airport to learn whether or not trips were operating. When I learned that they were, I went downtown to the reservations office and found that, with the help of Mr. Callahan there, both Grace and I could get on a trip which departed at noon. I contacted Grace immediately.

We arrived in Chicago about an hour late, proceeded to Margaret's (Grace's sister's) apartment, and are now ready to collapse into bed.

Chicago, Ill., Jan. 6, 1946   2100

Once more I was up early and off to the airport to see about reservations for Grace and me westbound. I found that I could get Grace on a flight late this afternoon and that I could get on almost any flight that I chose.

Tonight I'm all alone in Margaret's apartment. She is due in from Washington but has not yet appeared. I'm catching up with many personal chores which I've neglected for too long. Tomorrow I'll have a busy day with the company at the airport.

En route Chicago–Cheyenne, Jan. 7, 1946   2300

Margaret arrived back from Washington last night after I was in bed and asleep. I was up early this morning, and since I couldn't get a cab I had a jolly time getting my heavy baggage to the airport on the streetcar.

At the airport I had a busy day. There were so many people to talk with and much information I wished to obtain that I was on the run all day long. I had lunch with Mr. Patterson, Herlihy, and Ahrens and I practically wore my vocal cords out, answering all their questions. Then I posed for many pictures for publicity purposes for the company.

My trip was late, so we were not under way until 1915 hours.

Camp Beale, Calif., Jan. 8, 1946   2200

I arrived in Cheyenne after midnight this morning. The trip I was on did not stop at Sacramento, so I got off of it at Cheyenne and waited for a later trip which was scheduled to stop. I couldn't get a hotel room, so I got the *Johnsons* out of bed and made them put me up. Fortunately, my trip this morning also was late, and I had a good sleep and then a good opportunity for a visit with the Johnsons.

We made short stops at Salt Lake City and Reno. At Sacramento I had considerable difficulty in obtaining information about reaching Camp Beale. The army was not at all helpful, but at length I got on a bus and two hours later reached this enormous, bleak, active post, which is located north of Sacramento in the broad valley. Here there was much more confusion, but finally I signed in and received a billet.

Atherton, Calif., Jan. 9, 1946   2330

It seems literally days ago that I rolled out of bed at Camp Beale this morning to get an early start at processing for separation from the army. It was a beautiful, clear, cold dawn through which I walked to breakfast. At 0730 hours I started through the processing line, and from that time until I caught my bus at 1530 hours I was practically on the run constantly. The army handled me in a surprisingly thorough and efficient manner and completed the processing almost on schedule. There were such things as initial interviews, finances, orientation, property accountability, physical exam (a joke requiring ten minutes), officers' reserve corps oath, terminal leave pay, etc.

At the end, I had just time enough to catch the crowded bus to Sacramento. At Sacramento I had to change buses for San Francisco, and at San Francisco I had to change buses and bus depots for Menlo Park, with

I am released from active duty as a colonel.

no taxi available to haul my heavy baggage. Finally I arrived home half an hour ago, unannounced, because the telephone company strike prevented me from telephoning on ahead. At any rate, I'm home from the war at last, and tomorrow is my last day in the army.

Atherton, Calif., Jan. 10, 1946 2230

I had planned to spend this day at home, quietly renewing my acquaintance with Jimmy and Johnny. However, over a late breakfast, Roger Egeberg telephoned from San Francisco that he had only a few hours there and wanted Gracie and me to have lunch with him. We drove up in a hurry, had a delightful reunion over many old-fashioneds, and poured Roger aboard the train at 1630 hours. We returned home to spend a leisurely evening together before the fireplace with the boys.

On this day I terminate my active duty in the army. Until March 17 I will be on terminal leave but will have no duties. It is with mixed emotions that I leave the army. More than anything else, I'm glad to return to civilian life and to my family. However, but for the army I could never have had any of the exciting experiences I've had in this war. I've had a grandstand seat for the performance, for which I can never be sufficiently grateful to General MacArthur and General Sutherland. But for them I never could have experienced many of the exciting episodes that occurred during this devastating war. Since the war had to occur, I could never have been happy sitting on the sidelines as a civilian. For two years of my life, the army has given me in exchange broader acquaintances, broader tolerances, and a rich store of memories and experiences.

I shall close this journal here, because life now will be more routine and more exacting of my time. Someday I may once more start keeping an account of my activities, not so much for their interest as for a pleasant task to be performed every day. But I trust it will not be another war which prompts me to use the pen again.

24

After the War

My life after 1945 did not quite conform to the pattern I had planned. We purchased a house in Palo Alto, and I fully expected to go back to my occupation as an airline pilot. But my company had different ideas. Before my terminal leave from the army expired in March, 1946, I was asked by United Air Lines to move to Washington, D.C., to organize an effort to bring some order into the rapidly deteriorating and chaotic situation in air traffic control. Someone was needed who understood the requirements of the airlines, the military, and the private pilots.

This effort required nearly three years. We devised and obtained agreement to the basic air traffic control system that is in use today. Although this system is the frequent target of sensation-seeking reporters, it has well withstood the tests of safety and has not produced the catastrophes periodically predicted by many. No one yet has devised a better scheme. For our work, President Truman awarded the group the then-coveted Collier Trophy.

In late 1946, a daughter, Margaret Deborah, was added to our family while we resided in Washington.

I returned to United Air Lines in 1949 and for the next few years was engaged in the introduction of a new generation of propeller-driven aircraft into the airline fleet. The jets were still on the drawing board. During this period I was twice called back to duty by the Air Force. The first occasion was to write the policy for the Civil Reserve Air Fleet (CRAF). This is an agreement between the Air Force and the airlines that provides for installation at the factory of special military equipment in any new aircraft purchased by the airlines. This ensures that these aircraft will be immediately usable by the military in the event of an emergency.

The second occasion for my recall to active duty was in the winter of 1952, when the Military Air Transport Service (MATS) had a series of unfortunate airplane accidents. The mission was to fly with the pilots and go to various MATS installations around the world, inspecting flight procedures, maintenance practices, administration effort, etc. The accident rate dropped appreciably, and I trust the work was productive.

I also served as technical advisor to the State Department at international meetings on aviation on three occasions during this period. United was very tolerant of my absences.

The jet transport airplanes arrived on the scene in the late 1950s. It fell to my duty to fly the acceptance flights on each of these airplanes at the factories and then to serve as chairman of the committees responsible for integrating each of these aircraft types into the airline fleet.

My beloved Gracie expertly ran the household while I was constantly busy with my intriguing problems. She was a graduate of the University of Wisconsin, a collegiate champion tennis player, a registered nurse from the University of Wisconsin Hospital, and a part-time nurse to returning wounded soldiers at Dibble Hospital in Menlo Park, California.

We and the Roger Egebergs bought a large cattle ranch on the California coast near San Simeon in 1949. We still own the ranch, where I now make my home, and our grown families spend many happy times there.

In 1962 I was elected to the office of vice-president engineering by the directors of United Air Lines. This officer and his staff are responsible for the determination and issuance of all standards and procedures by which the airplanes and their ground support equipment are procured, operated, and maintained.

In late 1963 I lost my Gracie to cancer. My three children and my new job then made even more demands upon me. But Grace had ingrained into the children a fine foundation upon which to build. Now they and their spouses are successful professionals.

In 1965 I married Alta McElroy, a widow who had four grown children. Ours has been another happy union.

I retired in 1971 from United Airlines after more than thirty-seven years of service. I still am busier than I want to be with consulting, ranching, a bit of writing, grandchildren, and a few very close friends with whom I can relax completely and even affectionately insult on occasion without losing their friendship.

Except for the tragic loss of my Gracie at the zenith of her career, life generally has been very good to me! I've done the best I could with what I had.

25

Postscript

THE GENERALS

When I said good-bye to Mrs. MacArthur and General MacArthur on December 11, 1945, in the American Embassy in Tokyo, I had little hope that we would continue to have a personal relationship for several more decades. When the country's hero and my hero returned to the United States in April, 1951, I had the good fortune to be able to greet the couple when they landed at the San Francisco airport.

He had been relieved of his command by President Truman and was on his way home. My family and I went to the San Francisco airport hoping to greet him. Arriving there, we found that an enormous crowd had gathered and the arrival area had been cordoned off. I asked to be allowed inside the fenced zone but was told all of that area had been reserved for dignitaries—mayors, congressmen, governors, etc. I forced my way to the fence and luckily was opposite the door of the airplane when it parked. When the general came down the boarding ramp, he spotted me at the fence. He ignored his escorts and the dignitaries, came over and grasped my outstretched hands, and greeted me in a most heartwarming manner. I suppose I gloated a bit and probably cast a sneer or two in the direction of the uncooperative and impatient politicians.

I was privileged to serve as the pilot of General and Mrs. MacArthur on a couple of trips within the United States as they journeyed about, receiving the unparalleled plaudits of their countrymen.

General L. J. Sverdrup generously made it possible for all of us who were on General MacArthur's immediate staff to meet with the general each year on his birthday (January 26). General Sverdrup hosted a party annually for us at the Waldorf-Astoria Hotel in New York. The climax of each of these parties was an informal talk by General MacArthur.

[The only time, to my knowledge, that General MacArthur ever openly denounced President Truman and the other unnamed powers in Wash-

As a civilian I once more had the pleasure of flying the MacArthurs in the summer of 1951 on some of their tours when they were receiving the plaudits of their countrymen. At Cleveland, Mrs. MacArthur, the general, and I are flanked by members of my crew. Courtesy United Air Lines.

ington who participated in the action to relieve him of his command in Korea was the occasion of the first private birthday banquet.

He talked for an hour, giving us his version of what had occurred when his troops reached the Yalu River, which divided Korea from Manchuria. He said that his intelligence sources, as well as the information that Washington had provided him, agreed that a very large Chinese military force was encamped in Manchuria just north of the Yalu. Various estimates placed the number of men in this army at as many as 600,000. MacArthur was not too worried about this force crossing the wild, icy, turbulent river because we had complete command of the air and there were only six usable bridges across the river. If the Chinese did start to cross, our bombers could destroy these bridges within an hour, thus neutralizing their offensive capabilities. Moreover, he had assurances from Washington that the Chinese would not enter the war except to defend their territory on the Manchurian side of the river if we attacked there. But, contrary to all predictions, the Chinese did start to send troops across the bridges. MacArthur immediately ordered the Air Force to destroy the bridges by bombing. He said that within two hours of his issuing his orders they were countermanded by Washington. Thus the bridges were not destroyed; the Chinese sent thousands of troops across into Korea, inundated our extended defense lines, and eventually caused us needlessly to suffer the loss of many hundreds, even thousands, of American soldiers. He summed it up by saying that if you doubted that there was an element of complicity in high places, how could you explain our willingness to accept those casualties when we could have saved those American lives by bombing the bridges?

He went on to say that if this was modern diplomacy/warfare, he could not comprehend it, and that in his fifty-two years in the military he had always been taught, and he fervently believed, that the only reason for fighting a war was to win it. It was contradictable and inconceivable to fight a war not to win. If this was what was expected of him, perhaps it was just as well that he had been retired from active duty, he said. Quite obviously he was still smarting as much from the indignities heaped upon him by the *method* in which he was relieved from his command as from the act itself.]

On one of these occasions, January 26, 1960, Gen. Tom White, chief of staff of the Air Force, requested me to present to General MacArthur my command pilot wings, which had (symbolically) flown him throughout World War II. Thus we would be making him an honorary command pilot in the Air Force. This I did. General White, in return, presented me with a scroll signed by all attendees at the party. Attached to this scroll was a pair of command pilot wings that (again symbolically) restored me to flight status. The signatures on this scroll probably encompass the most illustrious collection of military signatures on any single document in existence today. General White jokingly said that the wings I pinned on

At the 1957 birthday party for the general I greet Mrs. MacArthur. Also present were *(from left)* Arthur MacArthur, General MacArthur, General Sverdrup, and Colonel Egeberg. Courtesy General Sverdrup.

Above: General Sutherland and I reminisce about the war. *Below:* General MacArthur and I exchange war-time stories. Photographs courtesy General Sverdrup.

Above: General MacArthur gathers again with his principal commanders, Generals Krueger and Kenney and Admiral Kinkaid. They were often referred to as MacArthur's KKK. *Below:* I present my Command Pilot wings to General MacArthur, making him an honorary Command Pilot in the Air Force. Looking on are former president Herbert Hoover; Gen. Thomas White, chief of staff, Air Force; and General Kenney. Photographs courtesy General Sverdrup.

The assembled officers restore me to flight status by presenting me with this autographed plaque and an attached set of Command Pilot wings. Courtesy General Sverdrup.

General MacArthur probably were made of pewter, but that he would guarantee that those I received in return were made of sterling silver.

General Sutherland, who was in poor health, had not attended these annual banquets prior to this one. For the 1960 gathering, I made a special plea to him and he responded, thus making the affair a most complete one.

[Since the war I have been asked on numerous occasions by friends and acquaintances two simple questions: What kind of man was Sutherland? What kind of man was MacArthur? The answers are not simple.

To most people General Sutherland was an enigma. He was a reserved, private man who almost never talked about himself. In close association with him it took me two years to learn a few facts about his life. He was the son of a United States senator and hinted that he had not had a particularly happy early life. After being graduated from Yale, he entered the army by way of the National Guard and served in France during World War I. Apparently, somewhere along the way he attracted the attention of General MacArthur, for while serving as an officer in China in 1938 he was transferred to Manila to work under MacArthur in the effort to build up the defenses of the Philippines. In July, 1941, when MacArthur was named Commander in Chief, USAFFE (United States Army Forces in the Far East), Sutherland was named his chief of staff. When MacArthur left the Philippines in early 1942, Sutherland was one of the twelve men he took with him to Australia. Sutherland remained MacArthur's chief of staff until he departed from Tokyo just before Christmas in 1945.

In many ways General MacArthur was not an easy man to work for. He demanded near perfection, he worked long hours, and he sometimes failed to realize that his immediate staff had few facilities for relaxation. Sutherland and his every move were highly visible to MacArthur because Sutherland worked with him on a minute-to-minute basis. This was not true of most others in GHQ. It was intriguing to observe the interrelationship between the two men during the planning process of an operational move. After all the intelligence data, such as enemy force distribution, landing beach conditions, seasonal weather prognoses, and prospects of enemy reinforcements had been obtained and studied, Sutherland usually had the task of determining and recommending which of our units were best equipped to participate. This included air cover and naval effort required, size of attacking force (regiment, brigade, division), supply problems, and the like. Sometimes this involved trips to contact unit commanders. Then Sutherland would report back to MacArthur, who made the final decision. From this point on Sutherland worked closely with General Chamberlin (G-3) to ensure that detailed military planning and coordination were effected. Usually two or three prospective operations would be in the planning stage at any one time. Thus, Sutherland was figuratively on the firing line all the time. Furthermore, some of the commanders appeared to resent having to deal with Sutherland when they would have preferred by reasons of prestige to deal with MacArthur directly. Obviously Sutherland's position was not one in which he could earn plaudits from his peers. And he did not do so.

His natural manner was to be abrupt, which did not create friends. Then, in Australia, he met and became deeply involved with an Australian woman. In some irregular way, even though she was an Australian citizen, she was commissioned in the American army as a captain in the Women's Army Corps. Unfortunately, her temperament was such that she irritated many people. When she wanted something, she did not hesitate to let all those involved know she was a special friend of General Sutherland's. Unlike some other Australian women who had similar relationships in GHQ, she was not sufficiently discreet to maintain a low profile. When GHQ moved to forward areas, she went along. She became the perfect gossip target for Sutherland's detractors and ultimately played a major role in the schism that finally developed between MacArthur and Sutherland.

General Sutherland was an intense individual in everything he did. He loved to fly the various airplanes with me, and this became his major active recreational outlet. But he did not relax and enjoy the flights: he was always attempting to learn something new or to improve his abilities. He had a prodigious memory for details. But he was unable to relax. I am sure he would have liked to become "one of the boys," but position as well as disposition would not permit this. He had difficulty going to sleep at night, and often he would telephone and ask me to come to his quarters for a nightcap. The subjects we discussed generally related to the military situation, airplanes, or world politics. He did most of the talking. After an hour or so he usually said he thought he could go to sleep, and I would depart. He was a lonely man, needing someone with whom to converse.

I came to the point where I greatly admired the abilities of this self-effacing man who really carried most of the burdens of the day-to-day conduct of the war. In a protective sense I developed a feeling of partial responsibility for the mental and social well-being of this dedicated administrator.

On the long flight home from Tokyo back to Washington by way of Brisbane, we were in the air almost fifty hours. General Sutherland spent most of that time in the cockpit, occupying the copilot's seat. He talked to me at great length. Much of the discourse was about his relations with General MacArthur. There was no doubt that he was very bitter about the way he had been treated after the outcome of the war was no longer in question. In the early stages of the conflict MacArthur had relied heavily upon him. Sutherland had responded to this confidence and responsibility by working ever harder. There had been some disagreements, but nothing of major consequence. Then there was the incident at Hollandia, when Sutherland had made a strategic decision about the bypassing of Mindanao because MacArthur could not be reached to seek his concurrence. According to Sutherland, from that point on everything was downhill for him. Nothing he could do seemed totally to please MacArthur. Decisions that were normally within Sutherland's province were criticized by the commander in chief.

Sutherland believed that MacArthur's violent reaction against his (Sutherland's) relationship with his Australian WAC friend was completely out of order because what he did with his private life should, in his opinion, have been his own affair. And there were several other similar liaisons in GHQ that MacArthur did not protest, at least publicly. When I suggested that perhaps the WAC's aggressive behavior toward others in GHQ may have had something to do with the commander in chief's dislike for her, he would not agree.

He went on to say that when MacArthur was faced with a job of outlining the detailed procedures for the surrender ceremony with the Japanese envoys who were to arrive in Manila, he did not hesitate to call Sutherland back from vacation in Washington because he needed him. He instructed Sutherland to study protocol and past precedent and produce a proper ritual that would be both dignified and impressive. After the surrender, Sutherland remained in Tokyo with little to do. Finally he took his aborted vacation in Australia, then returned to Tokyo expecting to be assigned in some capacity with the occupation forces in Japan. Again no assignment was forthcoming. At length he approached MacArthur, asking to be relieved of his job as chief of staff so he could return to the United States. MacArthur readily agreed—too readily for Sutherland's sense of pride. Sutherland said he did not receive even a "thank you" in recognition for all of his work. Perhaps MacArthur relented a bit, because when Sutherland asked him for the use of *Bataan II* to return to the States he readily consented.

Sutherland said MacArthur never gave him a complete explanation why he had fallen into disfavor. As a result he ended up a bitter and disillusioned soldier.

Many qualified people have tried to categorize or describe the complex individual known as General MacArthur. In my opinion most have failed to succeed because they have tried to analyze him through the results of his actions or through occasional glimpses of one or more of his quick reactions to some particular person or situation. This, my own personal assessment of him—prejudiced, perhaps—is based on an extended period of watching him during highly stressful activity as well as during times of complete relaxation. I have seen him momentarily blow his top over some minor, irritating event, and I have seen him remain absolutely calm in the face of tense developments that would panic many men.

There is no question but that the general was an egoist, but one without the negative implication that the word often carries. He believed in himself. He knew that he possessed a superior intellect and an almost perfect memory. In a subtle way he seemed mentally to challenge anyone who doubted. If in discussions with any of his counterparts he thought they were wrong, he was quick to grab the initiative and often buried any contrary opinion with myriad incontrovertible facts. It was almost as though he had specially prepared himself on that one particular subject in advance and knew all the aspects of it intimately. Thus he sometimes appeared to be dictatorial when in truth he was simply more knowledgeable. General Sutherland was the one man he did not, or could not, overwhelm in the give-and-take type of discussion. I believe this was because their dialogues usually pertained to the prosecution of the war, and in that area Sutherland was as well versed as the commander in chief. General MacArthur listened carefully to his staff briefings and staff opinions. At times he disagreed, but I never saw him become abusive or inconsiderate.

To those of us who were in contact with him frequently, he was a gentle man. He was stern, almost never engaging in "small talk," but always kind and helpful. He did not order one to do things — rather, he would suggest that thus-and-so would be a good way to do them. He accomplished this with such understanding and skill that one always wanted to do the best job possible. He was completely devoted to his wife and son, although when duty required it he showed no reluctance to part with them.

He possessed a quick temper that he kept under control most of the time. However, when a person or situation startled him or interrupted his train of thought, he was prone to abrupt outburst. I never heard him resort to profanity, and I once heard him remark that he did not think much of those who did use it because they were not sufficiently motivated to acquire a vocabulary that would enable them to express their thoughts forcefully. He almost never joked face to face with people — not that he lacked a sense of humor. His type of humor generally related to unusual past events or ridiculous plights he had encountered. Although he was reserved and at times appeared to be shy in crowds, he delighted in after-dinner informal conversations among friends, where he seemed naturally to take center stage. Although he would take an occasional drink, alcohol played no significant part in his life. His favorite relaxation was to watch a good movie in the evening at a private showing in his home. Only once did I know him to attend a large entertainment event outside his home during the war.

It is my opinion that he had some feeling that he was a man of destiny. He personally took chances that I thought were unacceptable for one in his command position. He seemed to believe that he was especially protected so that he could fulfill a mission. Although he was not religious in a parochial sense, he certainly believed that all events proceeded in an orderly manner because they were the results of overriding forces set in operation by a higher authority.

Although the general certainly was not an effusive, outgoing individual, neither was he inclined to moodiness. On only two occasions did I observe him to be noticeably introspective and withdrawn to a degree approaching depression. The first of these was when he was on his way to Honolulu to meet with President Roosevelt in a conference, the purpose of which was unknown to him. It is my opinion he had convinced himself the meeting might well result in the president's relieving him of his command. The second occasion was the interval immediately following the detonation of the atomic bomb over Hiroshima. Perhaps better than most people he could visualize the disruptive effects upon the structure and institutions of society. He had long been an avid student of world politics, world affairs, and world demographics. He could foresee violent changes that would occur in an uncertain world. Certainly he realized that the techniques of war that he had studied all his life would undergo revolutionary changes to an extent not yet predictable.

The general appeared to be in excellent health. He worked seven days a week, put in long hours, and seldom missed a day at the office. Even if he occasionally did not feel well, I doubt he would have let that be known because that might have been interpreted by others as a weakness. He did not appear to require spectacles for ordinary work, but he often wore sunglasses, and it is possible these had corrective lenses. He seldom wore them in the office, however. The thing that surprised all of us was that his physical fitness always seemed excellent. He took no exercise except for the almost continuous pacing he did in his office. On the occasions I accompanied him ashore after the beach landings, he outwalked most of us and never seemed out of breath. Regardless of the air temperature and humidity, I never saw him perspire. He was meticulous about his dress, yet somehow managed to attain that kind of unexplainable semi-rumpled, confident, at-ease look in his uniform. He was not a tall man, but his erect bearing made him appear so. In his later years he became somewhat stooped.

He possessed that indefinable characteristic of leadership. This quality appeared to be a delicately balanced mixture of aloofness and accessibility, severity and friendliness, exactitude and leniency. Those who were closely associated with him were fiercely loyal. This was not a loyalty of fear but a devotion born of the utmost respect and the fervent desire not to commit any act, or be deficient in any manner, that might endanger his esteem.

Possibly the most criticized characteristic of General MacArthur was his desire for recognition. It is true he wanted most publicity dispatches and military orders to be issued over his name. Conversely he did not want his subordinate commanders to issue their own press releases. Those who tried to do so soon learned better. Most of his staff played this game according to his desires, but a few were slow to learn. General Kenney made a few errors in this way but quickly became more prudent. On the other hand, General Eichelberger was probably the most aggressive and ambitious high-ranking officer in the theater, and it was common knowledge that he also coveted the limelight. There were those who thought he might not have had to wait so long to be told that he finally would have an opportunity to command an army—the Eighth—if he had been a bit more discreet. Some of the criticism General MacArthur received was due to the way his own public relations personnel handled the news. They used the general's name more often than necessary, and they seldom arranged for him to hold conferences with the news reporters. But I do not believe he particularly desired to meet the press anyway.

He said the press was prone to sensationalize the bad news and seldom treated good news with the same enthusiasm. For example, the press was always eager to emphasize the casualty lists, usually with the implication that they were heavy. Conversely, it almost never suggested how much larger these lists might have been if less sophisticated strategic and tactical procedures had been employed. He felt that the news media had a recognizable, built-in, negative bias. I once heard him make a remark that I frequently have thought of since. He said to Col. Larry Lehrbas, one of his public relations advisors, "Never get in an argument with the press. Those people sometimes make outlandish or provocative or on rare occasions even untrue statements in an effort to start a controversy. If you argue, they keep the controversy going in their own one-way medium where you can't reply and there is no end to it. They always have the last word as far as the public is concerned because you can't edit what they choose to write. On the other hand if you ignore their statements there is little they can do but let the issue die and label you as being uncooperative."

Early in the war many soldiers and sailors picked up such uncomplimentary refrains as "Dugout Doug." It is safe to say that 75 percent of those detractors were never as much, or as often, exposed directly to real combat hazards and physical danger during the war as was the general. Moreover, if those same detractors had had a less capable and casualty-sensitive commander, many of them would have been sacrificed needlessly in the war.

The general's military achievements have been recognized and widely proclaimed throughout the world. His theater of direct command by the end of the hostilities probably encompassed a geographic area greater than that of any other army commander in history with the possible exception of Genghis Khan. It extended from New Zealand to Australia to Borneo to the Kurile Islands. He presided over a conglomerate force of zealous but sometimes jealous personalities and units of Army, Navy, Air Force, and Marines. He had some petty moments, but he had many more moments of superb performance.

Sometimes overlooked in his military performance, however, is the fact that he accomplished so much with a minimum loss of men, particularly when his operations are contrasted with other protracted campaigns of similar magnitude. His basic strategy was to "bypass the enemy and let him rot in the jungle. Never face him head-on unless absolutely necessary." It paid off handsomely in terms of reduced casualties.

In my opinion his place in history as a military genius will be overshadowed by his postwar accomplishments in Japan. There, in a period of two or three years, the transformation of a relatively backward, ingrown, semifeudal society into one of the world's leading cooperative democracies was a prodigious feat. And he did this in the face of considerable opposition from powerful men in Washington, some of whom appeared to want him to chastise severely the defeated nation rather than to cooperate with the civil establishment.

I was not to see General MacArthur again after 1963. For all of us who had admired—even revered—this great and incomparable American, it was indescribably difficult to accept his demise when the end came in early April, 1964.

In my humble opinion, it will be a long, long time before our nation again produces a greater military genius, a greater idealist, or a greater patriot than General Douglas MacArthur.]

Appendix

DOCUMENTS FROM THE CAREER OF
COL. WELDON E. RHOADES

420 A.

U. S. ARMY AIR FORCES
THE AIR TRANSPORT COMMAND

OPERATIONS AUTHORIZATION ORDER
(Military Operation)

SECRET

By Authority of
The Commanding General
Air Transport Command
/3 nov   and
Date   Initials   Division

1. _____ Headquarters, ATC, Washington, D. C. November 13, 1943_____

2. _____ Operations Authorization No. 28_____

3. _____ W. E. Rhodes - United Air Lines Civilian_____

You will proceed with Aircraft C-54-A (UAL) No. 276 from Washington, D. C. to Miami, Florida, thence via the Caribbean Wing to Borinquen, Puerto Rico, remaining at Borinquen over night, departing the second day from Borinquen via the Caribbean Wing to Belem, Brazil, departing the third day from Belem via the South Atlantic Wing for Natal, Brazil, departing the fourth day from Natal via the South Atlantic Wing and Africa Middle East Wing to Dakar, thence to Marrakech, French Morocco where further instructions will be received. You are authorized to proceed from that point to any point so directed by the passengers or the designated officer so charged with this responsibility. Armed guards will be provided for aircraft while on ground.

Substantial variation from the above itinerary is authorized if directed by the person or persons so designated. Aircraft will at all times operate according to ATC operational procedures in effect in each Wing through which this aircraft passes. Cargo or passengers aboard this aircraft will not be removed or adjusted prior to their destination.

The pilot will report daily the position of the aircraft to the Commanding General, Air Transport Command, Washington, D. C. by priority cable.

Authorized crew members in accordance
with ATC Regulation No. 55-1:

Pilot - W. E. Rhodes
Co-Pilot - W. H. Gehlaar
Navigator - R. C. Walker
Radio Operator - R. F. Wolfe
Purser - Robert A. Schmidt
Engineer - Henry Strzelecki
2nd Engineer - Ray Carroll

By order of COMMANDING GENERAL
Air Transport Command

JAMES G. FLYNN, JR.
Lt. Col., Air Corps,
Act. Asst. Chief of Staff,
Operations.

Military orders for starting the round-the-world trip in the C-54.

498A.

UNITED AIR LINES
TRANSPORT CORPORATION
INTRA-COMPANY CORRESPONDENCE

From ___ General Office - Flight Operations ___ Place ___ Chicago, Illinois ___

To ___ San Francisco - Pacific Operations ___ Date ___ December 27, 1943 ___

Attention ___ Captain Weldon F. Rhoades ___ Reference ___

Subject ___ PERSONNEL: Military Leave of Absence ___

•

cc - S. V. Hall - SF   R. F. Ahrens - CG   W. D. Williams - CG

J. O'Brien - SF   J. W. Eberly - SF

You are aware that we have been contacted by General MacArthur in regard to allowing you to leave UAL for extended military duty directly under or as a portion of General MacArthur's staff.

As discussed with you during my recent visit to SF, it will be agreeable with UAL to grant you a military leave of absence. Your seniority will, of course, continue to accrue during the period of such active duty in accordance with leaves granted to a large number of our Captains now on active duty with the armed forces.

I would suggest that you contact Mr. O'Brien and Mr. Reeder in regard to company material which you now hold and which has been charged to you. Their advice as to the proper handling of this material will be entirely satisfactory to this office.

We wish you every success while on this mission and trust that you will return to UAL immediately following the close of hostilities.

W. J. Addems

W. J. Addems

WJA:F

UGIA. 150M. 12-41. CG11012V. Printed in U. S. A.

Notification of General MacArthur's request for my services.

Samples of the counterfeit Japanese pesos I was to deliver to the guerrillas on Mindanao.

GENERAL HEADQUARTERS
SOUTHWEST PACIFIC AREA

SECRET

AG 210.453 (25 Jul 44)

APO 500
25 July 1944

SUBJECT: Orders.

TO   : O and EM concerned.

Following-named O and EM WP Honolulu, TH, and such other places without and within the continental limits of Australia as may be necessary on temp dy for purpose carrying out instructions of C-in-C. Upon completion will return to proper sta:

MAJ WELDON E RHOADES 0277377 AC
S Sgt Frank P Cicerello 12024208

Travel by mil or commercial aircraft (par 3b, AR 55-120, 26 Apr 43), army or naval transport, commercial steamship, belligerent vessel or aircraft, Govt motor T and rail is directed. EWM.

Alws of not to exceed 65 pounds personal baggage while traveling by air atzd.

In lieu of subs flat per diem $7.00 atzd in accordance with existing law and regulations. TCNT. TDN. 65-*** P 432-02,03 A 212/50425.

By command of General MacARTHUR:

B. M. FITCH,
Colonel, A.G.D.,
Adjutant General.

SECRET

Secret orders to take General MacArthur to Honolulu to meet with President Roosevelt.

694 F.

United Air Lines

June 9, 1944

GENERAL OFFICES
UNITED AIR LINES BUILDING
MUNICIPAL AIRPORT
CLEARING STATION
CHICAGO, ILLINOIS
JB

Dear Major Rhoades:

On April 11th, following a directors' meeting, I walked into my office to be greeted by a group of employees who presented to me in your behalf a beautiful silver plaque in recognition of fifteen years of service.

Words failed me on that occasion, as they do now, in truly expressing my deep appreciation of this expression of friendship.

I had hoped to write a personal letter to each individual whose name appears on this plaque but when I found there were 677 I realized that the job would never be finished. Therefore, I must resort to a form letter, but I assure you it carries with it the deepest feeling of appreciation and gratitude.

I am a very fortunate individual to be associated with such a grand group of capable and thoughtful associates.

Sincerely,

W. A. Patterson

WAP:A

THE BUSINESS ROUTE OF THE NATION

Letter from W. A. Patterson, president of United Air Lines, congratulating me on my fifteen years with the company.

7 8 8 A

S E C R E T

GENERAL HEADQUARTERS
SOUTHWEST PACIFIC AREA

AG 323.35 (14 Oct 44)

APO 500
14 October 1944

STAFF MEMORANDUM)
               :
NO............51)

MOVEMENT OF ADVANCE ECHELON GHQ

1. Personnel listed in Annex "A" will depart GHQ 16 October.

2. The above personnel will embark on the USS NASHVILLE with the exception of Major General Charles P. Stivers, Lieutenant Colonel Joseph R. McMicking, Tec 5 Bernard E. Geeslin and Tec 5 Galera E. Sagon who will embark on a destroyer to be designated.

3. All personnel with the exception of the Commander-in-Chief's personal party, with all baggage, will leave GHQ at 0715I 16 October and will embark at Naval Post Office Jetty, Hollandia, at 0900I.

By command of General MacARTHUR:

R. K. SUTHERLAND,
Lieutenant General, United States Army,
Chief of Staff.

OFFICIAL:

B. M. FITCH,
Brigadier General, U. S. Army,
Adjutant General.

1 Incl:
   Annex A

DISTRIBUTION:
   C of S
   G-1
   G-2
   G-3
   G-4
   Director COIC
   Pub Relations O
   Hq Comdt

S E C R E T

Orders to board the cruiser U.S.S. *Nashville* for the Leyte landing.

7845.

ANNEX "A"

General Douglas MacArthur, 057
Colonel Lloyd A. Lehrbas, 0900274
Lieutenant Colonel Roger O. Egeberg, 0400234

Lieutenant General Richard K. Sutherland, 04623
Major Weldon E. Rhoades, 0277377
CWO Paul P. Rogers, W2114821

G-1:
  Major General Charles P. Stivers, 04667
  Lieutenant Colonel Joseph R. McMicking, 0888171
  Tec 5 Bernard E. Geeslin, 34883688

G-2:
  Colonel J. Paul Craig, 019395
  Major Robert P. McCampbell, 0405338
  Captain Edward E. Barker, Jr., 01284081
  T Sgt Paul H. Phelps, 37162609

G-3:
  Colonel Herbert B. Wheeler, 06801
  Colonel Courtney Whitney, 0398227

G-4:
  Colonel John L. Ballantyne, 015005

COIC:
  Major Lloyd D. Burton, Jr., 01284097

S Sgt Francisco J. Salveron, 10641013
Sgt Marcos Abug, 10647018
Cpl Vincent A. Pintang, 39556938
Cpl Francisco M. Balduena 37571446
Tec 5 Galera E. Sagon, 39544371

Press Pool:
  William Dickenson
  Earl Crotchett
  Frank Prist
  William Dunn
  Pvt Gae Faillace 12126982

Orders to board the cruiser U.S.S. *Nashville* for the Leyte landing.

WESTERN UNION

A. N. WILLIAMS
PRESIDENT

1201

CLASS OF SE~~~~		SYMBOLS	
This is a full-rate Telegram or Cablegram unless its deferred character is indicated by a suitable symbol above or preceding the address.		L Day Letter	
		NL = Night Letter	
		LC = Deferred Cable	
		NLT = Cable Night Letter	
		Ship Radiogram	

The filing time shown in the date line on telegrams and day letters is STANDARD TIME at point of origin. Time of receipt is STANDARD TIME at point of destination

```
PZA10.      LB54F INTL=PZF SANSORIGINE VIA MACKAYRADIO 14
:LC MRS W E RHOADES=                              15 1010=
     :49 GREENOAKSDRIVE ATHERTON (MENLOPARKCALIF)=

PAPPY GOT PROMOTED=

     WELDON RHOADES.==




          :49.==
```

Telegram to my wife Grace informing her of my promotion to lieutenant colonel.

1114A.

SOUTH EAST ASIA COMMAND HEADQUARTERS.

18th July 1945

Dear Rhoades,

Thank you so much for flying our
party back from Clark Field to Nichols Field
during my visit to General MacArthur's
Headquarters.

I must say the "Bataan" is certainly
a lovely aircraft and the flight was a great
experience.

Yours sincerely,

Louis Mountbatten

Thank-you letter to me from Lord Louis Mountbatten.

RADIOGRAM

VIA

PHILIPPINE PRESS WIRELESS, INC.

Soriano Bldg.   MANILA, P. I.   Plaza Cervantes

COM9 KJE8 BB

AUG 12 A.M.

PALOALTO CALIF 23 1945 AUGUST 10TH 1129PM

NLT WELDON RHOADES

GENERAL HDQTRS MANILA

THINKING OF YOU WISH COULD SHARE NEXT FEW DAYS CONGRATULATIONS LOVE

FROM BOYS AND ME

GRACE RHOADES

100AM 12TH

Radiogram from my wife Grace at the end of hostilities in the Pacific.

天佑ヲ保有シ萬世一系ノ皇祚ヲ踐メル
大日本帝國天皇裕仁此ノ書ヲ見ル有衆
ニ宣示ス
朕茲ニ本年八月十六日帝國政府ニ對シ
瑞西國政府ヲ通シテ傳達アリタル亞米利加
合衆國政府ノ通告第二項ニ記セラレタル聯合
國最高司令官ノ指令スル打合ヲ朕ノ名ニ於テ
爲スノ權限ヲ陸軍中將從四位勳二等河邊虎四
郎ニ付與ス

The text of the Japanese Imperial Message: HIROHITO, By the Grace of Heaven, Emperor of Japan, seated on the Throne occupied by the same Dynasty changeless through ages eternal,

To all to whom these Presents shall come, Greetings!

We do hereby authorise Lieutenant-General Torashiro Kawabe, Zyusii, Second Class of the Imperial Order of the Sacred Treasure, to make, on behalf of Ourselves, any arrangements directed by the Supreme Commander

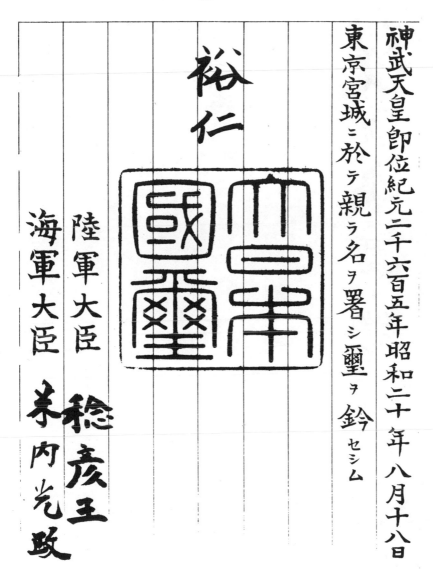

神武天皇即位紀元二千六百五年昭和二十年八月十八日

東京宮城ニ於テ親ラ名ヲ署シ璽ヲ鈐セシム

裕仁

陸軍大臣

海軍大臣

稔彦王

米内光政

for the Allied Powers, as stated in the second clause of the message of the Government of the United States of America which was conveyed to Our Government through the Government of Switzerland on August sixteenth of this year.

In witness whereof, We have hereunto set Our signature and caused the Great Seal of the Empire to be affixed.

Given at Our Palace in Tōkyō, this eighteenth day of the eighth month

of the twentieth year of Syōwa, being the two thousand six hundred and fifth year from the Accession of the Emperor Zinmu.

SEAL OF   Signed: HIROHITO
  THE
EMPIRE   Countersigned: Naruhiko
                                                        War Minister
                                                     Mitsumasa Yonai
                                                        Navy Minister
                                                     Mamoru Shigemitsu
                                                        Minister for Foreign
                                                        Affairs

COPY

27 Aug 45

FROM: CINCAFPAC - RESTRICTED

TO : WARCOS - PRIORITY

Active duty assignment of Lieutenant Colonel Weldon E. Rhoades referring
your WX 54454 was secured by personal request of General MacArthur to
president of the United Airlines for duty as personal pilot to CINC.
In view of exceptional amount of flying which will be required in Japan
immediately after arrival of forces of occupation it is essential that
Rhoades be retained for approximately 3 months. In addition to piloting
the CINC during this period he will, in his capacity as Commanding Officer
of Air Detachment and Chief Pilot for GHQ, give GHQ pilots essential training
in cold weather flying. It is the personal request of General MacArthur that
Colonel Rhoades retention for approximately 3 months be authorized and that
Mr. Patterson, President of United Airlines, be informed of this special
request and its approval.

Approved by:

R. K. SUTHERLAND,
Lieutenant General, U. S. Army,
Chief of Staff.

OFFICIAL:

B. M. FITCH,
Brigadier General, U. S. Army,
Adjutant General.

COPY

(65-35A)

Radiogram from General Sutherland to the War Department requesting extension of active duty for me.

1194A

SURRENDER CEREMONY

1. SCAP PERSONNEL

General J. W. Stilwell
General W. Krueger
General C. Spaatz
General G. C. Kenney
General C. H. Hodges

Lt General A. E. Percival
Lt General J. M. Wainwright
Lt General R. L. Eichelberger
Lt General R. C. Richardson, Jr.
Lt General R. K. Sutherland
Lt General J. H. Doolittle
Lt General B. McK. Giles
Lt General N. F. Twining
Lt General W. C. Styer
Lt General C. H. Gairdner
Lt General E. C. Whitehead

Maj General R. J. Marshall
Maj General J. M. Swing
Rear Admiral J. J. Ballentine
Maj General J. L. Frink
Maj General S. J. Chamberlin
Maj General C. P. Stivers
Maj General S. B. Akin
Maj General H. J. Casey
Maj General C. E. Le May
Maj General W. F. Marquat
Maj General W. B. Kean
Maj General B. J. Valdes
Maj General W. O. Ryan
Maj General L. J. Whitlock
Maj General L. J. Sverdrup
Maj General V. E. Bertrandias
Maj General C. A. Willoughby
Maj General P. B. Wurtsmith
Maj General F. D. Merrill
Maj General C. E. Byers

Brig General L. C. Beebe
Brig General W. E. Chambers
Brig General T. D. White
Brig General B. F. Fellers
Brig General J. L. Holman

Brig General W. E. Crist
Brig General G. R. Denit
Brig General D. R. Hutchinson
Brig General B. M. Fitch
Brig General C. E. Barnwell
Brig General H. E. Eastwood
Brig General L. A. Diller
Brig General C. Whitney
Brig General E. R. Thorpe
Brig General F. S. Bowen

Colonel H. B. Wheeler
Colonel D. Larr
Colonel S. F. Mashbir
Colonel H. B. Whipple
Colonel F. C. Gideon
Colonel R. O. Egeberg
Colonel Q. S. Lanier
Colonel J. B. Pugo

Lt Colonel W. E. Rhoades
Lt Colonel T Dooley

Sgt. H. Carroll

2. U. S. NAVY

To be designated

3. LIST OF ALLIED REPRESENTATIVES

A. CHINA

General Hsu Yung Chang
Vice Admiral Yang Hsuan Chang
Lt General Chu Shih Ming
Maj General Wang Chih
Colonel Li She Cheng
Colonel Wang Pei Cheng

B. UNITED KINGDOM

Admiral Sir Bruce Fraser and party

- 1 -

List of personnel to attend the surrender ceremony on board the battleship U.S.S. *Missouri.*

1194 B.

<u>SURRENDER CEREMONY</u>

C. UNION OF SOVIET SOCIALIST REPUBLICS

   Lt General Kuzma Nikolaevich Derevyanko
   Maj General Nikolai Vasilevich Verenow
   Rear Adm Andrey Mitrofanevich Stetsenko
   Capt Nikolai Michailovich Karamishev
   Lt Nikolai Nikolaevich Tulinov
   (   )

D. AUSTRALIA

   General Sir Thomas Blamey
   Lt General F. H. Berryman
   Rear Admiral George D. Moore
   Air Vice Marshal Jones
   Air Vice Marshal Bostock
   Commodore J. A. Collins
   Captain J. Balfour

  CANADA

   Colonel L. Moore Cosgrave

F. FRANCE

   General B. J. LeClerc
   Lt Colonel Repiton-Preneuf
   Major Langlois
   Major Musse

G. NETHERLANDS

   Admiral C. E. L. Helfrich
   Lt General L. H. Van Oyen
   Colonel C. Giebal
   Cmdr A. A. Fresco
   Lt Commander A. H. W. Van Freytag-Drabbe

H. NEW ZEALAND

   Air Vice Marshal Isitt

4. JAPAN

   3 Army
   3 Navy
   3 Government
   2 Representatives

5. WAR CORRESPONDENTS

- 2 -

List of personnel to attend the surrender ceremony on board the battleship U.S.S. *Missouri*.

1188ⁿ

RESTRICTED   C O P Y
PRIORITY   29 August 1945

TO   : CINCAFPAC
FROM : WASHINGTON
NR   : W 56236

    ANSWERING YOUR MESSAGE C 10098, 27 AUGUST 45. RETENTION OF
LT COL WELDON E. RHOADES FOR AN ADDITIONAL 3 MONTHS AUTHORIZED.
APPROVAL OBTAINED FROM MR PATTERSON.

                                    COMGENAIR

RESTRICTED
PRIORITY
                                          C O P Y

                                      (65.35B)

Authorization from the War Department and United Air Lines to extend my
active duty.

1300A.

R E S T R I C T E D

GENERAL HEADQUARTERS
UNITED STATES ARMY FORCES, PACIFIC

Special Orders)   APO 500
          :   14 November 1945
No.........158)   - E X T R A C T -

2. Announcement is made of the temp promotion of LT COL WELDON E
RHOADES 0277377 AC to the gr of COL AUS eff 14 Nov 45 with rank from same
date.

          By command of General MacARTHUR:

                                        R. K. SUTHERLAND,
                              Lieutenant General, United States Army,
                                        Chief of Staff.

OFFICIAL:

          R. M. FITCH,
Brigadier General, U. S. Army,
    Adjutant General.

R E S T R I C T E D

Orders promoting me to colonel.

!?32

                                GENERAL HEADQUARTERS
                        UNITED STATES ARMY FORCES, PACIFIC   6035
                                                                 AGPO

                                                                 APO 500
AG 201-Rhoades, Weldon E. AGPO   15 Dec 1945

SUBJECT: Order.

TO   : COL WELDON E RHOADES 0277377 AC, Advance Ech GHQ AFPAC APO 500.

        1. Above-named off, now at this station, WP Brisbane, Australia; Honolulu,
T.H.; Washington, D.C. and New York, N.Y. on TDY for purpose carrying out instructions. Off will accompany LT GEN RICHARD K SUTHERLAND, who is traveling under
separate orders. Upon compl of TDY and when so directed by LT GEN SUTHERLAND off
is reld from present asgmt and further dy in this theater and is atchd unasgd Sep
C No 42, Camp Beale, Calif. WP and report to CO for relief from AD under WD RR.
ASRS: 89. CO Sep C will notify this hq of EDCMR by rad. PCS. Auth: WD Ltr, PRI,
16 Aug 1944.

        2. Tvl by mil, naval or commercial acft (par 3b (2) AR 55-120 C15) to and
within the US is dir, except where other means of auth tvl are equally or more expeditious, and is necessary for the successful accomplishment of an urgent mission
directly related to the emerg. Tvl by army or naval transport, belligerent vessel
or acft, commercial steamship and govt MT, rail and any other means of transportation auth. TDN. Transportation Corps will furnish necessary transportation.

        3. Provisions of par 25 and 26, AR 35-4820, 19 Apr 45 apply. 65-*** P431-
02 A 212/60425. 65-*** P432-02 A 212/60425.

        4. Alws of 65 pounds personal baggage auth while traveling by air. Personal
baggage to be shipped limited to 135 pounds, marked with name, grade and serial
number and will be turned over to proper auth for shipment to US under provisions
of WD Ltr AG 524 (13 Aug) OB-S-D-M, 23 Aug 45, Subj: Processing of Baggage.

        5. Prior to departure off will have in his possession, WD AGO Form No. 8-117,
Immunization Register; WD AGO Form No. 66-2, AAF Officer's Qualification Record;
WD AGO Form No. 65 or 65-1, Officer's Identification Card; WD AGO Form No. 77,
Officer's Pay Data Card; record of lv accrued and granted, as prescribed in AR 605-
115; and will require physical inspection as prescribed by par 2, AFPAC Reg No 50-60,
30 Sep 1945.

        6. Off will notify correspondents and publishers to discontinue mailing let-
ters and publications and will advise them of his new address when so instructed by
his unit comdr at which time he will furnish unit mail clerk with home address or
other non-military address to which mail will be forwarded.

            By command of General MacARTHUR:

        Col Rhoades completes his
        TD at New York on 2 Jan. and
        will then proceed to direction
        in Par. 1.   J. H. LOWELL
                                                         Lt Col   AGD
                                                         Asst Adj Gen

Orders to return home and to be released from active duty.

GENERAL HEADQUARTERS
UNITED STATES ARMY FORCES, PACIFIC

GENERAL ORDERS)
:
NO.........394)

APO 500
14 December 1945

LEGION OF MERIT AWARD

By direction of the President, under the provisions of the Act of Congress approved 20 July 1942 (Sec. III, Bulletin 40, WD, 1942), and Executive Order 9260, 29 October 1942 (Sec. I, Bulletin 54, WD, 1942), the Legion of Merit is awarded by the Commander-in-Chief, United States Army Forces, Pacific, to the following-named officer:

Colonel WELDON E. RHOADES, 0277377, Air Corps, United States Army. For exceptionally meritorious conduct in the performance of outstanding services in the Southwest Pacific Area, from 12 January 1944 to 12 December 1945.
Address: 49 Greenoaks Drive, Atherton, Menlo Park, California.

AG-PA 201

By command of General MacARTHUR:

RICHARD J. MARSHALL,
Major General, United States Army,
Chief of Staff.

OFFICIAL:

for B. M. FITCH,
Brigadier General, U. S. Army,
Adjutant General.

Award of the Legion of Merit.

CITATION FOR LEGION OF MERIT

    Colonel WELDON E. RHOADES, 0277377, Air Corps, United States Army. For exceptionally meritorious conduct in the performance of outstanding services in the Southwest Pacific Area, from 12 January 1944 to 12 December 1945. In his capacity as Chief Pilot, General Headquarters, Southwest Pacific Area, and United States Army Forces, Pacific, Colonel Rhoades commanded the Air Detachment and was charged with the training of crews and the operation and maintenance of airplanes assigned to General Headquarters; he served as pilot during all journeys of the Commander-in-Chief. Through his outstanding professional knowledge and skill, his energy and attention to duty, the unit under his command maintained an unblemished record of operational safety and efficiency through the campaigns of New Guinea, Bismarck Archipelago, Southern Philippines and Luzon, and the occupation of Japan.

Address: Greenoaks Drive,
          Atherton, Menlo Park, California.

Award of the Legion of Merit.

1372

9 January 1946

SUBJECT: Appreciation.

TO:
Col. Weldon E. Rhoades, O-277377, AC
c/o United Air Lines, Mills Field
South San Francisco, California

1. It is desired to express to you the appreciation of the War Department for your continued service to National Defense by your acceptance of an appointment as an officer in the Reserve Corps. Your aid and that of the other veteran officers who, like you, are displaying an active interest by remaining in the Reserve will be invaluable in building and maintaining a sound and effective postwar Army. You and your comrades by your counsel, your leadership, and your wholesome influence on public opinion may well make the difference between mediocrity and complete success.

2. AR 140-5 and the other Army Regulations governing the Officers' Reserve Corps necessarily will be revised to conform with such statutes as may be enacted to govern the postwar Army. The revised regulations and other information concerning the Officers' Reserve Corps will be made available in the future.

3. As soon as the press of work permits, a formal commission evidencing your appointment will be mailed to you.

BY ORDER OF THE SECRETARY OF WAR:

EDWARD F. WITSELL
Major General
Acting The Adjutant General

"Thank-you letters" from the War Department and from President Truman.

1379.

WELDON E RHOADES

To you who answered the call of your country and served in its Armed Forces to bring about the total defeat of the enemy, I extend the heartfelt thanks of a grateful Nation. As one of the Nation's finest, you undertook the most severe task one can be called upon to perform. Because you demonstrated the fortitude, resourcefulness and calm judgment necessary to carry out that task, we now look to you for leadership and example in further exalting our country in peace.

Harry Truman

THE WHITE HOUSE

"Thank-you letters" from the War Department and from President Truman.

Radio Technical Commission For Aeronautics

Citation

Whereas, the Radio Technical Commission for Aeronautics has been awarded the Collier Trophy for 1948 "for the establishment of a guide plan for the development and implementation of a system of air navigation and traffic control to facilitate safe and unlimited aircraft operations under all weather conditions".

Now, therefore, this Citation is presented to

W. E. R. Boades

in sincere appreciation of his conscientious and effective collaboration in the work of RTCA Special Committee 31 which created the guide plan described in the citation above quoted.

Given Under My Hand and Seal
this 11th day of January 1950

J. Howard Dellinger
J. Howard Dellinger
Chairman. RTCA

Citation presented to me for my work in establishing a system of air traffic control.

𝔇epartment of 𝔖tate
OF THE
𝔘nited 𝔖tates of 𝔄merica

To all to whom these presents come, greeting:

This is to certify that   WELDON E. RHOADES

has been designated an Adviser on the United States Delegation to the

International Civil Aviation Organization Special Meeting on Airworthiness

and Operations - on Climb Requirements, to be held at Paris, France,

beginning September 14, 1950.

FOR THE SECRETARY OF STATE:

WASHINGTON, D. C.,

Warren Kelchner
CHIEF, DIVISION OF
INTERNATIONAL CONFERENCES

August 25, 1950
DATE

My official designation of participation in the ICAO meeting in Paris.

DEPARTMENT OF COMMERCE
CIVIL AERONAUTICS ADMINISTRATION
WASHINGTON 25

November 8, 1950

Mr. W. A. Patterson, President
United Air Lines
5959 South Cicero Avenue
Chicago 38, Illinois

Dear Mr. Patterson:

As you are aware, the United States Delegation has just recently
returned from a most satisfactory ICAO meeting on Climb Performance,
held in Paris, France.

We were fortunate to have with us on this Delegation a representative
from your company, Mr. Weldon E. (Dusty) Rhoades, and I would like to
take this opportunity, as Chairman of the U. S. Delegation, to express
to Mr. Rhoades, through you, my sincere appreciation of the very
splendid cooperation given us during this meeting. Mr. Rhoades'
wealth of experience from the air carrier operator's point of view,
was most valuable to us as the U. S. Delegation and to the General
Assembly meetings.

I would like to have you know that I considered Dusty Rhoades a very
valuable asset to our Delegation, and would welcome him as a member
of any future meetings we may have where this subject is being
discussed.

Yours very truly,

Original signed by
George W. Haldeman

George W. Haldeman
Chairman, U. S. Delegation
AIR/OPS ICAO Meeting

Thank-you letter to the president of United Air Lines for my work with the
International Civil Aviation Organization meeting in Paris, France.

Index

Flying MacArthur to Victory was composed into type on a Compugraphic phototypesetter in nine and one-half point Trump Medieval with two points of spacing between the lines. Trump Italic was selected for display. The book was designed by Jim Billingsley, composed by Metricomp, Inc., printed offset by Thomson-Shore, Inc., and bound by John H. Dekker & Sons. The paper on which this book is printed bears acid-free characteristics for an effective life of at least three hundred years.

TEXAS A&M UNIVERSITY PRESS : COLLEGE STATION